GOD IN THE RAINFOREST

God in the Rainforest

A TALE OF MARTYRDOM AND REDEMPTION IN AMAZONIAN ECUADOR

Kathryn T. Long

OXFORD
UNIVERSITY PRESS

OXFORD

UNIVERSITY PRESS

Oxford University Press is a department of the University of Oxford. It furthers
the University's objective of excellence in research, scholarship, and education
by publishing worldwide. Oxford is a registered trade mark of Oxford University
Press in the UK and certain other countries.

Published in the United States of America by Oxford University Press
198 Madison Avenue, New York, NY 10016, United States of America.

CIP data is on file at the Library of Congress
ISBN 978-0-19-060898-9

9 8 7 6 5 4 3 2 1

Printed by Sheridan Books, Inc., United States of America

To my brother and sister,
Keith Long and Jan Long Davis

Contempt imposes; grace discovers.
Contempt generalizes; grace is charmed by haunting particularities.
Contempt entraps; grace frees.

Marilynne Robinson
Key West Literary Seminar

Contents

Preface

WRITING A HISTORY of missionary interaction with the Waorani has been an exercise in seeing the Waorani primarily through the eyes of missionaries and anthropologists. This is nothing new. Since the nineteenth century, Americans have learned about non-Western cultures from the "indefatigable writing and speaking efforts" of missionaries.[1] In the case of the Waorani, missionary sources—especially, although not exclusively, from the Summer Institute of Linguistics—were indispensable, since missionaries were the first outsiders to make sustained contact with this Amazonian group. Missionaries were also among the few outsiders who achieved some fluency in *Wao tededo*, a language unlike any other and initially with no written form. Important missionary sources in Spanish included the published observations of Bishop Alejandro Labaca and the detailed history of the Waorani by the Capuchín missionary Miguel Angel Cabodevilla. Unless otherwise indicated, all translations from Spanish are mine.

In 1974 James A. Yost became the first anthropologist to study the Waorani, followed by Clayton and Carole Robarcheck in 1987 and Laura Rival in 1989. Their work, especially Yost's research, has been essential to my understanding of the Waorani. An increasing number of anthropologists have done fieldwork among the Waorani in more recent years. Publications by James S. Boster, Stephen Beckerman, and Flora Lu Holt have been especially helpful.

Rachel Saint (1914–94) and Elisabeth Elliot (1926–2015), pioneer missionaries among the Waorani, recorded their impressions from the day they arrived at the Wao clearing that came to be named Tewæno. Elliot's letters, articles, and other papers housed in the Billy Graham Center Archives at Wheaton College, as well as her book, *The Savage My Kinsman* (1961), describe Wao life on the cusp of the dramatic changes that accompanied outside contact. Rachel Saint's understanding of the Waorani was influenced by her relationship with the Wao woman Dayomæ, as reflected in their collaboration with the writer Ethel Emily Wallis on *The Dayuma Story: Life under Auca Spears* (1960), a book that contained early charts tracing relationships within Dayomæ's kinship group. Saint also included information about the Waorani in reports and letters to administrators with the Summer Institute of Linguistics, her sending agency. Many of these materials are in the Ecuador Branch Collection, part of SIL International's Americas Area Archives in Dallas, Texas. Others are in the William Cameron Townsend Archives, Waxhaw, North Carolina. Saint treasured her relationship with "Uncle Cam" and his wife, Elaine, and the Townsend Archives contain much of their correspondence related to the Waorani.

I was fortunate to have access to the personal papers of the late Catherine Peeke, an SIL linguist. Peeke analyzed the grammatical structure of *Wao tededo* for her PhD dissertation, completed in 1968.[2] Much of her adult life was spent in Ecuador, including twenty-five years assigned by SIL to work with the Waorani. By her retirement in 1992 at age sixty-eight, Peeke understood and spoke the Wao language better than any other outsider. While in Ecuador, she maintained an extensive correspondence with family, friends, and SIL colleagues, which included observations of the Waorani.

Yost, mentioned earlier, was an SIL staff member with a PhD in anthropology. He kept daily field notes, usually a few lines jotted into a small spiral notebook, from his arrival in Tewæno in 1974 until the day he and his family were flown out of the rainforest in 1982. On subsequent trips to Ecuador, he continued the notes. I had access to a typescript copy from the years 1974–79, including Yost's initial observations of Wao culture. Information from several interviews was helpful as well, as was the transcript of a 1987 interview in Ecuador with a group of Waorani by Yost and John Man. Literacy specialist Patricia Kelley provided essential explanations of Wao orthography and other issues, simplified for the nonspecialist. At my request, Yost and Kelley reviewed portions of the manuscript for factual accuracy. During two days of interviews at her home in Holzhausen, Germany, the late Rosi Jung, a linguist and medical worker, offered her perspective as the only European member of the SIL "Wao team."

Of course, many of the missionary sources that documented the Waorani were sources for the history of the missionaries as well. I also had access to letters and journals on the plans of the five men to contact the Waorani and the events that led to their deaths, particularly materials by Nate Saint from the late Marj Saint Van Der Puy and Nate Saint's letters in the Records of Mission Aviation Fellowship. These sources were in addition to the still valuable, published accounts, like Elisabeth Elliot's *Through Gates of Splendor* (1957), *Jungle Pilot* (1959) by Russell T. Hitt, and *Unfolding Destinies* (1990) by Olive Fleming Liefeld. In the interest of brevity, frequently cited sources appear throughout the notes in abbreviated form. An abbreviations list just before the notes provides the abbreviation and full citation information. The list also contains abbreviations and full citation information for frequently cited archival and manuscript collections, as well as the full names of individuals often cited in those collections.

The book is broadly chronological, although because of parallel story lines, some chapters overlap chronologically and have a more topical focus than others. Due to an already lengthy manuscript, I limited my research on the five "Ecuador martyrs" in order to focus on those missionaries and Waorani whose stories have rarely or never been told. I also limited my focus to Ecuador and the US. Much still could be written about the impact of the story in Great Britain, Canada, Latin America outside of Ecuador, and elsewhere.

I experienced the Waorani and their rainforest home firsthand during a three-week trip to Ecuador in 2005. The trip included visits, ranging from a few hours to five days, with Waorani in six clearings in the former protectorate. Despite language and cultural barriers, the opportunity to spend time with the Waorani, including some who appear in the pages of this book, was invaluable. Any errors or misrepresentations of Wao culture in the pages that follow are, of course, my own.

There is some risk in relying heavily on primary sources from members of a single organization, in this case, the Summer Institute of Linguistics. I chose to take that risk because the credibility of the materials could be verified and because SIL, which historically has shunned publicity, made many sources available for the first time. There also was no shortage of sources opposing SIL to balance the picture. I attempted to assess most charges against the missionaries, although my goal was not so much to defend missionaries as to get facts on the record. Some readers may find the book overly critical of missionaries; others may peg it as too sympathetic. Either way, I hope there is enough evidence for readers to make up their own minds.

Readers may notice that this history of missionaries and the Waorani includes little discussion of Wao cosmology or beliefs. In part, this was a function of sources. Few Waorani talked about such things, and when they did, there seemed to be little consensus about what specific beliefs people held in common. Some anthropologists suggested that this reflected the pragmatism at the center of Wao culture. Having a coherent belief system wasn't as important as living well in the present. "The Waorani believed that people had souls and that there was an afterlife where life was much like the life they knew, but no one spent a lot of time worrying or talking about it. What mattered was to make life work."[3] I do describe two types of people among the Waorani who were believed to have access to spirits: the *ido* and the jaguar father or mother.

An explanation of spelling and terminology is in order. The people first contacted by missionaries in 1956 called themselves Waorani (sometimes spelled Waodani or, in Spanish, Huaorani), meaning "the people." Outsiders called them *aucas*, a Quichua word for "savages," which many Waorani consider a pejorative term. Strictly speaking, Waorani is a plural noun, while Wao is a singular noun or an adjective (a Wao clearing). To avoid awkwardness in English, I occasionally use Waorani as an adjective as well. The noun Waorani is a broad term, referring to all people whose parents are both Waorani and who speak *Wao tededo*. Less often the word Wadani (or Waadani) is used to refer to "others," people who seem to qualify as Waorani but for whom no common kinship can be found. All non-Waorani are referred to as *cowode* (outsiders), historically thought to be cannibals.[4] I avoid the use of "auca" unless it has specific historical significance, such as in the term "Operation Auca." Because "auca" is not a proper noun, I normally do not capitalize it, except when quoting someone who did.

Wao tededo is a language that now can be written as well as spoken, but the orthography remains fluid. As a result, there are variant spellings of names, places, rivers, and so on in both published and unpublished sources. For consistency and to avoid confusion, I have tried to standardize the spelling of names and other proper nouns in *Wao tededo* as much as possible. On occasion, this included changing spellings when quoting primary sources to avoid the annoyance of alternative spellings in brackets and the repeated use of *sic*. However, I made no changes when quoting published materials. In other words, the name Yowe is always spelled the same way, unless I am quoting a published source, such as *The Dayuma Story*, where it is spelled Dyuwi. In the glossary at the end of the book the reader will find standard names and common variants (e.g., Yowe [Dyuwi, Dyowe]). As a historian and not a linguist, I also use a simplified alphabet. Spellings of Wao words in the book do not include the dieresis (ö) and therefore, among other things, do not indicate the nasal quality of *Wao tededo*. Except for "Waorani," which is the most common spelling of the word by English speakers, I use "d" rather than "r" (*Wao tededo* rather than *Wao terero*). I also use "c" or "qu" rather than "k." I have retained the letter "æ," which indicates a sound like the English "a" in "cat." It stands as a reminder that *Wao tededo* is not English or Spanish but a language with its own integrity. It also will help non-Waorani to more correctly pronounce the name of one of the central figures in this story, Dayomæ (die-yo-mæ, not die-*you*-muh).

Following the common practice for historians, I use the actual names of those involved, except for a very few occasions when it seemed appropriate to maintain the anonymity of certain Waorani or when Waorani were mentioned in passing by name in Yost's field notes. In some chapters I have broken with historical conventions in the way I have used names. Historians usually give a person's full name the first time the person is mentioned and use the surname from then on. Because several missionaries in this book share the same surname (Jim Elliot and Elisabeth Elliot, or Nate Saint, Marj Saint, and Rachel Saint), for clarity I sometimes repeat their full names or even use first names alone. This has its own challenges; for example, most people knew Elisabeth Elliot as "Betty," until she became a writer and speaker. In some contexts, the use of first names for missionaries also provides a certain symmetry with the Waorani, who traditionally had only one name, for example Rachel and Dayomæ. Their forceful personalities and central roles in this story also made each of the two women widely recognized by these names alone.

Acknowledgments

IN HIS *CONFESSIONS*, Saint Augustine describes God as "the most affluent giver of all good things." During the many years I worked on this book, and even in the midst of some difficult times, I have experienced an abundance of good things in the form of encouragement and support.

Wheaton College, especially former provost Stan Jones and former dean of humanities and theological studies Jill Peláez Baumgaertner, provided funding that supported my research and writing for more than a decade. Dr. Jones supplemented a Pew Evangelical Scholars Research Fellowship with salary support from Wheaton College to make possible a sabbatical during the year 2000, when the project first took shape. Dean Baumgaertner supported a second full-year sabbatical during the academic year 2011–12. In between, because of their efforts, I was the beneficiary of numerous faculty Aldeen Grants from Wheaton College that bought release time to facilitate progress on the book, even while I served as history department chair.

I am grateful not only for the Pew fellowship but also for a summer stipend award from the Louisville Institute for the Study of American Religion, which included support for writing time, as well as for a trip to Ecuador, during summer 2005. In addition, the Institute for the Study of American Evangelicals, directed by Edith Blumhofer, provided a generous stipend as part of the ISAE project "A Century of Change in American Protestant Missions." That grant also provided funding for an assistant to help with checking sources and with copyediting, and a cartographer to create maps for the book. Edith provided encouragement with numerous batches of Teddy Roosevelt's favorite ginger cookies as well. Larry Eskridge, associate director of the ISAE until it closed in 2014, was a perceptive conversation partner for discussing evangelical missions in the context of American popular culture.

Several people contributed to the book above and beyond any expectations I might have had. Mark Noll was a supporter from start to finish. Mark and Maggie Noll both read the manuscript and encouraged me to complete the book. Mark also responded with wisdom, grace, and practical suggestions to several panicked emails concerning research and other issues. Sarah Miglio read the manuscript and over many cups of coffee offered perceptive advice on interpretation and organization. Jonathan Sanchez worked part time for three years providing editorial assistance for both notes and text.

Grant Wacker recommended the manuscript to Oxford University Press and suggested the first round of cuts that made it tighter and better. Mike Hamilton, Dean Arnold, Tim Erdel, and Tom Headland also read the manuscript and made helpful suggestions. Rick Kennedy invited me to leave behind winter in Chicago for a few days to try out my ideas on students at Point Loma Nazarene University in San Diego. George Marsden did not read the manuscript, but, since my graduate student days at Duke, his influence has shaped the way I think and write as a historian. My colleagues in the history department at Wheaton College provided ongoing encouragement. Undergraduate and graduate teaching assistants at Wheaton helped with basic research and took on tasks that freed me up to write. I am grateful to Paul Bartow, Noah Blan, Alyssa Ericson, Matthew Neumann, Jon Obert, Michael Parks, Peter Swarr, and Amber Thomas.

A book of social and cultural history like this one would be impossible without archives and archivists. The staff at the Billy Graham Center Archives at Wheaton College are among the best. Thanks to Paul Ericksen, to retired archivist Wayne Weber, and especially to Bob Shuster, for their interest in the missionary-Waorani story and their help in making the holdings of the BGC Archives related to this story available to me. I am also grateful to Mission Aviation Fellowship and Christianity Today International, which deposited their papers in the BGC Archives and have opened them for scholarly use. Unpublished materials under copyright in those collections that are quoted in the book were used with permission. Keith Call and David Malone provided access to the V. Raymond Edman papers in the Wheaton College Archives.

One of the joys of traveling to Waxhaw, North Carolina, to the William Cameron Townsend Archives was meeting archivist Cal Hibbard. Cal was generous with his time, generous in giving me extended hours in the archives, and generous in sharing his knowledge of Townsend and the history of the Wycliffe Bible Translators. Joan

Spanne, then with the SIL International Language and Culture Archives, helped to facilitate a research trip to the headquarters of SIL International in Dallas. Don Hekman granted access to the Ecuador Branch Records, part of the SIL Americas Area Archives, even though the records had not been fully processed. Matt Welser provided a work station and otherwise made my visit a profitable one.

Quotations from unpublished materials in the Townsend Archives and the Ecuador Branch of the SIL Americas Area Archives are used with permission © SIL International. All quotations from unpublished materials in the private papers of James A. Yost and of the late Catherine Peeke that are under copyright by SIL International likewise are used with permission © SIL International. Materials under copyright by James A. Yost or by the estate of M. Catherine Peeke are used with permission. Permission to quote other unpublished materials in the book was requested on a case-by-case basis and is indicated in the notes.

I appreciate the organizations and individuals who provided photographs or digitized images and granted permission for their use. These include photos courtesy of Mission Aviation Fellowship; SIL International; the Billy Graham Center Archives from the McCully, Theodore Edward Jr. Photo File and from the Billy Graham Evangelistic Association Papers, World Congress on Evangelism Photo File; the Wheaton College Archives; and personal photographs © James A. Yost and © Patricia M. Kelley. I am also grateful for permission to include a Cornell Capa photograph, "Betty Elliot with Mintaka and Mankamu" © International Center of Photography/Magnum Photos. Thanks, too, to Last Refuge Ltd.

Maps were created by Alison DeGraff Ollivierre, Tombolo Maps & Design; the country, province, and city data for Ecuador courtesy of Dr. Marc Souris, Institut de recherche pour le développement; river data for Ecuador © OpenStreetMap contributors. The maps were designed to give the reader a general orientation to places and events mentioned in the book rather than precisely accurate locations. Map 1 is based on early copies of a map attributed to SIL linguist Catherine Peeke, although rarely credited to her, and reproduced widely in modified forms. SIL International does not claim the copyright. Map 4 was informed in part by maps from Mons. Alejandro Labaca, *Crónica Huaorani* (Quito: Vicariato Apostólico de Aguarico, Ediciones CICAME, 1988), 183–85, and Miguel Angel Cabodevilla, *Los Huaorani en la Historia de los Pueblos del Oriente*, 2nd ed. (Coca, Ecuador: Cicame, 1999), 418, fig. 402.

I have published several essays related to the missionary-Waorani story. Portions from some of these essays are used in original or reworked form in this book. All are used with permission of the publishers or permission was not required. Parts of chapters 1 and 2 and related notes first appeared in "In the Modern World, but Not of It: The 'Auca Martyrs,' Evangelicalism, and Postwar American Culture," in *The Foreign*

Missionary Enterprise at Home: Explorations in North American Cultural History, ed. Daniel H. Bays and Grant Wacker (Tuscaloosa: University of Alabama Press, 2003). Brief portions of chapter 2 were first published in "Missionary Realities and the New Evangelicalism in Post–World War II America," in *American Evangelicalism: George Marsden and the State of American Religious History*, ed. Darren Dochuk, Thomas S. Kidd, and Kurt W. Peterson (Notre Dame, IN: University of Notre Dame Press, 2014). Chapters 1 and 7 include paragraphs from "Cameras 'Never Lie': The Role of Photography in Telling the Story of American Evangelical Missions," *Church History* 72, no. 4 (2003). The epilogue drew from "More than Meets the Eye: History and 'The End of the Spear,'" *Books & Culture*, May–June, 2006, a review essay.

I interviewed numerous people, some of whom have since died, with connections to this story. Not all are quoted in the book, but the information they provided was invaluable. I am grateful to the following people for granting interviews: Cornell Capa, Rachelle Yost Dell, Kathy Saint Drown, Ruth Deyneka Erdel, Elisabeth Elliot Gren, David Howard, Thomas Howard, Donald Johnson, Rosi Jung, Patricia Kelley, Olive Fleming Liefeld, David and Marilyn Miller, Bruce and Joyce Moore, Gilberto Mincaye Nenquimo, Carolyn Orr, René Padilla, Catherine Peeke, Abe Van Der Puy, Marj Saint Van Der Puy, Lloyd and Linda Rogers, Steve Saint, Wallace Swanson, Daan Vreugdenhil, James A. Yost, Kathie Yost, and Yowe. Other people helped make the interviews possible through help with the logistics of travel or by providing hospitality that stretched available funds. Thanks to Sally Charles, Louis Gallien Jr., Kristine Larson, David and Margot Rox, and Susan Warner.

Martha Polo-Koehler was the perfect traveling companion for a three-week trip to Ecuador in July 2005. Thanks also to nurse Miriam Gebb, serving with Reach Beyond Mission, who met us in Shell Mera and went along to the Wao clearings. While friendly and welcoming, the Waorani who hosted us were not particularly impressed by a visit from a *gringa* historian. They were, however, happy to take advantage of the "mini-clinics" Miriam held to treat various minor maladies. Martha and I were grateful as well to have Miriam introduce us to many people she knew. I am thankful that research funding, especially for plane flights between clearings, stretched to cover Miriam's travel. Thanks also to Tæmænta, in charge of Wao tourism at the time, for approving and facilitating our trip.

Yowe and his family welcomed us to Tewæno. We were grateful for Cawetipæ, a young member of another of the original Tewæno families, who translated between *Wao tededo* and Spanish so that we all could communicate. Ana and Quenta offered hospitality at their family clearing. Epa and her husband, Tomo, and their children and grandchildren were especially kind when a shortage of airplane fuel in Ecuador meant that we stayed in their clearing for five days rather than the scheduled three.

We met Dayomæ for a brief chat at her home in Toñæmpade. Thanks to Mission Aviation Fellowship for air transportation to Wao clearings.

In December 2010 I was diagnosed with Parkinson's disease. I am grateful to doctors, physical therapists, my fellow Rock Steady boxers, and others who encouraged me to pursue the dream of completing this book, despite some bumps along the way. Special thanks to Carla Schemper, who reminded me that I did not have to finish the book, but who was unfailingly supportive when I said I did. Thanks, too, to Cynthia Read and her staff at Oxford University Press for their patience during the editing process and for insisting that the book be a manageable and readable length.

Finally, thanks to church friends and other "friends of the heart" not already mentioned, who supported this project in tangible and intangible ways. They include Finney and Pam Gilbert, the late Chris Mitchell, Tracy and Mary Stollberg, Ron and Carol Blauwkamp, the late Jim Caldwell, and Susan Caldwell. Nancy Underwood—that wonderful combination of coworker and friend—made my life and this project easier in more ways than I can express. Other than my family, probably no one is happier that I finally finished the book than George and Helen DeVries. Thanks for years of a special friendship.

Of the many good things in my life, my own extended family, including my sister and brother-in-law, Jan and Myron Davis, and my brother and sister-in-law, Keith and Meg Long, plus nieces, nephews, and a growing crowd of their spouses and children, top the list. I look forward to spending more time with you all.

GOD IN THE RAINFOREST

Introduction

WHEN JONATHAN EDWARDS wanted an example of ideal evangelical piety, he chose David Brainerd (1718–47), a young missionary who had been expelled from Yale in 1742 for challenging college authorities during the revival fervor of the early 1740s. His college career ended, Brainerd served for three and a half years as a missionary to Native Americans in New York, Pennsylvania, and New Jersey. His one ministry success before his death from tuberculosis was a revival among a small group from the Delaware tribe. From Edwards's perspective, however, Brainerd's true success was spiritual. As reflected in his diaries, the young man was a paragon of love for Christ, self-denial, and missionary zeal. After Brainerd's death, Edwards edited the diaries, taking some liberties to shape the narrative as a "case study of true holiness."[1] *An Account of the Life of the Late Reverend Mr. David Brainerd* was published in 1749 and became "one of the most influential missionary accounts of all time."[2] It defined the ideals of evangelical piety for nineteenth-century Americans, becoming a devotional guidebook for ordinary Christians and inspiration for young missionaries who followed Brainerd in self-sacrifice that often led to death on the mission field.

The *Life of Brainerd* also became the model for a popular genre of religious biography in America. It was the missionary narrative or missionary memoir, which presented missionaries as saints, heroes, or martyrs, or some combination of the three.[3] Memoirs or biographies of early nineteenth-century missionaries, including Samuel J. Mills, Luther Rice, and Adoniram Judson, along with Harriet Newell, Ann

Judson, and Ann Wilkins, among many others, helped to establish the genre. By the early twentieth century, independent, evangelical "faith missions," such as the China Inland Mission, the Gospel Missionary Union, and the Central American Mission, had their own missionary narratives to inspire and challenge. Among the most well-known was *The Triumph of John and Betty Stam*, the story of two Moody Bible Institute graduates, serving with the China Inland Mission, who were killed in 1934 by Chinese Communists. The Stams' total consecration to Christ made theirs the iconic missionary narrative for American fundamentalists. The emphasis on their triumph reflected a shift in the missionary narrative to incorporate the ideals of the "Victorious Christian Life" or the "Higher Christian Life," coming out of Keswick holiness, a movement with British and American roots that stressed Christian living on a higher plane.[4]

The narratives of Brainerd and early nineteenth-century missionaries idealized the values of Edwardsean "disinterested benevolence," whereby true holiness was demonstrated by a willingness to die without seeing converts or other results from missionary labors. Piety was proven by faithfulness amid apparent failure. In the twentieth century, absolute submission to the will of God continued to be an ideal of true holiness, but it carried the promise that God would grant spiritual power to those who trusted him and would vindicate their faith. Surrendering one's life to God did not guarantee success on the mission field or elsewhere, but it did promise ultimate victory.

Twenty-two years after the Stams were killed, five young men, American missionaries in the rainforests of Amazonian Ecuador, met a similar fate, speared by the violent and isolated Waorani people during an attempt to make peaceful contact. The story of Jim Elliot, Nate Saint, Ed McCully, Peter Fleming, and Roger Youderian, killed by the people they had hoped to evangelize, became the defining missionary narrative for American evangelicals during the second half of the twentieth century. It stood squarely within the tradition of the *Life of Brainerd* and other accounts but also reflected the context of modern America. Unlike most earlier missionary narratives, which spoke primarily to the faithful, the deaths of the "Ecuador martyrs" were covered on the front pages of daily newspapers, in a lead photo essay in *Life* magazine, and as a condensed book in *Reader's Digest*. This publicity happened before *Through Gates of Splendor*, Elisabeth Elliot's definitive account, was published in 1957 by Harper and Brothers, a respected mainstream publisher.[5]

Popular interest in the Ecuador missionary narrative reflected the increased visibility of theologically conservative Protestants, moving from separatist fundamentalism toward a "new" evangelicalism, open to engaging broader American culture. The founding of *Christianity Today* magazine in 1956 and the success of Billy Graham's Madison Square Garden Crusade the next year were indications of this shift. So, too, was public fascination with the idealistic and adventurous young missionaries, who braved the Amazon to give their lives for an obscure tribal group.

The narrative of missionaries and the Waorani also was unique because it had a powerful, unexpected sequel. In October 1958 Jim Elliot's widow, Elisabeth, and Nate Saint's sister, Rachel—aided by a Wao woman named Dayomæ—made peaceful contact with the Waorani who had killed their loved ones. This only added to the drama and inspirational appeal of the story. A few years later, sooner than anyone expected, a handful of Waorani began to profess belief in God. *The Dayuma Story: Life under Auca Spears*, a book that became the unofficial sequel to *Through Gates of Splendor*, introduced readers to the violence and fear that characterized Wao culture and to the power of the gospel that would transform it. It was a classic story of darkness and savagery transformed by the light of the gospel message, illustrated by Dayomæ's experiences.[6] Readers were assured that God was at work in the rainforests of Ecuador.

Elisabeth Elliot was more cautious than Rachel Saint in acknowledging conversions among the Waorani, and there were other differences between the two women. In November 1961 Elisabeth and her daughter, Valerie, quietly left the Waorani to return to the mission station in Shandia, where Jim and Elisabeth had served the lowland Quichuas. Elliot's departure left Rachel Saint as the only permanent missionary among the Waorani. By 1965 photos and news reports showed about thirty Waorani in Western dress, sitting under a thatched-roof structure, holding copies of the Gospel of Mark translated into the Wao language. A year later Rachel Saint took two Wao men to Berlin to attend the World Congress on Evangelism, and in 1971 Saint and three Waorani bore witness to their faith at fundraising and recruitment rallies throughout the American Midwest and portions of the South.

Most evangelicals assumed that these activities reflected the impact of the Christian gospel among the Waorani. A group of jungle killers had embraced Christ, rejected violence, put on clothes, become literate, and were reading the New Testament as Rachel and Dayomæ translated it. Some Waorani had become indigenous missionaries to uncontacted relatives. The deaths of the five missionaries had been vindicated by the redemption of the Waorani. This "indigenous conversion narrative," along with the original missionary narrative, became the accepted history of missionary-Waorani interaction and remained so for many evangelicals.

This book explores how that history became entrenched and, in its romanticized perspective, misleading—overlooking or minimizing complexities, controversies, significant achievements, and failures in Ecuador.[7] It also provides a more complete reconstruction than previously available of what happened during the four decades after the men were killed, focusing both on missionaries who came after the five slain men and on the Waorani. Apart from Rachel Saint and Elisabeth Elliot, these evangelical and Catholic missionaries have been forgotten in most versions of the story written in English. This is despite their contributions to the introduction of Christianity among the Waorani and to helping the Waorani survive their contact with the outside world. The missionaries included pilots from Mission Aviation Fellowship (known in Ecuador as Alas de Socorro), medical workers from Reach Beyond (HCJB Global), and traditional missionaries from Christian Missions in Many Lands (Plymouth Brethren) and the Christian and Missionary Alliance. On the Catholic side were Capuchín missionaries, among them Bishop Alejandro Labaca Ugarte and his coworker Inés Velásquez Arango, a nun from the Capuchín Tertiary Sisters.

The organization most associated with missionary work among the Waorani was the Summer Institute of Linguistics (SIL, now SIL International), known in Spanish as the Instituto Lingüístico de Verano, and JAARS, its jungle aviation service. SIL was represented in the United States by a separate, sister organization, Wycliffe Bible Translators. Rachel Saint was an SIL staff member, and, after the departure of Elisabeth Elliot, who was not affiliated with SIL, the organization assumed primary responsibility for the mission to the Waorani. SIL was a nongovernmental organization specializing in translation, linguistics, literacy, and community development. All SIL staff were evangelical Christians and were usually described by others in Ecuador as missionaries or generically as "linguists."[8] In addition to Rachel Saint, over the years the "SIL team" came to include linguists Catherine Peeke and Rosi Jung (also a medical worker), teacher and literacy specialist Pat Kelley, as well as anthropologist James A. Yost and his wife, Kathie. At different times between 1968 and 1992, these were the outsiders who lived and worked most closely with the Waorani. As a result, they are a major focus of this book.

The Waorani, of course, are another major focus. Here the story centers on Dayomæ and members of her kinship group, known as the Guequitaidi. Six Guequitaidi men killed the five missionaries, and Dayomæ's intervention was crucial to her extended family's later acceptance of Elisabeth Elliot and Rachel Saint. Dayomæ was the first Wao Christian and Rachel Saint's language informant. The ambiguous role Dayomæ assumed as cultural broker between her people and the outside world merits further exploration, as does her part in the indigenization of Wao Christianity and her close but mercurial relationship with Rachel Saint.

Much that has been written about missionaries and the Waorani during the second half of the twentieth century has fallen into one of two categories. On the one hand are the inspirational or hagiographical works described earlier that idealized the missionaries, particularly those who became famous, and emphasized the spiritual transformation of the Waorani. On the other are critics who have perpetuated the "black legend" that missionaries in the Americas have been uniquely effective in destroying indigenous cultures, with the Waorani as a prime example in the twentieth century. The Waorani remain somewhat stock figures in the background of both approaches. This book seeks a more nuanced approach.

The overarching argument is that the global expansion of Christianity as it happens on a case-by-case basis is complicated, even messy, much more so than either mythmakers or critics are willing to acknowledge. Missionaries make decisions with unintended consequences; indigenous people exercise agency in unexpected ways. Oil is discovered; isolated groups are pulled into global systems, moving, in Allison Brysk's apt phrase, "from tribal village to global village."[9] The missionary-Waorani story also is fascinating because for years the inspirational accounts and even the biting criticisms have eclipsed the quotidian actions of people in Ecuador, both missionary and Waorani. Christianity may be demonstrated as much by a willingness to spoon liquid down the throats of people suffering from influenza as from feats of missionary heroism. An old Wao warrior described himself as "a little believer" in the message of Jesus, meaning that he had a hard time understanding what the missionaries were talking about. Still, he learned enough over the years that he chose not to avenge his sister's murder, though he clearly wanted to.[10] His step in breaking a cycle of revenge may have reflected a spirit of sacrifice not unlike that of the missionaries he had killed years earlier on a riverbank in the rainforest.

Itota beyæ, tænonamai. On behalf of Jesus, do not spear.[11]

PART I

A Missionary Legend Takes Shape, 1956–1959

1

"Palm Beach" on the Curaray River

⟨ornament⟩ ───────────────────────────────────

TUESDAY, JANUARY 3, 1956, at 8:02 a.m., two minutes behind the meticulously planned schedule, a small yellow Piper Cruiser PA-14, dubbed "56 Henry" after its registration number, took off from the airstrip at Arajuno, a missionary station in the eastern jungles of Ecuador, a region known as the Oriente. The pilot, thirty-two-year-old Nate Saint, and his passenger, Ed McCully, twenty-eight, were among some twenty-three thousand North American Protestants working as missionaries in the mid-1950s, part of the wave of young men and women who had gone to the mission field during the *pax Americana* following the Second World War. About thirty of them staffed mission stations in this Ecuadorian rainforest at the headwaters of the Amazon. They often took advantage of sites developed—and later abandoned—by the Royal Dutch Shell oil company in an initial, fruitless search for petroleum between 1937 and 1950.[1] This evangelical missionary contingent represented a variety of nondenominational sending agencies, known as "faith missions." Their goal was to bring Christianity to indigenous people of the region.

Today's flight was not a regular "milk run" to drop off mail, groceries, or medicines at one or another of the missionary outposts. The small plane was headed over territory claimed by the fierce Waorani people, then known by the name their neighbors and enemies the Quichuas had given them: *aucas* (savages). Wao territory extended east from the foothills of the Andes, bounded on the north by the Napo River and on the south by the Villano and Curaray rivers (map 1). The area, an expanse of about 8,100 square miles, was their world. With their spears and their reputation as killers, the Waorani defended it against all outsiders.

This elusive and feared indigenous group had captured the imaginations of Saint, McCully, and three fellow missionaries: Jim Elliot, twenty-eight; Pete Fleming, twenty-seven; and Roger Youderian, thirty-one. The Waorani were seen as a tribe "untouched by civilization.... [a] people who had repulsed every attempt of the white man to contact them."[2] There were good reasons for the hostility. Their encounters with outsiders had not been positive. The rubber boom that swept the Oriente from the 1880s to 1914 had led to the kidnapping, torture, and death of Waorani by rubber traders who attempted to enslave them.[3] Waorani resistance was famous among Ecuadorians, to whom they were something "between legend and ghosts."[4]

To the young missionaries, what mattered most was that the Waorani had never heard the name Jesus Christ.[5] For serious young Protestants, the mission field represented the ideal expression of a dedicated Christian life, and pioneer work among "unreached peoples" was the pinnacle of what it meant to be a missionary.[6] The Waorani represented a pristine mission field, unsullied by outside vices or by misunderstandings of Christianity. The latter was particularly important for Elliot, Fleming, and McCully, representatives from Plymouth Brethren assemblies, groups that rejected formal church structures in favor of what they viewed as New Testament simplicity. "Ah, for a place where Scriptures have not been twisted!" Elliot had written a few years earlier, after a discouraging effort to form a Brethren assembly in Indiana. "Lord, send me to Ecuador!"[7] The Waorani were the answer to his prayers.

The plane flew east on the fifteen-minute hop across the rainforest from Arajuno to a sandy beach about two hundred yards long beside the Curaray. The strip of sand, called "Palm Beach" by the men, lay about six miles northeast of the cluster of Wao dwellings the men called "Terminal City" (map 2). It would serve as the missionaries' base camp, assuming Saint could land and take off successfully on the soft sand. He brought 56 Henry in under the fog and simulated an approach through the canyon created by tree-covered ridges on either side of the river. On the second pass, Saint landed. They were safely on the beach. Just as important, the sand was firm enough for Saint to take off again.[8]

McCully stayed behind as Saint returned to Arajuno for the other men and supplies. He made five flights that day, first bringing Elliot and Youderian, then ferrying food, radio equipment, and prefabricated boards and tin roofing for shelter. Like an all-male Swiss family Robinson, the men on the ground spent most of the day assembling their precut "house" thirty feet up in an ironwood tree overlooking the beach. It was a two-tiered affair with four plank bunks for sleeping and storing equipment. The tree house was designed to provide safe quarters at night for Elliot, McCully, and Youderian. Saint and Fleming would fly in each day and out again each night to avoid being stranded by flash flooding or possible attack. The missionaries also erected a pole on the beach, crowned with ribbons and a model of the plane, so the Waorani would identify them with earlier aerial gift drops over the nearby Wao settlement.

At the end of the day, on his return flight to Arajuno, Saint swung a few miles south over the Wao clearing. Using the plane's loudspeaker, he called out phrases meant to invite those below to the camp on the Curaray, but he observed that they looked puzzled. (The Waorani later said they had understood that the men were dropping gifts, but they could not understand their attempts at verbal communication.) Looping back over Palm Beach, the pilot buzzed his colleagues, again using the loudspeaker to report what he had done. He then headed out for the night.[9]

The three men on the beach that night and the two at the jungle station in Arajuno represented in microcosm the energy and idealism of conservative American missions. Youderian and Saint were World War II veterans whose call to missionary work came in the crucible of wartime service. Youderian made a personal commitment to Christ as a paratrooper in Europe, and Saint's faith deepened while he was a stateside crew chief supporting C-47 cargo planes. Elliot, Fleming, and McCully were a few years younger than the World War II cohort, though McCully had served a brief hitch with the US Navy. They were part of a postwar resurgence in missions interest among evangelical college students, Elliot and McCully at Wheaton College in Illinois, Fleming through the influence of campus parachurch groups at the University of Washington, and all three through their local Brethren assemblies.

RISK TAKERS FOR GOD

The three "Brethren boys," as Saint called them, had come to Ecuador sponsored by local Brethren fellowships at home. For his part, Saint was a pilot with the newly founded Missionary Aviation Fellowship, providing air support to the jungle missions. Youderian was affiliated with the Gospel Missionary Union, a Kansas City–based agency that had its origins in YMCA missionary work.[10] All these were faith missions, groups that did not guarantee their missionaries a salary on the field. Missionaries lived "by faith," trusting God to provide through the donations of individuals and congregations.

Members of faith missions were risk takers for God. They rejected what they saw as an overly cautious Christianity that was the norm for most Americans and were willing to put their lives on the line to preach the Christian gospel to those who had never heard it. The greater the risk, the more likely that the reality of God's presence and activity in the world would become evident.[11] The challenge was to distinguish between risk and recklessness by discerning the will of God each step of the way. The men involved in the Waorani project were relatively new to missionary work. Saint was the most seasoned, having spent seven years in Ecuador as a missionary pilot. Elliot and Fleming had arrived together in 1952 and were a month shy of completing four years' service. McCully and Youderian were concluding their third year on the field. Fleming and Elliot had come to Ecuador as single men; Fleming had broken an engagement with Olive Ainslie, whom he had known since childhood, and Elliot had backed away from a relationship with Wheaton College classmate Elisabeth Howard. However, by January 1956 all were married (including Fleming to Ainslie and Elliot to Howard), and all but the Flemings had at least one child, with a total of eight young children among them.

Elliot and Saint were the driving forces behind the group. Elliot, an intense, self-assured, spiritually focused young man, first heard of the Waorani during the summer of 1950 at the Summer Institute of Linguistics (SIL), a language training school for missionaries at the University of Oklahoma. Elliot later described the Waorani as the "one really savage tribe" left in Ecuador—a special challenge to an aspiring pioneer missionary.[12] Within a year he had recruited his friend Fleming and his college classmate McCully to missionary work in Ecuador, with the dream of contacting the Waorani.

Their dreams were deferred until September 19, 1955, when Saint and McCully took advantage of a clear day and some spare time to fly into Wao territory bordering Arajuno, McCully's mission station, to look for McCully's "neighbors." The semisedentary habits of the Waorani and their practice of building their thatched houses in small clearings on hilltops, rather than in settled villages, made them diffi-cult to locate. This time, however, fifty miles northeast of Arajuno, the men spotted a cluster of about fifteen clearings and houses—their first sightings of Waorani. Ten days later they located a half dozen Wao longhouses in the more accessible site they would name Terminal City. Saint, Elliot, McCully, and a second pilot, Johnny Keenan, decided that the providential discovery of a Wao settlement practically on McCully's doorstep signaled "the Lord's time to try to contact the Aucas."[13]

The missionaries expected God to "pull strings through circumstances."[14] Their job was to respond to his guidance. The Terminal City Waorani became the focus of a three-month effort to pave the way for the eventual ground contact. The men re-ferred to the project as visiting "the neighbors." Later writers dubbed it "Operation Auca," the name that stuck.[15] The men decided to keep the project secret from eve-ryone but their wives—from other missionaries, family members, even Saint's older sister, Rachel, herself a missionary in Ecuador. At the time, she was attempting to learn the Wao language from a young woman named Dayomæ, the only available Wao speaker not living with the tribe.[16] Again, circumstances tipped the scales. Nate and the others apparently made one failed attempt to arrange a face-to-face meeting with Rachel. In a letter written but never mailed, he told his sister that since they were unable to meet personally with her, he and the other missionaries had decided to continue their commitment to secrecy.[17] Nate also feared that if his sister knew their plans, she or others from SIL, her agency, might inform government officials, since SIL operated in Ecuador under government contract. The Ecuadorian government, in turn, might launch an armed invasion to subdue the Waorani, which would compromise any possible missionary outreach. On a personal level, Nate worried that "Sis" might attempt to protect him from the dangers of trying to contact the Waorani.[18] Of course, secrecy also kept Rachel and anyone else from calling into question any aspect of the men's plans. It reflected a blend of caution, heightened drama, and perhaps competition. The men may have been protecting the Waorani, but they also were protecting themselves from anyone who might challenge their pursuit of God's will. As a result, an isolated group of young missionaries set out to reach an even more isolated group of indigenous people.

CONTACT BY AIR

The missionaries' strategy for initial contact with the Waorani was by air. Saint had pioneered missionary aviation in Ecuador and was known within the missionary community for his creativity. He invented an alternative fuel system to serve as a backup for small planes flying in remote jungle areas. He also developed the bucket drop, a procedure for lowering a container from a plane to a fixed point on the ground below. The bucket might contain medicines or even an army surplus field telephone so that missionaries in remote areas could communicate directly with the pilot. Saint viewed Operation Auca as an opportunity to demonstrate "what air support can do to reduce the risk of initial contacts with dangerous, primitive people."[19]

The missionaries decided that offering gifts would be the most effective gesture of friendship. On October 6, 1955, they initiated the first of thirteen weekly gift flights over the Waorani settlement. Saint and whoever accompanied him—usually McCully, but sometimes Elliot—used Saint's spiral-line technique to lower gifts to specific areas of the Wao clearing. On the first flight, they offered an aluminum kettle, festooned with ribbons to make it more visible from the air, containing brightly colored buttons and a couple of pounds of rock salt. In his journal, Saint recognized that the Indians had never seen salt, nor would buttons be of much use other than as trinkets to people who wore no clothing. Subsequent gifts included more pots, machetes, shirts, trousers and shorts, an axe head and small knives, as well as close-up photos of the missionaries.[20]

By the fourth visit Saint had rigged a loudspeaker to the plane, and Elliot called out simple phrases in what he thought was the Wao language. ("I like you! I am your friend.") He had learned the phrases on a visit to Dayomæ. Dayomæ's native tongue had been corrupted, however, by the lowland Quichua language spoken on the hacienda where she had lived and worked for almost a decade. For example, because the Waorani were a kinship-based culture, they had no word for "friend." In the broadest sense, people were either Waorani, with some common ancestor, or *cowode* (a subhuman outsider). Nonetheless, the Waorani seemed to respond positively to the men's efforts. On the fifth trip, as the plane circled low into the clearing, McCully leaned out from the door and held out both hands. Several Waorani responded by extending their own hands. If he had had a ladder, McCully later wrote, he would have been tempted to climb down it and join them.[21] During the sixth gift drop, the Waorani tied a headband of woven feathers on a line from the plane, which had lowered a cooking pot. McCully described it as a "sign [from God] to proceed," an indication that some Waorani might want friendly contact.[22] Later visits brought additional exchanges: another headband, woven thread, a black bird, a parrot, two squirrels, smoked monkey tail, and other food.

As the flights continued, growing numbers of Waorani appeared for the gift drops. They may have felt that their reciprocal strategy of trading for goods was working. The missionaries, too, were caught up in the excitement. Saint wrote of the gift drops, "It is high adventure, as unreal as any successful novel." On film and in his journal, he carefully recorded each phase of the project, thinking he might someday publish "a booklet with pictures."[23]

GROUND CONTACT

The men regularly cautioned themselves not to run ahead of God's leading; they knew their undertaking was still dangerous. Nonetheless, by December they had begun to talk seriously about a ground approach. The Quichuas living near the mission station guessed what they were up to, and soon the word would spread. The first week of January would mark the last full moon before the rainy season began. In early December, Youderian had agreed to join the group, and, at a planning meeting two days before Christmas, Peter Fleming became the fifth participant. Using the military imagery common in evangelical circles after World War II, they set January 3 as their own D-day, a jungle beach landing in territory they hoped was no longer hostile.

Despite the risks, "God's leading was unmistakable." The smooth progress of the mission seemed to indicate God's protection. Not to have responded would have reflected disobedience and unbelief. Even when concerns surfaced, the men were confident. "Do you think I'd go if I thought we'd be killed?" McCully remarked during the discussions. "Look at Marilou. [She was pregnant.] I'm convinced that those Indians want to be friends. We have watched them and God has answered our prayers. Marilou and our two boys have lived here on Auca land for almost a year, and the Aucas haven't done anything to us."[24]

The January 3 landing proceeded without a hitch. The first night and the following day, Wednesday, were uneventful. The five continued to settle in, building a shelter on the beach, swimming, resting, reading, and fighting what Saint described as "47 billion flying insects of every sort."[25] McCully was more laconic. "Bugs are bad," he jotted in a note to his wife. Photos taken that day show a bare-chested Elliot displaying his catch of a fifteen-inch-long catfish and Saint reading *Time* magazine as he reclined in the middle of the shallow river, submerged but for head, hands, and a crossed leg to escape the insects. The atmosphere reflected a balance of anticipation and concern for the practical aspects of jungle camping. McCully made up a list of "things we need" for Marilou to send the next day. It included sunglasses, insect repellant, milk and lemonade (which the men consumed from glass gallon jars), and "sun helmet, if around."[26]

Thursday saw more of the same. McCully and Youderian chopped down trees that might obstruct plane landings or takeoffs. Later, braving the bugs, Elliot stood in the middle of the shallow river, notebook of Wao phrases in hand, and called out to the jungle.[27] Saint took off several times, circling the beach and gunning his engines to help pinpoint the site for any Waorani in the area. He need not have bothered. The Waorani knew where they were. The five Americans unknowingly had established their campsite at a point where a Wao ancestral trail crossed the river. Beaches that were wide enough for a plane to land also were ideal for trail crossings. The Waorani were accustomed to secretly observing the strange behavior of anyone who entered their territory, and several of them hunting in the area that Thursday heard what they described as the noise of a "big woodpecker hard at work."[28] Investigating, they saw the *cowode* cutting trees while their *ebo* ("wood-bee," or airplane) rested nearby. Returning to their clearing they shared the information with members of their kinship group who were present, probably no more than about two dozen people at the time. By most accounts, two sets of circumstances affected this group and their subsequent actions.

One was the search for Dayomæ, the young Wao woman who had fled during one of the periods of revenge killings characteristic of Waorani life. The "Terminal City" group happened to be the Guequitaidi (Guequita's bunch), Dayomæ's kinship group, including her mother, Acawo; her younger brother, Nampa; sister Guiimadi; aunt Mintaca, as well as her uncle Guequita and his wife, Mæncamo. Acawo was convinced that Dayomæ was still alive and assumed that she was the one sending all the gifts dropped from the plane. Acawo encouraged her daughter Guiimadi to go and ask about Dayomæ. Mintaca would go along as well.[29]

Guiimadi was of marriageable age, but Acawo opposed her daughter's most persistent suitor. He was Nænquiwi, feared and hated for his treachery and killings, even in a culture where revenge killings and other spearings were a fact of life. Nænquiwi had had two wives but had speared one in a fit of rage. Now he sought another, Guiimadi, in an increasingly tense standoff with her mother and brother. To add to the tension, Nænquiwi and Guiimadi were not in the correct cross-cousin relationship for a culturally appropriate marriage. Nampa was furious at the prospect of his sister's making a "wild" (improper) marriage. If, as Acawo suggested, Guiimadi and Mintaca left the clearing for a day, it might help to defuse the conflict.

FRIDAY ENCOUNTER

At dawn on Friday, January 6, the two women were on the trail walking toward "Palm Beach." Nænquiwi followed, continuing his pursuit of Guiimadi. By midmorning the three had reached the banks of the Curaray together. The young missionaries were standing on the beach opposite—McCully at one end, Elliot at the other, with Youderian, Saint, and Fleming in between. They alternated calling out their memorized Waorani phrases and waving gifts. Suddenly, as Fleming later recorded in his diary, "an Auca voice boomed out in a barrage of unintelligible, excited sounds to give us the long-awaited and much-prayed-for first contact with these savages."

With Guiimadi and Mintaca, Nænquiwi, who had spoken, stepped out of the jungle near McCully's end of the beach. Fleming's heart "jumped and thumped wildly as [he and the others] walked slowly to join Ed [who had waded into the river]." The exuberant Elliot yanked off his shirt and trousers and waded toward the Waorani. Hesitating a little as he approached, Elliot took their hands and led them back across the river. The men were ecstatic and wasted no time in getting out their cameras. A photo taken shortly after the initial encounter shows Elliot standing behind the two women on the beach, shorts still damp from the river, camera in hand and a grin of sheer delight across his face. The Waorani appeared poised, though oblivious to the significance of the encounter. "They showed neither fear nor comprehension of what cameras are and some excellent shots were taken," Fleming reported. "The man was interested but not forward, completely unafraid, unembarrassed, and at home."[30]

Three months earlier, after the first gift drop, Saint had described the flight as an attempt to express friendship to the people below, people, he noted, who were "a quarter of a mile away vertically . . . fifty miles away horizontally . . . and continents and wide seas away psychologically."[31] That January morning when the three Waorani emerged on the Curaray beach, the vertical and horizontal distances had been bridged, at least for the moment. Linguistic and cultural chasms, however, remained, far deeper in many ways than the men in their enthusiasm imagined. The missionaries had memorized what they thought were some basic phrases in the Wao language.[32] However, the phrases turned out to be both mispronounced and mistranslated.

Linguists would later determine that *Wao tededo* (the Wao language) was a linguistic isolate, that is, a language independent of any other. As a result, the missionaries' knowledge of lowland Quichua was no help. They were also unaware of certain cultural practices. For example, it was an aggressive act to directly ask someone his or her name. (The inquirer might be checking on kinship ties in the context of a revenge vendetta.) Better to ask indirectly, "What is his name?" Nor did the Waorani use words of greeting or farewell. Individuals simply came and went as each one pleased without verbal indicators. Despite earnest attempts at communication and a friendly atmosphere, the Waorani and the missionaries did not understand each other when they met on Palm Beach.

In the accounts that include the Waorani search for Dayomæ, it is clear that the missionaries had no idea what their visitors wanted. When Nænquiwi had initially indicated that Guiimadi was seeking Dayomæ, the men thought he was offering the young woman, whom they nicknamed "Delilah," to them. "My theory," wrote Fleming in a statement loaded with cultural assumptions, "is that he [Nænquiwi] had been sent with the girl and her mother to give us the girl in exchange for paring knives and beads."[33] Nor did the Americans catch Guiimadi's repetition of the word "Dayomæ, Dayomæ, Dayomæ," perhaps because the Wao pronunciation differed from that used by the Americans. Though not physically present, Dayomæ was a factor in this first encounter, an indicator of things to come.[34]

The fact remained that three "savage Aucas" were present on the beach, apparently friendly. Just as in the days of the Apostles or pioneer missionaries, Christianity had made contact with people who had never heard of its God or its message. Nothing could dampen the enthusiasm of the five men as they offered prayers of thanksgiving and entertained their guests. The missionaries made as many gestures of friendship as possible. They offered their visitors lemonade and hamburgers and insect repellant, showed them *Time* magazine, and demonstrated such marvels of modern civilization "as rubber bands, balloons, and a yo-yo."[35] Careful to find angles that preserved standards of modesty acceptable to evangelicals in the United States, the men took photographs and even home movies of the encounter, the first time the Waorani had been photographed in their own territory.

Saint gave Nænquiwi, nicknamed "George" since the men did not know his name, three short plane rides, two of them over the nearby Wao clearing. Nænquiwi's eagerness to fly encouraged the missionaries to stage an elaborate pantomime to demonstrate how the Waorani could clear an airstrip for the plane near their own village. They planted sticks in the sand to represent trees and swooped their wooden model of the Piper Cruiser down to "crash" against them and flip over while the men made exaggerated expressions and gestures of consternation. Then the "trees" were cleared away with energetic axe and machete strokes by the missionary mimes, the sand smoothed, and the model plane brought in for a safe landing to cheers all around. The Waorani watched, but Elisabeth Elliot, who would narrate the film made from footage shot that day, later commented dryly, "I am afraid they didn't get the message."[36]

Throughout the day the Waorani seemed friendly, though maddeningly nonchalant toward their hosts. Near the end of the afternoon, Guiimadi's mood visibly changed. Somewhat abruptly, she turned and walked away into the forest, followed by Nænquiwi. Mintaca, the older woman, remained on the beach "talking" with Youderian well into the night. When the men awoke the next morning, she had gone.[37]

Cautiously by radio during the day—lest others monitoring the signals find them out—and more fully when Saint and Fleming flew back to Arajuno that night, the men communicated details of their successful encounter to their wives. Marilou McCully and Barbara Youderian got firsthand reports in Arajuno and took charge of the film and diaries the men sent for safekeeping. Unable to share the secret with others in Shandia, including Rachel Saint, who was there, Elisabeth Elliot rejoiced over what she knew was the most exciting day of her husband's life. In Shell Mera, the missionary aviation headquarters, Olive Fleming had listened over Marj Saint's shoulder during the day as Marj maintained flight contact with Nate. All saw the "astonishingly friendly" encounter as an answer to prayer and, once again, evidence of God's involvement in the project.[38]

"How could we not rejoice with them," wrote Olive Fleming. "Imagine, a savage Indian man riding over his village in a plane, shouting with glee all the way." Considering what appeared to be the childlike trust of the Waorani, Olive, a twenty-three-year-old missionary wife, "felt a little ashamed" over her own worries about the safety of Pete, her husband of eighteen months. "Perhaps I had not really trusted God to do the impossible." In the darkness of that Friday night, however, her fears returned in force in the form of a vivid nightmare. "I saw Nate's plane on the beach, and five dead bodies around it. It felt so real that I couldn't calm myself down. I had been excited for the men earlier that evening; my hope had been renewed. Why the dream?"[39] The dream was the only dark note in a triumphant day for the missionaries.

While Olive Fleming attempted to reconcile her tangled emotions with her trust in God, tangles of another sort were affecting the Wao community. The several available Wao accounts of events of the next two days, Saturday and Sunday, January 7 and 8, 1956, vary some in particulars. All come filtered through translators, most with some stake in the story.[40] However, enough common ground exists to sketch a basic narrative.

"LET'S GO AND KILL"

Following Guiimadi as she left Palm Beach and entered the forest, Nænquiwi did not act as the emissary the missionaries had hoped for. Instead the two Waorani spent the night in the jungle, and Nænquiwi returned to the Wao clearing more determined than ever to marry Guiimadi. "I'm just going to spear and kill all of you," he threatened the group, as the argument over the marriage broke out again. One participant recalled that "everyone was yelling and screaming." Finally, Guiimadi's brother Nampa said, in effect, "Okay, do it!" (Marry her!) Infuriated, he took Guiimadi and shoved her into a hammock with Nænquiwi, an act indicating marriage.[41] Still furious, Nampa swung his blowgun against a tree with so much anger that he broke it. Then he smashed his dart holder and his poison pot. "You've been threatening to kill me," Nampa told Nænquiwi. "Now I've married her to you, now I'm going to kill a c. [*cowode*]," an act of displaced anger. Preparing spears with his own signature pattern of macaw feathers and then smearing them with red achiote dye (to mimic both the color and the odor of blood), Nampa called to his uncle Guequita, "Come on, let's go and kill!"[42]

The Waorani believed that *cowode* were cannibals and that it was kill or be killed. Despite Mintaca's description of the men as friendly, the long history of outside aggression against the Waorani fueled their anger. The missionaries had some inkling of the changed mood at the Wao clearing. Saturday, January 7, had begun quietly. The day wore on, with no sign of visitors. Curious, Saint made three trips over the cluster of Waorani houses. On the first trip, he noticed that instead of coming into the open to greet 56 Henry, Waorani women and children ran for cover. To assuage their fears, Saint called out in Wao from the plane's loudspeaker, "Come . . . come . . . come!" and dropped gifts of a blanket, a pot, and a pair of nylon swimming trunks. He reported that the Waorani "seemed relieved." From Saint's perspective, the response to two subsequent flyovers that same day was more positive. On both flights, he spotted Nænquiwi in the clearing along with other men. By the third flight he reported that Nænquiwi was smiling.[43]

The missionaries were eager for further contact and an invitation to visit the Wao clearing. Already they were planning "to get the airstrip in [at the Waorani settlement] as soon as possible," although they cautioned themselves "to wait and see how God leads us, and them, too."[44] Neither the two men at Arajuno nor the three still on the beach rested well Saturday night. All anticipated a possible encounter the next day. At 8:45 the next morning Saint and Fleming again climbed into the little plane for the flight to the beach.[45]

Not long afterward, a group of six Wao men, carrying nineteen spears among them, and accompanied by four women, set out to kill the foreigners.[46] The men were Guequita, Nampa, Yowe, Nemonca, Mincaye, and Quemo. Guequita was about forty years old. The rest were in their late teens or early twenties. The women were Acawo, Mintaca, Dawa (Quemo's wife), and Meñemo (Nænquiwi's sister). Nampa and Guequita were key to carrying out the attack: Nampa's anger incited the others, and Guequita, an experienced killer, encouraged the younger men to spear. Guequita later said that he had hoped that if Nampa and Nænquiwi killed *cowode*, they would get over their anger and life in the clearing would become more tranquil.[47] In the end, Nænquiwi did not participate.

"they're on their way!"

As another few hours passed with no sign of Waorani, Saint took to the skies once more. He flew over the clearing but saw only a few women and children. On his way back, however, he spotted the ten Waorani—probably as they emerged from the dense jungle to cross the Tewæno River—heading for the beach. Almost before the wheels touched down on the Curaray sand, Saint was shouting to his friends that the Waorani were coming. At 12:45 he radioed his wife at Shell Mera. "Pray for us. This *is* the day! Will contact you next at 4:30."[48]

Later accounts from the Waorani describe what happened at about 3:00, when they reached the beach. Details vary widely in the different stories. The memories of some Waorani have shifted over the years, and all were affected by the chaos of the attack. In one plausible scenario, two Wao women—Acawo and Dawa—emerged from the forest as decoys. Two missionaries, perhaps Youderian and Fleming, approached to greet them. As they did, Nampa burst out of a thick stand of cane behind them and came running with his spear ready. One man turned and saw Nampa. He reached for a pistol in a holster or in a pocket as Acawo and possibly Dawa grabbed him. The pistol went off at hip level, pointing upward. Simultaneously Nampa reached the missionary, running him through with a spear as the gun was fired. The bullet hit Nampa under the eyebrow, beside the nose, and he collapsed on the sand beside the fallen missionary. Meanwhile, Nemonca, coming from downriver, speared the second man. (Another account has only one missionary greeting the women, while the other is killed trying to get into the plane, perhaps to use the radio.) A third missionary, identified by the Waorani (Yowe and Guequita) as Elliot, crossed the Curaray and stood on a log shouting, "E airani!" ("Leave off!" or "Stop!") "We aren't going to kill you!" Quemo pursued him across the river and killed him. Back on the camp side of the river, Mincaye and Yowe killed McCully, while Guequita and Nemonca speared Saint.[49]

The attack was rapid and chaotic. Specific identifications of who killed whom have varied over the years as the Waorani have remembered that day. During attacks, several Waorani often would spear the same victims to share the responsibility.[50] A bloody 1961 description by Mincaye had most of the missionaries dying from multiple spearings.[51] The men did have weapons—their records indicated two or three pistols, a couple of .22 rifles, and a carbine.[52] They had decided to use the guns only to frighten—or, in an extreme emergency, to wound—the Waorani as a means of self-defense.[53] Some apparently fired into the air. However, after the initial surprise and the struggle with Nampa, the various accounts agree that the missionaries made no effort to defend themselves. Nampa, the one Wao man shot by the missionaries, initially survived, but according to several accounts, later died from the wound. Quemo's wife, Dawa, may have received a superficial injury, a powder burn or slight graze from shot pellets, either while she was hiding or while participating in the scuffle that wounded Nampa.[54]

It is impossible to know if the bullet that hit Nampa was fired intentionally in self-defense, as a reflex in response to the surprise attack, or by accident. The various versions agree that it happened in the context of a struggle. The specifics have been hotly contested over the years. Since 1974 critics have charged Rachel Saint and the Summer Institute of Linguistics with trying to conceal the gunshot and Nampa's death to make the missionaries look more heroic. The earliest published accounts contained significant inaccuracies, but neither Rachel nor SIL denied the shooting.[55]

The attack was over in minutes. Nate Saint's watch stopped at 3:12 p.m. The roll of film in his camera concluded with shots of the Friday visit. The Waorani ripped the fabric off the plane before leaving the site. Beginning in 1989 some of the Waorani who had participated in the attack reported seeing some sort of supernatural apparition at the time of the men's deaths—singing and lights or figures in the sky along a ridge above the river.[56] None of the earlier accounts mentions the vision. With Nampa barely conscious, the group spent the night at the top of the ridge. At daybreak they left, later burning their homes and disappearing into the jungle.[57]

BREAKING THE SILENCE

In Shell Mera, Marj Saint waited for the 4:30 radio contact. The ongoing silence indicated that something was wrong. Worried, she told Olive Fleming, "Nate would never leave the plane there overnight."[58] The women maintained the secrecy of the project until the next morning, when Johnny Keenan, Nate Saint's fellow missionary pilot, accompanied by Roger Youderian's wife, Barbara, flew over the Curaray beach. They saw no sign of the missionaries, only the skeleton of the plane. Once Keenan radioed back this information, the secret was out, and news of the men's disappearance spread quickly. Missionaries in the 1950s might still have answered the traditional call to take the gospel to the ends of the earth, but those geographic reaches were remarkably accessible in an emergency. Radio communication and aviation had done much to lessen the isolation compared to only a few years earlier.

The presence of missionary radio station HCJB, based in Quito, and the existence of an airfield at Shell Mera sturdy enough to receive heavy aircraft (a legacy of the Shell Oil Company) made the missionary stations of eastern Ecuador among the most accessible jungle outposts in the world.[59] HCJB served as a key conduit of information, both for search and rescue and for providing news about the missing men. The station's signal, transmitted at 50,000 watts, could be heard around the world.[60] First thoughts Monday morning were of search and rescue. Larry Montgomery, a missionary pilot with Wycliffe Bible Translators and a member of the air force reserves, suggested contacting the US Caribbean Command, headquartered in the Canal Zone, only about eight hundred miles by air from Shell. The head of the Caribbean Command was William K. Harrison, a two-star general and devout Christian, who knew some of the missing missionaries. He opened his home in Panama to traveling missionaries, and Pete and Olive Fleming had stayed there in 1954 on their way to Ecuador after their marriage. The following year Harrison had visited Jim and Elisabeth Elliot at their Shandia station.

The general authorized his chief of staff, Col. Robert May, to coordinate an effort by the US Air Rescue Service, in conjunction with the US Air Force attaché in Quito and the Ecuadorian military. By Wednesday two USAF C-47 cargo planes, transporting a dismantled helicopter, had landed at Shell. The Caribbean Command would have responded to the needs of any Americans within its area of operations, but Harrison's high profile as a conservative Christian and his acquaintance with the missing men facilitated a rapid response. It also added to the drama and significance surrounding the men's fate.[61]

HCJB's founder and director Clarence Jones made the first announcement to American audiences about the missing men during the broadcast of the station's popular *Back Home Hour* at 6:45 Monday evening, a little more than twenty-four hours after the attack. Jones's report beat the first notices over the Associated Press wires, not out until Tuesday. It also preceded the arrival of telegrams to some of the families, who, until they heard Jones's report, had not known their sons were engaged in the risky venture.[62]

NEWSPAPERS CARRY THE STORY

On Tuesday, January 10, in addition to the first AP report, news about the missionaries appeared in the *Chicago Daily News* and the *Milwaukee Journal*. On Wednesday, newspapers across the country ran the story, on page 1 in the early editions of the *Los Angeles Times*, the *Kansas City Times* and *Star*, and the men's hometown press. For the next four days, from Wednesday, January 11, until Saturday, January 14, Americans followed the missionary drama in Ecuador. Most of the stories were from AP reports, based on phone interviews, press releases, and broadcast bulletins from HCJB. Robert Savage, a missionary and spokesperson for HCJB, fielded phone calls from ABC, CBS, NBC, and other news organizations.[63] Initial accounts held out hope for the survival of at least some of the men, bolstered by reports published Thursday, January 12, that a commercial pilot had spotted two of them, waving a white shirt in a call for help.[64] Hopes were dashed as subsequent news stories confirmed the deaths of all five and the burial of four of the bodies near the small beach where they had spent their last days.

Newspaper accounts carried angles of interest beyond drama and tragedy. The missionaries were celebrated for using technology to contact "savage, stone-age tribesmen." The role of aviation attracted attention at a time when Americans had begun to travel by plane in record numbers. Early AP stories identified the men as "flying missionaries," while *Time* magazine described how they had used a plane to prepare for their face-to-face encounter.[65] Underlying both popular and evangelical interest in the missionary story and heightening its drama were a number of contrasts, including the contrast between the "stone-age" primitivism of the Waorani and the technology and civilization of the missionaries, as well as the contrast between the savagery attributed to the Waorani and the "wholesome, small-college boy" image surrounding the five young men.[66]

The Waorani were among the most feared indigenous peoples of South America. Even so, publicity surrounding the missionaries' deaths both sensationalized and dehumanized them. They were mistakenly identified as headhunters and described as having "the instincts of jungle beasts [combined] with human intelligence."[67] Newspapers also printed false reports that the attackers had mutilated and decapitated the bodies. Since 1949 press coverage of both mainline Protestant and Catholic missionaries had focused largely on the atrocities and suffering they had experienced at the hands of Chinese Communists. Though Communism played no role in the deaths of the Ecuador missionaries, press accounts of the tragedy drew from familiar themes of missionary courage in the face of savagery and danger.[68] The editor of one Christian magazine made an explicit connection: "No braver answer to the blatant denials, the blasphemous physical and mental tortures of atheistic

Communism has been offered in our time than the martyred dying of these five young Americans for the One Whom they adored and to Whom they gave that last full measure."[69]

Photographs of the Ecuador five featured in the press showed young men who were a far cry from the starch and formality of the Victorian missionary. Ed McCully was pictured in an open-collared shirt rather than suit and tie; Nate Saint exuded the confidence of a young pilot, with a grin on his face and a billed cap shoved back on his head. The AP wire service also circulated photographs of the men with their families, pictures that mirrored millions of other postwar couples doing their best to produce the baby boom generation. The images communicated lives full of promise, lives dedicated to missionary service, lives that had been tragically cut short.[70] These young men and their wives exemplified the postwar idealism that characterized missionaries and humanitarian workers alike and that invested other young Americans abroad, such as a Catholic medical doctor named Tom Dooley in Laos, with a kind of celebrity status.[71]

As the images and stories of the young missionaries found a prominent place in the American press, their widows and friends in the Ecuadorian jungles faced the realities of loss. Initially, the wives clung to the hope that at least some of the men might have survived. They waited and maintained their faith in God with a fortitude that sometimes seemed to border on stoicism. If tears were shed or doubts harbored, the women did so in private. Olive Fleming, the youngest of the wives, looked back years later at her private struggles: "At one point, I pled with God to bring Pete back for the Quichua work. Then, realizing that I really wanted him back for *me*, I felt guilty, as if it were somehow selfish to miss my husband. My thoughts leaped from one extreme to another as I tried to understand why this had happened. I couldn't believe God would allow the sacrifice of five men for only fifty Indians."[72]

By Thursday, however, it was becoming clear that no one had escaped. Maj. Malcolm Nurnberg of the USAF Mission in Ecuador flew to Palm Beach in an army helicopter. On the beach, he found nothing, but from the air he spotted four bodies, caught at various points downstream among the debris of the shallow river. Meanwhile, a search party of missionaries, Ecuadorian soldiers, and Quichuas was making the overnight trek to the site on foot and by canoe. As they went, they met a smaller party of Quichuas on their way back. They were from Arajuno and had known McCully. They had found McCully's body on the beach at the edge of the water the day before and were returning with his watch. That evening, as Nurnberg met with the wives and described what he had seen from the air, two more bodies were identified. "This one had on a red belt of some woven material." Peter Fleming. Another was clad in a T-shirt and blue jeans. Only Roger Youderian had blue jeans.[73]

On Friday morning, January 13, the ground party reached the deserted beach. Only the tree house and the airplane remained. The rotten smell from a large pot of beans, tipped over during the attack and now scattered on the sand, reinforced the reality of decay. At 12:15 the helicopter arrived once again, this time to help the ground crew locate the bodies. Four were recovered and identified from wedding rings and other personal effects. The fifth, that of McCully, apparently had been washed away after its identification by the Quichuas two days earlier and was never found. All five men were now confirmed dead.

In the helicopter with the military crew was Cornell Capa, a photographer on assignment for *Life* magazine. First from the air and then on the beach, Capa picked up the photographic record of Operation Auca. His initial shots were of death: a partially submerged body, white rubber soles of tennis shoes visible, and a spear protruding from the right hip; the darkness and torrential storm that shrouded the quick burial service on the beach. Capa's older brother, Robert, a well-known war photographer, had been killed in Indochina just two years earlier. In the gray dawn of D-Day, June 6, 1944, Robert Capa had made gritty black-and-white photographs of American troops landing on Omaha Beach. Now his brother recorded the aftermath of the missionaries' small, self-described D-day on a patch of Ecuadorian sand. Cornell Capa's photos looked like they, too, came from a war zone, as Ecuadorian soldiers stood guard, rifles ready to repel a feared Waorani attack. The darkness of the storm created an eerie atmosphere that to some of those in the search party represented the cosmic battle between light and darkness, good and evil. Certainly darkness reigned in the pictures Capa took that afternoon and his later description of the scene:

> The rain was coming down in buckets; my handkerchief served no more to clean my water-soaked lenses. Suddenly I saw a struggling group of men carrying the last of the missionaries to his common grave. He was on an improvised stretcher, made out of the aluminum sheets that had covered the tree house where the men had lived.
>
> . . . The pallbearers struggled against a muddy bank that led to the grave. I just made it in time to see the lifeless legs disappearing into the hole. Grim, weary missionaries looked for the last time at their friends, whom they could no more identify.[74]

Missionary Frank Drown, who led the search party, conducted a brief burial service from memory in the pouring rain.

Capa accompanied the search party overnight on their return, before a helicopter picked him up and ferried him to Shell Mera. Still emotionally raw from the loss of a revered older brother, he captured poignant images in black and white of young widows, babies and Bibles cradled in their arms. In one photo, Stevie Saint stands alone on the porch of his home only two weeks before his fifth birthday with the parrot, a gift from the Waorani in more hopeful times. Both are silhouetted against an empty sky where 56 Henry would never again appear.

Capa's work was published two weeks later as a ten-page documentary essay in *Life* magazine, "'Go Ye and Preach the Gospel': Five Do and Die."[75] It served as summary and climax to the intense publicity surrounding the men's deaths during January 1956. The *Life* essay was the first in a popular publication to explicitly describe the men as "martyrs," and it took full advantage of the magazine's "visually assertive" style. The opening two-page spread juxtaposed a Capa photograph of the five widows around the kitchen table at the Saint home in Shell Mera against a full body shot of Nænquiwi, "a savage Auca, his ear lobes distended by wooden plugs," taken by Nate Saint. Everything necessary to communicate faith, grief, idealism, and treachery—American goodness against savage ignorance—was present, or absent. The kitchen with its refrigerator, its cabinets, the windows over the sink, could have been any ordinary American kitchen in the 1950s.

The women listen to missionary doctor Art Johnson describe their husbands' burial. A pregnant Marilou McCully bows her head, her hand over her eyes. Barbara Youderian and Marj Saint gaze in exhaustion at Johnson over the heads of the young sons they are cradling. Jerry Lee Youderian is twenty-one months old; Philip Saint just a year. Olive Fleming and Elisabeth Elliot hang on to the doctor's words. All are composed, and the scene is compelling in its ordinariness. Women around a kitchen table with a clutter of plates and half-eaten sandwiches. Next to them visually is the Waorani warrior: naked, powerful, serious, and enigmatic. Present by their absence are the five men—husbands to the women, missionaries to the Waorani—now gone. The visual power of this opening spread was so great that *Life* was willing to airbrush the photo of Nænquiwi, adding a loin cloth to his *come* (hip-cord or G-string), so that the photograph would be more acceptable both to fundamentalists and to *Life*'s family-oriented readership.[76]

These and images on the following pages were made more powerful by the decision to draw heavily from Pete Fleming's and Nate Saint's diaries, plus brief quotations from Jim Elliot's journal, for the text of the article. This allowed the men to communicate their own idealism, adventurousness, and sense of mission. They had, as *Life* faithfully reported to an America still generally sympathetic toward such ideals, gone to preach the gospel to those who had never heard it, trusting God for the outcome. The essay touched a chord among *Life*'s readers, who praised it as "'the most inspiring article ever in *Life*,' and '*Life*'s greatest reporting feat.'"[77] Nearly four decades later Cornell Capa remembered the story as his "most rewarding assignment," one that elicited "a deluge of enthusiastic letters."[78] Through this article and subsequent work, Capa, a self-described "nonobservant Hungarian Jew" and humanitarian, would rank second only to Jim Elliot's widow, Elisabeth, as the martyrologist who provided images and highlighted themes that would define the deaths of the five missionaries for American popular culture.[79]

<h2 style="text-align:center">"WIVES CARRY ON"</h2>

The final two pages of the *Life* essay had the subtitle "The Wives Carry On, Trusting That Aucas Will Still Be Saved." On Sunday, January 15, a week after their husbands were killed, the five women attended an 11:00 memorial service in Shell Mera with other members of the missionary community. Those present found solace in the Bible and assurance that the men had not died in vain.[80] Later that evening another memorial service, held in Quito, was broadcast by HCJB to American listeners via the *Back Home Hour*. As a part of that broadcast, Clarence Jones announced the establishment of the Five Missionary Martyrs Trust Fund to aid the widows and children. Within a few months contributions to the fund would top fifty-six thousand dollars.[81] Other services would take place in the men's hometowns and elsewhere, and on February 16 Ecuadorian president José Velasco Ibarra held a ceremony in the presidential palace to honor the sacrificial work of Protestant missionaries in his country, particularly the efforts of the five slain men.

Amid the tributes and ongoing publicity, life inevitably went on. The five widows faced decisions about the future, as well as the immediate task of helping their young children accept the death of a father. Choices were most pressing for Marilou McCully, entering her ninth month of pregnancy. She decided to return to the United States for the baby's birth; the other widows accompanied her to the house Ed had built a year earlier at Arajuno to help pack her personal belongings. Within a short time, the house stood empty. Marilou, with sons Steve, four, and Mike, one, flew to her parents' home in Pontiac, Michigan. She worried about the impact of all the upheaval on the boys. Stevie was old enough to express a sense of loss. "I know my daddy is with Jesus," he said, "but I miss him, and I wish he would just come down and play with me once in a while."[82] Beth Youderian, also four, had trouble comprehending what had happened to her father. When Barbara Youderian returned to her home station among the Jívaro (Shuar) people, Beth climbed out of the plane looking expectantly toward the small group of missionaries waiting for them. "Bethy thought her daddy would be here to meet her," Barbara explained. "Although I've told her many times all that has happened, she was sure she would find Roj in Macuma."[83]

In the 1950s evangelical missionaries rarely left their posts for reasons other than furlough, ill health, or failure. For young women, the death of a husband did not mitigate God's call to the mission field. In fact it may have made that call more intense. If their husbands had given their lives to preach the Christian message to the Waorani, surely the wives should continue that work in some way. Nor were single women an oddity among Christian workers abroad. Among the personnel of conservative faith missions, women outnumbered men nearly two to one.

Four of the five widows decided to remain in Ecuador. Elisabeth Elliot and ten-month-old Valerie returned to their mission station among the lowland Quichuas. Elisabeth taught school, provided basic medical services, and continued to translate portions of the Bible into Quichua. "I came to Ecuador to serve the Lord and not Jim," she later told Cornell Capa. "With him gone, my duty did not change."[84] Barbara Youderian and her children joined a medical missionary, Dorothy Walker, to establish a missionary presence at Congaimi, a small jungle station among the Jivaroan peoples. Marilou McCully, who returned to Ecuador with her three sons in December 1956, and Marj Saint, also with three small children, left the jungles for the city of Quito. Marilou took charge of a boardinghouse for missionary children, while Marj ran the HCJB guesthouse, welcoming as many as a dozen visiting missionaries or church workers and their families at any given time.

Olive Fleming, with limited language skills in Spanish or Quichua, few ties to Ecuador, and the awareness that her missionary calling had been in the context of marriage to Pete, struggled to find a niche. After spending most of 1956 in the United States, then returning briefly to Ecuador to help Marilou McCully settle in with her children, she decided that her future lay elsewhere. She ended her brief career as a foreign missionary in March 1957, leaving Quito for good after unpacking and giving away many of the wedding gifts she and Pete had left in storage when they had moved to the jungle just months before his death.

It was a difficult decision. Supporters back home questioned the move: it held overtones of a retreat unworthy of her husband's death and of their understanding of God's will. "Some even quoted the [Bible] verse, 'No one who puts his hand to the plow and looks back is fit for the kingdom of God.'"[85] Bolstered by friends and her own sense of divine guidance, Olive Fleming returned to the United States, where she eventually accepted a job as secretary to the president of Shelton College, a small school in northern New Jersey. In June 1959 she married Walter Liefeld, a young pastor pursuing a PhD at Columbia University, who was an alumnus of the college.[86]

In death the five missionaries to the Waorani had become national figures. Americans, especially evangelicals, were drawn to the story of these young men: their faith, their American ingenuity, their pioneering adventures, their willingness to risk their lives, and the courage of their wives. At the same time, most published reports in the popular media ended on a tragic note. Even the *Life* essay, with its overtones of valor and martyrdom, chronicled the final months and days before the men were killed. As Elisabeth Elliot observed, "To the world at large this was the sad waste of five young lives."[87] The spiritual significance of the Ecuador missionaries' deaths was still not clear, their transformation from victims to martyrs incomplete. That transformation would take place in the months to come.

2

The Home Front

STORIES THAT ESTABLISHED the slain missionaries as icons of evangelical spirituality appeared over a period of about a year and a half. As daily papers ended their coverage, *Life, Time,* and *Newsweek* picked it up. The *Life* essay marked the culmination of coverage in mass-circulation papers and news magazines. Religious newspapers and magazines, with their longer production schedules, were just gearing up with articles for evangelical readers. Nearly all the major independent fundamentalist or evangelical periodicals featured the story in either their February or March 1956 issues, including the *Sunday School Times, Christian Life, Moody Monthly,* and *Youth for Christ.* In August a "condensed book" version appeared in *Reader's Digest.* In late May 1957 Elisabeth Elliot's *Through Gates of Splendor* was published, becoming an immediate bestseller and followed quickly by biographies of Jim Elliot and Nate Saint.

Most articles in secular papers hesitated to describe the men as martyrs, but the conservative religious press had no doubts. Using language familiar from missionary memoirs, evangelical magazines and newspapers proclaimed the men "midcentury martyrs" and "valiant saints," heroes who bore witness "to the power of the Christian faith which makes men willing to follow God's leading even unto death." When the *Sunday School Times* published a collection of news releases from Ecuador, the article was titled "Five 'Valiant Saints, Their Hope They Knew,'" a phrase taken from "The Son of God Goes Forth to War," a Reginald Heber hymn celebrating Jesus Christ, "triumphant over pain." Like the apostles of old, the five

Ecuador missionaries had "mocked the cross and flame," counting brutal death as nothing to follow the Savior.[1]

There were reports that one of the wooden lances used to kill the men had pages from a Spanish New Testament wrapped around it, an observation that tacitly reinforced the idea of hostility toward the Christian gospel, even though the Waorani had no concept of Christianity, of missionaries, of the Bible, or even of writing. The reports were based on a Capa photo of a lance that had been wrapped with a gospel tract used as a grip. Apparently the missionaries had used the tract to wrap and protect one of the gifts they had dropped from the air, and the Waorani reused it. Their attack had nothing to do with Christianity. It was a culturally conditioned act of rage.[2]

Despite the honor given the men as martyrs, finding triumph in apparent tragedy wasn't easy. Friends and family grappled with loss and pain. Fred Elliot, Jim's father, wept in anguish over the death of a son. "Why couldn't God have taken me instead?" he asked his wife. "He was so young. He had a whole lifetime of service to give the Savior. Why did he have to die?"[3] The themes of heroism, boldness, bravery, and sacrifice in evangelical newspapers and magazines were a response to persistent questions: Why did it happen? Why would young men with so much potential risk their lives and ultimately die for a small rainforest tribe nobody cared about? Why did God allow them to be killed?[4]

The evangelical press addressed the lingering doubts. The men were not foolish. Theirs was not "the fool-hardy courage of five young adventurers on a spur-of-the-moment escapade."[5] Reports from Ecuador emphasized the "thorough, ingenious, and remarkable preparations [the men made] to establish contact with the Aucas." Their motives were pure, grounded in a profound desire "to bring to the Aucas the transforming power of the Gospel of Jesus Christ."[6] Nor were the Waorani ultimately to blame for what had happened. In a radically faith-centric view of a premodern Amazonian culture, evangelicals viewed the Waorani as unwitting pawns in the cosmic spiritual conflict referred to in the New Testament. "Christian missions is not a game. . . . It is a warfare, a deadly earnest struggle against the powers of darkness."[7] The idea that the Waorani were a group caught up in an especially powerful manifestation of the battle between good and evil became an ongoing theme. Even so, ultimate victory remained certain. The deaths of the missionaries would prove once again, in the repeated paraphrase of the church father Tertullian, that the "blood of the martyrs is the seed of the Church."[8] The sacrifice in Ecuador would bear fruit for evangelical Christianity among the Waorani, in the US, and in other parts of the world.

It had already served as a wake-up call at home. In a tribute to his younger brother Nate, missionary Phil Saint observed, "Back in the homeland many Christians are taking stock of their own lives." Material possessions, such as "the shiny new car sitting in the driveway," the "fancy clothes," or the "hours spent sitting comfortably before the television set bring a haunting sense of spiritual delinquency."[9] Young people especially were reevaluating their lives. Magazines printed encouraging reports of renewed dedication, such as the five hundred students who committed themselves to the mission field at Northwestern College in Minneapolis, Roger Youderian's alma mater.[10] Such responses reflected the extent to which the evangelical rank and file throughout the United States had been caught up in the unfolding story of Operation Auca. This "was something new in missionary history," suggested one writer. "The jungle was brought right into the front rooms of folks at home."[11]

Other families may have struggled with loss, as Fred Elliot had done, but rarely in public. T. E. McCully, Ed's father, used his platform as executive director of the Christian Business Men's Committee to tell the story of his son's faith and to affirm his own trust in God. Letters and poems from Elisabeth Elliot affirmed the "triumph of Christ."[12] *Moody Monthly* magazine pointed to the "brave, bold, Christ-honoring faith" of Nate Saint's entire extended family—his wife, mother, father, sister, brothers, and even his seven-year-old daughter, Kathy.

While the military searched for her father, Kathy spent the hours "giving tracts to little native boys at Shell Mera." While doing so, she noticed one of the US soldiers smoking a cigarette, an action that convinced the child he was not a Christian. In response, Kathy positioned her record player near the soldier and his colleagues and began to play gospel records, including "Jesus Loves Me." The report concluded that "having played the records for some time, she returned them to the house, saying 'Now, he knows, too.' "[13] Kathy was mimicking the intense drive of American evangelicals in general, but particularly of the missionary community, to use the written and spoken word to communicate the gospel message. During the postwar period, evangelicals had renewed efforts to reach the entire world for Christ. The deaths in Ecuador inspired them to keep going. "Tears, Yes . . . but Triumph, Too!" was the title of an article containing the widows' reminiscences a year after the killings, emphasizing their confidence that God could give meaning to apparent tragedy.

"It would be easy to wish it were all different," Marj Saint wrote, "to wish that Nate were here with me and that Ed, Jim, Pete and Roger were with their wives." But, continued Saint, to wish such things would be to give up all that had been accomplished by the impact of the men's deaths.

It would mean my saying to little Carol who lives in Ohio, "Sorry, Carol, but the decision you made to take Christ as your Saviour last January is all off now because we are not just willing to give up our loved ones yet." And I would have to write to Gladys in Pennsylvania and say, "Go ahead with your plans to be married and live a quiet normal life in the USA instead of continuing with your decision to break your engagement and go to men and women in the foreign field who have never heard of Christ or salvation. The families of the five of us just can't get along without them."[14]

DISSENTING VOICES

Amid these expressions of meaning through faith in Christ, only a few dissenting voices spoke out in the pages of the Protestant press. The most controversial came shortly after the men's deaths in a brief editorial, "Five Missionaries Die Needlessly," in the *Christian Century*, a mouthpiece for the liberal wing of what was then mainline denominational Protestantism. The editorial reflected ongoing tensions between the mainline missionary establishment and independent evangelical missions. The tensions had their roots as far back as the late nineteenth century but had intensified as faith missions proliferated during the 1930s and 1940s.[15]

The *Century* acknowledged that the five men themselves had given "the last full measure of devotion in martyrdom" and did not explicitly criticize their efforts.[16] However, the editors infuriated evangelicals and offended many in their mainline readership by using the tragedy as a springboard to condemn the independent faith missions movement the men represented, a movement that sent them to "their unnecessary deaths." The independents, the *Century* charged, were shallowly conceived and hastily organized groups, exporting "hundreds of poorly trained young missionaries to the ends of the earth." This slipshod, hurried approach compared poorly with the mainline practice of demanding "historical, cultural, anthropological and linguistic training" and of placing new recruits in the field together with experienced staff. While recognizing that missionary activity held a certain amount of risk, the editorial contended that denominational missions, in contrast to their independent cousins, did "not court danger needlessly, or lose many lives through blundering or thirst for publicity."[17]

The *Century* editorial was only about three hundred words long, but heavy-handed, and even loyal readers responded with letters of indignation. Mainline Protestants, writers suggested, should examine themselves before throwing rocks at the competition. A Presbyterian described the editorial as "shameful." Another reader suggested "that if he were around today young Jesus ben Joseph *might* be acting just as foolishly as these men did!"[18]

A letter from Clyde W. Taylor, executive secretary of the Evangelical Foreign Missions Association, an umbrella association for conservative faith missions, disputed the suggestion that the missionaries to Ecuador were "the symbol of ill-trained workers identified with shallow independent Christian enterprises." Taylor pointed out that the missionaries were college graduates with "training in linguistics and anthropological studies," all, that is, except for the specialized worker Nate Saint, an experienced pilot. Taylor suggested that the real issue lay not in the realm of missionary methods but of theology. The theologically liberal *Century* "seized upon an hour of martyrdom" to express its hostility toward the evangelical message promoted by the independent agencies.[19]

Jack Murray, pastor of the Church of the Open Door in Philadelphia, agreed. In his radio broadcast, "Modernism and the Missionary Martyrs," Murray accused the modernists (liberals) of "sending out missionaries to teach people how to brush their teeth; how to plant carrots; how to have prettier bathrooms; how to read books; and how to get along with their neighbors, instead of proclaiming the matchless message of God's grace." In contrast, the five missionaries had died for the true gospel message and were "without fault before the throne of God" (quoting Revelation 14:5).[20]

Comments of this sort may have discouraged thoughtful criticism from within evangelical circles since questioning the men's actions might indicate a tendency toward liberalism or a possible defense of humanitarian work over preaching and evangelism. Few evangelicals even tried to analyze what had happened, at least not publicly. One who did was Robert B. Taylor, editor of *Practical Anthropology*, a fledgling journal for Christian anthropologists. Approaching the topic gingerly, Taylor acknowledged the "superior ability" of the missionaries and the care they took "in planning and executing their endeavor." At the same time, Taylor suggested that since God worked through human agency, it was appropriate to evaluate the missionaries' actions from a methodological perspective. He asked if a "greater degree of anthropological orientation or knowledge would have helped."[21] While stressing that anthropology was no panacea, Taylor insisted that if the field represented a worthwhile science, it should have something to offer missionaries seeking to contact hostile groups.

His modest proposals included a suggestion that future missionaries receive culturally oriented anthropology training. Such training would encourage and prepare them to learn as much as possible about a culture before seeking to enter it. Taylor also proposed that missionaries attempting pioneer work focus on language and do as much language study as possible. Throughout his comments Taylor's tone was diffident, and he took an agnostic stance toward the question of the actual use of anthropology by the dead missionaries. He simply wanted training in anthropology to be a part of "any further attempt to reach the Auca Indians or any other similar difficult group."[22]

Even this quiet plea for an examination of the men's methods met some resistance, expressed in letters to the editor. While agreeing with Taylor's suggestions, Don Burns, director of the Summer Institute of Linguistics in Ecuador, wrote that the only adequate perspective was the divine one. Humanly speaking, perhaps the men should have gone more slowly. However, Burns noted, "the heart of the martyr is deeply pressed with the urgency of the hour." Another letter also agreed with Taylor but claimed that the men in fact had done these very things. Taylor inserted an editorial note of his own, emphasizing that he had not intended to condemn the missionaries. He had gone to college with three of the men, had been a housemate with one, and had no "critical spirit" toward them or their endeavors.[23] The initial public analysis of Operation Auca ended there, carried out by offended modernists and a lone Christian anthropologist. Given the stress on God's providential leading and ultimate triumph in Christ, it was difficult even for friends to critique "the heart of the martyr."

It became increasingly clear that Elliot, Fleming, McCully, Saint, and Youderian would be remembered as martyrs and missionary heroes. But there was not yet a book-length narrative memorializing the men. From the time of their deaths, there had been calls for an authorized version of the story. Abe C. Van Der Puy, Ecuador field director for the World Radio Missionary Fellowship, the parent agency of station HCJB, seemed the logical choice to write it. Van Der Puy's press releases during the search efforts had provided information for the Associated Press and others. He had access to Nate Saint's detailed account of Operation Auca, as well as to excerpts from journals kept by Jim Elliot and Pete Fleming. Van Der Puy dedicated himself to the project during the weeks after the men's deaths, and by late February 1956 had nearly finished a manuscript.

SECOND ONLY TO THE BIBLE

Nate Saint's older brother Sam had agreed to represent the widows and their interests in the US, and Van Der Puy passed along their hope that the book would have a wide circulation in the secular world.[24] This ambition was realized and the story of Operation Auca given new impetus when Clarence Hall, senior editor of the *Reader's Digest*, came calling. Although the *Digest* published a hardbound Condensed Books series, which accepted some original manuscripts, Hall was interested in Van Der Puy's manuscript for the condensed book section at the end of the monthly magazine.

With its themes of real-life adventure, heroic Christianity, and stalwart faith, Operation Auca was perfect *Digest* fare. For missionaries interested in reaching a large audience, the *Digest* was in a class by itself. In terms of distribution, it was the next best thing to getting one's story inserted into the Bible. With net paid average sales of more than ten million copies monthly, the *Digest* enjoyed a circulation greater than any other publication in the history of type, the Bible alone excepted.[25] Unfortunately Van Der Puy's manuscript was not written in the dramatic style the magazine wanted.[26] With deadlines looming, Hall, himself a devout Christian, stepped in as ghostwriter. Van Der Puy offered his notes and research, and the widows supplied their husbands' journals. Hall wrote the *Digest* piece, which was published in August 1956, under Van Der Puy's name, despite his reluctance, and with the title he had suggested, "Through Gates of Splendor."[27] Even though Hall wrote the "condensation," the *Digest's* founder and publisher, DeWitt Wallace, paid the missionaries $20,000 for their story, twice the normal rate.[28]

The brief story emphasized action, an "extraordinary campaign" to take the Christian faith to "one of the most feared and savage Stone Age tribes left on earth."[29] Nate Saint was the key figure in the account, most often aided by Ed McCully. Saint's aerial exploits led to one success after another until the climax of the story: the first friendly meeting with the Waorani on the Curaray beach. Then came the mystery of the men's deaths. Finally, Hall provided a brief recap of the "astonishing response" to their sacrifice. Not only had the church in the United States reacted, but in Ecuador even Quichua and Jívaro Indians were signing up as evangelists and missionaries.[30]

The *Reader's Digest* selection informed readers that Van Der Puy's book would soon be published by Harper and Brothers. However, when the book appeared eight months later, its author was the young missionary widow Elisabeth Elliot. In November 1956 she had flown to New York City, thinking she was going to help with the final editing of the book-length version of "Through Gates of Splendor." When she arrived at the office of Harper's associate book editor Mel Arnold, however, he pointed her toward a typewriter and told her to write something. Surprised, Elliot asked Arnold what he wanted her to write. It didn't matter, Arnold responded, anything would do. Elliot complied, providing a vivid description of her adventures on a bus trip in Ecuador. Arnold pulled the sheet from the typewriter and read it. He informed Elliot that Harper's did not yet have a manuscript telling the story of her late husband and his friends but that during the next six weeks she would write it. The publisher would provide a suite in a nearby hotel and editorial assistance.[31]

Although the task was unexpected, Elliot possessed the eyewitness perspective and literary skills for the job. She needed longer than six weeks to complete a final manuscript, but she met the publication deadline. With permission from Van Der Puy and the *Digest*, the book used the same title as the "condensed" version, but the text was Elliot's own. Her version of *Through Gates of Splendor*, a spiritual "multibiography" of the five men, became an immediate bestseller. This was the inspirational book people had been waiting for. Part of Elliot's genius was including all five men in a single account. She drew heavily from their unpublished writings, shaped into a fast-paced narrative and given dimension through descriptions that vividly evoked the local color of missionary life in the Ecuadorian jungles. Elliot's writing was nonsectarian but deeply evangelical.[32] In her hands, the five "Ecuador martyrs" became missionaries not only to the Waorani but also to Americans on the home front, in the tradition of earlier books by or about missionary heroes or heroines.[33] Supported by Jim Elliot's biography, *Shadow of the Almighty* (1958), and Nate Saint's story, *Jungle Pilot* (1959), *Through Gates of Splendor* established the legacy of Operation Auca for American evangelicals.

Elisabeth Elliot abhorred religious jargon and was cautious in her use of the word "martyrdom," which appears only once in *Through Gates of Splendor*. Yet she had nearly perfect pitch when it came to expressing the nuances of evangelical spirituality. Elliot came from a family of writers and editors who considered the influential *Sunday School Times* "the family paper." Her great-uncle Charles G. Trumbull had been the foremost twentieth-century American proponent of Keswick ("Higher Life") teachings, which stressed a victorious Christianity.[34] Elliot drew from her familiarity with Keswick to be sure that the spiritual emphases in the book rang true to conservative Christian readers. At the same time, she used language that made sense to anyone in the broader public who might pick up the book.

Elliot followed traditional martyrologies in allowing the dead men to speak for themselves. Except for one, each of the nineteen chapters of *Through Gates of Splendor* contained quotations, often extensive, from the letters or diaries of the men. The exception was chapter 18, the story of the search efforts, appropriately titled, "Silence." The quotations included clear expressions of the all-out Christian commitment the men shared. Their comments represented updated versions of the call to total surrender or consecration characteristic of Keswick piety. Ed McCully wanted to "live a life of reckless abandon to the Lord"; Nate Saint found joy in leaving "the old life of chasing things that are of a temporal sort"; Roger Youderian sought to "live following Him [Christ] every second of my life."[35]

To Americans who in the mid-1950s had rediscovered their fascination with the frontier West, Elisabeth Elliot presented the men as "missionary pioneers—always looking to the regions beyond immediate horizons." Again, she exercised a deft touch. Roger Youderian had privately nicknamed the project "Operation David Crockett," a label with perhaps too much of the Indian fighter and not enough of the spiritual. Elliot kept the pioneering emphasis but dropped "David Crockett" in favor of "Operation Auca."[36]

GOD AS THE ULTIMATE AGENT

In the history of Christianity, accounts of martyrs almost always were designed to teach as well as inspire. *Through Gates of Splendor* was no exception. Although Elliot's text and the more than sixty photographs included in the book amply portrayed the activism of the young missionaries, her version of Operation Auca shifted the emphasis of the narrative from the *Reader's Digest* account in at least two ways. First, her narrative had a much stronger providential focus. More than the story of an event, it was a story of God at work through five men. Second, Jim Elliot became a prominent figure in a way he had not been in earlier published reports.

The most significant protagonist in *Through Gates of Splendor* was God himself, the ultimate agent behind all that happened. Elisabeth Elliot's explanation for the men and their decisions was that they took every step in obedience to God. To make that case, she frequently noted divine activity. "God *had* led Jim" since his childhood, she emphasized. After college graduation, Ed McCully entered law school. "But God . . . had other plans." Within a few years McCully, his wife, and their infant son were on their way to Ecuador, "where God had indicated he wanted them to spend their lives." September 1955, the month Operation Auca began, was "the month in which the Lord began to weave five separate threads into a single glowing fabric for His own Glory."[37] Most important, Elliot expressed the widows' conviction that "this was not a tragedy," but rather "was what God had planned."[38]

In addition to emphasizing divine involvement, Elliot broadened the context of Operation Auca to recognize her husband's significance. Jim's role had been less obvious in earlier versions largely because the voluminous journal he had kept since 1948 contained very little about the project to contact the Waorani. During the fall of 1955, when the men launched their effort, Jim had his hands full with the demands of his work among the Quichuas at Shandia, which was flourishing. He had been married for only two years, and much of the reflection he once poured into his journal he now discussed with his wife. The Elliots were new parents; life was busy. Jim had neither the time nor the need to maintain his journal as faithfully as he had in the past. He left almost no written account of the specifics of Operation Auca. Only two journal entries, dated October 29 and November 26, 1955, in addition to a few letters to his parents, mentioned the subject.

Yet Jim was a key figure in the project. He had recruited both McCully and Fleming to missionary service in Ecuador. Of the three "Brethren boys," Jim was the one who had first heard of the Waorani and had begun to consider peaceful contact. Once Operation Auca was under way, Jim was the most eager to encounter the Waorani face to face. Most important, it was his life as his widow re-created it from letters and the journal that provided the depth and passion that elevated Operation

Auca from a missionary project to a divinely inspired quest. For the *Life* magazine article, shortly after the men's deaths, Elisabeth Elliot had provided spiritual aphorisms from Jim's journal and letters that provided a framework for the heroic piety behind the endeavor. For example, in the face of Wao hostility, Jim affirmed a mandate from God. "Our orders are: the Gospel to every creature." It was Jim who articulated the faith of a man prepared to meet his Maker: "When it comes time to die, make sure all you have to do is die."[39]

Jim was not alone in his willingness to make the ultimate sacrifice. When the freighter carrying him and Fleming from the US arrived at the harbor of Guayaquil, Ecuador, the two men together quietly sang the hymn "Faith of Our Fathers," with its refrain, "Faith of our fathers, holy faith. We will be true to thee till death."[40] Having survived one serious plane crash, Nate Saint, too, understood the risks of his vocation. He "had always regarded himself as 'expendable' for the cause of Christ."[41] The other two men shared these sentiments as well, although all thought they had taken adequate precautions against a Wao attack.

Elisabeth Elliot assured her readers that these men were not social misfits. Jim was a champion wrestler, with a flair for the dramatic and the ability to recite "The Face on the Barroom Floor" and "The Cremation of Sam McGee" for his college classmates. McCully was the president of his class in college, a football star, a prize-winning orator, and a devoted husband and father. Fleming was a thoughtful scholar. Youderian had demonstrated his bravery during the Battle of the Bulge. Saint, an accomplished aviator and inventive mechanic, could put together bits and pieces to rig indoor plumbing and generate electricity for his jungle home. After the men's deaths, a letter described one of them as "the ideal of what a Christian should be." That description fit all the men profiled in *Through Gates of Splendor*. The book provided American evangelicals with case studies of true holiness, and the response was overwhelmingly positive.[42]

Through Gates of Splendor was a brief book that created its own world. There were no overt references to missionaries of the past or any but the most cursory discussions of social and cultural contexts apart from those defined by the lives of the five missionaries. Readers were not told that other missionaries besides the five men had hoped to contact the Waorani. In addition to Rachel Saint, Wilfred Tidmarsh, the senior Plymouth Brethren missionary in Amazonian Ecuador, had a longtime interest in the Waorani. Years before his younger colleagues arrived, he had begun developing a vocabulary list of Wao words, based on information from a Quichua Indian who had been captured by the Waorani and subsequently escaped.[43]

In March 1952, only a month after Pete Fleming and Jim Elliot had arrived in Ecuador, Tidmarsh talked with Fleming about a strategy for contacting the Waorani. With some modifications, the five missionaries of Operation Auca followed the broad contours of Tidmarsh's plan. Yet they did not tell the senior missionary, whom they (and others) considered something of an eccentric, what they were doing. God's will for Operation Auca apparently included neither Tidmarsh nor Rachel Saint, and *Through Gates of Splendor* gave no indication it could have been otherwise. The challenge of contacting the Waorani was the God-appointed destiny for only five men.

A CLASSIC OF EVANGELICAL SPIRITUALITY

Elisabeth Elliot pursued the inspirational and educational purposes of her book with absolute commitment. *Through Gates of Splendor* elevated the genuine and exceptional spirituality of the young men but tended to downplay aspects of their humanity, including any weaknesses they might have had. For example, she described Jim and Pete's trip from Quito, where they had been studying Spanish, to Shandia, their jungle station, as the journey of an intrepid missionary pair, rubbing shoulders with the locals as they headed toward their assignment. Her narrative described in detail what the men would have seen as they traveled by crowded bus over the Andes and down to the eastern rainforests. "Purple orchids nodded out over the road as the bus swayed and jerked along the narrow shelf of road, a precipice on the right, a steep wall of rock shouldering up on the left." The pair arrived in Shell Mera, met Tidmarsh, flew with him on the next leg of the trip, then hiked several hours to Shandia. "We have arrived at the destination decided on in 1950," Jim wrote. "My joy is full. Oh how blind it would have been to reject the leading of these days."[44]

Elisabeth Elliot had condensed a journey that spanned almost two weeks into a single day. On their trip from Quito, Jim and Pete were not exactly isolated pioneers. They had traveled over the mountains with eighteen Ecuadorian schoolboys, whom the fledgling missionaries would supervise for a week-long church camp at Shell Mera before heading to their own station. More poignantly, Jim left Quito fighting tears because he was leaving Elisabeth, with whom he was deeply in love but to whom he was not yet engaged. She still planned to pursue her own missionary work in a different part of Ecuador. Fidgety schoolboys, Bible camp, and the pains of courtship had little direct bearing on the heroic call of a jungle missionary and so did not find their way into *Through Gates of Splendor*.[45]

Finally, there was a certain dissonance in the book between the piety attributed to the missionaries and the actual procedures of Operation Auca, which often seemed like a bit of a lark. In their flights over the Wao longhouses, the men would circle different dwellings and watch people dash from one to the other, trying to anticipate where gifts would fall. On their third visit, choppy skies and a brisk northeast wind made it difficult for Saint and McCully to lower a machete with any degree of precision. After watching the Waorani attempt to position themselves as the machete swung wildly at the end of the long dropline, Saint wrote, "Several times when it was lowering near them they would scramble helter-skelter in that direction. It is really great sport." Saint seemed oblivious to the possibility that this was not sport for the Waorani or to how possession of the machete might affect relations among them.[46]

On subsequent flights, the missionaries determined which of the Wao houses in the small clearing dubbed "Terminal City" gave them the most enthusiastic welcome. One older man carried off a gift machete "with relatively little ceremony or enthusiasm." Later the man appeared "with his two women." Saint admitted that the missionaries "didn't feel that he warranted too good a gift, so we tossed him a pair of 'store-bought' trousers."[47] On one level, Saint and McCully—and sometimes Elliot—were just young men releasing tension, playing games from the air. Still, their habit of projecting motives and personalities on the people below risked objectifying the Waorani, seeing them primarily as targets of conversion.[48]

Attitudes toward the Waorani went unquestioned in *Through Gates of Splendor*. The indigenous people were secondary, shadowy figures. Most important was the book's portrayal of the drama of missionary life and its spiritual challenge. "And how it is written!" exclaimed one reviewer. "You . . . find yourself right in that little plane over the rain-jungles of the Andes; you live . . . the dangerous, thrilling life of a missionary." Even more celebrated was the book's devotional appeal. *Christianity Today* described it as "a spiritual experience" wherein the reader was allowed "to look into the diaries—and indeed into the hearts—of these missionary heroes and see their devotion to Christ, their utter death to self, their compassionate desires to reach those who have never heard the Gospel."[49]

The title of Elisabeth Elliot's 1961 book, *The Savage My Kinsman*, reflected a radical change of perspective and suggested that, had the five men established peaceful relations with the Waorani, they, too, might have displayed a different level of cultural awareness. Nonetheless, from its publication in 1957 until at least the end of the twentieth century, *Through Gates of Splendor* remained the defining narrative for Operation Auca among American evangelicals. Within eight months of its publication, more than 175,000 copies had been sold. One evangelical reviewer noted, "As far as circulation is concerned [it is] the leading missionary book of this generation."[50] The book was published at an ideal moment, during what seemed like a flurry of favorable media attention focused on evangelicals. Most prominent was the extensive publicity surrounding Billy Graham's Madison Square Garden Crusade, which opened May 15, 1957, two weeks before the book appeared. In mid-June a photographer snapped a picture of Graham's wife, Ruth Bell Graham, reading *Through Gates of Splendor*, with the book jacket clearly visible.[51]

In addition, on June 5 Rachel Saint was featured on Ralph Edwards's popular NBC television series, *This Is Your Life*. An estimated thirty million viewers saw Saint and her Wao-language informant, Dayomæ. A month later Saint and Dayomæ, described as "the first Auca Indian of Ecuador ever to visit the United States," appeared in New York at the Graham Crusade before an audience of nineteen thousand people. During their few minutes at the microphone, Saint expressed her desire to translate the Bible into the Wao language, and Dayomæ told a Bible story in her native tongue.[52]

Through Gates of Splendor was followed in quick succession by two biographies that appealed to ongoing interest in the Ecuador missionary story. *Shadow of the Almighty*, Jim Elliot's biography, did not match the blockbuster popularity of *Through Gates of Splendor*, but still held its own. A blend of biography and memoir, it further established Elliot's legacy as a missionary hero and model of evangelical spirituality. The book also popularized an entry from Elliot's journal that would become synonymous with his life: "He is no fool who gives what he cannot keep to gain that which he cannot lose." Elisabeth Elliot used a slightly edited version of the phrase at the beginning and the end of the prologue to *Shadow of the Almighty*, as well as once again in the book's epilogue. Written on October 28, 1949, the comment was part of Jim's reflections on a story in chapter 16 of Luke's gospel, where Jesus urged prudence in using the riches of this world to ensure one's future in the next. It echoed a similar saying by the Puritan preacher Philip Henry, not surprising given Jim's wide-ranging reading of inspirational biographies and other spiritual classics. There is no evidence that Jim ever highlighted the phrase or returned to it. Elisabeth, however, recognized the power of the words as Jim's "credo" and a call to radical Christian commitment.[53]

The phrase became a slogan for aspiring missionaries, appearing on the frontispiece of later editions of *Through Gates of Splendor* and inspiring at least two songs by popular evangelical musicians. It tops the list of quotations attributed to Jim Elliot on the internet and figures prominently in a mural in the student center at Wheaton College, his alma mater. It became the American evangelical equivalent to Dietrich Bonhoeffer's statement "When Christ calls a man, he bids him come and die."[54]

CONTRASTING SPIRITUALITIES

In 1959 *Jungle Pilot*, Nate Saint's story, joined *Through Gates of Splendor* and *Shadow of the Almighty* as the third volume in the trilogy that shaped the memory of the five missionaries killed in Ecuador. Because of the book and his aerial exploits, Saint became the second most well-known member of the group, after Jim Elliot. Written by the evangelical journalist Russell Hitt, *Jungle Pilot* followed the successful format of *Shadow of the Almighty*, which, in turn, resembled *Through Gates of Splendor*. The first editions of the biographies looked like twins: the same size and style, similar subtitles, excerpts from Bible verses at the beginning of each chapter, and fourteen pages of photographs in each volume.

Yet the lives of Jim Elliot and Nate Saint were in many ways a study in contrasts. Saint's biography suggested a style of fundamentalist piety that broke with the introspective, progress-of-the-soul spirituality common to accounts of missionary heroes and of which Elliot's story would prove to be a classic. One reviewer described Saint as the "Brother Lawrence" of evangelical missions, a reference to the seventeenth-century French monk who practiced the presence of God while working in a monastery kitchen. There was merit to the comparison. Saint, more comfortable around tools than books, had no desire to be a preacher and at first viewed his role in missionary aviation as a second-string position.[55]

Elliot's piety sometimes bordered on the pretentious; Saint's written reflections often included a wry take on himself and others. For Elliot, Christian devotion required a willingness, even an eagerness to die; Saint was known as one of the most cautious men in the jungle. Elliot was profoundly shaped by the spiritual practices of the Plymouth Brethren. Saint was a product of classic northern and eastern fundamentalism. His initial profession of faith had taken place during a teen summer camp in the Poconos run by Percy Crawford, one of the early leaders in the fundamentalist youth movement. Saint accepted the premillennialism of fundamentalists, followed the movement's behavioral codes, and by adulthood had experienced the "consecration" or surrender considered formative by many in the movement.[56]

However, in other ways Saint was not a stereotypical fundamentalist. He did not express feelings of alienation or militancy toward American culture or mainline Protestants. He demonstrated little concern for doctrinal issues apart from the bedrock convictions that God's love and care were constant and that people were lost eternally if they did not believe in Jesus Christ. He took a realistic stance toward daily Christian living and seemed not to worry much about his inner life.

Although *Jungle Pilot* included its share of inspiration and adventure, it was overshadowed by Elisabeth Elliot's two books. Elliot was an exceptional writer, and, perhaps more important, her books came out first. The story of Operation Auca had been told before Saint's biography was written. *Jungle Pilot* influenced evangelical readers, but in smaller numbers than the two earlier volumes. Saint did become a revered figure within the circles of Mission Aviation Fellowship. His story, both in *Through Gates of Splendor* and *Jungle Pilot*, helped to fuel MAF's rapid growth during the 1950s and 1960s.[57]

Looking back in 1996, *Christianity Today* noted that the story of the five missionaries and the Waorani had served as a "primary narrative for the young evangelical movement, reinforcing and illustrating to the world our core ideals." Ten years later the same magazine listed *Through Gates of Splendor* as number nine in a selection of fifty books that had transformed American evangelicalism during the previous half century.[58] The book helped define what it meant to be an evangelical during this period. Even so, neither *Through Gates of Splendor* nor the two biographies had the impact on missionary recruitment that readers often assumed. The men died at a time when interest in career missionary service already was booming.[59] That said, *Through Gates of Splendor*, *Shadow of the Almighty*, and *Jungle Pilot* encouraged and affirmed the spiritual aspirations and sense of calling that led waves of young people to the mission field or to other forms of full-time Christian work. By the time *Jungle Pilot* was published, however, a new chapter in the story of evangelicals and the Waorani had begun, one that involved the living rather than the voices of the dead.

PART II

Tensions and Competition, 1956–1958

3

A New Departure

THE THEME MUSIC sounded, and the announcer reminded the television audience that it was time for "*This Is Your Life*, a program for all America." The camera focused on the host, Ralph Edwards, standing next to two guests: the translator and missionary Rachel Saint and her young Wao language helper, Dayomæ. Saint and Dayomæ had arrived in California from Ecuador only a few days earlier. Saint had dragged her feet for months, reluctant to make the trip to the US herself or to bring Dayomæ, finally succumbing to persuasion and pressure from her boss, William Cameron Townsend. This evening, June 5, 1957, she had come to the Burbank studios thinking she and Dayomæ were to meet Edwards for an interview.

Instead they found themselves standing in a television set that reproduced a stylized jungle clearing, including a bamboo hut, tropical plants, and Andean curios. It was an odd juxtaposition: two women used to living in isolated, tropical settings now dressed in their best for an American appearance—Saint clutched white gloves and her purse throughout the program—and finding themselves transported to Hollywood's version of the Amazon. As the lights came up and the studio audience applauded on Edwards's cue, Saint and Dayomæ looked poised but slightly dazed.

"You've been out of the country for several years," Edwards began. "Have you ever heard or seen a television program called *This Is Your Life*?"

"No, I haven't. I've heard *of* it," Saint replied.

"We figured you wouldn't," Edwards said. "That's why we've gone much more obvious in our detail than we would [have]. . . . You and Dayomæ weren't necessarily brought up here from South America just for conferences and lectures but because we wanted to tell your inspiring life story.

"Tonight," he announced, "Rachel Saint of Pennsylvania, Peru, and Ecuador, *this is your life*."[1]

For the next half hour a stream of family, friends, and coworkers came out the door of the bamboo hut onto the stage to greet Rachel and Dayomæ and tell of Rachel's life, following the program's traditional format. Millions of Americans saw Saint celebrated as a courageous member of the Summer Institute of Linguistics (SIL), an organization with close ties to the Wycliffe Bible Translators (WBT). SIL members went to "primitive" jungle peoples and learned their languages in order to encourage literacy and translate the Bible. The "aucas" were one such tribe, and one of the five young missionaries they had massacred only a year earlier was Rachel's younger brother Nate.

Reflecting cultural expectations of the time, the program celebrated both the adventurous side of life in the rainforest and the inspirational nature of Wycliffe's goals. Viewers met Carlos Sevilla, the "Daniel Boone of Ecuador," and Chief Tariri, leader of the headhunting Shapra tribe in Peru.[2] Sounds of jungle drums and film clips of tribal peoples from a Wycliffe promotional film served as transitions between the various segments of the show, with the implication that the indigenous people on film were Waorani or Shapras. "This will give the anthropologists fits!" wrote one Wycliffe worker in a tone of bemused resignation after she had watched the program's use of the clips.[3]

Rachel, a woman who before her Wycliffe training "used to cringe at the sight of the tiniest, harmless spider," had ventured into the wilds of the Peruvian forests to spend six months among the Shapras with the pioneer missionary Loretta Anderson while Anderson's usual colleague was on furlough. Their work was not in vain. Tariri, the former headhunter, appeared in the Burbank studio as a Christian, an example of the success of the Wycliffe approach. With Anderson translating, Tariri, dignified in native dress, confirmed that "his heart was happy after he had received Jesus." His wife, Irena, the only obviously reluctant participant in the program, looked trapped and terrified in the glare of the television lights and sound of audience applause.[4]

Now, Edwards told the audience, Saint had "picked the hardest assignment of all," working among the "auca Indians" of Ecuador. Although Saint hadn't yet made actual contact with the tribe, Don Burns, the SIL director in Ecuador, confirmed that, based on her Shapra experience, she was trusting God for the ability to "reach the savage aucas . . . and give them the Word of God in their own mother tongue."[5]

Despite the accolades, Rachel Saint seemed an unlikely candidate for *This Is Your Life*. About to celebrate her forty-third birthday, she had not yet begun her life's work among the Waorani, nor had she done any actual Bible translation, other than helping Dayomæ to learn a few simple Bible stories. Saint had spent twelve years as a young adult working at the Keswick Colony of Mercy in New Jersey, "drying out drunks," as she told a later interviewer. In 1948 she attended SIL training at the University of Oklahoma, the first step toward becoming a Bible translator. In 1949, following jungle camp in southern Mexico, she went to Peru, where she served first on a two-month temporary assignment with the Piro people along the Urubamba River. That same year she visited her brother Nate and for the first time heard him mention the Waorani. Then, in 1951, came a stint in Lima, studying Spanish, followed in 1952 by a year as an interim coworker with Lorrie Anderson among the Shapras, where Rachel met Tariri. During 1953, she continued working in SIL's Lima office.[6] Another visit to Ecuador and more tales of the Waorani began to convince her that they were "the tribe the Lord had for me."[7]

Rachel was not a strong linguist, although when she appeared on *This Is Your Life* she was learning to speak *Wao tededo* from Dayomæ. What Saint did have was tenacity and a desire to take the Christian gospel to tribal peoples.[8] She also had the benefit of Cameron Townsend's promotional skills and support. Working with Edwards, Townsend orchestrated the television show from his home at SIL headquarters in Peru. It was his idea to include Carlos Sevilla and his idea to bring Tariri and his wife, along with SIL staff member Lorrie Anderson, to serve as Tariri's interpreter. It was even his idea to have Anderson and Saint tell the fascinated audience how they had made *masato*—the food drink of the Shapras—for Tariri while his wife was ill, a process that involved chewing boiled manioc and spitting it into a pot.[9]

At several points in the program, the unflappable Edwards almost lost control of participants who spoke four different languages and who included tribal people with no concept of television. Rachel seemed determined to introduce family and friends to Dayomæ rather than play to the studio audience and television cameras. Despite these challenges, "This Is Your Life, Rachel Saint," was a huge success. "The whole staff, including Ralph Edwards, said that this was one of the best programs that they have ever put on," wrote an excited Bill Nyman, Wycliffe's East Coast representative, to Townsend, founder of both the Wycliffe Bible Translators and the Summer Institute of Linguistics, and his wife, Elaine. Nyman was particularly pleased with the favorable presentation of Wycliffe's work. He wrote that Edwards gave the group "a few good boosts, and he did it in such a kindly and understanding way that you would think he was one of us." (Edwards was, in fact, a sincere Christian and lifelong Methodist.) For Nyman, the positive television exposure was a victory for the cause of Christ and for WBT. For the Burbank television producers, it represented a wholesome blend of sentiment, sensationalism, and inspiration.[10]

A NEW VERSION OF THE "AUCA EPIC"

Decades later, however, it is clear that "This Is Your Life, Rachel Saint" meant much more than this. The program, along with the events leading up to it and those that would follow, signaled a new departure in the ongoing story of evangelical missionary outreach to the Waorani, as well as a different interpretation of the significance of that story. It introduced the American public, particularly evangelicals, to two women—Rachel Saint and Dayomæ—and two closely identified organizations, the Wycliffe Bible Translators and the Summer Institute of Linguistics. Within a few years SIL, supported in the US by WBT, would become the American organization most closely identified with the Waorani. With the broadcast of "This Is Your Life, Rachel Saint," a second version of the "auca epic" began to unfold. *Through Gates of Splendor* and the extensive publicity since the men's deaths focused on the five slain missionaries. To Americans who were aware of the story, Waorani history began on January 6, 1956, when three Waorani made peaceful contact with the five men. *This Is Your Life* presented a different account.

In this version, the first chapter began years earlier, with Dayomæ's decision to flee the violence of her people. It emphasized her key role as language informant and cultural link between the Waorani and Rachel Saint, who had met Dayomæ in February 1955, before Operation Auca took shape. The two stories intersected at various points. Nate Saint was Rachel's younger brother, and the deaths of Nate and his friends only increased Rachel's sense of purpose. A little more than a week after the men were killed, Townsend wrote Rachel, expressing his sympathy and acknowledging her prior concern for the tribe. "My first prayer after hearing the news was that you would have the privilege of leading to the Lord the man who killed your brother."[11]

On an institutional level, SIL's public announcement via "This Is Your Life, Rachel Saint" of its commitment to work among the Waorani reflected divisions among evangelical organizations in Ecuador regarding publicity, strategy, and missionary philosophy. The response of these groups to Wycliffe's television success was muted. No one wanted to openly criticize the broadcast, and some appreciated the value of "fine [Christian] testimony" on network television.[12] But there were misgivings. Mission Aviation Fellowship (MAF) president Grady Parrott was troubled that the program seemed to suggest that Rachel Saint was the only missionary attempting to contact the Waorani. Edwards briefly mentioned Nate Saint as one of the five men killed, but "no where else was there any indication that anyone [else] had any part." Instead the program implied "that Rachel had first hazarded her life working among the headhunters in Peru . . . and now, [she] was working among the savage Aucas."[13]

This Is Your Life and the speaking engagements for Saint and Dayomæ that followed bore the stamp of the controversial, entrepreneurial genius of Townsend, a visionary whose specialized organizations broke new ground in their approach to missionary outreach. Townsend viewed interest in the Waorani among Americans at home as a sign from God that this tribe could be a powerful public relations tool on behalf of Bible translation. To American evangelicals, the missionary-Waorani story often was portrayed as a seamless unfolding of God's purposes. The reality was more complex as various individuals and groups tried to obey God's leading, even when his directives seemed to put them at cross purposes with one another.

The five men who organized Operation Auca did so as friends, with little concern for institutional affiliations. In part, this reflected the Plymouth Brethren background of Elliot, Fleming, and McCully, who were independent representatives of their home assemblies. Also, long before the Waorani project, the various evangelical missions working in the rainforests of Ecuador made an informal agreement to divide the territory and its people among themselves. It was a way to maximize their efforts and to avoid competition. The Christian and Missionary Alliance, as well as the Gospel Missionary Union, worked in the southeastern jungles, along the Pastaza and Bobonaza rivers, among the Shuar and Achuar peoples. Brethren missionaries took the central and northern area, where various groups of lowland Quichua peoples lived. Wao territory also lay in their domain, one reason why Elliot, McCully, and Fleming felt a particular interest in the tribe. When, at Nate Saint's suggestion, the other missionaries invited Roger Youderian to join them, they were "borrowing" him from the southern jungles, an action that brought the Gospel Missionary Union, his sponsoring organization, into the picture.

According to the policies of Mission Aviation Fellowship, Nate Saint's participation should have been limited to providing aviation services that would enable the others to carry out their plans. Yet because aviation was so central to the project, Saint assumed a prominent role, something he was eager to do. During the year before Operation Auca, Nate had longed for "additional outlets" beyond his daily flight routine.[14] Operation Auca provided a new, more direct ministry dimension to his work. MAF was in the forefront of the Wao project and maintained that role after his death. As a result, when the men were killed, three missionary groups or agencies were left with a direct stake in the project: Gospel Missionary Union, the Brethren, and MAF. SIL was not involved.

A LINGUISTIC AND CULTURAL AGENCY

The Summer Institute was a relative newcomer to Ecuador. In 1952 SIL signed a contract with the Ecuadorian government to begin linguistic work in the country, which it did the following year. SIL's arrival introduced a new dynamic into the missionary community. Now there were three types of groups with North American evangelical roots working among the indigenous peoples of Ecuador. First were the *traditional* faith missions and denominational missions, such as the Gospel Missionary Union, Christian Missions in Many Lands (Brethren), and the Christian and Missionary Alliance. They pursued traditional missionary activities, such as evangelizing the population and establishing churches. Second were *specialized* faith missions, like the World Radio Missionary Fellowship (later HCJB Global) and Mission Aviation Fellowship, both openly Protestant but each with a particular ministry focus: shortwave radio station HCJB and healthcare for the former, air support for jungle workers for the latter. Third was SIL, an organization staffed by evangelical Protestants but not an actual missions agency.

Both World Radio and MAF had negotiated contracts with the Ecuadorian government, and each sought to maintain good relationships with the various regimes that came to power. This could be challenging in a traditionally Catholic nation characterized by a weak state. Among other gestures of goodwill, World Radio included public service programming in the HCJB schedule and allowed the state access to the station during times of national emergency, such as the 1948 Ambato earthquake. For its part, MAF occasionally transported government officials and provided rescue services for soldiers in the rainforest. Personnel for both groups considered themselves missionaries, serving in specialized capacities.

A UNIQUE APPROACH

The Summer Institute of Linguistics entered Ecuador to engage in translation and literacy work, as well as in community development among indigenous peoples. Their work placed priority on the translation of the Bible but included other linguistic and research goals as well. The organization existed as a scientific, service agency, able to work with governments in some countries that might not have welcomed traditional Protestant missionaries. Although legally separate, SIL and WBT shared interlocking directorates and common goals. WBT operated primarily in the homeland, as the overtly religious arm of the duo. It presented the need for Bible translation to churches, raised funds, and recruited potential linguists. To become a full-time SIL worker, recruits first had to be accepted by WBT, a process that included a willingness to adhere to a theologically conservative statement of faith. They also had to trust God for their individual financial support, much as workers with the traditional faith missions did. Once they were given assignments outside the US, usually in linguistics, literacy, or development work, the WBT recruits became SIL staff members.

The different identities of WBT and SIL looked good on paper and were a creative way to work around the suspicions some evangelicals had toward science and the suspicions some Latin American governments had toward missionaries. However, in actual practice the distinction was not always clear. The approach was the brainchild of Townsend, familiarly known as "Uncle Cam," an energetic leader with a passion for Bible translation. Uncle Cam had such a knack for relating to Latin American politicians that one admirer described him as a "champion medal-recipient," referring to the numerous humanitarian awards Townsend garnered from governments during the first thirty years of SIL work in the Americas.[15]

Townsend was also a promotional genius, willing to buttonhole anyone he thought could further the cause of Bible translation work. This often put him at odds with traditional faith missions who were shy about publicity and tended to focus their buttonholing on the Almighty through prayer. Whatever God's ultimate purposes, in the short term Townsend's approach seemed to bring in contributions, while the more traditional faith missions were often short on funds. These groups also resented what they viewed as a tendency toward pride in Townsend's eagerness to court publicity.

Nonetheless, Uncle Cam's faith in God, his obsession with getting translators to people without a Bible in their languages, and his public relations savvy propelled the growth of SIL from fewer than fifty linguists in Latin America in 1942 to more than five hundred some fifteen years later. The latter figure represented one of every four conservative American missionaries serving in Latin America in the 1950s and one of every ten American Protestants of any stripe doing religious work in the region. Faith missions, whose numbers tended to be much smaller, easily could feel overwhelmed when SIL entered a country, particularly one as small as Ecuador.[16]

NATE SAINT'S CONCERNS

In 1953, when SIL Ecuador director Robert Schneider and his staff arrived in Quito, their initial tasks were to survey language groups throughout the country, including the tribes of the Amazonian region, and to select a site for a "home base." For the latter, they chose land bordering Limoncocha, a lagoon near the Napo River in the northwestern part of the rainforest (map 3). On several occasions during this initial phase, the SIL staff found themselves at odds with the existing missionary community. Nate Saint was involved in some of these conflicts, in part because Shell Mera served as the jumping-off point for Americans exploring the eastern Ecuadorian jungles. SIL personnel occasionally stayed at the Saint home, and Nate was the pilot for many of SIL's initial jungle surveys. At first Nate expressed only occasional concerns about the group in his regular reports to MAF headquarters, but on November 2, 1954, he unburdened himself in a lengthy letter to Grady Parrott.

Saint's main complaint centered on SIL's unwillingness to use MAF air support for the translators they planned to place in the eastern rainforests. Instead the organization would bring in its own pilots and planes, known as JAARS.[17] From Saint's perspective, SIL was introducing a duplicate air service. This represented a waste of resources—personnel, equipment, and funds—especially grievous since both MAF and JAARS were supported financially by donations from American evangelicals.[18]

There were various attempts at reconciliation, and Saint repeatedly expressed his respect and admiration for individuals associated with SIL. "My own sister, as you know is a member of the group," he reminded Parrott in the November letter.[19] But he found himself in constant disagreement with SIL's policies. He objected to the JAARS decision to purchase a Helio Courier (a small, fixed-wing airplane that could land on a very short airstrip), which he viewed as expensive and unnecessary. Just a month before his death, he complained bitterly about the willingness of JAARS to ferry Roman Catholic priests to their own missionary posts in the rainforest.[20] SIL maintained cordial relationships with Catholics as part of their nonsectarian stance and pro-government policies in countries such as Ecuador, where Catholic church-state ties ran deep.

This policy, however, angered Protestant missionaries, who often were the targets of Catholic persecution. It was not unusual for missionaries or their converts to be heckled or pelted with stones as they organized activities in towns and villages. In Latin America of the 1950s, evangelicals considered Catholicism a false religion and Catholics returned the favor. When reporting on Operation Auca, Saint wrote Charles Mellis at the MAF home office, "We are keeping the thing [outreach to the aucas] from SIL especially because of their policy on publicity and because of their relations with the govt and the Roman Catholics."[21] Some of these tensions remained in the background even after Operation Auca abruptly ended on Palm Beach.

GIFT FLIGHTS RESUME

After the deaths of Elliot, Fleming, McCully, Saint, and Youderian, their widows and the three missionary groups they represented committed themselves to picking up where the men left off.[22] In *Through Gates of Splendor*, Elisabeth Elliot wrote, "The prayers of the widows themselves are for the Aucas. We look forward to the day when these savages will join us in Christian praise."[23] Yet except for Elliot, circumstances made it difficult for the other women to play a direct role in Wao contact. Instead the missions represented by the slain men continued the project in an ad hoc fashion. At a meeting shortly after the men's deaths, an "auca committee," consisting of Johnny Keenan (MAF), Keith Austin (Gospel Missionary Union), and Elisabeth Elliot (Brethren), was formed, although it seems never to have functioned in any formal way.[24] Following Nate Saint's example in taking the initiative, Keenan made at least two exploratory flights in February 1956. The Waorani had deserted the old village not far from Palm Beach that the men had named Terminal City, but Keenan found new clearings about a mile upstream. He shifted his focus—and the gifts—to these houses.

In April Waorani began to appear outside their homes in the new location, once again waving to the plane as Keenan, assisted by Austin, made occasional flights to drop gifts.[25] In late May a senior MAF pilot, Hobey Lowrance, and his wife, Olivia, arrived in Shell Mera as interim replacements for the Saints. Lowrance and Keenan began to alternate regular gift flights every three weeks, using the spiral line technique Nate Saint developed. Austin became a regular passenger to help with the aerial contacts. He also administered a special "auca fund" that financed the flights. Elisabeth Elliot remained intensely interested, but she had no role in these efforts.

Although Elliot was respected as one of the widows, because she was a woman with a small child she was not welcome as a participant in her own right. She had wanted to accompany Keenan on the gift drops, as Austin did, and was willing to face any potential dangers, but both Keenan and MAF president Parrott refused.[26] Despite Elliot's competence—Lowrance was convinced that she "could take care of herself as well or *better* than the average man"—MAF was unwilling to risk criticism should a plane go down in Wao territory with a woman aboard. Yet Elliot was the only one left in the group who had even a rudimentary grasp of a few Wao phrases.[27]

Lowrance tried again, suggesting that Elliot might be the logical person to go in the plane and use a PA system to call out phrases to the Waorani below, as her husband and the others had done. MAF officials reiterated their opposition.[28] Elliot should not go along unless the missionary community in the Oriente supported the idea as the only way to keep the project moving forward. Besides, Parrott and Mellis feared the Waorani might respond negatively to a woman's voice, "since we know primitive peoples never hold a woman in [a] place of . . . importance."[29] Actually, this was not true of the Waorani, who had a radically egalitarian culture.

In August the Brethren missionary Wilfred Tidmarsh returned to the rainforest with his wife, Gwen, to pursue his own dream of contacting the Waorani.

Although generally respected for his years of service, Tidmarsh had a prickly relationship with other missionaries. As Lowrance put it, "He's always involved in misunderstandings with other missionaries, both because of his peculiarities, and equally because of their prejudices." When it came to the Waorani, Tidmarsh, too, had been shut out of Operation Auca and its aftermath. "He was unjustly neglected," suggested Lowrance. "Says nobody informed him of the incident, nor anything since that time."[30]

By late 1956, with replacements on the field, "Project Auca," consisting of regular flights over the small cluster of new homes not far from the deserted Terminal City, was under way. Twelve or thirteen Waorani outside one home regularly greeted the flights. Despite their response, more than eight months passed after the missionaries' deaths with little obvious progress. Evangelicals in the US prayed and waited for news.

Elisabeth Elliot continued working with Quichuas at the Shandia station, keeping her own counsel.[31] Tidmarsh settled at Arajuno. The Waorani seemed content to greet the plane and accept gifts, with no apparent desire for anything more. Everyone agreed that the next step would require the ability to communicate with them. Missionaries—most obviously Tidmarsh and Elliot—had to learn the Wao language. But there was a snag. Dayomæ was the only known person outside the tribe who spoke *Wao tededo*. Her ties to Rachel Saint placed her in the middle of the web of misunderstandings and miscommunications between SIL and the evangelical missions.

TENSIONS OVER DAYOMÆ

When Nate Saint and his colleagues were killed, Rachel Saint found herself in an awkward position. Her own desire to contact the Waorani clearly predated their efforts. By the time Nate and Ed McCully first spotted Wao settlements in late September 1955, Rachel already had spent five months in initial language study with Dayomæ and had established a relationship with her.[32] Now the five men were dead and their small cache of language notes destroyed on the Curaray beach.

Rachel seemed the obvious person to pursue further linguistic analysis and eventual contact with the tribe. Of course, she, too, was a woman, but in contrast to Elisabeth Elliot, Rachel was middle-aged, single, and had no children. Only a few weeks after Nate's death, his widow, Marj, suggested to Rachel that she "should be the first one to go into the Aucas—that now it was time for a woman to go."[33] But despite her availability, Rachel represented SIL and policies opposed by at least some of the slain men and their wives.

For example, as part of information released in January 1956, during the initial search for the missing men, Abe Van Der Puy had mentioned Rachel's translation work. Rachel asked that she be identified as working under the auspices of the Ecuadorian Ministry of Education, a request that met with "a storm of protest" from some of the widows. They wanted Operation Auca to be viewed strictly as "a GOSPEL project, a MISSIONARY venture," without confusing the issue by introducing SIL.[34] After the men were confirmed dead, Rachel stayed for two months at Shell Mera to help her sister-in-law and to be on hand should any Waorani come out of the rainforest near Arajuno or elsewhere. Although she never expressed it publicly, she was deeply hurt and angry over the way she had been treated by the five men and their wives. She continued to feel shut out.[35]

In March 1956 Rachel went to Quito to attend an SIL staff meeting. During her absence and without her knowledge, Van Der Puy arranged for Dayomæ to visit Elisabeth Elliot at Shandia for a few days. Elliot's work with her was facilitated by the fact that Elliot spoke Quichua, Dayomæ's second language. Rachel did not and had worked from a strictly monolingual approach. (She and Dayomæ communicated only in *Wao tededo*, as Rachel attempted to learn the language.) The missionaries involved in the ongoing Project Auca hoped that Elliot could increase her limited knowledge of the Wao language and perhaps persuade Dayomæ to record a greeting that could be played on a loudspeaker at the Arajuno station, inviting any Waorani who might be within earshot to a friendly meeting with the missionaries. Elliot also broached the possibility that Dayomæ herself might wish to ride in the plane and invite the nearby Waorani to Arajuno.[36]

After the fact, Van Der Puy told SIL that he had organized the meeting. He had done so while Rachel was gone, he explained, in order not to impinge on her time with Dayomæ.[37] Although the SIL staff doubted that Elliot, with only a summer of linguistics training, could make much headway in a week, word later circulated in the jungle missionary rumor mill that Elliot "got as accurate data in the three days as Rachel had in the three months."[38] This did nothing to mend the breach between SIL and other missionaries, or to shore up the relationship between Elisabeth and Rachel. The missions involved in Project Auca resented SIL's "possession" of Dayomæ; the linguists, in turn, took exception to the way the missionaries seemed to work behind Rachel's (and SIL's) back. The possessiveness Rachel eventually would display toward the Waorani may have had roots in the way she felt marginalized during this time.

The irony behind this tug of war was that if Dayomæ "belonged" to anyone, it was to neither the SIL translators nor the missionaries of Project Auca but to Carlos Sevilla, her patrón. In March 1944, along with two other girls, she had fled tribal violence among the Waorani and had encountered a group of Sevilla's Quichua workers

tapping rubber along the Curaray. Some months later they took her to Sevilla's hacienda at Ila, on the banks of the Anzo River, an upper tributary of the Napo, where
she was given clothing and work as a laborer on the plantation.[39] She would have
been about thirteen or fourteen years old at the time. Within a few years she had
learned to speak Quichua and had begun to absorb Quichua dress and customs. In
1952 she gave birth to a son, Ignacio, whose unacknowledged father was thought to
be Sevilla's eldest son, Vicente, if not the patrón himself.[40]

Either way, as biographer Rosemary Kingsland later noted, Ignacio's presence on
the hacienda was awkward, and Don Carlos soon had Dayomæ ensconced in an arranged marriage to a Quichua husband, Miguel Padilla, who moved with his new
wife and her son to a nearby Indian settlement on the upper Curaray. A year later
she bore a second son, Padilla's child, but the new baby and his father died in a measles epidemic, leaving behind a seriously ill Dayomæ and Ignacio. The two returned
to Hacienda Ila, where they lived with Padilla's aunt and where Rachel Saint and
her colleague Catherine Peeke found Dayomæ when they came to the hacienda in
February 1955 in search of a Wao language informant. When Rachel first began her
study of *Wao tededo*, Dayomæ continued as Sevilla's peon, working in the fields for
the patrón, who granted her a brief period each day for language study.[41]

Due first to ill health and then her brother's death, Rachel was gone from Hacienda
Ila for nearly nine months, from June 1955 to late March 1956. During that time,
the publicity surrounding Operation Auca had alerted Sevilla to Dayomæ's value.
Cameron Townsend had already grasped the same point. A little more than a month
after the missionaries' deaths, he wrote Rachel that a donor had promised two hundred dollars "to enable you to employ Dayomæ full time and buy her liberty from her
present patron so that you can take her to some convenient place in civilization to
concentrate on informant work." Rachel should stay away from anything that might
look like "a race for getting to the Aucas first," advised Townsend. Her job was language
study and Bible translation, Wycliffe's "distinctive and non-competitive" ministry.[42]

Thinking about Rachel and Dayomæ, Townsend came up with the idea that
would eventually lead to "This Is Your Life, Rachel Saint." Why not take advantage of the American interest in Ecuador and pioneer missions to bring Rachel and
Dayomæ to the US in May 1956 for a television appearance, several mass meetings,
and media interviews? He mentioned the idea to SIL Ecuador director Don Burns.
"It must not be a strenuous program or it would wear Dayomæ out, but if it is prop-
erly planned it can reach millions upon millions of people."[43]

The urgency to free Dayomæ grew with the news that the patrón had sold Hacienda
Ila to a Catholic priest who might wish to keep some of the workers along with the
property. Sevilla, however, would hardly release a young Wao woman who had already
received a modest amount of publicity and who was seen as key to further contact

with her people. On March 20, when Rachel and her new coworker Mary Sargent returned to Hacienda Ila, they found Dayomæ eager to greet them. Shortly afterward the whole entourage moved to Sevilla's new home, Hacienda San Carlos, still on the Anzo River.[44] Uneasiness about Dayomæ's servitude persisted, as Rachel spent much of the next year at the hacienda. She resisted requests to bring Dayomæ to the US or to involve her in overtures to her people. Rachel consistently was more cautious regarding the prospect of contacting the Waorani than most of the missionaries behind Project Auca. In part, she simply reflected the standard SIL policy of a taking a "slow approach."[45] But she also had begun to understand at least some of Dayomæ's dark stories of tribal violence. Although Rachel acknowledged positive aspects of Wao culture, she was convinced that in the context of warfare the Waorani were deceitful and sly, sometimes waiting years for the perfect opportunity to revenge a wrong.[46]

The missionaries coordinating the MAF gift drops were, of course, aware of the violent reputation of Wao warriors. No one could forget the spearings on Palm Beach. Still, the people, mostly women, who emerged from their homes to wave at the plane overhead did not seem especially frightening. After making aerial gift drops, Lowrance reported, "Their seemingly friendly response causes us to feel something of what the five fellows felt. . . . A compelling urge to land and greet them."[47]

THE PURPOSE OF PUBLICITY

In addition to tensions over SIL's nonsectarian approach and the group's claim to Dayomæ, missionaries in Ecuador were also miffed about the way SIL used publicity, an approach shaped largely by Townsend. Uncle Cam was convinced that God intended the impact of the five missionaries' deaths not for the Waorani alone, "nor just for the three organizations involved, but for 2,000 Bibleless tribes and for every organization and movement that tends toward the reaching of the unreached for Christ."[48] Efforts by any group, including the cooperative ventures of Wycliffe and SIL, to ride the waves of publicity would only multiply the good influence of Operation Auca as money was raised and workers recruited to carry out God's work in the world.[49] Townsend also believed that God helped those who did their part to obey his will. Using a football metaphor, Uncle Cam explained that the five men "ran interference . . . for a worldwide advance in behalf of primitive tribes. Wycliffe would be fumbling indeed, if it didn't follow through for the touchdown that includes 2,000 tribes [without the Bible]."[50] These convictions lay behind Townsend's persistent suggestion that Rachel Saint, and perhaps even Dayomæ, come to the US for speaking and fundraising work on behalf of SIL in Ecuador.

More cautious voices prevailed. SIL staffer John Lindskoog, filling in for Burns as director in Ecuador, warned that aggressive PR work on the heels of the Palm Beach tragedy would only intensify missionary sentiment against Wycliffe. Lindskoog imagined what people would say: "There goes Wycliffe again. They didn't have a thing to do with this expedition but now they are capitalizing on the publicity. . . . And here on the field they're a compromising bunch who won't even identify themselves with evangelical missionaries."[51] In the end, Townsend bowed to the counsel of Burns and Lindskoog, and to Saint's refusal to leave Ecuador, though he never changed his mind about what needed to be done. The promotional efforts simply were postponed until 1957. Almost all the publicity that eventually would surround Rachel and Dayomæ had its genesis with Townsend.

Most of the traditional faith missions and the individuals directly involved in Operation Auca and the subsequent Project Auca viewed the story of the missionaries and the Waorani primarily as a narrative with a spiritual message to Christians. They were wary of publicity for any other purpose.[52] After a conversation with Philip and Katherine Howard, Elisabeth Elliot's parents, Jim Truxton of MAF commented, "Maybe I'm wrong—but it was interesting that both Dr. and Mrs. Howard pretty well felt the same way—that the story is a 'sacred' challenge to Christians. Anything else takes second place."[53]

Certainly the two perspectives overlapped. Townsend wanted Christians to commit themselves more fully to God's work, especially to God's work among "Bibleless tribes." And the traditional missionary agencies' cooperation with *Life* magazine and the Harper publishing house reflected an openness on their part to telling the story to non-Christians. But their beliefs about the fundamental value of the story differed. Meanwhile, thousands of praying Americans awaited "news of the five martyrs' wives" and of the longed-for salvation of the Waorani.[54] No one wanted to move precipitously, yet there was a sense of urgency. It was based in part on evangelistic goals but also on the ever-present concern that somebody else would get there first. "We ask [in prayer] for those whom God has prepared to be sent to the Aucas and *only* those," wrote Elisabeth Elliot in a *Christianity Today* article commemorating the first anniversary of the men's deaths. "A well-meaning but misguided effort could ruin further opportunities to enter the tribe."[55]

UNEXPECTED VISITORS

The magazine's readers did not know that publicity surrounding Operation Auca already had attracted both Christians and adventurers of all sorts to the Ecuadorian rainforests. In late August 1956 Lowrance had written of the seemingly endless stream of visitors, "Seems the whole world wants to horn in. If they realized what a small group they [the Waorani that had been sighted] are . . . just 4 houses down in a valley, it wouldn't sound so glamorous."[56] Tourists came anyway—writers, ministers, curious evangelicals, and adventurers—all of whom wanted to be flown over Palm Beach and the new Wao clearing. Among them was Clarence Hall, the editor from *Reader's Digest*, who managed to squeeze in a couple of hours of fishing before leaving the rainforest. Magnum researcher Jozefa Stuart arrived in November to gather details and check facts for Elisabeth Elliot, then in New York, finishing *Through Gates of Splendor*.[57]

Lowrance wrote despairingly of two inexperienced Yale "fly boys," students at the college, who had learned to fly the year before and were now touring South America in their Tri-Pacer. They had landed in Shell Mera after some terrifying moments lost in the clouds that blocked the Ambato-Shell mountain pass on their trip across the Andes from Quito. Lowrance reported the young men arrived "somewhat shaken up," a state that may have contributed to their acquiescence to Lowrance's refusal to let a strange plane fly over Wao territory.[58]

Much more persistent were a Canadian psychologist named Robert Tremblay and an unidentified friend. The two showed up in Quito and announced that they were going to the Waorani, "to take them the gospel," though Marj Saint, normally generous in her assessment of others, commented, "It is quite obvious he [Tremblay] doesn't have it to give." Rebuffed by evangelicals, the pair moved to the small town of Tena, center of Catholic work in the northeastern jungles, to offer their services.[59] It was not the last the evangelical missionaries would hear of Tremblay.

Tremblay was barely gone when a travel writer, Jane Dolinger, arrived from Miami, eager to chronicle her own white-woman-in-the-Ecuadorian-Amazon adventure story. Even before the trip, Dolinger was more fascinated by the shrunken heads of the nearby Jívaro people than by the Waorani, whom she referred to by an earlier name, Aushiri. But she and her husband acknowledged that the timing of their "expedition" to Amazonian Ecuador had been sparked by the widespread coverage of the missionaries' deaths. Dolinger met Marj Saint and Barbara Youderian; later she and her husband, Ken Krippene, interviewed Rachel Saint and Mary Sargent at Hacienda Ila. Despite the missionaries' fears of what Dolinger might write, the book from her Ecuador travels mentioned them with respect. Most of *The Head with the Long Yellow Hair* focused on Dolinger's jungle adventures hunting hidden treasure (supposed "Inca emerald mines"), observing secret Jívaro head-shrinking rituals, and finding an elusive shrunken head with long, blond hair.[60]

Most heart-wrenching for the jungle missionaries was correspondence with William Youderian, Roger's father, about the elder Youderian's hopes of making contact with the Waorani. William Youderian did arrive in Shell Mera in April 1957.

However, to everyone's relief, instead of attempting to go into the rainforest, he worked on the construction of the Epp Memorial mission hospital in Shell Mera, another project that had been important to his son.[61]

COMPETITION WITH CATHOLICS

Outside visitors could be thorns in the flesh. However, pressures from others, particularly Roman Catholics, because of their proximity within the sparsely settled Oriente, were more worrisome. Most of the evangelical missionaries in the rainforests viewed themselves in competition with Catholic missions for the souls of the various tribal peoples. In the case of the Waorani, worldwide attention had intensified the rivalry. Reports of Catholic plans to contact the Waorani abounded, and evangelicals jockeyed to position themselves in locations where they would "find" the Waorani first, should any decide to leave their group. In September 1956 some Quichuas passed on a rumor that two priests had built a small "hut" or shrine over the men's grave on the Curaray, containing pictures cut from newspaper accounts. A month later stories began to circulate that the priests were "organizing an expedition to go into the auca village."[62] "They claim to have 'Christianized' the Aucas 40 years ago!" reported Lowrance indignantly.[63]

The willingness of Carlos Sevilla on occasion to aid the priests also made the Protestants nervous. Sevilla had pioneered in Wao territory in the early twentieth century, establishing cotton and rice plantations on the upper Curaray before the Waorani had driven him out. During certain seasons of the year that seemed safer than others, he still sent Quichua workers into Wao territory to fish or tap rubber trees. Some of these Quichuas had guided the two priests to Palm Beach.[64] By February 1957 Sevilla was proposing to Dayomæ that she return to her people and encourage some of them to come out of the rainforest, a prospect that worried Rachel Saint and Cameron Townsend. It also increased Townsend's determination to get Dayomæ away from Sevilla and off the hacienda, perhaps even out of the country.[65]

In December 1956 Townsend had written letters to Ralph Edwards in Hollywood and Sevilla in Ecuador. To Edwards, Townsend emphasized Rachel Saint's role reaching the Waorani and inquired about the possibility of presenting "Miss Saint and the Auca woman who teaches her to TV audiences in the U.S.A. without any flavor of commercialism." Of course, he noted, "Rachel would like to carry on her work quietly but funds are needed for the project, for a Base and for equipment. We also need to interest young people in the U.S.A. in volunteering for our worldwide scientific and missionary program."[66]

At the same time, Townsend reminded Sevilla, to whom he had earlier spoken by radio, of a possible trip to the United States that would include Sevilla himself. Townsend appealed to the patrón's sense of national pride in asking him to give Dayomæ more free time to work with Rachel. It was important both for the impression that would be made in the US as well as for the success of the overall Waorani project that Rachel become fluent in the Wao language. Townsend's plea and promise of travel worked, at least for a few months, and Rachel was able to intensify her language study.[67]

With interest on all sides, it sometimes seemed that evangelical efforts to cultivate friendship with the Waorani might backfire. "It would be easy to despair of having the Aucas come out," wrote Lowrance. "*Everybody* seems to be waiting for them." The Waorani, for their part, remained in the jungle, oblivious to the furor surrounding them, and giving no hint of what their next move would be.[68]

4

The Next Steps

IN MARCH 1957, while the Waorani remained isolated in the rainforest, Elisabeth Elliot and Rachel Saint—the two American women who would become most associated with the Waorani by the outside world—met in Shell Mera. It was their first lengthy conversation since Rachel had stayed with Elisabeth at Shandia while Jim Elliot was gone for the final days of Operation Auca. "It [the meeting] gave us both the first opportunity to air out a lot of misunderstandings," Saint commented.[1]

There was plenty to talk about. For example, despite misgivings, Elliot had supported the decision by the five men to exclude Saint from any knowledge of Operation Auca. Elliot also helped her husband gather language material from Dayomæ without Saint's knowledge in preparation for the Palm Beach expedition. While the men were camped on the riverbank and Saint was with Elliot at Shandia, Elliot monitored the radio using earphones so that the project remained secret. Saint discovered her brother was missing at the same time the rest of the world did. In addition, when she read portions of *Through Gates of Splendor* in manuscript form, Saint was distressed that the book paid little attention to Dayomæ and her significance.[2]

For her part, Elliot experienced a growing sense that God wanted her to be actively involved in contacting the Waorani. During the year since her husband's death she had lived intimately with the ideals of radical obedience as expressed by Jim in his journals. She turned to the journals while writing *Through Gates of Splendor* and especially while working on the manuscript that would become *Shadow of the*

Almighty. Like her late husband, Elliot, too, was willing to risk her life in obedience to God. She had wanted to go to Palm Beach during the original Operation Auca.[3] After Jim's death, she even arranged for her brother-in-law Bert Elliot, and his wife, Colleen, missionaries in Peru, to care for her toddler, Valerie, should Elisabeth herself be killed.

Elliot's greatest asset related to the Waorani contact was her linguistic ability. In early 1957 she needed Saint's cooperation to learn from the work Saint had already done and to have access to Dayomæ. But Rachel continued to be deeply loyal to Townsend and SIL, an obstacle for Elliot. "The up-shot was she hoped we could have fellowship with each other even if we do not agree about mission policies," Rachel wrote. The two women parted and left Shell Mera with that hope.[4] Shortly after that conversation, Rachel and Dayomæ flew to Quito, where Rachel talked with her sister-in-law Marj and with Marilou McCully, and more tensions from the previous year were resolved. Rachel was relieved. Particularly in light of efforts by outsiders and by Catholics, she wrote, "We who know Him [Christ] must stand together in faith at least, for the tribe."[5] Like Rachel and the men's widows, most of the evangelical missionaries and the SIL staff involved with efforts to contact the Waorani hoped for unity among themselves. Unity, however, proved elusive.

ENCOURAGEMENT TO RETURN

Rachel was fortunate to find at least a temporary resolution in her relationships with the widows, since she faced new challenges elsewhere, first on Carlos Sevilla's hacienda with Dayomæ and then from within her own organization. Sevilla, Dayomæ's patrón, continued to pressure Dayomæ to return as an emissary to her people. The young woman, whose attitude toward such a proposal seemed to vacillate, first broached the subject herself to Rachel in early February 1957, after Dayomæ had seen an aerial photograph of the Wao clearing. "Let's go down the Curaray," she suggested, "You, and Cathy [Peeke] and me. Not now—I've been away from my son now, but when he has school vacation, let's go."[6]

A few weeks later Sevilla gave Dayomæ "an official OK" if she wanted to return to her people. However, his idea was that Dayomæ go alone, while Rachel waited for her at the hacienda. Neither Saint nor Catherine Peeke, her interim coworker, quite understood the patrón's motives. Was this a subtle suggestion that it was time for the linguists to leave Hacienda San Carlos? Was it Sevilla's bid to help the Roman Catholics or to become a more central player himself in the drama around the Waorani? Or were Sevilla's suggestions simply the next move in negotiations with Cameron Townsend over Dayomæ's future? After Townsend's December overtures asking Sevilla to allow Dayomæ to travel to the United States and inviting the patrón to make the trip, Sevilla responded with his own *lotería*, the "prize" he would like to win as a result of the negotiations. He wanted Townsend to arrange for his youngest son, Carlos, to study in the US.[7] The possibility that Dayomæ might disappear back into the jungles could increase the pressure on Townsend.

Sevilla's proposal disturbed Rachel. She worried about the danger to Dayomæ. Would the young woman, now an adult wearing the clothing and hairstyle of a Quichua, be recognized after a thirteen-year absence? If not, she risked her life in approaching her people. Was she a genuine Christian? Although Dayomæ responded with interest to Bible stories and could, in turn, repeat the Christmas story, the creation account, and numerous other Old and New Testament narratives, Rachel was not yet sure that Dayomæ was spiritually prepared to meet death, should something go wrong.[8]

Dayomæ also remained crucial to SIL's language work and its involvement in any efforts to reach the Waorani. Then there was the issue of air support and cooperation with MAF should Dayomæ and later Rachel successfully contact the Waorani in an isolated location. SIL did not yet have a permanent base in Ecuador. Any air support, should Dayomæ or others need it, would have to come from MAF, further complicating an awkward situation. Townsend wasn't about to support the venture since, by early 1957, he was moving full speed ahead on plans for Rachel and Dayomæ to appear on *This Is Your Life*. The trip would lead, he hoped, to Dayomæ's eventual emancipation from Sevilla's control. In early May 1957, a few weeks before Rachel and Dayomæ left for the United States, Townsend cautioned Rachel to "avoid making any promises to Don Carlos about what Dayomæ will be doing after her return." When SIL's Ecuador jungle base camp was ready, Townsend thought it would make an ideal home for the two women.[9]

A year after Townsend first proposed Rachel Saint's appearance on *This Is Your Life*, SIL Ecuador director Don Burns agreed to support the idea, including Townsend's plan to bring Tariri, the Shapra tribal leader from Peru.[10] The formal request from Ralph Edwards to feature Rachel's story came in early May 1957, and Wycliffe regional representatives found themselves scrambling, with only about six weeks to arrange speaking engagements across the US for Rachel and Dayomæ.

AN EXTENDED STAY

When the two women flew from Quito to Los Angeles in late May 1957, they were embarking on an experience that would profoundly affect them both. The trip to the US was especially difficult for Dayomæ. She faced enormous challenges, including susceptibility to new diseases, strange food, and a language barrier, to name a few. Within twenty-four hours of her appearance with Edwards, she was in bed at the Hollywood Roosevelt Hotel with a severe case of tonsillitis. Rachel canceled a scheduled appearance that night before two thousand people at the Church of the Open Door in Los Angeles and contacted a doctor. He wrote a prescription, and Dayomæ had improved by the next morning. The incident was later recounted as one of Dayomæ's early professions of Christian faith. With Rachel interpreting, the doctor, cancer specialist Ralph Byron Jr., whom Rachel met in the hotel, told Dayomæ of his own faith in Jesus Christ. Dayomæ responded that she, too, thought of Jesus day and night.[11]

Despite the positive impact of Dayomæ's encounters with American Christians like Byron, Rachel had serious doubts about staying in the United States beyond the three months granted on Dayomæ's visa. By June 20, when the two had been in the country only a little more than three weeks, Rachel was already writing Wycliffe executives Bill Nyman and John Newman, opposing any attempt to extend Dayomæ's visa, which would expire on August 28, 1957. She reported that Dayomæ was "both sick and homesick at times—and sleeping off the excitement for hours at a time." In addition, she had "left a young son behind." What Rachel wanted most was to conclude their public appearances and spend the remaining weeks at the Oklahoma University linguistics institute with other SIL workers.[12]

Neither quiet weeks in Oklahoma nor a return to Ecuador came to pass. The two women had become famous and their public relations value to Wycliffe Bible Translators was enormous. For example, their appearance at Billy Graham's Madison Square Garden Crusade had provided an important opportunity for Wycliffe to publicize the need for Bible translation, to strengthen the group's ties with the Graham organization, and to raise funds for SIL's struggling work in Ecuador. The freewill offering from the meeting totaled $4,247.47, most earmarked for SIL's jungle base at Limoncocha, for which, as Townsend remarked, "so little had come in" before. He later acknowledged that money from the Crusade "was the main gift that helped us build our central Base in the jungles of Ecuador."[13]

Until the summer of 1957, fundraising for Ecuador, both for the jungle base and for airplanes—particularly for one of the Helio Couriers Townsend loved—had been slow. Precise information about the amount of money contributed to Wycliffe due to Rachel and Dayomæ's appearances is difficult to determine, although letters to Townsend indicate gifts of at least $12,247. A conservative estimate of the actual total would probably be closer to $15,000 or $16,000. About $2,500 of that amount went to cover travel expenses for Rachel and Dayomæ, as well as for Tariri, his wife and baby, and linguist Lorrie Anderson, who accompanied the Shapra family. Another $3,400 went to Rachel and Dayomæ for a future home at the Limoncocha jungle base, for school fees for Dayomæ's son, and $100 for a sewing machine "so Dayomæ can make her own clothes."[14]

On July 22, just days after he received news of the success of the Madison Square Garden appearance, Townsend wrote Sevilla, requesting permission for Dayomæ to remain in the US until October 12 to participate in ceremonies surrounding the dedication of an airplane given by the citizens of Kansas City for SIL's work in Ecuador. Harry Truman would be there, Townsend told Sevilla, as well as Ecuador's ex-president Galo Plaza. Rachel and Dayomæ would add to the pro-Ecuador senti-ment of the occasion, particularly "in encouraging people to contribute the money necessary to purchase the airplane."[15]

In the end, the Kansas City plane wasn't dedicated until January of the next year, but Townsend's optimistic projection served to delay the two women's departures. Then negotiations with Sevilla to release Ignacio (Sammy), Dayomæ's son, heated up, and Dayomæ herself became seriously ill with malaria and influenza. News from Ecuador during the coming months would cause Rachel to question decisions made for her by Townsend and SIL's new Ecuador field director, Robert Schneider. Even so, she and Dayomæ remained in the United States working on the Wao language at Wycliffe's center in Sulphur Springs, Arkansas, until May 1958. In the meantime, Dayomæ would be baptized as the "first Auca Christian," and events in Ecuador would shape the direction of future missionary work among the Waorani.[16]

WAORANI ATTACK AGAIN

In August 1957, while Rachel and Dayomæ were in Sulphur Springs and Elisabeth Elliot at Shandia, Wilfred Tidmarsh and Quichuas from the Arajuno missionary station built a bamboo hut on a promontory at the junction of the Curaray and Oglán rivers. The site was about a mile upstream from a small Quichua settlement on the Curaray and about fifteen miles from Arajuno (map 2). Tidmarsh wanted to establish a missionary outpost closer to the Wao settlement than Arajuno.[17] His plan was to spend weekdays at the hut, supervising the Quichuas, who were clearing the jungle for an airstrip nearby, and continuing his study of the Wao language, with a vocabulary list and the few other materials available. Weekends he would return to Arajuno to join his family and to help conduct religious services for the Quichuas there.

On Monday, September 23, after following this strategy for more than a month, Tidmarsh slipped on the muddy trail from Arajuno to the hut and dislocated his shoulder. Helped by the indigenous workers, he returned home. The accident probably saved his life.[18] On October 1, while Tidmarsh remained in Arajuno, recuperating, the Waorani sacked his hut. They took clothing, blankets, knives, pots, and tools, and scattered the rest—bottles of medicine, nails, lamps, books, and papers. The door of the hut had been pulled from its hinges and two crossed lances left behind, blocking the opening.

The Waorani had made contact with the missionaries at last, but the gesture was hardly friendly, and the incident placed a chill over the entire endeavor. Tidmarsh professed to be undaunted by the episode. He would move his operations to the nearby Quichua settlement until the airstrip near his hut could be completed and a stronger house constructed. Both MAF and SIL officials—in a rare moment of agreement—felt these plans were rash. They believed the Wao attack was a sign from God to pull back and proceed only with great caution. It clearly was a sign from the Waorani.

Grady Parrott wrote Hobey Lowrance to be careful in providing air support for Tidmarsh. "Any casualty at this point could bring a reversal of public opinion which Satan could use for bringing disrepute upon the Lord's work down there." Parrott also mentioned a note from SIL pilot Larry Montgomery hoping that "a needless other chapter might not be written."[19] These reactions reflected another tension at the heart of Project Auca, one that affected attitudes toward Elisabeth Elliot as well as toward Tidmarsh. Everyone involved supported the evangelical imperative to contact and Christianize the Waorani, but it had to be successful. God had allowed the first deaths, but no one thought his purposes included a second tragedy.

Townsend sent Tidmarsh a strongly worded letter of caution. Uncle Cam was convinced that Bible translation was an essential prerequisite for friendly contact, and he was not about to allow God's plan for the Waorani to be thwarted by some overzealous missionary. "The next move to the Aucas," he wrote Tidmarsh, "must be a fruitful move." Another life laid down might demonstrate the heroism of the missionary but would accomplish little toward Christianizing the Waorani. It might even cause the Ecuadorian government to prohibit all missionary effort directed toward the group.[20]

"The eyes of the world are upon that tribe," Townsend continued. "The stage has been set through the sacrifice of five missionaries, the extraordinary coverage given that heroic effort by the secular press and now Betty Elliot's inspiring book, for the greatest demonstration in history of the power of the Gospel in the savage heart." Yet the power of the gospel could not be demonstrated until portions of the Bible were translated into *Wao*. Rachel was making progress, and Dayomæ herself had become a Christian, so she could participate. Within two years Scripture portions and "a born again Auca taught in the Word" would be available for the tribe. "Won't you please wait?" Townsend pleaded.[21]

Members of the missionary community in Ecuador shared Townsend's concerns, and some considered Tidmarsh a loose cannon when it came to contacting the Waorani. But they still resented Uncle Cam taking it upon himself to intervene. It sounded once again as if Wycliffe and Wycliffe alone—through its translator, its Wao informant, and its JAARS pilots—held the key to the Christianization of the Waorani. In a sense they were right. Townsend did see Wycliffe playing an essential role because he was convinced that Bible translation was a prerequisite to any effective missionary work among tribal peoples. He also believed that Tidmarsh was "a consecrated, capable man, but on the wrong track."[22]

Townsend's letter might not have been controversial had he stopped with his call for a moratorium on attempts to contact the Waorani. Instead Townsend added a mild threat. If Tidmarsh continued to forge ahead with what SIL considered "premature efforts," Townsend would instruct Bob Schneider in Ecuador and Rachel Saint in the US to provide no more linguistic data or other language help to support the project.[23] This did nothing to mend fences between SIL and the Ecuador missionary community. None of the missionaries, least of all the hard-headed Tidmarsh, wanted to be told what to do by Townsend, even if Townsend were right.[24]

Tidmarsh lost no time in circulating the letter, and MAF's Hobey Lowrance, Elisabeth Elliot, and Abe Dyck of the Gospel Missionary Union all reacted strongly. Lowrance paraphrased what the letter communicated to the missionaries in Ecuador: "We [SIL] are the ones to do the job. . . . When we've written the language and translated the Gospel, we'll call you. May be two years, maybe more. We have the only Auca informant. . . . You'd better play ball with us, or you'll get *nothing* more."[25]

The advantage in the competition to contact the Waorani shifted dramatically less than a month later with the unexpected arrival of three Wao women at the Quichua village on the Curaray River not far from Tidmarsh's ruined shack. Their appearance set off a month of intense controversy as the uneasy balance of power between the various missions working in Ecuador and SIL was renegotiated.

The three women appeared at the edge of the small cluster of six Quichua homes about six in the morning, Wednesday, November 13, 1957. The inhabitants heard voices calling out from the edge of the clearing and responded by greeting the women, clothing them in the usual Quichua dress of loose checked blouse and navy-blue skirt, and offering food. Shortly afterward the youngest of the three fled back into the jungle, but the other two women remained in the home of a man named Dario Santi, accompanied by two older Quichua women, who befriended them, and a crowd of curious neighbors. A few hours later two Quichua men who had worked with Tidmarsh appeared in Arajuno. Tidmarsh had gone to Quito, but Elisabeth Elliot and her two-year-old were there, staying with his wife. After talking with the two men, Gwen Tidmarsh shouted the news to Elliot. Two Wao women were at the Quichua settlement.[26]

MINTACA AND MÆNCAMO

That news marked a turning point in Elisabeth Elliot's life.[27] Since Operation Auca, she had longed for a direct part in contacting the Waorani. As much as any of the five men who died on the Curaray beach, Elliot, too, wanted to be a pioneer missionary, or, as Lowrance described it, to "be in on the action."[28] But the doors had not opened. She was a married woman—first a wife, then a widow—and the mother of a small child. In the minds of most evangelicals, wives and mothers were called to different sacrifices than those exemplified by missionary heroes and martyrs.

Elliot disagreed. When God's will was clear, obedience was required, regardless of gender, marital status, or maternal ties. She was also sure that when it came time to obey, the specifics of the next step would be obvious. In this case they were. She would accompany the Quichua men back to the village to meet the two women. Valerie would stay behind since there was no one to carry her over the muddy tracks of the old oil road that narrowed into a jungle trail to the Quichua village.[29]

Having decided to go, Elliot moved from a supporting role as wife and martyrologist to an actor in her own right in the unfolding story of missionaries and the Waorani. It was an exciting moment, both a test of faith and a once-in-a-lifetime opportunity. She grabbed her pencil and language notebook and was so eager to leave she hardly knew what else to take. Gwen Tidmarsh helped to fill the small Quichua carrying bag with basic necessities, and the young missionary set off with the two Quichua men. Elliot realized she might be facing death in much the same way her husband and his friends had. The Quichua villagers thought the Waorani women might be decoys—perhaps like the Waorani who first visited the men on Palm Beach—and a full-scale attack might follow. But Elliot was living the epilogue to *Through Gates of Splendor*. She was the one who had written of the five missionaries' faithfulness to God, even unto death. Could she do less?[30]

At 5:00 in the afternoon the two guides and Elliot arrived at the village to find the Wao women still in Santi's house, surrounded by the villagers. Although neither woman wore balsa ear plugs, both had the large holes and distended ear lobes characteristic of the Waorani. One woman's ear was torn in a distinctive way, and Elliot recognized her from Nate Saint's photographs as the older of the two women who visited the men on Palm Beach. Dubbing the women "Molly" and "Sue" (not for weeks would Elliot learn their names were Mintaca and Mæncamo), Elliot immediately sat near them and began to take notes, hoping to learn as much as she could about their language in case the women suddenly decided to return to the forests.

After dark that night, as the Quichuas and their Waorani guests slept, Elliot took advantage of the weak glow of a small kerosene lamp to record the events of the day. They seemed an almost fantastical unfolding of God's purposes. Only a year earlier she had been in a New York City hotel room, finishing *Through Gates of Splendor*. Now she faced the possibility of leaving the relatively settled missionary station at Shandia and bringing Valerie to live with the Quichua community and the two Waorani women in more rustic conditions than she had ever before experienced. But with primitive jungle life came the incredible prospect of a relationship with the Waorani. As she contemplated the possibility, Elliot experienced something akin to spiritual euphoria. She understood the danger, even that first night. Nonetheless, she remained convinced that if one was sure of the will of God, all would be well.[31]

The next afternoon Tidmarsh arrived with a tape recorder, and he and Elliot managed to record a tape of the two women speaking that was broadcast on HCJB's *Back Home Hour* the following Sunday night. Evangelicals in the US who were following the Waorani saga knew about this development almost immediately, as if it were the next episode in a serial. A few days later Tidmarsh and Elliot made a second tape after showing the women photographs from *Through Gates of Splendor*. The women seemed to respond to the photographs and talked of killings, of an enemy named Muipa (Moipa), and other instances of tribal violence.[32]

On Tuesday, November 19, 1957, six days after the women first appeared, Elliot left the Curaray village to go back to Shandia and prepare to return for a more permanent stay. When fears surfaced, she found strength in the Bible. Writing her understandably concerned parents, Elliot encouraged them to read Psalm 118. God had spoken to her through the psalm, giving her the confidence she needed.[33] The following Saturday, November 23, she and Valerie—the toddler strapped to a wooden carrying chair on the back of Fermin, a Quichua Christian—set off for the Curaray. They arrived at dusk, but their stay proved brief. The following morning the Waorani attacked a Quichua man and his wife who had started downriver in a canoe, killing the man and his dog and taking his wife captive. The whole settlement was in an uproar, although there were no further attacks that day.

Elliot continued to trust in God's protection, but she was obviously shaken. Eighteen spears were removed from the body of the dead man, while Valerie played nearby. Combined with the mourning wails of the Quichua women and the loud, emotional, and unintelligible response of the Wao woman Mæncamo, the scene was surreal. "I felt, for a short time," Elliot confessed, with what was perhaps the height of missionary understatement, "that I had had enough of the Aucas. I would have been very glad to get out of the jungle, away from all that it meant."[34]

Although she did not leave the jungle, she did leave the village the next morning to return to Arajuno, accompanied by Mæncamo, with whom she was still unable to communicate except in the most rudimentary fashion. A week later the Quichuas, still fearing further violence from the Waorani, decided to abandon their settlement. They, too, arrived at Arajuno, en route to a new site on the Puní River, out of Wao territory. They left Mintaca with the Tidmarshes, Elliot, and Mæncamo.

RELOCATING TO SHANDIA

The MAF pilots and Tidmarsh convinced Elliot to take Mæncamo and Mintaca to Shandia. The site was well outside of Wao territory and was an established Brethren mission station. The location would serve to isolate the women from contact with Catholic priests, Carlos Sevilla, or even the Ecuadorian government.[35] Elliot coaxed the two into a small MAF plane for the hop from Arajuno to Shandia. Once in Shandia, all four—Mæncamo, Mintaca, Elisabeth, and Valerie—moved in with the family of Elliot's Quichua maid and companion, Eugenia. The Wao women obviously were more comfortable among the Quichuas than in a missionary household, and Elliot wanted to stay with them to hear as much of the language as possible.[36]

The MAF–Plymouth Brethren contingent in Ecuador finally had language helpers and contact with the Waorani in the persons of the two women. However, the death of the Quichua man dampened the initial excitement that accompanied this turn of events, and Elliot was finding language study to be excruciatingly slow. The Wao kinship group on the Curaray seemed as violent and hostile as ever. After the spearing, Elliot cabled Cornell Capa to cancel a planned trip to photograph the encounter between the missionaries and Mintaca and Mæncamo for *Life* magazine as the next dramatic step in Project Auca. The missionaries in Ecuador were too edgy to want publicity just yet. Meanwhile, Rachel Saint and especially Dayomæ, still in Sulphur Springs, Arkansas, were nearly frantic to know who the two women were and what news they might have of Dayomæ's family.

The presence of Mintaca and Mæncamo evened out the balance of power between SIL and the missionaries in Ecuador. Suspicions, misunderstandings, personality conflicts, and honest disagreements continued to dog the two groups, but now they needed each other more than ever. Elliot and Tidmarsh needed translation and other language help from Rachel and Dayomæ, while the latter pair wanted both news and the additional language information the two Wao women might provide. Perhaps, despite the layers of resentment that had continued to build during October and

November 1957, the two groups—or at the very least the five women most directly involved—would be able to work together.

ON THE MARGINS AGAIN

In contrast to the excitement in Ecuador when Mintaca and Mæncamo appeared, in Arkansas Rachel was experiencing a sense of déjà vu. Even with Dayomæ by her side, once again—as during Operation Auca and in the months after the men's deaths—Rachel found herself on the margins of missionary contact with the Waorani. No one bothered to call or cable with the news about the two women. Rachel found out the morning after the *Back Home Hour* had broken the story to the American short-wave audience. The broadcast reaffirmed evangelical hopes that God would make possible missionary contact with the Waorani. Mintaca and Mæncamo represented partial fulfillment of those hopes. After the evening radio program ended, Grady Parrott stayed awake most of the night, "rejoicing and thinking of the happening."[37] Phone calls crisscrossed the country among those most directly concerned. Marilou McCully called her parents, who, in turn, called Elisabeth Elliot's parents. Sam Saint called his sister Rachel the next day, as did Katherine Howard, Elliot's mother. Parrott called Marj Saint, who was in the US on furlough. And Rachel, after talking with Sam, called Marj. After two perplexing, often frustrating years, the Waorani had come out. Rachel, however, was a bystander for the second time. "It was of course quite disappointing to me to once again hear of these things when the world did," she wrote Townsend.[38]

CONFLICTING LOYALTIES

Saint found herself caught in a conflicting tangle of loyalties and obligations: to SIL and the wishes of Townsend, to Dayomæ, to the missionaries in Ecuador and their safety, and to her own desire to participate in the outreach to the Waorani. All of this was complicated by living in Sulphur Springs, a village in the "backwash" of the Ozarks. Her immediate response on hearing the news was to begin packing and to call for information about flights to Ecuador. After all, no one knew how long the two Waorani women would remain away from their homes, and "it would be sad to lose a real opportunity." Rachel and Dayomæ were the only ones with any immediate hopes of communicating with the women and perhaps obtaining information about Dayomæ's family and the longed-for details of the missionaries' deaths. In addition, Katherine Howard, in her phone call, expressed anxiety over her daughter's safety. She thought Rachel and Dayomæ's presence might be helpful.[39]

Tickets from Miami to Quito were easy to obtain, but there were no immediate connecting flights from either Tulsa, Oklahoma, or Springfield, Missouri. Also, Dayomæ at first resisted the trip. She had been out of bed for only two days after a serious case of influenza, and she was too weak for jungle trails. She also expressed some reluctance to leave the security of Sulphur Springs to face again the risks and fears of Wao tribal life. She understood that going back to Ecuador meant she would be called on to return to her people. Rachel reminded her "that Jesus did not say he didn't want to leave Heaven though it was a beautiful place." Dayomæ responded that as long as the killer Moipa was dead, "she would go to every Waorani house— stay a long time—and tell them all about the God who created man and women and said not to kill them."[40]

However, Dayomæ's willingness to follow the example of Christ was not to be tested at this particular moment. Rachel was getting mixed signals from Ecuador about whether she and Dayomæ should return. Meanwhile in the US the Wycliffe board of directors said no, as did Townsend, from Chiapas, in southern Mexico. Marj Saint, Rachel's informal link with the Ecuador missionary community, her-self remained open to Rachel's return. But Marj reminded Rachel of the consensus among the missionaries, that SIL had erred in many of its attitudes and decisions surrounding the Wao project. Wycliffe's Ken Watters pointed out that if she hurried back to Ecuador it would look like SIL wanted these new language informants as well and would exacerbate the already shaky relationships. Watters and Bill Nyman of Wycliffe's US home office felt Saint should return only at the direct invitation of Tidmarsh and Elliot, and even then she would need Townsend's permission.[41]

In a further complicating factor, Dayomæ's son, Ignacio, arrived in Quito from the Sevilla hacienda only a few days after the Wao women emerged from the rainforest. Once papers were secured, "Sammy" (as the missionaries nicknamed him) could join his mother in the US, which would, in effect, permanently sever her ties with the patrón. Rachel and Dayomæ's return to Ecuador "would probably scuttle the whole effort [to free Dayomæ and her son]."[42]

Rachel felt a strong pull toward Ecuador. She toyed with the possibility that she and Dayomæ might return to the country—but not to the rainforest—just to be on "stand by" in case they were needed. Then Dayomæ could easily talk with the other two Waorani women by shortwave radio. "Just because Betty [Elliot] does not think she needs our help is no reason to not make it available if it turned out she did."[43] Rachel had not known about it when her brother Nate and the others first contacted the Waorani. In hindsight, as one SIL staff member pointed out, she "must have thought that maybe, just maybe, her language materials might have made a different story out of that contact." This time she did know about Elliot and Tidmarsh. Should she still do nothing? After Katherine Howard called, Rachel was "like a lion in a cage." However, the fact remained that Dayomæ was hardly well enough to travel.[44]

Townsend, on his return from Chiapas, made the final decision. He remained convinced that God had brought Rachel and Dayomæ to the United States in order to provide them with an unhindered opportunity to pursue language study. Rachel's greatest obligation was to perform the task set before her, "giving God's Word at the first opportunity to the Aucas." Even if Mintaca and Mæncamo were Dayomæ's relatives—a relationship that had not been confirmed—the possibility of a reunion paled before the Waorani need for the Bible in their language. Townsend did, however, agree that Rachel and Dayomæ could once again provide translations of Wao tapes and other language assistance to Tidmarsh, since some friendly contact with the Waorani had been made. As for concerns over Elliot's safety, Townsend pointed out, "Betty and Dr. Tidmarsh evidently feel that God has led them to look to Him for protection—not to you and Dayomæ." Only if Katherine Howard sent a written request could Saint consider offering help. Otherwise, Townsend wrote her, "I fear you will be misunderstood." Until such a request arrived, "I expect you to continue right where you are working on the all-important task of putting the Message of Salvation into the Auca language."[45]

Rachel and Dayomæ remained in Sulphur Springs, though Rachel continued to have misgivings. "I still wonder why we are here & not there," she wrote. "Perhaps the Lord has a purpose, but it is hard for me to see."[46] Dayomæ had other concerns. News from Ecuador stirred unsettling memories and left questions unanswered. She and her Quichua husband, Miguel, had lived near the settlement on the Curaray where the Wao women first appeared, and he and their infant son were buried there. Dayomæ also worried about her son Ignacio's adjustment to the altitude and cold temperatures of Quito. Did he have a blanket? Enough food? Warm clothes? Isolated in Sulphur Springs, she could only make her requests known to Rachel. Dayomæ also made a tape recording to be played for the two women. In it she identified herself and asked repeatedly, "Who are you two?"[47]

DAYOMÆ IN CRISIS

Rachel and Dayomæ did translate several tapes that Tidmarsh and Elliot sent them of Mintaca and Mæncamo speaking *Wao tededo*. However, Rachel worried that the repeated inquiries from Tidmarsh and Elliot about "Moipa," apparently a notorious killer, and about the deaths of the five men would frighten the two Wao women. "I believe they would normally fear revenge—even by deceit and a show of friendliness on your part," she wrote, "and it may scare them unnecessarily."[48] The tapes, with their repeated accounts of Wao spearings and news that both Dayomæ's older brother Waawæ and younger brother Nampa were dead, traumatized Dayomæ. She responded with fits of weeping and anger.

Rachel took the young woman out for long walks and told her Bible stories that spoke to issues of anger and vengeance. The Old Testament account of David's refusal to take revenge when his life was threatened by Saul became one of Dayomæ's favorites. The two women lived in an atmosphere of intense emotion from November 1957 to February 1958. Years later the anthropologist David Stoll would suggest that Dayomæ, throughout her early years with Rachel, was "a rebellious language informant" who feared the prospect of returning to the Waorani. According to Stoll, only because Rachel "rigorously conditioned Dayuma" was she eventually able "to undertake a programme she feared."[49]

Stoll accurately captured a recurring pattern of unwillingness on Dayomæ's part to return to the Waorani, as well as the intensity of her relationship with Rachel during their stay in the US. For the first nine months of the trip, until Ignacio arrived in early March 1958, Dayomæ could communicate directly with only one person: Rachel Saint. The task set before them was translating the Bible into the Wao language. If Dayomæ had learned English or associated more freely with other Americans, it might have further compromised her ability to remember the Wao tongue of her childhood and early adolescence. Apparently no one questioned Saint's or Townsend's right to keep Dayomæ in what amounted to linguistic isolation. But the language work clearly came at an emotional cost.

Did Rachel "condition" Dayomæ? The word carries overtones of a kind of manipulation that would have been abhorrent to Rachel and the Wycliffe Bible Translators. Rachel, too, chafed under the isolation of Sulphur Springs. She responded to Dayomæ's emotional crisis with the resources available to her: the Bible and its teachings. And she very much wanted to believe that Dayomæ had become a Christian. Dayomæ seemed to respond to Rachel's overtures, setting aside her anger toward the Waorani who killed her brothers and expressing a new desire to tell her people about God. In a tape recording she made in *Wao tededo* for Mæncamo and Mintaca in late January 1958, Dayomæ told the two women at some length about God's son, who in "exchange he died" and "now, high in the sky He lives."[50]

Rachel was ecstatic. She reported that the tape was "as far as we know . . . the first time an Auca Indian has given the Gospel to her own people in their own language."[51] The tape and Dayomæ's increasing receptivity to Bible stories and evangelical Christianity indicated the beginning of a shift in her status from hacienda peon and language informant to Christian convert and potential missionary. Rachel, herself more missionary at heart than linguist, devoted much of her energy to teaching her protégée Bible stories and lessons. This shift was accelerated by two events during spring 1958: the arrival of Ignacio from Ecuador in March and Dayomæ's baptism in April.

"Ignacio is here and ours is a happy household," Saint wrote Townsend from Sulphur Springs on March 3, 1958. "He now understands 'no' in four different languages, but still does not obey quickly in any!"[52] A few weeks before the boy left Ecuador, the Wycliffe organization arranged for Sevilla's daughter, Julia, to live with a family in California and pursue her college education.[53] Apparently it was the *lotería* the patrón wanted, and he allowed the boy to leave the country, complete with papers that certified his status as a citizen of Ecuador. With citizenship established and living in a distant land, both Dayomæ and her son were free of the Sevilla hacienda and its patronage system. Their place within WBT was less clear, however. Had they, in effect, traded one patronage system for another, even if a more benign one?

Dayomæ, and now Ignacio, lived under Rachel's tutelage and care as a part of WBT. Wycliffe covered the expenses of their travel and stay in the United States, though the bulk of that money came from donations given in response to the women's speaking engagements the previous summer and represented Dayomæ's "earnings" as much as Rachel's. In Sulphur Springs, Dayomæ worked as a language informant and translation assistant, although she had no formal status within the Wycliffe organization. When she learned she was no longer under Sevilla's control, Dayomæ questioned Rachel: "Who will feed us if we do not go back to the patrón?" God would provide, Rachel responded. "We belong to the Lord and serve him." God would take the place of the patrón and, as Saint later described it, Townsend would be acknowledged by Dayomæ as "our" chief.[54]

THE "FIRST AUCA CHRISTIAN"

In tandem with these developments, Dayomæ asked to be baptized. Rachel had told her the New Testament stories of Jesus's baptism and of the early converts to Christianity. "What good man of God can enter me into the water?" she asked.[55] Rachel's answer reflected the isolation of the two women from any local church connection in Sulphur Springs. She suggested V. Raymond Edman, president of Wheaton College and a former missionary to Ecuador. Saint had corresponded with Edman since the early 1950s. He and his wife met Dayomæ on a visit to Ecuador, and Rachel and Dayomæ stopped to visit the couple in 1957 during their summer speaking tour. Edman's son Norman lived in St. Louis, and Saint hoped Edman might combine a family visit to the region with a trip to Sulphur Springs to perform the ceremony.

Edman responded to the request with bigger plans, suggesting that it "would be most appropriate . . . to have the baptism in Wheaton."[56] He volunteered the services of W. G. LeTourneau, a Texas industrialist and wealthy Christian layman, to fly the women from Arkansas to Illinois in his private plane. The service took place on April 15, and both Christian magazines and the secular press took notice, largely in response to a widely circulated press release and photograph issued by Wheaton College at Edman's initiative. Dayomæ was baptized by immersion. That act joined her not only to the Christian church but also, according to the press release, to the sacrifice of the five slain missionaries, whose bodies were recovered from the waters of the Curaray River.[57] A widely circulated photo showed a white-robed Dayomæ, smiling broadly, her hair dripping, standing waist-deep in water at Edman's side.[58] Ignacio, increasingly known as Sammy, was too new to evangelical Christianity to make the profession of faith requisite for a believer's baptism. Instead he was dedicated to Christ during the same service, with Elisabeth Elliot's brother Tom Howard and her father-in-law, Fred Elliot, serving as sponsors for the boy.[59]

Dayomæ's baptism was seen as a sign of things to come for the Waorani. Her new public identity as "the first Auca Christian" soon expanded to include expectations for her role as a missionary to her people. "She wants to go back to her people with the news of salvation," proclaimed an article in *Christian Life* magazine, "though it would most certainly mean death for her."[60] In the 1960 biography *The Dayuma Story*, the Wycliffe writer Ethel Emily Wallis suggests that the baptismal service marked "the initial step in the homeward journey for the first Auca missionary to her own tribe."[61] The image of Dayomæ's new role was reinforced when she, Rachel, and Sammy did finally return to Ecuador about six weeks after the baptism.

To American evangelicals unaware of any tensions among the mission boards and organizations in Ecuador, Dayomæ's baptism indicated that God's sovereign purposes behind the Palm Beach martyrdoms were unfolding as anticipated. "The Holy Spirit is writing a Sequel to Martyrdom," announced the cover of *Christian Life*.[62] The familiar theme of triumph sounded again. "I feel like the fellows must be smiling up there inside the Gates of Splendor!" commented a Wheaton classmate of three of the men in response to the baptism.[63] Dayomæ represented the first fruits of Christianity among the Waorani. No one seemed to wonder about who she was in her own right. Only a brief note at the end of the press release provided a faint glimpse of the person behind the symbol. It mentioned that while in Wheaton, Dayomæ and her son visited the nearby Brookfield Zoo so that Dayomæ could fulfill a wish to "take a long look at an elephant."[64]

5

An Invitation to Meet Dayomæ's Kin

⸉ ──

AS THE PASTOR who baptized Dayomæ, V. Raymond Edman became a part of the missionary-Waorani story, a role he was eager to assume. Edman and his wife had gone to Ecuador as missionaries during the 1920s, hoping to work among the indigenous people of the eastern rainforests. Instead health problems kept them in the cities and eventually forced them to return to the US. Edman earned a PhD in political science in 1933 and spent the rest of his life in Christian higher education, serving as president of Wheaton College from 1940 to 1965.

"Prexy," as students affectionately called him, never lost his missionary zeal, and he became more an inspirational head pastor for Wheaton than an academic leader. When the five men behind Operation Auca were killed, Edman felt an immediate bond with them and their families. Wheaton College alumni had long been involved in Ecuador missions. Now Ed McCully and Jim Elliot, Wheaton graduates during Edman's administration, and Nate Saint, who had taken classes at the college, had given their lives for a tribal group Edman himself once hoped to reach. Philip E. Howard Jr., Jim Elliot's father-in-law, was a trustee of the college; Elisabeth Howard Elliot ironed Edman's shirts and cleaned his home to make spending money during her college years.

Yet Elisabeth Elliot felt uncomfortable with the attention Prexy gave to the deaths of the five missionaries. Even as an undergraduate, she had been uneasy about the president's well-intentioned sentimentalism and tendency toward embellishment. Entering college in 1944, Elliot thought the Gold Star chapels where Edman would memorialize Wheaton men killed in World War II were "too sentimental in the way he conducted [them]. It bothered me." Her reticent, deeply private side recoiled from Edman's open displays of emotion. "He used to get up in chapel and cry," she recalled, finding herself suspicious of Prexy's response to events that seemed to call for something beyond tears. When Elliot's husband and his friends were killed in 1956, again she felt the president overplayed the story in the college chapel and elsewhere.[1]

In a March 1956 college newsletter, Edman wrote that the Waorani worshipped salt as "one of [their] gods." The claim fit into his theme that the slain missionaries were "the salt of the earth," but it was totally false. Edman knew nothing about Wao cosmology. Undeterred, the president concluded the article with the kind of florid assertion that made Elliot cringe. "In their savage slaughter of these lads . . . they [the "aucas"] have tasted the salt of the earth, and will become thirsty for the Saviour!" Elliot was mentioned in the same article, along with "little Valerie in their thatched-roofed home . . . in the hours of the night when the . . . birds send their weird and plaintive call from the jungle fraught with fear and danger."[2] It was all too much for a twenty-nine-year-old widow who might idealize her husband but who abhorred sentimentality.

FIVE MISSIONARY MARTYRS FUND

To further complicate his relationship with the widows, Edman became chairman of the three-member board of the Five Missionary Martyrs Fund, an account organized soon after the men's deaths under the auspices of the Evangelical Foreign Missions Association to handle contributions that were pouring in for the widows and their children. Administered by three respected evangelical leaders—Edman; Clyde Taylor, executive secretary of the Association; and US Army General William K. Harrison Jr.—the fund was a well-meaning attempt to channel gifts for the families into a single account to assist with emergencies and the children's education. By May 1957, when contributions finally tapered off, the fund contained more than $65,000. The amount was substantial, though hardly excessive for four families with a total of nine young children.[3]

The Five Missionary Martyrs Fund was a sore point with the widows from the start. They felt that the fund had been imposed on them and that the conditions for how the money would be used had not been clearly communicated to donors or to the families. The widows opposed the idea at first. In the faith mission tradition, saving money for the future was often seen as evidence of a lack of confidence in God. But despite their concerns, the account was set up anyway. Early press releases indicated that the fund "would be administered for the benefit of the widows and for the education of the children."[4] Many donors assumed contributions would be passed along to the families as soon as the money came in, with the fund serving as a central clearing house for financial gifts. However, the widows and the directors differed in their understanding of the donors' intentions. The widows thought the money had been given with no strings attached. The board viewed the money as given in trust for specific purposes.[5]

The widows were in a difficult position. On the one hand, they had to respond to inquiries from eager donors about funds the families had not received. On the other, to get the money the women had to make specific requests to a board that evaluated them based on need. This placed the board in a paternalistic relationship with the widows, a relationship that both sides, but particularly the women, found uncomfortable.

The women favored dividing the total fourteen ways, with equal shares for the five widows and nine children. The children's money, given to help fund their education, could be held in trust by the board or given to the widows to invest for that purpose, while the widows could use their shares as they saw fit. "The purpose of the fund is to meet . . . emergencies that arise," Clyde Taylor responded, on behalf of the board, with the balance administered in such a way that it would potentially provide for the bulk of the children's college education. "All three of us very much dislike being put in the position of watchdogs," Taylor emphasized. However, "we cannot completely throw off our responsibility."[6]

The women continued to disagree with the board's approach. One of her sons had been diagnosed with a degenerative bone disease, wrote Marilou McCully, but even should she need more money, she would not turn to the fund, because she was the only widow who had already made a request. It seemed unfair to ask for more when the other widows had received nothing.[7] Misunderstandings and correspondence continued for nearly a decade, until December 1966. By that time approximately half the fund, which had grown to nearly $92,000 in principal and interest, had been dispersed to the widows.

A few months earlier a frustrated Elisabeth Elliot, seeking her daughter's share of the remaining funds, had threatened legal action as a last resort.[8] An equally irritated Clyde Taylor, then supervising the fund largely alone because of Edman's ill health, threw in the towel and suggested to the other two board members that a legal way be found to disperse the remaining funds, about $47,300, in equal shares to the children. This was done early in 1967 and concluded a painful episode for all concerned.[9]

In response to a letter from Marj Saint, the irenic Edman had suggested as early as 1960 that the Five Missionary Martyrs Fund be closed and the money divided.[10] For unknown reasons, the board retained control for another six years. Despite Edman's good intentions, his role with the fund further distanced the Wheaton president from Elliot and the other widows. Quietly marginalized from the slain men and their stories despite the Wheaton College connection, Edman cultivated his link to the Waorani story through Rachel Saint and Dayomæ. He would later claim that it was in Wheaton, when Rachel and Dayomæ visited after their appearances on *This Is Your Life*, that Dayomæ became a Christian.[11]

Aided by the Wheaton College news bureau, Edman became a tireless publicist for Rachel, Dayomæ, and the Waorani. His work stood second only to the public relations efforts of the Wycliffe Bible Translators. Regular college news releases informed local papers and popular evangelical magazines about Dayomæ's activities, as well as the ongoing missionary work with the Waorani. In addition, Edman almost single-handedly created the Sunday school version of the Waorani narrative, writing sentimentalized stories such as "When the Aucas Laughed at Dayuma" and "'His Face Was Like the Daybreak'" for the *Sunday Digest*, published by the evangelical David C. Cook company.[12] Edman's unflagging optimism and unquestioning piety fit Rachel Saint's approach to evangelical missions better than Elisabeth Elliot's. During her stay in the United States, Dayomæ acquired Edman as an eager friend.

AN INVITATION TO RETURN

After Dayomæ's baptism, Saint's desire to return to Ecuador finally triumphed over her willingness to defer to Townsend's understanding of God's will on the matter. Her residency papers to live and work in Ecuador would expire if she did not renew them before May 30, 1958. Ignacio's permission to stay in the US was running out as well. Dayomæ had become increasingly eager to see her aunts and impatient over delays.[13] Despite her objections to some Wycliffe policies, Elliot had invited Rachel and Dayomæ to live in Shandia with her, Mæncamo, and Mintaca, so the five women could collaborate on language study. Saint was eager to respond to Elliot's offer.

Rachel also had become concerned with potential problems of cultural reentry for Dayomæ and Sammy.[14] Although Dayomæ was eager to connect with her family, she also enjoyed the attention and safety of life among American evangelicals. The stories her aunts told on tape of spearings and of the deaths of Dayomæ's brothers— and Dayomæ's memories of the violence of her own childhood—made her dread the prospect of going back to the rainforest. The combination of anticipation and terror kept her emotionally on edge. Rachel's solution was to purchase plane tickets that would have her and her "tribe" back in Quito on May 22.

The year Rachel and Dayomæ spent in the US was a momentous one for WBT. The two women arrived in obscurity and became minor celebrities. The Wycliffe side of the Waorani story had begun to be told and would only grow in influence. For many evangelicals, Rachel and Dayomæ became the link between Wycliffe and the hope of peaceful contact with the Waorani. The Waorani, especially Dayomæ, became the face of Townsend's cause: the two thousand "Bibleless tribes" around the world without the Christian Scriptures in their own languages. In a missionary prayer letter written a few months after Nate Saint's death, Rachel commented that the deaths of her brother and his friends were an indication "in a very personal way [of] the value God has put on this tribe."[15]

By mid-1958 many American evangelicals had also taken a personal interest in the tribe and prayed faithfully for them. Linguistic and missionary success among the Waorani came to symbolize not only the sacrifice and heroism idealized in *Through Gates of Splendor* but also the anticipated triumph of the gospel among unreached tribal peoples throughout the world. Rachel and Dayomæ demonstrated the power of the Wao story in other, more concrete ways as well, such as the funds they helped raise for the construction of SIL's Ecuador headquarters and base camp at Limoncocha. The base was rustic, but the airstrip and some homes were ready. While the Wao story never became a financial "golden egg" for WBT or SIL, during the years to come it still could be counted on to inspire recruits and to enhance fundraising.

The publicity surrounding Rachel and Dayomæ also lent needed legitimacy to the work of Townsend, Wycliffe, and SIL, whose unconventional methods and brash approach still were met with skepticism by many evangelicals. The Christian witness of Tariri on *This Is Your Life* and Dayomæ's baptism in Wheaton demonstrated that linguistic work did in fact accomplish the traditional evangelical goal of winning converts. The message of legitimacy was further confirmed in May 1958, when Billy Graham agreed to become a member of the WBT's board of directors. Graham's initial contact with Townsend and Wycliffe had come through his interest in the Waorani story. The evangelist later invited Townsend to speak on the need for Bible translation during Graham's 1968 San Francisco Crusade.[16]

LOW-KEY REUNION

At the end of May, four days after Rachel, Dayomæ, and Sammy arrived at the new Limoncocha base in Ecuador, they were joined by Elisabeth Elliot, Wilfred Tidmarsh, Mæncamo, and Mintaca. Cornell Capa had flown from New York City on the same plane with Rachel and Dayomæ to photograph the reunion. However, there was a minimum of visual drama. At the first meeting Mintaca simply remarked, "That's Dayomæ." Mæncamo, in contrast, greeted her niece with a rapid-fire account of Waorani warfare, and told her, "They speared your brother Wawae [Waawæ]." Hearing this, Dayomæ wept. The next few days were low key as heavy rains closed the Limoncocha airstrip. The three women spent hours in hammocks around a ground fire, eating and catching up through rambling accounts of the history of Dayomæ's kinship group since she left.[17] Dayomæ, for her part, embraced her role as an indigenous missionary, dramatizing for the two women her adaptations of the Bible stories she had learned from Rachel.

Hoping for a breakthrough in learning to speak *Wao tededo*, Elliot had been eager for the reunion. The six months she spent with Mintaca and Mæncamo at Shandia had been frustrating, and she was discouraged by her limited progress in communicating with the two.[18] The Wao women, of course, had no concept of their roles as language informants. Even the idea that an outsider could not "hear," that is, "understand," their language was foreign to them.

In a later description, Elliot provided a vivid portrait of herself leaning over Mæncamo's shoulder, trying to transcribe the sounds of *Wao tededo*. Mæncamo would speak, often with her mouth full and her head turned away, sometimes in a whisper, as Elliot, notebook in hand, tried to see the woman's mouth. To further complicate matters, Mæncamo, by far the more talkative of the two Wao women, had only a few teeth and, as a result, spoke with a slight impediment, although Elliot did not realize it at the time. Despite the discouragement, Elliot pushed on, and by late May she was catching snatches of conversation and communicating through simple phrases. One day when the women were discussing their return to their families, they invited Elliot to go along; at least that was what she understood. The two promised to serve as intermediaries and protectors and assured Elliot that their people would not spear her.[19] Even before she flew with Mintaca and Mæncamo to Limoncocha at the end of the month, Elliot had become convinced that she personally would go to the Waorani. The questions were when and with whom. Also, what about the ongoing complications?

COMPLICATING FACTORS

One complication was that Tidmarsh remained in the picture, doggedly pursuing his own plans. He still hoped to reestablish his outpost on the Curaray, and at some level he considered Mæncamo and Mintaca "his" more than Elliot's.[20] He continued studying the Wao language from tapes of the two women speaking, though the method would have posed a formidable challenge to even the most accomplished linguist. At his urging, MAF resumed "friendship flights" over the Wao clearing, and Tidmarsh toyed with plans to entice more Waorani out of the jungle via messages broadcast from the planes. Yet he admitted to one MAF pilot, Dan Derr, that he "wouldn't know what to do with them if they came."[21] Tidmarsh remained something of a wild card in the Waorani project. If Elliot had attempted to return to the Wao settlement on her own with Mintaca and Mæncamo, Tidmarsh might have taken it upon himself to join in, with unpredictable results.

Much more troubling, however, were the presence and increasingly irrational actions of a Canadian adventurer named Robert Tremblay. Described by his family as a psychiatrist formerly on staff at the St. Jean de Dieu Hospital in Montreal, Tremblay apparently had been restless since returning home from overseas service during World War II. He had made at least one trip to Africa and later hitchhiked most of the way from Canada to Ecuador with the goal of studying "primitive peoples."[22] The Waorani were the group he had in mind. Given the cold shoulder by evangelicals due to his erratic behavior (at one point he planned to parachute into a Wao village), Tremblay had contacted Catholic missionaries, who also backed away from his obsession with the Waorani. In February 1958 he wrote the Ecuadorian government, accusing the evangelicals of holding Mintaca and Mæncamo against their will. He later claimed that because of a previous accident, Nate Saint was mentally imbalanced when he flew for Operation Auca. More outrageous accusations followed, the Ecuadorian press had a field day, and finally even the government got fed up. The provincial governor in the Oriente region asked Elliot to bring Mintaca and Mæncamo to Tena, the provincial capital. She did so, and the two women obtained citizenship papers, affirming their right to move freely in the country. By April, Tremblay, armed to the teeth, had moved into Wao territory.[23]

He started out near the shack Tidmarsh had built, not far from the confluence of the Curaray and Oglán rivers. "On the way over he stopped [at Arajuno] and threatened to shoot Doc T. [Tidmarsh]," Hobey Lowrance reported. "He told the Indians [Quichuas] that he would machine gun the evangelical plane if it came near him (he apparently has a sub-machine gun), or will use it on the Aucas if they attack him."[24]

In early June the Canadian hired four Quichuas to take him down the Curaray. At that point accompanied by George Kiederle, a German expatriate, Tremblay established a camp on a bend in the river about a mile below the site of "Palm Beach." He apparently remained there several weeks, until he decided to move once again, this time to a deserted Wao clearing. At Tremblay's request, Kiederle and the Quichuas left him there. The Canadian remained alone in a Wao house.[25]

The Waorani, hidden in the rainforest, observed the *cowode* for several weeks. They considered him entertainment more than a threat. Probably because of Tremblay's long hair and beard, the Waorani nicknamed him "Kogincoo," their word for a hairy saki monkey, a small primate that looks much larger than it is because it is covered with hair. Tremblay continued to be unpredictable and fired his weapons with no apparent provocation. He remained in the Wao clearing, barricading himself in a house each night. Uneasy about his presence, on at least one occasion the Waorani tried unsuccessfully to kill him. Sometime later they heard a gun go off inside a house where Tremblay had remained for several days. The next morning, after hours of silence, two Wao women slipped up to the house and found the Canadian lying beside his guns with part of his head blown off. He apparently had committed suicide.[26]

Newspapers in Canada and the US carried Tremblay's disappearance and presumed death as another example of a "victim" of the fierce Waorani.[27] Insufficient evidence exists to provide a plausible explanation for Tremblay's need to court death in Amazonian Ecuador. Perhaps he suffered from what today would be called posttraumatic stress resulting from wartime service. Whatever his motivation, while Tremblay was still alive in Wao territory, it would have been the height of folly for any missionary to venture there. Tremblay's misadventures could easily have antagonized the Waorani and been disruptive to any strategy for entering the area.

INITIAL PLANS

Elisabeth Elliot was determined to accompany Mintaca and Mæncamo to the jungles. It was "not because she thought it was safe," reported Rachel Saint, with a certain amount of exasperation, but because Elliot realized the Wao women would not wait much longer to return home. Elisabeth asked Rachel and Dayomæ to go along, but Rachel felt that this was "premature." "Dayomæ had told me that just the three of them (Aucas) should go back first, without us 'foreigners,' but Betty forced her into saying she [Elliot] could go along," Saint wrote Townsend. Dayomæ had acquiesced, Saint added, because Elliot said that "God told her to go." For her part, Elliot believed that Mintaca and Mæncamo intended to return permanently to the Waorani, so to accept their invitation meant to go with them when they left.[28]

A decision was postponed when Elliot took a few weeks off from language study and the months of day-to-day responsibility for the two Wao women. She talked confidentially with MAF pilots Dan Derr and Johnny Keenan about tentative plans to enter the tribe in August, suggesting that Mintaca and Mæncamo would not stay away from their families any longer. In the event Rachel and Dayomæ did not make the trip, Elliot would be able to carry only the bare necessities for herself and Valerie and would have a special need for MAF air support. Derr and Keenan assured her that MAF existed to serve missionaries and that they would never leave her and her child isolated in the jungles. They did, however, ask her permission to quietly consult Grady Parrott at MAF's Fullerton, California, headquarters.[29]

Parrott was not as sanguine as his colleagues in the field. Together with MAF executive committee members Jim Truxton and Charles Mellis, Parrott continued to question Elliot's judgment and her discernment of God's will. Elliot's plans, "wading right in with Valerie, presuming upon God's protection," he wrote, came close to "*tempting* God."[30] Parrott's words reflected practical wisdom. There was a rational basis to the ongoing fears that any further tragedies would jeopardize the whole project and seem to a watching world like a demonstration of evangelical stupidity. Mission Aviation Fellowship did not want to risk that outcome. Middle-class assumptions about gender typical of the 1950s were also at work. "Were they [Elliot and Valerie] going under the leadership of the father of the home, there might be acceptance," Parrott conceded. "But under God's providence this is not the case."[31]

DIFFERENT PERSPECTIVES

Elliot returned in early July to Limoncocha, encountering tensions almost immediately. She had forged a cross-cultural relationship with Mintaca and Mæncamo, as had Rachel with Dayomæ, and now the relational equilibrium was shifting. In her eagerness to find her mother, Dayomæ challenged Rachel Saint's apparent hesitation to enter the tribe. Saint saw Elliot behind Dayomæ's new assertiveness. "Dayomæ for the first time was telling me I was afraid to go to the tribe—and Betty was not," she wrote Townsend.[32] At the same time, Rachel believed that Mintaca and Mæncamo were eager to return to their homes in part because they were unhappy at Shandia. "They had no game at Shandia and not much of anything else they liked."[33] From Elliot's perspective, all the women were ready to return home, while Rachel and SIL were dragging their feet.

Language work proved another sore point. Apart from Dayomæ's profession of Christian faith, the publicity surrounding Rachel and Dayomæ in the United States had centered on Rachel's project of translating the Bible into the Wao language and Dayomæ's role as language informant. Ralph Edwards had told thirty million Americans that Rachel was "learning the language . . . and developing an alphabet so she can give them the gospel written in Auca [Waorani] words." In collaboration with Saint, the linguist Kenneth Pike had prepared a brief article, "Notes on Warani Auca," with an eye toward publication. Wycliffe's *Translation* newsletter informed supporters in the United States that "the Auca language has now been reduced to writing, and Bible translation is underway."[34]

Elliot arrived in Limoncocha with boxes of file cards containing language notes from her work with Mæncamo and Mintaca to question those assertions. She believed that Dayomæ's ability to speak *Wao tededo* had been corrupted by her age when she fled the group and more than ten years as a Quichua speaker, never using her native tongue. Dayomæ's intonation was off; she used Quichua syntax; and she spoke a truncated form of Wao. "Betty says she talks like a first grade reader," Saint wrote. Elliot also challenged the claim that Saint was "doing Bible Translation in Auca." Elliot's accusations obviously hurt. "Betty says that Dayomæ's Auca is like her talking to Valerie (4 years old) . . . that one could never do a real translation using just Dayomæ, that she was not using idiomatic meanings, and that my texts had a lot of Quichua influence in [them] and would therefore be valueless."[35] The implications were clear. Wycliffe's publicity was a house of cards, built on the flimsy basis of a flawed language informant.

Saint conceded some truth to Elliot's comments but insisted that the basics of Dayomæ's speech were sound. Mintaca and Mæncamo understood Dayomæ, and she communicated with them much better than either of the Americans did. "I listened the other day while Dayomæ told her aunts the whole story of the crucifiction [*sic*] and the Resurrection," Rachel wrote in August. "After two months of talking with her aunts, I feel the differences [in Dayomæ's command of *Wao tededo*] are expanded vocabulary, and more realistic explanation of the capturing of Jesus in the garden— but basically [the stories were] the same. M and M's remarks and reactions fully persuaded me that they were listening, and understanding with intense interest." Dayomæ had forgotten some aspects of the Wao tongue, but not its essential core. "True, her intonation was lost, true many adverbs were not remembered, true, the repetitive forms she did not use much, but I insist that . . . the kernel of it [Wao] is in Dayomæ's speech."[36]

Saint also doubted that Elliot's own understanding of the language was advanced enough for her to make a valid critique. She suspected that Elliot's intense drive to contact the Waorani lay behind her comments. On several occasions, Elliot had misunderstood Mintaca and Mæncamo—most seriously, Saint suggested, their invitation to enter the tribe. Saint questioned one of the foundations of Elliot's sense of calling. "In Christian honesty, I must tell her if she says her two women have invited her to go to the tribe with them . . . actually what they said was 'go halfway' with us. She did not yet know the word 'halfway' in the language, but understood the rest."[37] From Saint's perspective, it was Elliot who was building her hopes on the shifting sands of miscommunication.

DIFFERENT APPROACHES

The friction between Rachel and Elisabeth had roots in the past experiences they shared, in the different groups they represented, and in the different personalities of two strong and determined women. It was exacerbated by their pivotal and, despite protestations to the contrary, competing positions in 1958 as the only two American evangelicals in contact with Waorani and with any facility in the Wao language.

Each woman brought strengths and weaknesses to her knowledge of *Wao tededo*. Elliot had a keen ear and analytical mind, and thus the better pronunciation and grasp of language structure, helped along because her informants had never spoken anything but *Wao tededo*. Saint had more experience grappling with the practical uses of the language because of her role as Dayomæ's interpreter. Living arrangements during the weeks at Limoncocha reflected their different approaches. Elliot wanted a place to study, while Saint hung her hammock in one of the shelters the Waorani used. "I want to be where I can hear the girls whenever they talk and she wants a quiet desk," Saint wrote, "so I guess it is the best arrangement for the present."[38] Yet the upshot of this more relational approach was that Elliot was right concerning Bible translation. Saint had not yet done any formal translation work. She was, however, ahead of her time in the way she taught the gospel to Dayomæ through oral Bible stories.

Saint explained the situation to Townsend in early August. She had "taught Dayomæ in Auca anything in the gospels that is in story form, and almost everything that is in story form." Then Saint had moved on to narrative passages in the Old Testament. "These stories I repeated, following the Scriptures verse by verse, until she could tell them back to me, as she has done, quite a few of them, on tape. . . . She would lie in bed at night and recapitulate, fixing these things in her memory."[39] Evangelical missionaries in Asia had long used indigenous "Bible women" to read and teach the Scriptures to their neighbors. Rachel employed classic storytelling techniques, appropriate for the oral tradition to which Dayomæ was accustomed, to create a Wao Bible woman.

"If you ask me how many verses I have translated for the ABS [American Bible Society]," Saint admitted to Townsend, "I would have to say none. Betty says, all I have are Bible Stories, and no translation—perhaps it is all a matter of terms. I told her I made no pretense at having anything ready for the Bible Society. . . . I have done no desk work on translations." Saint also told Townsend she had tried to correct the statements about the Wao language in the *Translation* story, but her changes were ignored.[40]

Rachel's approach to language study with Dayomæ reflected her own inclinations, but also the strain between her identity as a translator and as a missionary, a tension she had embraced when she became a part of WBT and, subsequently, SIL. The purpose of SIL was clear: staff members were engaged in scientific research, literacy programs, practical service, and Bible translation among indigenous peoples as stipulated by the government contracts under which they worked. They were linguists who served missionaries by providing language aids and translating portions of the Scriptures. Saint understood her role as an SIL staff member.

However, Saint also had a missionary heart. And her relationship with Dayomæ had grown from that of linguist and informant to spiritual teacher and disciple. Dayomæ had been adopted as an ex officio member of the Wycliffe organization, but she was under no government contract. She could return to her people as a Christian missionary, and many American evangelicals—including many staff members of Wycliffe and of the Summer Institute—believed she had been providentially chosen to do just that. According to Saint's reports, Dayomæ's primary reasons for reentering the jungles were to see her mother and to tell her extended family about God. "Dayomæ has no thought of staying in the tribe," Saint wrote, "though she talks of teaching them God's Word (in a short time, she thinks)."[41]

Rachel, who still longed to work among her brother's killers, was caught, as she had been for most of 1958, between the dual tasks of translation work and of preparing Dayomæ for her missionary role. At the same time, she was the head of the motley "household" at Limoncocha, responsible for making sure the needs of all the Wao women and Sammy were being met. The energetic Townsend thought she could—and was—doing it all. Under pressure, however, Saint usually fell back on her strengths: cultivating relationships with indigenous people and Bible teaching. And, as Elliot had noted and Saint freely admitted, Bible translation work suffered. It was a pattern that would be repeated in the years to come. One of the ironies of the reluctant partnership between the two was that, although officially Saint was the linguist and Elliot the traditional missionary, their apparent giftedness seemed just the opposite. Elliot had a knack and a temperament for acquiring languages, while Saint exuded the activism and unquestioning commitment associated with evangelical missions.

For their parts, SIL directors encouraged Dayomæ's missionary activities. When Rachel and Dayomæ had returned to Ecuador in May, they had been flown from Quito to Limoncocha in the *Spirit of Kansas City* Helio Courier, purchased with funds donated by people from that city. After Dayomæ's reunion with her aunts, Bob Schneider wrote to H. Roe Bartle, mayor of Kansas City, Missouri. He told Bartle that the *Spirit of Kansas City* had been used to carry Dayomæ, "the first Christian from the savage Auca tribe," to Limoncocha, where she continued to work with Rachel Saint "on the translation of the New Testament into Auca." The airplane also made possible the "dramatic meeting" between Dayomæ and her aunts, "which enabled Dayomæ to tell these women for the first time in Auca history that God has a Son, Jesus Christ, who died for them."[42] The *Spirit of Kansas City* did more than facilitate linguistics work; it served missions.

Schneider also wrote Saint, suggesting that the three Wao women should return to their family group first, before the two Americans went in. They should do so "to tell their people of their friendly reception . . . but most of all to bring a witness of Christ" to the tribe. Of course, this could not happen until Mintaca and Mæncamo "have been led to the Lord by Dayomæ." Until that happened, Schneider thought the Wao women should remain at Limoncocha, unless God indicated a different approach. "We are united in prayer that your combined efforts with the three Aucas and Betty will result in a more rapid evangelization of the tribe," he concluded.[43]

Townsend agreed. He also optimistically assumed Dayomæ had learned to read, presumably in *Wao tededo*, and would "be able to feed on the Word [the Bible] by herself."[44] In Townsend and Schneider's ideal scenario, Elliot would accept SIL's invitation to live and work with Saint at Limoncocha, along with the three women. All five would remain there a year or two, while the Bible was translated and Mintaca and Mæncamo became Christians. Then the three Waorani women would reenter their tribe as literate Bible women, carrying at least a portion of the Christian Scriptures in the Wao language. The tribe would be Christianized, missionaries would arrive to help, and God's purposes behind the Palm Beach killings would be accomplished. Through it all, SIL would maintain its identity as a "scientific, cultural, and linguistic" organization.[45]

MINTACA AND MÆNCAMO DECIDE

That vision for the future ignored the agency of the Wao women themselves. In the end, they set the timetable. By July, Elliot had begun to back away from her original plan to go in August, since Mintaca, Mæncamo, and Valerie had all been sick. Grady Parrott also had visited Elliot in Limoncocha to counsel caution. She was, he reported, still sure that God wanted her to "personally go into the Aucas" but could not speak with the same confidence about timing. Elliot also had mentioned, he added, that her parents were "besides themselves" over her plans.[46] Then, as August ended, Mæncamo announced that the kapok was ripe, and she was going home. "I told my people that if I did not return in the kapok season, I would be dead." She and Mintaca told Elliot she could come halfway and wait for them at the Oglán-Curaray junction, but then they decided even that was too dangerous. She might be "eaten by the pumas," they told her. The real reason may have been uncertainty in the wake of Tremblay's death.[47] It would be better for Elliot to wait in Arajuno.

With the moment of decision and risk at hand, Dayomæ hesitated once again. "She has a deep desire to teach her people God's Word, to see her family again, and to try to bring harmony within the tribe and with the outside world," Saint assured friends in the US. "On the other hand, she knew full well the darkness into which she was entering."[48] As one way to overcome the fear, Saint suggested Dayomæ write Edman, asking for prayer. With Rachel's help, Dayomæ did so. Edman alerted evangelicals within the Wheaton College network, and Americans, accustomed to praying for the Waorani, rallied for the next episode.[49]

On September 3, a JAARS plane ferried Elisabeth and Valerie Elliot, the three Waorani women, and other passengers from Limoncocha to Arajuno. Three puppies came along as pets for the Waorani. At 9:30 that morning, Dayomæ, Mintaca, and Mæncamo headed down the old road toward the Curaray River. They were loaded with trade goods to facilitate a positive reception.[50] Elliot and Valerie settled in to wait, despite a reluctant welcome from Tidmarsh, who was upset to be excluded as this phase of the Waorani project was launched from his doorstep. Meanwhile, Saint, who was caring for Sammy, went to stay with Bobbie Borman and her son, Randy, among the Cofán people while husband and father Bub Borman was away. The Bormans were SIL linguists working in the rainforest to the north of Limoncocha.

Five days after the women had gone, Dan Derr flew Elliot over the Wao clearing. Elliot had the "bucket drop" walkie-talkie system that Nate Saint had developed and was hoping to find Dayomæ. However, even though the plane circled the clearing numerous times, there were no obvious signs of the women. Elliot thought one gesturing figure might be Mæncamo, but she was not certain. Elliot called her name out the window and shouted some phrases that she, Mintaca, and Mæncamo had agreed upon. There was no clear response. The September days passed in silence. Johnny Keenan made a second flight, with Tidmarsh and Elliot along as spotters, and then a third. None of the women, who had promised to wear clothing so the missionaries could better identify them from the air, appeared. Rachel called Shell and Arajuno by radio each day, waiting for word.[51]

In the absence of news, a rumor spread in the US that Dayomæ had been killed. One day Sammy found Rachel distressed, holding some postcards. They expressed sorrow over Dayomæ's death, the first Rachel had heard of the rumor. She did not know what to tell the boy, except to follow her in praying fervently.[52] Sammy's prayers, wrote Rachel, were, "Don't let the tiger kill them, or the boa wrap them, or the snakes bite them."[53] Back in Arajuno, spirits were low. With no sign of the Wao women, Tidmarsh decided to accompany his wife to Quito for dental work. The Tidmarshes radioed Marj Saint, asking if she would stay with Elliot and Valerie. On the afternoon of September 23, as Marj arrived in Arajuno, she commented,

"Wouldn't it be wonderful to see three Auca women coming down the airstrip."[54] Two days later her wish and her sister-in-law's prayers were answered.

THE WAORANI RETURN

The morning of September 25, Elliot was doing the laundry when a Quichua man from the Curaray River area approached her. In response to her inquiry, he casually commented that the Wao women had come back and had brought other Waorani with them. They would arrive soon.[55] The whole contingent—Dayomæ, followed by Mintaca and Mæncamo, along with two other women, three girls, and two boys— created a sensation among the local Quichuas when they reached Arajuno.

Elliot had to teach a group of Quichuas that afternoon, and Marj Saint was needed at the radio, so they asked the Waorani to stay in one of the empty buildings at the missionary station, with Dayomæ in charge. "They had to do something with the Aucas, realizing that the nearby priest would pay any price to get even one of them," another missionary later wrote. As word spread, crowds of Quichuas gathered around the building. Dayomæ stood in the doorway and announced, "If you want to see an Auca, look at me, I'm one."[56]

Rachel arrived the next day with Sammy, and the persistent photographer Cornell Capa soon appeared, cameras in hand, still in pursuit of a *Life* exclusive. The Waorani had come with an invitation for both Saint and Elliot to enter the tribe. Conflict again surfaced as Saint announced her plans to fly back to Limoncocha with Dayomæ, to debrief her in a less chaotic atmosphere. Saint also was concerned about the fast pace of events. Part of her dilemma was that Elliot, an independent Brethren missionary, could make an immediate decision to accept any invitation the Waorani might extend. After three years of prayer, anticipation, and trepidation, Elliot was eager to go, daughter Valerie in tow. Marj Saint offered to take Valerie to Quito, but Elliot refused, saying, "Where I go, Valerie goes."[57] As an SIL staff member, in contrast, Saint needed approval from Ecuador director Schneider and from Townsend.

The next few days involved a furious exchange of information, as Dayomæ recounted events of the previous weeks. After three days on the trail going in, she had been too tired—or perhaps too fearful—to go on. Or she may have wanted a site more accessible to the outside world. The three women had stopped and cleared a spot along the Tewæno River, a few hours' walk from the cluster of houses where Dayomæ's kin lived. The next morning, Mæncamo continued to the group's current site, to tell Dayomæ's mother and her family that Dayomæ had returned. Later that day, Dayomæ's mother, Acawo, and other family members accompanied Mæncamo to the location along the Tewæno. There they gathered, away from the usual flight paths of the missionary planes and in a location hardly visible from the air.[58]

DAYOMÆ TAKES CHARGE

Once sure of the welcome from her mother, her uncle, and other family members, Dayomæ quickly assumed the role of cultural broker or mediator in the Tewæno clearing. She wore clothing and explained the ways of Quichua and missionary alike to her kin. She had brought two bottles of medicine into the jungles, and, when Acawo became ill, Dayomæ suggested she might have worms. She told the Waorani to wash their food and not to defecate in the rivers.[59] Also, as the missionaries had hoped, she recounted stories about God. For the first time in her life, Dayomæ had authority in her own right, and she exercised it with enthusiasm, a change the missionaries noticed when she returned to Arajuno. "Dayomæ really feels her oats, being of course the translator and go-between," commented one observer.[60] From always being the peon or underling, Dayomæ was beginning to become the boss (*patrona*).

With the Waorani promising the missionaries they had nothing to fear and with Dayomæ, Mintaca, and Mæncamo to help overcome the communications barriers, Saint and Elliot prepared to meet Dayomæ's kin. One missionary wrote home, "This seems to be the break the world has been praying for."[61] Events moved rapidly. The Waorani arrived on September 25, and SIL officials gave their final consent on October 3. Three days later the women left.[62] There was some strain over who would provide air support. MAF had serviced missionary attempts to reach the Waorani since Nate Saint and Operation Auca, but SIL staff like Rachel were usually supported by JAARS planes.[63] In a spirit of cooperation, however, JAARS remained in the background, and MAF continued to provide air support. The day before the group left, Keenan, Elliot, Dayomæ, and JAARS pilot Bob Griffin flew over Waorani territory so that Dayomæ could point out their destination to the two pilots. All the Americans were encouraged to discover that the new settlement was more accessible to outsiders by air and water than either of the two previous clearings occupied by the Wao kinship group. They also were heartened to see signs of homes under construction for the two women, as the Waorani had promised.[64]

On Monday, October 6, 1958, the group set out for Tewæno. In addition to the two missionaries and the Waorani, the party included five armed Quichua men who acted as carriers and intended to go only as far as the Quichua settlement on the Curaray. Valerie rode in a wooden chair on her Quichua friend Fermin's back. It had been just eleven days since Dayomæ, Mintaca, and Mæncamo had returned with their invitation. Exactly thirty-three months had passed since the five men had made contact with the Waorani on Palm Beach. Rachel Saint and Elisabeth Elliot left as reluctant partners, drawn together by the legacies of the slain men, by the Wao women they had befriended, and by the stubborn assurance each had that God wanted her in the rainforests of the Waorani.

PART III

Life in Tewæno, 1958–1968

⁓————————————————————————————

6

Peaceful Contact

THE FIRST DAY on the trail was deceptively routine for the band of travelers, who set out on the three-day trek from the mission station at Arajuno to the Waorani clearing on the Tewæno River. They followed the familiar, rigorous old oil road as they began the fifteen-mile walk to the Quichua village at the junction of the Oglán and Curaray rivers. This was near the place where Elisabeth and Valerie Elliot met Mintaca and Mæncamo in November 1957 and where the Waorani killed the Quichua fisherman, riddling his body with spears. This time the group arrived in the afternoon and were greeted by Quichuas who had returned to the site, including Maruja, the wife of the slain fisherman. She had been held by the Waorani until only a few weeks earlier, when Dayomæ had arranged her release.

From an emotional standpoint, the Quichua settlement turned out to be a discouraging place to spend the night. Maruja was more than happy to provide details of her husband's murder and her own captivity. She created a brief turmoil when she insisted that the Waorani expected her to return and would spear them all if she did not. She would go back, Maruja added, if the price were right—a deal Dayomæ indignantly rejected.[1] When Elliot asked what Maruja thought of their plans to go to Tewæno, she responded, "In my opinion . . . it will not be long before you are all dead and eaten by vultures."[2] The grim prediction assumed further weight as the former captive offered more details about the death of Robert Tremblay. After he committed suicide, she said, the Waorani made a necklace of his teeth, a claim that was never substantiated.[3]

In the months before he died, Tremblay had built a ramshackle "fortress" near the Quichua settlement as a starting point for entry into Wao territory. Still standing, the two-story house had a big aluminum-covered cross out front; it was rumored that the Canadian salvaged the sheet metal from Palm Beach during a trip down the Curaray.[4] The widow Maruja, the decaying Tremblay fortress, and the old aluminum all represented the reality of death that seemed to greet outsiders entering Wao territory. It had a chilling effect on the usually resolute Elliot, who briefly harbored second thoughts about what she and her daughter were doing. To Elliot, the Waorani "were the personification of death," a death she was prepared, but not eager (despite the suspicions of some), to face.[5]

Dayomæ shared none of the hesitancy. She took offense at any hint the Americans might back down. That night, Rachel, Dayomæ, and the Quichua men set up camp at Tremblay's house, while Elisabeth and Valerie stayed with a Quichua family. The next morning, the departure down the Curaray was delayed as Dayomæ haggled with their owners over the fitness of the three dugout canoes the group would use. Once under way, the excitement of spear fishing lifted everyone's spirits, and the day passed uneventfully. Dayomæ remained clearly in charge, "really calling the signals," Rachel noted, "telling the Quichua men what to do." The young woman obviously relished the role. "What a character," Rachel wrote. "She is so happy."[6]

By late afternoon, the party had reached the mouth of the Añangu River, where they camped for the night. The next morning, they bucked the current as the Quichuas poled the canoes up the shallow river. The spear fishing continued until the group stopped for a break near the mouth of an even smaller stream, the Tapir River. Then it was time for the last leg of the trip, a three-and-a-half-hour hike through the rainforest, with no trail that the Americans could discern.[7]

Originally the five Quichua men planned to turn back near the end of the river portion of the journey, but Dayomæ convinced them to accompany the group all the way to the Wao clearing. Elliot supported the decision for pragmatic reasons. With the Quichuas along, there was someone to carry Valerie and the heavy radio equipment. This was no small benefit as the group cut their way through the jungle, following the lead of Mæncamo and Dayomæ. Saint was more apprehensive about the decision. To her, the presence of Quichua men and their guns increased the potential for violence.[8] She also was concerned that once the men knew the way to the Wao clearing, word would get out and more visitors would follow.

That afternoon the group emerged into a modest clearing at a bend in the Tewæno River, where the Waorani had begun to build a few shelters, little more than thatched roofs supported by poles. A Wao man and two women waited for the foreigners, although their arrival elicited little or no emotion. The three were Quemo (Mæncamo's brother) and his wife, Dawa, as well as Dayomæ's sister Guiimadi. Guiimadi was the girl the five missionaries had nicknamed "Delilah" at Palm Beach. Other members of Dayomæ's extended family had returned to the gardens near their previous clearing to get food and await news of the women's arrival.[9]

DAYOMÆ'S ROLE

For Elisabeth Elliot and Rachel Saint, entering the clearing on the Tewæno was a moment of great excitement and vindication of their faith in God. Like the five missionaries before them, they met three seemingly friendly Waorani, a man and two women. But there were significant differences this time around. First and foremost, Elliot and Saint had come with Dayomæ as cultural broker, someone to bridge the divide between the Waorani and outsiders.[10] Their relationships with Mintaca and Mæncamo also helped. Although news reports and a November 24, 1958, *Life* magazine photo essay emphasized the missionaries' success in making peaceful contact with the tribe, particularly the presence of Valerie among her father's killers, Dayomæ clearly was the key element in making the entry possible.[11] Even so, Saint and Elliot were pleased to discover that they could understand at least some of what the three Waorani said, though much of the rapid speech went over their heads.[12]

For Elliot, the date of their arrival had additional significance. October 8, 1958, would have been Jim Elliot's thirty-first birthday, and Jim and Elisabeth's fifth wedding anniversary. That backdrop made Valerie's response to Quemo, the first Wao man she had ever met, all the more poignant. Less than a year old when the Waorani killed her father, Valerie knew he was dead, but Elliot had not explained to the three-year-old the circumstances surrounding the death. Even so, Valerie had made a connection between the Waorani and her father. As she watched Quemo, her reaction was one of confusion. "He looks like a daddy," she said. "Is that my daddy?" To Valerie, the Waorani were neither savages nor death personified. They were people, like the lowland Quichua she had known since birth. Elliot later wrote that Valerie "was ready to accept as her own father the man who had helped to kill her father." The comment planted the seed for the theme of Elliot's next book, a photo essay presenting the Waorani as "kinsmen" rather than killers.[13] Some days later, after the other men in the kinship group had arrived and Valerie had met them, Elliot mentioned that these were the men who had killed her father.[14] Valerie prayed nightly for them and for the other Waorani she knew by name.

The next few days were uneventful. Quemo went to the downstream clearing and alerted Dayomæ's mother and other family members that the women had arrived. In response, the Waorani made their way to Tewæno a few at a time. Dayomæ's kinship group numbered fifty-six, of whom only seven were adult men. About twice that many were adult women, wives and widows, while the rest were children.[15] They were the Guequitaidi (Guequita's bunch), after Dayomæ's uncle Guequita, the most influential man in the group. They represented about 10 percent of the total known Wao population at the time, a population divided into four mutually hostile kinship groups. Each group was scattered over a portion of Wao territory, which it controlled (map 1).[16]

The Quichua men remained at Tewæno for three days before returning to Arajuno. The MAF plane made food drops on October 9 and 10, and Saint and Elliot were able to establish clear radio contact with the plane overhead. On October 9 Elliot wrote one of her first letters from Tewæno to family and friends. Her opening paragraph, later expanded for *Life* magazine, described a peaceable kingdom where she and her daughter lived in harmony with the men who had killed her husband and Valerie's father.[17]

Saint was equally content. In one of several letters that circulated to SIL staff in Ecuador, she described the quiet poise of Dayomæ's sisters Guiimadi, Oba, and Ana. On the evening of October 9, Dayomæ's mother, Acawo, arrived in the clearing, carrying the three puppies Dayomæ had brought her. By the end of the evening, she had accepted the designation of Rachel as a member of the family. Dayomæ had earlier given Rachel the Wao name "Nemo," after a deceased relative. The name meant "Star," but for the Waorani, its significance lay in the kinship connection it represented.[18]

DAYOMÆ AS A BIBLE TEACHER

Initially, both Saint and Elliot were painfully aware of their need to listen, observe, and learn in order to relate effectively to the Waorani. Dayomæ, however, picked up her role as Bible woman where she had left off in September. On October 12, the Sunday after the group had arrived, she held an informal "church service" for about twenty Waorani. She told simple Bible stories she had learned from Rachel, "punctuated," Elliot later observed, "with admonitions to shut up."[19] Dayomæ's actions were completely foreign to Wao culture, where there were no such things as required group activities or one person taking the floor to speak while others remained silent.

News of the women's safe arrival and welcome spread rapidly through the Ecuador missionary community, although both the missions agencies and SIL maintained a moratorium on news to the outside world until they gained more confidence that nothing would go wrong. The moratorium also reflected an agreement between Elliot and MAF with Cornell Capa and *Life* to grant the magazine exclusive rights to the story of successful contact with the Waorani. *Life* editors cared little if news notes made their way into the Christian press, but they insisted no pictures appear until the magazine published its photo essay, in both national and international editions. The *Life* story appeared on November 24, 1958, followed by a news report, without photographs, in the *New York Times* three days later.

The only real challenge to the agreement with *Life* came from the irrepressible President Edman at Wheaton College. In response to a *Chicago Daily News* query about how the missionaries would spend Thanksgiving Day 1958, Edman patched together a brief radio interview with Elliot that provided material for an imaginative news release and a *Daily News* article on the "world's strangest Thanksgiving dinner," complete with a generic aerial photograph of a thatched roof shelter that was identified as the Tewæno home of Elliot and Valerie.[20] In fact it could have been any of millions of thatched dwellings around the world.

Elliot and Saint spent seven and a half weeks in Tewæno on their first trip. Rachel would later compare arriving in the clearing with reaching the Promised Land. For Elliot, too, it was a fulfillment of God's promise. In the nearly three years since Jim's death, she had hung on to a phrase from the Psalms: "Who will bring me into the strong city? . . . Wilt not thou, O God?"[21] It seemed that God had indeed broken through the impregnable barrier of Waorani resistance.

At the same time, life in the modest clearing at Tewæno could feel a bit anticlimactic. The site hardly qualified as a "strong city." Also, Elliot and Saint might have been the first outsiders to be accepted by the Waorani, but they were not, strictly speaking, pioneer missionaries entering a pristine field, as Jim Elliot had dreamed. Dayomæ had prepared the way during her visit in September. She was the first to talk to the Waorani about God and already had introduced changes the missionaries had not anticipated. First and foremost was the Tewæno site itself. It was a new clearing, chosen by Dayomæ, but familiar to her kinship group since it was located on the site of an old, abandoned Wao settlement. Tewæno was located four or five hard hours' walk over trails through the rainforest from the Guequitaidi's most recent homes near the Terminal City location where they had lived when they attacked the five men.

The new location had advantages. It was more accessible to the outside world, convenient both for the missionaries and for Waorani such as Dayomæ, who wanted more contact with Quichuas. At the same time, it was more distant from the traditional enemies of Dayomæ's kin, another Waorani group usually referred to as the *ænomenani*, the "downriver" people, also known as the Piyæmoidi (Piyæmo's bunch). The missionaries probably were safer at Tewæno than living near Terminal City. Nonetheless there were difficulties. The Waorani had cultivated gardens with manioc and banana trees at their previous location. No fields had yet been cleared in Tewæno, so food was scarce.

Elliot expressed some uncertainty over Dayomæ's decision to relocate the community.[22] A few Waorani seemed reluctant to move, and many of the others seemed to commute between the two locations, alternating a few days in Tewæno with a few cultivating crops or gathering food near Terminal City.[23] The population at Tewæno fluctuated during the women's first visit from a high of about thirty to a low of seven or eight. Some days the "strong city" was little more than a deserted clearing. On one Sunday in late October, for example, Elliot recorded that only six boys and Dayomæ's mother attended the Sunday meeting.[24] Along with Dayomæ, the Americans, and one additional boy, they were the only people in Tewæno that day.

CULTURAL CHANGES

Other changes Dayomæ introduced were designed, at least in part, to encourage her people to imitate the outside world. At Capa's urging, Elliot had photographed the Waorani from the day she entered the tribe. One of her pictures taken that day showed Valerie sitting on a log with Mæncamo and her brother, Quemo, the little girl scrutinizing the Wao man. When Valerie commented to her mother that Quemo looked "like a daddy," she wasn't simply referring to his anatomy. Quemo had a rough butch haircut, close-cropped all around, courtesy of the shears Dayomæ had brought her mother in September, rather than the traditional bangs and ear-length hair of male Waorani. With his short haircut, Quemo looked like a "civilized" Quichua or an American father.

Dayomæ had cut the hair of all but two of the males in the group, both to combat lice and to adapt to outside norms. In a letter to Marj Saint and Marilou McCully, Elliot reacted in mock horror to Dayomæ's efforts to bring the Waorani into the twentieth century, lamenting the Wao woman's determination to give haircuts, encourage clothing, and get people to remove their balsa earplugs.[25] After more than a decade living among Quichuas and a year in the United States, Dayomæ was not simply an indigenous Bible woman, as the missionaries had thought, or a cultural broker to facilitate the arrival of outsiders. The cultural bridge went two ways, and Dayomæ became a key change agent among her people. She was painfully aware of the stigma of Wao "savagery" and much more concerned than the missionaries themselves that the Waorani embrace outside ways, particularly those of the Quichuas.[26]

Within four days of her return in October, Dayomæ had arranged a marriage between Epa, a young Wao widow, and Mariano, a Quichua man.[27] This action directly challenged appropriate kinship requirements and flew in the face of Wao beliefs that the children of such "mixed" marriages would never be accepted as

Waorani. Some of Dayomæ's actions toward the Quichua men who accompanied the women to Tewæno suggested that she might have hoped for a Quichua husband as well.[28]

Elliot viewed Dayomæ's efforts with some skepticism. Was wearing clothes practical for people who lived in open shelters in the rainforest, particularly when they had no idea how to care for them? The Wao women and children who had come to Arajuno in September had, at Dayomæ's request, been given clothing by Wilfred Tidmarsh. Those who wore the shorts and skirts after they returned home simply kept them on until they rotted. Rachel took a somewhat different stance. Proud of Dayomæ's leadership, she supported most of her innovations, and she was pragmatic rather than dogmatic on the issue of clothing.

Several things may have motivated Dayomæ's push to clothe the people in the Tewæno clearing. First, she knew that the Quichuas in the area were quick to use clothing as a measure of "civilization," and Dayomæ was fiercely committed to improving her own lot in life and, in the process, to civilizing her family members. "Savages" were naked and risked being shot by outsiders. Second, there were rules of obligation in Wao culture. If Dayomæ had clothes, which she did, it was expected that she share them with her relatives.[29] Finally, as Rachel pointed out, clothing offered some protection against gnats and other insects.[30]

Rachel continued to differ from Dayomæ in one key area: she frowned on the prospect of increased Wao contact with outsiders. The Quichua carriers had gone home but returned several times while Elliot and Saint were there. Rachel worried about the implications of potential sexual liaisons and other problems.[31] For the rest of her life, she would fiercely oppose changes in Wao culture coming from the outside world, except for changes that she believed were mandated by the Bible.

LIFE IN TEWÆNO

During October and November 1958, however, the immediate challenge both women faced was understanding and adapting to Wao culture as expressed in everyday life. Even by the rigorous standards of SIL, which expected linguists to live in jungle settings with tribal peoples, Saint and Elliot were radical in their attempts to live as the Waorani did. Rachel shared a thatched dwelling with a Wao family—Guequita, his wife, Mæncamo, and three children. She placed her air mattress on bamboo slats not far from the fire, near the hammocks and an old piece of dugout canoe that served as beds for everyone else. The Elliots occupied a small shelter nearby—Elisabeth in a hammock like most of the Waorani, with Valerie on a "bed" of bamboo slats below her mother.

Interruptions during the night were common. Sometimes Mæncamo awoke and began chanting for no discernable reason, or she would start the fire and cook herself a meal. Wao women also expressed friendship by rousing the missionaries with gifts of monkey meat. "Nemo!" came the call, after Rachel was asleep one night. She sat up. "Without a word, Nemonca's wife handed me a monkey-leg, cooked, hairs half burned off, skin and toenails on!"[32] It was the third time Rachel had been awakened that night, and her second gift of meat. Elliot had similar experiences.[33]

Not all the interruptions seemed quite so benign. One night the dogs Dayomæ had given her family began to bark. "I awoke just in time to hear old Guequita say 'Tiger!'" Rachel wrote. "And he sprang to his feet from that horizontal position in the net as if he were a tiger [jaguar] himself!" On a separate occasion, Mæncamo decided the dogs' cries meant that the group's downriver enemies had come to attack. "She hurried out to a big log and for fifteen minutes cried out orders to the unseen foe!" Nothing further happened on either occasion.[34]

Meals were another challenge in cultural adaptation. The Waorani ate rapidly and with plenty of sound—"a great slurping and sucking." In three or four minutes a group of men could demolish a pile of plantains and a pot of meat without a bare minimum of the social niceties expected by Westerners.[35] When men were in the clearing and the hunting was good, monkey meat was standard fare. Elliot found it disconcerting to watch the creatures, shot with a blow gun and poison darts, first singed to remove the hair, then boiled. They looked too human.[36] The Waorani considered monkey heads a great delicacy, and skulls were licked and sucked with enthusiasm, including in a "mouth to mouth" position. After five or six weeks, Rachel confessed she had overcome her "prejudices" enough to eat some of the brains herself. However, she still "left the sucking of the eyes to Acawo."[37]

Not ready to go completely native in their diets and unwilling to burden the Waorani with three more mouths to feed, the women did get a weekly food drop from the MAF plane. There was tea and instant coffee for the adults and powdered milk for Valerie, along with other staples. The women also purchased bananas and frozen beef from the outside. They shared these with the Waorani as a way of compensating for the monkey meat and other Wao food they ate. The MAF pilots even parachuted a live hen so the women could have fresh eggs.[38]

ONGOING RISKS

Although they had been accepted into the kinship group, neither missionary was sanguine about the ongoing risk of living among the Waorani. Rachel's awareness of the danger took the form of a vivid nightmare. It occurred in mid-October, when

Mæncamo's brother Dabo arrived at Tewæno and joined his sister's family for the night. He "slept on a piece of the canoe under one of the hammocks," Rachel wrote, "his longish tousled head of hair not a foot and a half from mine!" About four-thirty in the morning, she dreamed she was in New York City, "and the 'villain' had a face like *Dabo*!" She screamed, waking Dayomæ in a nearby shelter, who, in turn, roused Rachel from her dream.[39]

Elliot reported no dreams, but she mentioned thinking often about the Tylee family—Arthur, Ethel, and their baby daughter, Marian—who served as pioneer missionaries during the late 1920s among the Nhambiquara people in western Brazil. In 1930, after the Tylees had spent more than two years with them, the Nhambiquara attacked, killing Arthur and Marian and leaving Ethel for dead (she survived). The story served as a reminder that five or six weeks of peaceful coexistence with Waorani provided no guarantee of safety.[40]

This seemed especially true as the women faced aspects of Wao culture that were more deeply troubling and difficult to understand than a taste for monkey brains or fish heads. Elliot wrestled with what seemed like a penchant for indifference and even cruelty among the Waorani. Normally an exceptionally articulate woman, she struggled to conceptualize what it meant to be a missionary in the light of certain incidents—episodes that seemed reprehensible, even sinister, to an outsider.[41] The Waorani laughed at cruelty toward children and animals. They talked in great detail about violence and the vengeance killings that had nearly destroyed their kinship group, and they seemed inured to death and suffering.[42] The elusive "neighbors" of Operation Auca were proving to be an even more formidable missionary challenge than Elliot had anticipated, despite her confidence in God's call to live with them.

Saint rarely pondered Wao cruelty, at least not in letters. In part, she was less reflective by temperament. She also had been prepared by years of listening to Dayomæ's stories of brutal vendettas among the Waorani and by her earlier experiences living among the Shapra people in Peru. Perhaps most important, however, she found an adequate framework for understanding the Waorani in the literal biblicism characteristic of fundamentalism. The tribe lived in spiritual darkness, under the sway of witch doctors and demons. Their perversity and violence were characteristic of the heathen condition.[43]

To Rachel, as for many evangelicals, this was a credible and adequate explanation for Wao behavior. At the same time, the Waorani among whom she lived were Dayomæ's family and, by adoption, her own. Their lives would—and could—be transformed in much the same ways Dayomæ's had been, through faith in Jesus Christ. The trajectory of Dayomæ's life hinted at God's ultimate plan of redemption for the Waorani. While Rachel's letters contained stories of thatched huts and monkey meat, she focused almost from the start on the spiritual receptivity of

Dayomæ's extended family rather than on their cultural practices—sinful or otherwise. While Elliot described the vast gulf between tribal culture and Christianity, Saint reported a group with at least some curiosity about God and a certain recognition that the killing of the five men on the Curaray was a mistake.[44] To Rachel, Tewæno was the spot God selected for the new Wao community, and Dayomæ the person he had chosen "to carry the name of Jesus to her people."[45] Like Cameron Townsend, Rachel had absolute confidence in the transforming power of the Bible, even the oral Bible stories Dayomæ recited. "She gathers the whole group together every Sunday . . . instructs them not to laugh, and teaches them little by little about God, the Creator and His Son, Jesus."[46]

Rachel knew that her own tasks were to improve her ability to speak and understand the Wao language, to continue teaching Dayomæ whenever she could, and to try her best to talk with the Waorani about God. It is unclear whether she realized at the time that Wao cosmology had no concept of a supreme God. The name she and Dayomæ chose for God was Wængongui, a creator figure in Waorani legends. Through the Old and New Testament stories Dayomæ told, Wængongui gradually would come to assume the character of the Christian God.[47]

CONTACT ILLNESSES

Rachel's confidence in God's purposes, in the Bible's impact, and in the genuineness of Wao receptivity helped her to deal with the deaths of two Wao women from contact illnesses, infections that reached the Waorani through their encounters with outsiders. These deaths raised the troubling issue of the eternal destiny of people who died as an indirect result of missionary efforts to contact the tribe but who had not yet had the opportunity to hear the full Christian gospel. One woman, Mimaa, caught a fever and respiratory infection when Dayomæ, Mintaca, and Mæncamo first returned to Wao territory. She had died before the missionaries themselves reached Tewæno. Learning of the death, Rachel took comfort in the knowledge that Mimaa had paid attention when Dayomæ had talked about God. Perhaps this indicated an inner spiritual receptivity.[48] The second woman, who died after the missionaries arrived, was Omænquede, one of Guequita's wives. On occasion, Rachel visited her house to chat. During one visit, she heard Omænquede repeat to her mother the story Dayomæ had told about the birth of Jesus. A few days later Omænquede, too, came down with the cold that was making the rounds and died shortly thereafter. Once again, Rachel found peace in the knowledge that Omænquede had been one of the first Waorani, apart from Dayomæ, to tell others about Christ.[49]

The story of Nænquiwi ("George"), while not a contact death, troubled Elliot. A participant in the bitter cycles of revenge killings among the Waorani, he had been speared by Yowe and Nemonca, two members of Dayomæ's extended family, after he had threatened others in the group.[50] Yet he was the man who welcomed the five missionaries to Palm Beach, studied the model airplane they brought, and sampled the food they offered. In the Gospel of Matthew, Jesus told his disciples that the one "who receives you receives me" (Mt. 10:40). The five slain missionaries had gone out in Christ's name, and Nænquiwi had received them. Elliot did not know that he also encouraged the subsequent attack, though he did not participate. She wondered if it were possible that he might be in heaven. Saint found this and other speculations deeply disturbing. She wondered about Elliot's seeming reluctance to talk to Dayomæ about God or to attempt a few words on the same subject with other Waorani. Were these signs that Elliot's acceptance of evangelical doctrines was on "shaky territory?"[51]

Saint's absolute commitment to the impact of Bible teaching—and her confidence in the clarity of the evangelical message of salvation—made it difficult for her to understand Elliot's questions and concerns, particularly since the Waorani seemed to be responding to Dayomæ's Bible stories. But Elliot wondered if such stories, repeated by rote, could even begin to communicate the truth of Christianity to people whose language apparently had no adequate vocabulary for matters of faith. She wrote family and friends requesting prayer that she and Rachel might be able to demonstrate or embody the love of God to the Waorani.[52] Saint worried about Elliot's "tendency to reach the Aucas with love—instead of [with] the Message of the Word" and feared that her questions indicated deeper doubts about basic evangelical doctrines.[53]

Although Saint and Elliot read the Bible and prayed together daily, they seemed to struggle almost as much in communicating with each other as each did with the Waorani. Two months in the rainforest had not brought about the unity that those who knew of their differences hoped for. On the contrary, this first trip to Tewæno was the only time during the three years both women lived among the Waorani that they entered and left the settlement together. From then on, although their stays in Tewæno still overlapped, sometimes for months at a time, the two came and went independently. It was a pattern Elliot initiated. She thought one of them should be with the Waorani at all times.

Saint's model was the traditional SIL practice of two people working as a team. Elliot briefly considered relocating altogether, establishing herself at the Wao settlement near Terminal City while Saint remained in Tewæno. In the event Elliot moved, Townsend encouraged Saint to bring a Wao family to the SIL base at Limoncocha and pursue language work there. Saint mentioned the possibility of finding another SIL coworker but in reality leaned on Dayomæ to fill that role.[54]

Neither Saint nor Elliot talked publicly about the other, and the strain between them was eclipsed by the general welcome and joy that greeted their return to Arajuno on December 2. To Saint's barely concealed dismay, six Waorani accompanied Elliot to Arajuno. From Elliot's perspective, the choice belonged to the Waorani. They were free to come if they wished.[55] Four were men: Dabo and Monca, both adults, and teenagers Quenta and Come. Two days after they arrived, pilot Johnny Keenan, with his wife, Ruth, made the regular "vegetable run" to Arajuno. Despite official MAF reluctance, in May 1957 Keenan had invited Elliot to fly with him on a gift drop over the Wao clearing, an experience that had strengthened her desire to meet the Waorani face to face. Now it was Keenan's turn for a close encounter with the Waorani he had flown over so often.

"KILL A COW BUT NOT PEOPLE"

"They were all laughing and eager to know our names," Keenan reported, "especially [the name of] the one who flew the big *ebo* ('beetle')." Dabo and Monca followed the pilot wherever he went, Dabo talking almost constantly, completely unfazed by Keenan's inability to understand anything he said. Before the couple left, Elliot gave Keenan a spear Monca had made, telling him it was the last one the group had left. As Keenan walked out the door of the house, carrying the spear, Dabo spoke to him (Elliot translating). "You be very careful with that thing and don't kill anyone with it," he said. "It's alright to kill a cow but not people." Dabo's statement was widely publicized in the missionary community and later in the US. To evangelicals, it was a miracle—and sign of answered prayer—to hear a savage Waorani saying, in effect, "Thou shalt not kill" to an American missionary pilot. Although Dabo knew next to nothing about Christianity at this point, he had picked up on the sanction against spearing that was part of the message. The Wao men also passed time by tossing a volleyball around with local Quichuas, people who until recently had been their sworn enemies. "You can't help but love them and long for the day when they will become children of God," Keenan wrote.[56] It was a comment borne of a brief encounter. Dayomæ's relatives were no longer killing Quichuas around Arajuno, but they had not yet embraced Christianity. Elliot still struggled with doubts that the Waorani understood what genuine love was all about.[57]

While the Waorani were in Arajuno, Rachel and Dayomæ traveled to Quito, where they would spend most of the next two months with Sammy. SIL director Bob Schneider took Rachel and Dayomæ to the Ecuadorian minister of education to report on their activities. Rachel also spoke to the missionary community in Quito and gave one interview to a *Time* correspondent, Jorge Jurado, although she and Dayomæ maintained a low profile. This was partially due to insistent cables from Capa and Rachel's brother Sam reminding her, Elliot, and MAF not to give any interviews since "worldwide publication of Auca story with Betty's text and pictures [has] been contracted exclusively to a number of magazines and newspapers." Not until the end of December would all the stories be published.[58]

The seven-page photo essay appeared on November 24, 1958, in the US edition of *Life*. It represented a collaboration between Elliot and Capa and, as such, focused on Elliot's part in the peaceful encounter with the Waorani. It contained thirteen photographs, mostly of Elliot, Valerie, and the Waorani, with only one close-up of Saint and no pictures of Dayomæ. Little Valerie provided the human interest angle for American audiences, with Elliot as the quietly heroic young missionary who not only had given God her husband but now risked her own life and that of her only child. All this highlighted Elliot's part in the story and omitted the critical role Dayomæ played as the bridge between the outsiders and the Waorani.

DAYOMÆ'S STORY

Schneider made plans, with Sam Saint's approval, to shift the focus in Ecuador to Dayomæ, a move that dovetailed with ongoing SIL public relations efforts in the country. Ecuadorians, he believed, would be fascinated by a Wao woman who had decided to "return to her people, tell them of Christ and guide them into Ecuadorian civilization."[59] Schneider also was encouraged by news that Mel Arnold, the religious book editor at Harper and Brothers, would arrive in Ecuador on December 7 to contact both Saint and Elliot about new books for Harper's missionary series. By late 1958 Harper's had two books in production to follow the success of *Through Gates of Splendor* and *Shadow of the Almighty*. One was *Jungle Pilot*, the other *Two Thousand Tongues to Go*, a history of the Wycliffe Bible Translators, which had grown out of a *Reader's Digest* "condensation" in much the same way as had *Through Gates of Splendor*. Harper's had only recently begun to also produce books by Billy Graham. Arnold was eager to enhance his line and wanted exclusive rights to books about the Waorani work. He first visited Elliot at Arajuno and persuaded her to write some sort of "Auca notebook," a journal or photo essay about her observations of the tribe.

Arnold also wanted Rachel and Dayomæ to coauthor a book. There were rumors among SIL staff that Harper's considered "a book by Rachel as the 'book idea of the year.' "[60] Apparently Elliot suggested the precise angle of the book to Arnold. Why not let it be Dayomæ's story—a history of the Waorani through the lens of her life experience?[61] This would bring Dayomæ's contribution to the fore and would provide Rachel with an opportunity to tell the complete story of Wycliffe's part in the Waorani project. Arnold met with Saint for the better part of two days to convince her to take on the book and to suggest how she might begin to organize her notes.[62]

Saint had rebuffed earlier book requests, viewing such projects as obstacles to her missionary and linguistic work. She responded more positively this time around, in part because of Townsend, always an influential figure in her life. Townsend still was concerned about the financial needs of the SIL branch in Ecuador, particularly finding the money to develop the Limoncocha base.

"I've wondered if Harper Brothers wouldn't pay ten thousand dollars in advanced royalties . . . to permit work on the Base to continue," he wrote Schneider, a letter Rachel also read. Because Rachel was an SIL staff member, under established policies profits from her book would go to the organization. However, Townsend did recognize the need to provide some compensation for Dayomæ: not money per se—he probably did not think she needed any—but "such items as a home for herself and son at our Base, the education of her son, health insurance, etc."[63] Much later the fact that Dayomæ received no share of the actual cash royalties would be a sore point between SIL and her son, Sam.

Saint was "staggered" and not a little frightened at Townsend's plans, which in addition to the royalty advance assumed that she could knock out a book in two or three months. But, perhaps for the first time, she *was* interested in writing something, especially if it could be done with Dayomæ and without hindering her work in the tribe. After months of keeping quiet in deference to the "missions who contracted with LIFE," it was time "to tell some of the stories that have been welling up inside." She was confident that she had enough material to write what Arnold was already calling "the Dayuma story." She also thought that collaborating with Dayomæ to write about the Waorani had potential benefits for Wycliffe's overall tribal work. She was "perfectly in accord" with Wycliffe's policies concerning remuneration from books, "though I well realize that the sum total may mount up." Saint, too, expressed concern for Dayomæ and Sammy, whom she had essentially supported since they left the Sevilla hacienda. "Some protective arrangement for them would be good—especially if anything should happen to me."[64]

There was only one problem. Saint hated debt, and the idea of Townsend's borrowing against the royalties of her potential book left her in a panic. "Just the thought of it," she wrote him, "almost caused my mind to go blank." Besides, what if Townsend got the loan and Saint was killed by the Waorani before the book was completed? She shared this concern with Schneider in Quito, who took it in stride. "That would make a better story!"[65] By the time Mel Arnold left Quito in mid-December 1958, he had commitments for two books about the Waorani: *The Dayuma Story* and the "Auca notebook," which would become *The Savage My Kinsman*. Townsend apparently did not borrow against potential book royalties. Instead SIL Ecuador solved some of its financial difficulties by making a deal with the Ecuadorian Ministry of Defense for the development of the Limoncocha airfield. Nor did Saint actually write *The Dayuma Story*. She and Dayomæ returned to Tewæno in February 1959 and spent the next four months there, paying little or no attention to writing.

EDITORIAL HELP

Arnold and Harper's were getting anxious, and so was Uncle Cam. In July 1959, while Dayomæ and Rachel were out on a break, Townsend flew Ethel Emily Wallis to Quito to offer editorial help. About a year earlier he had commandeered Wallis, an SIL staff member and linguist among the Mezquital Otomi people in Mexico, to be the author of *Two Thousand Tongues to Go*. She proved that she could write competently and, just as important, quickly. Rachel turned over personal letters, reports, and tapes of the Waorani and gratefully let Wallis shape them into a book, supplemented by extensive personal interviews with Rachel and Dayomæ.

The manuscript that resulted carried Wallis's name but was still very much Rachel Saint's book, done in part as a labor of love for Townsend. "Every time Dayomæ's patience wore down," Saint wrote Townsend, "(when I needed accurate details to share with Ethel—and the readers) my only recourse was 'Ethel is writing it for Uncle Cam!' . . . It simply could not have been accomplished as it has turned out without the Chief."[66] The result represented Saint's, Townsend's, and SIL's side of the Wao story.

The Dayuma Story, subtitled *Life under Auca Spears*, covered roughly the years from Dayomæ's childhood in the 1930s and early 1940s through the end of 1959, more than a year after peaceful contact had been established. During that year, Rachel and Dayomæ spent a total of about seven months in Tewæno, broken up by several trips out to Quito or Limoncocha, including the first seven-week stay. Rachel added a brief epilogue to the finished book, updating readers on the situation among the Waorani as of February 1960.

Elliot's *The Savage My Kinsman* had a narrower chronological focus. The body of the book itself was a pictorial essay that covered Elliot's life since her husband died in 1956, including her first year among the Waorani at Tewæno. She had lived there a total of about nine months, interrupted by several trips to the outside, until she left Ecuador in October 1959 for a year's furlough in the United States. It was Elliot's first real furlough since arriving in Ecuador in April 1952. While in the US, she wrote the book, her third, based largely on letters and reports she had written during her time with the tribe. *The Savage My Kinsman* was published in 1961, less than a year after *The Dayuma Story*. Neither Elliot nor Saint read each other's manuscript before publication.[67] During that first year in the tribe, they were together in Tewæno for about four and a half months, and alone with the Waorani for the remainder of the time each spent there.

Although the two books represented strikingly different approaches to the story, they shared some common characteristics. In its own way, each offered an innovative perspective on evangelical missions among tribal peoples. Each also sought to portray the Waorani as genuine human beings rather than dehumanized symbols of savagery. Each conveyed to the reader an assurance that he or she was reading about God's hand over the affairs of missionaries and the people they sought to reach. And each offered a response to the persistent question from American evangelicals: "What happened to the aucas after the five missionaries were killed?"

These similarities might be easy to miss in two books that reflected two sharply different personalities and perspectives. In fact the books were so distinct that someone reading them back to back might have found it hard to believe that significant portions of each recounted experiences that both American women, as well as Dayomæ, shared: the peaceful contact with the Waorani and the first year of missionary life among them. It was obvious that the two women saw, heard, understood, and experienced what it meant to be a missionary in very different ways. The same was true for how they interpreted the ongoing "auca" epic to American audiences.

7

A Parting of the Ways

THE DAYUMA STORY: Life under Auca Spears was a classic evangelical account of sin and redemption, played out in the rainforests of Ecuador. The book presented the history of the Waorani through the lens of Dayomæ's life. It included details about her childhood in the rainforest, her knowledge of Wao legends and customs, her experience of the darkness and violence of her people, as well as her escape to the outside world and encounter with Rachel Saint. Readers learned about her conversion to Christianity, her return to the jungle as a missionary in her own right, and the surprising interest of her kinship group in the Bible stories she told.

The book portrayed the Waorani as people isolated in their own small corner of the world. Aspects of their lives reflected traces of edenic innocence: unashamed nakedness, children splashing in clear streams, a profusion of beauty in the tropical flowers and plants of their rainforest home.[1] But far more powerful than these glimpses of paradise were the fear, superstition, and violence that dominated Wao existence. The Waorani were caught in never-ending cycles of sin and death, expressed through endless tribal spearings and retaliations, through burying the dead while they were still alive, and through infanticide. They were "ruthless killers," and their savagery had "not been exaggerated—if anything it has not yet been told."[2] The front cover of the dust jacket described them as "the world's most murderous tribe." Subsequent research would support many of these claims. Going back five generations (approximately from the late nineteenth to the mid-twentieth century), more than 41 percent of all Wao deaths were the result of spearings in the context of feuds between different kinship groups. Adding deaths that could be attributed to encounters with outsiders, more than 60 percent of Wao deaths during this period were violent ones, making the Waorani one of the most violent cultures on earth.[3]

Against the background of Wao depravity, Dayomæ became a symbol of survival and hope. Her life demonstrated the potential of the Waorani once they escaped "Auca darkness." Even as a child, Dayomæ had wondered about God. She later plied Rachel with questions: Who were Jesus and Mary? Would Jesus come back to earth again? What did "resurrection" mean? As Rachel responded with Bible stories, Dayomæ embraced Christianity. Her newfound faith, undergirded by extensive Bible teaching, put to rest her childhood terrors. Overcoming her fears of "the forest of death," Dayomæ became a missionary to her people, and, after initial skepticism, she was welcomed.[4]

The book also published for the first time a Wao perspective on what happened at Palm Beach. It put the attack on the five missionaries in the context of the Wao fear of outsiders and long tradition of revenge killings. By the time the Guequitaidi, Dayomæ's kinship group, encountered the five foreigners on the Curaray, they had nearly been destroyed through a particularly bloody period of warfare—among themselves, with other Waorani, and with outsiders. The attack was another chapter in that bloodshed. The book incorporated the killings into Dayomæ's own story, suggesting that the three Waorani who first went to Palm Beach—Nænquiwi, Guiimadi, and Mintaca—were searching for Dayomæ. When they did not find her, they concluded that the foreigners had killed her, as well as other Wao women who had fled to the outside. Nænquiwi, supported by Guiimadi, convinced the men in the group that the foreigners were evil and would murder other Waorani unless they were killed.[5]

Critics pointed out that the book's account of the spearings did not include the participation of Dayomæ's brother Nampa. His death came later, from having been crushed by a boa while hunting, a version of events Dayomæ would believe throughout her life. Culturally she had no choice. To say otherwise would have jeopardized her relationship with Rachel and could potentially have led to retaliation.[6] Instead, in response to the attack against the missionaries by her kin, and because Rachel and Elisabeth did not seek to avenge their loved ones' deaths, Dayomæ became the person who took the name of Jesus to the Waorani.[7] In an epilogue Saint wrote in March 1960, just before *The Dayuma Story* was published, she reported that four Waorani, two men and two women—Yowe, Quemo, Dawa, and Guiimadi—had responded to Christianity. The Waorani seemed amazingly—even miraculously—able to comprehend the gospel through the Bible stories Dayomæ had shared.

"HOW PRAYER HAS BEEN ANSWERED"

The Dayuma Story represented everything evangelicals wanted to believe about the Waorani in the aftermath of Operation Auca. Frank E. Gaebelein, a Harvard-educated fundamentalist and headmaster of the Stony Brook School for Boys on Long Island, endorsed the book. Gaebelein assured readers that *The Dayuma Story* not only revealed "the motivation for the massacre of the five martyrs of Ecuador" but also provided "thrilling evidence of the power of the Gospel to transform the primitive, fear-ridden Aucas into Christian believers at peace with one another," demonstrating "how prayer has been answered in the evangelization of the Aucas."[8]

Readers apparently agreed with Gaebelein. Ethel Emily Wallis's writing was predictable, tending toward clichés. She was, after all, writing against a deadline and describing places, events, and people not firsthand but based on Dayomæ's descriptions, translated by Saint. Nonetheless, by December 1960, the Harper edition had sold more than forty thousand copies, with an additional thirteen thousand purchased through book club subscriptions.[9] *The Dayuma Story* joined *Through Gates of Splendor* and *Shadow of the Almighty* as the most popular of the Harper missionary classics. By May 1962, Ken Watters, the treasurer of Wycliffe Bible Translators, reported income of twenty-five thousand dollars from the book's sales.[10]

The Dayuma Story's greatest appeal to popular audiences was its dramatic evangelical witness and its description of what happened to the Waorani after the missionaries' deaths. The book aspired to more, however, and it reflected some of the tensions inherent in the identities of WBT and SIL. Aimed toward American and British audiences, the book presented Rachel as a missionary with WBT, "a mission team devoted to sharing God's Book with neglected tribespeople the world over."[11] Though primarily a missionary story—of native missionary Dayomæ and her missionary mentor, Rachel—the book did cover some of SIL's scientific concerns. There were two chapters devoted to Wao legends, as told by the elders of the tribe, and a series of charts at the end of the book tracing the interrelationships of Dayomæ's kinship group. Additionally, the decision to make Dayomæ, an indigenous woman, the central figure challenged the usual evangelical practice of featuring the missionary heroism of people like themselves.

The Dayuma Story was significant for both Wycliffe and Saint. For Wycliffe, it was vindication of their innovative methods. The impact of Bible translation was such that even the oral translation of Bible stories was enough to convert a group as distant from God as the Waorani. Townsend was convinced that *The Dayuma Story* also legitimated Wycliffe's approach before anthropologists. After reading the book, "they will have to say, this is the power of God."[12] For Saint, the book justified her call to work with the Waorani. Dayomæ's story was Rachel's story, and

Rachel's story was Wycliffe's story. All were linked to the five missionaries' deaths not only through Rachel's brother Nate but also through the Waorani themselves. Dayomæ's kin—her uncle, her half brother, her sister's husband, and others—had killed the five men. Now, in answer to prayer, the transformation of the Waorani that evangelicals longed and prayed for was taking place through Rachel and Dayomæ.

In April 1959 David Kucharsky, news editor of *Christianity Today* magazine, wrote Abe Van Der Puy in Quito, seeking information about the contact with the Waorani. "This is *not* a matter of publicity," he wrote. "Thousands upon thousands of people have been praying for this tremendous project, and they are hungry for information," which "creates additional interest and sends up additional prayer."[13] The Waorani had become the missionary project of choice for American evangelicals and *The Dayuma Story* the true sequel to *Through Gates of Splendor*.[14] While *Through Gates of Splendor* established the five men as enduring icons of evangelical spirituality and sacrifice, *The Dayuma Story* established the Waorani as enduring icons of God's response: tribal people miraculously transformed out of the depths of spiritual darkness. Both accounts would have a tenacious hold on the imagination of North American evangelicals and essentially represent all of what many knew about Protestantism in Latin America.

The response to Elliot's next book was less enthusiastic.

THE SAVAGE MY KINSMAN

The Savage My Kinsman is a book-length photo essay radically different in image and tone from the standard evangelical missionary story. Harper's initially suggested an "Auca notebook," representing Elliot's impressions after living a year with the tribe, but Capa convinced her to tell her story through photographs as well as words. Elliot and Capa had become friends during Capa's work as photo editor of *Through Gates of Splendor* and through their collaboration on the November 1958 *Life* article about friendly contact with the Waorani. Unlike those who looked askance at Elliot and her independent attitude, Capa admired her. He taught her to use a camera and convinced her of its value.[15] *The Savage My Kinsman* became another collaboration. Capa's photos of Elliot and her work in Shandia as she waited for an opportunity to live with the Waorani dominated the first three chapters; Elliot's own photos carried the rest.

The result was a 160-page book with more than 120 photographs. It represented documentary photography that broke new ground in communicating the story of evangelical missions. For nearly a century prior to Capa's work in Ecuador, missionaries had used photographs to document their activity and successes in foreign lands—to provide evidence of their work for those back home. Capa introduced a different approach, one that portrayed the human connectedness of his subjects. Elliot followed suit. As the title suggested, photographs and text in *The Savage My Kinsman* emphasized the common humanity of missionary and Waorani. This was powerfully reinforced in the book's final photograph: a shot from behind of a Wao man and Valerie Elliot walking hand-in-hand along the Tewæno River on a spear-fishing expedition. This depiction of a powerfully built Waorani guiding the trusting child over the rocks in the stream presented both as created in God's image. Throughout the book, most of Elliot's photographs portrayed smiling people, living in community and content with their way of life. While their small clearing could look bleak when captured in black and white, these were not the images of people unusually depraved, living in darkness, in contrast to what Americans, especially evangelicals, had come to believe.

While *The Dayuma Story* maintained a kind of missionary triumphalism, *The Savage My Kinsman* reflected Elliot's awareness of the cultural barriers to effective missionary outreach, emphasizing her own cultural distance from the Waorani more than any apparent defects of Wao culture. In her text, Elliot introduces the book as a response to questions from American readers: "Who are the Aucas and why did they do what they did?" But in answering those questions, Elliot raises others: What does it mean to be a missionary, and why do they do what they do? Implicitly, the book also served as a reply to questions about Elliot herself. Who was Elisabeth Elliot, and why did she do what she did?

The Savage My Kinsman was perhaps the most detailed observation of an Amazonian people group undertaken by a missionary in the Americas. A 1961 *Library Journal* review recommended that the book be required reading for Peace Corps candidates.[16] Elliot observed the ways the Waorani adapted to their environment and suggested that, in cultural terms, Wao life compared well to life in the outside world—not always better, but not necessarily worse. Their hammock was "the most versatile piece of furniture ever devised." True, they had no written language, wore no clothing, and used banana leaves and their fingers instead of plates and silverware. But they also wasted little time on housework and tolerated the frequent rains with little discomfort, while the foreigner scrambled to protect paper, camera, clothing, and other clutter. Traditional Wao life had no need for the trappings of Western culture that so often accompanied the missionary message.[17]

Elliot did not dodge the more shocking aspects of Wao culture but refused to indulge in a sense of Western superiority. The book attempted, almost relentlessly, to present a balanced picture. Sometimes the Waorani were "a lovely contrast" from the outside world; sometimes they were "depressing."[18] The Waorani delighted in tales of endless killings. They killed because others killed them, their own version of "an eye for an eye." Yet Elliot reminded readers that a glance at *Time* magazine revealed news of a murder, a sex scandal, and two airplane bombings as the United States began the year 1960. "What do we mean when we speak of one people as being more 'needy' than another?" she asked. "What do we mean by 'savage'?"[19] The Waorani were not better or worse than Americans, just very different in the way they thought and lived.

Regarding the obvious language barrier, Elliot admitted that she understood only about 30 percent of what the Waorani were saying. She had begun to recognize that they spoke a language rich in onomatopoeia but apparently poor in expressing abstraction, which made it difficult to communicate concepts like love and faith.[20] Like her previous two books, *The Savage My Kinsman* had a missionary message for the people back home, the culture within which Elliot *was* a gifted communicator. The Christian public, like Elliot herself, needed to reject the view that saw missions as a one-way street, where superior Western Christians sent the gospel and their way of life to inferior "savages." Rather they needed to see the Waorani as "human beings, made in the image of God." With this recognition should come "a new acknowledgment of Jesus Christ, of our common need of Him."[21]

The Savage My Kinsman also emphasized a central theme in Elliot's inspirational writing and a concept foundational to her own self-understanding: the essence of Christianity was obedience to God. The only reason the five slain missionaries entered Wao territory was because "they believed it was what God wanted them to do." The heart of Jim Elliot's spirituality was his delight in obeying God. Elisabeth Elliot explained her own actions since her husband's death in terms of the same search for guidance and willingness to follow when it came. "Obedience, if it is a good reason for dying, is just as good a reason for living."[22] She was aware of some of the far-fetched rumors surrounding her determination to contact the Waorani: that she had borne the child of a Wao man, that she was mentally imbalanced, and that she was an alcoholic.[23] And, of course, there were the fears of Saint and others that Elliot was doctrinally unsound.[24]

Elliot's response was to describe herself as someone who simply followed step by step the direction given her by God through circumstances and, most important, through the Bible.[25] Although avoiding the heavy-handedness that might have offended a non-Christian reader, she appealed to the Bible, poetry, and hymns to support her beliefs. Even though her conclusions were radical, they were expressed in language that reassured readers of Elliot's fundamental orthodoxy as an evangelical Christian.[26] Readers seemed less convinced by another aspect of Elliot's emphasis on obedience: her proposal that evangelicals drop their four-year fixation with the Waorani and instead pay attention to what God wanted them to do with their own lives, a point she had already made in a *Christianity Today* interview.[27] This suggestion was largely ignored.

Published in early 1961, *The Savage My Kinsman* was generally well received in the secular press, while among evangelical reviewers and readers the response was mixed. Both Elliot's opinions on missions and her photographs were problematic for many. The pictures were the most obvious concern. With some chagrin, Elliot wrote her parents that a Christian bookstore in Arizona had classified the book as, in effect, pornography.[28] "Some of my very good friends were shocked by the photographs of unclothed Indians," wrote Russell Hitt in *Eternity* magazine, although Hitt himself defended the pictures. More shocking, he suggested, were Elliot's conclusions about missions and culture.[29] Another reviewer agreed. Alan Fletcher, writing in the *Sunday School Times*, referred delicately to the issue of nudity, suggesting only that "some may be distressed by the occasional, casual exposure of the human figure." Fletcher, too, stated that Elliot's text gave "a rude jolt" to the "notion that white, Christian civilization is necessarily superior to others."[30]

It is difficult to assess exactly how photographs, text, or more probably a combination of the two affected the book's popularity. Clearly Elliot had distanced herself from the triumphalism of her earlier bestsellers. She was unwilling to make optimistic predictions about the evangelization of the Waorani, although she acknowledged Dayomæ's missionary role and cautiously examined the Waorani response to it. Despite the excellence of the photography, perhaps American Christians did not want to see images of the Waorani as happy and human, in need of Christ but no more so than the reader's non-Christian neighbor, or even the reader herself. This was not the iconic story readers expected. "Somehow in this book Betty Elliot lets us see how all of us are naked before God," wrote Hitt in his review. "The filthy rags of our own culture aren't sufficient."[31] It may have been a disquieting revelation.

BACK TO TEWÆNO

When Elliot returned to Tewæno in September 1960, after a year's absence, the trip from Arajuno took ten minutes rather than three days. During the first half of the year, at Dayomæ's urging, the Waorani had finished clearing land for an airstrip. On July 22, the JAARS pilot Don Smith had landed the first plane because Saint's air support had come from SIL while Elliot was gone. Smith invited MAF's Johnny Keenan along as a courtesy gesture. The landing strip would have a growing impact on life in Tewæno in the years ahead, most notably in terms of increased contact with outsiders and an increasing availability of outside goods, like machetes, medicines, and clothing. It also helped to draw Waorani to the clearing and to solidify Tewæno's status as a permanent, settled community.

After sitting in an oceanside apartment in Ventnor, New Jersey, writing her book emphasizing the humanity of the Waorani, Elliot found her reunion with the actual inhabitants of Tewæno a bit jarring. She might have believed that the outside world had little to offer the Waorani, but they nevertheless were busy acculturating. At Dayomæ's initiative, the teenagers and adults in the clearing began wearing clothing, although Elliot remained unconvinced that their ragtag appearance was an improvement. A handful of Waorani began to express interest in Christianity, but Elliot questioned what they really understood. The measure of belief often seemed to be how much of Dayomæ's stories people could remember and repeat.[32]

Elliot returned to Tewæno apparently ready to do what she had advocated in *The Savage My Kinsman*: to live quietly, seeking Christ, serving the Waorani, and continuing language study. In November she asked some Quichuas to build her a more permanent house. She had said all she wanted to say and wanted no more publicity. When Dan Derr began to land MAF planes at the Tewæno airstrip, Elliot chided him for taking pictures of the Waorani and suggested that MAF need not publish information about this new phase in their air support. Derr accepted the admonition in good humor, but it obviously rankled. Why should Elliot object to photos, he wrote Charles Mellis, when she herself had just finished a film (the brief documentary *Through Gates of Splendor*) and a book about the Waorani, full of photographs?[33]

Elliot did seem curiously oblivious to the power of the epic missionary story she helped to create. The train had left the station, and, despite her wishes, it would not turn back. Near the close of *Through Gates of Splendor*, she had written, "Thousands of people in all parts of the world pray every day that 'the light of the knowledge of the glory of God' may be carried to the Aucas."[34] In late 1960 many continued to pray. They felt a personal connection to the Waorani, reflected in the popularity of *The Dayuma Story*, and as they learned of religious interest among the Waorani, there was a feeling that God was working miracles in Tewæno. People wanted to know more.

In August 1959 Donald Grey Barnhouse, longtime minister of the Tenth Presbyterian Church in Philadelphia and a noted evangelical author, editor, and radio preacher, had visited Ecuador. He asked JAARS pilot Bob Griffin to fly him over Wao territory. Griffin obliged, taking Barnhouse over the Tewæno clearing. But when Barnhouse asked to see Palm Beach as well, Griffin was unable to comply since he did not know the location of the Curaray sandbar. "Dr. B. seemed very disappointed," reported Dan Derr, ". . . and told Bob that his main reason for coming to the Oriente was to see P.B."[35] Palm Beach and Tewæno were pilgrimage points for

American evangelicals. If they could not see them in person, then they would visit them via magazine articles and books.

Elliot also misjudged, or did not wish to recognize, the extent to which the publication of *The Dayuma Story* and the signs of Christianization among the tribe further increased the importance of the Waorani to SIL. To Townsend, the Waorani were becoming a showcase work for the organization. In a letter to Allyn R. Bell Jr. thanking him for a Pew Foundation grant, Townsend provided an optimistic report of spiritual life at Tewæno. He emphasized Dayomæ's role, then added, "Some of the other Aucas are now worshipping the Lord. . . . The Aucas even have had testimony meetings. One of the killers of the 5 missionaries 3 years ago [*sic*] preached a half-hour sermon the other day to the rest of the tribe."[36] With testimony meetings, worship, and a sermon, Townsend's description made the handful of Waorani who had begun to remember and repeat Dayomæ's prayers and Bible stories sound very much like a fledgling American church.

ECUADOR'S PRESIDENT MEETS THE WAORANI

Americans were not the only ones fascinated by the change in the Waorani. SIL's work among the tribe contributed to the warm relationship Townsend and the linguists in Ecuador experienced with that country's president, José María Velasco Ibarra (1893–1979), during his brief fourth term, from August 1960 to November 1961. Velasco Ibarra was a classic Latin American populist, whose ideological commitments proved remarkably flexible and whose ongoing appeal lay more in his charisma and oratorical skills than in specific accomplishments. Scrupulously honest, Velasco enjoyed power more than wealth, and he opened his office door to peasants as well as to the Ecuadorian elite. In these respects, he resembled Townsend's longtime friend, former president Lázaro Cárdenas of Mexico.

In 1960 Velasco Ibarra had been elected to maintain peace and stability, as Ecuador struggled with the realities of a prosperous "banana boom" gone bust and consequent social unrest. He defined Velasquismo—his ideology—as "a liberal doctrine, a Christian doctrine, a socialist doctrine," or, as one historian commented, "something for everyone."[37] Velasco had been the president who first welcomed SIL to Ecuador, and the organization lost no time in renewing old ties. In a meeting on September 23, 1960, SIL's Ecuador director Don Johnson reminded Velasco Ibarra of their past connections and reviewed SIL's current projects in the country. Johnson and a coworker, Glen Turner, included a summary of Rachel Saint's work. At the mention of the Waorani, the two men reported that the interview "suddenly came alive." Velasco Ibarra was incredulous at the idea of an airstrip alongside a Wao village. When Johnson and Turner assured him that this was indeed the case and that the Waorani "had been tamed [*hechos mansos*] by the Word of God," the president responded, "Why haven't you invited me in to visit them?"[38] They responded that it was not yet considered safe for men to enter the tribe.

Buoyed by the interview, Johnson and Turner, in consultation with SIL's president Kenneth Pike, decided to invite Velasco Ibarra to Limoncocha. If he could not go to the Waorani, a few might be flown out to him. The resulting encounter was a high point of SIL-government relations in Ecuador. It took place on February 13, 1961, as part of the annual Día del Oriente (Day of the East), a holiday celebrating Ecuador's Amazonian region. The festivities began in Tena, the provincial capital, where Velasco Ibarra and his entourage of forty-five people, including the vice president, cabinet officials, and some thirty military officials, along with Townsend, were feted with a reception and luncheon. At midafternoon they flew to Limoncocha, landing just ahead of a torrential storm, which washed out all plans for a welcoming ceremony. The somewhat damp national leader was shown to his room, where he talked at length with Bob Schneider and Townsend. Townsend was encouraged by the president's interest in "spiritual things," that he "wanted to know how the Indians reacted to the Gospel, etc."[39]

The comment provided a natural transition to the Waorani, so Townsend called in Saint and three indigenous people—Dayomæ and a couple, Quemo and Dawa— flown from Tewæno for the occasion. They were natural choices. Both Quemo (Mæncamo's brother and the man who had been in the Tewæno clearing when the missionaries first arrived) and Dawa had been in Limoncocha on two previous occasions, so they were familiar with the base. Both were featured in the epilogue of *The Dayuma Story* as examples of Wao receptivity to Christianity. Almost exactly a year prior to the meeting with Velasco Ibarra, Dawa had been the first Wao after Dayomæ to profess faith, and Quemo, the first man to "talk about Jesus" (the "sermon" Townsend had referred to). Quemo also had participated in the Palm Beach killings.

With Quemo and Dawa seated on the floor of the president's room, Velasco Ibarra asked, "What can a primitive man like this one . . . comprehend about God?"

"Mr. President, just ask him," Saint responded, and offered to translate.[40]

"Who is Jesus Christ?"

Quemo responded, "Jesus Christ is the One who came from heaven and died for my sins. He made me stop killing, and now I live happily with my brothers."[41]

Velasco Ibarra was stunned and impressed, convinced by Quemo's expression that the words translated were his own. "The Word of God in the savage's own language is the power that made the change," Townsend later wrote, particularly when Bible translation was backed up by "God's love in word and deed."[42]

After the Día del Oriente, the Velasco Ibarra government maintained cordial ties with SIL. Velasco Ibarra himself paved the way for Townsend and other SIL officials to meet with Janio da Silva Quadros ("Jango"), the president of Brazil, who also had been elected in 1960 and shared some of Velasco's populist tendencies. With Quadros, as he had with Velasco Ibarra, Townsend used the Waorani as an example of the changes that occurred among tribal people when they "learned about God and became Christians."[43] Velasco Ibarra also met with SIL's president Pike in May 1961, where Pike broached Saint's concern that the Waorani needed land that was officially theirs. In the two and a half years since Dayomæ's kinship group had been at peace, Quichuas already had begun to cross the Curaray and Arajuno rivers and settle in what had been considered Wao territory. Saint was concerned that enough land be protected for the Waorani to have sufficient area to hunt and to continue their practice of migrating between various clearings and the gardens of manioc and bananas they had planted. Velasco Ibarra responded favorably to the proposal.[44]

A RELIGIOUS POPULIST

The Ecuadorian president obviously admired the SIL linguists and liked Townsend. After his visit to Limoncocha, Velasco Ibarra invited Townsend to a presidential luncheon in Quito later that year. Despite attempts by critics to present SIL in Latin America as a group in league with the CIA and in step with conservative American political agendas, Uncle Cam was always most comfortable with populists like Velasco, Cárdenas, and Quadros. He was himself a religious populist, concerned about the lives of tribal peoples and adept at commandeering elites to accomplish his purposes. At the August luncheon, the guests discussed the Cuban Revolution and the threats of guerrilla warfare in neighboring Colombia. Ecuador supported Castro's Cuba, though largely in the name of Latin American nationalism. For his part, Townsend had written President John F. Kennedy, urging him to refrain from sending troops to Cuba and calling on him to involve the governments of the hemisphere in addressing the problem of Russian military influence. Reports documenting the relations between SIL and Velasco Ibarra also suggest that the president had a genuine interest in the religious side of SIL's work. He continued to marvel at their success among the Waorani, whose purported savagery was legendary in Ecuador. "Can you imagine an Auca teaching the Bible!"[45]

At the same time, Velasco Ibarra appreciated SIL's influence in assimilating tribal peoples into Ecuadorian society, an expected goal in the 1960s. Quemo and Dawa had arrived in Limoncocha wearing clothing and imitating Dayomæ by talking about "the Chief of the land," even though "chief" was a new concept to the Waorani.[46]

Velasco honored Townsend and Ecuador SIL for their role "in saving individuals living on the margin of human existence and integrating them into their fatherland and a spiritual life."[47] With guerrillas in Colombia and renewed tensions between Ecuador and Peru over their shared jungle border, the government benefited from the presence of linguists in the rainforest, introducing tribal peoples to Christianity and civilization.

From SIL's perspective, doors were opening, and the Waorani seemed to be a master key. However, with the Cuban Revolution and the US response accelerating Cold War tensions throughout Latin America, the times were against populists. Neither the US government nor most militaries in the region wanted leaders who appealed to workers, peasants, or the indigenous. Velasco Ibarra would be deposed in November 1961 through a US-backed military coup; Quadros in Brazil had resigned in August. As it had in the past, SIL would navigate its way through changing regimes.

Velasco Ibarra's shifting political fortunes were worlds away from the small Wao clearing at Tewæno. By August 1961 Saint was describing continued evidence of spiritual growth. "Now almost anyone in the whole group of 75 with whom we live can tell us, without hesitation, the name of God's son," she wrote. Quemo and Yowe, another of the Palm Beach killers, had become male leaders of the "growing group of believers." When Dayomæ was unavailable to teach, one of the men would "very simply teach something from the Word and lead in prayer." Some Waorani had begun to pray over their meals of manioc and wild pig, although this did not become a common practice. Saint reported that eighteen Waorani had "publicly asked the Lord to cleanse their hearts."[48]

Much of the Christian teaching at Tewæno focused on concrete changes in a few specific Wao customs. Missionaries and Wao Christians alike pushed prohibitions against such practices as infanticide, burying alive the infirm, and, of course, spearings. A lower priority, but still evident, were instructions about sexual relations and against polygamy. By far the most important emphasis and the heart of the gospel for the Waorani was *Itota beyæ, tænonamai.* (On behalf of Jesus, do not spear.) Saint and Elliot arrived in Tewæno at a time when some Waorani already wanted to stop the terrifying and seemingly endless bloodshed. Aside from the many casualties, they realized that the violence was causing kinship groups to fragment and hide across a wide area of jungle, making it difficult for kin to find each other and to find appropriate spouses.[49]

However, as anthropologists later found, there was no effective mechanism in Wao culture for ending the vendettas. Christianity provided such a mechanism. It was particularly useful because the Waorani who killed the original five missionaries were members of Dayomæ's extended family, and Elliot and Saint were kin to the slain men. By Wao standards they should have come to Tewæno seeking revenge. Instead they arrived with gestures of goodwill and, through Dayomæ, spoke of God, a divine being of forgiveness and peace. If the missionary women, whom the Waorani originally believed were *cowode*—"barely human cannibals"—did not seek to avenge their kinsmen's deaths, perhaps the message they brought would provide a way out for the Waorani as well.[50]

This message was reinforced when Guequita, Dayomæ's uncle and a respected warrior, announced that he would no longer spear and that if he was killed, he did not want his family to avenge his death. In an interview years later Guequita said that when his wife Mæncamo (with Mintaka) met Elliot and Saint, it was the "first really good meeting" Waorani had experienced with *cowode*. After the missionary women moved to Tewæno, "they lived well here, and we lived well with them. They spoke lots about God. We listened and we understood. . . . We decided not to kill each other anymore."[51]

With SIL and MAF planes making regular trips to Tewæno to deliver supplies and mail and the Waorani showing evidence of Christian faith, visitors, including some men, began to arrive. At first they were people with a special connection to the Wao mission. The families of the five slain missionaries maintained and deepened their bond with the tribe. Most came on brief day trips, although Elliot's brother David Howard stayed a week and ten-year-old Stevie Saint, Marj and Nate's son, spent six weeks of his summer vacation with his Aunt Rachel. Marj Saint and her younger son, Philip, arrived to celebrate Valerie Elliot's birthday. Ed McCully's family—Marilou and her youngest, Matt, along with Ed's father, T. E. McCully— and Barbara Youderian flew in for a day in early November 1961. The group ate lunch—beans, homemade bread, fried plantains, corn-on-the-cob, lemonade, and pie—at Elliot and Valerie's home.

T. E. McCully, six feet tall and 230 pounds, was the largest outsider the Waorani had seen. They compared foot and girth measurements, discovering that two Wao men could fit inside McCully's buckled belt. Far more important to McCully, of course, was the opportunity to meet five Wao men who had participated in the Palm Beach killings. "I was able to put my arms around them and tell them that I love them—especially now that they had come to know my God," he wrote later in a magazine article.[52] In August Townsend, his wife, Elaine, and two of their children visited for a few hours.[53]

The Wao response to Christianity and increasing acculturation made translation work especially important. For all the talk of the impact of the Word of God among the Waorani, progress toward a written translation of the New Testament was slow. Before going to Tewæno and with the help of Ken Pike, a noted linguist, Saint had prepared a preliminary article on Waorani phonemics, a study of the essential letters necessary for a written alphabet.[54] SIL staff members Catherine Peeke and Mary Sargent had also done some initial work on the language from outside the tribe. Not until May 1961, however, did Pike officially approve an alphabet and authorize Rachel and Dayomæ to begin translation of the Gospel of Mark. Meanwhile, Elliot had continued her own language study. She, too, was working on an alphabet and, in 1961, wrote two literacy primers for the Waorani.[55]

A DIFFICULT TIME

Although Saint, too, had built a permanent house, and both women had settled in Tewæno, they still had been unable to forge a working relationship, much less any kind of friendship. Shortly after her return to Tewæno, Elliot had commented to Dan Derr that *The Dayuma Story* portrayed the Waorani as "Rachel's tribe."[56] Decades later Elliot remained convinced that the heart of their differences had to do with Saint's possessive attitude toward the Waorani. "From day one, the Aucas belonged to Rachel," she asserted, "and I was an interloper."[57]

Elliot also felt increasingly uneasy with the approach used by Rachel and Dayomæ to teach the Waorani about Christianity, which seemed to pressure them to respond in certain ways. As an example, Elliot described Dayomæ's leadership of Sunday meetings. One Sunday, after talking about the Old Testament figure Samson, Dayomæ put an unsuspecting teenage girl on the spot and quizzed her before the others about when she was going to profess Christian faith—with no explanation of how this related to the message. Clearly uncomfortable, the girl finally followed Dayomæ in repeating a few set phrases about believing. Dayomæ then accused a young man of impregnating a woman and insisted he improve his behavior. He responded that he would, in a litany repeated several times. The next morning, when Saint and Elliot met for daily prayer, Saint praised God for the way that both the girl and the young man had witnessed publicly to their faith. Elliot struggled to believe that either response was heartfelt. While recognizing both Saint's sincerity and her ability, despite barriers, to communicate an impressive amount of Bible teaching to Dayomæ and others, Elliot simply did not share Saint's perspective on spiritual life among the Waorani.[58]

For her part, Saint doubted that Elliot could appreciate God's work among Dayomæ's kinship group because of Elliot's own spiritual inadequacies. Saint was appalled at Elliot's description of a trip she, Valerie, and several Waorani took to visit Palm Beach and the missionaries' grave. Elliot's account appeared in a letter published in the *Sunday School Times*. Standing on the beach looking at a huge fallen tree, Elliot reflected on what might have been, on how God could have caused a tree to come down or otherwise have kept the men from landing. When she saw the unmarked, common grave, she remembered two lines from a Wordsworth poem on love that Jim Elliot had quoted.[59]

Saint responded to the article with anguish and tears, suggesting that it called into question Elliot's belief in the resurrection of Christ.[60] Elliot's musings on the river-bank did not reflect a genuine, evangelical trust in God. To Saint, such examples, and the questions raised in *The Savage My Kinsman*, were evidence that Elliot was not spiritually qualified to be a missionary to the Waorani. The two were at an im-passe, isolated in the rainforest and at loggerheads with one another.[61] Even more perplexing to Elliot, the two women had been supported by an outpouring of prayer from around the world and still had not been able to resolve their differences.[62]

Despite her prayers and determination, all she had risked, and the challenge of analyzing the Wao language, Elliot struggled with a growing awareness that she did not enjoy living and working in isolation, estranged from Saint. Only a few months after making peaceful contact, Elliot had confided to friends that every time she faced the trail back to Tewæno she did so with a sense of dread. She stuck it out, convinced that she was being obedient to God.[63] But by the time she returned from her furlough in the latter months of 1960, the project of Christianizing the Waorani seemed to be in motion, regardless of her direct contribution. For more than five years, even before her husband's death, she had prayed for the Waorani and had longed to live among them. Now the answer to those prayers seemed somehow flat.

In the end, issues related to translation work precipitated Elliot's decision to leave Tewæno. In September 1960 Rachel and Dayomæ had participated in a language consultation at Limoncocha with Ken Pike. Pike, a nationally known American lin-guist, often organized such meetings with SIL translators to supervise their work and, more important, use his expertise to help them solve translation problems. Elliot was not invited. Few questioned her absence, perhaps because she had just returned to Ecuador after a year out of the country.

A second conference took place eight months later, where Pike approved the Wao alphabet, and again Elliot was not included. Her letters from Tewæno gave no indica-tion that she expected an invitation, but she apparently expressed disappointment to Marj Saint and Marilou McCully.[64] Elliot's family and friends were perplexed. Many years later Elliot's brother David Howard remembered his own frustration: "Here was one of the world's leading linguists [Pike], and there were only two people in the world outside the tribe who knew the language, Elisabeth and Rachel. And they didn't even invite Elisabeth."[65]

The incident passed, and Saint did not tackle the translation of Mark for another six months. In November, when Saint announced her intention to begin a trial translation, Elliot asked to collaborate with her and Dayomæ. Saint refused. She later explained that it was because she wished to work with Dayomæ on a monolingual basis. Elliot and Dayomæ both knew Quichua and could do translation work bilingually, Waorani to Quichua, which Saint could not. It would be frustrating for her to be left out of those conversations and "impossible to get the monolingual reactions later."[66] She suggested that Elliot begin work independently on another book of the Bible. Elliot thought the reason for the refusal went deeper, rooted in Saint's reaction to the differences between them.

Two days later Elliot handed Saint a single typewritten page, announcing her decision to leave Tewaeno and the Waorani. She asked Saint to let her know if the statement was fair. The sheet contained a low-key summary of what had been a wrenching experience for both women. From Elliot's perspective, two issues had divided them, especially during the preceding year: (1) Saint's belief that Elliot was not a suitable spiritual mentor and teacher for the Waorani, and (2) Saint's unwillingness to collaborate on translation work. Saint would not compromise, and, therefore, Elliot saw no reason to remain in Tewæno. She concluded that God was leading her to leave the clearing.[67]

As with nearly everything else, the two had conflicting perspectives on the question of why Saint would not collaborate on language work. Elliot said it was because of disagreements over what each considered essentials or nonessentials of Christian faith.[68] In a letter to Townsend, Saint disputed this explanation. She refused, she told Townsend, because she wanted to work monolingually with Dayomæ. Although she did not say so to Elliot, she also believed that "translating Mark is a poor place to try to start working together with an informant in a language." She added that Elliot had previously questioned the value of research Saint and Pike had done on the Wao language and thus "felt it best to do my own work."[69] Saint chose not to directly respond to either Elliot's letter or her decision, but to Elliot's dismay, Saint broke the news to the Waorani before Elliot could do so. It was a final disappointment since Elliot had anticipated closure with the Waorani on her own terms.[70]

Perhaps both versions of the rift were true. Certainly from the early days of attempting to analyze *Wao tededo*, Saint had lived in Elliot's shadow. Part of the panic that she had experienced at the prospect of writing *The Dayuma Story* may have come from the thought of competing with Elliot's success as an author. Even in late 1961 Saint still felt the need to defend her linguistic efforts. There seemed to be a general impression in Quito, she wrote, "that the Auca linguistic work would fold up without her [Elliot's] help."[71]

Pike referred to these same attitudes when he defended the decision to work with Saint alone at the language consultations. "It would have been much more difficult . . . to have tried to have helped Rachel if Betty had been at the table at the same time. Rachel moves on these materials slowly—but I think solidly under guidance."

Rachel, he suggested, needed to stand on her own two feet "without danger of accusation of having had the work done by someone else."[72] Despite Pike's support, however, Saint struggled with Bible translation, and her inability to collaborate with others would have long-term consequences.

A STORY OF LOSS

Elliot also faced the shadow of the past when Saint refused her request to work jointly with Dayomæ. In 1953, during Elliot's first year as a missionary in Ecuador, she served as a linguist among the Tsáchila people (then called Colorados) in the jungle on the western side of the Andes. After a sluggish start analyzing Tsafiki, the unwritten language of the Tsáchilas, she had met Macario, a bilingual informant whose ability to speak both Spanish and Tsafiki enabled Elliot to decipher the perplexing language.

Only a few months later, Macario was murdered as part of a village vendetta, and Elliot's progress on a Tsafiki alphabet slowed to a crawl. With painful effort she finished a phonemic alphabet before she left the Tsáchilas to marry Jim Elliot. A few weeks after she left, however, she received word that a suitcase containing all her Tsafiki language materials—the fruit of a year's labor and at the time the only written alphabet that existed for the language—had been stolen from the top of a bus. It was never recovered.[73]

Elliot would later write about the experience in her 1975 book, *These Strange Ashes*. She did not mention, however, the parallels between the Tsáchila experience and her translation work among the Waorani. Again, there had been the hope of working with a bilingual informant—Elliot and Dayomæ were the only two people who spoke both Quichua and Wao—and the promise that it would accelerate the process of unraveling the complexities of the Wao language. But Dayomæ was Rachel's informant, and Rachel had said no. The refusal and the closed door to language collaboration meant that once more Elliot's language work lay in ashes. It was hardly surprising that she chose almost immediately to leave Tewæno. By late 1961 she had spent nearly a decade in Ecuador. She had learned four languages, married, borne a child, been widowed, and lived in three different jungle cultures. In the American evangelical world, her reputation as a writer and missionary heroine had been established. But in Ecuador, her missionary experience had been characterized by loss.

Twenty years later, when she wrote an epilogue for a new edition of *The Savage My Kinsman*, Elliot had gained some perspective. The woman who popularized Jim Elliot's sentiment, "He is no fool who gives what he cannot keep to gain what he cannot lose," acknowledged that perhaps both she and Saint were fools of a sort in their intensely spiritual, conflicting desires to obey God.[74]

"There are times, I confess, when the whole Tiwaenu [*sic*] scene strikes me as high comedy," she wrote, "though I haven't forgotten the tears. Imagine us—two such different women, different from each other, positively freakish to the Aucas, with a small blonde girl . . . depending upon them for everything and thus becoming three nuisances . . . lining people up to take pictures, shutting them up to listen to God's word, criticizing their morals, objecting to the rude noises they made during Dayuma's Sunday morning 'sermons,' and generally turning upside down their whole view of life and the world. Imagine!"[75]

Nevertheless, Elliot refused to deny the calling she and Saint had embraced. Despite their ineptitude, missionaries still stood "with Christ for the salvation of the world." This task was not one to be evaluated in "'either/or' terms—either it is flawless, and therefore a success, or it is flawed, and therefore a miserable failure."[76] However, back in 1961 the painfulness of Elliot's decision to leave Tewæno loomed large.

Elliot's letter of November 6, 1961, set off a flurry of communications between family, friends, and officials of SIL and MAF. Rachel and Elisabeth flew to Quito on November 17, where they met with Marj Saint, Marilou McCully, and two SIL officials, John Lindskoog and Don Johnson. The meeting did nothing to ease tensions or change Elliot's resolve. Saint flew back to Tewæno the next day, while Elliot, never one to hesitate once a decision had been made, arranged for four flights with SIL pilots to transport her possessions from Tewæno to Shandia. By December 1 she and Valerie had resettled among the Quichua at Shandia, where they would live for another two years before returning to the United States.

Few people who knew the two women were surprised by the turn of events. They knew that Saint and Elliot struggled over the years with personal differences, theological disagreements, institutional conflicts, and starkly contrasting views of the role of a missionary. Those close to Elliot accepted her explanation for the final break, that Saint and SIL did not want her to be a genuine colleague in translation work.[77] Saint's supporters cited the difficulty of two people who did not share the same institutional commitments working together on the mission field, compounded, as Townsend wrote, by "Betty's ideas that Rachel considers unsound." SIL Ecuador director Don Johnson wrote sadly about the frailties of human nature.[78] Townsend spoke more bluntly: "I can't be very optimistic about our being able to get two strong minded heroines to cooperate closely."[79]

In time, a few writers would embellish the conflict, citing such things as Elliot's supposed defense of polygamy on the grounds that the Bible did not prohibit it and disagreements over whether wine or grape juice should be served at communion. Many years later Elliot dismissed these examples as apocryphal.[80]

However, Townsend's comment contained an element of truth. Both Saint and Elliot were steeped in evangelical traditions of pioneer missionary heroism. Yet most of those pioneer heroes and heroines fulfilled unique roles, either alone or as unquestioned leaders. They were rugged, spiritual individualists. The very qualities that brought Elliot and Saint to Tewæno made it hard for them to work together there.

Neither woman spoke publicly about Elliot's departure, preferring simply to acknowledge that there were differences between them. There was no publicity; Elliot's letter circulated only among those with some involvement in the Wao project. As a result, most American evangelicals had no idea Elliot had left Tewæno until she and Valerie returned to the US. By then her books and essays, and the articles others had written about her faith and courage, forever associated her with the Waorani and provided her with a unique public platform as a speaker and writer on missions and spirituality. Nonetheless the pain of her experiences with Saint in Tewæno ran deep. Four decades later, in her mid-seventies, Elliot's explanation for the conflict remained unchanged. Yet she also valued the memory of the last time she saw Saint, a chance encounter on an airstrip in Ecuador. "I was able to give her a hug. She was very stiff, but she did manage to allow me to hug her."[81]

Elliot's departure in November 1961 had little obvious impact on life in Tewæno. It certainly did not seem to hinder the spiritual advance. Everett Fuller, a medical doctor at the HCJB hospital in Shell Mera offered to hold a medical clinic in Tewæno. He and another hospital staff member, David Sanford, arrived on November 22, 1961, only a few days after Elliot had left. To Fuller's surprise, Dayomæ requested that he baptize those Waorani who were ready to publicly proclaim their faith. Fuller and Sanford spent the night in Tewæno. The next morning, Thanksgiving Day in the US, Fuller talked with the Waorani about the significance of baptism, with Saint translating. Then he and Sanford baptized nine Waorani, including four of the Palm Beach killers, in the Tewæno River. The ceremony became another milestone in the "triumph on the Tewæno," the beginning of a visible Wao Christian church. The triumph seemed a little bittersweet to those who were not invited. Fuller and Sanford, a new missionary, had been chosen almost by happenstance, "kind of a blow to many whose hearts have been in this thing from the start," wrote Dan Derr wistfully.[82]

No one seemed to notice that the fledgling Christian church still had no access to written Scriptures. Its members were not literate, knew nothing about any other ordinances or sacraments of the church, particularly the celebration of the Lord's Supper, and their understanding of Christianity was mediated primarily through Dayomæ's experiences in the US. All this mattered little in light of nine Waorani publicly identifying themselves as Christians. Photographs of the ceremony recorded the classic image of a male Western missionary standing waist-deep in a river with an indigenous convert.[83] This traditional missionary vision triumphed in Tewæno at almost precisely the moment when SIL, a very nontraditional organization, one that did not consider itself a mission, assumed full responsibility for linguistic and religious work there.

8

The (Apparently) Idyllic Years

WITH THE NUCLEUS of a Wao church established and the conflict with Elisabeth Elliot behind her, Rachel Saint was at last on her own among the Waorani. She was the only permanent foreign missionary presence at Tewæno from Elliot's departure in December 1961 until the linguist Catherine Peeke and a nurse, Rosi Jung, became regular residents in 1970. Peeke did spend extended periods in the clearing during the 1960s doing research for her doctoral thesis on Wao grammar. In 1962 another SIL staff member, Mary Sargent, lived in Tewæno for three months as a literacy expert and trial coworker with Saint. The collaboration with Sargent was unsuccessful, however, and Saint, working with Dayomæ, remained alone in Tewæno.

Finally, at forty-eight, Saint was fulfilling her life's work as she envisioned it. In many ways, she stood in the late Victorian tradition of missionary heroines: independent, strong-willed, utterly committed to the salvation of souls, certain of the call of God in her life, and dedicated to the ideal of re-creating New Testament Christianity among previously unreached peoples. In contrast to common missionary stereotypes and later accusations raised against her, she was not prudish. She wanted the internal violence—the complicated vendettas that led to spearings—stopped. She could be harsh in her judgment, describing "Auca morals" as "shot through with immorality," referring to what she considered promiscuity.[1] But in almost every other way, she sought to retain Wao culture, sometimes more than did the Waorani.

Initially, Dayomæ's extended family, the Guequitaidi, seemed to be following the presumed patterns of a New Testament church. A second group of nine Wao adults and teenagers were baptized in 1962, bringing the total of baptized believers to eighteen. Among them was Mincaye, the last of the five living Palm Beach killers to seek baptism.[2] Translation work on the Gospel of Mark was nearing completion. Saint reported that a few Wao Christians had begun to express interest in taking the Christian message to other Waorani, still scattered and isolated in the rainforest. In Ecuador and in publicity to audiences abroad, the years 1961 to 1968 seemed almost idyllic in their success. Efforts to Christianize the Waorani would never again be as straightforward or "simple" as they seemed during this period.

DAYOMÆ'S MARRIAGE

Dayomæ remained the crucial link between Rachel and the Waorani. She was Rachel's language informant, de facto coworker, and informally adopted younger sister, and the established Bible woman for the group. Although Dayomæ never learned to read, she taught Bible stories and other lessons she learned from Rachel to the Waorani at regular church gatherings. She continued to be an important broker of change and of Christianity among the Waorani. When Dayomæ returned to her people in 1958, she arrived with knowledge of the outside world, with trade goods— pots, machetes, cloth, a small sewing machine—and with the patronage of Rachel, who supplied many of the goods. Dayomæ represented the early indigenization of Wao Christianity, but she herself wanted to leave much of her traditional culture behind.

Dayomæ's openness to new things was typically Wao. Theirs was a traditional culture with very little concern for tradition. "Tradition was not something to be bound to, and people were not criticized for being different or doing things differently," observed the anthropologist Jim Yost.[3] The transitory nature of life in the rainforest bred a pragmatism and an intense curiosity that readily accommodated new ideas, even competing and contradictory ones, if useful. There was no need to worry about the future or calculate the impact of change "because rot, mold, and death will all take over quickly anyway."[4]

Dayomæ's decisions regarding marriage were illustrative. Her first marriage, arranged on the hacienda, was to Miguel Padilla, a Quichua who died during a measles epidemic in the early 1950s. When looking for a second husband, Dayomæ turned again to the Quichuas. During the first trip to Tewæno in 1958, when six Quichua men accompanied Elliot, Saint, and the Waorani, Dayomæ expressed interest in the "outsider" men.[5] In 1962 she had decided to marry a Quichua when Rachel stepped in. Rachel opposed Quichua influence over the Waorani and was against the idea of a Quichua husband for the woman God had chosen to bring them the gospel.[6]

Dayomæ did not share Rachel's understanding of the ways of God, and the two quarreled loudly before Dayomæ capitulated. Elliot had observed similar arguments in the past ("knockdown, drag-out, screaming at each other"), but had said nothing.[7] Although quarrels made people nervous, most Waorani preferred loud talk to quiet conversations. (Both Rachel and Dayomæ often raised their voices even when they weren't mad.) Loud exchanges meant everyone knew what was going on. People who spoke softly might be arranging a marriage or planning a spearing raid.

In the end, Rachel and Dayomæ made up, as they always did. Whether because of Rachel's objections or because Dayomæ wanted to be sure her children would be accepted as Waorani, when a wedding did take place, on August 31, 1962, it was between Dayomæ and Come, one of Guequita's sons and a culturally appropriate match. Come was savvy as well, sending his mother to ask for Rachel's consent to the marriage. The action also was a nod to the traditional Wao custom of arranged marriages. Adding a touch from the outside world, Rachel helped Dayomæ make "a special ivory-white dress."[8]

"WHAT HAPPENED TO THE AUCAS?"

By the early 1960s Saint was beginning to accustom herself to the publicity surrounding the Waorani and her place in their story, though she did not seek the limelight. She was pleased when the *Philadelphia Bulletin* used her name in a crossword puzzle. Strangers sent "many, many letters" that made their way to Ecuador. They inquired about the Waorani, Saint reported, "as if they had known them personally or been here to visit," and promised to pray for other Wao groups yet to be contacted.[9]

In response to the interest, *Translation*, Wycliffe's magazine, devoted its Summer–Fall 1964 issue to updating readers on what happened to the "aucas." The issue featured a photograph of about forty Waorani, many smiling and all clothed, grouped in front of a neat longhouse. There were profiles, with brief Christian testimonies, of the "five living killers of Palm Beach," all of whom had become earnest believers. In other articles, readers learned that the Waorani had daily prayer meetings, that the "first Christian Auca wedding" had taken place, and that the Waorani in Tewæno recently had taken in a teenager named Oncaye from an unreached group of "downriver Aucas." She might become the needed contact person for Waorani-to-Waorani evangelism. The Waorani even had their own "statement of faith," the single sentence "Following Him we will go!" In short, the Waorani story was "a twentieth-century demonstration of the power of God," an example for American evangelicals of the redemption God could bring to other indigenous peoples throughout the world, "who are still without Christ and the one Book that tells of Him."[10]

The Waorani living in Tewæno during the mid-1960s numbered between seventy and eighty, mostly women and children, representing about 15 percent of the total Wao population. Tewæno was a "neighborhood cluster" of Wao extended families living in and around an airstrip and beside the shallow Tewæno River.[11] Most were Guequitaidi, the group that had first welcomed Elliot and Saint in 1958. A few were a splinter group from the Piyæmoidi, a different Waorani kinship group. In response to the violent internal vendettas that characterized Wao life, most Piyæmoidi had fled north, to a region between the Tiputini and Tivacuno rivers (map 1). Missionary writings referred to this group as the "downriver Aucas."[12]

COMPLICATING FACTORS

As early as 1964 there were indications that the vast Wao territory would not remain an isolated enclave where Rachel, Dayomæ, and the Waorani of Tewæno could replicate primitive Christianity in a pristine fashion. Since 1958 a Capuchín mission established in the village of Coca had assumed responsibility on behalf of the Catholic Church for much of Wao territory. The friars also were interested in contacting the Piyæmoidi, approximately one hundred downriver people scattered in the rainforest south of Coca. In 1965, when Rachel and the Christian Waorani at Tewæno launched what became known as "Operation Contact" to find the "downriver Aucas," they were targeting the same Piyæmoidi who were in the sights of the Capuchíns. Saint was convinced that the Capuchíns, as Catholics, had no genuine concern for the spiritual well-being of the Waorani.[13] A quiet competition ensued, although Saint and SIL had better airplanes, better language skills, and better government support, due to their contractual relationship with the state.[14]

Oil company activity also picked up. In March 1964 Ecuador's ruling junta leased Texaco-Gulf 1.43 million hectares (about 3.5 million acres) of eastern rainforest, mostly to the north of Wao territory. Even so, the prospect of future oil concessions on Wao lands increased the government's desire to move hostile Waorani and their spears away from areas of potential seismic exploration. At the same time, the Tewæno Waorani began to ask for formal title to their lands. The stage was set for the establishment of a Waorani "protectorate" (reservation) in the area around Tewæno. The protectorate, consisting of about 620 square miles, was not legally established until January 1969. From 1966 on, however, Tewæno Christians assuming the role of evangelists would contact other Waorani and encourage them to come to the area to

learn about God. Part of becoming a Christian came to mean relocating to the protectorate. Between 1968 and 1971 the Waorani population in the protectorate grew
from about 80 to nearly 350, with generally negative effects on Wao culture, on the
tranquility of Tewæno, and on efforts at Christianization.

Aside from Catholics and an Ecuadorian government hungry for oil, Saint faced
other, smaller, but perhaps no less significant challenges. Her hopes that the Waorani
would reject violence yet retain the integrity of their culture were at cross purposes.
Violence against outsiders was one of the key factors that enabled the Waorani to
maintain social and cultural isolation. Once the killing stopped, the Waorani and
other nearby groups began to lose their fear of each other. Also, despite Saint's continuing opposition, some Waorani in Tewæno married lowland Quichuas. Others
journeyed to haciendas on the rainforest's edge to work for "whites." And there were
a handful of professed Christians in Tewæno who slipped back into old ways or
slipped away from the clearing altogether.[15] Nonetheless Saint remained determined
that the Waorani would become the kind of evangelical New Testament church
North American audiences thought they were. That determination may have been
a key factor shaping her actions in what critics have described as "the 'kidnapping'
of Oncaye."[16]

THE KIDNAPPING OF ONCAYE

The incident involving Oncaye occurred against the backdrop of violence attributed
to bands of Waorani during the first half of 1964. The attacks were against
Europeanized or "civilized" Quichuas who lived in hamlets and rural areas near the
village of Coca, destined to become an oil boom town. Isolated incidents had been
reported before: one man wounded in 1958, another killed in 1960, two in 1961,
two in 1962. The next year had been quiet. Then, from January to May 1964, seven
people were reported killed and another attacked.[17] According to the Catholic version of the story, in late February, about the time hostile Waorani killed a Quichua
woman named Olimpia Avilés, residents of Coca reported seeing Waorani in the
area dressed in bathing trunks.[18] Supposedly these intruders knew a few phrases
of Spanish; fingers pointed back to the residents of Tewæno. Rumors spread that
Dayomæ had said the Waorani would destroy the town of Coca, even though most
Tewæno residents were still women, children, and young teenagers. Sensationalistic
newspaper reports kept anxiety levels high.[19]

The Capuchíns complained to the government about the Wao attacks, but to
no effect. A detachment of eight Ecuadorian soldiers in Coca was supposed to be
enough to protect the village. The murder of Ceferino Noteno on May 18, 1964, was

blamed on Waorani, and a search party of twenty-four soldiers and settlers went out to look for them. Expecting to find a large group, they instead stumbled across two Wao women hiding along the river. In the confusion, a member of the search party fired a shotgun. One woman was killed, the other—an adolescent named Oncaye—was wounded.

Oncaye received medical attention at the Capuchín Mission Hospital in Coca. A local official then gave custody of the girl to the Madres Lauritas, an order of nuns, for care. The people of Coca and the Capuchíns saw Oncaye as a potential emissary to the Waorani in the region. The evangelicals had Dayomæ and others at Tewæno; the Catholics would have Oncaye. After the initial shock, the teenager seemed to respond positively to the nuns' care. "Her first frightened words: 'I am a woman! I am a woman!' gave way to smiles for the children who maintained a friendly chatter with her" (she knew some Quichua words).[20]

At about 6:00 in the evening on May 21, Saint entered the picture, arriving by plane with the head doctor from the Pastaza military hospital in Shell. She explained that, as the only nonnative Wao speaker in the region, she had come to help. After talking with Oncaye—and not translating for the nuns—Saint insisted that the girl be flown to the military hospital for further care. The nuns were adamant that they, too, would go. The next morning, once Oncaye was aboard the plane, Saint climbed in and told the SIL pilot to take off. Coca residents surrounded the aircraft to keep it from leaving. Finally, Saint climbed out, insisting that "she was the one called to accompany her [Oncaye] and teach her something of God."[21] Two plane flights later, everyone involved—nuns, Oncaye, Saint, and the military doctor—had been transported to the hospital.

A delegation from Coca then sent a request to the military junta governing Ecuador asking that Oncaye remain in the custody of the Madres Lauritas. The Capuchín missionaries agreed, making their case in person before the junta. The junta apparently did not want to be caught between a US organization and the Ecuadorian Catholic Church and tossed the decision back to Col. Jaime Paz y Mino Salas, the officer in charge of the Pastaza hospital. Events at the hospital, described in Saint's notes, had all the makings of a soap opera. The colonel gave Saint permission to spend the first night in Oncaye's hospital room. At 1:00 in the morning she was "awakened by the familiar voice of the Monsignor."[22]

"Came to whisk her away, I knew it!" Saint wrote. "I roused myself and quickly stepped into my shoes and planted myself at the bedside, flanked by Dawa and Gaacamo [relative and sister of the wounded girl]. When the nuns came in, over Protest, were they ever surprised. The priest admitted that they had come to take the girl to the waiting car, sick and groaning as she was. . . . I insisted . . . [that] we would let her go only if the Colonel himself told us."[23]

The Capuchíns, of course, had a completely different take, suggesting that misunderstandings due to Saint's limited command of Spanish led her to falsely accuse them.[24] Saint was convinced that Oncaye's place was in Tewæno since four of her sisters—from the splinter group of Piyæmoidi—already lived there. She also hoped that Oncaye would help the Tewæno Waorani make peaceful contact with her other family members. "It was not a religious question at all but purely a sociological matter," wrote Don Johnson, the director of SIL Ecuador, referring to Oncaye's family connections in Tewæno. As they washed their hands of the problem, the junta in Quito were probably the only people in Ecuador who might have supported Johnson's line of reasoning. Everyone else seemed certain that the fight over Oncaye was a contest between SIL and the Capuchíns to see who could get to the downriver people first, even while Johnson emphasized SIL's good relationships with individual priests living near Coca.[25]

Through sheer force of personality and because SIL had a good relationship with Colonel Paz y Mino, Saint was able to take Oncaye to Tewæno. Reunited with her sisters, Oncaye eventually did help locate the other Piyæmoidi. The Catholics resented what they saw as Saint's attitude that Oncaye was her personal property and that evangelicals had exclusive rights to the various groups of Waorani. They also believed that Saint was oblivious to their concerns about the violence along the Napo River.

The story of Oncaye as told to evangelicals in the US through Saint's letters, magazine articles, and the 1973 book *Aucas Downriver* was quite different. Catholics were nowhere to be seen. In *Aucas Downriver*, Oncaye appears as an answer to prayer and as a means for the Waorani to fulfill the missionary imperative. God had told the Waorani to go to the "downriver people," but they didn't know how to overcome the animosity between the two groups. Saint encouraged them to pray for a contact such as Dayomæ had been. In this version, Saint is convinced that God will send someone to the Waorani at Tewæno. When word came that "a wounded Auca girl had been found," Saint was asked to go see her.[26] When Saint arrived, the "girl was still gravely ill." She was also deeply distressed, "furious at the people who surrounded her."[27] Oncaye could not remember how she got to the hospital. She simply woke up there, to be reunited with her sister who spoke to her of God. From Saint's perspective, Oncaye was "'the key to the whole downriver situation.'"[28]

This version of the Oncaye story had none of the complications of missionaries competing over indigenous people or dealing with deep-rooted patterns of violence. It was simply another example of God at work to further the spread of the gospel among the Waorani. A year and a half later, Rachel wrote "Ten Years after the Massacre" for *Decision* magazine, commemorating the deaths of Saint, Elliot, McCully, Youderian, and Fleming. Ten thousand copies of the article were reprinted in a widely distributed tract. After a glowing summary of the successes at Tewæno, the tract concluded with the baptisms of Kathy and Steve Saint. The ceremony took place in June 1965 on the same beach where Quemo, now an elder in the Wao church, had helped to kill their father nine years earlier. Oncaye was baptized on the same occasion, connecting her both to the death and resurrection of Christ and to the sacrifices of the slain men. The Waorani, Rachel wrote, "were ready to risk their lives, as Nate and Jim and Roger and Pete and Ed had done, for Jesus' sake." For her part, Rachel "thanked God and took courage."[29] She would need it. Throughout the mid-1960s the Waorani in Tewæno continued to represent successful missionary-indigenous contact. Within a few years, however, life and faith in the small clearing would change dramatically.

THE GOSPEL OF MARK

Between 1962 and 1965 Dayomæ worked with Rachel to translate the Gospel of Mark into *Wao tededo*. On Easter Sunday, April 18, 1965, printed copies were dedicated and distributed in Tewæno. Photographs showed the Waorani, sitting in their open-sided, thatched church, peering intently at the booklets. Rachel's description of the occasion was optimistic as usual, but it was difficult to know who, if anyone, could read the booklets. Some had memorized verses, which they recited. Quemo prayed an extended prayer, affirming, "All of us honestly accept Your Carving. . . . We shall always believe and obey."[30] A news release distributed several weeks later reported that twenty-one of the seventy Waorani in the village were believers, "living exemplary Christian lives."[31]

In November 1965 V. Raymond Edman arrived from Wheaton College with his wife and another couple to hold a "Bible conference" for the Waorani. With Rachel and Dayomæ translating, Edman taught lessons from Mark's Gospel. He baptized eleven more Waorani and followed the baptism with the first communion service celebrated in the Wao church, using boiled manioc as "bread" and banana drink as "wine." At the same service, Edman, a fellow visitor named George Traber, and Quemo commissioned the first three Wao "missionaries" (Yowe, one of the Palm Beach killers; a young man named Toñæ; and Oncaye) who committed themselves to search for other, potentially hostile Waorani whom they would invite to Tewæno to hear the Christian message.[32] For the rest of his long life, Yowe would take this commission seriously. Toñæ would pay for it with his life.

This fledgling missionary outreach, dubbed "Operation Contact," would eventually extend to include all the major Wao kinship groups, scattered throughout their rainforest territory. With air support from JAARS, Operation Contact became a major focus of Rachel's energies and ambitions. It was her opportunity to fulfill the dreams of her brother and his friends that all Waorani would hear the gospel. Rachel also convinced a handful of Tewæno believers to make the project their own.

THE BERLIN CONGRESS

In January 1966, ten years after the missionaries' deaths, the Waorani around Tewæno were living peacefully and had a church with more than thirty baptized believers. To cap a decade of progress that seemed to vindicate the sacrifices of 1956, Harold Lindsell, an evangelical leader representing Billy Graham and Carl F. H. Henry, invited two representatives of the Wao church to attend the Berlin Congress on World Evangelism the following October.

Come and Quemo became the first Wao men to leave the rainforest. Dressed in white shirts, suits, ties, topcoats, and fedoras, with their hair combed and parted Western style, the two men captured the imaginations of the press and many delegates. With Saint translating, they gave their Christian testimonies before the assembled group of twelve hundred delegates and sang a Wao hymn/chant. As the session concluded, an African delegate in the audience jumped up on the platform and, to the shock of the two Waorani, hugged each man. "It just about broke up the meeting," noted Wycliffe executive George Cowan. "I overheard one delegate say he had just done what they all wanted to do."[33]

As one of only a handful of women delegates to the Berlin Congress, Saint assumed a supporting role. She downplayed her significance as translator, nurse (Quemo spent his first four days in Berlin in bed), and financier (she paid a portion of the men's expenses from her own pocket). Staying in the background also was a way to avoid criticism as she, too, struggled to navigate unfamiliar cultural waters. She bristled when Thomas Klaus, a Native American delegate, told her not to call Quemo and Come "boys." "How would HE know that 'boys' was the affectionate term used for the Colony men at Keswick, & I was using it in that sense," she wrote Townsend.[34] However innocent, her response shows her isolation from both the civil rights and emerging nationalist movements of the 1960s.

Regardless of the occasional cultural blunder and her quasi-invisibility as a woman, Saint was still the missionary who brought Quemo and Come to Berlin. And she was overwhelmed by well-wishers after their presentation.[35] Townsend put it best: Rachel Saint, he wrote, was "one of the outstanding missionaries of our time."[36] Rachel might have demurred, but she did believe, along with the rest of the evangelical world, that God had begun a dramatic work of Christianization among the Waorani.

AN ATTEMPT TO CONTACT THE PIYÆMOIDI

Although 1966 was the year Saint received worldwide attention for accompanying two Wao men to the Berlin Congress, she was preoccupied for most of the year by events in the rainforests of Ecuador. In January she wrote that hopes were high among the Tewæno Christians for peaceful contact with the Piyæmoidi. She, too, was optimistic, believing that publicity in the US surrounding the tenth anniversary of the Palm Beach killings would result in "better prayer backing" than had supported two initial attempts a year earlier.[37] At first it looked like she was right. Yowe announced in early 1966 that God had told him to try again "when the moon was a small sliver." He had been a part of two groups that attempted to find the Piyæmoidi on two separate occasions in 1965 but turned back both times.[38]

Shortly after Yowe's announcement, JAARS pilot Don Smith located a Wao house some eighty miles north of Tewæno. Smith took Dayomæ, Yowe, and Oncaye on a flyover to see the house, and Oncaye identified her mother in the clearing below. Despite the possibility of a reunion, the teenager was a less than enthusiastic volunteer for the proposed "missionary journey." To Saint, the underlying problem was spiritual: invisible warfare against the devil, symbolized by the huge bushmaster snake Oncaye had accidentally stepped on a few weeks earlier. However, the immediate reason was less dramatic: a young man in Tewæno wanted to marry her, even though Saint believed their kinship relationship meant the marriage would be inappropriate. Convinced that Oncaye was God's instrument for peacefully contacting the Piyæmoidi, Rachel intervened to stop the relationship, as she had with Dayomæ. Invoking her "right" as a surrogate mother to Oncaye and with Dayomæ at her side, Rachel gathered some Tewæno Christian women to pray. By the time they finished, both Oncaye and her older sister Boica, with Rachel listening in, had told God they would risk their lives, if need be, to go "on the downriver trail."[39] Once again, they joined the two male Tewæno Christians, Yowe and Toñæ, who had accompanied them the year before.[40]

The four Waorani were willing to face danger, but they also had begun to learn the value of planes and technology in navigating a rainforest that was an environment perfectly designed to keep feuding Waorani hidden from one another. Before leaving on foot, the four requested a second flyover with Don Smith so they could gain a better sense of terrain and rivers between Tewæno and the clearing where they thought Oncaye's mother lived. Smith also promised to fly the route every other day to orient the ground party. The Waorani carried medicine for snakebite, as well as a walkie-talkie so that they could pick up and transmit messages on the Limoncocha frequency. Rachel gave the two men long-beam flashlights. Yowe brought a knotted string so he could tell when it was Sunday and time to rest and call in on the radio.

Working with Dayomæ on the translation of the Book of Acts, and therefore immersed in the story of the early Christian church, Rachel gave the rainforest "missionary journey" biblical significance. She wrote densely typed reports, chronicling every detail. The Waorani were more relaxed. The day before the four left, it rained heavily and the shallow Tewæno River became a torrent. After the Sunday church gathering some Wao men and boys, including missionary Yowe, amused themselves by plunging into the river and riding the current to a place where they could come ashore, walk back, and ride again. It reminded Saint of boys sledding after a snowstorm. "And me," she wrote, "I watched my happy family and prayed that all of us would hear His voice and never think of our own selfish happy security." For Saint, the moment was both a source of gratitude and a warning against spiritual complacency. The Waorani were simply "living well," in peace and freedom from fear.[41]

Yowe, Toñæ, Boica, and Oncaye left the next day. Despite their preparations, the trail disappeared in places, and they were lost twice during the first week. Finally, they found a trail Boica knew, which led to terrain familiar to Oncaye. There was optimism during the radio check-in the first Sunday. Two days later brought more excitement and an unscheduled radio transmission. They had found footprints. The goal was to locate relatives—Oncaye's two brothers and mother, as well as Yowe's kin sister Bogænæi—and invite them to Tewæno. Another two days passed before a dramatically different radio transmission. Through static, the names Titæda (Oncaye's mother) and Bogænæi were heard, along with the phrase "They are all speared dead." Then silence.[42]

Anxieties rose in Tewæno as days passed without word. Had the four missionaries been speared? Were Piyæmoidi warriors on their way to Tewæno? A group of Guequitaidi—Quemo and his big dog Yæte, Monca, Mincaye, and Quenta, plus Come, who went partway—headed toward a favorite fishing spot where they hoped to encounter Yowe and the others on their return. The waiting continued until, a few days later, Come rushed into the Tewæno clearing, shouting that "the downriver group [was] coming." With visions of enemies on the doorstep, Saint switched on her radio to alert the SIL staff in Limoncocha to Tewæno's danger. There was little anyone could do except pray as the late afternoon gave way to darkness.

Next to arrive that night were the four Tewæno missionaries who returned safely, along with those who had gone to meet them. Saint tried to piece together what happened. Along with Oncaye's mother's footprints, the four had found signs of an attack. There was human blood, pieces of the fiber grips from broken spears, and many male footprints. The next morning Oncaye and the others picked up her mother's trail again and followed it to a small house where vultures were already at work and the stench was overpowering. Saint pressed for details. To the Waorani, the circumstantial evidence was obvious. "They are all dead . . . all of them!"

Faced with the evidence of violence, the four had turned back. That night, as they prepared to sleep, they realized they were being followed. The four slipped away and headed quietly up the trail, but their path would be easy to follow. Using their flashlights, the Wao missionaries scarcely stopped during the next three days and nights until they encountered the Tewæno group at the fishing site and all returned home. Tewæno remained on alert for a few days, although Saint went to bed each night remembering a Bible verse that promised safe rest and slept soundly. The former killer Guequita stayed in his house across the Tewæno River, unfazed. "Praying to God, I will swing in my hammock!" The danger passed, and Tewæno returned to normal. Dayomæ and Rachel took up the Acts translation where they had left off.

COMMITMENT AND ISOLATION

Saint described the latest Piyæmoidi episode in detail to SIL's Ecuador director John Lindskoog and her SIL colleagues. Her preoccupation with the Piyæmoidi reflected the depth of her immersion in Wao life. She referred to the Christians in the Tewæno clearing as "the dear ones," her family.[43] Yet her commitment masked isolation and a loss of perspective. With no colleague to confirm or to challenge her perceptions, Saint was living in a world all her own. It was shaped by her sense of calling as a missionary and by the traditional Wao belief that the world extended only to the limits of the rainforest. Saint's concerns increasingly were shaped by the same boundaries.

Saint's identification with the Waorani also made it hard for her to accept others' suggestions, even those of John Lindskoog. For example, because the Guequitaidi were increasingly in contact with outsiders—Quichuas and others—Lindskoog suggested they be vaccinated against communicable diseases. "If we wait too long on this we will be sorry," he wrote, in what proved a prescient statement.[44] Apparently Saint did not respond. She disapproved of encounters between the Guequitaidi and nearby *cowode*, who wanted to trade with them. She seemed to think if she ignored or opposed the contacts, they would go away. Given the curiosity of the Waorani and the population density of their lowland Quichua neighbors, this was wishful thinking.[45]

Saint remained absorbed with the challenges of finding the Piyæmoidi, even though another attempt would not take place until January 1967. She was aware of the ongoing bloody vendettas among the groups that were not yet contacted. At the same time, there were rumors of more oil exploration, stories of Marxist guerrilla activity in neighboring Colombia, and word of continuing Catholic activity.[46] These circumstances made it difficult for Saint to concentrate on the details of a translation workshop at Limoncocha. "Here all our waking thoughts—and prayers are for possible contact," she admitted. "We need prevailing prayer for OPERATION CONTACT right now."[47]

The anticipated oil exploration became a reality in Wao territory during 1967. Texaco's Lago Agrio oil field came in about one hundred miles north of Piyæmoidi lands. By August, workers, guarded by forty armed soldiers, made an initial foray into Piyæmoidi territory. They saw no Waorani, but Quichuas along the Napo were not so fortunate. At least three spearings took place, and some of the blame, however groundless, reverted to Tewæno.[48]

Against this background, Tewæno Christians tried twice more—in January and in October 1967—without success to contact the Piyæmoidi, who clearly were reluctant to be found. In October Saint maintained an almost twenty-four-hour vigil every day for two weeks, praying and standing by the radio as Quemo, his wife, Dawa, plus Oncaye and Yowe entered downriver territory yet again. Saint's translation work suffered as a result. Translator and SIL consultant Bruce Moore already was uneasy about what seemed a very free rendering of Acts into the Wao language. Then Saint missed a January 1968 translation workshop in Limoncocha because she could not leave Tewæno.

"We are in constant binds here due to R. being the only Auca worker and the tribe being so dependent on her," Branch director Lindskoog wrote Cameron Townsend. Lindskoog still hoped to find a coworker for Saint and perhaps a married couple as well to join the Waorani work.[49] However, Lindskoog and Moore's misgivings were put on hold a month later with the news that after three years of trying, the Piyæmoidi had been contacted at last. The right set of circumstances converged: HCJB engineer Marion Krekler and pilot Don Smith had created a transmitter that would allow two-way communication. Limoncocha administrator Don Johnson suggested they hide it in the false bottom of a gift basket so it would not be destroyed. Oncaye and Rachel flew with Smith over a clearing where Oncaye had spotted family members. The basket was parachuted down, and Oncaye found herself talking to her brother Cænto. She invited him to meet in peace along the trail.

THE FIRST PIYÆMOIDI ARRIVE

"Bring me a foreigner's ax, and I will go," Cænto responded.[50] Don Smith's ax, sharpened and polished, was packaged and dropped into the clearing that same day. Ground contact took place four days later, and members of the Guequitaidi and the Piyæmoidi, who had fled one another's spears more than twelve years earlier, met peacefully. Oncaye discovered that her mother, Titæda, still lived. Yowe's half sister, Bogænæi, had been speared in January 1966. Twelve Piyæmoidi were welcomed to Tewæno. This was more than the Guequitaidi had expected (Quemo had prayed for three newcomers), but the new arrivals were not a major threat since only two were grown men. The women and children represented mouths to feed until they could plant their own gardens, but they had kin in Tewæno who would help provide. One of the two men, Oncaye's unmarried brother Tewæ, was given a wife from among the Guequitaidi women, reaffirming kinship ties.

Dayomæ and Rachel continued to be dominant personalities in the community. In what is clearly an understatement, Rachel downplayed their influence: "My age, in this situation, and my neutral position helps me to bridge the gaps between the two groups, related as they are," she wrote, "and Dayomæ still calls the signals from her unobtrusive position as Come's wife and church leader."[51] The new arrivals suffered from contact illnesses, primarily secondary pneumonia from colds, but all survived. Under normal circumstances it would have been time for a breather. But Rachel and the Waorani who worked with her felt compelled to contact other Piyæmoidi. Only a month after the first successful encounter, SIL began conversations with oil companies who would be in Waorani territory. A Texaco official informed Lindskoog that a seismographic crew would move into Wao lands south of Coca the following October. "I do not believe they will postpone this work," Lindskoog wrote Saint. To avoid bloodshed involving the remaining Piyæmoidi, he advised her to "proceed with all wise haste."[52] "Wise haste" proved difficult to maintain.

SIL flights searching for the remaining Piyæmoidi resumed. What began as an evangelistic project was also beginning to focus on Wao relocation. Now it was the new arrivals, such as Oncaye's brother Cænto and their mother, Titæda, who rode along to invite their family members to Tewæno. Cænto had expressed reluctance to set aside spearings and revenge. He may have been in the plane seeking family allies rather than recruiting relatives to live in peace. Either way, the call was answered in June 1968, when ninety-three Piyæmoidi arrived at the Tewæno clearing, shattering the tranquility of the small settlement.[53] Tewæno would never be the same.

PART IV

Relocation, 1968–1973

9

Big Oil, Waorani Relocation, and Polio

⌒──

NEARLY ALL THE downriver people straggling into Tewæno in June 1968 were suffering from contact illnesses, most with severe, flu-like respiratory infections. Some
arrived under their own power; others were carried in by Tewæno residents. All were
too sick to build shelters or find food. They arrived at the beginning of a month of
heavy rain, which created "the worst mud we have ever had," Saint wrote. She and
Dawa became nurses in a clearing transformed into a sloppy, damp, makeshift clinic.[1]

Some of the new arrivals stayed with family members. Forty others lay in hammocks
or on bamboo slats underneath the high raised floor of a large structure that served
as Saint's home, her radio room, and the community schoolroom. Several ground
fires kept people warm, while Saint hung blankets around the edges to cut the damp
wind off the river. For three weeks she and Dawa administered antibiotics, spooned
liquid down throats to keep their patients hydrated and nourished, and gave sponge
baths to bring down fevers. SIL staff in Limoncocha supplied antibiotics and sup-
plemental food. Saint's use of antibiotics pointed to the gravity of the situation. She
typically preferred homeopathic remedies because she feared the Waorani would
have adverse reactions to Western medicines. Rachel and Dawa saved lives to the
point that some of the recovering Piyæmoidi began to threaten to kill Tewæno
residents, their traditional enemies. In response, Quemo, Yowe, Dabo, and other
Christian men loudly announced the rules of the new dispensation: "Here ... God
wants us to have only one wife—It is the God who made us who does not want us to
spear our fellow men."[2]

The order of their announcement reflected another source of tension in the community: efforts by the different Waorani family groups to find spouses for their children. At least nine cross-cousin marriages (children of a father's sisters marrying children of a mother's brothers)—the approved Wao marriage pattern—took place between the Piyæmoidi and the Guequitaidi almost immediately after the flu crisis was over.[3] Conflicts came when Piyæmoidi men wanted more than one spouse or sought sexual relations with the wives of Guequitaidi men, practices widespread in Amazonia and approved under specific rules in traditional Wao culture.

Waorani marriage practices allowed polygyny (more than one wife) and polyandry (more than one husband). However, Saint had emphasized the teachings of the Ten Commandments to the believers at Tewæno, particularly the commandments prohibiting murder and adultery. These teachings were generally accepted because they contributed to peaceful relationships within family groups. Christianity had come to mean faithfulness to one spouse and no more spearing adults or killing unwanted infants. The newcomers, of course, did not share these beliefs.[4]

Saint also taught that believers should marry only other believers, but as the Piyæmoidi joined the Guequitaidi, she quickly realized that this was unrealistic for all but a few. Yowe and Oba, among the more active Christians in the community, asked to send their daughter Ayebæ to Limoncocha for several weeks to avoid unwanted marriage pressures. The rest of the Tewæno believers, Saint wrote, set out the rules: "They could have our girls, but each could have only one and was to remain faithful to that one." Recognizing the foreignness of this concept, she added, "Only the Lord's working in their hearts will ever accomplish this." Exhausted, Saint looked on the bright side. The customary gatherings or "fiestas" that served as the setting for marriages were curtailed due to a shortage of bananas and manioc to make festive drinks. "Providence, God's own sweet providence," Saint wrote with relief. While she did not object to fiestas per se—they had continued after she arrived at Tewæno—she did object to what she viewed as the immorality that accompanied them. Traditionally such parties were the occasions for a variety of sexual encounters, still governed by cross-cousin relationships. To Saint, these were the non-Christian activities of the old days, "when any party was license to appropriate your wives sisters [sic]."[5]

A CHANGED COMMUNITY

Other changes rocked the Tewæno clearing. As a precautionary measure, the few "outsiders" in the village, except for Saint, were flown out when the main group of Piyæmoidi arrived. Traditionally only people who spoke the Wao language and both of whose parents were Waorani were true Waorani. All others were *cowode*, including Dayomæ's eighteen-year-old son, Sam, whose father was not Wao, as well as Quichua men in the village who had married Wao women. Tensions eased a little in mid-August, when a Piyæmoidi family group dissatisfied with life in Tewæno returned to their home downriver. This left a total of eighty-five new residents and a bit more peace.

Still, the character of the community had changed. Catherine Peeke, a linguist who lived in Tewæno for short periods during the early 1960s, immediately noticed the difference on a brief visit to the village. When Peeke and pilot Bruce Linton landed, the newcomers clustered around the plane, while the Tewæno residents Peeke knew held back. Saint began introductions but was preoccupied with keeping herself positioned among the Piyæmoidi men she considered most volatile as they met the two *cowode*. Although unafraid herself, Peeke understood Saint's concern. Those who had been involved in killings had a different look about them, she observed. "And the overwhelming number of unfamiliar faces was a shock."[6] The familiar faces had changed, too. Oncaye and Dawa, who had borne the brunt of caregiving and peacekeeping among relatives, looked "thin and worn," as did Quemo. Saint, in contrast, seemed in good shape physically, though she was clearly distracted as she chatted with the visitors.

Life in Tewæno had become difficult and would remain so for the foreseeable future. Waorani scattered throughout the rainforest typically maintained two or three living sites, each with its own garden where they planted manioc, their subsistence crop. Families would rotate between the different sites. This semisedentary pattern kept them from exhausting resources at any one location; it provided them with ongoing sources of food as gardens matured in sequence; it made them more difficult for enemies to locate; and it offered them places of refuge should they have to flee an attack.

When the Piyæmoidi came to Tewæno, they left their gardens and living sites far behind. They were unfamiliar with the new territory and did not know where to establish new clearings and gardens. Tewæno residents urged the newcomers to live near the airstrip in the center of the settlement, making it easier to enforce the new behavioral standards. This strategy did maintain the peace, though not without serious challenges. It also resulted in food shortages, recurring waves of illness, and distorted power relationships between the Piyæmoidi and those Waorani with experience relating to the outside world.[7]

Efforts at Bible translation and basic literacy work languished as Saint faced crisis upon crisis after the downriver people arrived. She rarely acknowledged discouragement and held her ground with the stubborn faith that God could work miracles, even in what seemed like a contact disaster. During another flu epidemic in April

1969, she had 104 people—more than half the population around Tewæno—on antibiotics.[8] The situation was compounded by her refusal to ask for help, due to the danger of spearing. The months after the Piyæmoidi arrived marked one of the few times Saint expressed concern for her own safety. In an undated handwritten note during this period, she told John Lindskoog that she was thinking of inviting her youngest brother, Ben, a pastor, to visit Tewæno. "He is immense—6 ft 4 & I don't know how much more—& broad. I figured it might be good for the tribe to know I have a brother that size—& 5 more living."[9]

Despite the problems, Saint never questioned the need to contact the remaining Wao family groups and bring them to the area around Tewæno. They still were "unreached" people, living in a culture of fear and violence. The close-knit Wao kinship structure meant that there were Wao believers in Tewæno related to the family groups still scattered throughout the rainforest, representing perhaps another three hundred people. And the other motivating factors—ever advancing oil crews and ongoing Catholic missionary activities—remained unchanged.[10] Further contact efforts seemed inevitable. However, Saint had her hands full. She needed someone else to serve as liaison between Waorani, jungle pilots, SIL directors, and oil company officials. Beginning in October 1968 that person was a slim, middle-aged linguist and newly minted PhD, Catherine Peeke.

CATHERINE PEEKE

Born in 1924, the youngest of six children, Minnie Catherine ("Cathie") Peeke grew up on a North Carolina farm near Asheville. In high school, she was fascinated by languages and decided to study Latin on the hunch that it would be easier than home economics.[11] Peeke was active in the Weaverville Presbyterian Church and wanted to be a missionary. The Presbyterians helped to fund her education, first at Columbia Bible College (SC), then at King College (TN). However, when she graduated from King in 1947, she found that the options for single women missionaries in the denomination were limited to child evangelism, nursing, and secretarial work. None of them matched the quiet young woman's gifts, so the mission board suggested Peeke apply to the Wycliffe Bible Translators. She was accepted and attended the Summer Institute of Linguistics at the University of Oklahoma in 1949.[12]

By 1950 Peeke was living along the Pastaza River in northeast Peru, working with colleague Mary Sargent among the Shemigae (Andoa) people, whose language was part of the Zaparoan language family. That project was curtailed, and in 1953 Peeke became a charter member of SIL's Ecuador Branch. Peeke and Sargent attempted further translation work in the Záparo language. Seeking native speakers, Peeke accompanied Rachel to Hacienda Ila in 1955 when Rachel first contacted Dayomæ. "I was still working on Záparo," Peeke remembered, "while she worked with Dayomæ. I did learn some of the [Wao language], because of hearing it." When SIL determined that there were not enough Záparo speakers to make a translation project feasible, Peeke became the Branch linguistic consultant, assisting various translation teams in the country.[13]

As part of her work, Peeke gained familiarity with *Wao tededo*, going over word lists with the missionary Wilfred Tidmarsh in 1957. In 1959 she consulted with Rachel on Rachel's early translation efforts. When Elisabeth Elliot left in late 1961, some SIL administrators hoped Peeke would join Saint full time in Tewæno.[14] Peeke sensed a different calling: to pursue a PhD in anthropological linguistics from Indiana University. Her dissertation topic, however, kept her connected to Saint and to the Waorani. It was an analysis and technical grammar of the Wao language, based on Peeke's own research, Saint's translation work, and Elliot's language notes, among other sources. Peeke spent two and a half months with the Waorani in 1962 and made shorter visits to Tewæno annually for the next three years. Wangi (Peeke's Wao name) became a familiar figure to the original inhabitants of Tewæno. Nonetheless Peeke spent most of her time between 1962 and 1968 outside Ecuador.[15]

She received her PhD in June 1968 and by July was back in Ecuador, just after the large group of Piyæmoidi had arrived in Tewæno. Peeke was assigned to work with the Waorani, but because of safety concerns, she lived at Limoncocha for the next year, participating in Wao relocation efforts. After a furlough, she became a resident of Tewæno, which would be her home among the Waorani until she retired. Peeke was the first permanent worker among the Waorani who was not related to one of the slain missionaries. She was deeply loyal to Saint, but also quietly savvy about avoiding an assignment as Saint's coworker. Peeke was able to view the Waorani with a certain objectivity that Saint never attained, which enabled Peeke to become one of the most insightful interpreters of Wao culture.

SEARCHING FROM THE AIR

In October 1968 Peeke began what became her project for the next few years: finding and mapping the locations of the approximately three hundred Waorani still isolated in the rainforest. She got involved just as Operation Contact was changing from a Rachel Saint–Tewæno mission into a full-fledged SIL relocation project in cooperation with oil companies. Peeke was the only outsider other than Saint who could speak *Wao tededo* and thus coordinate flights that included pilots and monolingual Waorani on board who had been recruited to talk to their estranged relatives on the ground. The Baiwaidi and the Wepeidi—the two groups yet to be contacted—lived south of Limoncocha and east of Tewæno (maps 1, 3), and flight distances there were greater than for the Piyæmoidi. Peeke, lighter in weight than Saint, later remarked that "the skinnier the passenger, the greater fuel load could be carried" aboard the six-passenger Helio Courier planes.[16] As an additional bonus: she never got airsick circling jungle clearings.

Within a few months of leaving the world of American academia, the forty-four-year-old linguist was spending hours in the air, searching for Wao clearings and plotting their locations. A single month might involve up to thirty hours of flying. By January 1969 thirty-three Wao sites had been located and included on a map Peeke had created. The flights involved moments of adventure surrounded by hours of tedium, discomfort, disappointment, and sometimes danger.[17]

Peeke described the experience. First came fifty miles or more over endless, "rather boring" jungle canopy. Then passengers and pilot would spot a tiny clearing. "This was our goal; all things were 'go' for the Waorani aboard the plane to call from the loudspeaker [mounted on the wing], and for me to drop the parachuted basket [with hidden transmitter] and then record whatever those on the ground might say into the transmitter as they clustered around the basket to claim their gifts [small aluminum kettles, drinking bowls, combs]."[18]

"Flying in low over the postage-stamp clearing, the pilot would . . . slow the . . . Heliocourier [sic] to a near stall, swoop down . . . and motion for me to push out the basket, complete with small white parachute. . . . More circling to give them time to retrieve the basket. Now came the questions from above, via the transmitter: 'Whose son are you? Who is your mother? Your grandfather?'—for no one would ask the impertinently direct question, 'What is YOUR name?' "[19]

FINDING THE PIYÆMOIDI

Peeke and the Waorani in the plane tried to hear and understand the answers to these questions. Sometimes the clearings were empty or no one responded. Sometimes the circling and diving or the bumpy weather brought the passengers—Waorani and the occasional outsider other than Peeke—home with airsickness.[20] Some critics of the Summer Institute of Linguistics in Latin America have portrayed it as a kind of juggernaut—the missionary equivalent of a military force that could come in and sweep through the jungles. In the case of the Waorani, the relocation effort was modest. It was carried out by Saint and Peeke, a few pilots, and probably fewer than fifteen Waorani in all, assisted occasionally by oil company helicopters. Initially the expenses were borne by the "Auca fund," an account within SIL created years earlier for Saint to receive charitable donations designated for the Waorani. She used the money for medicines; literacy materials; cloth, pots, and other goods; sewing machines; and school expenses in Quito for Dayomæ's son Sam. Since 1965 expenses for Operation Contact had also been paid from the fund, which was never large.[21] The Piyæmoidi relocation in January and June 1968 and the medicines needed to fight contact illnesses depleted the account.

By late 1968 the Ecuadorian government had granted concessions in traditional Wao territory to four oil companies: Texaco, Anglo, Minas y Petróleos, and Petroleras Yasuní (map 3). Some Waorani were living within twenty-five miles of oil company trails, a potentially volatile situation. Since the oil companies showed no signs of curtailing exploratory activities, SIL was under "considerable pressure to accelerate our efforts to contact and pacify the remaining savage groups."[22] This pressure kept SIL in the air during 1969. Despite the urgency, however, Peeke had second thoughts about the whole project.

After one of her first flights, Peeke was struck by the vastness of the rainforest. "The utter remoteness bears in upon one," she wrote, "and the impossibility of attracting people to come over such distances is very real." This did not, of course, mean that the project was impossible, and Peeke responded to her own doubts with passages from the Bible, such as Jesus's promise to draw all people to himself, even as she voiced concerns about the timing and consequences of relocation.[23]

"The resistance of almost the entire Christian community [in Tewæno] to further advance is a matter for deep concern," she emphasized to SIL's Ecuador director John Lindskoog. "Are we to let oil companies dictate the Lord's program when the Church here is not mature enough to accept the challenge? The problems are incalculable, and this would not be bad if the Lord's people were ready to trust Him in the face of them. But *they are not*, with a few exceptions. . . . Many openly complain of the attempts made to . . . bring in more people to help eat up the food, and some grumble in private, and some merely retreat from the problem by living on another clearing."[24]

If the residents of Tewæno were resisting further relocation efforts, what about the potential new arrivals? What implications did the SIL project have for them? Peeke hoped that it would bring them into contact with Christianity, "drawing them out of the path of conflict and toward the sound of the Gospel." The promise of peace associated with Christianity was the most significant thing SIL and the Tewæno community had to offer. "I suppose we are all very much aware that we are not offering the people any better way of life from the material standpoint," she wrote. "For what are a few machetes and kettles compared to the unrestricted game reserve they have always enjoyed? And we are offering them unknown territory for known, a foreign land instead of home, dependency for self-sufficiency, subjection to outside powers instead of resistance, and hunger where there has been plenty."[25]

SIL, OIL, AND THE STATE

Although others have quoted Peeke's reflections, rarely have SIL's critics acknowledged that the earliest misgivings came from within the organization.[26] Why did her concerns seem to fall on deaf ears? Probably because neither Lindskoog nor other members of the SIL executive committee in Ecuador could see a better solution. They were convinced that if SIL pulled out of the project, either the Catholics would fill the void or the Waorani would be cleared out by Ecuadorian soldiers with machine guns.[27] SIL's actions were necessary "if the lives of the downriver Aucas were to be saved so that they could hear the gospel."[28] Could Christian Waorani have instead gone to live with their uncontacted relatives in the various smaller centers of population scattered throughout the jungles?[29] The high level of violence among Waorani who had not yet chosen to stop spearing made this a dangerous alternative, as the murder of the Tewæno missionary Toñæ in 1970 would confirm. There were no good alternatives, and the Waorani paid a price for survival.

In addition, while Peeke and the other SIL staff were motivated by the desire to see the Waorani embrace Christianity and peace, SIL was a linguistics agency under contract to the Ecuadorian government. That same government controlled subsoil mineral rights in Wao territory and had authorized the oil exploration. It made sense for SIL to cooperate with the government and the oil companies. In January 1969 Lindskoog began asking the companies to help underwrite expenses of the contact flights. All four companies with concessions in Wao territory apparently promised at least some financial support. On January 24, Lindskoog sent Hans Tanner of Texaco expenses for a "reconnaissance flight" over the Texaco concession south and west of Limoncocha. The flight lasted four hours and nine minutes. Texaco could pay for it as a tax-exempt donation to SIL's office in the US.

Lindskoog assured Tanner that SIL staff were "not at all interested in personal gain, but are simply endeavoring to continue this strategic Auca contact program."[30] Peeke encouraged the fundraising, suggesting that Lindskoog come up with a fair policy to share expenses. The flights benefited SIL, but others gained, too. "Every geodetic survey party, every flight-service organization, and every oil company, all stand to profit by any peaceful contact . . . with any of the Auca houses."[31] By late March, Anglo had sent a check for ECS$10,000 (about USD$400); Texaco and Minas were helping as well. All requested monthly updates on the relocation project.

The bulk of oil company support for SIL's work occurred between 1969 and 1972, the most active contact years. Texaco and Anglo were the main contributors, with the largest gift on record a check for ECS$100,000 from Anglo (about USD$4,000), given November 26, 1970, when SIL was working most intensively in the Anglo concession.[32] In return, Lindskoog and Peeke occasionally consulted with the companies on how to avoid clashes with Waorani. Peeke also supplied copies of maps pinpointing the various Waorani clearings so the companies could avoid them.

As these activities indicate and as critics have charged, SIL collaborated with companies whose concessions were in Wao territory. They did so most intensively, however, before the full environmental, economic, and social impact of oil production in the rainforest was understood. Also, from the linguists' perspective, officials on the ground (in contrast to those in faraway board rooms) seemed genuinely concerned about the safety of their workers and of the Waorani. On one occasion, three helicopter pilots along with Peeke and JAARS pilot Bruce Linton, risked their lives to rescue a Wao family.

HELICOPTER RESCUE

Dabo, a Piyæmoidi man who had come to Tewæno in June 1968, established a living site with his extended family some distance north of Tewæno in what was described as the "panhandle" of the Texaco concession. In March 1969, when Texaco workers were set to enter the panhandle, Saint sent word for Waorani in the area—Dabo's group and others—to return to Tewæno. Most did, but Dabo, his mother, Awænca, and his young brother, Cowæ, were seriously ill with influenza and too weak to travel. Dabo's condition worsened, and there was concern he would die. Three pilots working for Texaco volunteered to stage a rescue effort. Linton went along to help navigate and Peeke to communicate with the Waorani. The rescue was complicated because the Waorani had not cleared enough space around their house for a helicopter to land.

Flying over the site, the pilots saw a small strip of beach on the bank of a nearby stream. The bank on the other side rose twenty-five feet into the air, topped by towering jungle growth. It was challenging, but if the undergrowth on the beach could be cleared the helicopter might be able to land. Someone, of course, had to explain this to the Waorani. Peeke had "appalling" visions of herself descending a one-hundred-foot rope ladder. Fortunately the pilot could get close enough to the ground that no ladder was needed. "One could almost step out," Peeke noted. "So I magnanimously offered to go tell the people to complete the work [clearing the beach]. . . . Woody [a pilot] got me out . . . and I experienced that momentary feeling of desolation as . . . I was alone on the beach."

Peeke shouted, and several healthy teenagers and children appeared who made short work of the underbrush. A chilly rain had begun and Peeke realized, "a bit too late, that they were all expecting to be flown out, and I was very sorry to have to tell them that this was impossible, after they had worked so hard." All stood back and watched the helicopter land in what Peeke described as "extremely marginal" conditions. It then took about twenty minutes to load the sick Waorani and their possessions. After "another tricky performance" in the driving rain, the pilot got the helicopter safely out of the small ravine. Peeke was obviously relieved when the aircraft landed on a sunny airstrip in Tewæno, where the Waorani could get antibiotics and care. It was a public relations coup for the pilots, who now had "200 new Auca friends."[33]

THE PROTECTORATE

The prospect of relocating several hundred Waorani brought new urgency to the question of land and land titles. Dayomæ had first asked for a legally recognized land reserve for the Waorani when she met Ecuadorian president Velasco Ibarra at Limoncocha in February 1961. A few months later SIL executive Kenneth Pike visited Velasco Ibarra and reiterated the request. On August 20, 1961, the president issued a decree creating an exclusive zone for the Waorani to engage in "agriculture, cattle, hunting, fishing, etc."[34] The area, which came to be known as the protectorate, was bounded on the north by the Nushiño River and on the south by the Manderoyacu River and included other, smaller rivers feeding into the Curaray. The Curaray itself ran through the heart of the land (map 3). The protectorate represented about 8 percent of traditional Wao territory.

Underlying Velasco Ibarra's decree was a vision of "civilized" Waorani that presupposed a transition to sedentary village living, like that practiced by the Quichuas and other indigenous groups with long histories of assimilation.[35] Article 3 stipulated that the Ecuadorian Institute of Agrarian Reform and Colonization (IERAC) would work together with SIL to relocate Waorani families to sites in the reserve that could be organized into judicially recognized communities.[36] When that happened, IERAC would award land titles to properties appropriate for the needs of each community. Any colonization by outsiders would be prohibited until Waorani resettlement was complete. In addition, Article 6 obligated mineral and agricultural companies working near Waorani lands to help support economic and social development programs to benefit the Waorani.

SIL Ecuador viewed Waorani relocation to the protectorate as a positive step toward assimilation. Lindskoog bristled at the suggestion that "the Auca Indians were cleared off the land by the Wycliffe Translators in order to make way for Shell Oil [*sic*]." Contact, Lindskoog explained, had been initiated by Christian Waorani to reach their estranged family members. Relocation, in turn, was necessary because three or four hundred people were controlling 5 percent of Ecuador's land. (Other estimates suggested as high as 7 or 8 percent.) "With millions of land-hungry people searching for a way to better their lot," he wrote, referring to the homesteaders who accompanied the oil boom, "there would have been many years of bloody conflict" over Wao lands. The protectorate was not a "corral" but an area where the Waorani could pursue their traditional way of life in peace while transitioning to a more sedentary pattern, "developing skills in agriculture and animal husbandry."[37]

Lindskoog's explanation, and the policies he defended, reflected the prevailing ideal of incorporating indigenous people into the modern nation-state, creating a settled population of small farmers. This was before research in the mid-1970s identified the semisedentary, hunter-horticulturalist pattern characteristic of Waorani life. Lindskoog's analysis also came prior to the rise of modern indigenous movements that redefined the concept of "civilization" and emphasized the value of traditional indigenous cultures.

SIL staff did realize that while Velasco Ibarra's decree had set aside the protectorate, the Waorani still had no legal title to any of it. As long as the Waorani were not in communities, the legal status of their land was precarious, and they were vulnerable to squatters and to changing government policies. In 1967 Saint and Lindskoog petitioned the executive director of IERAC to adjudicate the Waorani claim to the protectorate. Gustavo Medina López, IERAC director of colonization, responded that once SIL conducted a precise survey of the land in question, as the institute was doing with other indigenous lands, granting title would be a simple procedure.[38]

Despite Medina López's assurances, progress on legal status for the protectorate moved slowly. Lindskoog and Saint made their request just as the oil boom got under way. There was some uncertainty about how the oil concessions and exploratory work would affect the future location of Wao communities. "It would be ironical," Lindskoog mused, "if we should be accidentally concentrating all of the Aucas in the exact spot where Anglo intends to drill."[39] His fears were assuaged in January 1969 when IERAC officially recognized the Waorani right to the protectorate, reaffirming the 1961 decree. The protectorate would remain in effect until the Waorani were able to gain title to their own plots within the zone.

Saint worried that the stipulations associated with the protectorate would be used to cheat the Waorani of additional land that was rightfully theirs, confining them to small plots. But the IERAC pronouncement bought the Waorani time and assured their place in the protectorate against further relocation. Legal titles would ultimately be granted to Wao communities in 1983, and in 1990 the Waorani would be awarded an additional two thousand square miles of land (about one-third their original territory) as an expanded Waorani Ethnic Reserve.

THE BAIWAIDI

By early 1969 the Waorani protectorate seemed secure, and oil companies with concessions in Wao territory were cooperating with relocation efforts. Gifts were dropped by parachute over clearings where peaceful ground contact had not yet been made. These included the living sites of the Baiwaidi, Dawa's family members, and the Wepeidi, who were scattered along a ridge near the Gabado River. The geography for both areas, as in much of Wao territory, included ridges covered with rainforest and cut through by multiple meandering rivers and streams.

The Wepeidi, or "ridge people," had historic ties with the original Tewæno inhabitants, having split from the Guequitaidi twenty years earlier. However, as the smaller and closer of the two groups, the Baiwaidi seemed the logical next group to contact, although there were risks. In the past, the Guequitaidi and the Baiwaidi had speared one another's family members, and the most feared killers of the two groups—Guequita and Baiwa (also called Bai)—were still alive, although Guequita was among the first to embrace Christianity and peace. And it had been only a year since the people of Tewæno received the Piyæmoidi.

According to Saint, during that year most of the Piyæmoidi had "heard the gospel." In July 1969 her brother Ben arrived. A pastor who weighed 230-plus pounds, he was an imposing figure among the Waorani during the two and a half days he stayed to preach and to teach the Bible. He was the only male outsider Saint had allowed to spend a night in Tewæno in more than a year. She reported that Ben and Yowe baptized fifteen people, three of whom were from the Piyæmoidi. The other twelve were original Tewæno residents. Despite ongoing waves of influenza and depleted food supplies, it seemed as if Rachel, the Christian Waorani, and the Tewæno community had turned a corner.

Saint once again called for prayer but seemed cautiously prepared when she learned that the Baiwaidi, a group of fifty-six people, had begun the overland trek to Tewæno. She was adamant that only God's power and the resolve of the Tewæno Christians would make assimilation possible.[40] What she could not predict was that this particular episode would become a defining moment in her life.

POLIO

The Baiwaidi clearings had been spotted in early 1968 but not positively identified until late that year. It was obvious from the start that the Baiwaidi were interested in the trade goods that came from the contact flights. One recorded interaction included a chorus of voices from the ground: "Throw me down a lot of beads"; "Bring me an axe tomorrow!"; "Bring me more (glass) beads when they ripen on the bushes"; "Throw me down an aluminum bowl"; "Throw me down a machete!" The demands were so numerous and insistent that later, as the tape was being played and replayed and analyzed by Rachel, Dayomæ, Dawa, and others in Tewæno, they heard a small voice call out in the same intonation, "Throw me down a cookie that I might eat it!" It was Dayomæ's three-and-a-half-year-old daughter, Eunice, blind since birth. Napping nearby, Eunie overheard the clamor and chimed in with her own request.

In tandem with the desire for goods was the hope of peace. Some in the group, most notably Bai himself, claimed they wanted to end the spearings. Saint was cautious. A splinter group that had fled the Piyæmoidi just before they moved to Tewæno appeared to have joined the Baiwaidi. This meant that Baiwa's group could contain people with vendettas against both the Guequitaidi and the Piyæmoidi, an explosive situation. And the problem of contact illnesses remained acute. Still, Saint felt the familiar urgency to pursue the relocation, especially since an oil trail ended near Baiwaidi homes.[41]

While Ben Saint was visiting Tewæno, Quemo, along with Dawa and Oncaye's sister Onguimæ, went on foot to the Baiwaidi clearings. Quemo's last contact with the Baiwaidi years earlier had been to kill his enemies among them and to steal Dawa. Nonetheless the three convinced the Baiwaidi to come to Tewæno. It took five weeks for the group to complete their migration, a journey marked by periods of near starvation. Like other Waorani, they subsisted mostly on manioc, so leaving their gardens behind resulted in genuine hardship. The rainforest was not, as outsiders often imagined, filled with food for the taking.[42] Saint tried to arrange for planes to make food drops, which were unsuccessful. In mid-August the newcomers arrived. For the next two weeks Rachel and Dawa were on the go almost constantly, helping the Baiwaidi settle in and watching for tensions that might threaten the fragile peace among the kinship groups.

On August 30, Dawa was called to help nurse Æmoncawæ, a young Piyæmoidi man whose family had settled along the Curaray River, several hours' trek to the north of Tewæno. She arrived with medicines for influenza, but he died the following night. On September 2 Saint received word that her mother, Katherine Proctor Saint, had died. Amid her personal grief, she faced a growing crisis. Æmonkawæ's death was only the beginning, as increasing numbers of Waorani living nearby became seriously ill. Saint described the symptoms over the radio to Lois Pederson, a registered nurse and manager of the Limoncocha clinic, and to Peter Rae, a physician at the missionary hospital in Shell Mera. The tentative diagnosis, later confirmed, was polio.[43]

The origin of the polio epidemic that swept through the Waorani living near Tewæno during September and October 1969 is uncertain. Outbreaks were reported earlier in the summer among the Shuar people, who lived far to the southwest of the Waorani. Almost simultaneous with the Wao epidemic, new cases were reported among the Shuars and jungle Quichuas.[44] First affected among the Waorani were Piyæmoidi families living along the Curaray River. Saint believed they contracted the disease from a group of Quichuas who had been traveling down the river and had made several stops. She routinely blamed Quichuas for nearly all contact illnesses, but there was logic to her reasoning since she so tightly controlled—and prohibited—almost all other outside access. Dayomæ's son Sam, nineteen at the time, blamed the outbreak on missionary contact. There was even some speculation that food packages dropped into Tewæno to help with shortages might have been contaminated. No credible evidence supported either rumor.[45]

Saint rejected initial offers of help. It was too dangerous for either Lois Pederson or Wallace Swanson, a physician from the HCJB hospital in Quito, to be flown in, even though they believed that "lives could be saved by some rather simple techniques."[46] Saint refused to administer oral polio vaccine to Waorani who had not yet contracted the disease, afraid that any adverse reaction to the vaccine would provoke violence. She was not swayed by assurances from physicians that the probability of a reaction was rare. Nor should seriously ill Waorani be airlifted to the Shell hospital because the culture shock would be too great and the weather too cold. Saint maintained that there was no alternative but to "ride it out." Her continued insistence on absolute control during the first three weeks of the epidemic pushed Lindskoog's patience with his famous and stubborn colleague to the limit. Lindskoog knew, of course, that a contributing factor to the epidemic was Saint's earlier refusal to allow anyone to vaccinate the Waorani.

"I am well aware . . . that people will wonder and inquire 'why didn't someone do something about this?'" wrote Lindskoog in frustration. "I have pushed as hard as I can without flatly telling Rachel that I intend to override her opinions."[47]

Saint soldiered on, although she apparently contracted a mild form of the disease and was quite weak herself. With Dawa's assistance, she did what she could for the first three weeks. Hardest hit were the Piyæmoidi and the newly arrived Baiwaidi, both because of their greater susceptibility to contact illnesses and because their defenses had been weakened by hunger. By September 20, six people had died, creating a dangerous situation because of the anger experienced by grief-stricken family members. Traditional Wao culture had no category for natural or accidental death. The Waorani believed that all deaths, whether a result of disease, snakebite, or other circumstances, ultimately had a human agent behind them. The typical response to death was not simply sadness but rage, satisfied, in turn, by killing someone else. Family members would try to determine who was the source of a death—what *ido* (a person with malevolent spiritual powers) had sent spirits to cause it—and then exact vengeance on that person.[48]

REVENGE SPEARINGS

This happened during the polio epidemic after Æmoncawæ, the young man who was the first to contract polio, died. His half brother Eniwa responded with rage against Piyæmo, from the Piyæmoidi group, believed to be an *ido*. Eniwa and two other young men attacked Piyæmo's family and speared his son, Nænquemo, the first such killing in the protectorate in twelve years. In response to Nænquemo's death, another revenge spearing occurred, this time of Eniwa's sister. The young woman had returned to Tewæno after spending time as a house servant in Quito. She had difficulty readjusting to Wao culture and had alienated other Waorani, which made her an easy target. "Lose a good man, kill a worthless girl," was Saint's summary of the killers' attitudes.[49]

The perpetrators of both spearings were young, between twelve and nineteen.[50] In 1965 Eniwa had been baptized in the Curaray, along with Steve and Kathy Saint. He had reaffirmed his faith in July, when Ben Saint visited Tewæno. Eniwa's action might have launched an all-out vendetta had he not mysteriously dropped dead after a seizure a few days later. Rachel viewed the death as "the judgment of God."[51] Some health workers suspected tetanus, and later there were rumors that he had been poisoned.[52]

The polio deaths, ultimately numbering sixteen—three Baiwaidi and thirteen Piyæmoidi—resulted in more than a few outraged relatives. This was Saint's rationale for barring outsiders. The Waorani, she explained, would "bash in everything that belonged to the person [who had died], and burn the house down, and furiously rant around and, in the case of the men, pick up their spears to kill."[53] The polio epidemic pushed Saint's customary role as enforcer of the Christian ethic of peace to its limits. She went from warrior to warrior, telling them not to spear. The family of Tidonca, Oncaye's half brother, was particularly hard hit. Grief-stricken and enraged as his fifteen-year-old-son lay dying, Tidonca sharpened a spear and talked of killing his daughter. When the son died, Saint confiscated the spear and hid it in her own house. In a similar instance of rage, Dawa's half brother Babæ, one of the newly arrived Baiwaidi, was furious when his wife died. He made a long spear, planning to kill some other man so that he, Babæ, could have the man's wife. Saint seized that spear as well and broke it to get it out of the house. These were risky actions in a volatile situation, yet Saint's courage and refusal to accept revenge killings served as a powerful example of the Christian gospel of peace.[54]

Concerned about the ongoing crisis, Lindskoog flew Swanson and Pederson into Tewæno on September 24 without consulting Saint. Over the next few days, the two improvised ways to help ill Waorani survive paralysis. Swanson rigged a "hammock apparatus that worked like a teeter-totter, moving their [the ill Waorani's] diaphragms up and down."[55] For those less severely ill, Pederson created exercise regimens with bunches of bananas as weights to stretch paralyzed muscles. She also improvised walkers using bamboo poles so that victims could begin to regain mobility. Pederson was familiar to at least a few of the Waorani. She staffed the clinic in Limoncocha where some had been flown for care.

Swanson did not spend nights in Tewæno, but Pederson remained in the clearing for several weeks, relieving some of Saint's burden and providing therapy for Waorani who were in recovery. The condition of nine patients was so critical that within a few days after Swanson evaluated them, they were flown to the HCJB hospital in Shell Mera. Seven survived, some despite severe paralysis. In a blow to relocation, half of the Baiwaidi left Tewæno to return to their old homes, preferring to take their chances with oil crews rather than polio. The new territory, to which they had come with much anticipation, turned out to be "full of disease and low in food supply."[56] Both the Piyæmoidi and the Baiwaidi thought "they were coming to heaven" when they arrived at Tewæno, mused Catherine Peeke. "They found out they weren't when they got polio."[57]

As news of the polio outbreak spread, medical supplies—vaccine, crutches, wheelchairs, therapy equipment—arrived from the US. In November, after the crisis had passed, a rehabilitation center was established in Limoncocha. Nine polio victims were flown there from Shell Mera and Tewæno for therapy. Medical personnel from the US, as well as HCJB missionary nurses and doctors, provided care on a rotating basis. Rosi Jung, a new SIL staffer from Germany who had been trained as a midwife, also joined the therapy team. In the end, Piyæmo lost most of the use of his legs and would need crutches; his son Cawiya also required a cane or crutches. Two other Piyæmoidi men, Nanca and Nænæ, were paraplegic; and Dayomæ's half sister Enæ suffered from severe respiratory problems.

CARING FOR ENEMIES

Grief and the desire for revenge still surfaced among the Waorani in the protectorate, especially among men who had lost spouses or children. However, despite the tragedy of lives lost or forever changed through paralysis, the polio epidemic did serve to demonstrate the difference Christianity had made in the lives of some Wao believers. Yowe, for example, spent weeks working in Tewæno with people disabled by the disease, including one of his own daughters. Lois Pederson had taught him basic therapy techniques, and he kneaded muscles and raised and lowered legs among the less seriously injured. Since Yowe no longer had time to hunt, Guequita provided meat for both his and Yowe's families.[58] These were countercultural activities in a society where the obligation to help others extended only to immediate family groups. Also, some enemies who were vulnerable should have been killed but were not.

However, the crisis did highlight an issue that had been developing for years: Saint's unwillingness to let anyone else live and work with "her" tribe. Lindskoog summed up the problem: "Rachel has been unwilling to accept a partner, consequently Rachel is the only voice speaking for the Auca tribal work."[59] In a crisis or conflict, there was no one to provide a second opinion. For example, Saint did not understand the degree to which hunger was a problem among the newcomers. For many Piyæmoidi and Baiwaidi, hunger more than polio would shape their memories of these years.

As the number of Waorani living near Tewæno increased, it was impossible for Saint to handle relocation work, medical care, literacy, and translation on her own. "We must . . . assign more personnel to the Auca work and let Rachel herself choose whether they will form a team with her or if we will set up a separate and parallel team."[60] This was the basis for Lindskoog's decision to ask Catherine Peeke to accept a permanent assignment with the Waorani, and to add Rosi Jung in 1970, literacy instructor Pat Kelley in 1972, and anthropologist Jim Yost and his wife, Kathie, in 1974. Although Saint's considerable influence would continue to be felt in Tewæno for another decade, the polio epidemic marked the beginning of the end of her role as sole proprietor of SIL's work with the Waorani.

A WAORANI MARTYR

Once the danger from polio subsided, SIL resumed plane flights and gift drops over the clearings of the Wepeidi. Many of the approximately 250 people scattered on the ridge were related to each other and to both the Guequitaidi and Piyæmoidi groups in Tewæno. One Tewæno Christian committed to contacting these people was Toñæ, whose half brother Wepe was a feared warrior and whose half sister Omade lived in the ridge area as well.[61] Toñæ's mother, Meñemo, and his father, Coba, had belonged to a kinship group that had been wiped out in the ongoing violence. Coba was killed. Despite historic animosity between the two kinship groups, the Guequitaidi in Tewæno had let Meñemo and her son live with them. Toñæ was about twelve when he arrived in Tewæno. At first the boy was aloof toward outsiders, but he embraced Christianity as a teenager and was mentored by Saint.

During the 1960s, up to the polio epidemic, Saint—occasionally assisted by Sam Padilla—held literacy classes on an intermittent basis. They were largely ineffective. Saint's training in literacy work was minimal, and even to grasp the concept of reading and writing involved a dramatic cultural paradigm shift on the part of the Waorani. Despite these barriers, young Toñæ learned to read and write. In early 1970, by then married and with a baby daughter, he was the only functionally literate Wao. Saint and others had high hopes for him as the Tewæno schoolteacher. However, Toñæ was also actively involved in the contact flights. As early as February 1969, he had identified one of the clearings where Wepe lived and, from the plane overhead, talked to members of the family group in the clearing below. During a flight in November, after the worst of the polio epidemic, he also found his half sister Omade's clearing.

Toñæ recognized that it was no time to bring more people to the protectorate. As the early months of 1970 passed, he decided that he would go to his relatives on the ridge. He explained, in a note to Saint written in the Wao language, "In Tewæno God said to me: Go! When you have gone and evangelized them all, whosoever agrees in faith shall come to Limoncocha. After they come out, when God's message has been thoroughly taught them, then we shall take them on to Tewæno. After we have taken them there, and they have believed well in God, we shall praise God for His working."[62]

On April 27, 1970, Toñæ was flown by helicopter to a garden area a short distance from Omade's clearing. Carrying a twenty-pound radio that at the time was considered "portable," the young man safely jumped from the hovering helicopter, dusted himself off, and walked toward the clearing. He was welcomed first by Wepe and later by Omade and their family members. Checking in by radio each day with Saint, Toñæ reported that he had told his relatives about God. He had emphasized the need to live in peace, not only because of the teaching of God's son named Jesus, but also after the example of the Old Testament warrior David, "God's man who did not spear his enemies." Toñæ read from the Gospel of Mark and encouraged his relatives to end their hostilities against other Waorani and outsiders. He also requested occasional gift drops of trade goods.[63]

After about six weeks, something went wrong. According to later accounts, Toñæ's half brother Wepe incited the murder. Angered that Toñæ, who had left a pregnant wife and small child in Tewæno, would not accept a second wife, Wepe convinced Omade's sons that Toñæ was not a relative after all but an outsider, an imposter.[64] Toñæ's decision to adopt the haircut and clothing of the *cowode* lent credibility to the accusation. Omade's husband, Nampawæ, lured Toñæ into the forest, where his sons attacked Toñæ from behind. Still conscious, Toñæ told his assailants that they could harm his body but that he would go to God's house. "We'll help you go, then," they said, using their spears. The killers later expressed surprise at Toñæ's confidence in the face of death.[65] Eventually they and others of the Wepeidi would turn away from vengeance killing, in part because of Toñæ's example.

Although Toñæ's death occurred in late June 1970, it would be almost a year before his family and the rest of the Tewæno community knew what had happened. They suspected tragedy, but the Wepeidi clearings on the ridge remained too dangerous for outsiders to enter. Repeated sightings from the air of Wao males who looked much like Toñæ gave rise to false hope. When the Wepeidi finally acknowledged the murder, Toñæ was honored as the first Wao Christian martyr. His death was a great loss. A young, literate Wao who had demonstrated clear promise as one who could help his people successfully confront the outside world was gone.

Toñæ's death also represented a setback in the strategy to contact the Wepeidi as oil companies closed in on their ridge area, located on the border between two different concessions. One company (Minas y Petróleos) was building trails and helicopter pads to the north and west of the ridge; another (Anglo) was located to the south (map 3). The ridge area with a sizable Wao population was caught in a squeeze between the two. "Anglo has nowhere else to go as an alternate—this is all there is left for them to do," Peeke reported to Saint after a September meeting. "The net is closing in until there is absolutely nothing they can do now but move ahead."[66]

After nearly two years of intensive efforts to facilitate peaceful contact, Peeke feared the worst, noting that the oil companies "really couldn't care less if they ... sort of wipe out a tribe." Attempting to be charitable, she emphasized, "That is ... the companies don't [care]; I think these folk who are locally involved really do care." But there seemed to be no easy solution. The Wepeidi and oil workers would soon be living and working in very close proximity.[67]

10

Early Anti-Mission Sentiment

———————————————————————

DESPITE THE INCREASING presence of seismic crews in Wao territory, 1971 began on an optimistic note for the Summer Institute of Linguistics in Ecuador. The previous December, oil company helicopters and motorized canoes had facilitated the return to Tewæno of twenty-eight Baiwaidi who had fled the polio epidemic. Although they would be slow to settle in, they were back.[1] There had been increasing contact between Waorani in the protectorate and oil workers and other outsiders, but so far with no violence or new waves of illness.[2] With John Lindskoog due to leave on furlough in June, Don Johnson was elected Branch director. Johnson was upbeat in his annual report for the Ecuador Branch of SIL, written early in the year.

"Never in our history [in Ecuador] have we enjoyed a better image," he claimed. In 1970 SIL had, for the first time, been included in the national budget of Ecuador. The Ministry of Education had provided strong support for the organization. Translations in the various indigenous groups where SIL had a presence were going well, though Wao translation work had been slowed by SIL's role as peacemaker between the Waorani and oil workers. Even so, Rachel and Dayomæ had finished a draft translation of Acts.[3]

One sign of renewed confidence related to the Waorani was Rachel's reluctant willingness to participate in a series of American "Auca Update Rallies." These were mass rallies on behalf of Bible translation, each shorter but similar in scale to a

Billy Graham Crusade, that took place in twenty-three cities from Dallas north to the Midwest, then south again, between late February and early April 1971. They were sponsored by Wycliffe Associates, volunteers who supported Wycliffe Bible Translators by engaging in fundraising and other activities. The rallies featured a sophisticated multimedia presentation on the history of Bible translation, followed by the story of missionary contact among the Waorani. The main draw, however, was Rachel herself and the three Wao believers who accompanied her: Dawa, Quemo, and Guequita. Sam Padilla, now twenty-one, went along as an unofficial advance man.

In a typical rally, the multimedia show concluded with the house lights darkened. When they came back up, Rachel had taken center stage. *Esquire* magazine writer Jerry Bledsoe described her appearance. She was "a plump, grandmotherly woman, with graying hair stretched into a bun, piercing blue eyes, and a face that fairly radiates." Rachel told audiences about the most recent happenings in the rainforest, then, "with her certain flair for drama, she introduced the Aucas." Rachel's approach was simple: "I want to introduce you to the man who killed my brother Nate. He is now my brother in Christ." Guequita came forward. With Rachel translating, Guequita, Quemo, and Dawa talked about the difference Christianity had made in their lives. Guequita told of his years as a killer, leading Waorani spearing raids, and how Jesus had changed his heart.[4]

The rallies reflected William Cameron Townsend's conviction that Rachel and the Waorani were among the best public relations representatives Wycliffe had ever had. Between 1968 and his death in 1982, Townsend shifted his focus from Latin America to the Soviet Union, but he never lost his assurance that God had provided Rachel and the Waorani story to advance Wycliffe's overall mission. Nor did he budge from his idealized vision of SIL's Waorani work.

Townsend visited Tewæno briefly on two occasions, in 1961 and in 1967, before the traumas of relocation had rocked the clearing. He repeatedly affirmed his view that Rachel was "a great missionary and a remarkable translator."[5] Ever the visionary, Townsend was not troubled by what he considered short-term setbacks. As soon as the first peaceful contact had been made with the Piyæmoidi in 1968, he was sure it was time for a sequel to *The Dayuma Story*.[6] Even at the height of the polio epidemic, Townsend kept pressing for another celebratory book. He himself would provide $250 toward writer Ethel Wallis's expenses, he assured Lindskoog. The beleaguered Ecuador team put him off.

Although Townsend romanticized Rachel and the Waorani, he and Wycliffe had an unerring sense of the ongoing North American interest in an inspirational version of the missionary-Waorani story. On February 22, Rachel and her entourage were interviewed on the *Today* show in New York City. Not since the five missionaries were killed had the Waorani received so much publicity. Thousands attended the update rallies, where they were challenged to support WBT financially or to join the ranks of the rapidly expanding organization.

It was clear that American evangelicals were captivated by Rachel's charisma and by the power of the narrative she and the Waorani embodied. Audiences wanted to see the Wao warrior who speared Nate Saint standing next to Rachel on stage. They were fascinated by the three Waorani who had lived in a culture of killing and hate but who now professed their love for Jesus and told of changed lives. Amid these powerful testimonies of transformed lives, it was easy to miss the irony that for a tour ostensibly designed to promote Bible translation, the Waorani had only the shortest gospel, Mark, translated and published in their language and that none of the Waorani on stage—or in Tewæno—could read.

The tour was grueling, despite the warm reception and flood of positive publicity. Rachel and the Waorani spoke sixty-six times in all, including interviews and before small groups, as well as at the large rallies.[7] This represented an average of more than one event a day, every day, for six weeks. Dawa, Quemo, and Guequita tired of the strange culture. Young Sam Padilla grew disillusioned with day after day of interviews. He was visiting the United States, but all he got to see were "freeways, the television and radio stations, the newspapers, and the churches."[8] When the tour concluded, the group spent ten days at the JAARS compound in Waxhaw, North Carolina—sick with the flu.

After returning to Ecuador, it was increasingly obvious that Rachel's vision was hampered by cataracts. Catherine Peeke had gently urged her to take a furlough the year before, suggesting she leave "the tribe with all of its problems in [God's] hands" while she took "a time of rest."[9] Rachel had resisted the idea. After twelve years with the Waorani, the idea of a missionary furlough may have become a foreign concept. She viewed herself as Dayomæ's kin "sister" and, along with other older women, a "grandmother" or matriarch among the Waorani at Tewæno. Taking a furlough from one's family did not make sense, especially when the situation at Tewæno still seemed precarious. (Later SIL staffers would comment that the situation always seemed precarious to Rachel.) Then she started stumbling over roots and stumps as she walked through the clearing. Impaired vision, rather than the urging of colleagues, sent her back to the US during the summer of 1971, where she had cataract surgery on her right eye. After six weeks her vision had improved enough that the left eye would have to wait. The Waorani needed her.[10]

THE BARBADOS DECLARATION

Only a few weeks before the Auca Update Rallies began, a small group of anthropologists met on the island of Barbados for the Symposium on Inter-Ethnic Conflict in South America, jointly sponsored by the World Council of Churches and the Ethnology Department of the University of Bern (Switzerland). At the end of their meeting they issued the Declaration of Barbados, dated January 30, 1971. It called for the liberation of the Indians of the Americas from domination "by a colonial situation which originated with the conquest and which persists today." A hallmark of this colonialism was the assumption that lands belonging to aboriginal groups were "free and unoccupied territory open to conquest and colonisation."[11]

According to the declaration, governments, religious missions, and anthropologists shared the blame for the oppression of indigenous societies, although governments and religious missions were most culpable. Missions, whether Catholic or Protestant, were hostile to indigenous cultures "conceived as pagan and heretical." In addition, "a religious pretext has too often justified the economic and human exploitation of the aboriginal population." The declaration called for churches to suspend all missionary activity among indigenous peoples. Until that happened, religious groups should back away from evangelism and cultivate respect for tribal cultures. They should no longer use trade goods to "blackmail" indigenous people, and they should "suspend immediately all practices of population displacement or concentration" as strategies for evangelization and assimilation.[12]

There was no indication in 1971 that officials from WBT or SIL were concerned about the Barbados Declaration or had an immediate reaction to it. The charges were nothing new. Missionaries had long been accused of destroying indigenous cultures and coercing conversions, particularly in Latin America, where cross and sword had arrived together in European conquest. Nonetheless the declaration represented a new era of anti-missionary sentiment that would have a profound impact on SIL. At the same time, the Barbados call for Indian liberation reinforced the beginnings of the modern indigenous movement that emerged in Latin America and throughout the world during the last three decades of the twentieth century.

Attitudes toward indigenous groups and toward missions that had been taken for granted would increasingly be challenged—and the declaration provided a convenient catalogue of both hypothetical and actual misdeeds. It legitimized critics and offered a vocabulary for their concerns. The declaration denied any possibility of authentic indigenous Christianity or genuine missionary contribution to the lives of indigenous peoples. Instead the document presented "indigenous" and "Christian" as mutually exclusive, rejecting Catholic or Protestant groups committed to any form of direct or indirect evangelization as an aspect of their mission. Though not a missions organization, SIL was an obvious target.

This was illustrated in an unintended outcome of the update tour. The success of the Wycliffe rallies caught the attention of Jerry Bledsoe, a writer for *Esquire* magazine. As a result, in late 1971 Bledsoe traveled to Ecuador, made a brief visit to Tewæno (for as long as Rachel would allow), and wrote "Saint," an article profiling Rachel and her work with the Waorani. The essay poked fun at the missionaries, particularly their fear that *Esquire* was, as Bledsoe put it, a "nudie magazine" and might not be an appropriate venue for an article about Rachel. *Esquire's* reputation notwithstanding, the essay was entertaining, accurate, and generally sympathetic to Rachel ("the most famous missionary of our time") and SIL.[13]

It did, however, reach readers who normally paid little attention to missionaries and Bible rallies. Some were more eager than Bledsoe to criticize Wycliffe and SIL. One such critic was Laurie Hart, a writer who used Bledsoe's work as the main source of information for a section on the Waorani in "Pacifying the Last Frontiers: [The] Story of the Wycliffe Translators," an influential article that appeared in 1973. It was published by the North American Congress on Latin America (NACLA), a loose coalition of individuals and groups who "opposed the obstructionist role of the United States in Latin America" and supported "the necessity of a far-reaching social revolution" in the region.[14] Hart's piece was the first of what would become a chorus of publications in the 1970s and 1980s describing the Summer Institute of Linguistics in Latin America, Southeast Asia, and elsewhere as the epitome of all that the Barbados Declaration condemned.[15] Like "Pacifying the Last Frontiers," many of these anti-SIL articles would use the Waorani as evidence to support their critiques. Just as they had become icons for the success of evangelical missions, the Waorani would be used in this new context to symbolize missionary excesses and failures.

Hart did not mince words. Conflating WBT and SIL, she accused Wycliffe of giving "a new façade to the old process of pacifying and pillaging native peoples."[16] She and others created what proved to be a persistent stereotype of the two groups as agents of Yankee imperialism and destroyers of native cultures. In Ecuador and else-where, from the mid-1970s into the twenty-first century, the Spanish acronym ILV (Instituto Lingüístico de Verano) became shorthand for abusive missionary prac-tice. This was true whether such practices were actual or imagined, whether SIL had addressed problems or not, or whether linguists and support staff with the Institute even remained in the country.

Repeated suggestions that SIL was a front for or otherwise collaborated with the CIA were simply untrue.[17] However, the sheer number of SIL staff in Latin America (more than one thousand by the late 1960s) and their dual identity as linguists under contract to governments and also as missionaries reporting back to a largely evangelical constituency in the US made them an easy target.[18] Unfortunately, too, some SIL staff members could be their own worst enemies. In addition to information from *Esquire*, Hart's section on the Waorani included a lengthy quotation from a February 1971 prayer letter from Bill Eddy. Initially a JAARS airplane mechanic from Limoncocha, Eddy was asked to serve as a public relations coordinator between the various oil company headquarters in Quito and Peeke, Saint, and others participating in Waorani relocation.

Like all SIL and JAARS staff, Eddy received financial support—his salary—from contributions given by churches and individuals in the US. To maintain communication and encourage giving and prayer, he wrote periodic newsletters that were printed or mimeographed and mailed to his supporters, standard practice for faith missions. To communicate the excitement and significance of his new assignment, Eddy wrote a letter that presented what was at best a simplistic description of what SIL was trying to do. "With the discovery of a vast reserve of oil under the eastern jungle twenty-one companies are working 1500 men there," he wrote. "As they advance we fly ahead of them and explain to Aucas living in their path that they are coming. We persuade them that they should move out of the way. . . . As a result of this close coordination by radio and telephone . . . there has not been one life lost to date. PRAISE GOD!"[19]

Eddy's letter circulated widely and perplexed supporters of Wycliffe and SIL. "It seems incredible to me that any of your people could find themselves working so wholeheartedly on behalf of an oil company," wrote Fred Morris, a United Methodist missionary in Brazil. Morris suggested that "this kind of alliance is exactly what has made the missionary enterprise suspect." Parishioners from the First United Methodist Church in New Haven, Connecticut, sought further information. Was WBT in Ecuador clearing the "Auca Indians" from their land to benefit an oil company? The letter refrained from criticism, but church members expressed concern about what was happening in the rainforest.[20]

In response to Morris, Wycliffe's North American director, Benjamin Elson, emphasized, "Our interest is not in oil but in Aucas." He reaffirmed Wycliffe's belief that the oil companies saw only one alternative to relocation: "Ecuadorian government soldiers simply clearing the way by gunfire."[21] John Lindskoog sent two detailed letters to the Connecticut Methodists, emphasizing SIL's independence from big oil: "We are not nor have we been their 'agents.'" Lindskoog also emphasized the Waorani role in initiating both relocation efforts and negotiations over establishing the protectorate. Dayomæ was the first to seek "a territory which the Aucas could rightfully call their own." And it was the "deep and personal obligation" sensed by "several of the Aucas" in Tewæno—prior to the oil boom—that led to initial efforts toward additional peaceful contact and relocation.[22]

Lindskoog was candid in explaining why the newly contacted Waorani agreed to relocate. He had talked with Catherine Peeke about their reasons. "It was not materialistic interest—they [Baiwaidi and Wepeidi] had frequent contact with oil exploration crews and their material desires were satisfied. Nor was it a desire (as we might have wished) to 'become Christians.' But it WAS a desire to escape from the fear-dominated society in which they lived." Lindskoog emphasized that SIL was not trying to confine the Waorani but instead was helping them gain legal title to lands large enough for them to pursue their traditional ways of life as they transitioned to a more sedentary pattern.[23]

ERWIN PATZELT TAKES ON SIL

Changes in the wider world during 1971 were also beginning to reach Tewæno. Waorani contact with nonmissionary outsiders was increasing. Quichua squatters, following oil trails, made incursions into the protectorate. The Wepeidi increasingly encountered oil company workers on the ridge and soon became adept at securing trade goods from them. With Rachel away much of the year, Catherine Peeke and Rosi Jung were the staff in residence at Tewæno.

The "pacified" Waorani continued to fascinate outsiders, and a growing number of visitors made brief stops in Tewæno. There were Ecuadorian government and political officials, as well as Cuauhtémoc Cárdenas, son of Townsend's close friend, former Mexican president Lázaro Cárdenas. Others were visitors who had helped support SIL financially, as well as researchers in residence at Limoncocha. Peeke confessed on one particularly busy July day that she hoped no one would stay for lunch because roasted monkey leg was all they had.[24]

Not everyone who wanted to meet the Waorani was a fan of SIL. Erwin Patzelt, a German naturalist and photographer and a teacher at Quito's German high school, was captivated by the people. With Sam Padilla as translator and using an oil company helicopter, Patzelt had a peaceful encounter with the Wepeidi on August 1, 1971, helped along by an ample quantity of trade goods. Taking a page from the linguists' book, before landing Patzelt made gift drops of sixteen aluminum bowls, each containing rice, candies, mirrors, knives, and pocket combs and attached to small red parachutes. After a brief visit, the Waorani requested machetes on the next trip and managed to secure Patzelt's shirt and the helicopter pilot's cap as additional booty.[25]

Less than a week later Patzelt returned with the promised machetes as well as a rooster and three hens. His purpose was to provide the Waorani with "a new source of nutrition." Back once again on September 1, Patzelt found that the three hens already had been added to Wao cooking pots. The rooster had survived because the Waorani were fascinated by his crowing. Padilla took orders for the next trip.[26]

Patzelt flew into the ridge twice more before encountering Peeke on September 14. Furious at seeing the helicopter, Peeke landed in another helicopter nearby to confront Patzelt and Padilla. She "scolded them both roundly" for courting danger by visiting the Wepeidi. It had been about fifteen months since Toñæ's death and only six months since an oil company cook had been speared nearby, although not by the Wepeidi. Peeke herself had made a brief visit to the ridge for the first time barely a month before she met Patzelt there. After the encounter, Patzelt found the oil companies unwilling to facilitate his visits, choosing their working relationship with SIL over the opportunity to ferry a freelance naturalist and photographer.[27]

Undaunted, Patzelt brought Lt. Col. Carlos Espinosa, head of the Ecuadorian military's geographical institute, along for his next trip. When the oil camp manager refused them the use of a helicopter, citing SIL's policy prohibiting such excursions, Patzelt was ready. He spread the news that "not even a colonel of the Ecuadorian army was permitted to travel over national territory, all by order of the Wycliffe Bible Translators."[28] The naturalist later published a letter from Pedro Porras, professor of anthropology at the Catholic University in Quito, suggesting that the Summer Institute, "a group of foreigners," had "formed a country within our country . . . in which, under cunning pretexts, they maintain in the most strict isolation . . . our countrymen."[29]

SIL had served for more than a decade as the liaison between outsiders, including the Ecuadorian government and oil companies, and the Waorani. This relationship had been formalized through government contracts and the land decrees issued by the Ecuadorian Institute of Agrarian Reform and Colonization. It had been reinforced by Rachel's protectiveness. The few others who were familiar with Wao culture, including Peeke, cultivated a healthy respect for the violence that characterized it.

About this time Peeke prepared a basic Spanish-Waorani phrase list for the benefit of oil workers. The list included phrases to establish location ("Where is the river?"), phrases to ask for help and to request food and drink. Under the heading "Friendly Relations," Spanish speakers learned *Wao tededo* for "I am your friend"; "Don't kill me"; "Let me live"; and "Don't spear me." For an outsider, staying alive seemed to be the key indicator of friendly relations. Despite SIL's protective instincts, Lindskoog would acknowledge about a year and a half later that the Summer Institute had tried "to do what we have no right to do, and what, in fact, is not possible for us to do— that is, to take the whole Auca tribe as our responsibility, attempting to control their contacts with the outside world."[30]

SIL staff made some halfhearted attempts to mend fences with Patzelt, although they underestimated his influence. In February 1972 Patzelt asked SIL for permission to visit Tewæno and the Gabado ridge. The linguists agreed but waited for two weeks before letting him know. "We had given him time to get miffed again," admitted Peeke.[31] Finally, in March, both Patzelt and Colonel Espinosa visited Tewæno and then the Wepeidi on the ridge. The visit to the ridge was largely a photography expedition and occurred without incident.

In Tewæno, Patzelt wanted to add to his collection of jungle plants, so Dawa and other Waorani women found plants for him, which Peeke numbered and identified on tape for later classification. The Waorani also planned a fiesta so Patzelt could record their singing. Peeke and Jung had told the naturalist about Waorani wedding practices, and Patzelt expressed disappointment that he would not be able to record a traditional wedding song. "What's his problem?" Mincaye asked. Peeke explained, and Mincaye promptly left the clearing. "Get out of the way, they're going to have a 'wedding'!" Dayomæ announced. Dancing and singing ensued with Mincaye and his wife, Ompodæ, playing the role of happy and "surprised" bride and groom.[32]

Despite the visit, Patzelt never found any positive side to SIL, nor did he acknowledge help provided by the Tewæno Waorani. Instead, in a film, articles, and books, he helped to create a "black legend" concerning SIL and the Waorani that endured into the twenty-first century. The initial accusations in the early 1970s were a mixture of justified critique and hyperbole. For example, based on comments from a disillusioned Padilla, Patzelt charged SIL with exploiting the Waorani by using them for fundraising purposes, a valid critique.[33] Again, with Padilla as a source, Patzelt presented as a new revelation the assertion that the five missionaries killed in 1956 were armed. Even more important, he suggested that one had purposely shot and killed Nampa, Dayomæ's brother and Padilla's uncle. In this version, the missionaries, as well as the Waorani, engaged in violence on Palm Beach.[34] Although none of the slain missionaries was affiliated with SIL, decades later SIL was still responding to this charge.[35]

Passing years did not soften Patzelt's attitude. In 2002 he published a coffee table book featuring the Waorani, with photographs of traditional Wao life, a description of their history and customs, and travel narratives of his encounters with the Waorani since 1971.[36] However, fanciful stories continued to be included among factual accounts. For example, Patzelt wrote that Tewæno residents Oncaye and her brother Tewæ kidnapped their father, Wepe, with his wife and son, at gunpoint, presumably in 1971 or 1972, forcing them to go to Tewæno, where they were kept under guard and deprived of food so that Wepe would confess to Toñæ's murder. Yet the story was never mentioned in the numerous letters written by Peeke and others concerning the relocation of the Wepeidi and the death of Toñæ. Wepe and his extended family had, in fact, relocated to Tewæno at their own request in November 1971, on the first flight out after a small airstrip opened on the ridge.[37]

Further, when Patzelt visited Tewæno in March 1972, Peeke had asked Wepe to accompany the naturalist on a brief trip to the ridge. After plans were changed various times due to convoluted flight schedules, Wepe went fishing instead. However, he was among those dancing and singing in the fiesta that evening, hardly the activities of an emaciated prisoner.[38] Nobody was ever kept "under guard" in Tewæno. The concept was alien to the Waorani, and neither Peeke nor Jung had the time, means, or inclination to play sheriff in an already violent culture.

Patzelt also seemed intent on supporting charges from Zoila Wiñame—representing the recently established, rival Wao settlement of Dayono—that Tewæno was a "mission prison."[39] Wiñame was a member of Dayomæ's kinship group, a woman who, like Dayomæ, had fled from Wao violence. Wiñame did not return to the Waorani until 1968 and was even more assimilated into Quichua culture than Dayomæ had been. Her experiences in the outside world and ability to speak both Quichua and *Wao tededo* positioned Wiñame to challenge Dayomæ's leadership.

There *were* problems in Tewæno. Dayomæ, supported by Rachel, had established a patronage system that gave her considerable power and led to the exploitation of Waorani who were newcomers. People were pressured to stay in Tewæno, and those who came long distances by plane or helicopter found it difficult to return home. But the Waorani could always walk away, as demonstrated by the significant numbers who did just that. Nonetheless, Patzelt's accusations, as well as the decision by Wiñame and other disaffected Waorani to establish Dayono, were signs that life in the protectorate was undergoing irrevocable changes.

CHALLENGES IN TEWÆNO

Far from trying to round up supposed Waorani outlaws, Peeke and Jung had their hands full during 1971 and 1972 helping the Waorani survive the sustained contact with the outside world that was now a daily reality due to the oil companies' presence. Peeke continued to facilitate efforts to relocate the Waorani out of the path of oil exploration and to mediate encounters between Waorani and oil workers. She also assisted Jung, who was the first trained healthcare worker assigned to the Waorani.

"Omade, Omade! OMADE! OMADE!" Peeke and Jung grew accustomed to awakening in the Tewæno clearing to the sound of Jung's Wao name shouted with increasing urgency. From late January through mid-February 1971, a viral influenza kept Tewæno's 240 residents feverish, coughing, and aching. Jung and Peeke splashed through pouring rain and mud visiting each house two or three times daily to give injections and "chiding and cajoling to get people to finish out their course of pills and stay in out of the rain." Jung was supposed to be engaged in language study. However, Peeke reported that the two barely "found time or mustered strength to prepare our meals, and midnight calls were followed fast by early-morning requests."[40]

The decision to concentrate so many Waorani in the Tewæno clearing meant that contact diseases would sweep across the group. First Rachel, then Peeke and Jung, assisted by medical missionaries in Limoncocha and Shell, made Herculean efforts to ensure that the Waorani survived. Most of them did. Nonetheless, like some of the Baiwaidi after the polio epidemic, the experience of Tewæno as a place "full of disease" was another reason Wiñame's group left Tewæno in late 1971 to found Dayono, a clearing on the northwestern border of the Waorani protectorate.[41]

Since her arrival in Tewæno, Wiñame had engaged in a power struggle with Dayomæ, Dawa, and Rachel. Traditional Wao culture was egalitarian and independent, with no formal leadership structure. Leadership was exercised on a situational basis. If a man convinced others to join him hunting or on a spearing raid, he was the leader on that occasion. After Rachel and Elliot arrived in Tewæno—and especially during the years Rachel was the sole missionary—power began to shift to Dayomæ. She spoke Quichua and understood the ways of the outside world. Dayomæ's "sister" relationship with Rachel and her position as Rachel's language informant gave her access to trade goods. She controlled their distribution to others in a way that would benefit her family and increase her influence. Imitating the power structure she had experienced on the hacienda, Dayomæ created a patronage system in Tewæno with herself at the top.

Rachel was convinced—erroneously—that Wao culture was matriarchal and that Dayomæ was exercising a culturally appropriate role as Christian leader and matriarch. Dawa, another Rachel protégée and the first in the clearing to profess Christian faith after the missionaries came, shared some of Dayomæ's power. The three women had a vested interest in concentrating the Waorani in Tewæno and in controlling outside access to them. Rachel's concern was spiritual. Tewæno was a Christian village, the one place where new arrivals would hear the gospel message, become churched, and thereby resist worldly temptations. Dawa seems to have shared some of Rachel's concerns, while by the early 1970s Dayomæ was more focused on exercising her patronage role.

According to Wiñame herself, in 1970 she was forced to marry Dabo, the Piyæmoidi man who had been the subject of Peeke's dramatic helicopter rescue.[42]

Dabo was restless, and Wiñame began to question the existing power structure. Neither she nor her immediate family members were interested in Christianity as practiced in Tewæno. In an acrimonious parting with Dayomæ and Dawa, Wiñame moved to what would become Dayono. Initially, at least, it was a smart move since the site offered greater accessibility to visitors and their goods than Tewæno.

The accessibility enabled Wiñame to renew her links with Quichua culture and her contacts among the Quichuas—connections that were more familiar to her than her weaker identification with Wao culture. She also established her own patronage relationships with outsiders interested in contact with the Waorani unmediated by SIL. These included Patzelt and a contract oil worker named Nelson Villalba. In March 1972 four Waorani went with Villalba to Quito to see the president of Ecuador and to appear on television, actions that further declared their independence from Tewæno and SIL.[43] The leaders of the two communities vilified one another. To Rachel and the Tewæno believers, Dayono was a den of iniquity—a place where guns, alcohol, and illicit sex were readily available—and its inhabitants "rebels." The Dayono residents, for their part, spread the word about SIL authoritarianism and Tewæno as a place of confinement, accusations that cast a shadow over SIL's reputation in Ecuador.

TENSIONS ON THE RIDGE

Despite the problems in Tewæno, Waorani continued to relocate, drawn by trade goods, the promise of peace, and the prospect of uniting families. The first ridge people transported to Tewæno were Dawa's kin: her brothers Cogi and Yowe, Yowe's wife, Wedæ, and their five children. All were shuttled out by helicopter at the end of July 1971. The Waorani had initiated work on a Gabado airstrip about a month earlier, encouraged by gifts from SIL. It progressed by fits and starts during the next three months. Finally, on November 9, the two-hundred-meter runway (about 219 yards) was ready. Wepe and his family—all relatives of Oncaye—moved to Tewæno on the first flight out, again at their request. In all, twenty-eight people were relocated to the protectorate during 1971 and approximately fifty more in 1972, leaving about two hundred still living on the ridge. More Waorani wanted to move, but SIL slowed the pace so that Tewæno could better absorb the newcomers.

Substantial numbers of Waorani remaining on the ridge, however, did not guarantee isolation. Patzelt and a film crew flew out to visit these more "unspoiled" (less acculturated) people. Oil company crews continued their work nearby. The presence of oil workers and poor sanitation brought other unwelcome changes to the rainforest. Streams became contaminated and the ridge Waorani began to suffer for the first time from pinworms and other intestinal parasites. Jung and Peeke sent oral polio vaccine and antibiotics with Dawa and others to help the people resist disease.

By July 1972 peaceful contact had been made with the majority of Ecuador's known Waorani. Three hundred fifty people, including those in Dayono, lived in the protectorate and about two hundred on the ridge. Although there was no guarantee that spearings had ended, Waorani and the oil workers were coexisting. Only a few elusive splinter groups that had chosen isolation remained overtly hostile to the outside world. One was known as the Tagæidi, and another was a subgroup that would become known as the Taadomenani.

LITERACY INSTRUCTION

As the Waorani in the protectorate became more aware of the outside world, interest in literacy increased. This was especially true in Tewæno, where hopes for a teacher had been dashed with the death of Toñæ. SIL responded by assigning Pat Kelley, a teacher with dual US-Canadian citizenship, to develop a literacy program. Kelley had already spent two years in Ecuador on a short-term assignment with SIL, teaching the children of staff members at Limoncocha. While there, she shied away from the Waorani, feeling that the publicity surrounding them overshadowed the translation and language work SIL was doing with other indigenous groups in the country. However, when the Waorani requested help, Kelley said yes.

In February 1972, when Kelley arrived in Tewæno, there were no literate Waorani, and the reading readiness of her students varied widely. For many of the "down-river" and "ridge" people, the concept of reading and writing was unknown; they had never seen a pencil or paper. Others in Tewæno had leafed through old copies of *National Geographic* and had some understanding of what paper was. Some who had attended Toñæ's classes before his death had a few basic skills.

Kelley organized four groups that met daily in the large classroom built as a part of Rachel's house. Boys attended in the early morning, women at midday after working their gardens, then a girls' class, and, finally, men in the late afternoon or early evening after a day in the forest. Class sessions focused on reading readiness, arithmetic, reading, and writing. Most instruction was in the Wao language, with the addition of some basic Spanish conversation and numbers to help students with outside contact. More than 150 students came to school at least once the first year, although attendance leveled off at about forty. Of those, about half came regularly and the other half represented fifty or sixty students who attended on what Kelley described as the "revolving plan." Families would attend for a while, then leave on fishing or hunting trips, to be replaced by others who would then rotate in and out, reflecting the mobility characteristic of Wao culture.[44]

Kelley's goal was to create a core of literates—at least one per household. She also hoped to develop culturally appropriate literacy materials through insights she gained while teaching and through student participation. Those who were quick learners became co-instructors and helped in materials creation. During the next ten years, Kelley and her students (and later those of her students who became literacy instructors) developed a series of six primers in *Wao tededo*, as well as flip charts, instructional guides, arithmetic books, and grammar lesson plans. Kelley also encouraged native-authored literature, in which new literates wrote stories about hunting, animal life, a national holiday, sayings of the "ancient ones," and even the mysterious Tagæidi group. These were printed in small booklets. As early as 1974 Kelley also produced charts for keyboarding in Wao and Spanish for students who had expressed interest in learning to type.[45] After all, they had watched the linguists do it for years.

By 1982, when many SIL staff left Ecuador and Kelley ended this phase of her full-time work among the Waorani, seven communities—by then dispersed across the protectorate—were recognized by the Ecuadorian state as Centros de Alfabetización (Literacy Centers). They had Wao literacy instructors who were recognized, supervised, and received payment from the Pastaza Provincial Office of Adult Education.[46] Between 15 and 18 percent of the total Waorani population were at least marginally literate, and Kelley's goal of a literate member in each Wao family had been accomplished in 75 percent of the families in the clearings of Tewæno, Tzapino, Quiwado, and Waamono. Kelley, or Cawo, as she was known, had become popular among many Waorani for her adaptability, her identification with the people, and for making extended visits to remote clearings to hold classes. She was, as Rachel wrote early on, "a natural."[47]

All this still lay ahead during the initial years of 1972 and 1973, as did the extent to which literacy, schools, and even the orthography of *Wao tededo* would become political issues. Pressures to assimilate and power struggles among the Waorani led to the opening of Spanish-language schools in Dayono and another key community during the 1970s. Staffed by Quichua teachers, these schools taught reading and writing but also tended to denigrate traditional Wao culture. "On one occasion, they burned reading materials written by Wao authors from another village because 'the Huao [Wao] language is no good.'"[48] By contrast a Wao literacy instructor in that same clearing received native-authored items with the comment, "'*Cowode dibodo ba ï! Waa-pödï!*'—'(They're) just like *cowode* books! Nice!'"[49] In 1973, however, the Waorani who sat on balsa wood stumps in the Tewæno schoolroom simply wanted to learn to read.

A STRUGGLING CHURCH

The work of Peeke, Jung, and Kelley during the early 1970s involved community de-velopment, broadly understood, rather than linguistics. Rachel was still the only SIL staff member assigned to translate the Bible into *Wao tededo*. She also promoted reli-gious activities and instruction, especially the weekly church meeting. When Rachel left for the update rallies in February 1971, Peeke deliberately took a less involved approach to church services, in contrast to Rachel's assertive style, hoping that the Tewæno Christians would step forward and "assume more responsibility." They did not. "They were in no wise ready for that, especially since no one of the leaders could read God's Word for himself," admitted Peeke. Even as Rachel toured the US with Guequita, Dawa, and Quemo, celebrating the impact of Christianity on the lives of the Waorani, believers in Tewæno were struggling. "All sorts of petty jealousies, pride, gossip, and actual violence flared up, even among Christian leaders; and it took Rachel's return and more thorough teaching to bring them together in some semblance of confession and acceptance of one another."[50]

Many Waorani had not yet been taught basic Christian concepts, underscoring the need for progress in literacy and Bible translation so that they could read the New Testament. Initially, Christian teaching relied on stories told by Dayomæ as the tribal "Bible woman" or from Rachel. Yet Dayomæ could not read, and over the years she began to lose enthusiasm for teaching and translation work. The one aspect of Christianity that had the most profound impact on Waorani life—that Christians were peacemakers who no longer speared—threatened to become the sum total of faith for many.

Peeke noticed this phenomenon when she talked with Waorani on the ridge who wanted to move to Tewæno. "To decide for God is no more than to agree to make the long trip to Tewæno and to join forces with former enemies. . . . To say 'Yes!' to relatives who prepare fields and homes and invite them here, is to say, 'Yes!' to God."[51] When people arrived, the Christianity they encountered seemed a religion of negatives: don't kill, don't have more than one wife, don't marry someone who is not baptized, don't leave this clearing.

There were bright moments, sometimes bittersweet, when Christian faith seemed evident, such as in the note Toñæ wrote before going to the ridge and his testimony in death. The death of Dayomæ's six-year-old daughter, Eunice, was another such occasion. Doted on by her parents and SIL staff alike, Eunie knew by heart all the Bible stories from Mark. Blind and given only six months to live when she was born, the little girl certainly would have been killed in traditional Wao culture. Instead she had grown into a healthy, vivacious child with a quick mind who loved to swing in her hammock and sing Wao songs at the top of her lungs. When she drowned in the Tewæno River in June 1972, Jung and Peeke, both in Tewæno at the time, were devastated, along with the distraught parents, Dayomæ and Come. But Jung could remind the people that Eunie was with Jesus, seeing clearly at last. Peeke selected words from Acts 2 to read at the burial, and Yowe prayed. As the earth was tamped down, they comforted one another. "Our believing family will see her again. And she will see us clearly!"[52]

Peeke left for furlough in July 1972, and Jung soon after. Rachel returned after having been in and out of the Tewæno—mostly out—for more than a year. She worked to finalize the translation of Acts. She also was preoccupied with those she called the "rebel group" at Dayono and their effect on other Waorani. To Rachel, leaving Tewæno represented "running away from the Lord and the Aucas who risked their lives to try to reach them."[53] She also was convinced that the Catholics would use the new settlement to expand their influence. Wiñame had requested a school, and there was some debate about whether Christian and Missionary Alliance missionaries in the area would supervise it, or whether it would come under the auspices of SIL. Or, Rachel feared, the Daibæidi (Catholic missionaries) would come from nearby Josefina and take charge.[54] Wiñame continued making contacts on all sides to shore up her influence.[55]

"WE SIMPLY *MUST* GET THIS MONKEY OFF OUR BACK!"

Dayomæ, with her patronage system, and Rachel, who controlled outside access, remained the two most powerful people in Tewæno. However, during the 1970s most critics blamed administrators of SIL Ecuador for keeping the Waorani off limits to everyone but themselves. In an internal memo dated March 19, 1973, Lindskoog, once again SIL's Ecuador director, acknowledged the problems and outlined a new strategy. The Summer Institute continued "to be the target of considerable destructive criticism . . . regarding the Aucas," he wrote. "We cannot continue to follow a policy of exclusivism but we must . . . come up with a positive plan that deals objectively with our relation to these people, their relation to Ecuador and to the outside world in general, etc."[56]

In conversation with the SIL executive committee for Ecuador, Lindskoog formulated a new policy for the organization's relationship with the Waorani. SIL would no longer act as gatekeeper. The Waorani were not the "private property" of the Summer Institute, and it had "neither the obligation nor the right to keep people out" of Wao territory. SIL still had a "moral responsibility" to warn outsiders of the potential dangers of contact, but not to protect visitors against their will. This did not mean that SIL was required to help people wishing to contact the Waorani, simply that it would no longer stand in the way. Lindskoog suggested that SIL ask the Ecuadorian government to designate a governmental agency to monitor access to Wao territory. "We simply *must* get this monkey off our back!"[57]

The bulk of Lindskoog's message emphasized SIL's need to stop trying to control the Waorani and access to them. But his final paragraph struck a different note. SIL also had an obligation to publish some serious studies "at a Ph.D. level" on Wao culture, before the traditional culture was completely lost or modified through contact.[58] To accomplish this goal, Lindskoog chose Jim Yost, a new SIL staffer with a PhD in anthropology. Yost and his wife, Kathie, had been assigned to work among tribal peoples in Colombia. But Lindskoog convinced them to come for a year to do an anthropological study of the Waorani. The Yosts became the final and, they assumed, temporary members of SIL's newly formed "Wao team." They had no idea what they were getting into.

FIGURE 1 The "Brethren boys" (from left): Ed McCully, Jim Elliot, and Peter Fleming in Los Angeles, a few days before Elliot and Fleming left for Ecuador on February 4, 1952. McCully and his wife, Marilou, were enrolled in a missionary medicine course at the Bible Institute of Los Angeles. Archives of the Billy Graham Center, Wheaton, Illinois

FIGURE 2 Nate and Marj Saint, Kathy and Steve, in Ecuador, circa 1954. Mission Aviation Fellowship

FIGURE 3 Roger Youderian with Nænquiwi, Palm Beach, January 6, 1956.
Nate Saint photo/Mission Aviation Fellowship

FIGURE 4 Elisabeth Elliot, learning the Wao language with Mintaca and Mæncamo, 1958.
Cornell Capa (Betty Elliot with Mintaka and Mankamu, Tiwænu River, October–November 1958) © International
Center of Photography/Magnum Photos

FIGURE 5 The "first Auca Christian." V. Raymond Edman, Wheaton College president and former missionary to Ecuador, baptizes Dayomæ, April 15, 1958.
Special Collections, Buswell Library, Wheaton College

FIGURE 6 Rachel Saint in Tewæno with Quemo and Come, 1966.
Archives of the Billy Graham Center, Wheaton, Illinois

FIGURE 7 Rachel Saint with Quemo (left) and Come, in Berlin to attend the 1966 World Congress on Evangelism. Saint was determined that the two men would challenge the image of the Waorani as "savages."
Archives of the Billy Graham Center, Wheaton, Illinois

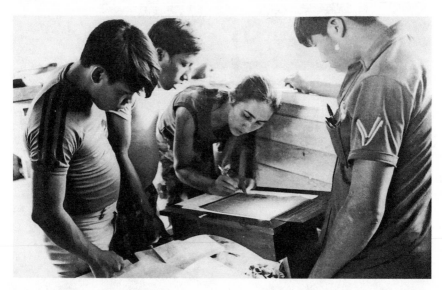

FIGURE 8 Three Wao literacy instructor trainees, (from left) Pegonca, Wini, and Amo, with SIL literacy worker Pat Kelley, in the late 1970s, learning how to produce reading materials written by Waorani.
© Patricia M. Kelley

FIGURE 9 Cæmpæde, one of the Waorani living along the Cononaco River, and anthropologist Jim Yost, 1983.
Adrian Warren photo/www.lastrefuge.co.uk

FIGURE 10 Rosi Jung (left) and Catherine Peeke in 1992 with the first copies of the Wao New Testament.
© SIL International

PART V

Access, 1974–1982

11

An Anthropologist Arrives

⌒——

WHEN JIM YOST, his wife, Kathie, and their eighteen-month-old daughter, Rachelle, first arrived in Tewæno on January 3, 1974, they discovered that at Rachel Saint's request the Waorani had constructed a small house for them. Fairly elaborate by Wao standards, the two-room structure with a big, open window was built off the ground to help protect from snakes and other hazards. There was no running water, but the Tewæno River was only twenty or thirty yards away. They brought a Coleman camp stove and lantern, although after the first few months they gave them up in order not to create a barrier between themselves and the Waorani. They used wood fires and candles instead.

The house was squeezed between homes occupied by Rachel on one side and by Dayomæ, her husband Come, and their family on the other, with about eight feet between each of the dwellings. It was close quarters, to say the least. The location reflected Saint's concern for safety, since Yost was the first adult *cowode* male, other than Quichuas, to establish permanent residence in Tewæno. The Yosts, whose family grew with the births of two more children (Natasha, b. 1975, and Brandon, b. 1977) during the years they spent with the Waorani, were also the first intact nuclear family of outsiders to live in the clearing.

Like Saint, Peeke, Jung, and Kelley, the Yosts were full-time staff members with the Summer Institute of Linguistics. A number of SIL linguists, Peeke among them, had significant academic training in anthropology, and at least ten had earned doctorates in the discipline. Jim Yost was something of an anomaly, however, as the first SIL staffer with a PhD in anthropology who served indigenous people in that professional capacity rather than as a linguist.[1] Yost had converted to Christianity in high school and decided to go to college—the first in his immediate family to do so—to become a missionary. Once at Northwestern Bible College in Minnesota, where he met Kathie, he gravitated toward anthropology. Despite the mistrust that historically existed between anthropologists and evangelical missionaries, by the late 1950s and early 1960s some evangelicals were recognizing that the discipline could provide useful insights. Yost was fortunate to meet one such person, George Jennings, who taught anthropology at Northwestern and encouraged the young man's interest.

At the same time, SIL, with its emphasis on work among indigenous people groups, seemed a good fit for the future.[2] Beginning in 1961 Yost spent three summers studying linguistics with SIL, assuming he would eventually work as a Bible translator. However, SIL's president Kenneth Pike and linguist Hank Bradley encouraged him to pursue a doctorate in anthropology and use that training on staff with SIL. Yost did, earning his MA and PhD from the University of Colorado and teaching along the way. In 1972, a year before he completed his degree, Yost filled out the last of his WBT/SIL candidate forms. He was an anthropologist, he wrote, interested in cultural change in Latin America. The SIL personnel department responded with skepticism, questioning the value of an on-site anthropologist for mission work. Furious, Pike intervened, and after a few twists and turns, Jim, Kathie, and their daughter were assigned to Ecuador.[3] Although Northwestern Bible College had also been Roger and Barbara Youderian's alma mater, the Yosts had only a passing awareness of the Waorani. Concerned not to prejudice Jim's findings, Lindskoog said little about previous tensions. Jim was to do fieldwork for an anthropological study of the Waorani, using Rachel as his interpreter. Jim and Kathie read the missionary books about the Waorani published up to that time and were off.

In line with his assignment, Jim saw himself as a Christian who was an anthropologist, rather than a traditional missionary. He and Kathie tried to model practical Christianity in their family life and their relationships with the Waorani, but Jim avoided overt missionary work. He attended church services but did not preach or teach except on rare occasions. And he resisted the urge to confront or try to change the Waorani. Instead he focused on participating, observing, and learning.

A CLASH OF STYLES AND PHILOSOPHIES

"If I had started preaching or using the knowledge they [the Waorani] were giving [me] in any way to challenge them on stuff, I would have undermined my purpose almost immediately. They wouldn't have shared with me the way they did."[4] Over time, Yost became more intentionally involved in applied ("action") anthropology, doing research, for example, to document the amount of territory the Waorani needed to sustain their traditional way of life. Even so, he still sought to encourage Wao independence. All this put him at the opposite end of the spectrum from Saint, who saw herself as an influential elder and spiritual teacher in the tribe—both in her own right and as she supported Dayomæ. Her approach was proactive and directive. In between were the other members of the "Wao team"—Peeke, Jung, and Kelley—who followed the more usual SIL pattern. They related to the Waorani in their professional roles as linguist, healthcare worker, and teacher, respectively, but they also took advantage of informal opportunities to read the Bible, pray, and try to help the people relate Christian belief to their lives. Yost's arrival set the stage for a clash of styles and philosophies. Over the years Saint had promoted a protective, authoritarian, and isolationist approach, while the newer members of the team favored policies that would equip the Waorani with the skills needed for encountering the modern world. All felt they were trying to act in the best interest of the people.

The tools of Yost's trade were a pencil or pen that he hung or taped around his neck and a small pocket notebook where he jotted brief field notes every day he was with the Waorani. Wadica (Yost's Wao name) sought to become an accepted participant-observer of Wao life. He also became a role model—the first male *cowode* most Waorani knew personally. Daughter Kigi (Rachelle) still remembers a young Wao man who wanted badly to assimilate to outside culture. He appeared one day with a pencil taped to his neck. If Wadica did it, it must be the *cowodi* way.[5]

Yost's notes provided detailed descriptions of the Waorani, first as they appeared to a newcomer who was just learning the language, then to an increasingly fluent cultural observer and speaker of *Wao tededo*. Yost filled more than fifty of the little books, plus larger notebooks and reams of files, documenting his observations between 1974 and 1982, the years when he, Kathie, and their family were on full-time assignment with the Waorani for SIL. Other notebooks tracked subsequent research and visits, as Yost pursued a range of projects after his full-time assignment ended.

Yost's early field notes became a vivid account of Wao life. They also reflected the issues and tensions faced by the Waorani and SIL staff members during the second half of the 1970s. If "pacification," or its more positive corollary, "reconciliation," characterized the period of relocation from 1968 to 1972, the idea of "access" best characterizes the years from 1974 to 1981. This was a time when numerous groups of Waorani left Tewæno to establish new clearings within the protectorate, most with better access to Quichua villages and Ecuadorian towns where the Waorani could obtain goods. A few settlements were established with an eye toward attracting tourists. In addition to Tewæno, by July 1980 there were five Wao clearings in the protectorate with more than fifty inhabitants each and another five clearings with populations ranging from seven to twenty-four.

THE *COWODE* WHO DRANK *TEPÆ*

In 1974, when the Yosts arrived, Tewæno was a village that still retained much of the character of a traditional Wao clearing. Men used blowguns for hunting, and in many houses the cooking pots were still clay, although women were beginning to acquire aluminum pots. Wearing some clothing had been the norm for years, but the Waorani still considered both men and women "dressed" (not naked) and with no cause for shame when they wore only the traditional cotton *come*, or hip-cord.

During the day, men hunted or fished while women worked in their manioc gardens and prepared food. Children played in the river or practiced the skills they would need as adults. Many, both children and adults, attended the literacy sessions Pat Kelley organized. Families or individuals occasionally traveled to gardens they had planted away from Tewæno or to other Wao clearings. The Tewæno clearing was located not far from the headwaters of the Tewæno River, so everyone bathed in clean water. At night, people swung in hammocks in their own houses or others', telling stories. The Yost children remembered their dad's spontaneous bedtime tales of eels and other jungle creatures. Sometimes the Waorani would sing. A few people had radios, but it was still common for the Waorani to chant before sleeping and again in the middle of the night if someone woke up. The practice had its roots in the days of hostility, when night was the traditional time for attacks. Singing let an enemy know that people in a clearing were alert. For his part, Yost chimed in with "Old MacDonald Had a Farm." The Wao language contained a strong onomatopoetic element, and Yost thought that his neighbors would enjoy "Old MacDonald" with its animal noises.[6]

For Rachelle Yost, who lived among the Waorani until she was almost ten, life in Tewæno provided the perfect childhood. She roamed the clearing freely since older Wao children were accustomed to looking out for the younger ones. She swam in the river and fished with the other kids. They caught grasshoppers on the airstrip for bait, attached some fishing line to a stick, put on a hook, and were off. Even if they caught only small fish, they felt proud to contribute to the dinner pot. "Or, if it was in the middle of the day, we'd borrow a little pot and start our own fire under the [raised] house and cook ourselves a snack."[7]

The Waorani kept pets, and the Yost children had their share: an otter, a Macaw and other birds, fish, and a marmoset (one of the world's smallest primates). The little monkey went everywhere with Rachelle, sometimes riding on her arm, at other times in her hair like the Amazonian version of a coonskin cap. Some days, Rachelle and her playmates would gather palm branches and build little houses on the airstrip, accumulating "thousands" of chiggers in the process. That led to another evening activity learned from the Waorani: the Yost family picking chiggers off each other before their bodies reacted to the little mites with angry, itchy bumps.

"They taught us how," remembered Kathie. "[The chiggers] were little teeny red pinpricks. It was worth getting them off!" It was easy for a child to fit in, and Rachelle, like Valerie Elliot before her, soon became bilingual. One day she and her friends were playing on the airstrip when the little girl looked up to see her father coming from the river and walking across the grassy field. She pointed and cried out, "Baado! Cowodi pompa!" ("Here comes an outsider!"), much to the delight of all Waorani within earshot.[8]

Not everything about the jungle was idyllic or easy to get used to. The Waorani had no concept of privacy or any rituals for greeting or farewell. Initially, Kathie found it unnerving to have her every move watched by curious observers and, at the same time, to feel strangely invisible since no one said hello or good-bye. In a village that fluctuated in size from a high of nearly two hundred to a low of about thirty—depending on whether literacy classes were in session and on who was off cultivating other gardens or visiting relatives—gossip was a highly developed Wao pastime. If she committed a cultural blunder, Kathie knew she would hear about it. ("Did you see what *she* did?" would make the rounds.) There were the inevitable misunderstandings as the Yosts learned *Wao tededo*. "Early on," Kathie recalled, "Jim wanted to go out to the gardens, and for him to go I had to go, too. I was carrying [Rachelle]. They asked Jim [something], and he didn't know what they asked. He said yes, and before I knew it they had taken Rachelle from me and loaded me up with a hundred pounds of bananas to carry back!"[9]

Along with bananas, the Waorani were generous in supplying the Yosts with meat and manioc. The North Americans didn't mind the food but struggled with the monotony of eating the same thing every meal. "I don't think the kids ever complained, but . . . eating the same thing seven days a week [was hard]," Kathie said. "I lost weight because I would always lose my appetite. We would supplement with carrots because they kept well, but then we all got sick of carrots." Due to mud and rain, it was hard to keep clothing clean and dry in the jungle. "We kept three outfits apiece [in Tewæno], and there were times when we were on our last thing, wearing it for the third day, and I still didn't have dry clothes."[10]

WINSOME AND CRUEL

As Elisabeth Elliot had observed nearly fifteen years earlier, besides spearings, the Waorani could have a cruel streak, demonstrated in their treatment of animals and, occasionally, children. Yet the Waorani were also loving and easy to live with. This combination of winsomeness and callousness was an apparent contradiction of Wao culture that non-Waorani struggled to understand. Although pets were common, the Waorani did not share the same concept of domestication as outsiders. Animals were kept to possess, display, and torment. Having pets taught children about animal behavior, and the animals helped rid living spaces of unwanted insects. But they were not trained or tamed for play.[11]

When play did occur, it was usually to the animal's distress, as when children found a baby hummingbird and threw it back and forth until it died. Or when a group of young boys used a captured sloth for target practice, shooting it full of blowgun darts before letting dogs maul it, then holding it over a fire, still alive. On his way home from an all-day hunt, a Wao man speared a large frog. Arriving in the clearing, he shook live coals over it. Everyone roared with laughter as the frog hopped into the dark, a living fireworks display. "Pretty, but morbid," wrote Yost, admitting that he too had laughed.[12]

That admission may have been a necessary self-check for a man who was doing everything possible to immerse himself in Wao culture. It wasn't easy. One roadblock was Rachel Saint. Yost quickly discovered that Saint had made him her neighbor in part to keep an eye on him. She had not been pleased with SIL's sending an anthropologist to Tewæno, acquiescing only when Lindskoog said she had no choice. Stuck with Yost, she set out to shape his observations. "R[achel] tell Come to move aluminum out of my pictures," jotted Yost, referring to corrugated sheets used for roofs. "Every day she manipulates people for me. My data becomes more suspect."[13] Rachel instructed the Waorani to react to the *cowode* in specific ways:

"You must protect him," she would admonish.

"Don't let him work hard."

"Don't go far or fast if he is along."

"Don't talk loud."

It was an anthropologist's nightmare. "The very reactions I need are unnaturally suppressed," Yost wrote.[14] Saint initially told Yost not to walk beyond the end of the airstrip or to leave the clearing with anyone except for two Wao men whom she trusted. The first time he went fishing with another group, he was "chewed out" roundly when he got home. After that, the thirty-two-year-old who had taught survival skills at the University of Colorado stopped telling her what he was doing. "It was the Waorani way."[15]

Yost went with the Waorani wherever he was invited and would try almost anything, though he took seriously the potential for violence in Wao culture. Out on the trail or spending the night away from Tewæno, he trained himself to stay alert. At night, "if there was a lot of noise I would sleep soundly. But if it was quiet, or if anyone would whisper or move quietly, I would be . . . immediately awake."[16] The Waorani consumed most of their carbohydrates in the form of thick liquids, sometimes made with mashed cooking bananas and sometimes with chewed manioc, slightly fermented (a drink called *tepæ*). Following the lead of Wao men, Yost downed gallons of *tepæ*. He also joined a crowd of Waorani who arose before dawn to wait for *atta* ants to swarm and to eat the dark red ones as a delicacy. "[You] must pick the large darker red ones from slightly smaller, lighter red ones. Not easy." There's "much jumping around, laughing and joking at someone getting bit." He joined the dances at wedding parties and other fiestas. He admitted in his notebook that it "felt good" when the Waorani talked about his exploits, especially his willingness to sleep in the forest.[17]

As Yost became more accustomed to Wao life, he accompanied the men hunting, not an activity for the faint of heart or short of breath. Waorani often would travel all day pursuing game, with few pauses. "No one ate or drank a thing today!" he wrote in amazement after one hunt. "We left at 6:00 [a.m.] and got home at 4:00 [p.m.]. I have never seen an adult drink plain water—why? They act surprised when I drink from the river. After that much exercise, you'd think they'd need it."[18] One of the more rigorous hunts was an hour and a half shorter but over a greater distance. Two Waorani and Yost covered about thirty miles "of *very* hard walking up and down [ridges] all day at a torrid pace." Each Waorani was carrying a seven-pound blowgun, and during the last four hours one man added the carcass of the fourteen-pound monkey he had killed, while the other split off to continue pursuing his game.[19]

"I had muscle cramps and spasms the last 2 hr." Yost admitted. He had to rest on numerous occasions, and the Wao man with the monkey carcass stayed with him. "When I sat he usually stood. When he sat I laid down. If he ever *laid* down, I would have long since been buried. He must be late 40's, my size, thin not muscular."[20] These and other such experiences were more than simply an opportunity for Yost to prove himself to the Waorani. They gave the anthropologist a vivid awareness of the amount of energy the Waorani expended to procure protein for their families. He also could see how the scarcity of game in the protectorate led to diminishing returns. Men used up more energy hunting than was represented by the protein they brought home once the meat was divided among family members. This knowledge proved useful in understanding how much land the Waorani needed to maintain a traditional lifestyle.

Such observations were important as the Waorani experienced increasing pressures from outsiders, particularly from the neighboring lowland Quichuas. The much more populous Quichuas wanted access to Wao land to hunt and fish and eventually to colonize. Some Quichuas established *compadre* (godparent) relationships with those Waorani adventurous enough to come out to villages, and there were a few more Quichua-Waorani marriages. But the Quichuas were not the only ones who wanted in. From 1974 on, anyone intrepid enough to try could visit Wao clearings without SIL intervention, subject only to the response of the Waorani in any given location.

Visitors came in what seemed like droves—Europeans and Latin Americans, as well as North Americans. There were tourists and adventurers, film crews, Ecuadorian functionaries, representatives from the United Nations, journalists, anthropologists, other researchers, and mission groups, both Protestant and Catholic, as well as encroachment from oil exploration. Books about the Waorani appeared almost immediately, beginning in 1975 with *Menschen im Regenwald: Expedition Auka* (Man in the rainforest: Expedition auca) by Peter Baumann with photos by SIL critic Erwin Patzelt.[21] Pat Kelley once joked about the number of different men who had boasted to her that *he* was the first white man to encounter the Waorani and live to tell the tale.[22] Now, it seemed, there was a new rush to visit and photograph Ecuador's last "savages."

Outsiders had conflicting expectations for the future. Some—usually tourists and adventurers—wanted the Waorani to remain "free" and uncorrupted, living in harmony with their environment. Other cultures changed, but the Waorani were expected to remain static and primitive or they would be "spoiled."[23] Unaware that they were encountering a native culture that was intensely pragmatic and had little patience with tradition for tradition's sake, these visitors viewed any change as an end to Eden.

For others, often Ecuadorian officials committed to integrating the Waorani into the national culture, change could not come soon enough. They wanted the Waorani to become "civilized" Ecuadorians. An official from the Ministry of Education made a brief visit to Tewæno in September 1975. "You've done so much," he told SIL staff. Yet Yost noted that the official was "horrified at how few clothes there are!—and [that was with] everyone all dressed up."[24] International consultants, such as UN representatives, pursued more specialized goals, including agricultural development and rainforest preservation.

THE CHALLENGE OF COLLECTIVE ACTION

Unaccustomed to worrying about the future, the Waorani were eagerly seeking the goods outsiders had to offer and, in many ways, emulating the Quichua culture around them. They traded blowguns, balsa ear plugs, hammocks, and exotic birds or monkeys for rubber boots, shotguns, aluminum pots, soap, butcher knives, radios, and blankets. Increasingly people switched from sleeping in hammocks near a fire to the Quichua custom of using raised wooden sleeping platforms and blankets. With blankets people did not have to stoke their fires all night and were also protected from insects. Yost noted the irony that "they sell the things that distinguish them as different so they can buy the things that make them more like those [from whom they] are buying! . . . Wiidä sell blowgun for boots today. I sit here bemoaning the changes, but to him it's the [same] excitement [as that] of getting that first car."[25]

While certain practices caught on quickly, cultural differences between Waorani and non-Waorani continued to run deep. Wao culture remained highly individualistic, highlighted when men and boys first began to take up the outsider sport of soccer, kicking a ball around the Tewæno airstrip. Early Wao soccer had no teams, and no one understood the concepts of winning and losing. Everyone participated, and each score seemed to be the ultimate goal of the game. Contact was rough, but nobody got mad, and there was no competitive spirit. It was just a bunch of men, literally *playing*.[26]

This independence frustrated efforts by Rachel and Dayomæ to sustain regular church services. The Tewæno Waorani were reluctant Sunday worshippers, in part because they had no history of this kind of communal activity. Extended families were self-contained units with no sense of community beyond the kinship group. In addition, family members were used to a great deal of freedom. There were no required activities. As a result, unless Rachel or Dayomæ gathered people for the church service and then directed it, the service floundered. The "congregation" had no idea of what it meant to worship together.[27] From the 1970s on, this form of individualism complicated efforts by outsiders—oil company officials, government workers, environmentalists—to relate to the people as a unified group. The Waorani lacked the cultural tools to pursue collective self-determination. They had no sense of a "whole"—no "chiefs," no concept of rank or status, no spokespersons, and no collective mentality.[28] These traits would leave them vulnerable to the agendas of those, outsiders and Waorani alike, who claimed to represent them.

There were dark sides to increased access. Outsiders brought illness. Vaccinations and ongoing healthcare kept further epidemics in check, except for an outbreak of measles followed by pneumonia that affected thirty-six people in 1977. Everyone recovered, but even with epidemics controlled, contact diseases remained a problem. There were occasions when Waorani died because of a cough or a sneeze that a tourist hardly noticed. Wao curiosity about the outside world was exploited on many levels. Young women whose inquisitiveness took them to Ecuadorian towns at the edge of the rainforest found themselves dancing in saloons and lured into prostitution.

Some Wao men offered their daughters as trade goods, in exchange for a plane ride or a bag of rice.[29] Other men who had little sense of the value of labor or the meaning of money worked weeks for oil companies only to be "paid" with a couple of used T-shirts. Quichua contacts supplied the Waorani with the latest "technology" for fishing: sticks of dynamite (referred to as "tacos") and DDT.

Waorani who were savvy about the value of money took advantage of those who were not, offering, for example, a two-dollar aluminum pot for a blowgun worth thirty or forty dollars and making an enormous profit in the artifact trade. As the Waorani gradually became more comfortable in Ecuadorian jungle towns, some would use their reputation as killers to intimidate townspeople, taking goods from stores or eating without paying.[30] One man walked to Shell Mera, wearing only his *come*. Embarrassed townspeople gave him clothes. He hid the clothes in the bushes, then repeated the scam numerous times on different streets, in the end returning to Tewæno with a bag full of slacks, shorts, shirts, and shoes.[31] At other times, the tables were turned, and the Waorani were harassed by Ecuadorians who viewed them as little more than animals.[32]

"A COMPLICATED MAZE"

The physical challenges of adapting to a rainforest environment provided an outlet for Yost in the face of growing professional concerns over the situation in Tewæno. His unease had begun the first day, when he and Saint flew from the SIL base at Limoncocha to Tewæno. As they flew over Dayono, the clearing established by Wiñame and her followers, Saint looked out the window. "That's where the 'rebel group' lives," she commented.[33] Yost was surprised. Since when did SIL take sides in conflicts between indigenous people, he wondered. The schism between Tewæno and breakaway groups of Waorani eager to establish their own contacts with the outside, particularly those in Dayono, was one of two issues Yost highlighted in his April 1974 "preliminary report" to Lindskoog. The other was the SIL policy of airlifting Wao families from the ridge—about one family a month—to Tewæno. The practice had its roots in the relocations of the late 1960s. It continued at the request of Waorani in Tewæno—particularly Dayomæ and Dawa, who wanted to bring in relatives—and of ridge people themselves, who had heard exaggerated stories about the attractions of the protectorate.[34]

Yost objected, in part because new families contributed to food shortages in Tewæno. Although Tewæno residents promised to provide for their relatives until they could plant their own gardens, these promises frequently were broken. That left the hungry newcomers with few alternatives. Too far away to return home, they could either beg or steal food from other Waorani, which created dependency and animosity. Or, disillusioned and embittered, they could leave for another clearing. "The most frequent accusation made at the weekly church service concerns the theft of food, a serious offense to these people," Yost wrote. The problem was exacerbated because the Waorani had not yet developed mechanisms of social control "to replace the threat of spearing." As a result, the culprits kept stealing, even though everyone knew who they were.[35]

Besides the immediate problem of food, Yost emphasized the long-term consequences of relocation and population growth. With some 350 Waorani out of a total known population of about 550 already in the protectorate, overhunting and overfishing were depleting the game supply, and further population growth would only put added pressure on the Waorani and their environment. Yost suggested a moratorium on relocation while SIL developed an intentional and careful strategy for change. SIL should work with the Waorani "where they presently live rather than inducing more strain . . . by transposing them into a new area." Such a plan should be flexible enough to respond to changes in government policy or oil company activity. Still, Yost considered it "unconscionable" to continue current practices "without considering future generations of Aucas."[36]

He had similarly strong views about SIL's stance toward the schisms between Tewæno and other Waorani. SIL should not play favorites. The Waorani "have a moral right to self-determination," and SIL should help them "make whatever transitions they want in a manner that is least destructive to them." SIL staff could offer "spiritual guidance" to any Waorani, wherever they chose to live, but SIL support should not be tied to religious conformity. "If we refuse to help them, we can hardly expect them to listen to the message we are trying to communicate." Specifically, SIL should try to lessen the animosity between Tewæno and Dayono. Yost noted that Dave Miller, the Christian and Missionary Alliance missionary working in Dayono at Wiñame's invitation, had contacted SIL for assistance, as had Pedro Chimbo, the local schoolteacher. SIL should pursue cooperation based on the needs of the Waorani, "not out of any desire to control them or make them become what we want them to become."[37]

As soon as she learned the contents of Yost's report, Saint weighed in. In a letter to Peeke, home on furlough, Saint disagreed with both the analysis and the proposals. There was no food shortage at Tewæno. "Food problems, yes, but not shortage. Game is abundant—d.r. [downriver] folks are good hunters & oil seems to drive them our way. *No one* has gone to other clearings because of a food *shortage*." Difficulties, she said, arose because of scheduling. For example, Kelley had been called away from her teaching for three weeks. People ate their food supplies while waiting for her to return. There was scarcity because they had miscalculated the time they would spend away from their gardens, not because of any inherent shortage. Ending the relocations would alienate the Waorani both in the protectorate and on the ridge. "The Aucas & Dayomæ in the Protectorate are up in arms about the thought of a freeze. Quemo & Dayomæ insist the land is enough."[38]

Nor did Saint support Wao self-determination, particularly by those in Dayono she considered unconverted. Waorani who interacted with outsiders away from the controls that governed Tewæno courted disaster. Wiñame was "letting the solteras [single girls] sleep with 'cowode' at Campana & Napo for pay—& then getting pills to keep them from getting pregnant," she alleged. Waorani from the ridge who left Tewæno inevitably got sick with contact illnesses and paid with their lives. Saint recalled one woman who had given birth to an "oil Co. baby" that was "thrown away at birth."[39] The Waorani needed spiritual guidance to face changing circumstances. That meant Saint's own leadership, since she was sure that the Waorani, at least those in Tewæno, viewed her as their spiritual teacher.[40]

Responding to Saint, Peeke repeated some of her long-standing doubts. Concentrating native peoples into a "reducción," as Jesuits and others historically had done in Latin America, was neither "feasible nor wise," however well intentioned. "This is the mission technique which has been so deplored, and with good practical as well as ethical reason." In the Bible, missionaries or evangelists were sent out. "Nowhere are we told to move the physical location of anybody but ourselves." Even when the "missionaries" were Waorani, the practice had been ineffective. "I show slides and talk about the exploits of these [*sic*] who braved the trails and the rivers to bring their people in; but always there is the nagging feeling that really this isn't what it's all about, since after they get them 'in,' they really aren't 'in' at all, but the same pagan sinners they were before."[41]

Peeke had gone along with the project, she admitted, because "it seemed reasonable in the case of those with strong family ties in Tewæno." But she had observed that family unification seemed to be motivated primarily by "matrimonial aspirations" rather than evangelistic zeal. "Not that there is anything wrong with that . . . in fact, it [culturally appropriate marriage] is now quite crucial to their continuance as a society." However, the relocated families generally did not flourish in Tewæno; instead they were "drug down" by their supposedly Christian kin. Peeke agreed with Yost "that we should hold off for a while." Peeke also challenged Saint's views on the availability of food. "You cannot tell me that there is no agricultural problem, for I have seen it."[42]

By 1974 there was no perfect policy for SIL on Wao relocation, and probably never had been. Lindskoog urged the Wao team to step back and try to make the best decision possible. At the same time, he encouraged them to use the issues Yost had raised to evaluate "the entire Auca operation with a cool and critical eye and together come up with policies that will guide us in present activities and future planning." SIL had made mistakes in the past, he acknowledged, "some of them doubtless serious." Nevertheless, it was time to learn from the past and to encourage the Waorani to "move ahead with an increasing degree of independence and confidence as they learn for themselves God's Truths and apply them and work them out within a purely Auca framework."[43]

Lindskoog's advice was good, but hard to implement. The issues Yost had raised were only part of a "very complicated maze" facing SIL in its involvement with the Waorani.[44] Yost documented additional problems in Tewæno that others were aware of, but no one had wanted to face. Christianity as practiced in Tewæno was ritualistic and lifeless; translation of the New Testament had come to a standstill; and, in October 1974, four Waorani from Tewæno were enticed into becoming hit men for a Quichua feud and speared three people.[45] Most painful and toughest to resolve was the reality that Rachel and Dayomæ ran Tewæno in ways that were unhealthy for all its inhabitants—the other SIL workers and Waorani alike.

12

Breaking a Pattern of Dependence

⌒───

FROM THE BEGINNING, the Summer Institute of Linguistics made exceptions for Rachel Saint and the Waorani. Everyone knew this was an unusual situation. Typically SIL assigned a pair of linguists, most often a married couple or two single women, to do indigenous language work. Rachel had gone to Tewæno in 1958 with Dayomæ and Elisabeth Elliot (who was not with SIL). When Elliot left in 1961, no one who knew Saint and Elliot was surprised that they struggled to work together. More perplexing, however, was the difficulty SIL had in finding a linguist to be Rachel's coworker. In June 1962 Ecuador director Don Johnson assigned staff member Mary Sargent as "Rachel's partner for the summer months." In 1956 Sargent had stayed briefly with Saint at the Hacienda Ila, and Johnson hoped that eventually Sargent and Catherine Peeke could work with Saint in Tewæno.[1] Peeke and Sargent did work alongside Saint in Tewæno during July and August 1962, but the anticipated team never materialized.

The question of a colleague seemed less pressing during the mid-1960s as reports from Saint indicated that Bible translation and Christianity were flourishing in Tewæno. The Ecuador SIL made another exception during this period by allowing Saint to coordinate "Operation Contact," clearly a missionary venture and not the work of a Bible translator. Uneasiness persisted among Ecuador SIL administrators over the slow pace of Rachel's translation work and her unwillingness to collaborate with anyone but Dayomæ. Even after Peeke finished her doctoral dissertation on the Wao language, Saint insisted on making final translation decisions. She rebuffed

Peeke's proposal to make changes in orthography, along with other corrections.[2] Peeke also spent months at Limoncocha, SIL's Ecuador jungle base, waiting for Saint's permission to relocate to Tewæno.

GATEKEEPER TO THE WAORANI

From 1961 to the early 1970s, Saint served as gatekeeper to the Waorani even among SIL staff. When John Lindskoog once again tackled the need for a coworker, this time thinking of new staff member Rosi Jung, he did so "without consulting Rachel as I knew what her answer would be—and it was."[3] On one occasion, JAARS pilot Roy Gleason was scheduled to fly visitors into Tewæno against Rachel's wishes. She reported by radio that the clearing was socked in, with clouds down to the treetops and limited visibility. All the other jungle stations were reporting clear skies, so Gleason decided to proceed with the flight. He checked in periodically, asking, "Rachel, has it cleared up yet?" She continued to report poor conditions and that Gleason would be unable to land. Suddenly, people in Tewæno could hear the motor and began to shout, "Rachel, the airplane's coming." Saint grabbed the microphone and declared, "It just cleared up."[4]

Incidents like this could be downplayed as personality quirks or as reflecting tensions between colleagues. Saint continued to draw from a reservoir of respect she had gained for her faith and determination in living among the Waorani. She enjoyed the backing of Cameron Townsend. She was famous in North America and Europe, especially to the large constituency who supported the Wycliffe Bible Translators. Although she sometimes acknowledged setbacks, she continued to release optimistic accounts of the Wao church. There were occasional bizarre charges from the US that she had taken up with Wao men, but they were easily dismissed.[5]

Perhaps most important, Saint had a strong sense of divine calling, and she could be persuasive in identifying her ideas and actions with God's will.[6] SIL staff were evangelical Christians, and some were wary about challenging a woman who seemed chosen by God to live among the Waorani, however flawed she might be. The situation worsened with the polio epidemic in 1969 and with complaints about SIL in the early 1970s from Erwin Patzelt and others. Saint's tight control over access to Tewæno fed rumors that if SIL was not letting people in, there had to be a reason. SIL Ecuador felt increasing pressure to defend itself against suspicions that something bad was happening in the rainforest. In addition, the in-migration of many Waorani to Tewæno between 1968 and 1972 overwhelmed Saint's capacity to serve as medic, linguist, missionary, and teacher.

When Peeke, Jung, and later Kelley joined Saint in Tewæno, they struggled with her overbearing manner in relating to the Waorani and her insensitive treatment of themselves, her coworkers. But each had her own demanding assignment, and no one was eager to confront the formidable Saint, the "senior missionary" among them.[7] Attempts to do so were rarely successful. The crisis reached a climax when Jim Yost arrived. Lindskoog originally asked him to collaborate with Rachel, who would be his interpreter. This quickly proved unsatisfactory, not only because of her efforts to choreograph Yost's observations but also because her very presence affected the Waorani. "She as a person intimidates. Her demeanor in questioning infl[uences] answers to be what she wants." She "is so involved she doesn't 'see' what is happening around her."[8] After sixteen years, Saint was so enmeshed in the lives of the Tewæno Waorani that objectivity was difficult, if not impossible, for her to achieve. Yost's field notes documented his growing alarm over how this affected the Waorani and its implications for SIL. Beyond his concerns about Saint's role in relocation efforts and in the conflict with the inhabitants of Dayono, Yost questioned her interactions with the Waorani, her relationship with Dayomæ, and the kind of Christianity she and Dayomæ had fostered.

Even though Rachel and Dayomæ argued frequently, Rachel believed she had a genuine kin relationship with Dayomæ as her adopted sister, and she embraced Dayomæ's family as her own. One rainy day, Rachel, nearly blind from cataracts, slipped on the wooden steps to Dayomæ's house. She yelled at Dayomæ for the poorly constructed steps. Dayomæ yelled back that the heavy-set Rachel was clumsy.[9] In a later incident, Rachel told Dayomæ to put her son Solomon to bed because the child was sick. Dayomæ got mad and refused. Rachel, in turn, called Dayomæ's husband, Come, and badgered him until he did it. "Intervening in marriage?" questioned Yost in his notebook. "Make him do what wi[fe] won't?"[10] Because Rachel was convinced the Waorani were a matriarchal culture, she probably saw herself playing the elder sister role in a family matter.

RACHEL AND DAYOMÆ AS POWER BROKERS

Despite the bickering, Rachel was absolutely committed to Dayomæ, both because of "kinship" ties and because she was convinced Dayomæ was a God-ordained trans-lator and tribal leader.[11] Rachel also depended on Dayomæ to offset her own lim-itations in language and cultural awareness. Dayomæ, a bright, ambitious woman, used Rachel to strengthen her position of power in the tribe. Few decisions were made without Dayomæ's approval. In March 1974, when several Waorani were asked to go to Limoncocha for a training course, all the names were cleared with Dayomæ first. "Why not clear it with the people not D? Just reinforces her power," observed Yost.[12] Rachel also supplied Dayomæ with trade goods—cloth, pots, sugar, rice, sewing machines, medicines—that Dayomæ used to keep newcomers who relocated to Tewæno in a kind of debt peonage. The biggest conflict between Saint and Yost was over Saint's commitment to reinforcing Dayomæ's power in ways that Yost viewed as exploitative of other Waorani.[13]

Dayomæ functioned, in effect, as a *patróna*, or female boss, in Tewæno. Having been a victim of sexual abuse and de facto slavery, Dayomæ replicated the kind of power dynamics she had experienced on the hacienda, but now *she* was in charge. And Rachel assumed a matriarchal role, controlling others by nagging them until they did what she wanted. When the Waorani purchased butcher knives, she insisted that they break off the point and the handle so the knife was harder to use as a weapon.[14] She pressured Tewæno residents to attend the weekly church service. She and Dayomæ would go from house to house telling people to come. Once they arrived, Rachel fussed over the structure of the service. She told some people where to sit and others which direction to face. One service, when no one volunteered to pray, she called on Come to do it, then instructed him on what to say. As he prayed, she added things he should include.[15]

Saint frequently scolded people. She was upset with one Wao woman because she thought the woman was neglecting her husband, who had a fever. The woman explained that when she had gone to the forest to work, the husband had not been ill. When the woman tried to walk away, Saint stepped in front of her to continue the lecture. The woman "finally walk[ed] off silently."[16] Seemingly innocuous events were blown out of proportion. In mid-March 1974 Dawa passed along the gossip that one young man had purchased some powder in Arajuno, which he brought back, mixed with lemon and water, and hid in the jungle for a week. Supposedly he was selling it to the children in the clearing. Convinced that the culprit was dabbling in moonshine or worse, Saint set out to shut him down. The questionable substance turned out to be Kool-Aid. The Waorani laughed at the youth's antics, but Saint was not amused.[17]

Saint's relational style reflected her own strong personality. Also, she viewed Dayomæ—who, as another SIL staff member wryly commented, had an "anger problem"—as the prototypical Wao. For Rachel, Dayomæ's actions defined Wao behavioral norms. Yet Dayomæ had her own personality quirks, and she had been shaped by her adolescent experiences at the Hacienda Ila, where ordering people around was standard practice.

OPPRESSIVE CHRISTIANITY

Yost's field notes also described what he characterized as "an oppressive type of Christianity."[18] Church services were highly ritualistic and reinforced Rachel's and

Dayomæ's roles among the people. Sermons were repetitive, incorporating the same memorized passages from Mark's Gospel or the same Old Testament stories week after week. People recited memorized verses "in [a] near monotone, [with] little emotion."[19] Old Testament stories, especially those featured on a series of picture cards, were popular. Dayomæ used the cards to illustrate her renditions of the lives of Abraham, Joseph, and Moses, the parting of the Red Sea, Elijah taken to heaven in a whirlwind, and the battle of Jericho. The stories were told again and again, week after week, in a set pattern in keeping with oral tradition.[20]

Church services also reinforced behavioral norms, what the Waorani called "living well." Living well in this context meant remaining in Tewæno and obeying community norms about settling near the airstrip and not killing or stealing. The Sunday gatherings served to remind various kinship groups that the heart of the gospel was "Do not spear" and to reassure everyone that killing would not begin again.[21] Those who "lived well" also were able, for a price, to obtain goods from Dayomæ. This framework reflected Dayomæ's skillful synthesis of traditional and modern practices to create networks of obligation.

Sin was described as "living badly": leaving Tewæno, distancing oneself from Dayomæ, or not responding to her demands. In other words, breaking the standards and relationships that were equated with faith. Church services provided opportunities to publicly accuse people who "did badly." Years later Yost would quip that "some churches have confession, we had accusation."[22] Sickness, a common problem for newcomers facing contact diseases, and snakebite were viewed as signs of sin. Church services, in short, became a form of social control and Christianity part of the patronage system Dayomæ had created. Rachel had become so accustomed to seeing the Waorani, including Dayomæ, through her own religious filters that she was oblivious to these distortions.

Saint insisted that the Waorani be protected from the outside world as well as from "their old immoral ways." That could happen only if they stayed under the tutelage of Tewæno Christians such as Dayomæ, Dawa, Quemo, and Yowe.[23] Her objective, at least during an interim period while the Waorani "learn[ed] to live in peace," was to maintain Tewæno and the surrounding protectorate as an isolated, Christian enclave.[24] Yost believed that Saint wanted to make the Waorani dependent so they would "be concerned about [their] souls and know [Christ] in their misery. Keep them 'protected' from the evils of the outside world lest they learn their ways."[25] In effect, she was advocating a distorted form of fundamentalism with her concern for separation from the world. Others on the Wao team, Yost thought, wanted to "teach them [the people] to interact with [the] outside in mature way[s] so [they] can *resist* evil."[26] When Yost submitted his initial report in April 1974, he focused on organizational issues rather than on personnel. Saint was mentioned only in passing. However, it was clear that Yost's recommendations challenged her at every turn. Yost followed up with a letter to Lindskoog, outlining his concerns about Saint. To Lindskoog, the analysis confirmed much of what he already knew. "I feel very badly that I have let it go this long," he admitted.[27] Over the years others had expressed concerns, but always in confidence, "not to be shared with Rachel." She would soon be leaving Tewæno for additional eye surgery in the US, and Lindskoog promised to confront her. "Only . . . if she changes her attitudes and actions, will she be allowed to continue in direct contact with the tribal people."[28] Personnel records are confidential, but Lindskoog apparently wrote Saint a letter in June, supported by SIL's Ecuador Executive Council (governing board), detailing changes that were needed. He also may have talked briefly with her.[29]

Saint responded with hurt and indignation that Lindskoog was "officially charging" her with insensitivity to the Waorani, discrimination against the Dayono group, and other actions unfavorable to SIL. Lindskoog asked her to remain in the United States an additional three months to work on these issues. She gave possible credence to only one point, the allegation that she was "possessive" of the Waorani. Even there, she blamed Lindskoog for not calling her to account earlier. She also resented being called on the carpet as she was leaving for surgery and to represent SIL at scheduled promotional events in the US. However, she wrote to Peeke that "the biggest blow" was that the directive kept her from "the translation & the spiritual training of the tribe," activities she insisted could be done only on site.[30]

The painful dispute between the Summer Institute of Linguistics in Ecuador and Rachel Saint would drag on for eight years before the two severed final ties in April 1982. While questions about the way Saint related to the Waorani remained crucial, SIL tried to focus the conflict on the more concrete issue of Bible translation. Once they reached the stage of actual Bible translation, many SIL linguists spent considerable time working outside their assigned indigenous groups to minimize distractions. This was one reason the organization had jungle bases in Ecuador, Peru, and elsewhere. Saint's entanglements with the Waorani clearly had slowed her progress. When she returned to Ecuador in late 1974, Lindskoog asked her to live and work at the Limoncocha base.

RACHEL'S DEFENSE

She refused. In January 1975 she wrote a letter to those involved in the conflict: Lindskoog, the Wao "team" (Jung, Kelley, Peeke, and the Yosts), and the

Ecuador Branch Executive Committee. The letter, two and a half typed, single-space pages, defended her desire to remain a permanent resident of Tewæno. The reasons centered on Dayomæ, on Rachel's work habits, her spiritual ministry, her relationships with the people, and her convictions about God's will. Rachel insisted that she must translate with Dayomæ. No one else among the Waorani was available who could do it, and only if Dayomæ died would Rachel consider an alternate. "God Himself has revealed to Dayomæ that the Auca translation is her responsibility."[31] Dayomæ would not want to come to Limoncocha, and it would be disruptive to her family. Yes, Rachel admitted, she and Dayomæ had conflicts. But those conflicts forced Rachel to consider more carefully biblical truths and how to explain them amid the nitty gritty of everyday life.

Saint also maintained that she worked best in the informal atmosphere of Tewæno, where Waorani who dropped by her house "would sit down and listen to the newest translation and answer questions about it." At the same time, newly translated material would immediately be available for the Wao church. The next to last paragraph in the letter focused on the emotional core of Saint's dilemma. "Separating me from the Aucas in some sense would be like telling Cathie [Peeke] she could not visit her family on furlough, or telling Jim and Kathy they had to leave Kigi [two-year-old Rachelle Yost] at the base, or telling John Lindskoog that he could never talk on the radio to his son in the Pacific. My relation to the Aucas has been close but wholesome," she insisted. "God has made it so."[32]

Saint approached the conflict as an all-or-nothing proposition: she must be allowed back in Tewæno on her terms or there would be no translation. She requested written responses from her colleagues, and all opposed her return. It was not easy. Peeke, who had known Saint the longest, overcame feelings of disloyalty to confront her with the reality of the situation. "The tragedy is that translation is not going forward and that the Wao church is stagnant," Peeke wrote. She reproached Saint for her unwillingness to submit to SIL leadership and her difficulty in listening to other points of view.[33]

Peeke also challenged the way Christianity was taught and practiced in Tewæno. While taking some of the blame herself, she pushed Saint to acknowledge the culture of condemnation that had become a part of life in the clearing. "You and I and the Christian leaders have tried to maintain an image of sinlessness while condemning others. . . . A great pain to me has been to see unconverted sinners told of their sins in a very condemning (not winsome) way. . . . They consequently move away without ever knowing the sweetness of the Gospel." Peeke also objected to Saint's refusal to allow others access to the Waorani. "We are under attack for the very attitude you represent." It was better that Saint stay away from Tewæno, "lest we indeed be found guilty of 'control' and 'paternalism' and 'imperialism.'"[34]

Saint remained at the Limoncocha base or in Quito throughout 1975. She and the Ecuador SIL were at a stalemate. They refused to let her back into Tewæno. She refused to translate, retire, or leave Ecuador, and spent much of her time defending herself. There was also the question of how much communication via radio or what kind of visits she could have with the Waorani. It seemed heartless to cut her off completely, but when she had contact she inevitably sought to influence the people in her favor. After one brief trip to Tewæno to retrieve some items, Saint wrote Lindskoog, "Dawa said to tell you that if you take away their spiritual teachers (meaning me) tell them [Lindskoog and others] not to 'cry' when Aucas kill outsiders."[35]

Rachel helped Dayomæ and her family get dental treatment at Limoncocha and in Quito. And, of course, they returned from such trips well stocked with goods.[36] Rachel also took a turn at trying to straighten out twenty-four-year-old Sam Padilla, who along with his mother was one of the few people who "managed" Rachel rather than vice versa. Rachel had paid for much of Padilla's education at two Bible colleges in the US. However, the young man neglected his academic work in favor of motorcycles and American girls. Part of the problem may have been that Padilla's formal education in Ecuador had ended with the seventh grade.[37] Although he had his mother's quick mind, he apparently made little effort to catch up. Instead of taking eleven credits during one semester at Florida Bible College, he enrolled for only four. Back in Quito, he had begun helping Erwin Patzelt and grew disaffected with SIL. "At this point I am not one bit interested in his further education!" wrote a frustrated Rachel. But she relented, primarily to get Sam away from Quito and out of trouble.[38]

THE TWENTIETH ANNIVERSARY

January 1976 marked the twentieth anniversary of the deaths of the five missionaries, and it came during the dispute with Saint. Branch officials struggled to meet North American expectations and still be realistic. In a draft letter, "The Auca Situation Today," Lindskoog tried to balance positive and negative aspects of Christianity among the Waorani. Although God had been at work, it was not, he insisted, "a unique success story."[39] Translation progress had been slow, and personnel might have created a culture of dependence, Lindskoog admitted, without naming any names.

However, when Lindskoog approved the official news release for SIL staff in Ecuador to send to constituencies in North America, optimism prevailed. The release reported that more than one hundred Waorani had become Christians during the previous twenty years. It acknowledged "obstacles of all kinds," including illnesses, deaths, and serious feuds. Even so, the tone was generally upbeat, in a spirit of "praise" and "rejoicing." Readers learned that Christian Waorani still wanted to take the gospel to their family members "in distant clearings . . . at great personal sacrifice." Young Waorani were "eager to learn farming, cattle-raising, and carpentry as well as the three R's."[40] Accurate to a degree, such statements clearly accentuated the positive. For example, some Wao men did want cattle, but as a status symbol. The animals did not thrive in the rainforest and had become a nuisance in the clearings where a few were raised. The one-page release also was one of the first mass-circulation documents from SIL in Ecuador that consistently referred to the group as "Waorani" rather than "Aucas."

When Yost and others complained about the tone, Lindskoog defended the release. Billy Graham's *Decision* magazine and HCJB were publishing their own reports, he noted, and it would be odd if the Ecuador Branch said nothing.[41] The exchange sparked an internal debate over the nature of honest communication with the homeland, and particularly over how to represent the Waorani. It extended to include Clarence Church, Wycliffe's US director. The official information about the Waorani sent to the US over the years had been uniformly positive, Church noted. Wycliffe had told the story they received. Now that Yost's reports were painting a different picture, what should they do? Retract the earlier books and articles? Tell Wycliffe backers, "The situation there is a mess"? Keep quiet and let people come to their own conclusions?[42]

Yost suggested that Wycliffe begin by encouraging all Wycliffe and SIL staff to take the Waorani out of the limelight.[43] Lindskoog, too, looked for ways to lower expectations. "People should be warned against the tendency of idolizing the Auca work and thus getting vicarious satisfaction to compensate for discouragements in the home church."[44] Lindskoog's comment touched on a reality that WBT, mission agencies, and others would find hard to acknowledge during the years to come. Saint had created a culture of dependency among the Waorani, but it was equally true that during the twenty years since the missionaries' deaths, segments of American evangelicalism, including Wycliffe, had become deeply dependent on the inspirational and emotional power of the Wao story. It had become a drama without parallel and proof of God at work in the world. Both patterns of dependency would be difficult to break. In Ecuador, however, Lindskoog still faced the immediate issue of Rachel Saint.

RACHEL SAINT AND SIL

"How do you fire your most famous missionary? Especially, how do you fire a missionary who is *the* image for a generation?"[45] Neither Lindskoog nor Don Johnson, his successor as Ecuador Branch director, knew the answer to those questions as they struggled to resolve the conflict. None of Saint's coworkers wanted a showdown—as one put it, "the gunfight at the OK corral." Yost was the most angry about Saint's impact on the Waorani, although all agreed that the situation was untenable.[46] Her colleagues spent hours listening to Saint's side of the story and seeking a workable solution.[47]

Rachel's brother Phil and later her brother Sam visited Ecuador to try to talk her into a compromise, but to no avail. SIL allowed her back in Tewæno for a trial period between January and May 1976, but the old patterns persisted, as did her inability to recognize them. The following August, the Ecuador Branch affirmed Lindskoog's decision to place Rachel on "probation" and to bar her from further direct tribal work.[48] Johnson supported his predecessor's decisions.[49] He prohibited Rachel from seeing Dayomæ or communicating with her since nothing seemed to have changed their volatile relationship.[50]

During the next few years, Saint made half-hearted attempts at translation from Quito, underwent additional eye surgeries, went on furlough, and tried a brief stint working with SIL in Dallas. But her belongings remained in Tewæno, as did her heart, and she tenaciously sought to return as her probationary period dragged on. She always insisted that those who opposed her were acting outside the will of God.[51] The conflict finally came to an end, almost exactly at the moment when it no longer mattered. In November 1980 the SIL personnel committee in the US upheld the decision by the Ecuador Branch that Rachel Saint be recalled from Ecuador to the homeland.[52] In May 1981 circumstances changed dramatically when Ecuadorian president Jaime Roldós Aguilera issued a presidential decree ending SIL's contracts in Ecuador within a year, an action that would greatly reduce the presence of SIL in the country. A few days later Saint requested retirement from WBT. Her ties with Wycliffe and with the Summer Institute ended in April 1982, when her financial accounts were closed. By then she was back in the Ecuadorian Amazon as a retiree, living next door to Dayomæ in the small village of Toñæmpade. It had been established only a few years earlier, independent of any SIL support.

There were ironies in Saint's return. The woman who had fought so hard to isolate the Waorani from external influences would live most of the rest of her life in a clearing specifically founded by Dayomæ and her son Sam to foster the tourist trade and access to the outside world. Waorani in more isolated clearings would have welcomed Rachel, but Toñæmpade was where Dayomæ lived. Saint's return was made easier by the reduced presence in Ecuador of the very organization she had represented for more than three decades. When she came back, SIL was in no position to object. If living with Dayomæ and her kin was victory, then Saint had "won" the conflict with the Ecuador SIL. On the other hand, SIL's success in keeping her away from the Waorani for the better part of eight years had facilitated significant shifts in population and power. Dayomæ remained an important power broker, but no longer the sole *patróna*. Rachel also continued to act like a matriarch, handing out spiritual advice, but her influence was much diminished. She had become the guest of the Waorani and not their proprietor. Many of them welcomed her return. When she died in 1994, she was buried in Toñæmpade.

FALSE STEREOTYPES

For all Saint's flaws, some of the persistent stereotypes and accusations leveled against her beginning in the 1970s were simply untrue. None of the Waorani considered her "Queen of the Aucas," nor did her Wao name, "Nemo" (Star), have special importance. The Waorani named people after relatives, and Nemo was the name of a deceased sister of Dayomæ. The literal meaning of the word had no more significance than modern English speakers would give the surnames Baker or King.[53]

Contrary to the prevailing sentiment among both Latin American governments and missionaries of her generation, and even within SIL itself, Saint was never an assimilationist. Her goal was not to transform the Waorani into good citizens of Ecuador. She strongly opposed violence and certain sexual practices. Otherwise she wanted the culture to survive, with its own integrity and not as a tourist attraction. She was fascinated by Wao legends and published several in Spanish and English translations.[54]

Unfortunately, however, she was unable to see the changes that already had come to Wao culture resulting from interactions with Quichuas, with oil company workers, and with the Summer Institute of Linguistics. She couldn't or wouldn't acknowledge the negative cultural impact of relocating so many Waorani to the protectorate. Nor did she realize that her aggressive efforts to limit Wao contact with the outside world would backfire by creating pent-up demand. By not recognizing these realities, Saint failed to help the Waorani confront them.[55]

While Saint controlled access to Tewæno during the 1960s and early 1970s, she never dominated the Waorani to the extent her detractors imagined. Dayomæ had no fear of challenging Rachel, as their frequent quarrels demonstrated. Dayomæ's role as Wao *patróna* created problems of its own, but it also served as a check on Rachel's power. Other Waorani might comply with Rachel's wishes, but they often did so as a calculated acquiescence, a trade-off for the *cowode* goods that had been associated with Rachel since her arrival. Some laughed at her scolding. Out of earshot, Wao men occasionally would parody her accent and her reprimands.[56] Others simply hid their intentions and actions (and the dynamite they used for fishing) from her.

The Waorani could have killed Rachel at any time during the many years she lived among them. This was especially true during the late 1960s and early 1970s, when the male population of the clearing increased. That they did not suggests they perceived significant benefits to her presence. There was medicine and trade goods, but more important, Saint regularly emphasized the need for peace in the name of God and helped enforce that ethic. During the polio epidemic and perhaps on another occasion as well, she stormed into the house of a Wao man who was threatening to kill, grabbed his spears from the thatched roof, and broke them. No one else could have done that and lived. This is not to defend her relational style. Her heavy-handedness contributed to divisions among the Waorani and to many dilemmas faced by colleagues who had to deal with the consequences of her actions. However, Rachel Saint was never the kind of cult leader in the rainforest that some critics implied.[57]

Finally, while her relationships with the Waorani got the most attention, Rachel did not discriminate. She had no qualms about telling her SIL coworkers, her brothers, the Ecuadorian military, or anyone else what to do. "You don't work with Rachel. You either work under Rachel or against Rachel, but there's no such thing as working with Rachel."[58] With the possible exceptions of Dayomæ and Sam, that comment held true whether your name was Oncaye or Yost. Rachel would mellow a little in her later years, but the stubbornness and spiritual self-assurance that made Rachel Saint a person who would dare to contact the Waorani and to live among them did not serve her well in the long run, either with the tribe or within SIL.[59]

13

¡Fuera de Aquí! (Get Out of Here!)

⌒——————————————————————————————

DURING THE MID-1970S, while the Ecuador SIL was trying to dislodge Rachel Saint from Tewæno, it also faced growing criticism from those who wanted SIL itself out of Ecuador and all Latin America. The controversy extended well beyond the Waorani, but opponents regularly invoked the group to support their arguments. For supporters and critics alike, the Waorani symbolized SIL's work among indigenous people in Latin America. In addition, the close relationship between the Ecuador SIL and Texaco and other oil companies during the Wao relocation made the organization an obvious target during a period of increasing nationalism and anti-US sentiment. The fact that both the oil companies and SIL worked under contract with the Ecuadorian government only strengthened the opposition.

The year 1975 marked the first, clear public expression of what would become widespread anti-SIL sentiment in Ecuador, a barrage of criticisms that would be most intense between 1980 and 1982. It began with a January conference on North American philanthropy, sponsored by the Pontifical Catholic University of Ecuador (PUCE), the institution that would produce the most stringent critiques. In 1972 PUCE had been the first university in Ecuador to establish an anthropology department, and many faculty members had been influenced by progressive ideas from Vatican II (1962–65), the Medellin Conference of Latin American Bishops (1968), and liberation theology.[1]

The conference aired a series of charges. Some had been raised before but had not captured public attention. All would become a familiar litany. SIL was in league with foreign capital, and their presence in the rainforest served as a way "to control future petroleum fields."[2] The organization had engaged in "cultural aggression" against the Waorani by relocating them to the Tewæno reserve. The Waorani lived in submission to Rachel Saint, who exercised authoritarian control. SIL controlled access to large portions of the eastern jungles, sovereign territory of Ecuador. Adding fuel to the fire, Erwin Patzelt complained once again that this territory remained closed to scientific investigations. Patzelt also repeated the "revelation" he had publicized in 1972, that one of the original five missionaries had shot and killed Nampa, a Wao man, during the 1956 spearings. Newspapers joined the attack, and the renewed attention reinforced the image of aggressive missionaries dominating tribal peoples.[3]

The Ecuadorian press devoted extensive coverage to the charges. Both the press reports and the attack from the PUCE conference caught the Ecuador SIL off guard. "Two years ago the problems . . . were not even dimly on the horizon—or at least we were not aware of them," wrote John Lindskoog, once again SIL's Ecuador director.[4] Lindskoog took comfort from the fact that the critique had originated with private individuals and institutions and not the Ecuadorian government. Only a few years earlier, the government had renewed its contract with SIL and, in a separate action, awarded Lindskoog the Order of Merit, one of the country's highest civilian honors. As a result, the SIL director underestimated the impact of students and faculty in PUCE's new anthropology department. They kept opposition to SIL alive until the political winds shifted in their favor with the end of military rule and the election in 1979 of Jaime Roldós as Ecuador's president.

¡FUERA DE AQUÍ!

Complaints against North American missionaries were reinforced by a noncommercial, yet widely circulated film, *¡Fuera de Aquí!* (Get Out of Here!; Llocsi Caimanta! in Quichua), produced in Ecuador in 1977. The work of an acclaimed Bolivian director, Jorge Sanjinés, millions of Ecuadorians saw the movie during the first five years after it opened.[5] Employing a documentary style but using the fictional village of Kalakala, the film featured guitar-playing US evangelical missionaries who arrived with sermons—and "a secret sterilization campaign" against indigenous women. The missionaries' preaching divided the community and set up the indigenous people to be exploited by a multinational mining company. The film was relentless in linking "religio-cultural colonialism with economic exploitation," while concurrently presenting politicians and the military as willing allies in oppressing the indigenous.[6]

The film never explicitly identified the missionaries with SIL, but many viewers did, since the charges it made paralleled those against the linguists. Posters advertising the film also made the connection. One featured a picture of an indigenous man from the film with the caption "POR LA LIBERTAD DEL OPRIMIDO, INSTITUTO LINGÜISTICO DE VERANO I.L.V., ¡FUERA DE AQUI!" (For the freedom of the oppressed, Summer Institute of Linguistics SIL, Get Out of Here!).[7] In addition to forced sterilization and economic exploitation, *¡Fuera de Aquí!* showed missionaries encouraging tribal peoples to boycott indigenous organizations that were becoming more visible and politicized in Ecuador during the late 1970s. Finally, the film promoted the idea that religious proselytization created conflicts that divided indigenous communities.[8]

The sterilization accusation was the most far-fetched and the most easily refuted. The indigenous groups where SIL linguists worked in Ecuador enjoyed healthy population growth, partially due to the healthcare SIL provided. A biomedical analysis of the Waorani in August 1976 by a team of seven researchers organized by the Duke University Medical Center found the group in excellent health, with normal reproductive rates.[9] Later data placed annual population growth at 2.25 percent between 1974 and 1976 and at 4.6 percent in 1978.[10] Yet sensationalism died hard, and *¡Fuera de Aquí!* may have inspired rumors persisting into the twenty-first century that SIL had controlled the Waorani and other indigenous groups by doing other things, such as adding laxatives to their food.[11]

The two other criticisms made by the film had more merit, though not in the exaggerated versions on screen. Most evangelical missionaries in Ecuador did view the emerging indigenous federations of the mid-1970s with suspicion, as too politicized and under leftist influence. Many, though not all, SIL staffers shared this perspective. In part, this was because early antagonism toward SIL came from the Shuar Federation and the leftist-oriented Single Front of Peasant and Indigenous Struggle (Frente Unico de Lucha Campesina e Indígena), in addition to the Catholic University.[12] Some missionaries simply wanted indigenous people to remain apolitical, as SIL workers assumed they themselves were. Protestant missionaries did make an exception for the Ecuadorian Federation of Indigenous Evangelicals (Federación Ecuatoriana de Indígenas Evangélicos), formed in 1980. The Federation was viewed by opponents as a lackey of SIL.[13] The Waorani did not participate in these early expressions of indigenous activism. Still in the initial stages of contact, they had no formal political structure.

The conflict between Zoila Wiñame and Dayomæ that led to the founding of Dayono in December 1971 left SIL vulnerable to the third charge in the film: that religious proselytization caused divisions among indigenous people. However, the split between the two women had more to do with a struggle for power in Tewæno than it did with Christianity or missionaries. Among other things, Wiñame resented Dayomæ's control over outside goods and over marriage arrangements. The Dayono group barely had settled into their new location when Wiñame recruited David Miller, an evangelical missionary serving with the Christian and Missionary Alliance, to help establish and staff a school for her clearing, which he did. Also, conflicts and schisms from spearing vendettas had been a part of traditional Wao culture long before missionaries arrived.

"TODAY'S WYCLIFFE VERSION"

Anti-SIL sentiment simmered both inside and outside of Ecuador between 1975 and 1979, although the Ecuador SIL retained a solid working relationship with the military government of Gen. Luis Durán. This ongoing relationship with the state did nothing to reassure critics. A second Barbados Conference in July 1977 was overtly anti-SIL, attacking the organization's work and adopting a resolution on "the colonialist policies of SIL."[14] About the same time, voices from the US began to weigh in. *The Other Side*, a magazine of the evangelical left in the United States, contributed "Today's Wycliffe Version," described as "a major report," written by the magazine's publisher, Philip Harnden.[15] Although Harnden did extend his research to include SIL activities in Bolivia and Brazil, the essay followed a familiar path. It began by focusing on the Waorani and on SIL's role in relocating them to the protectorate, then quoted heavily from Laurie Hart's "Pacifying the Last Frontiers," as well as Jerry Bledsoe's *Esquire* essay. The report also drew from an idealized picture of the Waorani in an article by Ethel Wallis, "Sharper Than Any Two-Edged Spear," published a year earlier by the Wycliffe Bible Translators to commemorate the twentieth anniversary of the 1956 deaths.[16]

In "Today's Wycliffe Version," Harnden wondered if WBT and its sister organization, SIL, had betrayed the legacy of the five slain missionaries. He accused SIL of encouraging the Waorani in an indiscriminate embrace of "civilization" and of being willing to accept favors from "anyone and everyone who can help them reach more souls." Where, the author wondered, were Christians who would refuse to cooperate with the "exploiters" and who would "stand beside [native peoples] and risk their own lives to demonstrate the fruits of the Spirit."[17]

Harnden seemed unaware that, however imperfectly, SIL workers among the Waorani were trying to be the kind of people he described. During the month before the essay was published, thirty-six Waorani in Tewæno had come down with the measles, and all subsequently contracted pneumonia. Rosi Jung, assisted by two nurses from the SIL clinic at Limoncocha, provided around-the-clock care to seriously ill Waorani for several weeks. The task was demanding and exhausting, but all survived.[18]

In addition, what it meant to "stand beside" the Waorani during the second half of the 1970s was not always clear. Sometimes it meant that SIL staff would cut back or stagger their presence in the protectorate to lessen the possibility of dependence. And during their stays among the people, they poured their energies into projects that were intended to help the Waorani face the outside world on their own. This led to an emphasis on healthcare, land issues, and literacy. Like others who shared the faith-mission heritage of SIL, the organization usually avoided defending itself publicly, preferring to let actions speak. In this case, however, the controversial decisions of the late 1960s seemed to define SIL Ecuador far more than later efforts to change course.

Harnden's analysis was also too simplistic in identifying the "exploiters." In addition to oil company workers, they could be lowland Quichuas, Ecuadorian *colonos* (settlers), well-meaning tourists, or Waorani taking advantage of other Waorani. Issues such as helping to provide the Waorani with national ID cards (what surnames to use and how to spell them) or determining the best approach to primary education (bilingual or monolingual) reflected the ongoing complexities of what it meant to support the Waorani. Often the missionaries were divided over the best course to take, as were the Waorani themselves.

"ACTION ANTHROPOLOGY"

Jim Yost wrestled with related questions as he sought to define his role as an anthropologist. He had come to eastern Ecuador to research Wao culture but had found himself living and working among people who were under increasing pressure to change. Taking refuge in pure research seemed irresponsible, so Yost turned to "action anthropology." Within the tradition of cultural anthropology, it offered an approach in situations "where people of radically different cultures come in contact" and where the power dynamics were uneven, that is, where a smaller group faced the danger of its culture being overwhelmed by pressures from a larger group with "technical and political advantages."[19] Action anthropologists sought to learn from the people with whom they worked and to help those in vulnerable cultures adjust in their own ways to inevitable change. The anthropologist's role was to educate, in the broad sense of the word, and to be willing to be a catalyst for action while respecting the freedom of groups to make their own choices. Ideally, the anthropologist helped all parties caught up in cultural pressure to understand the alternatives available to them and the possible outcomes of their choices. While an attractive model, it did assume the ability of the anthropologist to dispassionately adjudicate cultural conflict and change.

Action anthropology appealed to Yost in several ways, and it seemed to fit the Waorani situation. By 1978 it was clear that the Waorani in the protectorate—representing about 80 percent of the total Wao population—were increasingly susceptible to pressures from the neighboring Quichuas, from an influx of land-hungry highland settlers, and from multinational oil companies. Yost believed that the Waorani were heading toward a crisis that could threaten their survival. Action anthropology offered a framework for involvement. It focused on problem-solving in the present rather than on fault-finding in the past. And it acknowledged the role of values, particularly those of truth-telling and of allowing communities freedom to choose their own future.

The approach also contained risks. First, the theoretical framework behind action anthropology presupposed a sense of community or a basic decision-making structure the Waorani lacked. For people to choose freely, they needed a way to establish agreement and to resolve dissent or conflict. Second, having survived the violence that threatened to destroy them physically, the Waorani still might choose a way forward that could lead to cultural destruction. Yost recognized the intense desire on the part of many Waorani at the time "to become as much like the Quichuas as possible and, more than anything, to share in the goods that they see available to the Quichua."[20]

The anthropologist later would describe an incident that illustrated this desire. He had spent the night in a Wao clearing after accompanying hunters as they pursued peccary (wild pigs). Yost and Enæwæ, one of the hunters, lay on the raised palm floor of a thatched shelter, watching the night sky and listening to the "cacophony" of rainforest sounds. Nearby "a Wao chant [blended] inobtrusively into the mélange." As they waited for sleep, Yost and Enæwæ talked about the hunt and the prospects for the next day. The conversation eventually turned toward "the changes . . . [Enæwæ had] seen during his short lifetime. . . . [He mentioned] his aspirations—to own a shotgun, to learn to speak Spanish, to raise a herd of cattle." Yost was overwhelmed by the experience, both his rapport with Enæwæ and the natural and cultural setting surrounding them.

"I begin to drift toward sleep," he wrote, "when I realize how deeply immersed I have gotten into the Wao language and culture and let my mind roam in anthropologist thoughts. . . . Eager to share my insights I prod Enæwæ.

" 'Listen, the wiki [frogs] are talking Wao. They're saying odæ . . . odæ . . . odæ' (peccary, peccary, peccary)."

Enæwæ listened, "half indulgently, half amused for a few moments.

" 'No, they're saying wagada . . . wagada . . . wagada' (cattle, cattle, cattle), he snorts and rolls back over, indignant that I interrupted his sleep for such foolishness."[21]

Waorani like Enæwæ did not recognize the extent to which imitating the Quichua threatened their own identity. In the context of action anthropology, Yost hoped to provide information about "possible alternatives and their consequences," as well as to increase Waorani awareness of the value of their own culture. "The Waorani are not fools. . . . Given enough time they are going to choose a path that suits them."[22] Yost's fieldwork between 1976 and 1981 was aimed, at least in part, at helping them find that path. He coordinated collaborative studies documenting patterns of health and disease and engaged in research on Waorani land use. He also made a concerted effort to provide transportation back to their traditional neighborhood clusters to any Waorani wishing to leave the protectorate. At the same time, he continued his original ethnographic study of Wao life and culture.

HEALTH AND THE EFFECTS OF CONTACT

A major project, mentioned earlier, to measure the overall health of the Waorani, took place during August 1976. A medical team organized by the Duke University Medical Center examined 293 people (147 males, 146 females), drawn from all the main kinship groups and composing about 60 percent of the known Waorani population at the time. Those examined were young—80 percent were thirty or younger, 33 percent ten or younger—representative of the population after the recently ended spearing vendettas.[23] Overall findings concluded that the Waorani were "robust and appeared in excellent health," except for severe tooth decay. There was no evidence of cancer, heart disease, or obesity. By North American standards, Wao blood pressure was low, with no evidence that it increased with age. Apart from the polio epidemic in 1969, infectious diseases had played little part in Wao mortality, 90 percent of which had resulted from internal violence (spearings), conflict with outsiders, infant mortality and infanticide, and snakebite.[24]

Doctors speculated that the absence of cancer and heart disease might be related to diet, since most of the population still had "very limited access to salt, sugar, and other processed food." Other possibilities included "fewer toxins in the environment [or] a less stressful life style." They also acknowledged that a "diminished life expectancy" due to violence might mean that people simply did not live long enough to suffer from certain illnesses.[25] Serious tooth decay and tooth loss were endemic and seemed to have existed long before outside contact.[26]

The general good health of the Waorani reflected the isolation that had characterized their lives until only a few years earlier. Already, however, there were signs that outside contact could have negative health consequences. Three areas were of concern: (1) susceptibility to the viruses of the common cold, influenza, and pneumonia; (2) misuse and overuse of medicines; and (3) sanitation. Because of their remote living sites and relatively small population, the Waorani had had limited exposure to viruses prior to peaceful contact with outsiders. But since the relocation began in 1968, colds had "reached epidemic proportions" during certain months.[27]

The medical team speculated that respiratory infections peaked during the first quarter of the year in part because it was the dry season and the time when the fruit of the *chonta*, or peach palm, was ripe. Waorani would gather frequently for celebrations sustained by the consumption of large quantities of chonta fruit. The fruit was made into a drink, prepared much like manioc: first boiled, then mashed and chewed and mixed with water. People dancing, talking, and sleeping in close proximity, as well as sharing prechewed *dagæncapæ* (palm fruit drink) from common pots increased the spread of viruses. In addition, easier travel due to less muddy trails and lower river levels brought tourists into Wao territory and Waorani to visit the outside, both of which led to the transmission of cold viruses.[28] Even when not life-threatening, colds were misery in a culture that had no history of them and therefore no provision for them—no handkerchiefs, tissues, or even sleeves.

Because of the danger from contact illnesses, for years SIL distributed medicines without charge. Saint raised most of the money to pay for them, later supported by Peeke and other members of the Wao team. This approach, along with selfless efforts by SIL staff to care for the sick, contributed to Waorani survival. Only a handful of deaths over twenty years were due to colds, influenza, or pneumonia. As a result, however, the Waorani came to demand medicine, especially antibiotics, for almost any malady, no matter how minor. They were indiscriminate in self-medication, as likely to take tetracycline as aspirin for a headache.[29] If SIL staff refused to provide pills or injections, the Waorani would seek them elsewhere, often with even greater potential for misuse. In 1976 SIL implemented modest charges for medicine, hoping the Waorani would think about whether they really needed medication and, if so, choose only what would most effectively treat their condition.[30]

By 1979 the new policy had had mixed results. Many Waorani in the protectorate had become accustomed to paying for some of the cost of their medicines. However, a few of the Waorani who had been trained to dispense basic medicines engaged in price gouging or in other ways used their authority as a source of power. Waorani outside the protectorate, such as those living on the ridge, did not get needed medicines because they objected to the cost or weren't accustomed to a cash economy.[31]

THE ARTIFACT TRADE

The medicine policy also had the unintended effect of increasing SIL involvement in the Wao artifact trade. The main way the Waorani could get cash for medicines or other goods was through the sale of artifacts, mainly spears and blowguns. Someone—Peeke, Kelley, the Yosts, Jung, and occasionally pilots who served Tewæno—had to buy the artifacts for resale, or at least make sure they arrived safely in Limoncocha to be sold to SIL personnel or tourists. The Waorani used the money not needed for medicines to buy goods at a small "store" in Tewæno. The SIL staff had begun the store in the early 1970s to help the Waorani understand the concepts of buying, selling, and getting a fair price when trading with outsiders.

Over time, the store took on a life of its own, even after most Waorani were comfortable dealing directly with outsiders. In 1976 a frustrated Peeke wrote her colleagues that she did not consider running a store "a necessary service of Bible translators for Ecuadorian citizens [Waorani] who travel to Arajuno, Tena, etc."[32] Besides, she wrote in a later report, the store made it seem like the team had a commercial interest in the Waorani, which was not the case.[33] But with the Waorani facing ongoing healthcare costs, the SIL workers found that closing the business was easier said than done. In 1979 Peeke had exhausted her personal funds and still was unable to purchase all the artifacts Waorani wanted to sell to cover medical expenses.[34]

Besides respiratory diseases and the misuse of medicines, changed sanitary practices increased the incidence of intestinal parasites.[35] Traditionally the Waorani established their neighborhood clusters near the headwaters of small streams that flowed into the larger rivers of the region. The clean water was used for the drinks made from plantains and premasticated manioc or peach palm that were the staple of the Wao diet. People defecated in designated areas of the forest, usually quite near the houses but away from the water supply.[36] As the population became more concentrated, a few villages built latrines, following the example of SIL staff. Significant numbers, however, imitated some Quichuas by defecating directly into the streams or by constructing latrines that emptied directly into the streams. This "out of sight, out of mind" approach to human waste increased the risk of parasites and more serious illnesses, such as typhoid, for those living downstream in the increasingly crowded protectorate.

These and other findings from the 1976 medical evaluation established a baseline of health among the Waorani and highlighted the need for specific healthcare training and strategies. The researchers verified vaccination records not only for polio but also measles, yellow fever, DPT (diphtheria, pertussis, and tetanus), and BGC (tuberculosis).[37] They also analyzed the level of vaccination required for the Waorani to resist specific diseases and alerted SIL healthcare workers to potential danger from rubella as well as the probable future need for a malaria control program. The medical team also documented traditional medical practices and their connection to Wao cosmology, including beliefs about the role of the *ido* (a person who could curse others) in causing spirit-induced diseases.[38]

INDIGENOUS HEALTHCARE PROMOTERS

The SIL team offered the Waorani opportunities for basic training as healthcare promoters (paramedics) and, to a lesser extent, dental hygienists. Jung already had done some individualized training, but growing demand highlighted the need for a more structured program. Between 1979 and 1980 nurses Lois Pederson and Verla Cooper from SIL's clinic at Limoncocha helped train fourteen Wao health promoters who represented seven communities within the protectorate.[39] The training included ongoing mentoring and emphasized prevention as well as cure.

"When Ænkæde arrived at Limoncocha to help me with translation, the first thing he demanded was boiled water to drink, and wanted to know where he should throw his garbage!" reported Peeke.[40] Other Waorani learned to provide dental care, primarily how to encourage good dental hygiene and when and how to pull teeth—and when not to. Because of the training required and the dangers of working with mercury, filling cavities and other more complicated procedures were left for periodic dental clinics staffed by outsiders.[41] These efforts marked the beginning of ongoing healthcare training that eventually would be carried out by other agencies as the impact of outside contact on Wao health became ever more obvious.

Training indigenous paramedics and encouraging Waorani to use medicines more judiciously were official goals during the late 1970s. But SIL staff often were called on to respond to specific medical emergencies. That was Pat Kelley's experience in February 1978, when Wentæ, a Wao teenager about sixteen or seventeen, severed the femoral artery of his right leg in a spear fishing accident. His relatives carried him to the airstrip at Tzapino, the clearing where he lived. The next morning a small plane flew him, along with Kelley and Wentæ's aunt Dawa, to Limoncocha. SIL's DC-3 then arrived, having flown from Quito specifically to take Wentæ back to a hospital there.

Due to what might be considered miraculous circumstances (it was rare that unscheduled flights involving rainforests and Andes mountain passes could be coordinated so quickly), Wentæ was checked into the Vozandes mission hospital in Quito by 5:10 p.m. on the day after his accident. To save the teenager's leg, doctors did a graft to replace the six inches of artery that had been severed and damaged. The next two weeks were touch and go. Wentæ not only had survived the original accident and not bled to death, but with the help of the Vozandes staff and resident Ecuadorian doctors, he also lived through other brushes with death after the first operation. These included pulmonary edema, the rupture of the graft, the amputation of his leg, and a subsequent systemic infection as well as a localized infection on the stump of the amputated leg.

Dawa and Kelley spent days, and sometimes nights, at Wentæ's side. For Kelley, the experience meant trying to navigate a critical situation in two—sometimes three—very different languages and cultures. "The emotional load or price was heavier than anything else," she later reflected. "The initial incident, the decisions, the diagnosis, the possibilities or alternatives [including the issue of Wentæ's and Dawa's giving informed consent for the amputation] . . . attitudes, sounds and smells, infection, . . . pain, etc., etc." While the emotional load was draining, Kelley also faced the practicalities of providing plain boiled fish and traditional Wao banana drink several times a day to supplement Wentæ's diet, since he was unaccustomed to the standard hospital fare. Kelley became such a familiar figure around the hospital that one doctor jokingly threatened to make her "an honorary member of the intensive care ward."[42]

Dawa, a longtime Christian, emphasized to her nephew that God had let him live for a reason. Despite their faith, however, both Dawa and Kelley broke down at the prospect of Wentæ's amputation. How could he return to the rainforest, to the only life he had ever known, with only one leg? Although Kelley tried to stay positive, as she kept vigil at Wentæ's bedside the night before the amputation, the tears came. Wentæ woke up.

"Why are you crying?" he asked in *Wao tededo*.

"I'm crying for you," was her broken response.

"Don't you cry," he said firmly and quietly.

After doctors had removed his leg about six inches below the hip, Wentæ and Dawa prayed together. "Previously I lived well for you," Wentæ told God. "Then for awhile I lived saying no to you. Now . . . I will truly live responding to you."[43] After his release from the Quito hospital, Wentæ recuperated at Limoncocha for a few months until his stump healed and he could return home. Defying the odds, he managed to get around amazingly well. Two years later he was "walking for miles through the jungle on his crutches and spearing fish again."[44]

Not all accidents had happy endings. A few days after Wentæ returned home, Kelley was back in Quito with Violeta, a year-old Wao baby experiencing convulsions from a head injury. Doctors were unable to save the child, who died three weeks later.[45] These and other medical needs led Kelley to write her colleagues—all of whom were away from Ecuador during the first half of 1978—that instead of "holding down the fort," she was "holding down the hospital."[46]

SNAKES

While 1978 was Pat Kelley's year, all SIL staff working among the Waorani responded to medical emergencies at one time or another: broken bones, spear wounds from hunting or fishing, dynamite accidents, eye injuries caused by poorly made shotguns, measles that led to pneumonia, and, of course, cold viruses.[47] Team members, beginning with Saint, also routinely dealt with victims of snakebites and saved a number of lives through the use of antivenin and by training village health promoters to use it.

The 1976 medical research team confirmed what SIL staff suspected: the Waorani experienced an unusually high incidence of snakebite, especially during the rainy season. Almost 95 percent of adult males "had been bitten once and about half of the men had been bitten more than once."[48] Although the actual snake population varied from location to location, fifty-three species were observed in an investigation of a region just north of Wao territory. Of them, at least nine species (or about 17 percent) were venomous. Historically about 4 percent of all Wao deaths came from snakebite, significantly higher than the rates in adjacent indigenous populations and one of the highest percentages ever reported.[49]

Outsiders living among the Waorani also had to deal with the snakes. During her first year in Tewæno, Elisabeth Elliot calmly reported finding a coiled snake near Valerie's head while the child slept.[50] Years later Kelley wrote about one period of unusually frequent snake encounters in Tewæno, and for years Jung included a prayer for protection against snakes as part of her daily devotional.[51] In the end, none of the outsiders was bitten, likely because they rarely engaged in activities that carried an increased risk. Wao women often were bitten on the hands or arms while tending their manioc gardens. Men commonly were bitten on the foot or leg as they hunted in the early morning, walking quietly while focused on the forest canopy above.[52]

SIL's stated priorities during the late 1970s and early 1980s were translation, literacy, and healthcare, particularly the training of Wao health promoters. Yet it became increasingly clear that the most pressing issue affecting the cultural and physical survival of the Waorani was land. They needed enough land to pursue their traditional lifestyle, they needed titles to that land, and they needed ways to keep land-hungry outsiders from colonizing their territory. Ironically, however, as the Waorani were seeking greater territorial security to preserve their culture, many continued to be drawn by the pull of the outside world, particularly the practices of the nearby Quichuas. Critics charged SIL with ethnocide, but for some Waorani the desire to assimilate—to be like the Quichuas and to have what the Quichuas had—came from within.

14

Land, Literacy, and "Quichua-ization"

SUPPORT FOR WAORANI rights to their ancestral territories received an unexpected boost in the mid-1970s from a forestry project initiated by the United
Nations Food and Agriculture Organization (FAO). Between 1974 and 1976 two
FAO representatives, Allen Putney and Daan Vreugdenhil, worked with representatives from the Ecuadorian Department of National Parks and Forest Life to develop a conservation plan to protect Ecuador's most important native forests.[1] In
January 1976 Vreugdenhil and Jim Yost made an aerial survey of Wao territory as a
preliminary step in investigating the possibility of setting aside part of the land as
an ecological reserve or national park. A few months later Vreugdenhil returned to
do further research for a national park, accompanied by members of the Ecuadorian
Ministry of Agriculture and Ranching and of the French Office of Research and
Development Overseas.[2]

Yost, and occasionally Rachel Saint, served as guides and translators. The forestry
team met with representatives of the Wao communities of Tewæno and Tzapino to
discuss how much of their ancestral lands should belong directly to the Waorani
and the potential consequences of a national park. The Waorani wanted to extend
the boundaries of the protectorate eastward to encompass an additional large tract
of their ancestral lands. They sought to enlist the influence of Vreugdenhil and the
UN on their behalf.[3] The FAO forest protection project had no mandate or legal
authority to establish ethnic reserves or to adjudicate indigenous land claims, but
Vreugdenhil agreed to help however he could. As a result, the original proposal for

what would become the Yasuní National Park intentionally excluded a large expanse of Wao lands adjacent to both the protectorate and the park. The Waorani hoped to secure legal control of this area, where historically they had lived and hunted, even though large portions had been vacated because of oil exploration and the relocation.

In 1978 population counts indicated that approximately 525 Waorani, out of a total of fewer than 625, were living in the protectorate; in other words, an estimated 84 percent of the known Wao population occupied an area that represented about 8 percent of their ancestral territory.[4] Not only were oil companies working in areas recently inhabited by Waorani, but Quichuas and migrant farmers also were encroaching on the land. Texaco had just constructed the Via Auca, a road that bisected the northern portion of Wao territory, extending sixty miles due south from the town of Coca, parallel to the company's main oil pipeline into the area. Typically colonists followed such roads, exercising their legal right to homestead on either side. True to form, non-Waorani, including other indigenous people and colonists, quickly began to homestead along the Via Auca.[5]

To outsiders, it wasn't immediately obvious why additional land for the Waorani was so important. The 620 square miles of the protectorate seemed like plenty of room for a group of about six hundred, even with healthy population growth. To grant the Waorani rights to all 8,100 square miles of their ancestral territory seemed unnecessary or wasteful, even unfair, considering land shortages elsewhere in Ecuador. Official government land policies reflected a desire to integrate the region with the rest of the country, in part by encouraging migrants from the Ecuadorian Andes to homestead on "unoccupied" (indigenous) lands. However, fieldwork by Yost and Kelley between 1974 and 1977, as well as the research of the UN-Ecuadorian forest protection team, pointed to the need for a new approach.[6]

LAND AND CULTURE

While the standard government allotment of fifty hectares (about 124 acres) per family might be sufficient for small farmers, it would not support the semisedentary hunter-horticulturalist culture of the Waorani. Enabling Amazonian people to maintain their traditional ways of life required much more land than that necessary for physical survival. Yost argued that the land allotted to the Waorani "should be sufficient . . . [to] give them the option of maintaining their distinctive way of life indefinitely" without having to raise livestock or cultivate protein-intensive crops for survival.[7] In fact, traditional settlement patterns enabled the Waorani to inhabit land with some of the poorest soils in all of Ecuador—mostly clay, highly acidic, and with aluminum toxicity.[8] They planted their manioc gardens in ways that least disturbed the soil. Once a garden was harvested, the land was allowed to lie fallow for eight to twelve years before being planted again. The Waorani also moved between clearings two or three times a year, staggering their plantings so that they always had access to manioc ready for harvest.[9] This had the additional benefit of helping to preserve both the environment and the game in any given area, which would have time to replenish before the Waorani returned to plant and hunt again. These were sound practices—but required much land.

The expansive territory claimed by the Waorani also compensated for the fact that not all the area was equally habitable or productive. Significant portions frequently flooded during heavy rains, making them unsuitable for settlement or for hunting. In addition, the Waorani long had observed that certain areas were not good for gardens and didn't sustain the usual amount of game or of the nuts, berries, and other foods they gathered.[10] When these and other factors were considered, the land traditionally claimed by the group turned out to be an appropriate size to maintain their cultural heritage and identity.

Government action on land issues picked up with the election of Jaime Roldós Aguilera as president of Ecuador. During his brief tenure in office (1979–81), Roldós expressed greater support for indigenous peoples and their rights than had previous presidents. In August 1980 an Interinstitutional Commission of the Ministry of Agriculture and Ranching was established to coordinate various governmental agencies within the ministry that had authority over issues related to land and native peoples.[11] Supported by the American NGO Cultural Survival, the Ecuadorian commission initiated an Indian lands demarcation project to determine the territorial needs of the Cofán, Siona, Secoya, and Waorani.

Regarding the Waorani, the commission's work built on Yost's earlier research, supplemented by further investigations. Yost walked nearly four hundred miles in one seventeen-day period in 1980, tracing the boundaries of Wao land.[12] Two Ecuadorian officials—an anthropologist, Enrique Vela, who headed the commission, and Jorge Uquillas, a sociologist, consultant, and commission member—took an interest in the Waorani. In his role as liaison between the Waorani and the Ecuadorian government, Vela visited Wao territory several times between 1979 and 1981 to find out about land needs and boundaries.[13]

Jorge Uquillas worked within the Ecuadorian National Institute for Amazonian Colonization and the Institute for Agrarian Reform and Colonization to make sure legal foundations were laid for the allocation of Wao territory during the 1980s and 1990s. The proposal reflected many of the same ideas that were discussed with Vreugdenhil. First would be the protectorate, legally owned by Wao communities; a second, adjacent tract would be an "ethnic reserve," additional land for the Waorani to hunt and live that would also be a protected area for Waorani who chose to live in isolation from the outside world. The rest would become a part of the Yasuní National Park.

The authority of the Ecuadorian National Institute for Amazonian Colonization and the Institute for Agrarian Reform and Colonization, plus years of combined efforts and legwork by the Waorani, Vela, Uquillas, and Yost, with the support of Cultural Survival, culminated in a visit by President Osvaldo Hurtado, Roldós's successor, to Wao territory in April 1983. Hurtado awarded specific groups of Waorani title to the lands of the protectorate. He promised the establishment of the Waorani Ethnic Reserve and acknowledged the Waorani's right of access to the ethnic reserve and the Yasuní National Park. Uquillas, who was in attendance, had spent the previous week traveling to Wao communities to emphasize that it was the government commissions, Yost, and the Waorani themselves who had made the land grants possible.[14]

The status and boundaries of the ethnic reserve would be revisited in subsequent years, and in April 1990 the Ecuadorian government would grant the Waorani legal title to this land, more than 600,000 hectares (about 1.5 million acres) that represented "the largest reserve of indigenous land" in Ecuador (map 5).[15] The Waorani Ethnic Reserve and the adjacent Yasuní National Park included about 85 percent of Wao ancestral territory. Despite government recognition of their land rights, the Waorani faced ongoing and often losing battles to keep colonists out and to curb deforestation as migrants from other regions of Ecuador flooded into the eastern rainforests, as many as 350,000 people between 1970 and 1992.[16] Nonetheless efforts during the late 1970s and early 1980s were crucial in laying the groundwork to establish Waorani rights and titles to a significant portion of their ancestral territory.

LITERACY AND EDUCATION

By 1980 Waorani in some clearings could write government officials on their own, thanks to Kelley and the native literacy teachers she trained. These early letters, written in *Wao tededo* and translated into Spanish, expressed concern over land issues. For example, representatives from Toñæmpade wrote Enrique Vela, voicing frustration and impatience over government inaction as outsiders violated their territorial boundaries. Their representatives wrote, in part:

> Listen here, we are Waorani. . . . We emphatically reject the cowode coming in on our land. . . . They have . . . poisoned the fish in our rivers and our game is disappearing.

Listen, government, immediately write that this is Waorani land. . . . What in the world is holding you up?[17]

As this letter suggests, access to the outside world increased the need for literacy as the Waorani sought to support their land claims, sell their artifacts, interact with tourists and other visitors, and assume some responsibility for first aid and health-care.[18] During the ten years (1972–82) that Kelley worked to develop and implement a literacy program, the Waorani were overwhelmingly monolingual. In 1972 fewer than 2 percent knew any Spanish, a rate that increased to about 6 percent a decade later.[19] Since most people continued to speak only *Wao tededo*, Kelley's approach was primarily monolingual, although she continued to incorporate basic instruction in spoken Spanish. Despite Kelley's successes and her commitment to culturally appropriate instruction, the Wao literacy program faced numerous challenges. These included pressures to establish fiscal (government-sanctioned) primary schools where education would take place entirely in Spanish, the need to finalize an orthography (alphabet and spelling) best suited for reading and writing *Wao tededo*, and ways to cope with the inevitable changes literacy education brought to Wao culture.

The first fiscal school for Wao children opened in 1973 at Dayono, the clearing established by Zoila Wiñame and her followers after they left Tewæno. Wiñame contacted David Miller, a Christian and Missionary Alliance missionary, to request that he begin a school in the clearing. Miller already supervised numerous small churches and other Protestant mission sites up and down the Napo River, as well as six government primary schools at various locations along the river. In August 1972 Miller, his friend Dick Brown, and a Quichua pastor and schoolteacher named Pedro Chimbo made the rigorous forty-mile trip from the town of Dos Rios to Dayono. They clambered through virgin jungle, tried to dodge excrement thrown by irate spider monkeys in the jungle canopy, then took canoes and a raft down the Nushiño River. After meeting with Wiñame and other Waorani, Miller agreed to seek approval for a government school, with Chimbo as the teacher.[20]

The school began the following year with the first grade, adding a grade each year until the primary grades were complete. All instruction was in Spanish; pupils had to learn the language along with the subject matter. Miller made no apologies for Spanish-language instruction. His experiences with the bilingual approach among Quichua children had been "very negative," especially for girls. Quichua girls spent three years gaining literacy in their native language before starting first grade in Spanish. By the time they had finished the six primary grades, they had spent nine years in school, and many were old enough to marry. As a result, girls did not go on to high school and, from Miller's perspective, ended their education too soon. He did not want the pattern repeated among the Waorani.[21]

Miller also responded pragmatically to the possibility that Spanish-language instruction might lead to a devaluing and ultimate loss of *Wao tededo*. From his perspective, "many thousands of languages [had] been lost" throughout history. Some languages died; others became dominant. People learned them and went on with their lives. Miller "didn't see any problem" should the same thing happen to the Waorani. There was a clear philosophical divide between him and the SIL staff on this point. The Dayono community, however, wanted Pedro Chimbo and Spanish-language instruction.[22] The fiscal school was a point of pride, reflecting the desire of the Waorani in Dayono to be like the nearby lowland Quichuas.

Five years later a second fiscal school was established under similar circumstances. Waorani from the new clearing of Toñæmpade approached a Plymouth Brethren missionary, Lloyd ("Daniel") Rogers, to request a fiscal school. From his mission station at Arajuno, not far from the protectorate, Rogers had been working with the Ecuadorian government to establish schools in indigenous (mostly Quichua) communities. Dayomæ had contacted him repeatedly, asking for help. Rogers was hesitant, reluctant to compete with SIL literacy work. He also knew that Toñæmpade had been established by Dayomæ and others after SIL had begun to curtail its transport of trade goods into Tewæno. The new settlement was within easy walking distance to the spot on the Curaray River where the five missionaries had been speared in 1956. The Waorani wanted a school and airstrip to establish the legitimacy of the community and to attract tourists and goods. It was also a way for Dayomæ to shore up her influence in Rachel Saint's absence. The Ecuadorian provincial director of education encouraged Rogers to take on the school, observing that the Waorani also had contacted a local priest and that Catholic-Protestant competition in Toñæmpade might not be in anyone's best interest. In the end, Rogers agreed. A fiscal school, staffed by a Quichua teacher, opened in October 1978.[23]

Rogers was ambivalent about the impact of the school. As an evangelical missionary he believed that literacy—and literacy in Spanish, if that was what the Waorani wanted—was essential to healthy indigenous Christianity.[24] The emphasis on Spanish in the fiscal schools also opened the possibility that over time Rogers and subsequent colleagues could pursue religious work among the Waorani without the need for fluency in the difficult *Wao tededo*. Yet Rogers recognized that there were limits to the control missionaries could exert over government schools. He knew that government teachers, usually Quichua men (due to a government mandate that indigenous children be taught by indigenous teachers), could be bad influences in Wao communities, especially those teachers with minimal adherence to Christianity. Even exemplary teachers still opened the door to increased Quichua influence.

Venancio Grefa, the first teacher at the Toñæmpade school, proved dedicated and competent, although the task of using Spanish to teach monolingual *Wao tededo* speakers was daunting.[25] His assistant, a Quichua man married to a Wao woman, was sacked at the end of the first term for being a poor example for the children. The school year that began in October 1979 saw SIL working with Grefa and Rogers to create a modified bilingual approach. Pat Kelley and Catherine Peeke suggested that two Wao literacy trainees, Nancy, Dayomæ's daughter, who was fluent in reading and writing *Wao tededo*, and Miipo, a young man who had attended the Tewæno men's literacy class, be hired to help. They could teach a preparatory "first grade" (reading readiness and basic literacy) in the Wao language for Toñæmpade children who had not yet enrolled in the already crowded fiscal school. The two teachers could share a stipend from the Ministry of Education. However, a month after the plan was implemented, Dayomæ intervened, pressuring Miipo and Nancy to resign in favor of an aide of her choosing.[26]

The SIL staff let Rogers sort out the matter. A month later Miipo was back—no one quite knew why—facing a class of about twenty small children. Barely literate himself, Miipo was one of the least qualified of the Wao instructors. But as Kelley noted, he was the only one willing to take on a class at Toñæmpade, where Dayomæ called the shots. As its founders had hoped, the government school, frequent tourist visits, and plenty of contact with Quichuas drew Waorani to Toñæmpade. By the time Yost carried out a census in 1980, the community had a population of 119.[27]

Not everyone found the larger community attractive. Guequita, one of the original residents of Tewæno, rejected the cultural chaos and sexual laxity that Toñæmpade came to represent and refused to let his children attend the government school. He moved his family group, about fifty people, to an isolated clearing. However, they were open to literacy instruction in *Wao tededo*, and one of Kelley's trainees agreed to go. At the same time, the Pastaza Provincial Office of Education assigned four Wao literacy teachers to communities in the protectorate, and there was the prospect of two more Wao teachers receiving appointments.[28]

CHOOSING THE RIGHT ALPHABET

One of the crucial tasks Kelley faced during her decade as the Wao literacy field-worker involved collaborating with Peeke and the Waorani in establishing an appropriate orthography (alphabet and spelling) for written *Wao tededo*. The goal was to establish an alphabet that would "closely reflect the linguistic reality of the language" for native speakers.[29] The orthography in use when Kelley arrived in 1972, and which she used initially, consisted of fifteen vowels and fourteen consonants. As the Waorani learned to read and write, it became clear that this alphabet overdifferentiated the nasalization that was a prominent feature of the language. That is, the alphabet included inconsistent and multiple ways to indicate nasalization. This confused and overwhelmed both instructors and students because they were being cued to do things in their reading and writing they normally did automatically, just as English speakers would automatically change an "s" to a "z" sound when they read "pads," in contrast to "pats."[30]

In 1978, after several experimental revisions with Waorani input, Peeke and Kelley settled on a more straightforward alphabet consisting of five oral vowels, five nasal vowels, and eight consonants: eighteen letters instead of the original twenty-nine. This simplified alphabet reflected the reality of *Wao tededo* and worked well for native speakers. Objections came from non-Waorani, however, for whom the alphabet was underdifferentiated and who therefore were required to learn pronunciation rules until they internalized the system. Outsiders also had to master unfamiliar vowel sounds since the *Wao tededo* alphabet included several letters, mostly nasalized vowels, that were not a part of the Spanish alphabet.[31]

In essence, to simplify literacy for the Waorani and to maintain the integrity of *Wao tededo*, the linguists chose an alphabet that favored native speakers and their language. Peeke's research had indicated that *Wao tededo* was a "linguistic isolate," an independent language unrelated to any other language, whether Spanish or indigenous.[32] Kelley argued that acceptance of *Wao tededo* by national educators and other outsiders would demonstrate respect for "the uniqueness of 'the people' and the complexity of the language they all speak."[33]

Kelley also hoped that as the Waorani became literate, they would create their own record of their culture. The foundational literacy materials produced between 1973 and 1982 included a preprimer and a series of six primers. The preprimer focused on reading readiness, while primers 1 through 3 introduced all the letters and letter combinations of the Wao alphabet, as well as instruction in the basics of writing. Primers 4 through 6 emphasized reading and cursive writing; these books were structured around texts written by students or transcribed from oral stories. The Waorani wrote about snakebite, gathering leafcutter ants, all-night fiesta dancing, an alligator night hunt (which included the participation of Wentæ on crutches), a jaguar attack, and more.[34]

The emphasis on native-authored literature also reflected Kelley's curiosity about the flora and fauna of the rainforest. She got the people to identify different species of fish, birds, and other animals. It once took three tries, even working from a photograph, for Kelley to draw an acceptable *oba* (type of armored catfish) that her literacy students would approve as a primer illustration.[35] In contrast, the Spanish-language fiscal schools used a standard curriculum that included lessons emphasizing the shared culture of modern Ecuador. Amid the escalating pressures of the outside world, Kelley hoped that literacy in *Wao tededo* would help the Waorani to preserve their identity as a distinct people, and—central to the mission of SIL—that it would enable them to read and contribute to a Bible translation in their own, unique language.

ADAPTING EDUCATION TO CULTURE

Kelley became an itinerant teacher, holding literacy classes and training Wao instructors in various clearings so that the people could learn to read without having to travel. Her ease in relating to the Waorani made Kelley welcome in many clearings. Even so, teaching—or mentoring teachers—had its ups and downs. For instance, she arrived in one location to supervise a young literacy instructor who had just returned home after having been married. Classes hadn't been held for some time, and the school showed definite deterioration. A small chalkboard at the front of the room was streaked and separated from its plywood backing due to rain leaking through the roof and walls. Visiting Quichuas had stayed in the school when they had attended a fiesta in the clearing. Apparently they had opened a metal can storing school supplies and had taken or destroyed most of its contents. The few primers and notebooks that had been left on a bookshelf were disintegrating thanks to termites and wood ants.

Nonetheless classes began. A few days later a storm blew the thatch off the peak of the school roof. While the children's class watched and the downpour continued, the Wao instructor climbed up through the gap to retrieve and repair the thatch. Over the weekend, government malaria sprayers arrived to fumigate all the structures in the village. After they finished with the school, the instructor stepped in to survey the white film of DDT on the benches, the walls, even the inside of the roof. "It stinks!" he declared. Despite his new wife's efforts to clean off the residue, the smell lingered for days.[36]

By the early 1980s the literacy program had established *Wao tededo* as a language that could be read and written, with the beginnings of its own native-authored literature. Not only the primers but instructional guides, typing charts, arithmetic exercises, a first-aid and hygiene booklet, and other materials—all in *Wao tededo*—gave the Waorani some basis for autonomous literacy education and healthcare. Despite these achievements, however, when Kelley left Ecuador in 1982, monolingual education, even when some basic Spanish was included, faced an uphill battle. There were pressures from the Ecuadorian state, the Quichuas, and the Waorani themselves.

CITIZENS OF ECUADOR

Some of the different agendas were obvious during a 1980 visit to the Tewæno school by Ecuador's minister of education. The children were prepped to stand when the minister entered the school so he could instruct them to be seated (actions with no significance in Wao culture). Ñiiwa, the Wao literacy instructor, had a notebook listing the students in each class, as well as their attendance record. So far, all was in order. Then, Kelley reported, the school began to "lose points," first when the minister discovered that Ñiiwa did not give grades to the students. Kelley tried to explain that the instructor corrected student notebooks and kept track of the progress each one made as he or she completed the sequence of primers. Unconvinced, the minister persisted, "But doesn't he have any records of the grades and progress?"[37]

The visiting officials also wanted to be sure that the children knew they were Ecuadorians. "Did they know the colors of the flag, etc., etc." Intimidated, the children "weren't about to utter one peep."[38] When the officials insisted that the children respond, Kelley sought to salvage the situation by suggesting that the minister lead the children in the national anthem. They all trooped outside to gather around the flagpole and Ecuadorian flag that had been taken out of storage for the occasion. With the minister leading, all present managed to make it through the anthem— the minister leading in Spanish, the children and instructor trailing along behind. After the visit, a disappointed Kelley wrote that the minister probably thought "they don't know a dignitary out there when they see one and the señorita . . . speaks lousy Spanish [and] doesn't teach them how to keep grades."[39] Incidents like this reinforced the accusation that culturally appropriate, monolingual education did not have the structure or the content to help indigenous children assimilate into the broader culture of Ecuador.

Many Waorani were concerned about assimilation as well, although the outside culture they most wanted to emulate was not that of the Ecuadorian state but that of their next-door neighbors. As had been the case for Dayomæ many years earlier, for most Waorani the Quichuas symbolized what it meant to be "civilized." Fiscal schools were important to the Waorani not so that they could say "Somos Ecuatorianos" (We are Ecuadorians) but because, for the most part, Quichua children were educated in fiscal schools. The native-authored books produced under Kelley's tutelage may have been popular, but the Quichuas knew, and were not afraid to say, that "real" education took place in Spanish.[40] However, the Waorani as a group had not yet experienced the consequences of state-sponsored education. For example, fiscal schools required an increasingly sedentary life so that children could attend the required 159 days per calendar year.[41] And while children might gain facility in Spanish and other educational skills, they would have less time to master the ways of the rainforest, the basis of Wao culture and identity.

LIVING LIKE THE QUICHUAS

From the mid-1970s to the early 1980s, education was only one of many ways the Waorani were susceptible to the influence of their Quichua neighbors. Others, some already touched upon, included the location and style of housing, marriage patterns, the accumulation of manufactured goods, religious expression, and hunting practices. Yost wrote with concern of a "generally growing disdain for their own Waodani culture, in light of all which appears so desirable, and yet is so little understood, in the outside culture—primarily the Quichua."[42] Leading the way were Dayomæ, Wiñame, and a third woman, Olga, all of whom had spent their formative years among Quichua speakers.[43] It was no accident that as people began to leave Tewæno, among the earliest of the new clearings were three founded by these women. The locations were based in part on increased accessibility to the outside world. Waorani in other clearings depended upon these women as well, at least initially, to facilitate their communication with outsiders.[44] Less obvious, but also influential as cultural brokers, were a handful of Quichua men, among them Benito, Cochi, and Eusibio, who had married Wao women.

An early indication of the power (and peril) of Waorani-Quichua contact had come in 1974, when four Wao men were drawn into a Quichua feud. At the center of the conflict was a self-identified sorcerer, hated and feared in the Quichua community. Another Quichua man who had married a Wao woman and had lived in the Tewæno area for at least a decade persuaded the Waorani to act as hit men and kill the alleged sorcerer. Speared along with him were his wife and uncle. In effect, the Quichuas used the Waorani to carry out vigilante-style justice. Two of the Wao killers were baptized Christians and lived in Tewæno. One later expressed deep remorse for his participation; the other apparently saw no harm in killing a Quichua under these circumstances.[45]

Trying to understand the killings, Yost believed that the "Waorani were vulnerable because they were engaged in strengthening ties with Quichuas and may have felt obligated." At the same time, the "Waorani idolize [the] Quichua because they seem [to be the] next step up on the social ladder, yet not as strange as other outsiders." Finally, the request had come "through a very respected and trusted . . . bicultural person who acts as a representative agent of the Quichua culture to the Waorani."[46] Yost emphasized that he was not excusing the murders but seeking to understand what true justice might entail. Some people suggested the Quichua instigator used the Waorani to settle his personal accounts rather than acting on behalf of the community. Peeke later lamented that the Waorani continued to accept this man despite all the ways he had "wronged" and "cheated" them over the years.[47] Yet he continued to facilitate the contact with the Quichuas that they wanted so badly.

NEW STYLES OF HOME AND HEARTH

The headlong rush by Waorani in the protectorate to imitate the Quichuas was first evident in home construction and in the accumulation of goods. For years some Waorani had built their homes with the floor a few feet off the ground, Quichua style; now the practice began to spread widely. Also following the Quichuas, people added walls, platform beds rather than hammocks, blankets and sometimes mosquito nets, as well as sandbox stoves inside the house for warmth and cooking.[48] As houses became more substantial, so did the amount of goods to put in them. The 1970s saw more and more people acquiring aluminum pots, shotguns, radios, soap, and a variety of foods, among them new staples: sugar, salt, rice, and lentils. People continued to buy clothing, but now as much for adornment as to identify themselves as civilized.[49]

In the late 1960s, when they were still encouraging a sedentary life in the protectorate, SIL introduced the Waorani to chickens, ducks, turkeys, and a starter herd of a few pure-bred Brahmin cattle. Contact with Quichuas had boosted Waorani interest in these and other animals during the 1970s, after the SIL team had recognized the error of trying to raise cattle in the rainforest. Peeke wrote of "the damage cattle are doing to the crops. And the water supply. And the night's sleep," not to mention the misery of the "poor, skinny beasts" themselves. To further complicate matters, the Waorani did not raise cattle to feed themselves but to sell beef outside the protectorate for cash.[50] This meant the animals had to be butchered, and the meat taken out by plane to be sold. The pilots who served the Waorani did not consider the messy commercial beef transport part of their missionary job description, even when their agencies were reimbursed for the cost. All of this was far from the simplicity of Wao domestic life that Elisabeth Elliot described when she and Rachel Saint first arrived in Tewæno.[51]

"HIGH-TECH" HUNTING

The Waorani also took to shotguns, the novel and "high-tech" approach used by some Quichuas for hunting. In January 1974 there were only three shotguns among all adult Wao men; by the early 1980s the number had increased to sixty-six shotguns among 194 male hunters (or about one for every three men). Most of the guns were poor-quality, locally made 16-guage, single-shot breechloaders.[52] Shoddy workmanship notwithstanding, the guns were expensive, as were the cartridges. A Wao man would have to work for about two months to make enough tourist-quality blowguns or spears that he could sell to buy a gun. Despite the expense, shotguns were attractive for the aesthetic pleasure they offered, which Yost enumerated: "shiny, smooth metal, mechanisms that click, the polished wood stock, and that beautiful sense of power in the kick and boom."[53]

A study carried out by Yost and Kelley revealed that a shotgun was 1.5 times more efficient in obtaining meat (protein) for the Waorani than the traditional blowgun alone and 1.22 times more effective than the combined results of hunting with blowgun and spear. This was primarily because of the shotgun's versatility. A Wao hunter with a shotgun was more successful in killing large animals than a man with a spear, and the gun could also be used for hunting smaller animals in the canopy, such as monkeys. With shotguns, the Waorani spent the same amount of time hunting as before but brought home an increased amount of meat, in one village about 33 percent more per hunt.[54]

Because of their effectiveness in killing large land animals, particularly wild pigs, shotguns had an ecological impact, contributing to the scarcity of game in areas where guns were used frequently. However, their impact paled in comparison to the effects of two new technologies borrowed from the Quichuas for fishing. These were the use of dynamite and DDT. Sticks of dynamite, known as "tacos," were easy to buy or steal from oil company workers who used them in seismic explorations. When tourists began to visit Toñæmpade, some even brought dynamite as partial payment for food and lodging.[55]

To "fish," the Quichuas and then the Waorani would throw lighted sticks of dynamite into a river, stunning hundreds of fish that would float to the surface, where they could be gathered by the basketful. The Waorani were delighted by the abundance and unconcerned about the long-term consequences of depleted rivers and damaged ecosystems. Even when dynamite began to yield fewer fish, the Waorani continued to use it, fascinated by the explosions and by the satisfaction of possessing this new technology.[56] Peeke attempted to explain the long-term damage that would result, but her words fell on deaf ears. The fish wouldn't disappear while this generation of Waorani were alive, they told her, and their children would just have to fend for themselves. Their response reflected both the radical independence of the Waorani (every person must care for himself or herself) and the difficulty in comprehending the reality of environmental destruction by people not previously capable of such damage.[57]

The use of DDT to poison fish was much less widespread but more harmful. The Waorani already had a natural poison, barbasco, made from a jungle plant. Dumped into a pool or slow-moving water, barbasco would stun fish when it passed through the gills, then the fish would float to the surface for the hunters to collect. DDT did the same thing except that it was more toxic, which led to a greater yield of fish—at least until the fish in nearby rivers had been killed. On several occasions, Dayomæ bought the pesticide from the government "malaria men," who used it liberally to eradicate mosquitos. The Quichuas encouraged this more intense fishing because of its efficiency. Fortunately for the health of all concerned, fish caught with DDT had a bad taste, which limited its popularity.[58]

IMITATING QUICHUA CHRISTIANITY

The desire among Waorani living in the protectorate to imitate all things Quichua extended to the Quichua practice of evangelical Christianity. Attempting to foster a more indigenized faith, SIL encouraged Quichua pastors to preach to the Waorani, beginning with a 1975 Bible Conference in Tewæno led by Pastor Gervacio Cerda. Cerda preached in Quichua with Dayomæ translating. About two hundred Waorani attended, and, even during Cerda's sermons, people interrupted to confess sins or profess faith. The Waorani also tried to learn the words as Cerda and his family sang Quichua songs. On Sunday, at the close of the four-day conference, fifty people were baptized. SIL staff were cautious about the significance of that number. Some Waorani already were believers when they arrived at the conference but had not been baptized. Others, Peeke observed, might have done so for "social advantages." (Some Wao believers wanted their children to marry only other baptized believers, which was difficult given the limited option for spouses within traditional Wao norms.)[59] Even so, the Waorani had responded to a Quichua preacher. The trend toward a more Quichua-ized Christianity was reinforced by the two Quichua men appointed as teachers for the fiscal schools in Dayono and Toñæmpade—Pedro Chimbo and Venancio Grefa, respectively. Both were also evangelical pastors. By 1978 Quichua hymns had become a common feature of Wao church services.[60]

In 1981 European critics of SIL published a book titled *Is God an American?* The question was posed in the context of the Cold War, suggesting that when religiously conservative groups such as SIL identified Communism with Satan, they tended at the same time to bring an American view of God into tribal groups.[61] This was not the case with the Waorani. Their understanding of God was culturally more Quichuan than American. All this imitation of Quichuas put Waorani at risk of ethnocide, Yost observed gloomily, "but they *want* it."[62]

Even as the Waorani imitated Quichua culture, they were divided over whether they wanted actual Quichuas in their territory. In pursuit of social equality and financial gain, Dayomæ and the Toñæmpade community encouraged Quichua traders and visitors. Other clearings resented their presence.[63] For their part, the lowland Quichuas, who in some estimates of total population outnumbered the Waorani roughly thirty to one, sought land they could claim as squatters, along with cheap fish and meat from the game in the protectorate.[64] The second half of the 1970s also saw a brisk trade in Waorani selling meat from the protectorate to Quichua consumers.

MORE MIXED MARRIAGES

Of the many changes that took place, the most potentially disruptive to Wao culture were marriages between Quichuas and Waorani.[65] As already described, a few marriages between Quichua men and Wao women had taken place since peaceful contact in 1958. However, the trend accelerated between 1974 and 1981. Precise figures are difficult to find, but a conservative estimate would be between six and eight marriages. Yost's 1980 census of the Waorani listed nine outsiders (most probably Quichuas) living in various clearings inside the protectorate and nine Waorani (eight women and one man) living outside Wao territory.[66] Not all represented Wao-Quichua unions, but some certainly did. Dayomæ and her husband, Come, were key matchmakers in arranging many of the marriages, including one for their daughter Nancy. For Dayomæ it was a way to create ties that bound her family to the Quichuas.[67]

While marrying an outsider might have seemed a step up from what others viewed as the lowest rung of the social and cultural ladder in Ecuador, the nuptials came at a cultural price. Every Wao who married a *cowode* represented one fewer potential spouse within the tribe. For a small, traditionally closed society that had strict rules about appropriate spouses, losing even a few people was significant. It led to increased friction within kinship groups, "where the expectation would have been for weddings to have sealed inter-kin-group bonds among the Waorani."[68] Choosing a *cowode* represented a rejection of culturally prescribed patterns for Wao marriages. The children of these unions would have no defined place in Wao culture; traditionally, they were not considered Waorani. If these children tried to marry within the tribe, this would lead to the breakdown of the whole system of cross-cousin marriages, with devastating cultural consequences. There were other concerns as well. Wao-Quichua unions raised the possibility of some Quichuas gaining legal right to land inside the protectorate.[69] Peeke envisioned the relatives of Quichua spouses "pouring in" to the protectorate, while at the same time they would be "carrying out natural resources wholesale."[70]

EARLY INTERACTION WITH OIL COMPANIES

The Waorani, especially those in the protectorate, focused much of their attention on contacts with Quichuas during the 1970s. But increased access led to relationships with other outsiders as well. The list included oil companies, national and international tourist agencies, Catholic missionaries, and government entities, not to mention short-term encounters with researchers, filmmakers, and journalists. Their presence added to the complexity of the relationships between Waorani and non-Waorani.

For most adult Wao men, working for an oil company, known generically as *la cía* (short for *la compañía*) was their first experience with wage labor. For exploratory purposes, the Ecuadorian state had divided Wao lands into concessions (blocks of land), which, in turn, were awarded to multinational companies.[71] Much of the initial seismic exploration in the field was carried out by a French geophysical company, Compagnie Générale du Géophysique (CGG) under contract to Ecuador's state-run petroleum company, Corporación Estatal Petrolera Ecuatoriana (later Petroecuador). CGG would hire crews, including a few Wao workers, to cut a grid of paths through the jungle with holes every hundred meters along the way where charges of dynamite would be placed. The sound waves from the explosions were used to map the subterranean stratified rock structure.[72] While it created jobs for locals, the exploratory work was disruptive to indigenous people and wildlife living nearby. It also brought work crews and Waorani into proximity.

The official policy of most companies, including the CGG, toward the Waorani was to avoid conflict. They would do whatever was necessary to keep the Waorani from attacking crews in the field. This included a liberal distribution of goods. Although the policy had the long-term effect of encouraging the Waorani to view the oil companies as inexhaustible sources of largesse, it did seem to work. Only four fatalities from Wao attacks on oil company workers were recorded during the 1970s. One, on March 31, 1971, was a cook, working for the Occidental Exploration and Production Company (la Western). The others, on November 3, 1977, were three employees of the CGG. Both attacks were blamed on the elusive group known as the Tagæidi.[73] In contrast to most Waorani, the Tagæidi had chosen isolation from the outside world. The challenge was to keep this Wao group from killing oil workers who entered their territory so that the Tagæidi, in turn, would not be destroyed. Company officials wanted help. This time, however, they found it not with SIL but with Catholic missionaries, especially one dedicated priest, in a little-known chapter of missionary-Waorani history.

15

Catholics and the Waorani

THE KEY FIGURE behind Catholic efforts to contact the Waorani was Alejandro Labaca Ugarte, a member of the Capuchín order of missionary friars. A Spaniard from the deeply Catholic Basque region of that country, Labaca (1920–87) entered the Capuchín order in 1937, took his final vows in 1942, and was ordained a priest in 1945.[1] He served in China from 1947 until expelled by the Communist regime in 1953. Six months later he was assigned to Ecuador, where he spent the rest of his life. In January 1965, after serving for over a decade in various administrative positions, Labaca was named apostolic prefect of Aguarico—that is, the supervisor of a missionary region not yet established as a diocese by the Catholic Church. The prefecture of Aguarico encompassed about 11,200 square miles in the eastern rainforests of Ecuador, including the area on both sides of the Napo River from the town of Coca eastward to the Peruvian border, and extending south to include about 80 percent of traditional Wao territory.[2]

Shortly after he was named prefect, Labaca met with the papal nuncio in Ecuador, who asked Labaca in the name of the Holy See to assume responsibility for the "Auca problem" and for all of Wao territory, even though some of the land fell within the jurisdiction of the Josephine Fathers' mission.[3] The "problem," Labaca soon discovered, was that the Capuchín mission had not made peaceful contact with the Waorani and also that the Waorani were killing Quichuas and others living along the Napo with disturbing regularity. A dozen people had been speared in surprise attacks between 1958 and 1965.[4]

The new prefect wasted little time in getting started, renting a DC-3 in May 1965 so that he and two other priests could get aerial views of Wao clearings. Taking off from Nuevo Rocafuerte, they flew southwest for thirty-seven minutes to the Cononaco River, near where it was joined by the Shiripuno River, more than half the width of Wao territory, east to west. Near the junction of the Cononaco and Shiripuno, they saw a cluster of Wao houses and could make out eight or ten Waorani who emerged to look up at the sky. Then they turned north toward the small town of Coca. Along that route, they spotted a large longhouse. Encouraged by the sightings, Labaca organized two expeditions by canoe and over land, one in July 1965, the other in late August. However, he soon found out that it was easier to catch glimpses of the Waorani from the air than to encounter them on the ground. The expeditions saw some evidence of Waorani—an old spear, footprints, and some broken branches—but not the people themselves.[5]

After these disappointments, Labaca's sense of mission was renewed through his participation in the final stage of the Second Vatican Council, September 14 to December 8, 1965. During this period, delegates approved eleven of the sixteen documents that came out of the council. The last to be approved, after extensive revisions, was *Ad Gentes Divinitus*, the Decree on the Missionary Activity of the Church. Labaca was particularly moved by one section of the decree. It taught that, following Christ, missionaries should implant themselves among the people and culture to which they had been sent and should be attentive to "seeds of the Word which lie hidden among them."[6] The emphasis on incarnational mission and on potential "seeds of the Word" among the Waorani would shape Labaca's later missionary strategy.

While in Rome, Labaca wrote a letter to Pope Paul VI, expressing his desire to obey "the command of Christ to preach to all people, especially to [the] AUCAS." He sought the pope's advice about how far he should go in risking the lives of other missionaries, of local people, and his own life in this effort. Paul did not reply directly. However, during a group audience with the bishops of Ecuador, which Labaca also attended, the pope greeted him with a smile and the words "¡Animo, ánimo!" (Courage, courage!). To Labaca, that brief encounter represented a papal blessing on attempts to contact the Waorani, despite the risks involved.[7]

THE CAPUCHÍNS ACQUIRE A PLANE

Labaca also took advantage of his time in Rome to raise money to provide the Capuchín mission with a small plane, a Cessna 185, which arrived in Coca in March 1966.[8] Flying out of Coca, the missionaries began to map the locations of Wao clearings, determining land routes to the sites. They were doing so at about the same time that Rachel Saint and the Tewæno Waorani were beginning their efforts to find and relocate many of the same "downriver people" to Tewæno.[9] The Capuchín aerial investigations revealed that several Wao clearings, especially those near the Napo River, had been deserted and the houses burned. The Waorani were nowhere to be seen.

With their mission to the Waorani at a standstill once again, the Capuchíns faced a new, even greater challenge: *colonos* (settlers) from the highlands, flooding the Oriente looking for work in the oil fields and for land to homestead. Relatively easy access to the rainforest via oil roads from Quito to Lago Agrio, then from Lago Agrio to Coca, put the newcomers in the northern sector of the Capuchín mission. For the first half of the 1970s, the priests had their hands full meeting the social and spiritual needs of this population. In light of these demands, they relinquished the airplane as too expensive to maintain and operate. That decision marked the close of the first chapter of Catholic attempts to contact the Waorani.[10]

For about eight years, from 1968 to 1976, Labaca also focused his energy elsewhere. In 1970 he resigned from his post as apostolic prefect, citing physical and spiritual exhaustion. For the next few years he worked as a "simple, frail" missionary, fulfilling various assignments that eventually took him to Nuevo Rocafuerte, a town at the eastern edge of the Ecuadorian Amazon, where the Yasuní River flowed into the Napo, only a few miles from the Peruvian border. Between 1976 and 1980 Labaca sought once again to become a missionary to the Waorani. This time he would be successful, at least in the short term.

By July 1976 the French geophysical company CGG had teams engaged in seismic exploration very close to Wao clearings, near the headwaters of the Dicado River and its tributaries, about sixty miles west of Nuevo Rocafuerte (map 4). Dicado was the Wao name given to the upper reaches of the Yasuní River. The Waorani living there were a subgroup of the Wepeidi (Wepe's bunch), sometimes referred to by SIL as the "Ridge Aucas," because they previously lived on a ridge along the Gabado River where SIL had an airstrip. In the mid-1970s, when, at Jim Yost's urging, SIL curtailed flights from the ridge to Tewæno, the Wepeidi began to scatter. Those who moved near the Dicado River had experienced some contact with outsiders, and some had family members in Tewæno, but most had never been to the protectorate.[11] A little to the southwest, along the Cononaco, was the traditional territory of a different kinship group, the Tagæidi.

HARASSMENT FROM THE "ÆMIGOS"

Dicado Waorani soon became regular visitors to the nearby oil camps. They would approach the camps calling out "Æmigos, æmigos," the Spanish *amigos* (friends) with a Wao accent. However, the CGG workers complained that the "friends" harassed them and stole their supplies with impunity. The workers were concerned that relations might deteriorate, leading to violence. They were also terrified at the prospect of a surprise attack by the Tagædi.[12] The Capuchín mission volunteered to send Father Labaca to spend a few days with the oil workers.

On July 28, 1976, CGG flew Labaca to the area where the seismic crews were working. Just the day before, the Waorani had looted the camp, taking hammocks, blankets, mosquito nets, clothing, boots, hatchets, machetes, the entire supply of sugar, some rice, and cans of tuna and sardines. They also took more than 3,000 sucres of the workers' money. Labaca spent two days and nights with the nervous crew, most of whom were ready to walk off the job (except that company helicopters provided the only way out of the isolated rainforest). He listened to their complaints and offered spiritual encouragement, celebrating Mass for those who wished to attend. Labaca drew from the Gospel of Matthew to tell the workers that they were providing food for the hungry and clothes for the naked. They were, he told them, "missionaries [to the Waorani] chosen by God."[13] Although they remained on the job, the workers were unconvinced. They had signed up because of the wages offered, not for a higher calling, and simply wanted to return home alive.

During this visit and the first few days of his second visit, Labaca did not encounter the Waorani. This changed on Monday, August 9, 1976, when three men, clad in their traditional *comes* (hip-cords), arrived at the camp. Labaca learned that they were Pego, about twenty-five years old; Wane, about thirty; and Nampawæ, about seventy. The men accepted the gifts Labaca and the workers gave them—mirrors, combs, safety pins, needles, nets, and necklaces with a cross. Then the Waorani began rifling the men's possessions, especially Labaca's. The priest had come newly prepared for jungle living, with extra shirts, undershirts, socks, a rain poncho, sheets, a mirror, and a rubberized bag to carry everything. The Waorani took it all. The priest wryly remarked that the Waorani were helping him to live out his Franciscan vow of poverty.[14]

Labaca stayed for the next two weeks, until the crew moved away. Groups of Waorani continued to arrive almost daily. While Labaca's presence seemed to reassure the oil workers, it did nothing to curb the confidence with which the Waorani plundered the camp. One afternoon, five Waorani arrived just in time to share in the food and drink of the midday meal. Before leaving and despite the workers' protests, they dismantled one of two tents used for shelter and, with shouts and laughter, walked off with it. Almost immediately a torrential rainfall began, leaving Labaca and the oil crew to squeeze under the one tarp they had left.[15] The deluge continued throughout the night.

The next morning two of the same Wao men returned, right on time to view supplies that had arrived by helicopter. They ate hurriedly and left, carrying a bundle of hammocks and mosquito nets, just when a new group of five Wao teenagers arrived. The young men, Labaca observed, were impertinent and annoying. They took apart the chainsaw and fiddled with the radio transmitter, holding the microphone and calling out "Dicado, Dicado. . . . Pañacocha, cambio," imitating the workers.

Amid the chaos, Labaca decided to intervene. One youth was amusing himself by opening various cans and jars of food. If he did not like the smell or the taste, he threw the cans as far away as he could. When this happened to a jar of instant coffee, Labaca shouted at the boy and asked him to retrieve the jar. With sounds Labaca interpreted as grumbling, the young man brought the jar and threw it into Labaca's hand. Then he picked up a machete and pantomimed cutting off the priest's head. Next, he took a plastic plate from the kitchen and used the machete to smash the plate to smithereens in front of Labaca. The unflappable priest observed in his notes, "He seemed to want me to understand that the young Wao man is not willing to humble himself before anyone!"[16]

LABACA VISITS A WAO CLEARING

Most interactions were not as dramatic but instead consisted of the Waorani's ongoing pursuit of goods. On August 18, a day after his encounter with the young man, Labaca was thrilled when CGG authorized a pilot to take him for a half-hour visit to a Wao clearing. The clearing was about fifteen miles from the oil camp. As they approached the site, it was obvious that these Waorani were among those who had visited the camp: the purloined tent was pitched and attached to one of the houses. Upon landing, Labaca observed that the men were dressed in clothing from the camps. Among other gifts, the priest had brought dresses for the women, which they immediately put on. For their part, the Waorani offered the visitors feathers and feather crowns as gifts. At Labaca's request, the Waorani allowed him to enter one of their houses, although he later admitted that it was so dim inside he could make out very little. The other men took photographs outside, and after thirty minutes they took off without incident.[17]

This peaceful excursion paved the way for Labaca to make three longer visits to Wao clearings between December 1976 and February 1977. All were facilitated by oil company helicopters, in exchange for Labaca's ongoing work among the crews. The priest had conflicted feelings about this arrangement. At last he was fulfilling his missionary calling among the Waorani. He also felt genuine pastoral concern for the oil workers, many of whom were poor Quichuas who had not understood the potential danger of a job cutting paths through the jungle.[18]

Yet Labaca objected to the whole project of exploiting the petroleum under traditional Wao territory. He believed that all aspects of exploration should be suspended until the Waorani as a group could give informed consent to the government's plans.[19] This put him at odds with officials from both Corporación Estatal Petrolera Ecuatoriana (CEPE) and the CGG. It also provided an incentive for the Capuchín missionaries, initially Labaca and two other priests, to find an alternative way to reach the Wao clearings. The most logical was by motorized dugout canoe, traveling up the Yasuní River from the Capuchín mission station in Nuevo Rocafuerte. The missionaries made their first successful trip in April 1977 and motored up the river five more times between August 1978 and April 1980. They cut through fallen trees and navigated floodwaters but made all five trips successfully. Labaca still occasionally used oil company helicopters but no longer depended on them.

The priest's first overnight stay among the Waorani took place December 23, 1976. A helicopter dropped him off at the same clearing with the tent that he had visited before. It was home to two families, that of Iniwa and Paba, a couple who Labaca guessed were in their forties, with three children, and a somewhat younger couple, Ompodæ and Bogænæi, and their two children. This clearing was part of a "neighborhood cluster" of four related family groups that made up the Dicado Waorani. The Summer Institute sometimes referred to this group as "Nampawæ's bunch" after the oldest male in the group.

"ADOPTED" BY A WAO FAMILY

As would become his custom, Labaca arrived in the clearing laden with gifts. What he perceived as a warm welcome probably was as much for the goods as for the missionary. Once inside the longhouse belonging to Iniwa and Paba, Labaca distributed clothing, batteries (for flashlights), matches, and packages of food. Opening one package, he spread marmalade on pieces of bread and passed them around to be eagerly consumed.[20] Labaca spent the night in the same longhouse. He woke up about 1:00 in the morning to the sound of Paba chanting as she stoked the fire from her hammock. The scene was repeated twice more during the night, to Labaca's delight. He was sure the chanting had a religious component.

By morning Labaca had decided he wanted to be "adopted" by this family. Clad only in his underwear, he knelt before Iniwa and somehow communicated his desire. (Labaca knew only a few words of *Wao tededo* at this point. Apparently they included "mother" and "father.") Iniwa placed his hands on Labaca's head, forcefully rubbing his hair. Paba, Labaca's new "mother," did the same. The priest then disrobed completely, knelt and kissed the hands of his new "parents" and "siblings" before putting on his clothes. He saw himself entering a new life, one where he would, as the New Testament suggested, be clothed more and more with Christ.[21]

While the Waorani did incorporate outsiders into their families, as the Tewæno Waorani had with Rachel Saint and the rest of the SIL Wao team, the ritual of adoption Labaca described seemed more connected to Catholic rites than to any cultural practices of the Waorani. It also reflected an imitation of the actions of St. Francis, appropriate for a Capuchín priest whose order was a renewal movement within the Franciscan family.[22] Usually the Waorani incorporated an outsider into their kinship structure by giving that person a name, such as "Nemo" for Rachel Saint, that would establish the kin connection and accompanying behavioral expectations. It is unclear exactly what Labaca's Wao name was. Beginning with his second extended stay, he was called "Capitán Memo" (possibly Mæænmo), a name the Capuchíns believed indicated both affection and respect.[23] Labaca continued to pursue strong kinship ties with Iniwa and Paba as his "father" and "mother," a relationship the Waorani seemed to accept.

During Labaca's second stay, January 2–7, 1977, and his third a week later, January 14–15, 1977, he sought to fit into Wao culture, no small challenge for a fifty-seven-year-old who had lived the life of an administrator. He quickly learned he could not keep up with the Waorani in the rainforest. When on January 6, 1977, the helicopter did not arrive to pick him up, Labaca set out on an all-day trek to the nearest oil camp, guided by the Waorani. The priest barely made it, going up and down the steep ridges, favoring a bum knee, and trying to keep up with the Wao men, who set a pace he could not match. His legs shook, his head ached, he retched bile, and later he described the experience as his "Calvary."[24]

Two of the Waorani, Nampawæ and Adabæ, helped Labaca over the logs that spanned rivers, carried his things, and encouraged him until the three were met by another priest, José Miguel Goldárez, and a lay catechist, Mariano Grefa, who had landed by helicopter at the Wao houses. Not finding Labaca, they had set out through the forest, guided by Iniwa. Accompanied by Goldárez, Grefa, and the Waorani, Labaca stumbled into the oil camp where he and the others were greeted warmly and given coffee and food.[25] This was the only recorded occasion when Labaca made such a trek. Recognizing his limits, he never expressed interest in accompanying Wao men or women on their hunts.

LIFE WITH THE WAORANI

Instead Labaca volunteered to cut firewood and carry water, and on occasion he accompanied children to the river. And, of course, he always brought gifts. On his January 14, 1977, visit, he arrived with four dogs, eight hens, four roosters, peanut seeds, grapefruit, avocados, tomatoes, and a melon. Asked the names of the dogs, the priest was taken aback. He had not inquired. Lacking the knowledge to risk Wao names, on a whim, he turned to Chinese, and the dogs became Peiku, Taku, Huanku, and Shiasku.[26]

Labaca was idealistic in his assessments of Wao culture. He described the prototypical Wao woman as "the queen of the home, respected and loved."[27] He noted that the Waorani scrupulously respected one another's property, an attitude that clearly did not extend to outsiders. He continued to admire the chants the Waorani sang at night and entertained the household by his own clumsy efforts to imitate them. His goal was to "accept everything except sin" in Wao culture.[28] For Labaca, discerning the difference between sin and certain cultural practices was most difficult in areas related to male sexuality. For example, should he imitate Wao men in the use of the *come*, and how should he react to what he interpreted as homosexual practices among the men? During the day of Labaca's first overnight stay with the Waorani, he was the only person in the clearing who was fully clothed, as defined by outsiders. By nightfall his clothes were not fit to be worn—soaked with sweat and dirty from sitting on the floor of the longhouse. From then on, he removed his clothes when he entered the Wao clearing, tucked them away for his return, and remained clad only in swim trunks or underwear.

Labaca's experience with the *come* occurred during a later visit. The priest had gone alone to a stream to bathe. Once there, he also washed his underwear, socks, and towel. He laid them out to dry in the sun while he sat naked on the bank, reflecting on the Apostle Paul's call in the Book of Romans to "take off the works of darkness . . . [and] dress ourselves with the armor of faith."[29] The meditation was cut short by the unexpected arrival of two families, guided by Pego. No one seemed to think it unusual to see Labaca, without a stitch of clothing, sitting in the sun. There was, however, one problem. "You don't have a *come*," Pego told him. Pego borrowed the cotton cord used for that purpose and helped Labaca put it on. "Now we can go to the house." Labaca realized that by Wao standards, he was dressed. The priest admired the way the Waorani viewed their bodies without shame.[30] Although he usually wore his swim trunks, sometimes he, too, dressed only in the *come* as a way of identifying with and affirming the Waorani.

The priest liked the physical closeness of Wao life. He described one chilly night in a shelter with only a single fire. He was sleeping under a sheet of plastic, which gave him a little warmth. From about 1:00 on, the young men would take turns crawling under the sheet next to Labaca to share his body heat. The priest, as a good Franciscan, thought about how wonderful it was "to share even the warmth of the body with the poor."[31] Labaca may have described such experiences in his journal as a way of being transparent, considering the one thing he rejected in Wao culture was conduct he viewed as homosexual.[32] The second time Labaca met the Waorani, still in the oil camp, several young men made lewd gestures to the cook, the medic, and Labaca, gestures that Labaca interpreted as proposing homosexual acts. In fairness, the priest noted that never again was he approached that way.[33]

Labaca later observed that men in the same family group liked to play games involving erotic acts with one another. When Labaca refused to participate, the Waorani accepted his choice. The priest generally tempered his refusals with humor, and the incidents did not seem to affect his overall positive attitude toward the Waorani. Despite these sexual practices and their habit of stealing from outsiders, the Waorani were still innocent natives in Labaca's eyes, with the "seeds of the Word" hidden within their culture, as Vatican II had suggested.[34] As a missionary to the Waorani, Labaca had found his vocation. After one visit he wrote, "Perhaps never have I felt so vividly a follower of St. Francis."[35] He lamented that his limited knowledge of *Wao tededo* kept him from offering even a hint of the Christian gospel except when responding to questions about the crucifix around his neck. "This is Jesus. His mother is Mary," he would reply as he kissed the Christ.[36]

CONTACT SLOWED

By May 1977 Labaca had stayed in Wao clearings overnight or longer on four separate occasions. He also made a few brief visits to greet the people and to drop off gifts. His reception had been uniformly friendly. During his first visit by motorized canoe, lasting from April 27 to approximately May 10, the Waorani also accepted the presence of two other priests and the two Quichua pilots. The trip, wrote Labaca, marked the opening of the "stage of evangelization" for this group of Waorani.[37] He was keenly aware that he and the others needed to learn *Wao tededo*, and he had asked SIL for help. When Labaca left midyear for a few months' vacation in Spain, prospects looked bright for an ongoing Capuchín mission among the Waorani.

The picture changed abruptly the day after Labaca returned. On November 3, 1977, Waorani attacked a small group of CGG workers while they were cutting a path near the Tivacuno River, about twenty-five miles northwest of the Wao clearings Labaca had visited (map 4). Three workers were killed, each speared repeatedly. News of the attack spread quickly, making the front page of papers in Quito and throughout the nation. The identity of the perpetrators was unclear, but the best guesses came down to the Tagædi.[38]

As noted earlier, the CGG worked under contract with CEPE, the Ecuadorian state oil company. Company officials were anxious to find a way to maintain the pace of exploration, while also safeguarding both the lives of workers and the human rights of the Waorani. At least this was the official stance. Both the Capuchín Mission and SIL suspected that the real priority was Ecuador's need for oil revenues. Therefore, what mattered was keeping crews in the field.[39] At midnight on November 4, the night after the killings, Labaca was roused by Maj. Luis Gudiño, CEPE's security chief, accompanied by an official from CGG and one from Texaco. A group of workers still in the jungle had been threatened by Waorani. The workers' nerves were on edge as heavy rains began to fall in the darkness. The crew expected an attack before dawn, and they had frantically called in by radio to seek advice.

Labaca took the radio microphone, calmly identifying himself to the workers as Padre Alejandro, who knew something of Wao customs. He assured the workers that the Waorani too were afraid of the forest at night. They stayed in their houses with the doors secured with slabs of chonta palm wood. They would not attack.[40] In fact, Labaca was mistaken. The Waorani preferred to attack at night, and the reason the longhouses were so tightly secured was to slow down the perpetrators of a surprise attack.[41] However, the Waorani did value the element of surprise, so it was unlikely they would attack an oil camp where workers were awake and aware of their presence. Labaca contacted the workers again at 4:00 in the morning and then at 5:00 with short phrases they could call out in *Wao tededo*. The attack did not materialize.

During the next few days, with the workers safely evacuated and oil exploration suspended, a series of meetings took place between representatives of CEPE, officers of the Ecuadorian military, and staff from SIL and the Capuchín mission. At the first meeting, December 10, 1977, the Capuchíns took the lead. They reiterated a call they had made a month earlier in an open letter to the Ecuadorian government, asking the state to establish a special "Waorani region," a zone much larger than the existing protectorate. The proposed area represented about 40 percent of traditional Wao territory, and any attempt to usurp it would represent a violation of the human rights of the Waorani.[42] The region was smaller but incorporated some of the same land Jim Yost and others were asking the government to give to the Waorani as an ethnic reserve. The Capuchíns also suggested that, because of their knowledge of *Wao tededo*, the SIL Wao team should seek out the Tagædi or other splinter groups and try to make peaceful contact. In the meantime, while CEPE did not have to abandon its pursuit of oil, the corporation should postpone its work in Wao territory.

RELATIONS WITH SIL

Glen Turner, head of tribal affairs for SIL, supported these points. However, the CEPE representative insisted that the government could not wait, nor could the consortium it directed. They would put helicopters, planes, loudspeakers—whatever was necessary—at SIL's disposal so the linguists could locate and contact the reclusive Tagæidi.[43] Pat Kelley underscored the difficulty of the task, explaining that the group or groups in question were so isolated that the Waorani from Tewæno were unable to identify the makers of the spears used in the attack. Even other Waorani would approach this isolated group with great caution, assuming they could be found.

After the meeting, Labaca and fellow priest Juan Santos Ortíz de Vallalba sought out Turner and JAARS pilot Roy Gleason for informal conversation. It was not the first time they had met. SIL's Limoncocha base was near the parish of Pompeya, where both priests had served over the years. The previous February, Labaca had contacted both Gleason and Don Johnson to confirm that the Capuchín work among the Waorani did not encroach on the work of SIL. He also requested help in learning *Wao tededo*. Then, as in this meeting, SIL emphasized that it had no proprietary role with the Waorani, and the Capuchíns could pursue contact as they wished. This time around, the two organizations agreed to issue a joint request, once again asking the government to set aside more land for the Waorani. SIL would prepare the request and both groups would sign it.[44]

Full of the ecumenical spirit of Vatican II and Pope Paul VI, the Capuchín missionaries hoped to collaborate with SIL. Relations between the Catholic friars and the evangelical linguists were cordial. When Labaca visited Johnson in February 1977, Johnson had promised to organize a language course for him in Limoncocha, tentatively scheduled for late March. Yet despite the openness, SIL never seemed ready to actually collaborate. Trying once more, Labaca traveled to Quito in late January 1978, hoping to meet with Johnson during the annual meeting of the Ecuador SIL. The priest waited for two weeks before a dinner was organized. In addition to Johnson and Turner, guests included Jim Yost, Pat Kelley, and Catherine Peeke, along with Labaca and his colleague, Father Miguel Angel Azcona.

During a long and friendly exchange that extended into the night, familiar issues were discussed: the need for more land legally ceded to the Waorani and the most effective approach for contacting the still belligerent, isolated groups. When the Capuchín missionaries asked if the SIL Wao team thought it safe for them to resume contact with the Nampawæ-Iniwa group living up the Dicado, the response was no. The priests should wait until that section of Wao territory, bordering land where the Tagæidi were said to live, had calmed down.[45] The meeting was the last explicit effort by the Capuchíns to collaborate with SIL, although the Catholics' attitude toward the Institute then and in subsequent years continued to be one of friendship and charity.

For SIL, the timing was wrong. The Wao team, as well as Johnson, Lindskoog's successor as executive director of the Ecuador SIL, had their hands full dealing with the ongoing Rachel Saint dispute while also helping the Waorani in the protectorate adjust to increased contact with the outside world. The team was short-handed. Except for attending the Ecuador Branch annual meeting and therefore being present at the dinner, Peeke was in the US from October 1976 to October 1978. She would have been the logical candidate to help the priests learn *Wao tededo*. Jim and Kathie Yost were gone off and on for about a year during the same period. The Capuchíns, along with the Ecuadorian military and SIL administrators, consulted with each other about what steps should be taken regarding the Tagæidi. However, the frazzled Wao team lacked the time, energy, and staff in the field to pursue the kind of cooperative efforts the Catholic mission had envisioned.

RETURNING TO THE WAORANI

By July 1978 more than a year had passed since Labaca had visited the Waorani and about seven months since the oil workers were killed. Despite the risk, on August 1 the priest and two assistants headed up the Yasuní. They traveled through frequent downpours; otherwise the first two days were uneventful. At about 10:30 in the morning of the third day, the three men heard voices. Labaca began shouting Wao phrases, and within a few minutes they were face to face with four Waorani: a man, Cai, and three of his wife's grown children. Labaca knew them from earlier visits; all were part of the larger kinship group he had contacted.

As usual in a Labaca-Waorani encounter, the Waorani wasted little time in finding the gifts the priest had brought, including two dozen pairs of swimming trunks, as well as tubes of toothpaste and necklaces for the women. Cai and his family appropriated these goods before Labaca even encountered other members of their kinship group. Fortunately the priest had come well supplied. The rest of the two-day visit was spent in renewing relationships, sharing food, and presenting more gifts.

As Labaca and the two Quichuas prepared to return to Nuevo Rocafuerte, the Waorani asked Labaca to bring specific items on the next trip. They also encouraged him to bring women along. Labaca had told them of the nuns (*cowode* women) who lived in Rocafuerte. Of course, the Waorani had no concept of "priest" or "nun," and Labaca lacked the language skills to even begin to explain. In response to Labaca's inquiry, the Waorani assured him they would not spear the women but would treat them well.

Labaca led four more trips by river between November 1978 and April 1980. During the spring of 1979, he also made five brief visits by helicopter to Wao clearings, again assuming the familiar role of mediator between oil companies and the Waorani. Despite their bluster, since the 1977 killings CEPE and affiliated companies had postponed work in the region around the Yasuní River, as well as in areas where the Tagæidi might be living. In February 1979 seismic explorations resumed in force, filling the air with helicopters and the ground with men cutting trails where dynamite would be detonated at regular intervals. One project tackled by the crews was rehabilitating site 34-6, an overgrown helicopter landing pad near several Wao clearings. It was the place where Labaca had been dropped off during his early encounters with the Dicado Waorani. Shortly after oil workers arrived at the site, they found themselves surrounded by Waorani "amigos."

NUNS JOIN THE PROJECT

Labaca was called almost immediately. The Waorani had relocated since his last visit, and he arrived at their new clearings to find several people suffering from malaria. He transported one young Wao man to Coca for treatment, the first of the Dicado Waorani to visit a *cowode* town. He was Adabæ (Paba's son and a Labaca favorite). As word of the illnesses spread, two nuns volunteered to return with Labaca to help nurse the sick. The nuns, Inés Ochoa and Amanda Villegas, were Madres Laurítas, the same order that had cared for the wounded girl Oncaye fifteen years earlier.[46]

On February 27, 1979, a helicopter headed for landing pad 34-6 carrying the much-improved Adabæ, the two nuns, a doctor from the Coca hospital sent by the provincial director of health, two oil company officials who did not intend to stay, and Labaca. The overnight visit went off without a hitch. The doctor treated the sick, and one nun helped to administer medicines while the other cooked large quantities of rice for everyone. Labaca soon slipped into his role as water carrier and wood gatherer. He kept the fires stoked in Iniwa and Paba's longhouse through the chilly night and made sure that the pair, weakened by malaria, had plenty of firewood for the immediate days to come. For Labaca, the presence of the nuns and the uneventful visit represented "with the blessing of God, a great step forward toward the evangelization of the Waorani."[47]

Further evidence of that step forward was hard to find during the next few months. April through July 1979 was a tense time as oil workers again swarmed the territory of the Dicado Waorani. Labaca continued his helicopter diplomacy for about six months, trying to defuse tensions and avoid military intervention. The Waorani were suffering not only from malaria but also from influenza and other contact illnesses. Labaca brought medicines and occasionally doctors (and a dentist) to the Wao clearings. He always came with gifts. Probably the most surprising were a shotgun and ten cartridges for each family, distributed after most oil crews were gone. Until then, the Dicado Waorani had only one shotgun among them all, and they repeatedly requested more. Labaca believed that both CEPE and the army had given shotguns to other groups of Waorani and that this group deserved them as well.[48]

As the oil workers moved elsewhere, Labaca resumed his more unambiguous role as a missionary. Together with various companions—fellow missionary friars, nuns, and his trusted Quichua assistants—he made trips by boat up the Yasuní in June and November 1979 and in April 1980. Earlier, Labaca had explained that the goal of the missionaries was "to live together in friendship with [the Waorani], seeking to deserve to find with them the seeds of the Word. . . . We only want to live a chapter of Wao life, under the gaze of a Creator who has made us brothers."[49] Like Elisabeth Elliot urging evangelicals to view the Waorani as "kinsmen" rather than "savages," Labaca's affirmation of brotherhood with the Waorani was a radical Christian stance.

AFFIRMING WAO CULTURE

While Labaca valued Wao culture, he seemed unconcerned about the changes he and the other missionaries were introducing. Because of Labaca, the Dicado Waorani had dogs, chickens, rice, machetes and other tools, fruit trees, corn and peanut seeds, shotguns, and, of course, clothing. These goods represented the lure of the outside world, something else Labaca apparently didn't realize. He was so convinced of the "timid and reclusive" nature of the Waorani that he could not anticipate that they might soon want to travel downriver to Nuevo Rocafuerte. Nor did Labaca know that some of the Waorani he visited were still engaged in spearing raids against other Waorani. In 1978 Ompodæ and Pego killed two of the uncontacted Taadomenani, an act that would have tragic repercussions decades later.[50]

For Labaca, the high point of his April 1980 visit was the decision of two young Wao men, Adabæ and Æguinto, to accompany the missionaries back to Nuevo Rocafuerte. When Adabæ first expressed a desire to go, Labaca confided in his journal that perhaps, just perhaps, the boy might someday become a priest who could communicate Christianity to his people in a culturally appropriate way. Adabæ's mother, Paba, probably had other priorities when she urged Labaca to take the young man to Tewæno to visit relatives from whom he had been separated through tribal vendettas. She may have hoped Adabæ would find a woman in the appropriate cross-cousin relationship to be his wife.[51] Whatever the motivation of the various parties, the isolation of the Dicado Waorani, first broken by oil companies and the Capuchín mission, was coming to an end. For Labaca, it also marked a "new stage of genuine brotherhood among the peoples of this small parcel of God's Amazon."[52]

WAORANI COME TO NUEVO ROCAFUERTE

A year later, on April 6, 1981, thirteen Waorani, representing two families of the Dicado kinship group, arrived in Nuevo Rocafuerte on their own, with plans to live in the town.[53] The families, headed by Cai and Adabæ, had come to see Labaca, who, it turned out, was in Spain. The responsibility to care for the visitors fell on Juan Santos Ortíz, a priest who had spent years working among the lowland Quichua but knew little about the Waorani and spoke no *Wao tededo*. Santos Ortíz soon learned to cope. He made the most of creative pantomime, enlisted the services of Sister Inés Arango, who spoke a little of the language, and settled the Waorani in the mission guest house. They stayed until June 9, a period that included a month living among the lowland Quichua of Pompeya and a brief visit to the "big city" of Coca. While he made every effort to meet their needs, Santos Ortíz insisted that the families return to their homes along the Dicado River. Their response: "We want to stay here [Nuevo Rocafuerte] forever. This is a good place. Here."[54] Santos Ortíz understood the attractions of running water, electric lights, modern plumbing, not to mention gifts from local residents, but was convinced that these "people of the forest" were not yet ready to become permanent residents, living on their own in a strange culture. Still, he wanted the decision to be theirs.

The solution lay in compromise. Despite no experience with maps or two-dimensional representation, the Waorani could understand a map of familiar territory with surprising clarity. With the map spread out before them, Santos Ortíz asked Adabæ where he wanted to live. The young man put his finger on Nuevo Rocafuerte, then moved it along the Yasuní up to the area where he had been living. Then he moved it slowly back to position about halfway between the two points and said, "Near here is good."[55] Adabæ had indicated a location known as Garzacocha, a lagoon on the Yasuní located about seventy miles upriver from Nuevo Rocafuerte. It was isolated enough that the Waorani would be able to hunt freely and live by their customs. Yet they had access to the outside world since the site was only about a day and a half by canoe from the town. The other Waorani agreed on the site, which came to be known as Táparo Anameni (loosely translated as Palm Ridge).[56]

On June 9, 1981, the Waorani set off upriver, accompanied by Santos Ortíz, two faculty members from the Department of Indigenous Education of the Catholic University, two Quichua men to help those Waorani who had said they wanted "Quichua-style" homes, and two visiting teenagers, sons of the schoolmaster in Santos Ortíz's hometown in Spain. The group brought a chainsaw, hatchets, axes, an adze, machetes, a small generator, bedding, gasoline, and food supplies. Enduring the relentless rain storms, the outsiders accompanied the Waorani for three weeks as they established their clearing and selected sites for their homes. The two Quichua men also built a dugout canoe. The Waorani began to plant gardens of manioc and *plátanos*, and the men found that the hunting was good. By the end of June the Waorani had settled in.[57]

Táparo Anameni proved to be a good place for the Waorani. It remained small, although some family members did come from the upper reaches of the Dicado to build their houses nearby. When they wanted goods from Nuevo Rocafuerte, the Waorani took blowguns, hammocks, necklaces, feather crowns, and other items to trade. The locals knew them and treated them well. The Capuchín friars tried to ensure that the Waorani were not exploited by other outsiders. There were a few unfortunate instances of tourists visiting Táparo Anameni, causing the Waorani to "feel observed like animals in a zoo." It was curious, mused Santos Ortíz, that some of the same people who argued that the Waorani should be left in peace were first in line to satisfy their own curiosity.[58] Eventually the priests worked with local authorities to ban tourism up the Yasuní.

The Capuchín missionaries maintained their contacts and friendships with the Waorani of Táparo Anameni, as well as those who continued living farther up river on the Dicado. Labaca's involvement, however, was limited because he had been named superior for the Capuchín order in the Aguarico region. Santos Ortíz, on the other hand, spent extensive time with the Waorani in 1982 and 1983. He and others followed Labaca's strategy. "We were not in any hurry," wrote Santos Ortíz, "much less [did we intend] to make ourselves into agents of a cultural or religious invasion. Perhaps one day they will want to choose, and if they are ready and continue in the hands of the Good Shepherd, they will make the best choice."[59] The only cloud over this otherwise tranquil scene was ongoing concern over the small splinter group still hidden and hostile in the rainforest: the Tagæidi. Their story would unfold during the 1980s.

16

Leaving Ecuador

∽

DURING THE LATE 1970s and early 1980s, SIL, the Capuchín friars, and missionaries Lloyd Rogers (Brethren) and David Miller (Christian and Missionary Alliance) continued to support the Waorani in their increasing contact with the outside world. At the same time, other voices called for the Waorani to be left alone, especially those Waorani who had not relocated to the protectorate. One such advocate was Sam Padilla. Critics from the Catholic University and elsewhere also continued the drumbeat of anti-SIL rhetoric that contributed to the decision in May 1981 by President Jaime Roldós to end Ecuador's contractual relationship with SIL. Roldós's decree gave the organization a year to transfer its programs to Ecuadorians or, if that was not possible, to close them. Coincidentally 1981 marked the twenty-fifth anniversary of the five missionaries' deaths, bringing with it additional scrutiny and publicity. For SIL Ecuador, and especially the Wao team, these were difficult times.

SAM PADILLA

Sam Padilla grew up shaped by four cultures, but with no secure place in any of them. He spent most of his early childhood on Carlos Sevilla's hacienda, among Quichuas, and Quichua was his first language. In 1958, after not having seen his mother for nine months, eight-year-old Padilla was flown to the US, where he would spend four months with Dayomæ and Rachel Saint at a Wycliffe training center in Sulphur Springs, Arkansas. Returning to Ecuador, he remained at the Limoncocha base, where he was tutored with two other children, while his mother took Rachel and Elisabeth Elliot to Tewæno.[1] For the next year he spent time with Dayomæ when she came out of the rainforest and stayed with SIL families in Limoncocha while she was gone. In 1960 Padilla began his formal schooling in Quito. He lived in Quito between 1960 and 1966 except for visits to his mother's home in Tewæno during vacations. His separation from his mother and her culture reflected Dayomæ's intense desire that he receive a good education. Committed to transforming the Waorani from "savages" to "civilized" people, Dayomæ wanted her son to be a full participant in the outside world. This was a challenging goal in 1960s Ecuador, where anyone identified as an *indio* faced open discrimination.[2] Yet Padilla was not fully Waorani either. In traditional Wao culture, a child who had one *cowode* parent was not considered to be Waorani.

There was nowhere Padilla really belonged, nor did he have a stable family life. He did not do well as a Quito schoolboy, although he learned to speak Spanish and English, the latter from North American missionaries. He also picked up the basics of how to live as an urban Ecuadorian or, a later journalist would say, as a "sophisticated Auca."[3] Padilla was smart, but he had started over with first grade in Quito at age ten, so he was three or four years behind his peers. By sixteen he was playing hooky from both school and church and, as a teenager, was becoming "more and more demanding in money matters," according to Saint, who helped support him.[4] A year later he left school, having completed seventh grade, and went to Tewæno. He spent most of the next four years, from 1967 to 1971, among the Waorani. He built on the knowledge of Wao culture he had acquired during school vacations and, by his own account, finally learned to speak *Wao tededo*.[5] He took a brief and unsuccessful stab at teaching literacy to Tewæno children and worried Saint with his romantic attachments and apparent aimlessness.

Padilla was restless both in the outside world and among his mother's people. He wanted the comforts of "civilization" as well as the mystique associated with the Waorani. One solution was to work as a guide for adventurers and tourists. Beginning with Erwin Patzelt, it seemed like everyone who mounted an expedition in the 1970s and early 1980s to visit Wao clearings hired Padilla. In July and August 1971 he accompanied Patzelt on his initial trips to visit the ridge Waorani, living near the Gabado River.[6] Between 1972 and 1976, the years when Padilla attended Bible college in the US, he still managed to use his time in Ecuador on college breaks to help Patzelt.[7] To outsiders, Waorani from the Gabado ridge were the genuine "naked savages," usually described as the last remnant of a people doomed to extinction, or, at the very least, doomed to lose their identity.[8] In the moment, however, they were available to be photographed and observed by visitors arriving with trade goods as gifts.

A NEW IDENTITY

Throughout the 1970s Padilla became increasingly critical of SIL and of all missionaries working with the Waorani. When interviewed by Jerry Bledsoe in 1971, he had admitted that while he didn't mind living in the rainforest, he would "rather be outside [of Wao territory], because there's more things to do and see." He also conveyed a positive picture of Rachel and the SIL Wao team. "Rachel Saint, she's doing a great job. . . . Missionaries in Tewæno, they're trying to do the best they can helping the people [Waorani] so they won't be like they used to be."[9]

Seven years later Padilla's persona and perspective had changed dramatically. In a 1978 interview with *El Comercio*, Quito's most influential newspaper, "Sam Padilla" had become the "civilized name" of the Wao man Ceantu (more commonly, Cænto). According to the paper, Cænto spoke four languages and had lived in Quito and the US, but was most content in the jungle, helping those Waorani "who still had not had contact with civilization." Cænto was the self-appointed "representative of the Auca tribe" and stated flatly, "The worst enemy we have are the missionaries." Missionaries, he charged, made the Waorani wear clothes, took their blowguns, made them use shotguns, and, worst of all, read them the Bible, imposing customs and needs they had not had before. In short, mission work had "destroyed" at least five hundred Waorani.[10]

Cænto, in contrast, was working to save those few who were left. His description of these Waorani, including himself, was idyllic. "We live free, happy in our environment. It's true that we aren't rich, but we lack nothing." Elsewhere in the article, the reporter described Cænto's rainforest as "a world of freedom, without time and without fear."[11] The description may have provided a needed corrective to the usual emphasis on Wao savagery, but it traded one stereotype for another: barbarianism for the pristine primitive.[12]

Padilla Cænto's assertions angered SIL, although administrators followed a standard policy of making no official response. However, coming only three months after the release of the film *¡Fuera de Aquí!* and less than a year since the second Barbados declaration, Padilla Cænto's allegations reinforced other criticisms of SIL in Ecuador and in Latin America. Sam's comments also ignored his mother's role as a catalyst for change, and his claim to represent the Waorani was dubious since the very concept of representation was unknown in their culture. Perhaps most galling to those he criticized, his relationship with the ridge Waorani was less than altruistic. He wanted them to remain as they were to benefit his own business ventures.

PADILLA CÆNTO AND WAO TOURISM

Padilla Cænto saw the potential of tourism in the mid-1970s when he worked for Metropolitan Touring of Quito on their *Flotel*, a three-deck, flat-bottomed riverboat designed to enable wealthy clients to explore the Amazon rainforest in comfort. The experience inspired Padilla Cænto to begin a tourist business of his own. It would have two focal points: one would be the ridge Waorani, the other a new Wao village to be established along the Curaray River, near the Palm Beach site where the five missionaries were killed.[13] Already Padilla Cænto had begun to take small groups of tourists—two or three at a time—to the ridge. To accommodate larger groups, however, he needed a location with a bigger runway. A deserted oil camp along the Cononaco River, to the south of the ridge, had an appropriate airstrip. In early 1977 Padilla Cænto encouraged about forty ridge people to move to the site, a deal sweetened by promises of rice and canned tuna so people would have food as they planted their manioc gardens.[14]

As agreed, the Waorani relocated, even though Padilla Cænto's rice was slow in coming. These Waorani were the subjects of two books, published in the early 1980s: Swiss author Peter Broennimann's *Auca on the Cononaco* (1981) and British writer John Man's *Jungle Nomads of Ecuador* (1982).[15] Both Padilla Cænto and these supposedly pristine people captivated Broennimann and his wife, Wally, during four visits they made between 1977 and 1980. Broennimann was a fine photographer, and the lavishly illustrated book used the couple's experiences with the Cononaco group as a window into Wao culture. Although he never said so directly, Broennimann left the impression that the pair were the first outsiders to visit this endangered tribe. He explained their reception ("We are touched, patted, smelled; they explore our bodies") as an effort by the Waorani to confirm that the visitors were human beings rather than the legendary *cowode*, originally thought to be subhuman cannibals.[16]

Broennimann's descriptions of Wao life—houses, blowguns, hunting expeditions, and more—were well written, but he and Wally rarely asked questions or pushed for answers that might challenge their idealization of the Cononaco Waorani as isolated, innocent people of the rainforest. In Broennimann's eyes, any contact with the "Linguists" (his name for SIL) was never good. He hoped that a separate Cononaco Reservation might be secured, protected by Padilla Cænto and a small group of presumably secular guardians "who have thorough knowledge of the Auca's way of life."[17]

More entrepreneur than guardian, Padilla Cænto was busy trying to extend his business beyond the Cononaco. For his second attraction, Dayomæ and her followers left Tewæno and established a new settlement near the Curaray River. The village was first called Ochococha, a Quichua word, but was renamed Toñæmpade (Toñæ's stream or Toñæ's creek in *Wao tededo*). From the start, there were misunderstandings. Those who came with Dayomæ envisioned a Waorani commercial center that would draw visitors with goods, clothing, and other items. Padilla Cænto, in contrast, was planning a tourist attraction with the locals living like their ancestors, which meant getting rid of clothing, shotguns, and Quichua-style houses. The idea did not go over well. In the end, Padilla Cænto took wealthy tourists to the Cononaco, while Toñæmpade got the less lucrative and less demanding backpackers. Dayomæ provided food and housing, which meant that she was the only one in the village who benefited financially in any significant way.[18]

With his tourist projects launched and a new identity in place, Padilla Cænto (as Samuel Cænto) sent a letter to Alejandro Labaca, opposing Labaca's missionary work for many of the same reasons that he objected to SIL's. Missions deprived the Waorani of their identity, he told the priest, leaving them "with shotguns, surrounded by plastic and using money." Padilla Cænto asked Labaca to end his religiously motivated outreach and to work together with him and others who understood the real needs of the Waorani.[19]

The priest refused. Labaca insisted there was a deep difference in the way he and Padilla Cænto viewed the Waorani, especially when it came to tourism. Labaca accused Padilla Cænto of ignoring the wishes of the Waorani that Padilla Cænto act as a mediator between them and the outside world. Instead Padilla Cænto kept them isolated, except for the tourists he brought to their clearings. Tourists were the ones who gave the Waorani "American dollars, Swiss francs, [and] sucres" that did nothing to help them.[20] Labaca also stated that the Waorani with whom he worked had discovered the lure of oil company goods well before the Capuchins arrived. The Waorani also had first grasped the value of shotguns from observing the oil workers. "I tried to dissuade them when it came to weapons," he wrote, "but I had to respect their decision."[21]

Padilla Cænto's patronage of the Waorani along the banks of the Cononaco also was a complicating factor affecting Jim Yost's efforts to encourage some Waorani to return to the Cononaco from the protectorate. Catherine Peeke imagined a worst-case scenario: "You are playing right into [Padilla Cænto's] plans by throwing them [returning Waorani] on the mercies of his handouts for their livelihood. And the repercussions in published materials will be marvelous! How ILV [SIL] has abandoned and he has rescued."[22]

Peeke's fears did not materialize because very few Waorani left the protectorate in the late 1970s to return to places they had left behind. In July 1980, when Yost compiled a census of the Waorani, only 58 were in clearings along the Cononaco River. These were people most frequently visited by Padilla Cænto. Another 33 Waorani were living on the Yasuní River in contact with the Capuchín mission; 113 were in Dayono, where the Christian and Missionary Alliance worker David Miller continued to supervise the school; and 119 were in Toñæmpade, where Lloyd Rogers oversaw the village school. The remaining 325 Waorani lived in nine other settlements within the protectorate, with Tewæno the largest at 73. Although they had reduced their presence, SIL staff were in contact with many of these settlements, including Tewæno, Tzapino (population 68), Quiwado (66), and Guequita's clearing (53).[23] All known Waorani had at least some access to the outside world, except for the Tagæidi, who were not included in the census. Due to their location, the Cononaco Waorani remained the most isolated of the contacted groups.

OBSTINATE CRITICS

While Padilla Cænto's plans might have frustrated SIL and other missionaries working with the Waorani, he was not SIL's most serious opponent. The Catholic University (PUCE), specifically the Center for Research and Socioeconomic Studies (CIESE) in the anthropology department, continued to be a hotbed of criticism.[24] CIESE published an influential 1980 pamphlet, *Ecuador ILV/WBT: Entre el Etnocídio y la Alfabetización* (Ecuador SIL/WBT: Between ethnocide and literacy), followed in 1981 by *Los Obscuros Designios de Dios y del Imperio: El Instituto Lingüístico de Verano en el Ecuador* (The obscure designs of God and empire: The Summer Institute of Linguistics in Ecuador), written by Jorge Trujillo, an anthropologist and PUCE faculty member. A 1981 Spanish translation of a book written by a team of German writers, *Los Nuevos Conquistadores: El Instituto Lingüístico de Verano en la América Latina* (The new conquistadors: SIL in Latin America), also was published in Ecuador.[25]

The books and pamphlet dealt with SIL as a whole in Ecuador and in Latin America. However, as usual, SIL's work among the Waorani was featured to support various allegations. For example, the relocation of several hundred Waorani to the protectorate was a move the CIESE—echoing the first Barbados Declaration—considered "ethnocide."[26] In Trujillo's *Los Obscuros Designios*, SIL represented a convergence of the religious and economic domination of indigenous peoples. Just as colonial-era Spaniards had used the indigenous as a captive work force in the name of Christianity, SIL, too, wanted to convert Ecuador's indigenous peoples and incorporate them into the front lines of modern capitalism.[27] Chapter 2, "The Mythical Oriente and the Crazy Enterprise of Brother Townsend," focused on the Waorani.[28] The five slain missionaries—mistakenly identified at different points as all belonging to the Mission Aviation Fellowship or the Wycliffe Bible Translators— had engaged in a "battle" with the Waorani, a battle that justified the subsequent intervention of the Summer Institute.

SIL missionaries had "used" Dayomæ, had "sold out" to petroleum companies, had created a *reducción* (mission compound) in Tewæno, and were responsible for bringing polio to the settlement and for delaying treatment of the afflicted.[29] After contributing to Wycliffe's pursuit of spiritual and monetary gain through the Auca Update Rallies, Dawa, Quemo, and Guequita were left "forgotten in the reserva-tion [protectorate], reduced to begging and other humiliating efforts to survive, obligated to pose for tourist photographers."[30] The accusations were couched in a tone at once cynical and sarcastic.

The exploitation of Dawa, Quemo, and Guequita was a new addition to the list of offenses. Once again, truth and exaggeration were bedfellows. The 1971 Auca Update Rallies represented a clash between the promotional instincts of Cameron Townsend and other US staff and the best interests of the Waorani. While Rachel Saint and the Ecuador SIL succumbed to pressure from the home front for the ini-tial tour, both Saint and Peeke opposed the suggestion of a return trip, Peeke noting that the tour had been particularly hard on Quemo.[31] Dawa, Quemo, and Guequita all remained in the protectorate after their return from the US, but none became beggars or was forced to pose for photographs. *Los Nuevos Conquistadores*, a widely circulated book, contributed little new to the conversation but added to the critical mass of anti-SIL literature in Ecuador. Its greatest impact may have been visual. The book contained satirical cartoons lampooning the Summer Institute.

Years later the historian Miguel Angel Cabodevilla described the campaign against the Ecuador SIL throughout the 1970s and early 1980s as a conflict "characterized by a clamorous lack of dialogue between affected parties . . . where worthless or ab-surd things [were] mixed together with those [that were] sustainable." Cabodevilla suggested that the early criticisms had forced SIL to make needed changes in Tewæno, changes that were "not appreciated by its obstinate critics."[32]

SUPPORT FOR SIL

SIL had its defenders, ranging from a former Ecuadorian president, Galo Plaza Lasso (1906–87), to the newly organized Federación Ecuatoriana de Indígenas Evangélicos (FEINE). In 1952, during his presidency, Plaza had established the first contract between Ecuador and SIL. Son of a prominent Ecuadorian family with roots dating back to the Spanish conquest, Plaza was a rancher, a politician, and a respected diplomat. He had donated money to the Ecuador SIL and in July 1980 led a delegation to lobby in support of SIL during an interview with President Roldós.[33]

Although it would become a nationwide federation, FEINE was organized in November 1980 among evangelical Quichuas in the Ecuadorian highlands. The catalyst was a dispute between representatives of the PUCE and indigenous people sympathetic to SIL over orthography for the highland Quichua language. Opponents considered FEINE "the presence of the ILV [SIL] by another name," but FEINE's existence suggested that significant numbers of indigenous people supported the Summer Institute.[34] On October 7, 1981, less than a year after its founding, the federation led between five thousand and six thousand indigenous people in a march to the Ecuadorian Congress to present a statement in favor of SIL.

SIL also had support among journalists and columnists in *El Comercio* and other daily papers. It was backed by Ecuador's conservative political parties, along with business and agricultural groups. Nevertheless, the winds of change were blowing in a different direction. Political supporters of Roldós included the PCD (People, Change, and Democracy Party), the DP (Popular Democracy Party), and others on the left, all of whom opposed SIL. As mentioned in earlier chapters, the inauguration of Roldós in 1979 marked a new openness toward Ecuador's indigenous population. Advisers to the president questioned the idea of assimilation and of a hegemonic state in favor of what they described as plural nationalities, or "pluriculturalism," in Ecuador. They favored allowing indigenous groups to maintain their specific nationalities and cultures within the broader Ecuadorian state.

Many individual SIL linguists could embrace this vision, minus its leftist political rhetoric, despite promotional materials from the organization that still emphasized SIL's effectiveness in "la Obra Civilizadora" (the task of civilizing [indigenous people]).[35] While the idea of "civilizing" tribal peoples was standard fare into the 1970s, by the end of the decade it was being replaced by a celebration of indigenous uniqueness.

A DIFFICULT YEAR

On May 22, 1981, the president signed Decree No. 1159, which ended all contracts between SIL and the Ecuadorian state. Roldós did not expel SIL, as some reports claimed; he ended a contractual relationship. Various interpretations have been given to this act. The decree itself stated that after almost three decades of work by SIL, it was time for Ecuador to take responsibility for its indigenous peoples.

A sovereign state should not contract out something that important.[36] Roldós also was under political pressure to issue the decree. Activists behind the emerging indigenous movements in Ecuador feared that the religious control they attributed to the Summer Institute would be translated into political clout. If SIL influence were curbed, indigenous groups where linguists had worked could be more easily mobilized to support various political agendas.[37] Any hopes on the part of SIL that Roldós might be convinced to rescind or amend the decree were quickly dashed. The president died in a plane crash just two days after issuing the decree. As one of the popular president's last official actions, Decree No. 1159 was hard to challenge.

If Decree No. 1159, mounting criticism, challenges facing the Waorani, and the climax of the Rachel Saint conflict were not enough, 1981 also marked the twenty-fifth anniversary of the five missionaries' deaths, a milestone that could not have come at a worse time. The last thing the Ecuador SIL wanted was more attention focused on the Waorani. The Wao team also dreaded the prospect of having to host and to serve as interpreters for a small army of visitors. Each major anniversary—the first, the tenth, the twentieth, and sometimes even the five-year marks in between— led to renewed interest among American evangelicals. Each also brought a new wave of publicity, assuring people back home that the five men did not die in vain and that God continued to transform the Waorani.

The twenty-fifth anniversary followed this pattern, except for two things. First, international interest had increased. Europeans, as well as North Americans, were captivated by the Waorani. The BBC, Time-Life Britain, a Hungarian TV crew, and others arrived in the jungle. They were followed by print journalists, secular and religious, from the US. Second, it became clear to many visitors, even those sympathetic to SIL, that the spread of Christianity among the Waorani was not an epic story of ever-increasing spiritual success. Evangelical writers faced the dilemma that the Ecuador SIL had confronted five years earlier. How could they compose an honest report while not undermining the inspirational power of the story? SIL administrators in Ecuador and the Wao team wanted the evangelical world to have a more realistic picture of the Waorani. However, given the anti-SIL sentiment at the time, they were sensitive to anything that might support the critics, especially if it came from other evangelicals.[38]

Writers and publications took a variety of approaches to the anniversary. A journalist named John Maust spent three days in Tewæno and wrote an article for *Christianity Today* that focused on the dedication of the SIL staff—Jim and Kathie Yost, Rosi Jung, and Catherine Peeke—rather than on past events. Maust's article was balanced and informative and avoided controversy. It was published in January 1980, a full year before the twenty-fifth anniversary, as a news story rather than a tribute.[39] In contrast, *Christian Missions in Many Lands*, the magazine of the Plymouth

Brethren sending agency with the same name, published an homage to the five men and their faith that appeared in January 1981. The article, "High Stakes, High Risk, High Calling," by Ken Fleming, Peter Fleming's brother, was unambiguously triumphant, but the triumph had more to do with the inspiration of the slain men's lives than with the Waorani. "No other incident in the last thirty years has stirred the evangelical world to commitment like that on the Curaray [River]," Fleming wrote. He also stated that "the waters of the Curaray have received Auca believers in baptism." However, Fleming acknowledged that Lloyd Rogers and a few other Brethren missionaries who were just beginning to work with the Waorani in Toñæmpade did not yet have enough believers to organize an assembly (church) among them.[40]

UNSTILLED VOICES

The most painful incident to come out of the anniversary centered around a book by James and Marti Hefley, prolific journalists and inspirational writers. The couple—together and as individuals—had written more than thirty books, about two-thirds of which could be described as inspiring, true-life stories for a popular audience.[41] Familiar with Wycliffe and the Summer Institute as well as with evangelical audiences, the Hefleys seemed the perfect people to bring the Waorani story up to date. Jim Hefley thought so and successfully pitched the book idea to the Fleming H. Revell Company, an evangelical publisher.

With a contract from Revell and a modest advance to fund a trip to Ecuador, the Hefleys started work. As Jim interviewed Rachel Saint, the rest of the Wao team, Elisabeth Elliot, Marj Saint, and others related to the story, it was not long before the couple realized that this was not the straightforward missionary narrative they had expected. As evangelicals and journalists, they struggled to find an appropriate focus for the book. "Had we known all of the problems, we [probably] would not have done the book," Jim admitted. "But once we were committed and found them out, then integrity demanded that we face them with honesty and grace."[42]

The Hefleys devoted a significant portion of the manuscript to addressing the problems of the previous twenty-five years. Conflict on the mission field was not the main emphasis of the book, but it was an important theme. Elliot and Marj Saint reviewed the manuscript, since about half of the text had to do with the five men, their missionary commitments, their deaths, and what had happened to the families. Each woman suggested some changes but in general let the book stand. Neither had any direct stake in the controversies surrounding SIL. In contrast, the normally sanguine John Lindskoog, then serving as SIL's international director of communications, was furious. He believed the Hefleys had deceived him with a manuscript that was very different from their original proposal. Lindskoog thought the book should be revised to emphasize the positive, or the whole project scrapped.[43]

The Hefleys were shocked at the intensity of Lindskoog's response. In a series of letters to Victor Oliver, senior editor at Fleming Revell, Jim Hefley defended their work. He and Marti had not misled Lindskoog; they simply had not known how complicated the story really was. They felt Lindskoog was overreacting, attempting to censor the book, partly because he was still emotionally involved with events in Ecuador. SIL had not commissioned the volume or underwritten it financially, and therefore neither Lindskoog nor SIL should dictate editorial policies. Jim also defended the decision to include controversial content: "This idea of writing so that missionaries (or anyone else) always come up smelling like roses is unrealistic, wrong, dishonest, and unfair to people who buy books expecting to get the truth, at least from the writer's perspective."[44] Jim was defending journalistic integrity, Lindskoog an organization to which he was deeply committed.

The dispute continued for several months until William R. Barbour Jr., the president of Fleming H. Revell, brought it to a close. In June 1980 he informed the Hefleys that Revell would not publish the book. Barbour was candid about his reasons, citing personal loyalties as the deciding factor. He and his wife had supported the work of the Wycliffe Bible Translators, the Summer Institute of Linguistics, and Wycliffe Associates for the past six or eight years, he wrote. Also, his daughter and son-in-law were serving with SIL. Given those connections, Barbour was unwilling to risk publishing a book that might adversely affect the reputations of Wycliffe or SIL, although he acknowledged the validity of the Hefleys' position. At the same time, Barbour mentioned the number of people close to the story who had contacted him expressing concerns. It wasn't just Lindskoog.[45]

The Hefleys did not challenge the decision, nor did they highlight the controversial side of their manuscript when seeking another publisher. A revised version of the book, titled *Unstilled Voices* (possibly a double entendre), was published by Christian Herald Books, a respected evangelical publishing house, though not one with Revell's visibility and influence.[46] Released in 1981, with a dust jacket emphasizing the positive, the book slipped largely unnoticed into the evangelical world.

FISHERS OF MEN OR FOUNDERS OF EMPIRE?

The twenty-fifth anniversary passed without public incident. The criticism, however, was not over. David Stoll's *Fishers of Men or Founders of Empire? The Wycliffe Bible Translators in Latin America* was published in 1982 with comments both more acerbic and more perceptive than anything the Hefleys had offered. Written by a young freelance writer and aspiring anthropologist, the book would influence later critics of SIL, as well as opponents of Christian missions, even though it never became well known among rank-and-file evangelicals.[47] In *Fishers of Men*, Stoll argued that the close connections between WBT and SIL masked what was in fact the dual identity of the same organization. That dual identity set the stage for duplicitous relationships with constituencies at home and abroad. People at home thought they were giving financial support to missionaries; governments of foreign countries thought they were signing contracts with nonsectarian, scientifically oriented linguists and literacy workers. Yet in each case they were referring to the same people. Stoll called it "a sacred system of misinformation."[48]

Even more troubling, SIL—either intentionally or because of naiveté—supported right-wing dictatorships and attempted to convert indigenous people to conservative anti-Communism as well as to Christianity. Even when linguists distanced themselves from politics, the act of translating the New Testament in collaboration with native speakers resulted in the fragmentation and cultural destruction of indigenous groups. As such, the linguists were in fact, if not in intention, agents of internal colonization and cultural destabilization.[49] Stoll was an indefatigable researcher, who reportedly spent seven years working on the book. He led readers through a detailed analysis of SIL's history, followed by an investigation of controversies in Mexico and in several South American countries, including Ecuador. Packed with information, the book ended oddly. Instead of a conclusion, the final chapter traced "the rise and fall of Wycliffe's most famous mission," the Waorani.[50] Stoll's facts were usually correct and, despite a pervasive skepticism, his observations offered a more thoughtful challenge than most anti-SIL literature. Nonetheless, given the "versatile fiction" of its dual identity, SIL was incapable of doing anything right.[51] The staff were pleasant, with good intentions, but the organization was a disguised faith mission that unwittingly supported right-wing governments. Stoll's final chapter, "The Huaorani Go to Market," traced contact with the Waorani from the five missionaries' deaths, through the involvement of SIL via Rachel Saint, up to events of the late 1970s. As the chapter title indicated, Stoll framed the narrative in economic terms. Before peaceful contact, the Waorani "defied the world market" by defending 7 percent of Ecuador's territory against all intruders.[52] Then, responding to the allure of trade goods, the Waorani had been subdued and relocated to make way for Gulf and Texaco.

The Waorani, Stoll argued, had done "much to make the Wycliffe Bible Translators what it is today." This happened through a process of commodification in which Dayomæ and the Waorani as a whole gave SIL a powerful story that could become "a symbol of savagery and redemption for consumption in the United States."[53] Only a handful of Waorani had ever traveled with Rachel Saint to the US and to Europe, but because of the publicity surrounding them, the group had been "exploited symbolically, to raise funds and recruits" for SIL. In addition, images and narratives associated with missionary media hype had played a key role in stimulating tourism. Consequently, the Waorani were exploited as "ethnic curiosities."[54] While SIL was Stoll's main target, he also criticized Erwin Patzelt, other authors who published on the "last of the Aucas," and Sam Padilla.[55]

Stoll offered his own version of the history of the Waorani and outsiders since 1956. He attributed the deaths of the five missionaries in large part to "evangelical competition for the prize of the unreached tribe." It was Nate Saint and his friends versus Rachel. Stoll also described Dayomæ as a reluctant language informant who had to be "conditioned" by Rachel.[56] Stoll's version of the " 'kidnapping' of Onkaye" had Rachel competing with the Catholic Sisters of Mother Laura for the young Wao woman.[57] Ethel Wallis's 1973 book, *Aucas Downriver: Dayuma's Story Today*, was an example of "fairy tale optimism." Stoll also mocked advertisements for Sam Padilla's tourist ventures with the Cononaco Waorani as "adventures in ethnocide."[58] In contrast to most critical accounts, Stoll did acknowledge efforts by SIL to curtail patterns of dependence that had developed and to encourage Wao independence. Nonetheless the chapter represented a deconstruction of the "Auca legend" as it had been told for years in the US.

Fishers of Men was reviewed in a number of evangelical publications, primarily academic journals dealing with history or missions. Most treated it as flawed but important. The chapter on the Waorani was mentioned in a review by David Howard, Elisabeth Elliot's brother, but otherwise was eclipsed by the rest of Stoll's dense analysis. Even those who rejected Stoll's political argument—that SIL had sold its soul to repressive governments—paid little attention to the economic side of the equation, particularly as it related to the Waorani.[59] The most thoughtful response to Stoll's claims came from Jim Yost. Stoll had summarized his argument in an essay that appeared in *The Other Side*, the same magazine of the evangelical left that had critiqued Wycliffe and the Summer Institute six years earlier. Yost's rejoinder was published in the same issue as Stoll's summary.[60]

YOST RESPONDS

Yost tackled Stoll's main arguments head on. In his essay, Stoll assumed that Christian witness directed toward native peoples inevitably destroyed cultures. He also suggested that political action was essential—a first principle—to free indigenous people from exploitation and oppression. Yost countered that the "spiritual dimension" in the lives of indigenous people was of utmost importance, followed by education. He rejected the idea that "cultural isolates" would survive in the context of a late twentieth-century world that was "bent on the discovery, exploitation, and consumption of every last physical resource."[61] Change was inevitable. Only people with a healthy spiritual foundation and the ability to read and write could negotiate it successfully.

Responding to the charge that SIL's contracts with foreign governments kept it from speaking out against oppression, Yost argued that working under a "formal relationship" with a state did not mean that either SIL or individual staff members agreed with all government policies. The occasion could arise, he conceded, where he "might have to choose to leave a country rather than be a party to any form of oppression."[62] Yet most of the time, Yost and other SIL staff tried to bring about change from within. He pointed to his work helping the Waorani secure title to their traditional land, as well as to SIL's pioneering efforts in bilingual-bicultural education. Were these two initiatives examples of being co-opted by the state?

Finally, Yost took on Stoll's accusation of duplicity in the relationship between Wycliffe and SIL, the idea that the dual identity existed "to hide from supporters what the members are doing on the field (science, linguistics) and to hide from host governments that the members are Christians trying to translate portions of the Bible."[63] Evidence did not support the allegation, Yost argued. Based on the context of the formal contract or through informal discussions, host governments knew that in addition to other linguistic work SIL members planned to translate the New Testament into indigenous languages. In turn, most staff members were intentional about explaining the relationship between the two organizations to their constituencies in the US. Rather than to deceive, the two organizations existed in order to best communicate that members "were both Christians and scientists."[64] Having two organizations also encouraged members to embrace both sides of their dual identities. *The Other Side* did not solicit a rejoinder from Stoll, so the exchange was left hanging. Nonetheless it was one of the few occasions during the 1970s and 1980s when a representative of SIL engaged in print with the organization's critics.

END OF AN ERA

Presidential Decree No. 1159 gave the Summer Institute until May 29, 1982, to transfer its operations to various agencies of the Ecuadorian government. SIL turned over an extensive bilingual education program. Linguists, pilots, and support staff prepared to leave. The Limoncocha base was dismantled, a move with great symbolic importance. Some Ecuadorians viewed Limoncocha as their country's Panama Canal, a "large, foreign-controlled enclave which was an affront to national sovereignty."[65] To many people, Limoncocha *was* SIL in Ecuador. As a result, the Institute "pulled out all the stops" to rapidly conclude its work and vacate the facility. It was a "trying and traumatic time for all concerned."[66]

The nearly three decades in Ecuador when SIL operated under its traditional model of government contracts were ending. However, to the dismay of those who opposed SIL, the government allowed the Summer Institute to maintain a limited presence in the country. Four teams that had not yet completed translating New Testaments and other materials stayed, including Peeke, Jung, and Kelley with the Waorani. A small number of additional staff were seconded to mission agencies still operating in Ecuador so they, too, remained. SIL also retained property in Quito, with buildings that were used for administrative headquarters, a translation center, and housing. On a much smaller scale, the Quito headquarters replaced Limoncocha as a home base where linguists still in Ecuador could come for concentrated work or when they needed a break from jungle living.

Within a few years, roughly between 1984 and 1990, additional language teams and support personnel were able to quietly and legally return to the country to complete work that had been interrupted by the decree.[67] Although Ecuadorians had picked up some projects, SIL linguistic teams who had worked with different indigenous groups for years—sometimes decades—had the relationships and experience to collaborate with local people to finish dictionaries, literacy materials, and portions of the Old Testament. In 1992, the same year the Waorani New Testament was published, a low-profile Summer Institute of Linguistics would officially finish its translation work in Ecuador. At that time the organization left with the expressed thanks of President Rodrigo Borja Cevallos.[68]

But this lay in the future. In 1982, for SIL members like Jim and Kathie Yost, Decree No. 1159 meant leaving the only home their three young children (Natasha and Brandon, along with Rachelle) had ever known. Jim and Kathie found it "wrenching to face the reality of leaving the Waorani," even though Jim later realized it was a necessary departure. The Waorani needed him to leave, and he needed to leave them. However, it was hard to say good-bye. On the day in May 1982 when a JAARS pilot flew the last plane out of Limoncocha, he stopped in Tzapino to pick up the Yosts. They were the last SIL family out of the rainforest.[69]

PART VI

Transitions, 1982–1994

17

The Aguarico Martyrs

AS THE SUMMER Institute was reducing its personnel in the rainforests, the Capuchín friars, unaffected by Decree No. 1159, continued their mission among the Waorani. During the early 1980s, Juan Santos Ortíz led the effort, but by the middle of the decade, Alejandro Labaca, recently named bishop of Aguarico, renewed his involvement. Labaca was an outspoken defender of Wao rights, and he personally took charge of the search for the Tagæidi. The latter project would cost Labaca his life, along with that of his coworker Sister Inés Arango Velásquez. Among Catholics in the Spanish-speaking world, especially in Ecuador, Colombia, and Spain, Labaca and Arango would be recognized as martyrs who gave their lives for the Waorani. In the English-speaking world, however, few people have ever heard of them.

THE UNPRETENTIOUS BISHOP

Bells rang from the parish church in the town of Puerto Francisco de Orellana (Coca), amplified by loudspeakers and announcing the ordination of Alejandro Labaca Ugarte as the first bishop of the Apostolic Vicariate of Aguarico. The faithful filled the streets on Sunday, December 9, 1984, to see a procession that included twenty bishops in full regalia from throughout Ecuador, as well as catechists and local religious leaders representing the many small settlements in the vicariate. Toward the end of the procession came five Waorani, including members of Labaca's adopted Wao family. They walked alongside four members of his biological family who had come from Spain. The Waorani had not yet been evangelized in any conventional sense. The Capuchín strategy of living among the Waorani and sharing their lives meant that none yet knew enough about Christianity even to consider baptism. Nonetheless, Labaca chose Iniwa, his adoptive father, to be the principal godfather (*padrino*) for his ordination.

Affirming both his own roots and the diversity of his flock, the new bishop gave portions of his homily in Spanish, Quichua, Basque, and *Wao tededo*. The brief remarks included reflections on a familiar Labaca theme: finding the "seeds of the Word [Christ]" among the diverse cultures of the Waorani, Siona, Secoya, Cofán, Quichua, and Shuar people who lived in the vicariate. Their encounters with Christ should not be scripted by outsiders, Labaca emphasized, but should express their own, culturally specific ways of relating to God. He also called for a more orderly settlement of the Oriente, one that respected the rights of indigenous people and homesteaders alike.[1]

While pomp and ceremony were the order of the day for the ordination and investiture of the new bishop, Labaca never ceased being a people's priest who embraced the Franciscan ideal of poverty. He would don the bishop's vestments when appropriate, but he was a much more familiar sight in a short-sleeved shirt, untucked over plain trousers. He wore shoes or rubber boots, and his only jewelry was a wristwatch. He paid so little attention to his personal needs that at one point a group of nuns bought him a package of socks and undershirts as a gift. When they apologized for having to guess the appropriate size, Labaca allayed their fears. If the socks and shirts did not fit, he had plenty of people to whom he could give them.[2]

AN ADVOCATE FOR THE WAORANI

At the time of his ordination, Labaca's last extended stay among the Waorani on the Dicado River had been a month-long visit in August 1980. After that, the priest's responsibilities as superior of the Capuchín Mission, as well as a knee operation, kept him out of the rainforest. He did maintain contact with Waorani who came to Nuevo Rocafuerte or Coca. His work on behalf of the Waorani, both as an advocate before the Ecuadorian government and a participant in direct efforts to protect the Tagæidi, resumed shortly after he became bishop. These dual roles unfolded simultaneously. Labaca's initial push centered on land, a concern shared by Catholics and evangelicals. In June 1985 he wrote "Carta de los Derechos de la Nacionalidad Huorani [*sic*]" (Letter on the rights of the Waorani nationality), directed to the state and advocating for the rights of the Waorani to their ancestral lands.[3]

In November 1986 Labaca expanded the June 1985 letter to include a call for the state to grant and protect all rights to which the Waorani were entitled. These included the right to exist as a people with their own identity, language, culture, customs, and natural resources; the right to be considered a single nationality, made up of both scattered groups and those now settled in the protectorate; and the right to receive protection from the national government against homesteaders, illegal loggers, and poachers of game and fish. Because the Waorani were a minority group in danger of biological extinction, Labaca called on the government to recognize their rights to land sufficient for them to flourish free from any fear of relocation and forced removal. This also meant the government should give the Waorani collective title forever to their ancestral lands outside the Yasuní National Park—territories indicated in a map that accompanied the letter. Finally, the government should provide, free of charge, all legal documents—birth certificates, identity cards, marriage licenses—necessary for the Waorani to access their rights as Ecuadorian citizens.[4] Labaca believed that a certain amount of assimilation into the national culture was inevitable but that the Waorani should be free to set their own pace in a way that maintained their identity.[5]

This description of Wao rights was written as an open letter to the state, first published in the newsletter of the Aguarico Vicariate to express the official position of the Church. The document placed the Catholic Church on the side of the Waorani, although it was also an exercise in faith since Labaca understood that the national government exercised very little actual control over its Amazonian region. Other than a desire for its riches, politicians in the metropolis of Quito were distant physically and culturally from Amazonia. Those in charge of the region were officials of the state oil company (CEPE) and the military. They, in turn, made decisions that affected several competing groups: environmentalists, oil companies, missionaries, tourists, and often corrupt local functionaries.[6] Advocating for the Waorani was a delicate balancing act with no guarantees. This dynamic shaped Labaca's actions, especially regarding the Tagæidi.

A MINORITY WITHIN A MINORITY

The Tagæidi (Tagæ's bunch) were a small family group whose actions were a microcosm of the Waorani as a whole. Like all Waorani before contact, the Tagæidi had a reputation for treachery and violence and often were assumed to be more numerous than they were. According to other Waorani, there were about a dozen people in the group in 1968, when they broke away from the Piyæmoidi. Their isolation coincided with the beginning of the oil boom, and the Tagæidi established their reputation for violence against outsiders by killing workers in 1971 and 1977 and terrifying others. The traditional territory of the Tagæidi fell within what became Blocks 16 and 17 (map 4), concessions later leased by Ecuador to Conoco (Block 16) and Braspetro, the state oil company of Brazil (Block 17). Crews from the Compagnie Générale du Géophysique (CGG), with their seismic work, first crisscrossed these lands before the two companies arrived to drill.

Labaca believed the Tagæidi represented the smallest of the Waorani groups, a minority within a minority.[7] In 1984 his interest in making peaceful contact with the group was renewed after a Tagæidi attack on a motorized canoe carrying CGG workers down the Shiripuno River. The company had chosen the Shiripuno as a cheap supply route to work sites on the Cononaco. According to one account, in the process of clearing the river to make it easier to navigate, workers removed a large, fallen tree. Unknown to them, the tree trunk was a bridge used by the Tagæidi to cross the river to reach their manioc gardens. In retaliation, on the afternoon of December 27, 1984, only three weeks after Labaca had become bishop, the Tagæidi attacked a CGG canoe, seriously wounding the Quichua pilot. Despite his wounds, the pilot shot and killed one of the attackers, an older man, who some would later suggest was Tagæ himself.[8]

Labaca followed news of the attack, although publicity was minimized to avoid frightening workers doing seismic exploration. After six months, when CEPE had not responded to the issues raised by the attack, Labaca sought to mobilize the Ecuadorian Bishops Conference and the nation's press. He insisted that every effort be made to protect the Tagæidi, claiming, "One Tagæidi alone is worth more than all the oil."[9] The result of Labaca's campaign was an agreement signed between the vicariate and CEPE on October 15, 1985. It allocated five million Ecuadorian sucres (roughly USD$42,000) from CEPE's budget for the vicariate to use over a six-month period to fund helicopter flights and other efforts to locate and contact the Tagæidi. The bishop soon discovered that renting helicopters or small planes to conduct the search was neither easy nor cheap. He eventually made six flights between October 1985 and June 1986, all to no avail. Despite his public comments, however, Labaca was in no particular hurry to find the Tagæidi. Oil exploration had been suspended temporarily in their territory, and the presence of these mysterious Waorani was the best possible deterrent against poachers, settlers, and drug traffickers.

The arrival in Tagæidi territory in early 1987 of the oil companies Braspetro and Conoco, as well as Petrocanadá and Arco, gave new urgency to Labaca's quest. The Tagæidi recently had been spotted in Block 17, prompting Labaca to seek renewal of his contract with CEPE. He found the company strangely reluctant. Finally, in early May 1987, a new agreement was signed, authorizing Labaca to use what remained of his original budget in searches and contacts to be completed by November 30, a strict six-month limit. What the bishop would not discover for another two months was that CEPE was developing an alternate plan, one that counted on the services of an Ecuadorian anthropologist named Julio Enrique Vela.[10]

ANTHROPOLOGIST OR VIGILANTE?

Most information about Vela and his role in the project to contact the Tagæidi comes from two books written by Capuchín friars, one narrating the history of the Waorani, the other a combined biography of the lives and deaths of Arango and Labaca.[11] Clearly these are not neutral sources. Even so, it is striking that in books that maintain a charitable tone toward almost all who appear on their pages, Catholic and non-Catholic alike, Vela is presented as a charlatan and a villain.

Vela's contact with the Waorani began in the late 1970s, when he served as a liaison between the Waorani and the Ecuadorian government on land issues. In that capacity he frequently visited Wao clearings. The picture that emerged during this period was of a man of energy and enthusiasm, with a flair for the dramatic. Every time Vela visited, he was full of new ideas for community development. In one letter, Pat Kelley enumerated just a few of them: water pipes, a generator, a chain of Wao stores, and a plan for extracting and selling oil from petomo nuts (for hair growth).[12] On several occasions, Vela nearly drove Catherine Peeke to distraction when he commandeered her services as interpreter. From her perspective, Vela and the agencies he represented, were trying to accomplish a "total social-economic transformation overnight."[13] Peeke half-seriously threatened to resign if she had to set aside her translation work to help Vela with land surveys.[14] Vela was long on enthusiasm and ideas but short on follow-through. He was also an enigma to SIL administrators. "I never know quite how to read the guy," commented Branch Director Dave Underwood. He added, "I really like [him]."[15]

This was a far cry from the Enrique Vela the Capuchín Fathers described several years later. They blamed him for allowing the former SIL Limoncocha base to fall apart during the eighteen months he served as Ecuador's state-appointed administrator after SIL turned the facility over to the state. During the same period, 1982–83, Vela so antagonized the Quichuas living around the base that they demanded his removal. "Limoncocha administrator was expelled by the indigenous," announced the newspaper *El Comercio*.[16]

According to the historian Miguel Angel Cabodevilla, Vela's next move was to reinvent himself as an expert on the Waorani and as a political and social conservative, in tune with the priorities of then president León Febres Cordero. Vela became practiced in spotting "Communists" within the indigenous organizations emerging in the Oriente and even among the Waorani. In the same way that Febres Cordero campaigned for the presidency as a populist cowboy, an Ecuadorian "Marlboro Man," Vela presented himself as a pistol-packing veteran of the rainforest.[17] He surrounded himself with a group of hardened indigenous bodyguards, called the Casa Verde (Green House), but perhaps best characterized as "Vela's gang," all heavily armed. Vela's new identity gave some credence to the Capuchín friars' claim that among the staff of CEPE he was informally known as "el loco Vela."[18]

Despite the nickname, when CEPE needed someone to contact Wao groups, presumably including the Tagæidi, within oil Blocks 14 and 17, they ignored Bishop Labaca and hired Vela. Ecuador's deteriorating economy may have put CEPE under pressure to expand drilling. Oil prices had fallen from a peak of thirty-five US dollars a barrel in 1980 to a low of eleven dollars a barrel in 1986, at a time when oil represented between 60 and 70 percent of Ecuador's export earnings. Then, on March 5 and 6, 1987, a series of devastating earthquakes occurred in the mountains, resulting in a death toll of at least a thousand people and the destruction of thirty miles of oil pipeline. Ecuador lost six months of oil revenue. By July 1987 there was an urgent need to get things up and running and to increase production.[19]

Vela's plan seemed altruistic enough. His stated purpose was to "guarantee their [Tagæidi] survival in their original habitat."[20] The project was financed to the tune of twelve million sucres, contributed by the various companies that held concessions in the two blocks where the Tagæidi were purported to be living.[21] A number of government agencies participated in the planning. However, the process became so cumbersome that on July 9 the oil companies suggested that the group should simply call on Labaca, with his knowledge of Wao territory, his experience in working for the CGG, and his success in fostering peaceful relationships. In the end, they decided that Vela could implement his plan by land, while Labaca would reach the Tagæidi by air.[22]

When he learned of the project, Labaca was appalled at the decision to use Vela and his men. In May of the previous year, the bishop had visited an oil camp where terrified workers expected a Tagæidi attack. Labaca and Sister Inés Arango spent four days in the camp, calming the crew and confirming that the Tagæidi were not in the immediate vicinity. Vela had stopped by the camp before the missionaries arrived but reportedly had done little more than empty his revolver randomly into the jungle and ask to be flown out immediately.[23] From this and other experiences, Labaca thought Vela was trigger-happy and would not hesitate to shoot the Tagæidi. The bishop confided to a friend, "If I don't go [to contact the Tagæidi], [Vela and his gang are] going to kill them."[24] Looking back, Capuchín missionaries close to the bishop were convinced that Labaca's actions leading up to his encounter with the

Tagæidi on July 21, 1987, could be understood only in light of his conviction that if Vela found them first, the results would be tragic.[25]

During the first six months of 1987, Labaca's contacts with Waorani, though few, had been routine, conforming to expectations the priest had developed during most of the previous decade. In January, on one flight searching for Tagæidi, Labaca and a fellow priest came across houses they had not seen before. Two women made what Labaca interpreted as welcoming gestures, so he ordered the helicopter to land. The family were not Tagæidi but were friends of the Waorani on the Yasuní who had adopted Labaca. The bishop and the intrepid Sister Inés Arango returned on January 22 to spend two days and two nights with the family "to secure the bonds of mutual trust and friendship."[26]

Six months earlier, Labaca, Arango, and another nun, Sister Consuelo Rico, spent four days in the rainforest, camping near areas where the Tagæidi reportedly had been sighted. The first night out, as the three missionaries shared a small tent, Sister Consuelo asked Labaca, "And if they come and kill us?" The priest replied, "We will give each other an embrace and die together."[27] Rico was unprepared for such risky pioneer mission work, and after two nights she was flown out and replaced by a lay Quichua man. Two days later, with still no sign of the Tagæidi, the missionaries departed.

Although these encounters did not result in Tagæidi contact, both ended safely, reinforcing Labaca's natural optimism. While no one ever accused the bishop of being a jungle adventurer, one of his favorite verbs was *arriesgarse*, "to risk oneself," and he did want to give himself wholly to missionary work.[28] This idealism, coupled with more than a decade of taking risks in the jungles of Ecuador and surviving them, plus the need to beat Vela to the Tagæidi, may have caused him to lower his guard when the next opportunity arose.

SISTER INÉS ARANGO

The risks, along with the daily challenges of living among the Waorani in the rainforest, were among the reasons Labaca found it difficult to recruit missionaries, particularly nuns, to share in the project. Inés Arango was the only nun in the vicariate who expressed a specific calling to be a missionary to the Waorani. Born April 6, 1937, in Medellín, Colombia, Arango first entered religious orders as an aspirant at age sixteen. At eighteen, she took vows with the Capuchín Tertiary Sisters and three years later, in 1959, made her perpetual vows. From an early age, she was interested in mission work, but she spent nearly two decades teaching in Colombia before she became "a true missionary," assigned in March 1977 to the Apostolic Prefecture of

Aguarico.[29] This was about three months after Labaca had spent his first night in a Wao clearing. Nuns did not accompany Labaca to meet the Waorani until February 1979. Arango was one of a second pair who made the trip the following April.[30]

By July 1987, when Arango joined Labaca to contact the Tagæidi, she was a veteran of numerous trips to visit the families along the Dicado-Yasuní River who were friendly to Catholic missionaries. She had begun to learn *Wao tededo*. "I think I can make myself understood," she wrote in March 1987, while acknowledging that she spoke only "a little" of the language.[31] Her last visit with the people of Táparo Anameni, whom she knew well, was for ten days in June 1987, only about a month before her death.[32]

Although Arango had demonstrated that she could fend for herself, the usual practice among the Capuchín Tertiary Sisters and other religious orders was that at least two women would go together on missionary ventures. In addition, the idea of a bishop and a nun alone together in the rainforest was bound to raise eyebrows. This was particularly true when the bishop might end up wearing swimming trunks or a hip-cord. Also, as Arango acknowledged, very few nuns wanted to risk their lives for a group as small as the Waorani, and even fewer for the handful of Tagæidi. Life in any Wao clearing was rigorous, demanding "a strong stomach, good health, much love for them [Waorani], no fear of the rainforest . . . great physical endurance and besides this a good spirit that seeks the truth."[33]

At five feet two inches tall and eighty-eight pounds, Arango was physically slight but tough. In 1987 she was fifty, finally had found her calling, and had no time to waste. "I am happy living among them as a sister, loved and respected and esteemed, [people] I can help as much as possible," she wrote a friend, referring to the families at Táparo Anameni. She would live and die alone among them if need be.[34] There were Capuchín priests who might have accompanied Labaca; Roque Grández and Alain Sernier each rode with the bishop on flights during the January 1987 attempts to locate the Tagæidi. However, Labaca believed the Tagæidi would be more likely to attack two men than a man and a woman. It also was evident that Labaca and Arango were comfortable working together. Their relationship was a friendship between two deeply religious people drawn together by a common calling.

FINDING THE TAGÆIDI

Despite his years of searching and organizing exploratory flights, Labaca was not the first to find what looked like a Tagæidi clearing. In late March the Braspetro oil company, with the help of the CGG, organized reconnaissance flights over

Block 17. On one flight, they spotted a small group of Waorani who fit the description of the Tagæidi making threatening gestures toward the plane. Labaca was in Quito at the time, but, when notified, he advised that the next step should be to drop gifts.[35]

Labaca spent most of June following up on this lead and attempting to track the movements of the Tagæidi. There were longhouses in various sites between the Tiguino and Cachiyacu rivers in Block 17, south of the Shiripuno River (map 4). On July 17, Labaca reported that eight people had been spotted once again in the longhouse where gifts had been dropped in March. Their gardens were new, and they made gestures Labaca interpreted as an invitation for the helicopter to land. "All the signs have been very positive," he wrote in a report to CEPE, "and soon it will be possible to attempt a first friendly personal contact."[36] Events began to move quickly. Labaca planned to leave Ecuador August 2 to spend a month in Spain. He would be celebrating the golden anniversary of his novitiate—fifty years of religious life—with others who had entered with him in 1937. The bishop feared that in his absence, contact with the Tagæidi would turn violent.[37] He needed to make contact before leaving for Europe.

Members of the Capuchín mission were divided over Labaca's decision. Some felt it was premature and was being done only to satisfy the oil companies. These colleagues were not with Labaca at a final meeting on July 17 with directors from Braspetro and CGG, plus Enrique Vela, when the decision was made to go ahead. The group decided to make one more "friendship flight" the following day and plan for contact based on the results. When they did, a Wao man came out, picked up the gift packages, and made signals that seemed to be inviting them to land. The "positive signs" of recent flights encouraged Labaca's decision to enter the clearing, along with Inés Arango, on July 20.[38] He called Arango, then in Quito, and urged her to return as soon as possible. Both bishop and nun were aware of the risks, but the nuns of Arango's community described her as eager to participate. Asked on several occasions if she feared being killed, Arango's standard reply was "I'll die happy."[39]

Even when his Wao father, Iniwa, warned Labaca not to go, the bishop refused to change his mind. Sunday night before the flight, several of Labaca's closest friends tried once more to convince him to cancel. "Alejandro, if you go in there, they are going to kill you, and I'll have to go and recover your body," said José Miguel Goldárez, Labaca's most senior colleague. Labaca responded, "Well, if they kill me, you will [just have to] take charge of all this, right?" And the discussion ended.[40] Four days later Goldárez would remove seventeen Wao spears from the body of his friend.[41]

THE BEGINNING AND THE END

Their flight was scheduled for Monday, July 20, but the winch that would lower Labaca and Arango from the helicopter to the ground had broken, and the trip was postponed for a day.[42] At about 5:30 Tuesday morning, Labaca and Arango left Coca, as they had the day before, for the ninety-minute drive to the CGG base. It was due south down the dirt road that would come to be known as the Via Auca. They were driven by Roque Grández, one of the Capuchín missionaries. Clouds were low, and the three arrived to find that the flight would be delayed until the weather improved. At about 10:00 they were cleared to fly. Labaca and Arango got last-minute instructions on how to put the sling under their arms when they were lowered to the ground. Then they boarded the helicopter along with the pilot, the technician to handle the winch, and the director of the CGG base.

Everything began smoothly. After about thirty minutes in the air, the pilot located the Wao longhouse and circled it once before dropping the packaged gifts about two hundred yards from the house. A few Tagæidi emerged and went to pick up the gifts. They did not seem in a hurry and did not carry spears. The helicopter circled again, then came in near where the gifts had been dropped. It hovered about ten feet above the ground to drop off Labaca and Arango. The Waorani hid as the helicopter neared, and by the time the two missionaries touched ground, they were alone. When the helicopter circled one more time, the crew saw Labaca and Arango cupping their hands to their mouths and shouting phrases in *Wao tededo*.

Plans called for the chopper to do another flyover in twenty or thirty minutes. The pilot landed at an oil company refueling pad about five minutes' flight away. The crew got gas, waited a short while and took off again. Five minutes later, there was no sign of the Wao clearing. The pilot was lost. He may have been using the Tiguino River as his reference, then took off from the pad in the wrong direction and mistakenly followed the Cachiyacu. Whatever happened, the helicopter circled through the area repeatedly but never located the site and eventually returned to the CGG base. No one ever explained why the pilot didn't return to the landing pad and try again from there since the clearing was so near. No equipment was available for an afternoon flight. The missionaries were on their own.[43]

When a helicopter flew over the clearing early the following morning the site was deserted except for two bodies. Labaca, wearing a *come*, lay sprawled, arms outstretched against a log that was alongside the path from the longhouse to the jungle. A cluster of spears remained in the body.[44] At least one account would later describe Labaca's body as arranged in a way reminiscent of ancient indigenous practices in the Amazon.[45] However, there is no indication that any Waorani ever followed such practices. Based on the one grainy picture taken from the helicopter, if anything, Labaca's outstretched arms resembled the crucifixion of Jesus, a connection that would later be made explicit.[46] Although not initially visible from the air, Inés Arango lay near the right side of the longhouse, pinned to the ground by three Wao spears. She wore the simple white dress that was her habit but had removed her head covering and shoes—her usual practice among the Waorani.[47]

As news and the shock spread to Coca and communities throughout the vicariate, the Jungle Brigade of the Ecuadorian military made plans to recover the bodies the same day. They deployed three helicopters, including one equipped with artillery and another large enough to carry eighteen soldiers and two Capuchíns, Roque Grández and José Miguel Goldárez. True to his word, Goldárez, an expert in such risky recoveries, would bring home his friend's remains. The soldiers were heavily armed, but Goldárez insisted that no shots be fired. He was certain the Tagæidi had fled and gunfire would only increase fear among the troops.[48]

The recovery took place without incident. Goldárez removed the heavy, eleven-and-a-half-foot spears from the bodies. Both were riddled with puncture wounds from repeated thrusts. The coroner's report would confirm a total of twenty-five wounds of various sizes on Arango's body, counting both the wounds made when a spear entered the body as well as when it emerged; the report for Labaca's body listed approximately ninety such wounds.[49] Wrapped in a plastic sheet, each body was hoisted into the helicopter hovering above the clearing. Because of Arango's slight build, her body was easy to get into the helicopter. The bishop's body was harder to maneuver, both because of its size and because of the fear that all but paralyzed the ground troops. The helicopter flew so near the Wao longhouse that by the time the mission was accomplished, the structure had been blown apart by the draft of the blades.

AFTERMATH

The Capuchín missionaries described the deaths as martyrdoms, a word echoed by Antonio González, the archbishop of Quito, at a funeral mass on Thursday, July 23. The story was covered extensively by the Ecuadorian press but, except for the *Miami Herald*, received little notice in the US and none among American evangelicals. Many reports in the Spanish-language press in Ecuador and elsewhere paid homage to Labaca and Arango for giving their lives to befriend and serve the Waorani. The bishop was not "a martyr of the faith, because they did not kill him for being a . . . messenger of the faith," one priest was quoted as saying. "He should be considered a martyr to love [*caridad*]."[50] There were no calls for vengeance since most people assumed that the Tagæidi were protecting their territory.

In a pronounced cultural shift from attitudes of earlier years, at least one newspaper suggested that describing the group as "savages" was an expression of internal colonization on the part of white Ecuadorians.[51] Another report viewed the deaths as a tragedy and a lesson in the need to take into account "justice and respect for other cultures."[52] Blame generally was directed toward CEPE and the oil companies, both for encroaching on indigenous lands and for pressuring Labaca to establish friendly relations. CEPE's general manager Carlos Romo Leroux acknowledged the disruption caused by bulldozers and dynamite but insisted the real threat to the Tagæidi way of life came from the tens of thousands of homesteaders who followed the oil companies into the jungles. Protecting the Tagæidi meant keeping the *colonos* out.[53]

There were, of course, observers willing to criticize Labaca. It was no secret that some of his fellow missionaries felt his actions were hasty, taken in response to the perceived threat from Vela and his men. Also, while Arango and Labaca could both make themselves understood in simple exchanges, neither was fluent in *Wao tededo*. Later critics chastised the bishop for arriving by helicopter, for misreading gestures from the Tagæidi, and for ignoring a red warning stripe on the roof of the longhouse.[54] Like the missionaries killed in 1956, Labaca was overconfident in his ability to interpret the situation on the ground from an aircraft above. As for the warning stripe, none of the eyewitness accounts mentioned anything unusual on the palm leaf roof. Until the Tagæidi could give their side of the story, all explanations were speculative.[55]

After the deaths, CEPE announced a three-month moratorium (August–October) on oil exploration in Block 17, the area that included the clearing where Labaca and Arango were killed. By November, Vela and his men were actively sweeping the region, checking for Tagæidi. After dividing the block into various zones, Vela affirmed that the Tagæidi remained in only one part of the territory. The irate Capuchíns viewed the practice of confirming Tagæidi-free zones as ethnic cleansing, although there was no evidence of Waorani killed or driven out. In January 1988, when CEPE asked Petrobras to resume exploration efforts in the block, the government concurrently set aside 30 percent of the approximately five hundred thousand acres in the concession as Wao territory where there would be no drilling. For the first time, the government had declared a portion of traditional Wao lands off limits for drilling. It was hailed as a significant breakthrough in the state's efforts to protect both the Tagæidi and the oil workers, resulting in part from the deaths of Labaca and Arango.[56] It also represented the government's increasing awareness of the rights of all of Ecuador's indigenous cultures. It was not, however, the end of encounters—some of them violent—between Waorani and oil workers. Nor, in the long run, did it provide protection for the Tagæidi.

18

The New Testament in *Wao tededo*

⌒————————————————————————————————

WITH HIS ORDINATION as bishop, defense of Waorani rights, and death by
Tagæidi spears, Alejandro Labaca had been a public figure in 1980s Ecuador. In contrast, these years were quiet and safe for Rosi Jung and Catherine Peeke, the two SIL
linguists remaining in Tewæno. Yet, paradoxically, the decade from 1982 to 1992 was
pivotal for SIL's work among the Waorani. With little fanfare, linguists Peeke and
Jung accomplished a goal that had been set when Rachel Saint first met Dayomæ in
1955: the translation of the New Testament into *Wao tededo*.

A DESTINY FINALLY FULFILLED

Nearly a quarter of a century since she first heard the Wao language and a decade
after she returned to Ecuador from the US with a PhD in anthropological linguistics, Catherine Peeke (1924–2014) embarked on the translation task for which she
was uniquely qualified.[1] Although Peeke had been a part of efforts to contact the
Waorani from SIL's earliest days in Ecuador, she remained on the periphery for many
years. She was in and out of Tewæno between 1962 and 1965, doing research for her
doctoral dissertation, and coordinated Waorani relocation efforts from Limoncocha
between 1968 and 1970. But not until 1970 did she officially become a part of the
Wao team.[2] The logical assignment for Peeke would have been to collaborate with
Rachel Saint on translation. However, Saint resisted any suggestions for changing

the orthography she had created or the translation she had done. Peeke attempted to revise Saint's work on the New Testament Book of Acts but was challenged every step of the way.[3]

Recognizing that she and Saint could not work together effectively, Peeke backed away from Bible translation.[4] She continued to assist with the relocations, researched Wao genealogies, and helped Pat Kelley with early literacy materials and medical phrase sheets. She also spent more than half her time, roughly every other year between 1969 and 1978, in North Carolina caring for her elderly mother, who died in 1980. After Jim Yost arrived in 1974, Peeke collaborated with him on anthropological research. She also pursued her own projects, including collecting lists of vocabulary words in *Wao tededo*. Some she compiled, some came from Saint, and others from Kelley and Kelley's literacy students. Peeke worked on Wao names for birds based on a list of Amazonian birds generated as part of graduate research by an ornithologist and biologist named David L. Pearson.[5] Peeke's various lists were the beginnings of what by the 1990s would become a collection of more than four thousand Wao words that became the basis for a trilingual *Wao tededo*-Spanish-English dictionary.

In the midst of one project, Peeke tried to explain her activities to constituents from her home church, Weaverville (NC) Presbyterian. These were friends whose donations to the Wycliffe Bible Translators supplied Peeke's salary. Peeke told her "church family" she was recording the life stories of individual Waorani, seeking information about their culture, its social structure, and Wao beliefs about the spirit world. Apparently some people questioned the linguist's priorities. "You wanted me to tell the Church why I'm putting anthro projects 'ahead of translation,'" she wrote her sister, Libba. "I don't think that's exactly what I'm doing... [but] no matter how many other jobs I report doing, they go on happily talking about my 'translating the Bible for the Aucas,' and never seem to notice that I've never done that."[6]

Some of the misunderstanding came from Peeke's unwillingness to discuss the conflicts that had caused her to distance herself from Wao Bible translation. In addition, she had the sensibilities of both scholar and missionary, believing that her work in linguistics and anthropology was ultimately significant and relevant to effective Bible translation. Ironically, during the 1970s, when SIL was accused of misleading governments by promising to do scientific work when all it really did was Bible translation, just the opposite took place in Tewæno. Research in linguistics, anthropology, genetics, and medicine moved ahead, as did efforts at literacy and community development, while Bible translation stalled.

That changed in 1981. Rachel Saint's prolonged trip to the US—from early 1979 to February or March of 1982, shortly before she retired—opened the door for Peeke at last to be assigned to the Wao New Testament. She was in the early stages of the task when Roldós issued Decree No. 1159. Although a blow at the time, the decree proved to be a blessing in disguise, freeing Peeke to focus exclusively on translation. With Limoncocha closed and most SIL staff gone, it was clear that those who were left would no longer be able to handle community development or healthcare.

However, the government issued only two-year visas to Peeke, Jung, and other translators. This reinforced the understanding that those who remained in the country did so to finish specific tasks. The visas could be and, in the end, were renewed, but the uncertainty lent urgency to the translation project. Peeke did not face the job alone. Rosi Jung (1936–2015), the German medical worker and linguist, had also been assigned to Wao translation. The two women had worked together among the Waorani since 1970, but always with distinct responsibilities. In 1979 they joined forces and, despite numerous interruptions, devoted the next twelve years of their lives to translating the New Testament. They came to the task of translation by different paths but were an effective team.

THE UNLIKELY LINGUIST

Even in her seventies, Rosi Jung could remember the exact date of her first conscious prayer. It was December 16, 1944, and eight-year-old Rosi was in the cellar of her aunt's house as Allied bombs fell on her hometown of Siegen, Germany. The houses shook, and the adults around her cried and screamed. Rosi cried and screamed too, but she also prayed. "Oh God, protect us. I will be a good child forever and ever."[7] She and her family emerged unscathed.

Jung's mother had died in early 1944, and the little girl did not get along with an aunt who had come to care for her. Her father, though unchurched himself, thought Sunday School might help. He sent Jung to a nearby Free Evangelical Church. The first Sunday, she heard that God loved her. It was welcome and overwhelming news for a child grieving the loss of a parent and experiencing the fears of wartime. It became the foundation for a faith that ultimately drew Jung to Ecuador.

Her journey, however, was circuitous. In postwar Germany, the competition to enter a university or to find a good job was fierce, and Jung ended her public school education at age fifteen. She worked several unskilled jobs before spending two years at a Bible school. In 1959 she and a friend went to England for a year, working and learning English. Jung picked up the language quickly, an initial indication that she might have a facility for language acquisition. On her return, she enrolled in midwifery school in Tübingen, two years later receiving a diploma as a nurse midwife.

Throughout this time Jung was searching for a vocation that would give her a sense of purpose. While in Bible school, she considered the possibility of missionary work.

Later, in England, she read *Through Gates of Splendor* and felt that God might want her to serve a group of people like the Waorani. During the summer of 1964, Jung took classes with the German branch of WBT, and, after completing her midwifery degree, she spent a second summer in 1968 training with Wycliffe, this time in England.

To her surprise, Jung was accepted as a staff member by the German Wycliffe organization. The questions that remained were where she would serve and how she would raise the funds to support her work. Although "all German Wycliffe people [seemed] to get called to Africa," Jung was drawn to Latin America. She had heard of Rachel Saint's work with the Waorani, as well as other stories of Wycliffe in the region. When it came time to request a country assignment, Jung listed Peru, Suriname, and Ecuador as possibilities. In response, Ecuador Branch director John Lindskoog contacted her with two opportunities: working with Saint or caring for missionary children in Limoncocha. Uncertain, Jung tossed the ball back to Lindskoog. Where did he think she was most needed? At this point, in 1968, Lindskoog was urgently seeking a potential coworker for Saint. He invited Jung to take the position. While he indicated there might be some challenges, he did not tell her that Saint had rejected all previous candidates.

At last Jung had found her calling. However, in October 1968 she did not yet have the funds to complete her Wycliffe training and get to Ecuador. A woman Jung did not know coordinated a network of women's prayer groups in Reformed Churches throughout Germany. She began to circulate information about Jung through the network. Money from people Jung had never met began arriving at her door, the postal carrier literally pushing envelopes filled with cash through the mail slot. Women in the prayer groups provided the funds she needed for travel expenses and continued to sustain her financially as she served in Ecuador. What Jung viewed as God's unexpected provision became a touchstone during the difficult years ahead.

HELPING POLIO VICTIMS

Jung arrived in Ecuador on July 4, 1969. She studied Spanish in Quito until October, when she was asked to come to the HCJB mission hospital in Shell to help care for the most seriously ill Wao polio victims. Saint made a brief trip from Tewæno to meet her new colleague, but the two women did not work together until January 1970 in Limoncocha. Jung had gone to Limoncocha to take charge of the physical therapy program for Waorani who had suffered paralysis. Saint arrived and wanted to help, so the two women divided the patient load. Saint and Jung's working relationship was troubled from the start, partly because of Jung's unwillingness to cede all control to Saint. Jung respected her senior colleague and recognized her own lack of experience as a missionary. She had, however, assumed she could make some decisions and have opinions of her own. On furlough in the US, Peeke wrote Jung, advising her to go along with whatever Saint wanted. Forthright and open by nature, Jung found it hard to toe the line.

After the polio patients had returned to their homes, Lindskoog tried to salvage the situation by asking Peeke to be Jung's "partner" (official coworker) and giving Jung responsibility for the Wao healthcare program, a position she held from 1970 to 1978. The first three and a half years were particularly exhausting as the recently relocated Waorani experienced wave after wave of contact illnesses. Jung was always on call. "In a hospital, you end your shift and go home," she observed. "[In Tewæno] they lived all around you." Sick Waorani would moan or talk to one another, sometimes loudly. Jung found this particularly unnerving at night. Even when the patients were stable, one person might call out to another, "Oh, look! He's going to die any time now." "Oh, look, he's going to die." Jung, a light sleeper, found it difficult to ignore the cries, even when she was sure they were false alarms. She would pray, "Oh Lord, don't let him die," and try to sleep.

During Jung's first months on the job, Saint was in Tewæno, looking over her younger colleague's shoulder. This only added to the stress. Even when Saint was not present, the ongoing conflict over her role among the Waorani took a high emotional toll on Jung. Despite the pressure, and thanks in part to the availability of antibiotics, none of the adults Jung treated during her nine years in healthcare died. She lost one infant, but nothing would have saved the child.

In addition to treating the sick, Jung implemented many of the healthcare policies established during the 1970s. She standardized the vaccination program, keeping records and ensuring that the Waorani were vaccinated against yellow fever, polio, measles, diphtheria, whooping cough, and tetanus. She instituted a system of modest charges for medicine. She also began to train Waorani to handle first aid. She selected two women from the original Tewæno group: Ana, a half sister to Dayomæ, and Ayebæ, daughter of Yowe and Dayomæ's sister Oba. Both were eager to learn and proved to be excellent at handling basic medical complaints, taking some of the load from Jung. Additional indigenous healthcare workers were trained by nurse Lois Pederson at Limoncocha before the base closed. One thing Jung did not do was midwifery. The Waorani, she later observed, did fine delivering babies on their own.[8]

TRANSLATORS IN TEWÆNO

By 1978 Jung was ready for a change. She knew that Peeke was preparing to take on translation of the New Testament, and she asked if she could share in the project.

Peeke agreed, as did SIL administrators. Usual policy called for at least two people to work on any Bible translation. Jung took a refresher course in translation and by mid-1978 was translating the account of Joseph from Genesis. The Waorani loved the Old Testament stories Dayomæ and Rachel told over the years, and the strong narrative element made it a good place to "warm up" for New Testament translation, which was SIL's main goal. Peeke, meanwhile, worked on two gospels—a revision of Mark and a translation of Matthew—as the narrative texts that would ease her into full-time translating.

Jung had a rocky start—major surgery in mid-1979, her father's illness in 1980, and his death in 1981—that kept her away from the Waorani for roughly two years. However, by September 1981 she had returned and was finishing Joseph. In November she was ready to begin the New Testament Epistle of I Thessalonians. Spurred by the uncertainties surrounding Decree No. 1159, Peeke and Jung pushed ahead as quickly as they could during the next six months.

The two women shared a small house in Tewæno that had a kitchen–living area, a bedroom, and a porch. All were screened to keep out at least some insects. The floor was about three feet off the ground, which deterred but did not prevent snakes—or more often, rats—from entering. Housemates since the early 1970s, Peeke and Jung were opposites in many ways. Jung was a morning person, usually up and ready by 7:00. By 6:00 in the evening, she was done. Peeke loved to work at night, often typing by candlelight until nine or ten. She was such a deep sleeper that Jung was sure "you could have carried her [Peeke] away in the middle of the night." Jung slept lightly, drifting off to the usual chorus of night sounds. If the sounds changed, she would wake up.[9]

The two women were not afraid of the Waorani in Tewæno. Their door had no lock but was secured at night with a bamboo pole or a large hunk of petrified wood. Jung could remember the specifics of only one dangerous incident, though she acknowledged there might have been a few others. In the one episode, a Wao man became angry with a pilot who had been buying artifacts and had run out of money. The pilot managed to fly out safely, but the offended indigenous man continued to rage. Kelley, in Tewæno at the time instead of Peeke, suggested that she and Jung sleep in the same house. When Kelley arrived to stay with Jung, she had her machete in hand. "What are you going to do with that?" Jung asked. "I don't know," Kelley replied, "but that guy's not going to get me." The night passed uneventfully, and the episode blew over.[10] Before she moved from Tewæno, Dayomæ helped to enforce the norm of nonviolence. Yowe, one of the older men and a Christian, lived with his family in a house at the end of the airstrip. From there he kept an eye on Peeke and Jung's house.

DAILY LIFE AS A LINGUIST

The two linguists took turns cooking, each for a day at a time. Their stove consisted of three top burners, fueled by propane. The menus were simple: rice or noodles, carrots, cabbage, and onions—imported from the outside—supplemented by local bananas, both cooking and eating varieties, manioc, and chonta palm fruit (a vegetable). The women planted papaya, which flourished.[11] If the Waorani had success hunting, they often would give the women meat and fish. Monkey and wild pig were favorites, prepared in one of their two pressure cookers. Sometime Jung and Peeke would bring tins of cookies to share with the Waorani. The empty tins became the perfect storage containers to protect papers and other items from the humidity. A favorite pastime for the Waorani was watching the translators eat. This bothered Peeke, who felt it was impolite to eat in front of them, even though she couldn't invite a sizable portion of the village to dinner every night. Jung was more apt to respond. After the perennial questions "What are you eating, Omade?" and "What does it taste like?," she would sometimes reply in German or in English, "We're eating just the same thing today as we did yesterday."[12]

During a typical day of translation work, Peeke and Jung would spend mornings working with language assistants to do a first-draft translation line by line from the New Testament. To avoid distractions, Jung usually worked in their home, Peeke in the school or other available building. After lunch and a break, each woman would spend the afternoon writing up her notes from the morning and then doing research on the meaning of the next section to be translated. SIL supplied its linguists with exegetical helps—materials that discussed various interpretations of difficult passages or concepts. Depending on the availability of native speakers and on what phase of the translation process they were in, sometimes the women would also work with their translation assistants into the afternoon. Later in the day, after the sun went behind the treetops, Jung often walked up and down the nearby grass airstrip to get some exercise. This practice perplexed and amused the Waorani, who had no concept of walking for any purpose other than to get somewhere. A crowd of children followed along until the novelty wore off.[13]

BARRIERS TO TRANSLATION

Translating the New Testament—and in Jung's case, also a story from the Old Testament—required patience on the part of translator and native speaker alike. Significant barriers existed between the world of the Bible in its English translation and the world of the Waorani and their language, especially given their historic isolation. The translators had to find words in *Wao tededo* to express such concepts as specialized occupations (carpenter, fisherman, teacher); unfamiliar social relationships (servant/master, rich/poor, teacher/learner); common products (bread, loaves, wine); domesticated animals (sheep, goats, donkeys); and many others.

Most important, the translators had to settle on a word for God since, according to Peeke, "the Waorani had no concept of a god, much less a supreme God."[14] Rachel and Dayomæ had chosen what seemed to be the closest name among Wao legendary figures, Wængongui. Peeke noted that Wængongui seemed to be "a fairly harmless character" who "created this earth, the spheres, the vegetation, and, in some accounts, animals and man."[15] Then he went to the upper world. Peeke and Jung decided to keep the name, building on teaching already done by Rachel and Dayomæ. Identifying Wængongui as the Christian God and the greatest or supreme ruler over heaven and earth came only as the Waorani learned of his dealings with his people through the Old Testament stories introduced by Rachel and Dayomæ and repeated by other Waorani. The New Testament would further illuminate the character of the supreme God as the father who had a son, Jesus, whom he sent into the world. The name they used for Jesus was Itota, a Wao adaptation of the Spanish Jesús.

Often the translation difficulties involved trying to find the right word in *Wao tededo* instead of the almost right word. For example, Jung and a young Wao man, Pegonca, were working on the portion of the Joseph story where the Egyptian pharaoh had a dream of seven sleek, fat cows and seven gaunt, lean cows, symbolizing periods of abundance and famine.[16] Jung struggled to explain to Pegonca, who spoke only *Wao tededo*, the difference between the more general word "thin" and words such as "lean" and "gaunt" that signify starvation. Jung did not know how the latter two words or the idea behind them would be expressed in *Wao*. She and Pegonca went over and over the text trying to figure out the appropriate translation until at last Pegonca caught the nuance and suggested the correct words.[17]

Neither Peeke nor Jung was completely fluent in *Wao tededo*, and, as in the case of Jung and Pegonca, the translators might struggle to adequately communicate the meaning of a text to their Wao assistants.[18] This highlighted the essential role the Waorani themselves played in the translation process. Twelve Waorani made significant contributions to the translation, with four serving as principal Waorani translation "helpers," as they were usually called.[19] An additional dozen or so people pitched in on various occasions when their paths happened to cross those of the translators.

The twelve most significant assistants all had some direct connection with missionaries or the spread of Christianity. Dayomæ was one of them, and seven others were related to her, either directly or by marriage. These included Dayomæ's half sister Ana; Dayomæ's sister Oba; and three of Oba's nine children, along with two of their spouses. The children and spouses were son Pegonca and his wife, Conta; daughter Wanguincamo and husband, Ñiiwa; and daughter Ayebæ. Two other helpers, Onguimæ and Gaba, were children of Toñæ, the Wao martyr killed in 1970. Tæmænta, one of the principal assistants, was the son of Nænquiwi ("George") of Palm Beach. Enæ, a helper during the early years, was a half sister of Dayomæ and one of the polio victims whom Jung had nursed.

CONTRIBUTIONS FROM THE WAORANI

Of the four principal assistants, Oba and Tæmænta regularly worked with Peeke while Ana and Ayebæ helped Jung. Each brought strengths to the project. Oba was a consistent worker and, according to Peeke, excellent at correcting grammar. Oba was concerned that Peeke express the translation correctly but, Peeke added, "[She is] not at all perturbed if what I say makes no sense." On occasion, however, Oba, who had been baptized as a Christian in the early 1960s, displayed "some real insights."[20] Tæmænta, the "pastor" and community leader for the Quiwado clearing and a member of the younger generation, brought a genuine understanding of the Scriptures to his translation work. Tæmænta could read and write *Wao tededo*, which enabled him on occasion to write the correct translation himself as he and Peeke worked together. The biggest difficulties were the limits on his time. Tæmænta often worked as a day laborer for the oil company and had to squeeze translation consultations into his days off. Nonetheless, he was committed to the translation project, and Peeke considered him almost a language consultant, certainly her best translation assistant.[21]

Ana, one of Jung's principal translation assistants, was a health promoter and a church leader in Tewæno. On the younger edge of the "older generation" (Dayomæ and her contemporaries), Ana was one of the few in that group who was literate, poring over the Scriptures available to her. She was eager to take part in translation work and often spoke in church about the insights she gained. She also had a reputation for taking to heart the lessons learned.[22] Ayebæ, Jung's other key translation aide, also was a health promoter and did household work for the two linguists. Ayebæ was the best reader among the women.[23] Although she rarely responded to the content of the Scriptures as they worked, one exception was the account of Jesus healing a blind man in the Gospel of John. Ayebæ found the story exciting and told it back to Jung as if the linguist had never heard it. "For days, she kept thinking about it," Jung remembered. "She explained the whole chapter; she was thrilled."[24] Kelley remembered Ayebæ's amusement at the encounters between Jesus and the Pharisees.[25]

All the translation helpers were paid, usually a salary comparable to that earned by household help in Shell or a neighboring town. Jung wrestled over whether they should pay more, yet she realized that a higher rate could create disruptive income disparities. Translation work was less demanding physically than household labor, but required patience and concentration. The linguists rarely turned down anyone who wanted to help, even briefly, but they were never overwhelmed by applicants. Many Waorani saw little importance in Bible translation and were put off by the demands of the job. Others with some exposure to reading and writing *Wao tededo* criticized the work of the helpers and the orthography in use. A few dismissed Wao translation efforts in favor of learning Spanish.[26]

The translators and their assistants formed deep bonds during the years they worked together. When the linguists moved out of Tewæno in 1992, having finished the translation, Oba could not bear to come to the airplane to say good-bye. Peeke herself was devastated a few years later at Oba's untimely death during a 1994 chicken pox epidemic. The linguist poured out her grief in a poem written to remember her friend. Before bowing to the inscrutable purposes of the Almighty, the seventy-year-old Peeke wished she would have died instead of Oba. Jung, Peeke, and Kelley all experienced a second heartbreak in 2002 when Ayebæ died of hepatitis.[27]

THE PROCESS OF TRANSLATION

Translating the New Testament into *Wao tededo* was a painstaking process that followed a series of steps prescribed by SIL. These were necessary, if often tedious, and helped to explain why Peeke and Jung had completed a rough translation of the New Testament by October 1985 but did not finish the final manuscript for another six years.[28] Each step of the way the translators worked with their Waorani assistants to revise and refine their work. The process was fluid, with different portions of the New Testament in different stages of translation at any given time.

Peeke and Jung each worked on different books of the New Testament, with Peeke tackling those that were most challenging conceptually and theologically, such as the Epistle to the Hebrews. Due to her advanced knowledge of *Wao tededo*, Peeke also worked more quickly than Jung, translating the greater portion of the Scriptures.[29] Peeke initially pushed them both to work quickly so that they would have a complete draft translation in case their visas were not renewed. Having gone over the entire New Testament at least once with native speakers would have helped the linguists to continue the work outside of Ecuador.

Peeke's pace reflected the resolve of a woman who had waited for years to participate in this project and was determined to see it through. Sometimes her determination exceeded her physical capabilities. In 1984 she experienced a "collapse" and temporary numbness that she suspected might be light strokes. Tests found nothing wrong; the real culprit probably was exhaustion.[30] Jung could not match her coworker's pace or knowledge of *Wao tededo*, but she held her own with the difficult language. Her involvement in the translation was essential, both for the work she completed and because she was the only person qualified to check Peeke's use of the Wao language. The two were a team from start to finish.

Just as the nature of Wao language and culture made the initial translation difficult, so, too, culture and circumstances tested the linguists as they revised their work. First, they had to convince the Waorani to do comprehension checks. The linguists would ask a translation helper or other Wao to read or listen to a draft translation of some portion of the New Testament. Then Peeke or Jung would question the person to find out how much he or she had understood. Doing this for large sections of the New Testament was daunting, particularly because it was another activity that made no sense to the Waorani. Why would the translators quiz *them* about the meaning of material that the translators themselves had written?[31] In time, the translation assistants began to grasp what the linguists needed. "Pegonca, his wife Conta, Tæmænta, and Wanguincamo now give a fair expression of what they understand a passage to mean," Peeke reported. "At least, when they are quite blank, we can be sure it means nothing to them—so it's time to start again."[32]

Peeke and Jung alternated two months of translation work in Tewæno with two months in Quito, spending that time further revising what they had done and typing it into a computer. While most Tewæno sojourns were uneventful, interruptions in the translation schedule were common. On one occasion, the two women arrived to find that Wanguincamo had had all her upper teeth pulled as preparation for getting false teeth. She was, Peeke wrote, "somewhat indisposed," particularly when it came to speaking.[33] During a summer 1987 session, Ana was in Shell due to unexpected complications with her pregnancy. At the same time, Ayebæ had a baby whose needs led to frequent interruptions.

Although the Waorani might juggle translation work and babies, Peeke and Jung had their own hands full just trying to do the translation. The work involved "a lot of pointing, some acting out and a good deal of frustration."[34] All the while the linguists jotted notes on three-by-five cards or in spiral notebooks. When the *Presbyterian Journal* offered a romanticized description of Peeke engaged in translation with a "curious child on [her] lap," the linguist wrote a forceful correction. "*No way* would you catch one on *my* lap while I'm trying to concentrate on language work!"[35]

Peeke always downplayed her knowledge of *Wao tededo* and her accomplishment in determining its grammatical structure. *Wao tededo* was, she said, "difficult to speak [but] not so hard to analyze."[36] Even late in her career, she was quick to acknowledge how much she still did not know. In 1987 the anthropologists Clayton and Carole Robarchek, researchers with no SIL affiliation, arrived to do fieldwork among the Waorani. Peeke helped them with language learning in her spare time. After a month, the visitors were discouraged over their continuing inability to carry on conversations. "And all the while poor Rosi and I are thinking how little we can communicate and understand after all these years," Peeke wrote her sister.[37] Despite these limitations, Peeke maintained a lifelong fascination with and love for *Wao tededo*. In 1991 she lamented the unanticipated amount of time she needed to finish a journal article. Yet she quickly added, "I am enjoying doing it. . . . The Waorani have such neat ways of saying things!"[38]

CONTROVERSIAL WORDS

An important moment in revising the text of the Wao New Testament was a two-day consultation in August 1990 between the linguists and influential Waorani to check key terms used in the translation. The meeting had been precipitated by the news that Dayomæ and Dawa, still important figures among Wao Christians, had objected to certain words or phrases the translators had used. The two women argued that some of these terms were associated with jaguar fathers and therefore inappropriate. Jaguar fathers were Waorani believed to be in touch with jaguar spirits who helped hunters locate and pursue wild peccary. Traditionally the influence of jaguar spirits was relatively benign. Nonetheless Christians opposed association with such spirits.[39]

The most controversial words were *ëwoca-*, "to have God's Spirit," and *ëtawë*, "to have in (one's) being, heart, character."[40] Upon investigation, Peeke and Jung found that Dawa and Dayomæ were right; jaguar fathers did use these same words in talking about their experience with spirits. However, the translation assistants and other Waorani in Tewæno insisted that context was the decisive factor. The words were appropriate when used by believers or in the Bible to refer to the work of the Holy Spirit in someone's heart.

Dawa and Dayomæ also objected to a few other translation choices that were less controversial. Peeke, Jung, and their assistants were struggling to determine the best translation of certain difficult words or concepts. All were included on a list of key terms to discuss. Seeking consensus, Peeke and Jung invited Dayomæ and her daughter Nancy, along with Dawa and husband Quemo as special guests at the consultation, held in Tewæno. A few people from other settlements attended, and most of the adults and young people in Tewæno were there at least part of the time.

During the two days of discussions, the linguists began "gingerly," first seeking advice on the use of Spanish loan words and other relatively nonthreatening issues, before tackling the disputed terms. Conversations were harmonious until participants got to *ëtawë*. After some explanation from the linguists and debate by the Waorani present, most agreed that the word was appropriate when used in context. However, Dawa was visibly distressed and voiced her concern. Her objections were partly an expression of loyalty to Saint, who would have disapproved of the usage. "Rachel had done it one way, and now we wanted to do something different," remembered Jung, who had been tired and discouraged in the face of the seeming impasse.[41] It was late at night, and the group adjourned.

The next morning, talks resumed. Peeke and Jung were astounded when "Dawa quietly agreed, along with the others, that this [*ëtawë*] would be a good term to use."[42] Later they learned that Ayebæ had gone to her after the meeting. Without confrontation, she had a long discussion with Dawa, explaining that "the Holy Spirit enters us and remains, replacing demonic influences."[43] For the Christian, if the word referred to the Holy Spirit, it could not, at the same time, carry with it connotations of jaguar spirits. "Oh, is that the way it is?" responded Dawa, after Ayebæ's explanation. "That's the way it is," Ayebæ affirmed.[44] So Dawa changed her mind. There were no other objections, and the rest of the meeting went smoothly. "The visitors . . . seemed thoroughly pleased to have been brought back 'home' to Tewæno [flown by MAF] and relationships were cordial all the way around," Peeke reported. "They also seemed pleased to have direct input into the Scripture translation."[45]

THE POLITICS OF ALPHABETS

Having cleared the hurdle of key terms, Peeke and Jung spent the next year on final revisions, which included finalizing the alphabet for *Wao tededo*. This was important because pressure to change Wao orthography had surfaced once again. Beginning about 1988 there was renewed interest in a more Hispanicized alphabet, even though it might not correspond to *Wao tededo* as closely as the orthography the linguists were using.[46] Several factors were behind calls for a change. First, and probably most important, fiscal schools that offered instruction only in Spanish had spread among the Waorani. By early 1991 these schools had been established in six Wao settlements, and they seemed to be the wave of the future.[47] As a result, many, if not most, Wao children would learn to read first in Spanish rather than *Wao tededo*. This younger generation would be "more familiar with the Spanish orthography than with their own."[48] Moreover, as Spanish became the language of "educated" people, Spanish orthography would enjoy more prestige among the Waorani than a distinct alphabet for *Wao tededo*, despite Wao speakers learning to read more quickly with the latter. The closer the Wao alphabet was to the Spanish, the more legitimacy it would enjoy.

In addition, there were people in Toñæmpade still loyal to Saint and the alphabet she had developed, which represented the Spanish-influenced end of the orthography spectrum. These critics included a core group of Quichuas who had married into the tribe and found the *Wao tededo* alphabet, with ten distinct vowels, difficult to read. As a result, they had been vocal critics of any alphabet that challenged Saint's, as well as of printed materials produced using a different alphabet.[49] An alphabet closer to Spanish might mollify the dissidents. On the other hand, opposition to a Hispanicized alphabet most likely would come from indigenous organizations that had continued to gain visibility and influence since the brief regime of Jaime Roldós. They emphasized the distinct identities of indigenous people and could be expected to oppose a Spanish-influenced orthography in favor of something that reflected the unique structure and pronunciation of the Wao language—something like the alphabet that Peeke and Jung had been using.[50]

However, in December 1991, when a committee of the Ecuador SIL met to approve the final orthography for the Wao New Testament, neither the Confederation of Indigenous Nationalities of Ecuador nor the newly formed Organization of the Waorani Nation of Amazonian Ecuador (ONHAE) had expressed a position on Wao orthography. Informally, Nantowæ "Nanto" Huamoñi, the newly elected ONHAE president, expressed his preference for the Hispanicized version.[51] Peeke and Jung, along with Kelley, who still traveled regularly to Ecuador to encourage literacy among the Waorani, preferred an alphabet that reflected the uniqueness of *Wao tededo*. Most important, however, all three wanted a New Testament that people would read. Within reason, the orthography that best contributed to that end was the one they would choose, even if it reflected social and cultural preferences over linguistic precision. The dilemma in late 1991 was that no one knew which orthography would ultimately win acceptance among the Waorani, and the New Testament was nearly ready to be printed. In the end, at the recommendation of Peeke, Jung, and Kelley, the SIL translation committee in Ecuador approved the Hispanicized version as the orthography the linguists thought would be most widely accepted. It had some similarities to that used by Saint, with modifications to eliminate ambiguities and to clearly mark the vowel nasalizations, which were meaning-based and an essential feature of *Wao tededo*.

On January 13, 1992, not long after Summer Institute staff in Quito surprised them with a celebratory cake in the shape of a Bible, Peeke and Jung flew to SIL's international headquarters in Dallas, Texas, with their manuscript. It needed final proofreading, and Peeke and Jung made one last decision affecting the orthography: to use the letter "d" rather than the Spanish "r" (*Wao tededo* instead of *Wao terero*). It may also have been one small rebellion against the influence of Spanish orthography. Only because they had a master file of their manuscript on a computer disk were Peeke and Jung able even to consider a change in orthography at that late date.[52] Their circumstances demonstrated how central the computer had become in the translation process.[53] It was much easier to make changes that once would have required hours of typing and retyping.

After final manuscript preparation, which included Peeke and Jung rereading the entire Wao New Testament three more times to check for errors that might have slipped through, the linguists returned to Ecuador. Five hundred copies were printed in May 1992 for a population of about twelve hundred, of whom some 30 percent were marginally literate. At more than six hundred pages, the Wao New Testament cost approximately forty dollars per copy to produce, an expense that was underwritten by the International Bible Society, by Wycliffe Associates, and by contributions from church groups and individuals. The Waorani would pay two thousand sucres or about USD$1.25 per copy.[54]

NEW TESTAMENT DEDICATION

SIL's practice was to dedicate each New Testament translation when it was ready for distribution. The Wao New Testament was dedicated twice, once on June 11, 1992, in Tewæno, a service planned and attended primarily by Waorani, and a second time two days later in Shell for outside supporters, with Waorani participants in attendance. Peeke and Jung helped to plan the Shell event and provided support for the Tewæno planners. Dedication day in Tewæno included the entire community, some seventy residents. Most had made specific contributions to the translation project or had played supporting roles—even if they simply supplied Peeke and Jung with meat or cooking bananas. They were joined by an equal number of Waorani from other clearings, generally from among the 15 to 20 percent of the Wao population who were practicing Christians.

The ceremonies had a clear Christian focus, beginning with a baptismal service for thirteen young adults who had made professions of faith when outside visitors had organized vacation Bible schools in their clearings. They were baptized by a Quito pastor, Xavier Muñoz, together with Yowe and Quemo, unofficial pastors for the Tewæno and Tzapino congregations.[55] Most of those in attendance, and certainly the older Waorani, would have known that Yowe and Quemo had participated in the spearings that killed the five missionaries in 1956 and that both had been

Christian believers for more than three decades. The baptisms offered some hope that the Bible would be read by the younger generation, a welcome sign since many of the older generation, such as Yowe and Quemo, had not been able to overcome cultural barriers that prevented them from learning to read. Most young people, in contrast, were literate, but in the absence of the violence experienced by their elders they saw little practical reason to embrace Christianity. Peeke and Jung, of course, hoped that the availability of the New Testament would change that perception.[56]

The actual dedication service focused on the value of the Bible, with singing, Scripture reading, testimony, and a meditation on the written word, all led by Waorani, culminating with the distribution of the Wao New Testaments. There was a brief recognition of political realities when schoolchildren sang the Ecuadorian national anthem in *Wao tededo* and Nanto, president of ONHAE and himself a former student in the literacy classes in Tewæno, gave the prayer of dedication. Pastor and translation consultant Tæmænta had been scheduled as the main speaker at the Tewæno service, but unusually low river levels kept him from arriving by canoe. (He gave his message two days later in Shell.) In Tæmænta's absence, two gringos—SIL Ecuador director David Underwood and former director Don Johnson—spoke briefly. Forty copies of the New Testament were purchased by Waorani after the Tewæno dedication; by the end of the month sales had risen to more than one hundred.[57]

The Shell service two days later was like that in Tewæno but more specifically directed toward non-Waorani. More than two hundred people joined about forty Waorani. Some of the guests were local, some from Quito, some from the US, Germany, and other foreign countries. Rachel was there, along with Nate Saint's three children and seven of his grandchildren. Personnel from HCJB, particularly medical workers, and from Alas de Socorro (Mission Aviation Fellowship) were honored for their support of the Waorani and of Peeke and Jung. Representatives of other indigenous groups attended, and a member of the Cofán people spoke. The Shell service received little notice in the American evangelical press, but when it did, the focus was on the ties with the 1956 killings. "Jim Elliot's Legacy Continues" was the title of a brief report in *Christianity Today*, while an extensive article, titled "At Last: The Afternoon Service," in *World* magazine highlighted the Shell dedication as the fulfillment of the five men's desire the day they were killed to have a Sunday afternoon "service" with the Waorani. That article also noted that three of the original Wao killers—Yowe, Quemo, and Guequita—were present at the Shell gathering.[58]

In both Tewæno and Shell, Peeke and Jung maintained low profiles, standing at the back surrounded by stacks of New Testaments. The two translators confessed to feeling "more numb than elated" as the ceremonies took place. There had been so many steps in the process, Peeke said, that "you finally just take the last step."[59]

The women planned to tour Ecuador for a few weeks with a handful of family and friends. Afterward Peeke, sixty-eight, expected to retire, while Jung, fifty-six, would return to Germany to work at the Wycliffe administrative headquarters there. Both anticipated future short-term visits to Ecuador to help teach the Waorani to study the New Testament. Peeke also looked forward to tackling her Wao dictionary.[60]

CREDIT WHERE DUE

Peeke and Jung's tendency to downplay the credit they were due for translating the Wao New Testament succeeded almost too well. After Rachel and Dayomæ, there were no more legendary figures associated with evangelical missions among the Waorani. The "ordinary" *cowode* who were Saint's successors—the Yosts, Kelley, Peeke, Jung—avoided the limelight and rarely were recognized for their work. The same was true for those, such as Lloyd Rogers, David Miller, and others, who assisted the Waorani as one facet of their missionary responsibilities. If they were acknowledged, it often was as targets of criticism or as cast members with bit parts in the ongoing inspirational saga, a saga that as time went by had less and less to do with actual events in Ecuador. In fact, the Wao church was "no more glorious than the average Church at home," conceded Peeke.[61] And the missionaries who worked among the Waorani did not claim to be the stuff of heroic tales.

The staying power of the legend and the extent to which those not a part of it were forgotten was demonstrated once again in a 1994 fundraising letter signed by Martin Huyett, then president of Wycliffe Associates. Seeking financial contributions to support Wycliffe Bible Translators, Huyett returned to the story of the five slain missionaries, presenting their sacrifice as a valiant first step toward the translation of the New Testament into the Wao language. Huyett's appeal reached its climax with Rachel Saint and Elisabeth Elliot. He wrote:

> Over time, Elisabeth and Rachael [*sic*] learned the Auca language and were instrumental in translating God's Word for these people and teaching them to read.
>
> In 1992, the New Testament, translated in the language of the Aucas, was presented to a small group of about 800 people in the Amazon jungle.[62]

Peeke, who received one of the letters, made her own personal corrections in ballpoint pen. Without crossing out the references to Elliot and Rachel, she inserted, after "teaching them to read":

However, it was Catherine Peeke and Rosi Jung who began the translation work in 1979, and in 1992, the New Testament, translated in the language of the Aucas, was presented to a small group. . . . They [Peeke and Jung] have returned for 3 months in 1993 and 1994 to teach the Bible in the various clearings.[63]

Although recipients of the letter would never see the changes, Peeke's notes suggested that, even for her, modesty had its limits.[64]

19

David and Goliath

THE DEATHS OF Bishop Alejandro Labaca and Sister Inés Arango in 1987, the departures of Rosi Jung and Catherine Peeke five years later, and the death of Rachel Saint in 1994 signaled the end of an era of missionary-Waorani relationships that stretched back to the arrival of Elisabeth Elliot and Saint in 1958. In the 1990s and beyond, missionaries still worked among the Waorani, and SIL staff returned for short-term projects, but none would have the same pioneering experiences.[1] For the Waorani, centuries of isolation and separation from the outside world had ended, and they were experiencing the dramatic social and cultural transformations that began in the 1970s. They were caught up in the challenges of finding their place in modern Ecuador and the incursions of globalization. Transnational indigenous movements, multinational oil companies, and the wide-ranging interests of ethnobotanists, anthropologists, environmentalists, filmmakers, biodiversity experts, ecotourism companies, academic researchers, illegal loggers, adventurers, students, and tourists brought the world to Wao clearings and villages. The Waorani themselves expanded the boundaries of their world to include visits to nearby Ecuadorian towns. They returned greatly influenced by *cowode* culture.

Missionaries became only one voice among many, and not necessarily the most influential. North American evangelicals who still found inspiration in the Waorani story seldom realized that during the late 1980s and early 1990s oil companies, not missionaries, cast the longest shadow over the people of the Ecuadorian Amazon, including the Waorani. While the place of missionaries was changing, so, too, were attitudes toward oil extraction. The most dramatic shift occurred between 1987 and 1991, when Ecuador awarded Houston-based Conoco the service contract to develop petroleum resources in Block 16, located in the middle of traditional Wao territory.[2] Conoco's presence would focus international attention on the rainforests of eastern Ecuador and mobilize a new group of outsiders wanting to help save them. While the overt influence of Christian missionaries waned, other English-speaking outsiders arrived with their own sense of mission. The Conoco episode marked the transition.

BACKGROUND

As earlier chapters have described, between 1967 and 1990 Texaco became the principal oil producer for Ecuador. After 1971 it worked in an increasingly close contractual relationship with the national oil company, CEPE (later renamed Petroecuador). By 1976 CEPE was the majority financial partner in the Texaco consortium, the result of a series of moves by Ecuador designed to maximize the country's profits from petroleum. Nonetheless, Texaco remained responsible for actual work in the field, its efforts representing 88 percent of all oil produced in Amazonian Ecuador.[3] While Texaco was in charge, the majority of wells were concentrated in the Lago Agrio area, near the border with Colombia, and in two large fields at Shushufindi and Sacha, directly north of historically Wao territory. It was clear, however, that the Texaco consortium considered ancestral Wao lands south of the Napo River to be potential oil fields as well. The first indication was the appearance of work crews engaged in the seismic exploration of the area. The second was the construction of an access road in the early 1980s, the so-called Via Auca, extending a little more than sixty miles south from the town of Coca, bisecting Wao lands. The Via Auca provided a corridor for equipment and a pipeline to facilitate oil extraction.[4]

CONOCO AND BLOCK 16

In 1987 Petroecuador awarded Houston-based Conoco the service contract for Block 16, a concession of about half a million acres. The concession was located partially in the Yasuní National Park and partially in Wao territory outside the park, although the Waorani did not yet hold legal title to the land (map 4). After exploratory drilling between 1987 and 1989, Conoco estimated that Block 16 and areas immediately adjacent to it could contain as many as five hundred million barrels of recoverable oil.[5] This was welcome news to the Ecuadorian government, which continued to count on oil revenues to fund about 60 percent of its annual budget.[6]

Oil drilling in Block 16, however, had major challenges. One was the need to construct a new access road to the proposed drilling sites from the Napo River across
some thirty-five miles of national parkland and an additional thirty-five miles of
nonpark, ancestral Wao territory, all virgin rainforest. The Via Auca, marred on either side by homesteads and cleared land, was a graphic demonstration of the way
roads led to colonization and deforestation, outcomes that would be disastrous
both to the Waorani and to the national park. Another hurdle was how to drill an
estimated 120 oil-producing wells and to construct support facilities, including a
pipeline to get the oil out, while avoiding environmental damage to an area that
had been identified as one of the most biodiverse regions in the world. This designation was strengthened in 1989 when UNESCO declared the Yasuní National Park
a Man and the Biosphere Reserve, a region with special potential for research in
the natural and social sciences on the relationship between human beings and their
environment.[7]

The actions of Conoco, then a subsidiary of the American chemical company
DuPont, caught the attention of environmental groups in Ecuador and internation-
ally in a way that Texaco's years of drilling had not.[8] Indigenous organizations joined
environmentalists to oppose the project. North American groups with particularly
high profiles included Cultural Survival, the Natural Resources Defense Council
(NRDC), the Sierra Club, and the Rainforest Action Network.[9] Their opposition
represented a turning point for the ways the environmental movement perceived
threats to the world's rainforests. "Up to now, most of the concern about rain forests
has focused on slash-and-burn agriculture and cattle," commented Jacob Scherr, an
attorney with the NRDC. "But the driving force in the future will be . . . [the impact
of] minerals and oil."[10]

Initially, Conoco pledged to prove the critics wrong. It would be "the oil company of choice for work on environmentally sensitive operations, and eastern
Ecuador . . . [would be] its showcase."[11] This would happen largely through self-
regulation since the Ecuadorian government had just begun to express concern for
environmental standards.[12] The National Department for the Environment had
been established only a few years earlier, in 1984.[13] Conoco was the first oil company to develop and submit an environmental impact statement to the department,
although, as one critic observed, the company did not wait for approval from the
understaffed and underfunded agency before implementing the plan.[14]

To minimize environmental damage, Conoco's proposed road into Block 16
would begin on the south side (the Waorani side) of the Napo River, which was
nearly a mile wide at the designated location, and instead of a bridge the company would ferry its equipment across. As the road was constructed, park rangers
and indigenous guards would patrol it to discourage trespassers. As for the actual

extraction, the company planned to use directional drilling and to group the wells in cluster sites, about ten to twelve wells per site. During construction of a pipeline to get the oil out, Conoco Ecuador would work with scientists who would catalogue species and gather biological specimens for rainforest research. The company also was investigating safe ways to dispose of the wastes associated with drilling. In short, Conoco would "establish a model oil operation in Ecuador" that might "lead to new rain forest operating standards around the world."[15]

WHO REPRESENTS THE WAORANI?

Conoco faced one challenge seemingly more daunting than the logistics of environmentally sound oil extraction: determining "who represents the Huaorani."[16] The Conoco project was the first time in Ecuador that an oil company on a corporate level took steps to communicate with and to acknowledge the rights of indigenous people. However, in 1989, as Conoco was creating its plan, the Waorani still had no representative agency to speak for them. Given that reality, Conoco pursued two approaches. One was to consult representatives of the Confederation of Indigenous Nationalities of the Ecuadorian Amazon (CONFENIAE), along with Ecuadorian and US environmental protection groups.[17] The other was to hire anthropologist Jim Yost, then working as an independent consultant, to provide an overall assessment of the impact that a road and oil extraction would have on the Waorani living along the Yasuní River, who would be most affected by the company's actions.

During the late 1980s, CONFENIAE had stepped in to address the confusion over how to communicate appropriately with the Waorani. The organization was created in 1980 as an umbrella body to unite already existing groups representing various ethnicities in Amazonian Ecuador and to speak for those who did not yet have their own organizations. The Shuar and Quichua, by far the two most populous groups in the region, traditionally dominated the leadership. However, the organization also claimed to represent the much smaller Achuar, Waorani, Cofán, Siona, and Secoya peoples.[18]

Initially, CONFENIAE focused on land issues. Their efforts contributed to the decision in 1990 by President Rodrigo Borja to award the Waorani title to about 1.5 million acres of their ancestral lands that came to be known as the Waorani Ethnic Reserve.[19] While this was a victory for the indigenous movement, it also served the interests of the Ecuadorian state. In a clever bit of gerrymandering, the day before the ethnic reserve was established, officials had redrawn the boundaries of the Yasuní National Park so that significant portions of Blocks 16 and 22 (an adjacent concession where Conoco also planned to drill) were transferred to the Waorani Reserve.

The land titles given to the Waorani came with explicit stipulations that the state maintained its subsurface oil and mineral rights and that the Waorani could not impede government-approved oil exploration and extraction.[20]

For several years prior to the 1990 land grant, CONFENIAE had been pushing the Waorani to organize their own social and political organization, something Jim Yost had encouraged the people to consider as early as 1980.[21] From CONFENIAE's perspective, such a group would affiliate with them, reinforcing the larger organization's authority. The Waorani, however, were slow to engage in such a deeply countercultural activity. By default, CONFENIAE maintained its role as the organization speaking for the Waorani and, as such, entered the Conoco controversy. As a result, in early 1991 the Sierra Club Legal Defense Fund represented CONFENIAE and the Waorani in a petition before the Inter-American Commission on Human Rights, part of the Organization of American States.[22]

DAVID AND GOLIATH

The Sierra Club petition employed an innovative strategy: casting the environmental conflict as a case of indigenous tribes against a transnational oil company. At first, the legal team explored national laws and international treaties related to endangered species and national parks. But when they realized that Waorani were living in or near the areas in question, the focus shifted to international human rights and the rights of the indigenous.[23] The David and Goliath story of a small group of indigenous people facing down "Big Oil" in the Amazon, especially a group with the mystique of the Waorani against a company as well-known as Conoco DuPont, was more compelling to audiences in the US and elsewhere than endangered species or deforestation. This also redefined the historic narrative of the Waorani, at least to North American audiences. Instead of mysterious and feared aggressors, they became the underdogs.

CONFENIAE also established an alliance with the NRDC. Robert Kennedy Jr. served as that organization's staff lawyer and Scherr as director of its international program. Scherr and Kennedy learned about the Conoco conflict through a young lawyer named Judith Kimerling, hired in 1989 as the NRDC's Latin American representative. Arriving in the Oriente with the vague idea of "helping to save the rain forest," Kimerling was "appalled" by what she found. She spent the next two years traveling throughout the oil-producing areas of Amazonian Ecuador, documenting the devastating impact of oil extraction on people and the environment. Kimerling was the first to blow the whistle on environmental abuses committed by the Ecuadorian government and transnational oil companies. She was particularly outraged that companies like Texaco could pollute the rainforest using practices that had been prohibited in the US.[24]

In collaboration with CONFENIAE and another indigenous organization, the Federation of Native Communities of the Ecuadorian Amazon, Kimerling wrote *Amazon Crude* (1991), a book the *New York Times* called the "*Silent Spring* of Ecuador*.*"[25] The book alleged that Texaco had acted with impunity for two decades, ignoring standard, environmentally sound practices for oil extraction. It also included a section on "Conoco, the Huaorani, and Yasuní National Park."[26] The book was written shortly before Kennedy and Scherr asked Kimerling to show them the problems firsthand. In July 1990 the two men spent five days in the Ecuadorian Amazon. They observed examples of the pollution Kimerling had found, most attributed to Texaco or to Occidental Petroleum. Kennedy and Scherr were impressed with Kimerling's work, so much so that Kennedy wrote the preface for *Amazon Crude*, Scherr the foreword, and NRDC staff helped edit and publish the book. A few months later, in October 1990, Kennedy and Scherr wrote Edgar Woolard, chairman and CEO of DuPont, expressing their opposition to Conoco's plans.

The letter led to a meeting in November between Conoco and the NRDC. In "an abrupt about-face," Kennedy and Scherr left the meeting on Conoco's side.[27] They had been convinced that Conoco would be more environmentally responsible in extracting oil from Block 16 than any company that might replace it. As a result, during a follow-up meeting in February 1991, the NRDC made a unilateral decision to work with Conoco to establish a nonprofit foundation for indigenous peoples, sometimes referred to as the "Rio Napo Foundation."[28] Conoco committed $10 million to fund the foundation, in return for the NRDC's endorsement. In March 1991 Kennedy and Scherr contacted Valerio Grefa, a Quichua who was the newly elected president of CONFENIAE, for his support. Grefa and his vice president, Angel Zamarenda, upped the ante. In return for CONFENIAE's backing, Conoco should put $211 million in the fund, roughly a dollar for every barrel in Block 16, based on conservative estimates.[29]

Meanwhile, as word of the NRDC's deal leaked to other environmental groups in Ecuador and the US, there was outrage over "the sale of the Huao homeland." Scherr and Kennedy were vilified as "environmental imperialists." It was also obvious that the Waorani had taken no part in the negotiations.[30] Tensions already existed between the Waorani and Grefa, and CONFENIAE under Grefa's leadership did not speak for the Waorani. To further add to the confusion, that same month—March 1991—a letter written in Spanish and addressed to "General Manager, DuPont-Conoco Company, United States of North America" turned up at the offices of the Rainforest Action Network in San Francisco. The letter expressed opposition to the

Conoco project and objected to the exclusion of the Waorani from the discussions. It was signed by the officers of the Organization of the Huaorani Nation of the Ecuadorian Amazon (ONHAE), a fledgling Wao organization, founded only a few months earlier.[31] This letter was the catalyst that drew the writer and adventurer Joe Kane to Amazonian Ecuador.

A POSSIBLE SOLUTION

In 1989, the year that Kimerling arrived in Ecuador and two years before the Rio Napo Foundation had been proposed (and fallen apart after widespread criticism), and before the ONHAE officers had written their letter, Conoco hired Jim Yost, no longer with SIL, as a consultant on relations with the Waorani and Wao attitudes toward the proposed road to Block 16. Yost took the job with some trepidation, since he opposed the road because of potential damage to the Waorani. Nonetheless, he viewed the road as inevitable, given the worldwide demand for petroleum, and hoped that he might be an advocate for the one hundred or so Waorani who then lived in the Yasuní region.[32] Yost's initial assessment report for Conoco, written in April 1989, was a combination of basic principles for cross-cultural encounters with the Waorani, concrete guidelines for behavior, and general suggestions for the future. In addition to the report, Yost and his colleague Douglas McMeekin visited Wao communities along the Yasuní and Cononaco rivers and those near other oil concessions in the protectorate to survey their reaction to oil extraction and to the road. A summary of this survey was written in November 1989 for Unocal, a second oil company with a concession in Wao territory, but it also circulated to Conoco. Yost found most Waorani favored the road but opposed allowing outsiders to homestead, hunt, fish, garden, or otherwise settle their land.[33]

Yost made at least two more trips to Ecuador, in January and August 1990, as a consultant for Conoco. Especially in his August letter to Ed Davies, general manager of Conoco Ecuador, he emphasized the importance of working directly with the Waorani on an ongoing basis, establishing long-term relationships, meeting with them for extended periods in their territory, and avoiding any actions that could be considered deceptive or secretive. Yost acknowledged the existence of the newly formed ONHAE and suggested Conoco meet with Nantowæ, called "Nanto," ONHAE's president.[34]

At the time, Yost's efforts and suggestions seemed to have been ignored, although they later would form the basis of policies embraced by Conoco's successor, Maxus. Yost's letter to Davies was written a month after Kennedy and Scherr had made their first trip to Ecuador and about three months before the NRDC and Conoco officials met in New York City. The way the NRDC and Conoco tried to establish the Rio Napo Foundation—from the initial, top-down plan created by *cowode* in New York City to attempts to get CONFENIAE and ONHAE on board in Ecuador—violated nearly everything Yost had told Conoco Ecuador during the previous two years. Executives in the US had attempted a quick fix that supposedly would have helped the Waorani and assuaged the environmental community.

But in the end, no one was happy. Environmental activists berated both Conoco and the NRDC. Relationships with the Waorani were never initiated. Conoco faced not only the earlier petition in the Organization of American States but also another legal challenge from the Sierra Club Legal Defense Fund and from the Corporation for the Defense of Life, an Ecuadorian environmental law group. These two groups charged that the company had violated the provisions of the US Foreign Corrupt Practices Act by pressuring Ecuador's Tribunal of Constitutional Guarantees to reverse a ruling that oil production on national park lands was unconstitutional. The judges first ruled against oil development in national parks, but then abruptly reversed themselves four weeks later.[35] Despite these clouds over the company, the Ecuadorian government approved the Conoco project on September 20, 1991. However, three weeks later, in an unexpected about-face of its own, Conoco decided to pull out of Ecuador completely, including its projects on Wao land and in the Yasuní Park. It would sell its interest in the development of Block 16 to another member of the Block 16 consortium, Dallas-based Maxus Energy Corporation.

Conoco insisted that the decision was based on economics, but environmental groups claimed victory. However, the celebration was short-lived when it became clear that the project would continue under Maxus's leadership, supported by other, smaller partners that remained in the petroleum consortium.[36] This result seemed to vindicate the fears of Kennedy and Scherr that, if Conoco left, someone else, perhaps without the same deep pockets, would step in. The Waorani, whose land was at issue, appeared as little more than pawns of the Ecuadorian state and multinational companies. As told in a *New Yorker* essay that would become the standard narrative of the Conoco episode, a frustrated Kennedy uttered the ongoing question from environmentalists and oil companies alike: "Well, who *are* the Huaorani?"[37]

During the 1990s, a broad cross-section of both popular and academic audiences in the English-speaking world received answers to that question for the first time from people who were not Christian missionaries.[38] After the attention created by the Conoco controversy, for many people "saving" the Waorani meant saving the rainforest rather than converting its inhabitants. Among the most important of these new voices were the anthropologist Laura Rival, the environmental lawyer Kimerling, and the journalist Joe Kane. The three introduced the Waorani to academic and popular audiences beyond those in the evangelical world. They also questioned the work of SIL and other missionaries, reinvigorating the charge that missions damaged native cultures, especially Wao culture.

NEW VOICES, FAMILIAR PATTERNS

Laura Rival, then a graduate student in anthropology at the London School of Economics, arrived in Ecuador in January 1989, the same year as Judith Kimerling, to do fieldwork among the Waorani. During subsequent years, Rival would establish herself as the leading academic expert on Wao life and customs. Her initial fieldwork extended from January 1989 to June 1990. She was not the first non-SIL anthropologist to spend extended time with the Waorani. Clayton and Carole Robarchek, a husband-and-wife team from Wichita State University, spent a year doing fieldwork in 1987, with follow-up in 1993. However, they had a specific area of interest—dynamics surrounding peace and warfare—and were studying the Waorani against the backdrop of earlier work among the Malaysian Semai people. Rival was the first nonmissionary anthropologist to make the Waorani the exclusive focus of her fieldwork and to write a dissertation that included an ethnographic description of the Waorani as she observed them in 1990.[39]

Rival initially came to Ecuador as a student and collaborator with Blanca Muratorio, a specialist in the Quichua people of the Upper Ecuadorian Amazon.[40] Muratorio facilitated Rival's meeting with Pedro Chimbo, the Quichua man who had taught school in the Wao settlement of Dayono from 1972 to 1987. Chimbo introduced Rival and her young daughter, Emilia, who was with her, to the people of Dayono. They agreed to let the two live in the village if Rival helped teach school and secured funding for basic healthcare. Rival agreed, but she got off to a rough start. She felt that Zoila Wiñame resented her presence, and Emilia, who was attending school with the Wao children, contracted a severe case of malaria. Her need for medical care brought Rival's first fieldwork experience to a premature end. The pair stayed in Shell Mera while Emilia recovered. She eventually returned to France and her mother to Dayono. Over time, the anthropologist established positive relationships with the adult children of Ñamæ, one of the men who, with his extended family, had left Tewæno with Wiñame to found Dayono in 1971. Ñamæ's married daughter befriended Rival, and his two sons, Amo and Moipa ("Moi"), both of whom spoke some Spanish, became her most important cultural informants. Eventually she was adopted into the family.[41]

These relationships meant that when Ñamæ left Dayono in late 1989 to establish the new settlement of Cæwæidi Ono on the upper Shiripuno River, Rival went along. A large part of her field data came from watching this group create a new community, located outside the protectorate, in what would become the Waorani Ethnic Reserve.[42] Initially, they did so in a traditional manner, constructing Wao longhouses in the forest and planting manioc gardens. Cæwæidi Ono began with an extended kinship group of sixty-two people. By June 1990 the population had increased to 105, and by 1993 the number had doubled to 212.[43] By that time some people had begun to build Quichua-style homes, and the community included a schoolhouse, although apparently in poor condition.[44]

While Cæwæidi Ono was Rival's home base and her richest source of information on Waorani life and customs, the anthropologist also traveled to all the Wao clearings and villages in the protectorate, as well as to the more isolated groups on the Cononaco and Yasuní rivers. In some ways, the picture of the Waorani that emerged from her observations paralleled that presented by Yost in two influential 1981 essays.[45] Like Yost, Rival stressed the radical egalitarianism of traditional Wao culture, the respect for individuality, and the freedom given to children. Both recognized the importance of kinship ties and of marriage as a central ritual of Wao life. And both recognized that the Waorani were in the process of negotiating what it meant to be "civilized," trying at the same time to maintain their unique cultural identity. In their own ways, both Yost and Rival were activists. In 1990 and 1991, for example, each served independently as a resource for Waorani involved in founding ONHAE.[46] Both also weighed in on the controversies surrounding the Waorani and oil.

In other ways, however, the two anthropologists employed different methodologies and came to some radically different conclusions. Rival was interested in theoretical discussions informing anthropology, while Yost took a more direct, empirical approach.[47] The most significant difference between the two, and one that was never resolved, had to do with the basic identification of the Waorani and their culture. Yost described them as hunter-horticulturalists, while Rival insisted they were hunter-gatherers. "A correct understanding of Huao culture and society must start by considering them as nomadic hunters-and-gatherers, rather than horticulturalists," she affirmed.[48] For their part, in an essay published years later, Yost and his coauthors asserted that a number of Rival's publications were "irretrievably flawed by her erroneous insistence that the Waorani are hunters and gatherers."[49]

The conclusions each researcher reached concerning the role of manioc, a cultivated tuber, in the Wao diet illustrated their differences. From Rival's perspective, manioc was used primarily as the basis for *tepæ* consumed on special occasions (fiestas), although the drink was also a part of the daily Wao diet in times of peace and prosperity. She found that "a normal communal meal (is comprised) mostly of boiled meat or fish and a few vegetables, and it ends with a small bowl of fruit or manioc drink."[50] According to Rival, "While the Huaorani know how to cultivate gardens of manioc, banana and plantain and value the fact of having gardens, they . . . prefer to subsist on hunting and gathering."[51]

In contrast, Yost argued that manioc was the principal subsistence crop for the Waorani and that their reliance on manioc gardens contributed to their practice of maintaining two or three different living sites, each with a manioc garden at a different stage of maturity. The extended household (*nanicabo*) would travel between the different locations as the manioc was ready to harvest, planting new gardens in each place as they harvested the old in order to maintain an ongoing cycle. Yost acknowledged that at certain seasons of the year, *plátanos* (cooking bananas) and the fruit of the peach palm replaced manioc as the basis of the main carbohydrate-rich drinks consumed by the Waorani. Meat and fish served as sources of protein, while wild honey and fruits gathered in the forest supplemented cultivated items. Still, manioc was the backbone of the traditional Wao diet.[52]

In sum, Rival and Yost agreed on the foodstuffs that made up the Wao diet, but differed on their importance. Yost gave central importance to meat and manioc, thus classifying the Waorani as hunter-horticulturalists. Rival stressed meat and foods gathered from the forest, with manioc as a luxury food; accordingly she identified the Waorani as hunter-gatherers. This example may seem minor to nonspecialists, but the differences between Yost and Rival affected the picture of the Waorani communicated to the outside world and the credibility of each anthropologist's research. At least one later anthropologist avoided the conflict by splitting the difference and describing the Waorani as hunter-gatherer-horticulturalists.[53]

Although Rival's dissertation itself did not circulate widely, many of her arguments, including her depiction of the Waorani as hunter-gatherers, attained broad exposure through subsequent publications. In addition to her portrayal of Wao life and culture, a central focus of the dissertation was the impact of formal schooling on the social transformation of the Waorani. Rival argued that fiscal schools were the main conduit of modernity or "civilization" to Wao villages. Contrary to common assumptions, however, the Waorani learned what it meant to be "civilized" not primarily from the classroom. Rather "civilization" was demonstrated and inculcated by the practices or daily habits that accompanied the establishment of schools, such things as combing hair, brushing teeth, and engaging in group calisthenics.[54]

The Waorani as portrayed in Rival's fieldwork were not victims of cultural norms imposed by the Ecuadorian state. Certainly formal schooling changed the lives of students and parents alike, encouraging a sedentary lifestyle and identification with the inhabitants of a particular village rather than with the traditional kinship group. The Waorani found surrogate kin in teachers and other students. According to Rival, the Waorani were aware of these changes and chose to embrace them. At the same time, they continued to maintain a private sphere in the home and during school vacations where they could "borrow elements from modernity on their own terms" and so "remain autonomous in their choices on how to handle them."[55]

While Rival insisted that the Waorani were not victims of the state, she showed no hesitation in presenting them as victims of their contact with missionaries. A strain of antimissionary sentiment ran through the dissertation. Her most important informants were from families that had left Tewæno in 1971 as part of the bitter Dayomæ-Wiñame split. They had sought the assistance of Christian and Missionary Alliance worker David Miller but maintained old hostilities toward Rachel Saint and SIL. Communication may have been another problem. Catherine Peeke commented ruefully on her difficulty talking with Rival. The young anthropologist arrived unexpectedly in Tewæno on June 17, 1989, during a trip to visit all the Wao villages, collecting information. She had specific questions for Peeke. However, because Rival was a native French speaker and had learned British English, she had trouble understanding what Peeke called "my hillbilly accent" (from the mountains of western North Carolina) and ended up mostly interviewing Rosi Jung, who also spoke English as a second language.

This may have affected Rival's understanding of missionary-Wao history, since among the SIL staff Peeke was the most perceptive observer both of the Waorani and of her colleagues.[56] She also had the longest exposure to the Waorani and their culture. Whatever the reason, while some of the charges against missionaries in Rival's dissertation were true, many were not. For example, SIL did not found or support the village of Toñæmpade. It was Dayomæ's and Sam's project, with some help from Lloyd Rogers. Nor did Rachel Saint live there permanently until after she retired from SIL. Yost did not introduce the Waorani to shotgun hunting, although he happened to begin his work among the Waorani at a time when shotgun use was increasing dramatically.[57]

Nonetheless, when in doubt, Rival blamed "the missionaries." Consequently, through its influence on Kimerling and others, Rival's work helped to reinvigorate criticisms of missionary-Waorani contact. For example, in a reference to the initial contact between missionaries and the Waorani in 1956, Rival assumed the missionaries found Wao food objectionable because they offered Nænquiwi a hamburger rather than requesting food from him. This was "a clear sign of disgust and rejection" and represented the beginning of a pattern in which "SIL spent its time giving things away."[58]

While offering hamburgers may have been a culturally naive gesture, it had nothing to do with attitudes toward Wao food. It was simply an act of hospitality and an attempt at friendship with Waorani the missionaries viewed as visitors. Nor did it anticipate SIL's attitude toward trade goods since none of the missionary men involved was affiliated with SIL. Rival simply assumed missionaries would find indigenous food disgusting, in the same way she erroneously assumed that a Wao Christian woman in one of the protectorate villages "despised and condemned" chanting.[59]

In 1958, when Rachel Saint and Elisabeth Elliot first went to live with the Waorani, their goal was to share Wao food. For logistical reasons, they compromised and depended in part on weekly food drops from the outside. Still, a little more than a week after arriving in Tewæno, Elliot mentioned in a letter to her family that her lunch had consisted of boiled plantains (cooking bananas), monkey meat, and instant coffee.[60] During all the years she lived among the Waorani, Saint's customary breakfast was a bowl of *pæænæmæ* (plantain drink). Neither woman could overcome her aversion to sucking the brains and eyeballs from howler monkey heads, but they would try almost anything else. In the case of Peeke and Jung, neither drank *tepæ*, but both ate manioc and jungle meat when available. They and the Yost family found the Wao diet boring over long periods, but not an object of disgust.

Rival also blamed the SIL for promoting the end of Wao dietary taboos and for opposing dancing and chanting as "evil" and "savage," "a product of the devil."[61] Yet dietary taboos were of no concern to Saint or the other SIL staff. Most Wao taboos reflected what Yost described as the "'principle of association,' a belief that you are what you eat." In other words, if you ate a large animal such as tapir you would become slow and lazy.[62] According to Yost, Dayomæ began to dispel some of these beliefs after her time with the Quichuas. "That's not true," she'd say, "because when we ate it [a taboo food] with the Quichua, nothing happened." Or she would use the taboos to her own advantage, saying, "That's taboo for you, so bring it over to me." Over time, other Waorani caught on, especially as game became scarcer in the protectorate. "Hah," they would say, "we'll eat it ourselves." The Waorani weren't afraid to experiment and to make their own choices about what foods to eat. Missionaries had very little, if anything, to do with it.[63]

Especially after she moved to Cæwæidi Ono, Rival was captivated by the Wao practice of chanting. She recorded chants by a local jaguar father, by ordinary people as they went about their days, and by participants on special occasions such as fiestas. She also found that chanting as a daily practice by men, women, and children was much more prevalent in isolated clearings that had no school. She concluded that chanting was associated with traditional culture, along with "nakedness and pierced ears." Rival went on to assert that SIL introduced writing in its literacy programs in opposition to traditional chanting. For SIL, "chanting was 'savage,' a product of the devil. Writing was 'civilized.'"[64]

While Rival was correct that chanting came to be identified with traditional culture, it was largely because Quichuas, whom young Waorani wished to emulate, made fun of Wao music. As a result, chanting became less common during the 1980s in villages such as Dayono and Toñæmpade. During the mid-1970s, when the Yost family arrived in Tewæno, the inhabitants chanted often. In his field notes, Yost recorded only one time where chanting was questioned by an SIL staff member. In early 1974 Jung thought a Wao man was "chanting to demons." After checking, Rachel and Dayomæ discovered he was only singing about a toucan. They asked him to stop, but Dayomæ and other Waorani thought the incident was funny.[65] In 1965 Saint recorded four reels of tape, mostly chants at a fiesta given by Guequita, but also including some songs related to animal legends. Peeke deposited them in the Archives of Traditional Music at Indiana University, along with four other sound recordings, including more chants, from the late 1950s and early 1960s.[66]

An ethnobotanist and writer named Wade Davis spent about three weeks with the Yosts in a Wao clearing called Quiwado during the spring of 1980 to collaborate with Jim in researching Waorani use of medicinal plants. When he later described the experience, Davis mentioned in passing that he had participated in a Wao fiesta, dancing and chanting. Davis also observed Cowæ, a jaguar father, as he "empowered" poison darts that would be used in hunting. And Davis attended a lackadaisical church service, led by Wepe's daughter, a young Wao woman recently returned from working as a maid in a frontier town. It was she, not the Yost family in the back row, who told the people they were "savages." The "congregation" of Quiwado Waorani ignored her.[67]

Rival also accused SIL of separating families during the relocation efforts of the 1970s. "Several couples were 'divorced' de facto, as one spouse took the plane, and the other stayed behind." According to Rival's informants, this happened because "when the SIL missionaries landed, they [the Waorani] had only a few minutes to either climb in the plane or stay behind." If some Waorani were away hunting, they lost their chance and "were not given the opportunity to decide whether they wanted to join the mission or not."[68]

On occasion, there was confusion between the expectations of the Waorani and those of the SIL staff regarding who would be airlifted to the protectorate, but families were not split in the haphazard fashion described by Rival. Nor were people moved without prior notice or planning. The situation became more difficult in the mid-1970s as SIL (often against Dayomæ's wishes) tried to encourage people on the ridge to stay put. In one case, Peeke reported that SIL had agreed only to bring "Awa and [his] family, plus his mother, Guiima," to honor a promise Dayomæ had made. When the plane landed, Awa was furious that he could not include his grown son, Baiwa. Since Baiwa and his wife had no children, Peeke thought the two could fit on the plane if Guiima remained behind with other extended family members. "This seemed to satisfy everyone," Peeke wrote. "Old Guiima didn't seem to be one whit upset at not starting a new venture at her age."[69]

Unlike some later anthropologists, Rival was aware of the distinct missions agencies working among the Waorani: SIL, of course, but also David Miller from the Christian and Missionary Alliance; nurse Miriam Gebb from HCJB Global; and Lloyd Rogers with the Hermanos Libres (Plymouth Brethren). She apparently did not, however, understand the differences between the groups. Brethren missionaries, for example, practiced a rigid separation from the "world" in favor of the spiritual church. A comment Rogers made to Rival that the "jungle is dangerous and evil, full of snakes," while the "town, corrupted to the heart, is also an evil place," reflected Brethren rejection of the world.[70] In practice, however, Rogers believed that rapid integration into the national culture of Ecuador was the better of the two evils for the Waorani. Most of the time when Kimerling or Rival critiqued "missionaries" for telling the Waorani that their culture was sinful, they were referring to Rogers.[71]

Unlike Saint, who was determined to change Wao moral standards but who hoped to preserve much of the rest of their culture, Rogers wanted the Waorani to embrace "civilized" life, including attending Spanish-language schools and eating with utensils. Rogers pursued these goals from a large, American-style "lodge" he built in Shell, with inexpensive rooms available for indigenous Christians to rent when they came for medical treatment. The Hermanos also had an agreement with the Education Department of Pastaza Province. The mission helped to select qualified teachers, inspected schools, and provided uniforms and other supplies in return for permission to teach the children Bible verses in Spanish.[72]

Rogers and the Hermanos were quintessential fundamentalist missionaries, identifying Christianity not only with faith in Christ but also with a clear set of do's and don'ts. They followed what the historian Lamin Sanneh has described as "mission as diffusion," an approach whereby the culture of the missionaries is the "inseparable carrier of the message."[73] To embrace the gospel meant to also embrace the cultural standards of those who brought it to Ecuador. This could lead to a denigration of Wao culture. Nonetheless many Waorani in clearings with a government school appreciated Rogers's attempts to find teachers with some commitment to moral behavior and Christian faith—at the very least men who would not rape Wao schoolgirls.

For Rival, the appearance of her first academic essay on the Waorani in 1993 marked the beginning of more than two decades of prolific publications, work that eventually led to a position as lecturer in anthropology at Oxford University. As part of her own activism in Ecuador, she occasionally published on the Waorani in Spanish and English to popular audiences, as well as influencing the publications of others.[74]

20

Saving the Rainforest

⟶

WHILE LAURA RIVAL was doing fieldwork with the Waorani, Judith Kimerling continued documenting the environmental impact of oil exploration. Although she came to Ecuador on behalf of the Natural Resources Defense Council, Kimerling was fired when she objected to Robert Kennedy Jr. and Jacob Scherr's decision to cooperate with Conoco.[1] Unemployed, she remained in Ecuador, risking jail or expulsion from the country to draw attention to the destruction that accompanied oil extraction and its impact on indigenous people, colonists, and the rainforest. She did so primarily through her book *Amazon Crude*, but also through several extensively documented law essays and the adaptation of two essays into a 1996 book in Spanish, *El Derecho del Tambor*.[2]

When writing about missionaries, Kimerling relied heavily on Rival. As a result, her published work included accusations that missionaries (SIL) rejected Wao culture, telling the Waorani that they were "backward savages" and that their culture was "primitive and sinful."[3] Kimerling also repeated an account of Alas de Socorro's (Mission Aviation Fellowship) refusing to transport an indigenous mother and her dying baby to the hospital because the mother's village had participated in a CONFENIAE gathering where Alas de Socorro was criticized. According to Kimerling, the story illustrated the way missionaries used their services to "manipulate the people and deepen their dependency."[4]

Asked about the incident a quarter-century later, Gene Jordan, an MAF pilot flying out of Shell at the time, had no memory of any such occurrence and strongly questioned whether it happened as reported. "Maybe a flight was scheduled but the weather did not allow it to be completed. Maybe the airstrip was too muddy to land," he commented. There were "literally dozens of conditions that [might] preclude a safe landing" even to help a critically ill infant. These scenarios were all conjecture, but Jordan flatly rejected the idea that an MAF pilot would deliberately allow a child to die as manipulation or retribution. "Are we human? Absolutely. Have we made mistakes? Of course! But I have also seen MAF pilots go to extreme lengths . . . to provide help to the different people groups they serve."[5]

Kimerling also followed Rival in condemning missionary efforts to relocate the Waorani, even though Kimerling emphasized the role of the Ecuadorian state much more than Rival had. Kimerling pointed to the shocking degree of institutionalized racism in Ecuador during the late 1960s and early 1970s and " 'ethnocide' [as] a strategy of the national government to conquer Amazonia." Despite this awareness, Kimerling presented SIL's efforts to relocate the Waorani as part of the ethnocide rather than an attempt, however flawed, to save the Waorani from destruction. She also asserted that "many Huaorani died" because of pacification and exposure to contact diseases.[6] In fact, except for the sixteen people who died from polio, contact illness deaths among the relocated Waorani were quite low. While the approximately three hundred people in Tewæno did experience food shortages and emotional trauma at the height of the relocation, Duke University researchers in 1976 nonetheless found the Waorani in excellent physical health.[7]

Kimerling's books and essays alerted environmentalists in Ecuador, the US, and other parts of the world to the potential dangers of oil extraction in Amazonia. Her relationships with indigenous organizations marked the beginning of her long-term advocacy on behalf of the indigenous residents of Amazonian Ecuador, especially some Wao and Quichua communities. In the short term, Kimerling's work contributed to the pressure that eventually led to Conoco's decision to pull out of Ecuador. As suggested earlier, however, it was a hollow victory.

JOE KANE

If Rival defined the Waorani to anthropologists and other academics and Kimerling was the whistle-blower who alerted environmentalists to the devastating consequences of oil extraction in Amazonian Ecuador, the journalist and adventure travel writer Joe Kane was the popularizer who introduced secular American audiences to the Waorani. He wrote two widely read essays in the *New Yorker*, later expanded into a book, *Savages* (1995). The book was described as a "muckraking account of [Wao] confusion and exploitation."[8] Kane focused both US and international attention on the Waorani, their homeland, and Big Oil.

Kane earned his credentials as an adventure travel writer with his first book, *Running the Amazon*, which made the *New York Times* bestsellers list in August 1989.[9] The book was a first-person account of a multinational group of ten adventurers attempting to be the first to navigate the entire 4,200 miles of the Amazon, from its headwaters in Peru to the Atlantic Ocean. In March or April 1991, nearly two years after *Running the Amazon* was first published, Kane returned to the Amazon basin—this time to the rainforests of eastern Ecuador.

Like Kimerling, Kane, too, "wanted to do something to help save the rain forest."[10] He hoped to do so by writing about the Waorani instead of a river. "American oil companies coveted their land, American missionaries their souls, American environmentalists their voice . . . but no one knew what the Huaorani wanted. No one really knew who the Huaorani were."[11] Kane coveted their story. In a quest that in some ways harkened back to adventurers like Erwin Patzelt and Peter Broennimann, or even the five missionaries in 1956, Kane would report his encounter with the Waorani almost as if he were the first white man to meet them.

But he was not. Nor were the Waorani he met isolated "savages." Kane first made contact with the Waorani in the oil boom town of Coca, on the edge of their ancestral territory. The four men he met were in their mid-twenties (about a decade younger than Kane), who represented the first generation to come of age since peaceful contact. Nanto, Moi, Enqueri (Æncædi), and Amo were the elected leaders of ONHAE, serving as president, vice president, secretary, and treasurer, respectively. "They had been elected by their people to speak to the *cowode*—the cannibals, who included the missionaries, the Company, me, and everyone else on earth," wrote Kane, far overestimating their actual authority.[12] These Waorani were unusual among their people in the early 1990s because all spoke passable Spanish, and Æncædi could read and write Spanish to a limited degree. Moi had lived in Quito for a brief period and had worked with Laura Rival in Cæwædi Ono and other Wao clearings. These were young men who were comfortable interacting with *cowode* and knew how to relate to the outside world. Most important for Kane, he could communicate with them in Spanish.

Kane made two extended trips to Ecuador between March 1991 and September 1992 to get to know the Waorani and to chronicle their struggle against oil companies—first Conoco, then Maxus—that wanted to build an access road across Wao land. *Savages* focused primarily on this eighteen-month period, although the book extended into 1994 to cover the aftermath of Moi's 1993 trip to Washington, DC. He testified before the Inter-American Commission on Human Rights of the Organization of American States in support of the petition on indigenous rights filed nearly three years earlier by the Sierra Club Legal Defense Fund.

The picture of the Waorani that emerged from *Savages* was of a rainforest people with little time to adapt to a modern world rapidly encroaching on their land and their lives. The older generation—on the periphery of Kane's story—were affected in one of two ways. Either they isolated themselves and their families in the forest, or they were destroyed by "the Company" (Big Oil). Cæmpæde (Quemperi), the oldest man in a kinship group living along the Cononaco River, represented the first approach. Another older man, Babæ, who succumbed to alcoholism in a stiflingly hot shack along the Via Auca, reflected the second. The younger generation, too, was split. Nanto, Æncædi, and Amo represented an approach that moved toward what "they understood to be a *cowode* future that could be survived only by learning a *cowode* way of life."[13] Kane portrayed them as beleaguered by an outside world that was always poised to outmaneuver them. He also found them a little goofy, given to their own brand of Wao slapstick comedy. Moi symbolized the minority approach of those who wanted to find in traditional culture "the knowledge and skills that would help them navigate the present."[14] Moi maintained a "spirit of defiance" and did not crack jokes.[15] According to Kane, Nanto and Æncædi had grown up under the influence of Rachel Saint and SIL, an influence they found difficult to set aside.

Moi, in contrast, attended primary school in Dayono, under the Quichua teacher and pastor Pedro Chimbo. Missionary David Miller, the school supervisor, made only occasional visits, and he denied ever objecting to things he considered culture-neutral, such as Wao chants and wearing clothes.[16] Neither Miller nor Chimbo had the authority of a Rachel Saint. Moi, Kane told his readers, "had long since escaped Rachel's influence" and had become an apprentice of Mingatoæ (Mengatowæ), a Wao jaguar father.[17] However, there is no evidence Moi was ever under Rachel's influence. Kane offered little information about Amo, who died under suspicious circumstances while Kane was in Ecuador.

A STUDY IN CONTRASTS

To explore the contrast among the generation that represented the future of the Waorani, Kane chose Æncædi and Moi as the main characters for his book. Aside from speaking Spanish, both men were single. This gave them the flexibility to accompany Kane on the rainforest adventures that enliven the story. Kane is sympathetic to both, but Moi clearly emerges as the quintessential Wao, the last best hope for his people. Moi is the "natural leader," the "spiritual force" behind ONHAE.[18] When Nanto and Moi met Valerio Grefa, Quichua head of CONFENIAE, in Quito, Kane described the meeting. Moi arrived spear in hand, "a man-killing Huaorani spear—the longest and heaviest spears used by anyone in the forest, spears that take real muscle to wield." Moi intentionally brought the spear for shock effect, since in Wao culture men did not carry spears to threaten or intimidate, only to hunt or to kill enemies. Moi also wore his feather crown and quivers with poison darts for his blowgun. "Around his neck hung a single jaguar tooth. As for the look in his eyes—if, at that moment, you'd run across Moi in the bush, you'd have had only one thought: May the end be swift."[19]

The final chapter of *Savages* concludes with Moi's 1993 trip to the US and the broken promises that followed. Accompanied by Kane, Moi made a brief side trip to New York City (he carried his spear around Manhattan). While he was there, the photographer Richard Avedon shot his portrait for Kane's *New Yorker* story.[20] The portrait shows Moi from the navel up, wearing nothing but his dart holders, with his long, black hair framing his face and spilling over his shoulders. His expression is enigmatic as he looks squarely into the camera lens. His arms are crossed, one hand turned upward either questioning or in supplication. This was the noble savage, a man representing a people who had never been conquered and who asked only that their homeland be left alone.

Much as Dayomæ had come to symbolize the potential of Christianization among the Waorani to evangelicals a generation earlier, to environmentalists Moi symbolized the determination of the Waorani to save themselves by defending their rainforest home. The photograph appeared in the *New Yorker* and on the hardcover edition of *Savages*. It made Moi a minor celebrity and de facto Waorani spokesman to the outside world. For example, he had a leading role in the 1996 documentary *Trinkets and Beads*.[21]

If Moi was Kane's ideal Wao man, Moi's counterpart Æncædi was Kane's tragic example of Waorani ruined by missionaries. When Æncædi took Kane to visit Cæmpæde's kin along the Cononaco River, Kane noted, apparently as a flaw, that Æncædi was afraid. "Raised on radio and volleyball and El Señor (the Christian God), the Condorito [Æncædi's nickname] now found himself immersed in what the missionaries had taught him was the dark and demonic side of the Huaorani culture."[22] From the Cononaco, Æncædi led Kane on a harrowing journey: a seventy-five-mile overland trek through the rainforest to Block 16 (the oil concession under dispute) and then to Waorani living along the Yasuní River. Wandering through the jungle, sure he would starve to death, Kane recognized that his life was in Æncædi's hands. "I liked him very much but . . . I did not trust him at all."[23] Despite Kane's doubts, Æncædi got him safely through the rainforest.

Kane described Æncædi's home village, Toñæmpade, as a "shantytown," built around a radio and a toilet. The "pitiful shacks . . . seemed to huddle under the radio [which, according to Kane, broadcast a Bible story to start each day] . . . as if life were a choice between the forest and God."[24] The author seemed unaware that Toñæmpade's actual inception had centered more on a choice to pursue the tourist trade. Moi's home village of Cæwæidi Ono, in contrast, was to Kane the Eden of Wao traditional culture, a "pastoral setting" that "may well have been the prettiest of all the Huaorani settlements." It was filled with Waorani who cultivated a spirit of "independence and defiance . . . against the missionaries, the Shuar, the Quichua, the president of Ecuador."[25] Kane incorrectly described Moi's village as having been founded in "an act of rebellion against the evangelical missionary influence."[26] The description, however, fit an underlying theme in the book: missionaries ruined the Waorani, and defying missionaries would save them. Æncædi's flaws— according to Kane, he lied, stole Kane's provisions, and was susceptible to pressure from missionaries and to bribes from oil companies—were all laid at the feet of Rachel Saint and SIL. "Nanto and Enqueri [Æncædi] had grown up wearing Rachel Saint's uniforms and eating Rachel Saint's food and flying in Rachel Saint's airplanes and studying in Rachel Saint's school. They had learned that the way their parents hunted and the way they ate and the way they dressed and the way they made love were evil."[27]

Saint was always a formidable figure, even into her late seventies, her age when Kane met her. However, Kane's claims about the nature of her influence over Æncædi and Nanto did not fit their ages and experiences. If they were born around 1966, as the book suggests, they would have been of primary school age in 1972, when Pat Kelley began the literacy program in the Wao language, using materials that affirmed Wao culture.[28] The fiscal school in Toñæmpade did not begin until 1979, when Æncædi would have been about thirteen, and at that point Saint was out of the country until 1982. Æncædi may have been influenced by Lloyd Rogers's fundamentalism and Saint may have raised money to support the school. She had lived in Toñæmpade nearly a decade by the time Kane visited the village. She surely influenced Æncædi as a young adult but could not have dominated his entire life, as Kane implies. Ironically SIL staff such as Catherine Peeke viewed Toñæmpade not as a hotbed of missionary influence but rather as a place dominated by schoolteachers with "radical views and ambitions."[29]

Despite his capabilities, Æncædi, according to Kane, found it difficult to resist outsiders and the perks they offered. As the second president of ONHAE, Æncædi succumbed and signed an agreement with Maxus Energy. When Æncædi finally realized the consequences of "selling out" to Maxus, Kane claimed to see in his eyes "a look of real fear . . . as rare among the Waorani as his eyeglasses." Kane imagined that Æncædi's father had worn a similar look forty years earlier when he first saw the unfamiliar missionary plane. "His father had lashed out, but soon, tempted and terrified by that new and unfathomable power, he had surrendered—whether he knew it or not."[30] While Kane's imagined scenario may have brought a certain symmetry to his account of Æncædi's life, it did not ring true. Far from surrendering, Æncædi's father, Mincaye, became an astute observer of the *cowode* and learned to make the relationships work in his favor.

Contrasting Moi and Cæwædi Ono with Æncædi and Toñæmpade enabled Kane to balance two themes: first, missionaries, specifically the Summer Institute of Linguistics and Rachel Saint, were agents of ethnocide who wanted to destroy traditional Wao culture as "Satan-inspired savagery" and replace it with "a life based on school and church."[31] Second, the Waorani were exceptional, noble savages, the chosen people of the rainforest. "They lived in the forest's deepest reaches; they alone were truly warriors." Despite the harm done by missionaries, Kane concluded that the Waorani "believed, absolutely, that they ruled their land and controlled their destiny." After all, as Kane repeated numerous times, "they had never been conquered and never would be, because they were the bravest people in the Amazon."[32]

This assertion, and Moi himself, gave hope to Kane's book. It offered a redefinition of the saved and the damned, one the environmentalists would sorely need as Maxus took Conoco's place as the company that would build the road and drill the wells on Wao territory. The publication and brisk sales of *Savages*, as well as the efforts of Rival and Kimerling, gave the environmental movement a representative Wao (Moi), a book that told the Waorani story, a typical village (Cæwædi Ono), and, within a few years, a film (*Trinkets and Beads*).[33] Ironically these paralleled many of the ways evangelicals had publicized the Waorani in the 1960s. Environmentalists, too, needed a romanticized version of the Waorani for domestic consumption.

MAXUS ECUADOR INC.

"Waponi, amigo Waorani, boto Maxus." (Greetings, Waorani friend, I am Maxus.) Building a road through the Waorani Ethnic Reserve or installing Block 16 wells, this was the phrase oil workers memorized in case of an "unforeseen encounter with a Wao." It was part of Maxus's effort to express respect for the Waorani and to maintain peaceful relations. "Keep calm," instructions advised. "Remember that, in general, the Waorani are always armed with spears and shotguns for protection and hunting and that they speak loudly and make many gestures. You should not think that these are signs of attack. Do not show fear or make any gesture that might seem aggressive. Tell the Wao you are his friend and, looking at his face, repeat [the phrase above]." At that point the ideal, cool-headed oil worker was to follow the most welcome order of all: "Report to your supervisor so that he can talk to the Wao and resolve the situation."[34]

The chief of operations for Maxus Ecuador was William Hutton, coincidentally an avowed evangelical, whose presence reinforced the perception of missionary–oil company collaboration. With Hutton at the helm, a number of missionaries, including Rachel Saint prior to her death, supported the company as the best among available options. Actual collaboration was minimal, little more than maintaining the status quo in education and healthcare for the Waorani, now funded by the oil company.

In 1991, when Maxus assumed the largest percentage of the Block 16 concession, the Dallas-based company inherited Conoco's plans for what was considered an environmentally friendly approach to drilling, along with inheriting Conoco's enemies among environmentalists. These environmental groups continued to oppose both oil extraction in Block 16 and what came to be known as the "Maxus Road." Unlike Conoco, however, Maxus did not back out, despite never overcoming the negative publicity and committing public relations blunders of its own. And Maxus under Hutton did develop the wells in Block 16 following Conoco's plan, using up-to-date industry guidelines for oil extraction in tropical rainforests.[35]

Just as controversial as the Block 16 project itself was Maxus's relationship with the Waorani. Opponents of Hutton and Maxus Ecuador viewed the company as paternalistic and exploitative. In Kane's account, Maxus first bribed Nanto, then Æncædi (and then denied having done so), in an effort to gain ONHAE's support for both oil extraction and the oil road. In December 1991, less than a month after Maxus had taken over from Conoco, ONHAE met in its fourth *congreso* (assembly) and passed a series of resolutions, including one expressing opposition to any new activity related to oil extraction or road construction and one calling for a ten-year moratorium on all initiatives from outsiders so that the Waorani would have time to prepare themselves to confront the pressures of change.[36]

Neither Maxus nor the Ecuadorian government could wait. The week of October 26, 1992, about the same time that approximately two hundred Waorani were demonstrating outside the corporate offices of Maxus and Petroecuador in Quito, construction of the road to Block 16 and an underground pipeline alongside it began as scheduled. Kane reported that Nanto, Moi, and Luis Macas (president of CONAIE, the most powerful national indigenous organization in Ecuador) met with Ecuadorian president Sixto Durán that same week to present their case against drilling, again to no avail.[37]

With oil extraction in Block 16 a fait accompli based on the needs of the state, Maxus focused on winning support from the majority of the Waorani. By November 9, 1992, the company had initiated an ongoing relationship with ONHAE and had begun to develop a methodology for approaching all of the Waorani communities.[38] First, it provided funding for relatively small items that the Waorani wanted: food and transport for ONHAE assemblies, sponsorship of soccer tournaments, school supplies, outboard motors and gasoline, pipe to improve drainage around local airstrips, as well as rice, tuna, and other foods.[39] Second, the company attempted to create a more holistic, long-range development plan for the Waorani as a form of compensation, since the government of Ecuador and not the Waorani would share in any actual profits from oil. Much of the content came from the original Conoco plans.

The result was the Acuerdo de Amistad, Respeto y Apoyo Mutuo Entre las Comunidades Huaorani y Maxus Ecuador Inc. (Agreement for friendship, respect and mutual support between the Waorani communities and Maxus Ecuador Inc.), signed on August 13, 1993, in the Wao clearing of Quiwado by President Sixto Durán, ONHAE president Æncædi Nihua Æwænguimæ, and Maxus general manager William Hutton. Among its most important points, the document affirmed that the Waorani would no longer oppose petroleum exploration and extraction on their lands and would give up their call for a moratorium. For its part, Maxus would assist the Waorani in education, healthcare, and community development based on studies and requests submitted by individual Wao communities. Maxus also would support community-based plans initiated by the Waorani in ways that would not encourage dependency. A community relations team was formed shortly after the accord was signed, and Maxus promised USD$500,000 to fund the agreement during the first two years.[40]

With so much money in play, word quickly got around among other indigenous groups that ONHAE had become "la 'mimada' de Maxus" (Maxus's pet or spoiled child).[41] A report in the *Dallas Morning News* in March 1994 claimed that the company spent USD$260,000 on the Waorani during 1993 alone, the year the accord was signed.[42] While the company did provide significant funding for ONHAE as an organization and for its presidents during the next few years, investment in community development never came close to the extravagant amounts promised in the accord. Maxus did not have the deep pockets others attributed to it. The company had lost money in four of the previous six years and was $900 million in debt.[43] The Block 16 project, originally estimated to cost $600 million to $650 million, was running about 30 percent over budget.[44]

Looming losses increased the pressure to finish the access road and get Block 16 and two adjacent fields into full production. Maxus focused on these goals rather than on the time-consuming process of visiting Wao clearings and listening to residents who were new to the whole process discuss community development needs. It was easier to work through existing channels, such as Lloyd Rogers's supervision of fiscal schools. Maxus workers built school buildings, and company dollars provided educational materials and teacher salaries.[45] The company also helped to support medical work already under way by missionaries. When it came to training additional healthcare workers, however, Maxus's own doctors took the path of least resistance: they worked almost exclusively with the few young Waorani who spoke Spanish. This marginalized a significant number of older people who already had a foundation of basic healthcare training from both SIL and HCJB missionary nurses.[46]

Maxus's decision to collaborate with existing missionary programs raised the specter of the late 1960s and accusations that Big Oil and missionaries were controlling the Waorani. Hutton's evangelical faith and working relationship with Saint, highlighted in Kane's accounts, did nothing to dispel such beliefs. While the two shared certain values, Hutton turned to Saint because he apparently spoke little or no Spanish and certainly no *Wao tededo* and needed her to communicate with the Waorani and to know what was happening during ceremonies at Toñæmpade.[47]

The impact of Maxus among the Waorani was mixed at best, and its efforts toward environmentally sustainable oil extraction in Block 16 were far from perfect.[48] Still, the company outdistanced Texaco, Petroecuador, and its other predecessors in attempting to use best practices. Nevertheless, Maxus's inability to overcome its negative image as the oil company that exploited the Waorani would be summed up with the words "trinkets and beads." The phrase came from a disastrous off-the-cuff attempt at humor during a ceremony in Toñæmpade in the fall of 1993, not long after the accord had been signed between Maxus and the Waorani. This gathering was to sign an additional agreement, this time between ONHAE and the Ecuadorian Institute of Forests and Natural Areas. It would authorize the Waorani to help establish policies for the Yasuní Park and to serve as park rangers.

About three hundred Waorani, mostly village residents, attended the signing. Also attending were Jorge Barba, minister of parks, Alicia Durán Ballén, the president's daughter and his adviser on indigenous affairs, plus Rachel Saint, Hutton, and other officials. As part of the ceremony, the Waorani presented Durán Ballén with a feather crown and a woven armlet. In turn, the president's daughter removed her gold earrings and put them on the ears of Æncædi's mother. Durán Ballén turned to a young man near her, identified by Kane as Mark Wiznitzer, a staff member at the US embassy, and asked, with a smile, "Was that a fair exchange?"[49] It was a patronizing remark, spoken in English, and Wiznitzer replied, also in English, "Well, that's how we got Manhattan, trinkets and beads."[50]

He spoke almost in a mumble, and the exchange would have disappeared unnoticed except that another American nearby had a video camera and recorded the incident. When it later became part of a 1996 anti-oil documentary, the comment was emphasized with subtitles. Wiznitzer's attempt to be clever also provided producers with a title for the film, *Trinkets and Beads*. The young embassy worker had no connection to Maxus, but the phrase perfectly summed up what the producers wanted to communicate. While the film did not appear until 1996, it was clear by mid-1994, with the appearance of Kane's two *New Yorker* articles—one of which presented Maxus as sinister, the other as culpable for genocide—that the company had lost the PR campaign.[51] This may have been inevitable, given how hard it was to defend drilling in the Amazon. No matter how innovative Maxus tried to be, more passionate voices would point out that it would take twenty years of oil production from Maxus's wells "to meet the United States' energy needs for about thirteen days." Not only that; Kane pointed out, "Unless something changes, soon, it seems safe to assume that by the time that oil is gone the Huaorani will be, too."[52]

A PIVOTAL YEAR

For disputes over oil between the Ecuadorian government and environmentalists, as well as for specific events affecting the Waorani, Maxus, and evangelical missionaries, 1994 turned out to be a pivotal year. In January the government unveiled its intent to double the land in the Oriente where oil extraction would be permitted, immediately raising the ire of environmentalists. Groups such as the Rainforest Action Network and the Center for Economic and Social Rights charged the government with human rights violations because of the "dangerous levels of toxic contamination and related health problems in Ecuador's Amazon."[53]

Later in the year, the OAS Inter-American Commission on Human Rights received a long-delayed invitation to investigate human rights violations in the Ecuadorian Amazon, in part a response to the 1990 suit filed by the Sierra Club Legal Defense Fund. The commission focused primarily on the implications of environmental degradation allegedly perpetrated by Texaco during its two decades in charge of most oil operations in the region. Commission members also participated in a meeting with some fifty Waorani, led by Moi, in the oil town of Coca. The group objected to Maxus and complained that ONHAE did not represent them.[54]

The latter complaint pointed to a schism that had been growing since Moi and several other participants walked out of the February 1993 ONHAE meeting to protest what they perceived as the influence of Maxus over the event. In response, elected officials from ONHAE insisted that Moi and his followers represented a "dissident faction," while ONHAE represented the majority of Waorani. Nonetheless a political scientist doing fieldwork in Ecuador claimed that "international environmentalists and journalists consistently support the dissident Moi faction."[55] The split pointed to the continuing difficulties the Waorani faced in presenting a united front to the rest of the world and the tendency of outsiders to support the particular Wao representatives most helpful to them.

Oil production began in Block 16 in May 1994 and "reached almost 35,000 barrels per day that year before being limited by the available capacity in the Trans-Ecuadorian pipeline."[56] With the wells on line and the majority of the Waorani on board, but with public opinion running against the company, Hutton was replaced as general manager of Maxus Ecuador. This turned out to be a sign of even bigger changes to come. In 1995 the Argentine company Yacimientos Petrolíferos Fiscales purchased Maxus. (YPF, in turn, would be purchased four years later by the Spanish oil giant Repsol.) These companies continued to supply goods to the Wao communities as Maxus had. However, frustration increased among the Waorani as it became increasingly difficult to know with whom they were supposed to be dealing. The days of accords and ceremonies were past.

Toward the end of the year, on November 11, 1994, Rachel Saint, eighty, died of cancer in Quito, Ecuador. She was buried in Toñæmpade, her home for the previous twelve years. Subtracting time in Quito and in the US, Saint had lived with the Waorani, and specifically the Guequitaidi kinship group, whom she called the Iñanani (literally "these people here," her family), for more than three decades. Although she had not been affiliated with SIL since 1982, she had remained the iconic Christian missionary to many outsiders. As one of the first two people to make sustained peaceful contact with them, the Waorani, especially the older generation, continued to view Saint as a peacemaker or peace enforcer. She also still served as a convenient symbol for critics of missionary outreach. Her behavioral standards, which reflected the Ten Commandments, were unbending. She could be controlling and tactless, and she took orders from no one short of God himself.[57] Still, most Waorani remembered her fondly.

Rachel's death served as a catalyst for her nephew Steve Saint's renewed involvement with the Waorani (see the epilogue). Christian practice and missionary activity among the Waorani continued, even if the latter seemed fragmented. Wao Christians in the Quiwado clearing baptized twenty-one people in March 1996. About the same time, an additional seven were baptized in Nemompade, a small settlement begun by Steve Saint.[58] Lloyd Rogers collaborated with Compassion International to encourage education and Bible memorization in Spanish. During the 1990s, Rogers and his wife, Linda, began holding summer Bible camps near Quito and on the Pacific Coast. Wao children and teenagers who memorized a certain number of Bible verses in Spanish were eligible to attend.

Every year or eighteen months, Catherine Peeke and Rosi Jung arrived for extended visits to encourage the Waorani in various clearings to read the New Testament in *Wao tededo*. From mid-July to late September 1994, for example, they visited eight different communities. In six clearings they were "greeted enthusiastically" by people who responded to instruction in how to study different portions of the New Testament. In two other communities, people "reacted negatively to our focus on *reading* and *studying* the Book," Peeke reported. She explained that the less enthusiastic groups had hoped for something more exciting, like the planned activities of evangelistic teams that placed fewer demands on them to read.[59] Several times during the decade, Pat Kelley returned to teach literacy classes. In September 1996 Peeke and Kelley met in Shell with a group of Waorani to launch a Scripture recording project to produce an audio version of portions of the New Testament in *Wao tededo*, particularly for Waorani who could not read.[60] Despite the popularity of such projects, the known number of practicing Christians among the Waorani never exceeded more than about 20 to 25 percent of the population, lower than assumed by most evangelicals in the United States. Many of the most active were from Dayomæ's kinship group. Historically they had the greatest exposure to missionaries, and several had been among the nucleus of Bible translation assistants.

In April 1995 ONHAE briefly reversed its pattern of subservience to Maxus and staged an occupation of a drilling and pumping site in Wao territory. The occupation had the support of the other regional indigenous organizations, along with environmental groups in Quito and the US. To the disappointment of their supporters, though, the Waorani maintained the occupation for only a few days. They still had little practice in this type of political action or in collective action more generally.[61] Nonetheless Moi and other Waorani who shared his concerns remained key contacts for researchers and environmental activists who carried on the fight to protect the Yasuní National Park and the Waorani Ethnic Reserve from deforestation and contamination. Environmentalists and missionaries each maintained their own distinct networks among the Waorani, networks that rarely overlapped, at least not publicly.

Also, in 1994 Peeke wrote a series of reflections about the Waorani, about missionaries, and about oil companies in response to a letter from a North American university student. As had the student, Peeke defined "missionary" broadly, to include SIL staff like herself. She recalled attending a special fiesta one night in Tewæno with Oba, her friend and language consultant. As they watched the dancing, Oba turned to Peeke and exclaimed, "Just look at all of those young boys! In the olden days they would all have been speared before having a chance to grow up." Oba and Peeke were convinced that Christianity, as expressed by the phrase "Itota beyæ, tænonamai" (On behalf of Jesus, do not spear), had enabled the Waorani to break the deadly cycle of spearing vendettas that threatened to destroy them.

"They had experienced the harsh results of killing," Peeke explained, "and were ready to abandon it; the God of their new faith gave them power to forgive and to let live."[62] Although only a minority of the people became Christians, there were sufficient numbers to allow others to come safely to the protectorate in the late 1960s, to find spouses, and eventually to gain access to the outside world and to trade goods.

Of course, the story was never that simple. Relocation to the protectorate may have helped to preserve the Waorani as a people by curbing the spearing vendettas, avoiding potentially deadly clashes with oil crews, and fighting contact illnesses through the availability of medicines. Still, for a time Christianity was practiced as little more than a means of social control. And the overcrowding led to genuine dislocation and suffering, food shortages, and the polio epidemic.

"Learning to 'believe' is such hard work," Jim Yost jotted in his notebook in 1979. "It takes a long time, lots of practice, many mistakes in learning." That was true for those Waorani who accepted Christianity. Something similar might be said of those who arrived to live among them. Learning to be a missionary, too, was hard work. It also took a long time, lots of practice, many mistakes in learning.[63] Delays in translating the New Testament, an unwillingness to confront Rachel Saint, traumas of the relocation, and failings of the church were some of the mistakes. Missionaries, as Peeke pointed out, were "an imperfect, failing lot," who nonetheless were "motivated to make [Jesus Christ] known to those in need."[64]

In response to her undergraduate interlocutor, Peeke also asserted that there were no perfect *cowode* in the jungles of eastern Ecuador. "Missionaries are subject to much of the same blindness as that of anthropologists, environmentalists, government agents, tourists, and petroleum explorers." Unsurprisingly, however, Peeke defended the missionary presence. "I see both good and bad, but principally good."[65] She mentioned SIL's role in peaceful contact and also in healthcare training, literacy education, help in relating to outsiders, and, of course, providing the Waorani with the New Testament in their native language.

The resurgent emphasis on indigenous identity in Ecuador and elsewhere in Latin America at the close of the twentieth century had the potential to support the long-term survival of the Waorani, but the outcome was still uncertain. Despite their historic notoriety, the Waorani remained a relatively small indigenous group, surrounded by more populous, land-hungry neighbors who traditionally relegated them to the bottom rung of the social hierarchy. Devastation of their territory and adjacent lands due to oil extraction and attendant abuses, including deforestation and overhunting, showed no signs of abating. At the same time, this small group, in a remote but valuable region of Amazonian Ecuador, retained their fame as the subject of one of the most widely publicized and controversial missionary-indigenous encounters in the history of American evangelicalism. They and their story continue to capture the imaginations of the *cowode* beyond their rainforest and around the world.

Epilogue

THE TWENTY-FIRST CENTURY

⌐————————————————————————————————————

ELISABETH ELLIOT ONCE commented that she wrote her novel, *No Graven Image*, as a way of using a fictional story to deal with her experiences on the mission field, especially the three years she spent among the Waorani. Margaret Sparhawk, the heroine of Elliot's book, is a sincere young woman who struggles with the challenging and unexpected complexities she encounters in her efforts to live out the gospel among an indigenous people. Through Margaret's experiences, Elliot explored the idea that there is much more to missionary work than meets the eye, in fact, a great deal more than the folks back home ever imagine.[1]

Elliot's insight is helpful at the beginning of an epilogue. After learning about missionaries and the Waorani between 1956 and the mid-1990s, the reader might wonder what has happened since then. What is life like for the Waorani now that many participate in the modern world while trying to maintain their identity as people of the rainforest? How many Wao Christians are there? Do missionaries still work with them? What about the story of the five men killed on the banks of the Curaray River? What place, if any, does that story have among evangelicals during the initial decades of the twenty-first century?

This epilogue responds to these questions while recognizing the limits historians face in interpreting the recent past. It is too early for a historical assessment of the past twenty years. Many of the missionaries and other outsiders mentioned here are still alive, and the significance of their actions, particularly those of recent years, is not yet clear. As for the Waorani, the many challenges they confront can only be summarized.

A NEW FACE TO THE STORY

The most significant figure in the ongoing missionary-Waorani saga during the decade between 1996 and 2006 was Steve Saint, Nate Saint's elder son and Rachel Saint's nephew. Born in Ecuador in 1951, Steve spent his first five years in Shell, at the edge of the rainforest and the home base for Mission Aviation Fellowship in Ecuador. After Nate Saint's death, Marj Saint and her three children moved to Quito, where Steve grew up until he went to college in the US, although on several occasions he spent school vacations in Tewæno with his Aunt Rachel and the Waorani. After graduating from Wheaton College, Saint worked for a few years in Quito before returning with his wife, Ginny, to the US, where he became a businessman and entrepreneur.

When Rachel died in 1994, Steve Saint handled her affairs and in doing so renewed his ties with Waorani he had known growing up, mostly Guequita's kin. At their invitation, Steve, Ginny, and their four teenagers moved to the rainforest for a year. They worked with several Wao families to establish a new clearing called Nemompade, located beside a small stream of the same name. The stream was named after the grave site of Nemo, one of Dayomæ's ancestors, and the Wao name that later was given to Rachel. Centrally located in the old protectorate, Nemompade was to be a place where Waorani could provide medical and dental care for one another and acquire other technical skills that would enable them to participate in the outside world from a position of equality rather than dependency.[2] This focus became one of two themes Saint would highlight as he became the new face of the missionary-Waorani story before North American audiences. He also emphasized the power of Christian faith to bring about forgiveness and reconciliation, dramatized in the 2006 movie *The End of the Spear.*

Initially, however, Saint stressed that the greatest threat the Waorani faced was a crippling dependence on outsiders. According to Saint, the "harsh reality" he had discovered "was that the Huaorani church of the midnineties was less functional than it had been in the early sixties," when he was a boy. The church, he asserted elsewhere, was a "travesty," with no elders and an inability "to govern themselves as believers."[3] Well-meaning missionaries, "the overbearing, over-indulging outside Christian community," were to blame.[4] During the forty years since peaceful contact in 1958, missionaries had done next to nothing to help the Waorani to form a "self-propagating, self-governing, and self-supporting church."[5] In articles, interviews, speaking engagements, and a book, Saint pointed to the Wao church as a case study illustrating the dangers of dysfunctional relationships between missionaries and indigenous people.

Saint also founded the Indigenous People's Technology and Education Center (I-TEC) in 1999. Headquartered near Ocala, Florida, and described by one observer as "part technology start-up, part missionary agency," the purpose of I-TEC was to make technology available to indigenous people in ways appropriate to their circumstances and needs.[6] Projects included a powered parachute, which was a light aircraft that could be used to transport medicines, as well as one or two passengers, between Wao settlements. Saint also developed a solar-powered, portable dental chair with an electric drill. I-TEC subsequently added I-Fix, I-Med, and I-See, which covered maintenance and repair skills, basic medicine, and inexpensive eyeglasses, respectively.[7] More recently, I-TEC offered I-Film, helping indigenous people to tell their own stories on film.[8] The organization also coordinated "Wao Vision Trips," where outsiders could visit Ecuador, spending four or five days with Christian Waorani in a clearing near the village of Tzapino. The trips were designed to foster cross-cultural understanding and to provide income for the Waorani in an evangelical version of ecotourism.

Saint's diagnosis of the problem may have been accurate to a degree; certainly SIL had been aware of the perils of fostering dependence among the Waorani since at least the 1970s. But his analysis reflected little or no awareness of Waorani history during the approximately twenty-five years between his visits in Tewæno during the 1960s and reestablishing those relationships in the mid-1990s. Others questioned his assessment. According to Jim Yost, significant numbers of Waorani were practicing their faith, but in ways adapted to their culture. Historically, extended families (kinship groups) were the only social institution the Waorani had. "When I go back, late at night I hear grandmothers, fathers and mothers teaching their children and grandchildren scriptures in the quiet of the night and solitude of the home," Yost wrote. "I hear prayer coming from home after home throughout the night. There are no well-kept buildings, but genuine, strong faith still exists."[9]

In addition, the golden age of Saint's childhood was the period when the number of Waorani Christians was limited to a small group of Guequitaidi, living in Tewæno under the direct tutelage of Rachel and Dayomæ. The growth of autonomous Wao Christianity became more complicated with the relocations of the late 1960s and early 1970s, the delays in Bible translation, the challenges related to literacy, and the preference among some Waorani for a "Quichua-ized" Christianity. Foreigners had built a church in Toñæmpade that few used except for show, but blaming missionaries for the failings of the Wao church was simplistic, and it underestimated the vitality of indigenous believers.

Saint's account of healthcare among the Waorani reflected a similar historical amnesia. He paid little attention to SIL-sponsored, on-site village health promoter training, taught by Lois Pederson and Verla Cooper, with Jim Yost and Catherine Peeke translating. Miriam Gebb and Janet Jenkins, HCJB missionary nurses, trained approximately fifty Waorani as health promoters between 1991 and 1993, building on the skills older members of the group, such as Dawa and Ana, had learned from Rachel and Rosi Jung.[10] Steve Saint was accurate in observing that the default method of dental care among the Waorani was to pull decayed teeth. However, others had offered dental training to the Waorani before I-TEC. SIL had sponsored dental courses in Limoncocha, which at least a few Waorani had attended.[11] During the first decade of the twenty-first century, I-TEC arrived with innovative technology. They, too, soon discovered how hard it was for the Waorani to sustain basic healthcare. Solar-powered dental equipment did not automatically overcome complications such as the prevalence of hepatitis D in Wao territory during the late 1990s, potentially affecting dental care.[12]

"GRANDFATHER" MINCAYE

While Saint was drawing attention to the problem of dependency, he was also interpreting the story of his father and the other four slain missionaries for a new generation of North American evangelicals. Told very much as his family's story, Saint focused on the power of reconciliation and of ending cycles of violence. Both emphases were vividly demonstrated by the presence of "Grandfather" Mincaye, one of the Waorani who participated in the 1956 killings, with Saint at many of his speaking engagements. Saint believed that Mincaye, a teenager at the time, had played a direct role in killing his father.[13] Mincaye, who was Dayomæ's half-brother, was an early believer among the Guequitaidi. He was baptized by Rachel's brother Phil in 1962, a year or two after Steve had begun to visit Tewæno. Mincaye befriended the boy, who was nine or ten when the two first met, teaching him to hunt and fish alongside Mincaye's own young sons. The two renewed their friendship years later, after Rachel died. Mincaye, an increasingly outspoken Christian who was blessed with an extra measure of the personal charm characteristic of the Waorani, became a surrogate grandfather for Steve Saint's children. During visits to the US, he joined Saint in appearances before church groups and missionary conferences.

Saint and Mincaye became more well-known after unexpected encounters with two very different, but influential, evangelicals. First was Mart Green, founder and CEO of Mardel Christian and Education Supply stores and the son of Hobby Lobby's founder, David Green. Mart Green knew the Ecuador missionary story, but it took on new meaning in 1997, when he heard Saint and Mincaye. Green had been looking for ways to promote Bible reading, and Mincaye's comments, as translated by Saint, moved him deeply. This "violent society now lives in peace," Green noted, "and the answer is God's Word transformed their life." Like others before him, Green was undeterred by the fact that Mincaye, like most Waorani of his generation, could not read. In 1999 Green met with Saint to discuss the possibility of a feature-length film "about the power of God's Word," from the Wao perspective.[14]

Saint took Green to Ecuador to meet the Guequitaidi who would be the subjects of the film. After initially refusing to grant rights to the story, the Waorani reportedly changed their minds after hearing about the 1999 Columbine shootings in the US. According to Green, they said, "If our story can help North America, then you tell our story."[15] Green formed a production company, Every Tribe Entertainment, and hired filmmakers to produce what would become two movies about the missionary-Waorani story. One was a docudrama, *Beyond the Gates of Splendor*, released in 2005 and aimed at church audiences. The movie included interviews with the five widows, filmed before the deaths in 2004 of both Marilou McCully and Marj Saint. *Beyond the Gates of Splendor* was followed by *The End of the Spear*, a feature-length commercial film released in January 2006 to coincide with the fiftieth anniversary of the missionaries' deaths. Saint was a consultant on both and did the stunt flying, representing his father, for *The End of the Spear*. Mincaye was interviewed, along with other members of Dayomæ's kinship group, for *Beyond the Gates*. The lead Wao character in *The End of the Spear* was "Mincayani," a composite figure whose story included elements of Mincaye's life.[16]

About the same time he met Mart Green, Saint was contacted by a singer-songwriter named Steven Curtis Chapman after Chapman had read *Through Gates of Splendor*. They became friends, and Chapman devoted the middle segment of each performance of his 2002 concert tour to retelling the story of the five missionaries. The narrative was backed by songs composed and performed by Chapman, and the segment culminated with the on-stage appearance of Saint and Mincaye. It was in some ways reminiscent of Rachel's appearances in 1971 with Guequita. According to one reporter, the moment when Saint embraced Mincaye, "the Ecuadorian Indian who killed his father," was the climax of the concert. Only months after the September 11 tragedies, concertgoers responded to the Christian message of "redemption and forgiveness."[17] Two of the songs from this segment, one with Mincaye's Wao chant in the background, were included on Chapman's album *Declaration*, which went gold, selling more than five hundred thousand copies.[18]

In between traveling to Ecuador with Green and joining Chapman's concert tour, Saint, Mincaye, and Tæmænta (son of Nænquiwi, or "George," who met the missionaries on Palm Beach) attended Amsterdam 2000. This meeting, sponsored by the Billy Graham Evangelistic Association, brought together more than ten thousand evangelists from around the world. Although the conference bore some resemblance to the Graham-sponsored Berlin Congress in 1966 (attended by Rachel, Quemo, and Come), the globalization of Christianity was much more evident, with 209 countries and territories represented. In the 1960s Quemo and Come had gotten short haircuts and worn suits; three decades later Mincaye and Tæmænta wore toucan feather crowns and Mincaye inserted his balsa earplugs. Similar on both occasions was the response to the Waorani. In Amsterdam, after translating Mincaye's remarks, Saint asked all the delegates who had been "affected . . . in some significant way" by the missionary-Waorani story to stand. Thousands of delegates rose to their feet. Saint said that he issued the invitation to demonstrate that "what they [the Waorani] meant for evil . . . God intended for good." It also echoed the theme of triumph amid tragedy long a hallmark of the story. The last chapter of Saint's autobiography, also titled *The End of the Spear*, ended with this scene.[19]

Saint's frenetic pace—sometimes speaking five or six times a day, granting numerous interviews, publishing three books, establishing I-TEC—reflected his energetic personality and effectiveness as a communicator. It also was a way to cope with another tragedy. Having lost his father, Saint also lost a child. His twenty-year-old daughter Stephenie died of a cerebral hemorrhage on July 23, 2000, only a week before Saint traveled to Amsterdam. Saint's openness about his grief reflected a characteristic spiritual intensity.[20]

OTHER EFFORTS TO TELL THE STORY

Others contributed to keeping the missionary-Waorani story alive. Wycliffe Bible Translators sponsored a dramatic, modern-dance retelling of Dayomæ's story that toured from September 1996 to March 1997. The astronaut Patrick Forrester took a small piece of Nate Saint's plane—recovered from the banks of the Curaray River—on a 2009 flight of the space shuttle *Discovery* to "honor Nate Saint, the Saint family and all missionaries around the world."[21] Anthony Solis, a researcher, formed Veritas Ministries in 2014 with an ambitious agenda of producing several inspirational books about the story. In 2015 the artist Bradford Johnson explored the intersection between photography and painting in telling stories of the past, inspired by the missionary-Waorani narrative.[22] Children were another favorite audience. Numerous biographies of Jim Elliot and Nate Saint for young readers were published between 1998 and 2013, along with one of Rachel Saint. Valerie Elliot Shepard wrote *Pilipinto's Happiness* about her years growing up in the jungle. Her father was featured in a short, animated film for children, *The Jim Elliot Story*.[23]

The single most influential version of the missionary-Waorani story in the twenty-first century, however, was the film *The End of the Spear*. Released in January 2006 the film was panned by many secular critics but nevertheless grossed about $12 million. The DVD version, released in June 2006, also enjoyed healthy sales. The film retold the story of the missionaries' efforts to contact the Waorani and covered the history of violence characteristic of their culture. A new focus, central to the plot, was the account of reconciliation and forgiveness between Steve Saint's character and the composite character, Mincayani. This emphasis expressed a core belief of evangelicalism, even if the script was not overtly "Christian."[24]

The film opens with the words "From a True Story," while small print following the closing credits acknowledges composite characters and fictionalized incidents. Notably, the climax of the movie involves a dramatic scene that never happened. The character of the adult Steve Saint, played by Chad Allen, is tempted to avenge his father's death and kill Mincayani, but instead chooses reconciliation and forgiveness. Saint acknowledged that the scene was fictional and that he and Mincaye had never been estranged.[25]

Another scene also was open to debate. Beginning in 1989 several Waorani Christians who had participated in the killings began to talk about seeing supernatural phenomena—lights or music or angelic figures—above the trees on a ridge behind the riverbank as the men lay dying or shortly after their deaths. In *The End of the Spear*, a brief flashback shows angelic figures in the sky and light flooding the area. Radiance comes down and touches the dying Nate Saint.[26] The first reports of supernatural manifestations came from Dawa and Quemo when, along with Rachel, they had taken Olive Fleming Liefeld, her husband, Walter Liefeld, and the Liefelds' daughter, Holly, to see Palm Beach on the Curaray River. While at the site, the two Waorani talked once again about what had happened in 1956, with Rachel translating. As part of their narrative, Rachel said, "they heard singing." She explained that "as they looked up over the tops of the trees they saw a large group of people. They were all singing, and it looked as if there were a hundred flashlights ['bright lights']." After an indeterminate amount of time, "suddenly it disappeared."[27] Although cautious about the meaning of what Dawa and Quemo had said, Liefeld included the account in her memoir, *Unfolding Destinies* (1998).

At Liefeld's request, Steve Saint later interviewed other Waorani who had participated in the killings. Memories were vague, but Yowe and Mincaye also reported seeing something. Quemo later identified a specific piece of music from the original soundtrack of *Beyond the Gates of Splendor* as the "chanting" he had heard on the river bank more than forty years earlier.[28] Although they accepted the reality of the supernatural—it *could* have happened—others close to the story were not so sure that it did. Elisabeth Elliot expressed uncertainty because of the amount of time that had elapsed between the event and the reports. "I take it with a grain of salt because in all the time I was there [Tewæno], I never heard anything like that." Nonetheless, with typical candor she commented, "I wasn't there" (during the original attack or on the Liefelds' visit).[29]

Catherine Peeke also confirmed that she had never heard of angels on the Curaray until Liefeld's book came out. This was despite her work with the Waorani to select a word for "angel" in *Wao tededo* to use in translating the New Testament. Peeke did recall that a Wao man involved in killing the indigenous missionary Toñæ had told her that as Toñæ died, he said to his killers, "You may kill my body, but I will go to God's house." At the same time, "a gorgeous red macaw came soaring down from the sky toward him." From Peeke's perspective, this account suggested that the Waorani were willing to talk about unusual occurrences and would not have waited more than three decades to mention angels. In addition, a macaw seemed like a culturally plausible expression of the supernatural.[30]

More significant for *The End of the Spear* than whether angels were present was how the scriptwriters developed the film's central theme of reconciliation. On screen, reconciliation occurs as imagined by Hollywood rather than as it happened in the Ecuadorian rainforests. After hearing the Christian message of peace, the hardest work of reconciliation occurred among Waorani, as some let go of the need for revenge that fueled their internal spearing vendettas. A more accurate movie might have followed the old warrior Guequita and what it cost him to put down his spear. Or it could have extended the theme of reconciliation to missionary relationships. Such deeply committed and determined women as Elisabeth Elliot and Rachel Saint found it easier to forgive their loved ones' killers and live among them than to get along with each other.

The End of the Spear portrays recent Wao history as the history of the Waorani and the Saint family. During a *Christianity Today* interview shortly after the film was released, Steve Saint was asked about what had happened in Ecuador since the events covered in Elliot's book, *Through Gates of Splendor*. He responded that Elliot's book was "just chapter 1 of the whole story." Chapter 2 was Rachel going to live with the Waorani and encouraging them to tell other Waorani about the gospel message. "Chapter 3 begins 11 years ago when Aunt Rachel died, and the Waodani asked me to live with them."[31]

This is a very narrow slice of the story, although it is the one Saint could tell as his own. There are no chapters for SIL staff other than Rachel, or for Bishop Labaca and Sister Inés, or, for that matter, for other Waorani beyond the Guequitaidi. Between 2006 and 2012, the year he was seriously injured and partially paralyzed while working on an I-TEC prototype, Saint continued to visit Ecuador while accepting speaking engagements and directing I-TEC in the US. After the accident, his public appearances were curtailed, but he still spoke to audiences via online video clips and I-TEC. Mincaye told his own story in *Gentle Savage Still Seeking the End of the Spear* (2013), an English translation in book form of extensive oral history interviews with Mincaye, supplemented by additional comments from Quemo and Yowe.[32]

NEW CHALLENGES FOR THE WAORANI

Before the accident, while Saint and Mincaye were drawing crowds in the US during the early 2000s, the Waorani in Ecuador, especially the younger generation, were juggling tensions between their identity as Waorani and the pressures of modern life. As the new century dawned, the Waorani numbered between fifteen hundred and two thousand people, most under the age of twenty-four, scattered in three dozen small villages or clearings, up from about twenty communities a decade earlier.[33] Many lived in the established clearings of the old protectorate and others in the Waorani Ethnic Reserve. Two groups, the Tagæidi (Tagæ's bunch) and the newly identified Taadomenani (the lowlanders, or the meandering ones), remained in self-imposed isolation deep in the Yasuní National Park in an area known as the "untouchable" or "intangible" zone (map 5).[34]

The Waorani were still among the least acculturated of the indigenous groups in Amazonian Ecuador. However, except for the Tægaidi and Taadomenani, the Waorani increased their contact with the outside world and their participation in the market economy. It was not uncommon for young men to spend significant amounts of time in towns such as Puyo or Coca near the border of their traditional territories.[35] Market forces, new settlement patterns, and changes in socialization all provided the cultural context for Christianity as experienced by the Waorani and the handful of missionaries who worked among them.

Many in the younger generation had an advantage over their parents in that they were literate and could read *Wængongui nano apænegaino* (God his ancient spoken message, the Wao New Testament). By 2004 about ten young Waorani, not necessarily professing Christians, had at least some university education. Others had finished the equivalent of high school. Yet even with increased educational levels, the obstacles to the spread of an indigenous Wao Christianity were daunting. Spanish was the dominant language in school, on radio, and, of course, in all the provincial towns that the Waorani frequented, followed in importance by various dialects of the lowland Quichua language.

By the early 1990s alcohol abuse had become a serious problem among the Waorani; drugs and sexually transmitted diseases also had been introduced. Patterns of ongoing violent vendettas had largely ceased more than twenty-five years earlier, but not entirely. Isolated spearing raids have taken place since that time. Many incidents involved the influence of alcohol and were vengeance spearings in response to provocations by the Tagæidi and the Taadomenani. One such massacre, mostly of women and children, took place against the Tagæidi in May 2003.[36] In 2006, and again in 2008, the Taadomenani (by then reportedly joined by remnants of the Tagæidi) attacked illegal loggers operating in their territory. Three loggers were speared: two were killed, one survived.[37]

Conflict again broke out in 2013. In a contested and tragic series of events, the Taadomenani killed an elderly Wao couple, Ompodæ and Bogænæi, who had been among the first Waorani to welcome Alejandro Labaca nearly four decades earlier. The spearings took place on March 5, 2013, near the village of Yaadæntado, where the couple lived. An isolated clearing, it was located along the Maxus oil road, within the Yasuní National Park, about 140 miles from the town of Coca and in the same general area Labaca had visited.[38] Why the couple had been targeted is unclear. Whatever the reason, traditional Wao culture called for family members to avenge the deaths. The historian and Capuchín missionary Miguel Angel Cabodevilla and others sought government intervention, possibly with the payment of reparations, to defuse tensions within the dead couple's kinship group. Under Ecuadorian law, the government was responsible both for protecting its citizens, including the Waorani, from Taadomenani attacks and for protecting people groups in voluntary isolation, such as the Taadomenani.

Despite the pleas, there was no government response. Three weeks later a band of Waorani located and surrounded a Taadomenani longhouse. Using guns and spears, they systematically murdered an estimated twenty people (reported numbers varied widely), many of them women and children. Two little girls, about three and six, were captured by the attackers after their mother pled for their lives and hers. She was killed. The attackers took cell-phone pictures of the scene and some later bragged about what they had done. Despite this evidence, the government seemed to be "either actively hiding the story, or hiding from it."[39]

Eight months passed before Ecuador acknowledged the killings and arrested nine Waorani. All were imprisoned. Two were later killed, allegedly "trying to escape," and the rest eventually were released. The government's repeated unwillingness to act in the face of violence by and against the Taadomenani has raised questions about Ecuador's commitment to the long-term survival of this isolated group, as well as to charges of human rights abuses. For their part, the Waorani were divided over what role, if any, they wanted the government to play.[40]

PETROLEUM AND THE WAORANI HOMELAND

Tensions were heightened even more by a looming environmental crisis in Ecuador. In August 2013 President Rafael Correa ended the controversial Yasuní-ITT Initiative, in effect since 2007. This was a proposal to leave the petroleum reserves located under the Yasuní National Park in the ground in exchange for contributions from the international community to offset the revenue Ecuador lost by not drilling. While innovative, the plan had significant flaws and the anticipated donations never materialized. Although it provided a reprieve, if only temporary, for portions of the rainforest, Ecuador continued to be heavily oil-dependent.[41] When oil prices plummeted in 2014 and 2015, the country borrowed billions of dollars from China, much of it to be paid back in oil. With the end of the Yasuní-ITT Initiative, the state pushed for increased petroleum production, even when it meant drilling in or near pristine rainforest, and even when the cost of producing a barrel of oil was more than its price on the open market. The Yasuní National Park may have been recognized as the ancestral territory of the Waorani, one of the most biodiverse places on earth, and home to one of the few remaining indigenous peoples in voluntary isolation (the Taadomenani). But it also had oil, 846 million barrels' worth, according to some estimates.[42]

While oil extraction posed significant environmental risks, corollary activities, especially road construction, could be even more devastating. Roads within the park were prohibited by law, to little effect. As early as 2014 satellite imagery clearly showed that at least one illegal road had been constructed "into the core of the park," with others planned.[43] These roads served as open invitations to illegal loggers and settlers alike, both of whom contributed to deforestation. Undeterred, the government announced in April 2016 that it had begun construction on the first of a planned 276 wells in the ITT oil field, which overlapped the park (map 5). Earlier, in January 2016, Ecuador signed a deal with Andes Petroleum Ecuador, a consortium of two Chinese state-run companies, to explore two blocks (a half million acres) of rainforest that bordered the national park and the intangible zone to the south and east.[44] By mid-2016 the rainforest lands that had been the ancestral territory of the Waorani, and where many Wao communities were located, were surrounded by active oil wells and infrastructure to support extraction.

Few North Americans and even fewer North American evangelicals had ever heard of the Yasuní National Park or knew that it was part of ancestral Wao lands.[45] People familiar with the stories of Rachel and Dayomæ, of Jim Elliot or Nate Saint, were unaware of the amazing environmental diversity and species richness of the land. Just one section of Yasuní forest about the size of a football stadium contained "more than 650 different tree species . . . more than the total number of tree species found in the United States and Canada taken together." More than six hundred bird species had been observed in the Yasuní, about two-thirds the total number (925) in the US and Canada. Yasuní was a paradise for those who loved bugs: a single hectare (about two and a half acres) contained one hundred thousand species, "the highest documented insect diversity in the world."[46]

AGUINDA V. CHEVRON

The other widely publicized controversy dealing with oil in eastern Ecuador was *Aguinda v. Chevron*, the convoluted and long-running litigation against Texaco, first filed in 1993 and inherited in 2001 by Chevron after it acquired Texaco.[47] The suit sought compensation for environmental damage and its impact on the health of peasant farmers and indigenous people during the nearly two decades (1972–90) when Texaco was effectively in charge of the production and export of oil in Ecuador. Originally filed in a US court, the suit was dismissed in 2002 in favor of litigation in Ecuador. In 2011 an Ecuadorian court handed down an $18.2 billion verdict against Chevron, later reduced to $9.5 billion. Refusing to pay, Chevron, in turn, sued the plaintiff's lead lawyer, Steven Donziger (*Chevron v. Donziger*), other members of the legal team, and the plaintiffs in a US court for alleged "fraud and other misconduct," including "allegations of improper collusion between representatives of the plaintiffs and Ecuadorian governmental officials."[48] In March 2014 US District Judge Lewis Kaplan ruled in Chevron's favor, concluding, in essence, that Donziger and others committed fraud and extortion in order to get a favorable ruling in Ecuador.[49] The documentary film *Crude* follows this legal case, focusing on tribal groups such as the Cofán people, who were more directly involved than the Waorani.[50]

The original *Aguinda v. Texaco* was filed on behalf of indigenous groups, including the Waorani, and nonindigenous settlers who lived in areas alleged to have been harmed by Texaco's oil extraction activities. The Waorani themselves, however, were never plaintiffs, even though significant portions of their traditional territories had been affected by seismic exploration and oil wells carried out under the auspices of Texaco. In addition, the company had built the Via Auca roadway, opening Wao territory to settlers. Some Waorani also blamed Texaco, along with SIL, for the relocations of the late 1960s. For these reasons, in November 2012 a group of forty-two Wao leaders from five communities retained Judith Kimerling to file a motion to intervene on their behalf in the *Chevron v. Donziger* suit.[51] They sought to defend their rights should any of the *Aguinda* money ever reach the Ecuadorian Amazon and to remind the outside world that those who had suffered actual damages risked being eclipsed by feuds between lawyers and a multinational oil giant.

Since 2007 Kimerling had also worked with a grassroots alliance of Wao communities, known as Ome Gompote Kiwigimoni Huaorani (We Defend Our Waorani Territory), Ome Yasuní for short. Ome Yasuní wanted their voices to be heard when governmental entities or international NGOs made decisions concerning the Yasuní Park. According to Kimerling, the communities of Ome Yasuní are home to many older people with unhappy memories of leaving their lands in the late 1960s to relocate in the protectorate, and some associate missionaries (SIL) with Texaco.[52]

The Huaorani Ecolodge, a cluster of small thatched dwellings that accommodates a total of ten guests at a time, was established in 2008 to tap into ecotourism. It is located on the upper Shiripuno River near the small community of Cæwæidi Ono, which currently is home to about one hundred Waorani. The lodge was the brainchild of Moi Enomenga (of *Savages* and *New Yorker* fame) and a Welsh ecologist, Andy Drumm. The Ecolodge operates as a joint venture between Tropic Journeys in Nature, a company founded by Drumm, and the Cæwæidi Ono Association, founded and led by Enomenga and made up of Waorani from Cæwæidi Ono and other nearby communities.[53]

CHALLENGES OF POLITICS

Moi Enomenga has been recognized by outsiders for his work as an environmentalist and for seeking to preserve traditional Wao culture. To other leaders and aspiring leaders among the Waorani, his ongoing role in ONHAE, the political entity created to represent the Waorani to the outside world, has been more problematic. Most missionaries have stayed away from Wao disputes centered on ONHAE, renamed NAWE (the Spanish acronym for the Waorani Nationality of Amazonian Ecuador) in 2007. The instability of the organization has its roots in the egalitarianism of traditional Wao culture as well as the divergent needs of Waorani settlements scattered across the former protectorate and the Waorani Ethnic Reserve. For most of its existence, NAWE (and ONHAE before it) has been funded by Big Oil. Many Waorani are happy to have NAWE leaders negotiate with oil companies for the gifts of food and supplies they have come to expect as a form of rainforest abundance. Even so, distributing the expected oil company largesse does not give NAWE leadership the political authority that outsiders might expect.[54]

There are some indications that the Waorani are investing political authority in smaller, more localized groups, such as Ome Yasuní and the Cæwæidi Ono Association. According to Kimerling, "The Ome Yasuni communities regard NAWE as 'a social organization that should help the communities,' and not as a tribal authority or legal representative of the communities or their members."[55] Another group with growing economic and cultural influence is The Association of Waorani Women of Ecuador, founded in 2006.

One of the biggest challenges of the twenty-first century is for outsiders to recognize both the common ethnic identity of the Waorani and the internal differences among them. As one observer explained, small communities of Waorani "are grouped throughout the territory in a spectrum of acculturation from west to east," that is, from those closest to outside towns to those more remote. "These households have different access to education, markets, employment, forest resources, tourists, oil companies, missionaries, and health care."[56] Like the overall ecology of the rainforest, where plant and animal species tend to thrive when scattered over an expansive territory, the Waorani, too, flourish as people of the rainforest when their communities are widely distributed over their territory.

CHRISTIANITY AMONG THE WAORANI

Even during what seemed like an endless series of crises, there were indications that Christianity had begun to take root in some Waorani clearings and villages. Not surprisingly, Waorani who had been employed as translation assistants and their kin were among those most active in Bible reading. These included families in the clearings of Tewæno, Tadangado, and Acado, among other locations.[57] Extended families read the Wao New Testament together, reflecting a house church model; a few Wao men became traveling preachers and evangelists; and two Brethren missionaries, Reinaldo Bernal and Pablo Revelo, worked with Waorani students at the Bible Institute in the village of Damointado and at the high school in Toñæmpade. Lloyd and Linda Rogers moved from Shell to Quito during the 1990s, although they continued to encourage Bernal, a Colombian, and his wife and family in their work as full-time missionaries to the Waorani. Bernal also helped to organize a church in Puyo, Iglesia Cristiana Biblica Misionera Waorani, for Waorani who live in towns on the edge of their traditional lands.

One public indication of indigenous faith was a conference held January 6–8, 2006, in Toñæmpade, still the largest village in the former protectorate and near the site along the Curaray River where the five missionaries were speared in 1956. Wao Christians chose the location for a gathering to remember the men's deaths a half century earlier and the subsequent introduction of Christianity. About three hundred Waorani from at least eight, and possibly more, Wao clearings attended. Eighty-five visitors also arrived, from Australia, Ukraine, the United States, Canada,

England, and Peru, in addition to Ecuador. The dynamics of the conference reflected Wao leadership, with missionaries in supportive or peripheral roles.[58]

The three days included sermons, testimonies, and reminiscences, as well as prayer, songs and hymns, soccer games, and traditional dances. On Friday afternoon, January 6, a group of Waorani and their *cowode* guests walked to the place on the bank of the Curaray River where the five missionaries had their camp. Village children splashed in the river alongside relatives of the slain men, exactly fifty years from the day when Waorani and missionaries had made initial peaceful contact. On Sunday morning, the fiftieth anniversary of the date Wao warriors returned in anger to kill the men, the crowd gathered at the site to share boiled *plátanos* (cooking bananas) and grape drink in Christian communion. Ten Waorani were baptized.

Amid such signs of faith, the Toñæmpade setting also held reminders that the outside world and the lure of the marketplace continue to pose challenges for the Waorani and for Christianity among them. Teenagers in the village reflected the reach of advertising in the new millennium with clothing and shoes from Nike and Tommy Hilfiger. They might have enjoyed Christian songs in the form of traditional Wao chants, but they also identified openly with Western music from Green Day and Christina Aguilera.[59] Unlike their parents and grandparents, they wanted to learn English and imitate American popular culture. These Wao young people never experienced the level of violence and murder that turned their elders toward faith. They have struggled to find the meaning of Christianity for their generation. These generational differences may have contributed to disagreements among anthropologists and others over the extent of Christian commitment among the Waorani.

The place of future missionaries is also unclear. Outsiders still trek into Wao territory, among them Christians who come with visions of transforming the "savages" of their imaginations into believers. Others think they may be the ones to make peaceful contact with the Taadomenani. Visitors are common, but only a few people in recent years have made long-term commitments. Among them are Chet and Katie Williams, who have lived in Shell, Ecuador, for more than a decade, engaged in cooperative efforts with the Waorani to encourage Christian discipleship. The Williamses; Wao pastor Gilberto Mincaye Nenquimo and his wife, Silvia; Jim and Kathie Yost; Miriam Gebb; and others have formed Centa (the Center), an Ecuadorian nonprofit training center for tribal people, including the Waorani. Centa recently purchased ten acres that had housed the now-closed Nate Saint Memorial School in Shell, for the training center. Compassion International still has a presence in the Ecuadorian Amazon, channeling help through local churches. The Vozandes Hospital in Shell closed in 2014, although community development and mobile medical support teams, sponsored by Reach Beyond, the new name given to HCJB Global, operate in the area. In sum, evangelical missionaries can still be found among Amazonian peoples, including the Waorani, although there is a greater emphasis than in the past on collaborating with Ecuadorian nationals to meet felt needs. Despite the hopes of North Americans, Wao territory is not the "Bible belt of the Amazon," in one writer's memorable phrase. At the same time, Christian faith is present, even after the deaths of the first generation of Wao believers.[60] An analysis by the anthropologist Casey High, who describes the Waorani as "Christian" in the 1970s and "post-Christian" at present, is exaggerated on both counts.[61] Also, given the ebbs and flows of adherence to Christianity in other parts of the world, such characterizations after only sixty years seem premature.

As far as the missionary-Waorani story, perhaps it is time for critics to concede that SIL workers did help the Waorani end some patterns of internal violence and survive contact with outsiders. By the same token, it may be time for North American evangelicals and also missionaries to recognize that the Waorani do not live in a historical, cultural, or geographic vacuum, nor are they frozen in time. The deaths of Guequita in 1997 and Dayomæ in 2014, among others, underline the fact that these are not the same people who encountered missionaries in the 1950s. The Waorani are much more than the "supporting cast" for missionary heroism. They are people with a unique language, culture, and geographic location that—in common with all other cultures—reflects both the goodness and the brokenness of the created world.

The twenty-first century clearly is time, too, to retire the well-worn word "savages." Perhaps appropriate for shock value when Elisabeth Elliot wrote *The Savage My Kinsman* or as a double entendre in Joe Kane's *Savages*, in recent years the term has served primarily to sensationalize the Waorani and their lives.[62]

Will the availability of their language in written form support Wao identity in significant ways? Will increasing numbers of Waorani claim the Christian gospel for themselves and create an ever more indigenized faith? Can Christianity provide resources to help the Waorani become the real—and not romanticized—guardians and residents of their rainforest? Or, as some outsiders expect, will Christians become a remnant, little more than a legacy of past missionary efforts? The answers are unknown. During the 1960s and 1970s, some Waorani embraced Christianity to break the pattern of internal violence that threatened their existence and to gain access to desired trade goods. Younger generations have found it more difficult to appropriate resources from the Christian faith to support cultural identity and survival in the face of competition from other powerful external forces. However, those who can do so will make the history of Wao Christianity in the twenty-first century.

MAPS

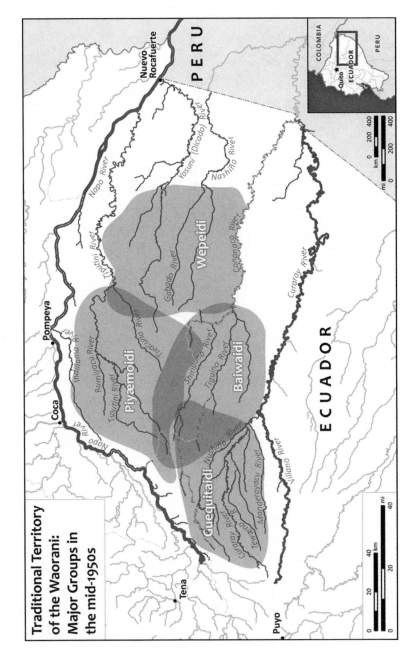

Traditional Territory of the Waorani: Major Groups in the mid-1950s

MAP I

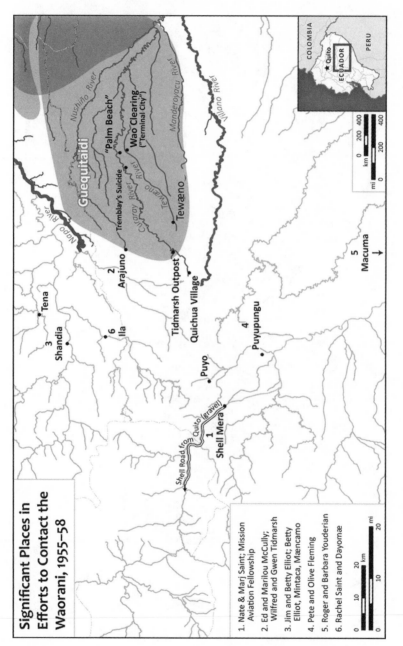

Significant Places in Efforts to Contact the Waorani, 1955–58

1. Nate & Marj Saint; Mission Aviation Fellowship
2. Ed and Marilou McCully; Wilfred and Gwen Tidmarsh
3. Jim and Betty Elliot; Betty Elliot, Mintaca, Mæncamo
4. Pete and Olive Fleming
5. Roger and Barbara Youderian
6. Rachel Saint and Dayomæ

Guequitaidi

"Palm Beach"

Wao Clearing ("Terminal City")

Tremblay's Suicide

Tewæno

Arajuno

Tidmarsh Outpost

Quichua Village

Tena

Shandia

Ila

Puyo

Puyupungu

Shell Mera

Shell Road from Quito (gravel)

Macuma

Napo River

Nushiño River

Curaray River

Tewæno River

Manderoyacu River

Villano River

COLOMBIA

ECUADOR

Quito

PERU

MAP 2

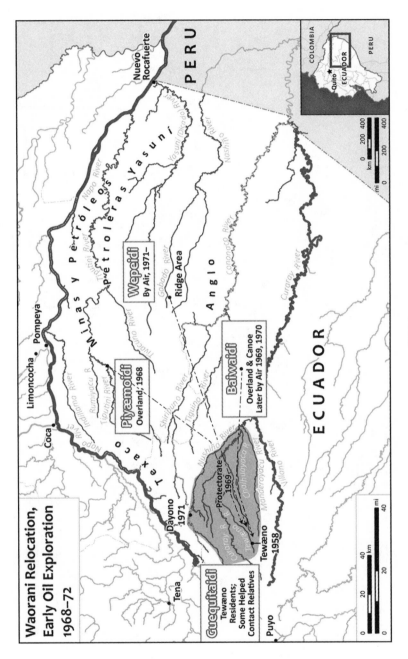

Waorani Relocation,
Early Oil Exploration
1968–72

Coca
Pompeya
Limoncocha

Tena

Puyo

Dayono
1971

Guequitaidi
Tewæno
Residents;
Some Helped
Contact Relatives

Protectorate
1969

Tewæno
1958

Piyæmoidi
Overland, 1968

Baiwaidi
Overland & Canoe
Later by Air 1969, 1970

Ridge Area

Wepeidi
By Air, 1971–

Nuevo
Rocafuerte

P E R U

E C U A D O R

A n g l o

M i n a s   y   P e t r ó l e o s

P e t r o l e r a s   Y a s u n í

T e x a c o

Napo River
Río Napo
Jivino River
Rumiyacu River
Tiputini River
Tivacuno River
Shiripuno River
Tiguino River
Cononaco River
Yasuní (Brod) River
Nashiño o Nashiño River
Curaray River
Villano River
Manderoyacu River
Cholmayaca R.
Cononaco River
Gabado River
Tiguino River
Nushiño River
Curaray R.
Tzapino R.
Chiquita R.

MAP 3

COLOMBIA
ECUADOR
PERU
Quito

km 0 200 400
mi 0 200 400

km 0 20 40
mi 0 20 40

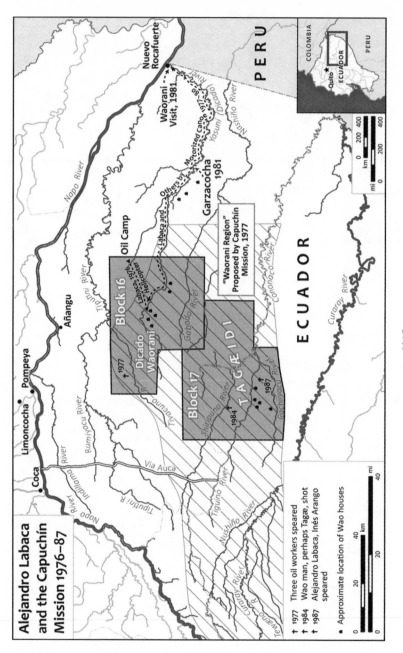

Alejandro Labaca
and the Capuchin
Mission 1976–87

Nuevo
Rocafuerte

Waorani
Visit, 1981

Others by Motorized Canoe, 1977–86

Garzacocha
1981

"Waorani Region"
Proposed by Capuchin
Mission, 1977

Oil Camp

Block 16

Labaca, 1976,
Helicopter

1977

Dicado
Waorani

Block 17

T A G Æ I D I

1984

1987

Añangu

Pompeya

Limoncocha

Coca

Via Auca

P E R U

E C U A D O R

COLOMBIA

Quito

ECUADOR

PERU

Napo River

Indillama River

Tiputini R.

Rumiyocu River

Tiputini River

Tivacuno

Gabado River

Shiripuno River

Cononaco River

Curaray River

Yasuní (Dicado) River

Noshiño River

Cachivacu River

Nushiño River

Tiguino River

Curaray River

Curaray R.

Ti...

0   200   400
km

0   200   400
mi

✝ 1977   Three oil workers speared
✝ 1984   Wao man, perhaps Tagæ, shot
✝ 1987   Alejandro Labaca, Inés Arango
speared

● Approximate location of Wao houses

0   20   40
km

0   20   40
mi

MAP 4

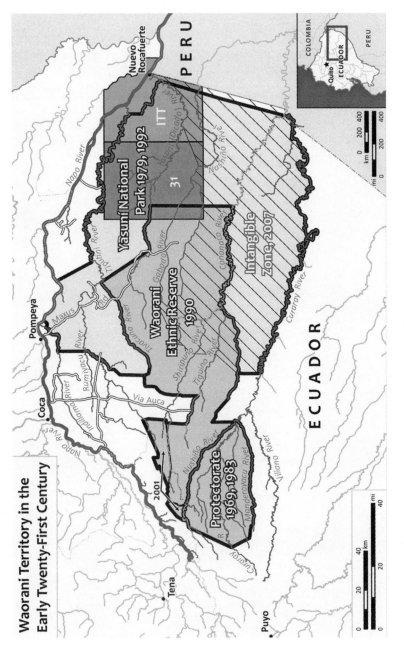

Waorani Territory in the
Early Twenty-First Century

MAP 5

⌒──

ABBREVIATIONS OF SOURCES

Amazon Crude   Judith Kimerling, *Amazon Crude* ([New York]: Natural Resources Defense Council, 1991).

Arriesgar la Vida   Rufino María Grández, *Arriesgar la Vida por el Evangelio* [Risking one's life for the gospel], 2nd. ed. (Coca, Ecuador: CICAME, 1997).

Cabodevilla, *LH*   Miguel Angel Cabodevilla, *Los Huaorani en la Historia de los Pueblos del Oriente* [The Waorani in the history of the peoples of the East (Amazonian region)], 2nd ed. (Coca, Ecuador: Cicame, 1999).

Crónica Huaorani   Mons. Alejandro Labaca, *Crónica Huaorani* [Waorani chronicle] (Quito: Vicariato Apostólico de Aguarico, Ediciones CICAME, 1988).

Dayuma Story   Ethel Emily Wallis, *The Dayuma Story: Life under Auca Spears* (New York: Harper & Brothers, 1960).

Fishers of Men   David Stoll, *Fishers of Men or Founders of Empire? The Wycliffe Bible Translators in Latin America* (London: Zed Press, 1982).

Gentle Savage   Menkaye [Mincaye] Ænkædi with Kemo and Dyowe as told to Tim Paulson, *Gentle Savage Still Seeking the End of the Spear* (Maitland, FL: Xulon Press, 2013).

Gates of Splendor   Elisabeth Elliot, *Through Gates of Splendor* (New York: Harper & Brothers, 1957).

JY field notes   James A. Yost field notes, James A. Yost Papers, private collection, copy in the author's possession, all notes used with permission.

Kingsland, *SAS*   Rosemary Kingsland, *A Saint among Savages* (London: Collins, 1980).

Kinsman   Elisabeth Elliot, *The Savage My Kinsman* (New York: Harper & Brothers, 1961).

"Literacy Materials"   Patricia M. Kelley, "Issues for Literacy Materials Development in a Monolingual Amazonian Culture: The Waodani of Ecuador" (master's thesis, University of British Columbia, 1988).

"People of Forest"   James A. Yost, "People of the Forest: The Waorani," in *Ecuador: In the Shadow of the Volcanoes*, English version by Pamela Gordon-Warren, Sarah Curl ([Quito]: Ediciones Libri Mundi, [1981]).

"Rage, Revenge, Religion"   James S. Boster, James Yost, and Catherine Peeke, "Rage, Revenge, and Religion: Honest Signaling of Aggression and Nonaggression in Waorani Coalitional Violence," *Ethos* 31, no. 4 (2003): 471–94.

SST   *Sunday School Times.* Note: SST used a dual page-numbering system. The number in parentheses on each page was the page number for that issue; the number next to it was the cumulative page number for each yearly volume of the paper.

"Social Trans."   Laura M. Rival, "Social Transformations and the Impact of Formal Schooling on the Huaorani of Amazonian Ecuador" (PhD diss., London School of Economics, University of London, January 1992).

"Twenty Years"   James A. Yost, "Twenty Years of Contact: The Mechanisms of Change in Wao ('Auca') Culture," in *Cultural Transformations and Ethnicity in Modern Ecuador*, ed. Norman E. Whitten Jr. (Urbana: University of Illinois Press, 1981).

Ultimos Huaorani   Juan Santos Ortiz de Villalba, *Los Ultimos Huaorani* [The last Waorani], 3rd ed. (1980; Quito: Colección Cicame, 1991).

Unfolding Destinies   Olive Fleming Liefeld, *Unfolding Destinies: The Ongoing Story of the Auca Mission* (1990; Grand Rapids, MI: Discovery House, 1998).

Unstilled Voices   James Hefley and Marti Hefley, *Unstilled Voices* (Chappaqua, NY: Christian Herald Books, 1981).

"Yasuní"   Matt Finer et al., "Ecuador's Yasuní Biosphere Reserve: A Brief Modern History and Conservation Challenges," *Environmental Research Letters* 4, no. 3 (2009), doi:10.1088/1748-9326/4/3/034005.

ABBREVIATIONS OF ARCHIVE COLLECTIONS

CTI Records   Records of Christianity Today International, Collection 8, Billy Graham Center Archives, Wheaton, Illinois.

EBC-SIL   Ecuador Branch Collection, Summer Institute of Linguistics Americas Area Archives, SIL International, Dallas, Texas.

Edman Records   Office of the President Records (V. Raymond Edman) 1918–72, RG/02/004, Wheaton College Archives and Special Collections, Wheaton College, Wheaton, Illinois.

EHE Papers   Papers of Elisabeth Howard Elliot, Collection 278, Billy Graham Center Archives, Wheaton, Illinois.

MAF Records   Records of Mission Aviation Fellowship, Collection 136, Billy Graham Center Archives, Wheaton, Illinois.

Peeke Papers   Papers of Minnie Catherine Peeke 1946–2006, Accession 08-36, Billy Graham Center Archives, Wheaton, Illinois (unprocessed collection).

TA   William Cameron Townsend Archives, Waxhaw, North Carolina (catalogues documents by folder numbers only and citations listed accordingly, i.e., TA#).

Yost Papers   James A. Yost Papers, private collection, copy in author's possession.

ABBREVIATIONS OF NAMES IN ARCHIVAL SOURCES

Derr   Dan[iel] A. Derr

E. Elliot   Elisabeth Howard Elliot (Gren)

Johnson   Donald F. Johnson

Kelley   Patricia M. Kelley

Lindskoog   John N. Lindskoog

Lowrance   Hobert "Hobey" E. Lowrance

Parrott   J. Grady Parrott

Peeke   M[innie]. Catherine Peeke

R. Saint   Rachel B. Saint

Schneider   Robert G. (Bob) Schneider

Townsend   William Cameron Townsend

Truxton   James C. Truxton

Van Der Puy   Abe C. Van Der Puy

Yost   James A. Yost

NOTES

PREFACE

1. Daniel H. Bays and Grant Wacker, "Introduction: The Many Faces of the Missionary Enterprise at Home," in *The Foreign Missionary Enterprise at Home: Explorations in North American Cultural History*, ed. Daniel H. Bays and Grant Wacker (Tuscaloosa: University of Alabama Press, 2003), 2.

2. M. Catherine Peeke, *Preliminary Grammar of Auca* (Norman, OK: Summer Institute of Linguistics, 1973), published version of Peeke's PhD diss., Indiana University, 1968, rev. 1971.

3. C. Roderick Wilson and James A. Yost, "The Creation of Social Hierarchy," in *Ethnographic Essays in Cultural Anthropology: A Problem-Based Approach*, ed. R. Bruce Morrison and C. Roderick Wilson (Itasca, IL: F. E. Peacock, 2002), 110.

4. For an explanation of the complex Wao social structure, see "People of Forest," 103.

INTRODUCTION

1. Joseph Conforti, "Jonathan Edwards's Most Popular Work: 'The Life of David Brainerd' and Nineteenth-Century Evangelical Culture," *Church History* 54, no. 2 (1985): 195.

2. George M. Marsden, *Jonathan Edwards: A Life* (New Haven, CT: Yale University Press, 2003), 333.

3. Amy Peterson [guest columnist/reviewer], "The Missionary Myth," Stranger in a Strange Land, *Books & Culture*, January–February 2015, 6, http://www.booksandculture.com/articles/2015/janfeb/missionary-myth.html; Dana L. Robert, "The Influence of American Missionary Women on the World Back Home," *Religion and American Culture* 12, no. 1 (2002): 66.

4. Joel A. Carpenter, *Revive Us Again: The Reawakening of American Fundamentalism* (New York: Oxford University Press, 1997), 81–82; see also Joel A. Carpenter,

introduction to *Sacrificial Lives: Young Martyrs and Fundamentalist Idealism*, ed. Joel A. Carpenter (New York: Garland, 1988), n.p.

5. *Gates of Splendor*. The Stams also received some newspaper publicity, although not comparable to the missionaries killed in Ecuador.

6. *Dayuma Story*.

7. Ann Rodgers, "Ecuadoran Tribe Transformed after Killing of 5 Missionaries," *Pittsburgh Post-Gazette*, January 8, 2006, www.post-gazette.com/ae/movies/2006/01/08/Ecuadoran-tribe-transformed-after-killing-of-5-missionaries/stories/200601080177, made a similar point in a different context.

8. SIL today views its staff as professionals—linguists, literacy workers, anthropologists—who are lay Christians and not missionaries. However, prior to the 1980s, the lines between missionary and linguist often were blurred in the field. Rachel Saint identified herself as a missionary and her assignment as missionary work, with Bible translation as one part of that work.

9. Alison Brysk, *From Tribal Village to Global Village: Indian Rights and International Relations in Latin America* (Stanford, CA: Stanford University Press, 2000).

10. "Rage, Revenge, Religion," 481.

11. Ibid., 482.

CHAPTER 1

1. Clayton Robarchek and Carole Robarchek, *Waorani: The Contexts of Violence and War* (Fort Worth, TX: Harcourt Brace, 1998), 95–96.

2. Elisabeth Elliot, *Shadow of the Almighty: The Life and Testament of Jim Elliot* (New York: Harper & Brothers, 1958), 129.

3. Blanca Muratorio, *The Life and Times of Grandfather Alonso: Culture and History in the Upper Amazon* (New Brunswick, NJ: Rutgers University Press, 1991), 100–106; Robarchek and Robarchek, *Waorani*, 89–91.

4. Cabodevilla, *LH*, 5.

5. Russell T. Hitt, *Jungle Pilot*, updated ed. (1959; Grand Rapids, MI: Discovery House, 1997), 272.

6. Joel A. Carpenter, *Revive Us Again: The Reawakening of American Fundamentalism* (New York: Oxford University Press, 1997), 82.

7. Elliot, *Shadow of the Almighty*, 140.

8. *Gates of Splendor*, 180.

9. Ibid., 182.

10. Missionary Aviation Fellowship in the United States became Mission Aviation Fellowship (MAF) in 1971. Dietrich G. Buss and Arthur F. Glasser, *Giving Wings to the Gospel: The Remarkable Story of Mission Aviation Fellowship* (Grand Rapids, MI: Baker Books, 1995), 27. Gospel Missionary Union has changed its name to Avant Ministries.

11. See, e.g., Peter Fleming's diary, quoted in *Unfolding Destinies*, 94.

12. Elliot, *Shadow of the Almighty*, 129, 177.

13. Hitt, *Jungle Pilot*, 276.

14. Elliot, *Shadow of the Almighty*, 129.

15. For "Operation Auca," see Abe C. Van Der Puy, "Through Gates of Splendor," *Reader's Digest*, August 1956, 57, 74; *Gates of Splendor*, 121, 128, 134, 217, also 140 for "visitation" of "neighbors."

16. There may have been two or three other Wao women or girls who also had fled tribal violence, but for a variety of reasons they were not accessible or suitable as language informants. "Twenty Years," 682.

17. Quoted in Hitt, *Jungle Pilot*, 260–61.

18. Nate Saint to "Sis" [R. Saint], October 2, 1955 [letter held until after Nate Saint's death], Nate Saint Papers, copies in the author's possession with permission of the late Marjorie Saint Van Der Puy. Excerpts from the letter are included in Hitt, *Jungle Pilot*, 260–61. Nate Saint's concerns that Rachel's close ties to the government of Ecuador, via the Summer Institute of Linguistics, might jeopardize the project were not included in the quoted portions. In letters to MAF headquarters, Nate mentioned rumors of an armed invasion of Wao territory by the government of Ecuador, as well as government relations with SIL, as reasons for secrecy. Nate Saint to Parrott et al., October 11, 1955, and Saint to Charles Mellis and Parrott, December 7, 1955, both in Folder 37, Box 4, MAF Records.

19. Saint to Mellis and Parrott, December 7, 1955, MAF Records. For Saint's innovations, see Hitt, *Jungle Pilot*, 149–54.

20. *Gates of Splendor*, 134–65, 172–73, describes the various gift flights. Elliot quoted liberally from Saint's journal.

21. Ibid., 145.

22. Ibid., 148.

23. Hitt, *Jungle Pilot*, 266.

24. *Unfolding Destinies*, 197.

25. "'Go Ye and Preach the Gospel': Five Do and Die," *Life*, January 30, 1956, 14.

26. Quoted in *Gates of Splendor*, 183.

27. Ibid., 185.

28. *Dayuma Story*, 172; Guequita, Yowe, Wato, Acawo, Ana, and other Waorani, English transcript of oral history group interview with John Man and Jim Yost, April 1987, Ecuador, 86f, Yost Papers (transcript includes group interviews as well as individual interviews) (hereafter Man-Yost interviews).

29. Wato, Man-Yost interviews; *Dayuma Story*, 173.

30. Quotations from Peter Fleming's diary in Abe C. Van Der Puy, "Five 'Valiant Saints, Their Hope They Knew,'" *SST*, February 4, 1956, 84 (4).

31. Hitt, *Jungle Pilot*, 262.

32. *Gates of Splendor*, 133, 159, 189.

33. Quoted in "Go Ye and Preach," 15.

34. Dayomæ denied that the missionaries had a picture of her that made her family think she had been killed or eaten. E. Elliot, "Free Translation of Ipa's Version of the Palm Beach Story" [tape made in November 1960, translated in April 1961], Folder 9, Box 4, EHE Papers.

35. Van Der Puy, "Through Gates of Splendor," 71.

36. *Though Gates of Splendor* (1967; Muskegon, MI: Gospel Communications, 2003), DVD.

37. *Dayuma Story*, 174; *Gates of Splendor*, 192.

38. *Unfolding Destinies*, 201.

39. Ibid., 201–2.

40. My account is based largely on the Man-Yost interviews, which included a visit to the site of the attack. Jim Yost was fluent in the Wao language, and neither he nor John Man was related to the slain men, both of which lend credibility to the transcript. It is supplemented by material in Steve Saint, "A Cloud of Witnesses," in *Martyrs: Contemporary Writers on Modern Lives of Faith*, ed. Susan Bergman (San Francisco: HarperSanFrancisco, 1996), 142–54. Saint included a similar account in Steve Saint, *End of the Spear: A True Story* (Carol Stream, IL: Tyndale House, 2005), 37–60. I also consulted three early, unpublished accounts by Epa, Mincaye, and Guequita recorded and translated by Elisabeth Elliot and included in her papers, Folder 9, Box 4, EHE Papers. The earliest published accounts of the attack appeared in Wallis's *Dayuma Story*, 173–76, 270–71 (1960 epilogue). The 1965 edition of the book included "Ten Years Later," by Rachel Saint, with more information. Rachel Saint also wrote, "What Really Happened, Told for the First Time," *Decision*, January 1966, 11. Other accounts include Kingsland, *SAS*, 76–95; *Fishers of Men*, 282–85. Spanish translations of the story plus interviews with some of the Waorani participants can be found in Cabodevilla, *LH*, 319–30. Other unpublished sources include Rachel Saint, "Rundown of Palm Beach additional [information]," December 7, 1962, copies in Yost Papers and Peeke Papers; see also (author unknown), "Excerpts from Life History Interview with Nemonca at Dayono," February 17, 1977, Yost Papers. Part of the importance of Rachel Saint's "Rundown" was that she understood the Waorani to say that Nampa did actively participate in the attack and was wounded in the struggle over a weapon, something she and Dayomæ later denied. Some variations in these accounts may have been because Saint was still learning the difficult Wao language. Dayomæ may have wanted to avoid directly accusing someone in Nampa's death, which culturally would have required revenge. For a recent oral history account from one of the Wao participants, see *Gentle Savage*, 167–78. Despite comments by Rachel Saint and others that the Waorani rarely mentioned the killings, this lengthy note suggests that numerous firsthand accounts do exist.

41. Man-Yost interviews, 5–6.

42. Ibid., 6, 86.

43. Van Der Puy, "Through Gates of Splendor," 71–72.

44. Note from Ed McCully to Marilou McCully, January 7, 1956, quoted in *Gates of Splendor*, 193.

45. *Gates of Splendor*, 194; Van Der Puy, "Through Gates of Splendor," 72. Both Van Der Puy's and Elliot's accounts correspond to and are based in part on typescripts of notes made by Nate Saint, as well as excerpts from diaries kept by Ed McCully and Peter Fleming, typescript copies in the author's possession, courtesy of Marjorie Saint Van Der Puy.

46. Yowe had four spears; Guequita five; Mincaye four; Nemonca four; Nampa two; and Quemo none. Before the attack Yowe gave him two. Man-Yost interviews, 86.

47. Jim Yost, written comment to author, April 2, 2015, based on Yost's conversations with Guequita.

48. *Gates of Splendor*, 194.

49. Yowe, Man-Yost interviews, 86f, 86.

50. Guequita, Man-Yost interviews, 84.

51. Elisabeth Elliot, "The Palm Beach Story, according to Mincaye, one of the killers. Taped, transcribed, translated—May, 1961," Folder 9, Box 4, EHE Papers.

52. Nate Saint carried a small .22 revolver usually loaded with blanks. See Hitt, *Jungle Pilot*, 254–55. "David Crockett" typescript, included in Saint's papers, summarizing logistics for the

project, has handwritten notes, suggesting that the men would take two .22 weapons, either rifles or pistols, a carbine, a .32 automatic pistol, and a .38 pistol. While on the beach, in the day before the attack, Saint writes of cleaning the .32 automatic. Nate Saint Papers.

53. Nate Saint journal, *TS*, December 10, 1955, Nate Saint Papers; see also Hitt, *Jungle Pilot*, 254, 264–65.

54. Guequita, Man-Yost interviews, 84; Yowe, Man-Yost interviews, 86f, see also 114–18; Saint, "A Cloud of Witnesses," 152.

55. Saint, "What Really Happened," 11. This brief article was abridged from Saint's epilogue to the 1965 edition of the *Dayuma Story*. It later became clear that Nampa actively participated in the killings.

56. *Unfolding Destinies*, 234–35.

57. Yowe, Man-Yost interviews, 86. There were steep ridges on both sides of the river; it is not clear exactly where they spent the night.

58. *Unfolding Destinies*, 203.

59. Kenneth L. Pike, "Report to General Direction, Board, and Branch Directors of the First Phase of Ecuador Trip, May 5–14, 1956," 3, TA#40026.

60. Alvin M. Goffin, *The Rise of Protestant Evangelism in Ecuador, 1895–1990* (Gainesville: University Press of Florida, 1994), 42.

61. Anne C. Loveland, *American Evangelicals and the U.S. Military, 1942–1993* (Baton Rouge: Louisiana State University Press, 1996), 50.

62. "Missionary Missing in Ecuadorian Jungle," *Milwaukee Journal*, January 10, 1956.

63. Robert Savage would go on to produce *Mid-Century Martyrs*, a filmstrip that was the first audiovisual presentation of the story, widely distributed to evangelical churches in the US. Stephen E. Savage, *Rejoicing in Christ: The Biography of Robert Carlton Savage* (Reading, VT: Shadow Rock, 1990), 245, 249–50.

64. "See 2 in Jungle," *Kansas City Star*, January 12, 1956. Portions of this analysis of newspaper coverage first appeared in Kathryn T. Long, "In the Modern World, but Not of It: The 'Auca Martyrs,' Evangelicalism, and Postwar American Culture," in *The Foreign Missionary Enterprise at Home: Explorations in North American Cultural History*, ed. Daniel H. Bays and Grant Wacker (Tuscaloosa: University of Alabama Press, 2003), 225–29.

65. "Bury Bodies of 5 Missionaries Savages Killed," *Chicago Daily Tribune*, January 14, 1956; "Ecuador: Mission to the Aucas," *Time*, January 23, 1956, 30; "5 Flying Missionaries Lost in Jungle," *Chicago Sun-Times*, January 11, 1956; "Killed by Aucas: One of Five Flying Missionaries from U.S. Is Victim in Amazon Jungle," *Kansas City Times*, January 11, 1956. By 1957 domestic airlines would surpass trains in the number of passengers carried. James T. Patterson, *Grand Expectations: The United States, 1945–1974* (New York: Oxford University Press, 1996), 314.

66. "Ecuador: Mission to the Aucas," 30.

67. Quoted from a US government report that formed the basis of a widely circulated AP story, taken here from "Auca Tribe Murderous," *Oregonian*, January 14, 1956; cf. Hal Hendrix, "Auca Indians Live in Trees and Chatter Like Animals," *Kansas City Times*, January 13, 1958. In Dewey Linze, "The Unsubdued Aucas: Behind the Murder of Five Missionaries," *Los Angeles Times*, January 14, 1956, and elsewhere, aucas were characterized as headhunters, confused with a neighboring tribal group, the Jívaroan peoples.

68. Christian missionaries were expelled from China after the founding of the People's Republic in October 1949. Their stories dominated press coverage of missions during the first

half of the 1950s. The "Go Ye . . . and Preach" editorial in the *Portland Oregonian*, January 15, 1956, connected the "Auca expedition" and the "barbarous treatment missionaries have received at the hands of Asian Communists."

69. Daniel A. Poling [editor, *Christian Herald*], "My Faith Today: Five Heroic Martyrs," February 12, 1956, Folder 11, Box 11, Edman Records.

70. For example, "Tell Missionaries' Last Jungle Days," *Chicago Daily News*, January 12, 1956; "Pilots Scan Jungle for 5 Missionaries," *Chicago American*, January 12, 1956; "Missionary Missing in Ecuadorian Jungle," *Milwaukee Journal*, January 10, 1956; Charles Regal, "Seattle Missionary, Four Others Feared Captured," *Seattle Post-Intelligencer*, January 11, 1956; "Five Missionaries Slain by Indians," *Portland Oregonian*, January 14, 1956.

71. *Deliver Us from Evil: The Story of Vietnam's Flight to Freedom* (New York: Farrar, Straus and Cudahy, 1956), Tom Dooley's dramatic (and embellished), first-person account of efforts to evacuate Catholic refugees from North Vietnam, first appeared as a condensed book in the *Reader's Digest*, April 1956. James T. Fisher, *Dr. America: The Lives of Thomas A. Dooley, 1927–1961* (Amherst: University of Massachusetts Press, 1997), 71–76; see also the review of Fisher's book by Scott Flipse, "Deconstructing Dr. America," *American Catholic Studies Newsletter* 24, no. 2 (1997): 14–15.

72. *Unfolding Destinies*, 206.

73. *Gates of Splendor*, 200, 233–35.

74. Cornell Capa and Richard Whelan, eds., *Cornell Capa: Photographs* (Boston: Little, Brown, 1992), 210.

75. "Go Ye and Preach," 10–19. Portions of the analysis that follow first appeared in Long, "In the Modern World," 229–30, and in Kathryn T. Long, "Cameras 'Never Lie': The Role of Photography in Telling the Story of American Evangelical Missions," *Church History* 72, no. 4 (2003): 841.

76. Cornell Capa, interview with author, May 16, 2000, New York City, confirmed the decision to airbrush the photo.

77. Andrew Heiskell, "Danger and Dedication," *Life*, May 13, 1957, 187.

78. Capa and Whelan, *Cornell Capa*, 152.

79. Ibid., 11, 152. Capa's follow-up articles for *Life* were "The Martyrs' Widows Return to Teach in Jungle," May 20, 1957, 24–33, and "Child among Her Father's Killers: Missionaries Live with Aucas," November 24, 1958, 23–29. He also served as photo editor for *Through Gates of Splendor* and collaborated with Elisabeth Elliot in producing the film with the same name. He encouraged Elisabeth Elliot to portray the humanity of the Waorani through her own photographs, later published along with some of his in *Kinsman*, with Capa as picture editor and author of the foreword. He later served as photo editor for several other books on evangelical missionaries in South America.

80. "Go Ye and Preach," 18–19; "Nate Saint's Last Message, Notes on Open Letters," *SST*, February 11, 1956, 102, 118 (2, 18).

81. "Editor's Note," *SST*, January 28, 1956, 66 (2); V. Raymond Edman to Mr. and Mrs. R. G. LeTourneau, May 7, 1956, "Five Missionary Martyrs Fund, 1956–1966" Folder, Box 5, Edman Records.

82. *Gates of Splendor*, 252.

83. Frank Drown and Marie Drown, *Mission to the Headhunters* (1961; Fearn, UK: Christian Focus, 2007), 187.

84. Capa, "Martyrs' Widows Return," 27.

85. *Unfolding Destinies*, 16.

86. Ibid., 19–20.

87. *Gates of Splendor*, 252.

CHAPTER 2

1. "Death Could Not Conquer," *Christian Life*, March 1956, 15; Reginald Heber, "The Son of God Goes Forth to War," in *Hymns for Praise and Service*, compiled by Homer Rodeheaver and George W. Sanville (Winona Lake, IN: Rodeheaver Hall-Mack, 1956), 53.

2. Cornell Capa photo and caption, *Gates of Splendor*, 230. For why the Waorani killed, see "Rage, Revenge, Religion," 471–94.

3. *Unstilled Voices*, 62.

4. "Why Did It Happen?," *SST*, February 4, 1956, 81 (1); "Death Could Not Conquer," 13.

5. "Death Could Not Conquer," 13.

6. Abe C. Van Der Puy, "Five 'Valiant Saints, Their Hope They Knew,'" *SST*, February 4, 1956, 83, 85 (3, 5).

7. Harold R. Cook, "Five Lives for the Aucas," *Moody Monthly*, March 1956, 32, referring to Ephesians 6:12.

8. "Death Could Not Conquer," 13.

9. Phil Saint, "My Kid Brother, Nate," *Moody Monthly*, March 1956, 56.

10. "A Stirred Public Responds," *Christian Life*, March 1956, 14.

11. Cook, "Five Lives," 29.

12. Elisabeth Elliot, "Through a Widow's Tears," *Youth for Christ*, March 1956, 13. The title was an editorial comment. Elliot herself did not mention tears.

13. "Brave, Bold Testimony of a Martyr's Family," *Moody Monthly*, March 1956, 7.

14. Marjorie Saint, "Tears, Yes . . . but Triumph, Too," *Youth for Christ*, March 1957, 11–12.

15. Joel Carpenter, *Revive Us Again: The Reawakening of American Fundamentalism* (New York: Oxford University Press, 1997), 29–30.

16. "Five Missionaries Die Needlessly," *Christian Century*, February 1, 1956, 132.

17. Ibid., 132–33.

18. Letters quoted are from Frederick C. Fowler, First Presbyterian Church, Duluth, MN, and Mrs. Harry W. Stone, Waldport, OR (emphasis Stone's), "Correspondence," *Christian Century*, February 26, 1956, 242.

19. Clyde W. Taylor, "Correspondence," *Christian Century*, February 26, 1956, 243.

20. Jack W. Murray, "Modernism and the Missionary Martyrs," transcript of a radio broadcast, February 12, 1956, "Auca Indians—Five Missionary Martyrs, Magazine Articles 1956" Folder, Box 1, Edman Records. Used with permission.

21. Robert B. Taylor, "Reflections on the Auca Tragedy," *Practical Anthropology* 3, no. 1 (1956): 1.

22. Ibid., 4.

23. "Letters to the Editor," *Practical Anthropology* 3, no. 2 (1956): 37–40.

24. Van Der Puy to Sam Saint, February 21, 1956, Folder 31, Box 59, MAF Records.

25. John Heidenry, *Theirs Was the Kingdom: Lila and DeWitt Wallace and the Story of the Reader's Digest* (New York: Norton, 1993), 239.

26. Writing for the *Digest*, probably the most heavily edited publication in the country, was a daunting task. Ibid., 111, 399.

27. Despite qualms, Van Der Puy allowed the use of his name at the *Digest*'s request to get the story out. He openly acknowledged Hall's authorship. Abe C. Van Der Puy, interview with author, June 27, 2000, Keystone Heights, FL.

28. Portions of the story of Hall's role in writing the *Reader's Digest* version of "Through Gates of Splendor" and the choice of Elisabeth Elliot to write the subsequent book appear in Kathryn T. Long, "Missionary Realities and the New Evangelicalism in Post–World War II America," in *American Evangelicalism: George Marsden and the State of American Religious History*, ed. Darren Dochuk, Thomas S. Kidd, and Kurt W. Peterson (Notre Dame, IN: University of Notre Dame Press, 2014). Used with permission.

29. Abe Van Der Puy [Clarence Hall], "Through Gates of Splendor," *Reader's Digest*, August 1956, 56.

30. Ibid., 75, 57.

31. Elisabeth [Elliot] Gren, interview with author, June 27, 2001, Magnolia, MA.

32. Elliot identified the men as "representing three different 'faith-missions'" and sharing a "common belief in the Bible as the literal and supernatural and perfect word from God to man." *Gates of Splendor*, 121.

33. Such as David Brainerd, Harriet Newall, William Borden, and John and Betty Stam. I am indebted to the historian and missiologist Dana Robert for describing these figures as missionaries to the home front.

34. Carpenter, *Revive Us Again*, 26.

35. *Gates of Splendor*, 51, 68, 75. For Keswick piety "at the very heart of the fundamentalists' missionary impulse," see Carpenter, *Revive Us Again*, 82.

36. *Gates of Splendor*, 95; cf. 127, 145, for references to "five pioneering missionary families" and to Saint, McCully, and Jim Elliot as "the three pioneers." See also "An Alabama reader," "The Ecuador Story," Notes on Open Letters, *SST*, August 11, 1956, 630 (2). Beginning with the "[Davy] Crockett Craze" in 1955, westerns rose to new popularity on television and on film, according to James L. Baughman, *The Republic of Mass Culture: Journalism, Filmmaking, and Broadcasting in America since 1941* (Baltimore: Johns Hopkins University Press, 1992), 87.

37. *Gates of Splendor*, 16, 50, 54, 121.

38. Ibid., 252.

39. "'Go Ye and Preach the Gospel': Five Do and Die," *Life*, January 30, 1956, 10–11.

40. *Gates of Splendor*, 27.

41. Ibid., 60.

42. Ibid., 18, 74, 253.

43. Truxton to D-1 [administrators], May 4, 1956, Folder 34, Box 62, MAF Records.

44. *Gates of Splendor*, 27–29.

45. Elisabeth Elliot, *Shadow of the Almighty: The Life and Testament of Jim Elliot* (New York: Harper & Brothers, 1958), 180–85.

46. *Gates of Splendor*, 181–82.

47. Ibid., 147, 149.

48. Michael Kress, "Objects of Conversion" (unpublished essay, written for a class taught by Mark A. Noll (HDS 2353), Harvard Divinity School, May 10, 1998), 2, copy in author's possession.

49. Norman R. Oke, "Book of the Month Review," review of *Through Gates of Splendor*, by Elisabeth Elliot, *Nazarene Minister's Book Club*, August 1957, n.p., Folder 4, Box 1, EHE Papers;

Larry Ward, "Five Martyrs of Auca," review of *Through Gates of Splendor*, by Elisabeth Elliot, *Christianity Today*, April 29, 1957, 35.

50. Review of *Through Gates of Splendor*, by Elisabeth Elliot, *Evangelical Christian*, February 1958, Folder 5, Box 1, EHE Papers. By February 1958 *Gates* had sold 105,000 copies exclusive of sales in connection with seven book clubs. "Tips for the Bookseller," *Publishers' Weekly*, February 17, 1958, 90, 92. For other sales figures, see "News and Trends of the Week," *Publishers' Weekly*, February 17, 1958, 21, and the advertisement in *Christianity Today*, July 8, 1957, 19. The book would remain in print almost continuously for twenty-five years; in 1996 two fortieth-anniversary editions were issued, followed by a fiftieth-anniversary edition released in 2005.

51. The photograph of Ruth Graham was reprinted in *Billy Graham New York Crusade News*, June 21, 1957, 1.

52. "Auca Spoken in New York," *Translation*, Fall 1957, 15.

53. Elliot, *Shadow of the Almighty*, 15, 19, 247; Matthew Henry, *The Life of the Rev. Philip Henry, A.M.* (London: William Ball, 1839), 35. In the context of giving to the poor, Matthew Henry quoted his father: "He is no fool who parts with that which he cannot keep, when he is sure to be recompensed with that which he cannot lose." The quote also appears in a 2012 biography of Matthew Henry by Allan Harman: *Matthew Henry, His Life and Influence* (Fearn, UK: Christian Focus, 2012), chap. 2, Kindle. See also "Jim Elliot Quote," Billy Graham Center Archives, Wheaton College, last modified January 9, 2016, www2.wheaton.edu/bgc/archives/faq/20.htm. There was no reason for Jim Elliot to have mentioned the inspiration for the quote in his personal journal, if he was even aware of the source. Nor was there any reason for Elisabeth Elliot to question her husband's authorship.

54. Songs are Scott Wesley Brown, vocal performance of "He Is No Fool," by Scott Wesley Brown, Phill McHugh, Greg Nelson, track 7 on *To the Ends of the Earth*, album and CD, released 1988, Word #7019082602, release #4568566; Twila Paris, vocal performance of "He Is No Fool," by Twila Paris, track 9 on *For Every Heart*, vinyl, LP, album, released 1988, Star Son Music, SSR 8102, release #516904. Quotation is from Dietrich Bonhoeffer, *The Cost of Discipleship* (New York: Touchstone, 1995), 77.

55. Joseph T. Bayly, "Common Sense and Danger: Auca Martyr Story," review of *Jungle Pilot: The Life and Witness of Nate Saint*, by Russell T. Hitt, *Eternity*, September 1959, 42.

56. Carpenter, *Revive Us Again*, 61.

57. *Directory of Foreign Missionary Agencies in North America*, rev. ed. (New York: Missionary Research Library, 1956), 30; *North American Protestant Foreign Mission Agencies*, 7th ed. (New York: Missionary Research Library, 1966), 27.

58. Editor's introduction to Steve Saint, "Did They Have to Die?," *Christianity Today*, September 16, 1996, 20; Editors (compilers), "The Top Fifty Books That Have Shaped Evangelicals," *Christianity Today*, October 2006, 55.

59. The number of "conservative evangelicals" serving as career missionaries increased from 9,216 in 1953 to 13,255 in 1956, an increase of 4,039 or 44 percent during the three-year period, about the same as the growth rate during the four-year period from 1956 to 1960, when the numbers grew from 13,255 to 18,724, an increase of 5,469 or 41 percent. Based on Robert T. Coote, "The Uneven Growth of Conservative Evangelical Missions," *International Bulletin of Missionary Research* 6, no. 3 (1982): 120, table 2.

CHAPTER 3

1. All quotations, as well as the description of the program, are from NBC's *This Is Your Life*, aired on June 5, 1957, from a taped copy of the program on VCR tape given the author by the late Loretta Anderson.

2. "Candoshi-Shapra" in *People of Peru*, ed. Margarethe Sparing-Chávez, 2nd ed. (Lima: SIL Peru, 2005), 92–93, http://www.peru.sil.org/es/resources/archives/30081. The Shapras are a small subgroup of the Candoshi people.

3. Quoted in a letter from Idella Newman to Ken Pike, June 11, 1957, TA#13893.

4. *This Is Your Life*, June 5, 1957.

5. Ibid.

6. Kingsland, *SAS*, 34; most of this paragraph is based on chapter 3 in Kingsland, 34–40. See also "Prayer Bulletin," October 1949, TA#41450; R. Saint to "Dear Folks—Townsends," May 17, 1950, TA#06607.

7. R. Saint, "Unreached . . . . and Unreachable?," February 9, 1955, unpublished typescript to friends and financial supporters, Folder 12, Box 11, Edman Records.

8. Unknown to "Dear Dick" [Pittman?], January 26, 1949, TA#06255; Kenneth L. Pike to Townsend, March 10, 1949, TA#06085.

9. Townsend to Ralph Edwards, December 3, 1956, TA#11945; Townsend to Dick Gottlieb, March 1, 1957, TA#13037; Robert B. Harris to Townsend, April 15, 1957, TA#13496.

10. William G. Nyman to W. Cameron and Elaine Townsend, June 7, 1957, TA#12616.

11. W.C.T. [Townsend] to R. Saint, January 17, 1956, TA#12140.

12. Marj Saint to Truxton and Parrott, June 17, 1957, Folder 30, Box 5, MAF Records.

13. Parrott to Lowrance, June 14, 1957, Folder 26, Box 5, MAF Records.

14. Nate Saint to Parrott et al., June 30, 1954, Folder 14, Box 4, MAF Records.

15. Cornell Capa, interview with author, May 16, 2000, New York City.

16. W. Cameron Townsend, "Retrospect and Prospect," *Translation*, Winter 1957–58, 3; also based on statistics from *Missions Annual—1958* (New York: International Foreign Mission Association), 27–40.

17. In the early years, the aviation arm of SIL was called the Jungle Aviation and Radio Service (JAARS), later, simply JAARS. A subsidiary of SIL, JAARS in Ecuador and elsewhere maintained the organization's airplanes, trained their pilots, and provided service to remote jungle locations.

18. Nate Saint to Parrott, November 2, 1954, Folder 14, Box 4, MAF Records.

19. Ibid.

20. Nate Saint to "Dear Charlie and Grady" [Charles Mellis and Parrott], December 7, 1955, Folder 37, Box 4, MAF Records.

21. Ibid. For examples of Catholic opposition to evangelicals in Ecuador, see Stephen E. Savage, *Rejoicing in Christ: The Biography of Robert Carlton Savage* (Reading, VT: Shadow Rock, 1990), 144–47.

22. "'Go Ye and Preach the Gospel': Five Do and Die," *Life*, January 30, 1956, 18.

23. *Gates of Splendor*, 253.

24. Elisabeth [Elliot] Gren, interview with author, June 27, 2001, Magnolia, MA.

25. Ruth Keenan to Grady [Parrott], April 25, 1956, Folder 50, Box 4, MAF Records.

26. Johnny Keenan to Parrott, May 7, 1956, Folder 50, Box 4, MAF Records; Parrott to Lowrance, June 1, 1956, Folder 2, Box 5, MAF Records.

27. Lowrance to Parrott and Charles Mellis, May 28, 1956, Folder 53, Box 4, MAF Records (emphasis Lowrance's).

28. Lowrance to MAF D-1 [Parrott], June 13, 1956, Folder 3, Box 4, MAF Records; G. Parrott to Marj Saint, February 21, 1956, and Parrott to Lowrance, June 1, 1956, both from Folder 2, Box 5, MAF Records.

29. Parrott to Lowrance, quoting Charles Mellis, June 18, 1956, Folder 2, Box 5, MAF Records.

30. Lowrance to MAF Exec. Committee, August 30, 1956, Folder 53, Box 4, MAF Records.

31. Lowrance to Parrott, August 30, 1956, Folder 53, Box 4, MAF Records.

32. Even before SIL entered Ecuador in 1953, based on conversations with her brother Nate, Rachel Saint was convinced she had been called to work among the Waorani. In October 1953, before Rachel had begun to work with Dayomæ, Peter Fleming considered studying the Wao language with her. Perhaps due to health problems, he did not pursue the idea. Ken Fleming, *Peter Fleming: Man of Faith* (1995; Dubuque, IA: ECS Ministries, 2013), 115–16.

33. R. Saint to Lindskoog, January 28, 1956, TA#12590.

34. Lindskoog to "Uncle Cam" [Townsend], January 27, 1956, TA#12385 (emphasis in original).

35. R. Saint to John and Carrie [Lindskoog], Friday [January 27, 1956], TA#12588; Donald H. Burns to W. G. Nyman, February 14, 1956, TA#12584.

36. Johnny and Ruth Keenan to Parrott, April 12, 1956, Folder 50, Box 4, MAF Records.

37. Van Der Puy to Don Burns, March 3, 1956, TA#12566.

38. Kenneth L. Pike, "Report to General Director, Board, and Branch Directors on First Phase of Ecuador Trip, May 5–14, 1956," TA#40026. Pike attributed the original comment to Elliot herself.

39. Date that Dayomæ fled is from a timeline developed by James Yost, confirmed by Catherine Peeke. Copy in author's possession.

40. Van Der Puy to David E. Kucharsky, September 13, 1959, Folder 6, Box 5, CTI Records; Kingsland, *SAS*, 67; *Fishers of Men*, 286.

41. Kingsland, *SAS*, 67–68.

42. Townsend to R. Saint, February 14, 1956, TA#12130.

43. Townsend to Don Burns, February 16, 1956, TA#12121.

44. *Dayuma Story*, 82.

45. Keenan to Parrott, April 25, 1956, MAF Records; Pike, "Report to General Director," TA.

46. R. Saint to Wesley Swauger, February 25, 1957, TA#14121.

47. Lowrance to D-1 [MAF Administration], October 17, 1956, Folder 53, Box 4, MAF Records.

48. Townsend to Saint, February 14, 1956, TA.

49. Townsend to Burns, February 16, 1956, TA.

50. Townsend to R. W. Wyatt, June 1, 1957, TA#12878; Townsend to Schneider, November 23, 1957, TA#12682.

51. Lindskoog to Townsend, January 27, 1956, TA.

52. Parrott to Marj Saint, February 20, 1956, Folder 2, Box 5, MAF Records; Charles J. Mellis to Truxton, April 17, 1956, Folder 1, Box 5, MAF Records.

53. Truxton to D-1, May 4, 1956, Folder 34, Box 62, MAF Records.

54. Taken from the title "What News of the Five Martyrs' Wives?," *SST*, May 19, 1956, 401–2 (1–2).

55. [Elisabeth Elliot], "The Prayer of the Five Widows," *Christianity Today*, January 7, 1957, 7 (emphasis Elliot's).

56. Lowrance to Parrott, August 30, 1956, MAF Records.

57. Marj Saint to Parrott, April 13, 1956, Folder 4, Box 5, MAF Records; R. Saint to Kenneth L. Pike, November 26, 1956, TA#12455.

58. Lowrance to GHQ [Headquarters], August 18, 1956, Folder 53, Box 4, and Lowrance to Charles J. Mellis, March 6, 1957, Folder 23, Box 5, both MAF Records.

59. Marj Saint to Parrott, April 13, 1956, MAF Records.

60. Jane Dolinger, *The Head with the Long Yellow Hair* (London: Robert Hale, 1958). The book includes graphic details, plus some tasteless photographs, of the process the Jivaroan people used to shrink heads. Published in Great Britain, the book was not sold in the US. See also Lawrence Abbott, *Jane Dolinger: The Adventurous Life of an American Travel Writer* (New York: Palgrave Macmillan, 2010), 71–80. Abbott's chronology of Dolinger's visit does not seem to correspond to MAF correspondence at the time.

61. The hospital, later renamed Hospital Vozandes del Oriente, was operated by the health-care division of HCJB World Radio. For William Youderian's proposed visit, see Lowrance to Parrott, August 30, 1956; Lowrance to R. J. Reinmiller, Parrott, and Charles Mellis, December 6, 1956; R. J. Reinmiller to William Youderian, November 21, 1956; R. J. Reinmiller to Keith Austin, November 21, 1956; W. P. Youderian to Lowrance, November 25, 1956; all in Folder 53, Box 4, MAF Records; also Lowrance to Parrott, April 2, 1957, Folder 23, Box 5, MAF Records. See Eleanor Boyes, *Bridge to the Rain Forest* (Colorado Springs, CO: World Radio Missionary Fellowship, 1995), 43, for Roger Youderian's role in the hospital construction.

62. Lowrance to D-1, October 8, 1956, Folder 53, Box 4, MAF Records.

63. Lowrance to Parrott, August 30, 1956, MAF Records.

64. Lowrance to D-1, October 8, 1956, MAF Records.

65. R. Saint to Wesley Swauger, February 24, 25, and 26, 1957, TA#14122, #14121, and #14120, respectively.

66. Townsend to Edwards, December 3, 1956, TA.

67. Townsend to Carlos Sevilla, December 27, 1956, TA#11924.

68. Lowrance to D-1, October 8, 1956, MAF Records (emphasis Lowrance's).

CHAPTER 4

1. R. Saint to Ken Pike, March 31, 1957, TA#14069.

2. Donald H. Burns to Townsend, March 6, 1956, TA#12350; R. Saint to Townsend, January 9, [1957], TA#12402.

3. Parrott to Marj Saint, February 21, 1956, and Parrott to Lowrance, June 1, 1956, both in Folder 2, Box 5, MAF Records.

4. Saint to Pike, March 31, 1957, TA.

5. Ibid.

6. R. Saint to Townsend, February 9, 1957, TA#13584.

7. Saint to Townsend, January 9, [1957], TA.

8. R. Saint to Wesley Swauger, February 24, 1957, TA#14122.

9. Townsend to R. Saint, May 10, 1957, TA#12916.

10. Don Burns to Townsend, April 10, 1957, TA#13010.

11. *Dayuma Story*, 96, 113. In *Wao tededo*, the same word means "to think" and "to believe."

12. R. Saint to Bill Nyman and John Newman, June 20, 1957, TA#13879.

13. Ken Watters to Townsend, July 19, 1957, TA#13341; Townsend to Kilo Kid [Henry C. Crowell], July 24, 1957, TA#12783; Townsend to A. L. Luce Sr., December 1, 1958, TA#14323.

14. Townsend to William and Etta Nyman, September 26, 1957, TA#12630; Watters to Townsend, July 19, 1957, TA.

15. Townsend to Carlos Sevilla, July 22, 1957, TA#12794 (translation mine).

16. "Triumph—Not Tragedy," *Missionary Tidings*, July–August 1958, 565.

17. W. G. Tidmarsh, "Auca News," typescript news release, n.d., enclosed with Lowrance to Parrott, October 15, 1957, Folder 23, Box 5, MAF Records.

18. Ibid.

19. Parrott to Lowrance, October 22, 1957, Folder 27, Box 5, MAF Records.

20. Townsend to Wilfred Tidmarsh, October 21, 1957, TA#12701.

21. Ibid.

22. Townsend to Ben [William G. Nyman Sr.], October 21, 1957, TA#12629.

23. Townsend to Tidmarsh, October 21, 1957, TA.

24. Other missions leaders also urged caution, but Tidmarsh remained undaunted. Lowrance to Parrott, October 31, 1957, Folder 23, Box 5, MAF Records.

25. Lowrance to Parrott and Truxton, November 15, 1957, Folder 23, Box 5, MAF Records (ellipses, emphasis Lowrance's).

26. This paragraph and the following account are based on a letter from Elisabeth Elliot to her father, Phillip Howard Jr., dated November 20, 1957, and published as "What I Learned from Two Auca Women: A Recent Letter from Betty Elliot," *SST*, December 28, 1957, 1007–9 (3–5). For a copy of the original letter, see Olivia Lowrance to Parrott, n.d. [received November 27, 1957], Folder 23, Box 5, MAF Records. Additional details are from *Kinsman*, 28–29, 34–35.

27. *Kinsman*, 30.

28. Lowrance to Parrott, August 30, 1956, Folder 53, Box 4, MAF Records.

29. Elliot, "What I Learned," 1007 (3).

30. *Kinsman*, 28–29.

31. Elliot, "What I Learned," 1008 (4).

32. Ibid.

33. Ibid.

34. *Kinsman*, 38.

35. Lowrance to MAF D-1 [administrators], November 21, 1957, Folder 53, Box 4, MAF Records.

36. *Kinsman*, 38.

37. Parrott to Lowrance, November 19, 1957, Folder 27, Box 5, MAF Records.

38. R. Saint to Townsend, November 18, 1957, TA#13203.

39. Ibid.

40. Ibid.

41. Parrott to Lowrance, November 19, 1957, MAF Records.

42. Donald H. Burns to Schneider, November 23, 1957, TA#13713.

43. Saint to Townsend, November 18, 1957, TA.

44. Nadine Burns to Townsend, November 21, 1957, TA#13200.

45. Townsend to R. Saint, November 21, 1957, TA#12686.

46. Handwritten comment on R. Saint "To All Concerned," November 24, 1957, TA#13711.

47. Dayomæ, "Reactions and Message," English translation transcript of tape recording, typed, dated, and translated by R. Saint, November 18, 1957, TA#13723.

48. Saint "To All Concerned," November 24, 1957, TA.

49. *Fishers of Men*, 285.

50. Dayomæ, untitled message to Mintaca and Mæncamo, English translation transcript of tape recording, typed, dated, and translated by R. Saint, January 23, 1958, TA#16232.

51. R. Saint, form letter to friends and Wycliffe supporters, February 8, 1958, TA#16199.

52. R. Saint to Townsend, March 3, 1958, TA#15339.

53. Saint, form letter, February 8, 1958, TA.

54. *Dayuma Story*, 154; R. Saint to Townsend, July 7, 1958, TA#14669. Saint wrote, "Since Dayomæ acknowledges you as 'our' chief, I think it is about time I clear with you some of the recent happenings." Dayomæ's use of "chief" reflected outside influences since the Waorani had no chiefs or word in their language for "chief."

55. *Dayuma Story*, 154.

56. Ibid.

57. Wheaton College News Bureau, "Auca Vengeance upon Martyred American Missionaries in Curaray Jungle Waters Has Counterpart in Baptismal Waters at Wheaton Church," news release, April 16, 1958, Folder 11, Box 11, Edman Records.

58. Cover, *Missionary Tidings*, July–August 1958.

59. Dick Pittman to Townsend, received April 21, 1958, TA#15275.

60. "Sequel to Martyrdom," *Christian Life*, May 1958, 9.

61. *Dayuma Story*, 156.

62. Cover, *Christian Life*, May 1958.

63. "Triumph—Not Tragedy," *Missionary Tidings*, 565.

64. Wheaton College News Bureau, "Auca Vengeance," Edman Records.

CHAPTER 5

1. Elisabeth Howard Gren, interview by Robert Shuster, March 26, 1985, Tape T2, transcript, EHE Papers. Used with permission.

2. V. Raymond Edman, "The Salt of the Earth," *Bulletin of Wheaton College*, March 1956, Folder 5, Box 11, Edman Records.

3. Clyde W. Taylor to V. Raymond Edman, William K. Harrison, May 24, 1957, Folder 11, Box 11, Edman Records. Because in practice, if not legally, the fund existed to meet the children's needs, Olive Fleming received only one disbursement of fifteen hundred dollars, which was given to each widow.

4. EFMA [Evangelical Foreign Missions Association] Missionary News Service, "Trust Fund Set Up for Families of Martyred Missionaries," news release, January 15, 1956, Folder 11, Box 11, Edman Records.

5. Clyde W. Taylor to Mary Lou McCully, Barbara Youderian, Elizabeth [*sic*] Elliot, Marjorie Saint, March 24, 1961, and E. Elliot to Clyde Taylor, July 15, 1966, both in Folder 11, Box 11, Edman Records.

6. Taylor to McCully et al., March 24, 1961, Edman Records. Quoted with permission.

7. Marilou McCully to Clyde Taylor, April 10, 1961, Folder 11, Box 11, Edman Records.

8. Elliot to Taylor, July 15, 1956, Edman Records.

9. Clyde W. Taylor to V. Raymond Edman, July 28, 1966; Clyde W. Taylor to E. Elliot, Marilou McCully, Marjorie Saint, Barbara Youderian, August 4, 1966; Clyde W. Taylor to William K. Harrison and V. Raymond Edman, December 7, 1966; Wade Coggins to V. Raymond Edman and William K. Harrison, January 18, 1967; all in Folder 11, Box 11, Edman Records.

10. V. Raymond Edman to Mrs. Nathanial [sic] Saint, October 18, 1960, Folder 11, Box 11, Edman Records.

11. V. Raymond Edman to Iva Mae O'Bryant [South Africa General Mission], February 18, 1959, Folder 12, Box 11, Edman Records.

12. V. Raymond Edman, "When the Aucas Laughed at Dayuma," *Sunday Digest*, December 8, 1963, 4; V. Raymond Edman, "His Face Was Like the Daybreak," *Sunday Digest*, February 2, 1964, 6.

13. R. Saint to Townsend, April 23, 1958, TA#15274.

14. Ibid.

15. R. Saint form letter to friends, May 21, 1956, Folder 12, Box 11, Edman Records.

16. "New Board Member," *Translation*, Fall 1958, 12.

17. *Kinsman*, 63; *Dayuma Story*, 158–60.

18. E. Elliot to R. Saint, April 9, 1958, TA#16092; E. Elliot to Townsend, R. Saint, and Sam Saint, April 13, 1958, TA#15285.

19. *Kinsman*, 47, 55, 59.

20. Elliot to Townsend, R. Saint, and S. Saint, April 13, 1958, TA.

21. D. Derr to Parrott, July 24, 1958, Folder 42, Box 5, MAF Records.

22. Hugh Doherty, "Montreal Doctor Missing 3 Months on Headhunters Quest," *Montreal Gazette*, May 13, 1958, Google News, https://news.google.com/newspapers?nid=1946&dat=195 80513&id=WUswAAAAIBAJ&sjid=b6gFAAAAIBAJ&pg=6827,2430981&hl=en.

23. Lowrance to Parrott and Truxton, January 31, 1958; Lowrance to Parrott, March 13, 1958; Lowrance to Parrott, April 16, 1958; all in Folder 54, Box 5, MAF Records. E. Elliot to "Dearest Family," February 19, 1958, and E. Elliot to "Dearest Mother" [Katherine Howard], February 24, 1958, both in Folder 6, Box 4, EHE Papers.

24. Lowrance to Parrott, April 16, 1958, MAF Records.

25. Derr to Parrott, July 24, 1958, MAF Records; R. Saint to Townsend, July 7, 1958, TA#14669; "Fear Canadian Is New Victim of Auca Tribe," *Chicago Tribune*, August 8, 1958.

26. Guequita, Quemo, and other Waorani, English transcript of oral history interview with John Man and Jim Yost, April 1987, Ecuador, 92–95, Yost Papers; *Gentle Savage*, 203–8; *Dayuma Story*, 190.

27. Doherty, "Montreal Doctor Missing"; "Fear Canadian Is New Victim"; "Jungle Indians Slay Explorer," *Ottawa Citizen*, October 4, 1958.

28. Saint to Townsend, July 7, 1958, TA; Derr to Parrott, July 24, 1958, MAF Records.

29. Derr to Parrott, July 24, 1958, MAF Records.

30. Parrott to Derr, July 30, 1958 [second letter], Folder 58, Box 5, MAF Records (emphasis Parrott's).

31. Parrott to Derr, misdated July 3, 1958 [July 30, 1958, first letter], Folder, 58, Box 5, MAF Records.

32. Saint to Townsend, July 7, 1958, TA.

33. R. Saint to Townsend, August 5, 1958, TA#15160.

34. Ralph Edwards, video recording, *This Is Your Life*, June 5, 1957; "Auca Language Study," *Translation*, Spring–Summer 1958, 13.

35. Saint to Townsend, August 5, 1958, TA.

36. Ibid.

37. Ibid.

38. R. Saint to Schneider, July 9, 1958, TA#15924.

39. Saint to Townsend, August 5, 1958, TA.

40. Ibid.

41. Saint to Townsend, July 7, 1958, TA.

42. Schneider to H. Roe Bartle, July 5, 1958, TA#15934.

43. Schneider to R. Saint, July 11, 1958, TA#15921.

44. Townsend to R. Saint, July 15, 1958, TA#14668.

45. Report by Philip W. Grossman, WBT Regional Secretary, August 28, 1958, TA#15796.

46. Parrott to Truxton, July 11, 1958, Folder 58, Box 5, MAF Records.

47. Quoted in Derr to Parrott, July 28, 1958, Folder 42, Box 5, MAF Records.

48. R. Saint to "Dear Praying Friends," September 2, [1958], misdated 1957, TA#13792.

49. *Dayuma Story*, 183.

50. Transcript of Marj Saint, "The Back Home Hour Broadcast at HCJB Sunday Night, October 5, 1958," Folder 62, Box 5, MAF Records; *Kinsman*, 64.

51. *Kinsman*, 64, 70.

52. Kingsland, *SAS*, 108.

53. R. Saint to "Dear Friends," October 1, 1958, Folder 12, Box 11, Edman Records.

54. Saint, "The Back Home Hour," MAF Records; Marjorie Jones Whitaker to Blanche S. Jones, October 2, 1958, Folder 12, Box 11, Edman Records.

55. Saint, "Back Home Hour," MAF Records; Whitaker to Jones, October 2, 1958, Edman Records.

56. Whitaker to Jones, October 2, 1958, Edman Records. Whitaker letter quoted with permission.

57. Quoted in Whitaker to Jones, October 2, 1958, Edman Records.

58. *Dayuma Story*, 185–86.

59. *Kinsman*, 74.

60. Whitaker to Jones, October 2, 1958, Edman Records.

61. Ibid.

62. Ibid.; Schneider to Cameron and Elaine Townsend, October 9, 1958, TA#15058; Schneider to "Dear Gang," n.d. (includes extensive excerpts of R. Saint letters, beginning with an excerpt dated October 7, 1958), TA#15050.

63. Derr to D-1, October 3, 1958, Folder 42, Box 5, MAF Records.

64. R. Saint to Schneider, October 5, 1958, in Schneider to "Dear Gang," TA (October 5 letter appears out of order in Schneider's compilation, following those dated October 7, 8, and 9).

CHAPTER 6

1. R. Saint to Schneider et al., October 7, 1958, in Schneider to "Dear Gang," n.d., TA#15050.

2. *Kinsman*, 81.

3. Saint to Schneider et al., October 7, 1958, in Schneider to "Dear Gang," TA. While the Waorani did enjoy telling the story of Tremblay and his fate, neither of the two Wao accounts translated into English mentions his teeth. See Guequita, Quemo, and other Waorani, English transcript of oral history interview with John Man and Jim Yost, April 1987, Ecuador, 94–96, Yost Papers; *Gentle Savage*, 203–7.

4. Saint to Schneider et al., October 7, 1958, in Schneider to "Dear Gang," TA.

5. *Kinsman*, 82.

6. Saint to Schneider et al., October 7, 1958, in Schneider to "Dear Gang," TA.

7. E. Elliot to Folks, October 9, 1958, Folder 6, Box 4, EHE Papers.

8. R. Saint to Mother and Dad, October 9, 1958, in Schneider to "Dear Gang," TA.

9. *Kinsman*, 82, 100.

10. "Twenty Years," 682, emphasizes the role of cultural brokers.

11. "Missionaries Live with Aucas: Child among Her Father's Killers," *Life*, November 24, 1958, 23–29; Tad Szulc, "U.S. Women Live with Killer Tribe: Widow and Daughter, 4, of Missionary Camp among Savages Who Slew Him," *New York Times*, November 27, 1958.

12. Saint to Mother and Dad, October 9, 1958, in Schneider to "Dear Gang," TA.

13. *Kinsman*, 83.

14. "Recent News from Betty Elliot," *SST*, December 13, 1958, 920 (6).

15. *Kinsman*, 69, 83.

16. "Twenty Years," 679.

17. Elisabeth Elliot, "Mother Tells of Poison Darts, Eating Burnt Monkey—and Hymns," *Life*, November 24, 1958, 26–27.

18. R. Saint to Mother and Dad, section dated October 10, 1958, in Schneider to "Dear Gang," TA.

19. *Kinsman*, 156.

20. Office of the President, Wheaton College, "Report on Operation Auca at Thanksgiving Time 1958," Thanksgiving 1958, Folder 3, Box 11, Edman Records; Lois Wille, "Strangest of Feasts—a Roast Monkey," *Chicago Daily News*, November 27, 1958.

21. Ps. 60:9, 10 (KJV); "Recent News from Betty Elliot," 920 (6). Jim Elliot had called out the first verse of this same psalm to his parents as he and Peter Fleming embarked for Ecuador. See *Gates of Splendor*, 13.

22. E. Elliot to Marj [Saint] and Marilou [McCully], October 13, 1958, with ongoing dated sections to October 28, 1958, TA#15651.

23. Maintaining two or three houses about a day's walk apart was customary for the Waorani, although they normally moved among them every few months. Stephen Beckerman and James Yost, "Upper Amazonian Warfare," in *Latin American Indigenous Warfare and Ritual Violence*, ed. Richard J. Chacon and Rubén G. Mendoza (Tucson: University of Arizona Press, 2007), 164.

24. "Recent News from Betty Elliot," 920 (6).

25. Elliot to Marj and Marilou, October 13, 1958, TA. In an autobiography published from an oral history interview, Minkaye Ænkædi blamed Elliot for forcing the Waorani to wear clothing. See *Gentle Savage*, 232. Evidence does not support this assertion; Dayomæ played a much larger role in promoting clothing as part of her efforts to "civilize" her people. On numerous occasions, Elliot voiced her conviction that the Waorani looked better wearing their traditional *come* (hip-cord). See, e.g., Elliot to Marj and Marilou, October 13, 1958, TA; also "Letter from Betty Elliot," *SST*, December 3, 1960, 948 (6).

26. "Twenty Years," 682.

27. Elliot to Marj and Marilou, October 13, 1958, TA.

28. R. Saint to Townsend, January 28, 1959, TA#17272. Rachel defended Dayomæ.

29. "Twenty Years," 689.

30. Saint to Mother and Dad, October 10, 1958, in Schneider to "Dear Gang," TA.

31. Saint to Townsend, January 29, 1959, TA.

32. R. Saint, "Night Life among the Aucas," typescript compilation of letters Saint wrote from Tewæno, October 27, 1958, TA#40015.

33. Elliot to Marj and Marilou, October 13, 1958, TA.

34. Saint, "Night Life," October 27, 1958, TA.

35. *Kinsman*, 120.

36. Elliot to Marj and Marilou, October 13, 1958, TA.

37. *Dayuma Story*, 238–39.

38. Typewritten note in Daniel A. Derr files, n.d., stamped as received December 20, 1958, Folder 42, Box 5, MAF Records; *Kinsman*, 126.

39. Saint, "Night Life," October 27, 1958, TA.

40. Elliot, "Mother Tells of Poison Darts," 27. Alternate spellings for Nhambiquara are Nambikwara or Nambiquára.

41. [Elisabeth Elliot], "Life among the Aucas," section dated "November 10, 1958," *SST*, January 24, 1959, 72 (4); see also Elliot to Marj and Marilou, October 13, 1958, TA, in the postscript dated October 28.

42. [Elliot], "Life among the Aucas," 72 (4).

43. Saint, "Night Life," October 27, 1958, TA.

44. Ibid.

45. Rachel Saint, quoted in *Dayuma Story*, 229.

46. Saint, "Night Life," October 27, 1958, TA.

47. See Catherine Peeke, "One Supreme God," unpublished summary, typescript copy sent to author as email attachment, March 3, 2005; "People of Forest," 111–13, offers a brief summary of Wao cosmology that does not include Wængongui.

48. Saint to Mother and Dad, October 9, 1958 in Schneider to "Dear Gang," TA.

49. *Dayuma Story*, 230.

50. For Nænquiwi's death, see *Gentle Savage*, 196–203.

51. Saint to Townsend, January 29, 1959, TA; also R. Saint to Townsend, December 12, 1958, TA#14923.

52. [Elliot], "Life among the Aucas," 72 (4).

53. Saint to Townsend, January 29, 1959, TA.

54. Townsend to R. Saint, January 26, 1959, TA#16886; Saint to Townsend, January 29, 1959, TA.

55. Elisabeth [Elliot] Gren, interview with author, June 27, 2001, Magnolia, MA.

56. J. C. Keenan to Truxton, December 7, 1958, Folder 49, Box 5, MAF Records.

57. [Elliot], "Life among the Aucas," 72 (4).

58. Cable from Sam Saint and Cornell Capa, no recipient name [Schneider], n.d. [December 5, 1958], TA#14948; Schneider to Cameron and Elaine Townsend, December 6, 1958, TA#14947.

59. Schneider to Townsends, December 6, 1958, TA.

60. Ibid.; see also Townsend to Schneider, December 3, 1958, TA#14316.

61. R. Saint to Townsend, January 24, 1959 [1960], misdated, TA#17281.

62. Saint to Townsend, December 12, 1958, TA.

63. Townsend to Schneider, December 3, 1958, TA.

64. Saint to Townsend, December 12, 1958, TA.

65. Quoted in ibid.

66. R. Saint to Townsend, May 6, 1960, TA#18970.

67. Saint to Townsend, January 24, [1960], TA.

CHAPTER 7

1. *Dayuma Story*, 37–41.

2. Ibid., 148, 182.

3. C. Roderick Wilson and James A. Yost, "The Creation of Social Hierarchy," in *Ethnographic Essays in Cultural Anthropology: A Problem-Based Approach*, ed. R. Bruce Morrison and C. Roderick Wilson (Itasca, IL: F. E. Peacock, 2002), 119; also Stephen Beckerman et al., "Supporting Information," 1, to "Life Histories, Blood Revenge, and Reproductive Success among the Waorani of Ecuador," *PNAS* 106, no. 20 (2009), doi: 10.1073/pnas.0901431106, http://www.pnas.org/content/suppl/2009/05/11/0901431106.DCSupplemental/0901431106SI.pdf.

4. *Dayuma Story*, 192.

5. Ibid., 173–76.

6. The various versions of what happened at Palm Beach are confusing. Neither Rachel nor Dayomæ were there, and Rachel was still learning the Wao language when *The Dayuma Story* was written.

7. *Dayuma Story*, 177, 229.

8. Frank E. Gaebelein, book jacket of *Dayuma Story*, 1st edition.

9. Mel Arnold to Townsend, December 8, 1960, TA#18708.

10. Ken Watters to Ethel Emily Wallis, June 29, 1962, TA#21243. The Ecuador Branch of WBT/SIL received $1,650 of these funds, with another $3,500 going toward planes for Ecuador and Bolivia. The rest was budgeted for other WBT/SIL expenses.

11. *Dayuma Story*, 25.

12. Cameron Townsend, "How Loving Service Opens Closed Doors" (chapel talk, University of Oklahoma, Norman, July 1960), unpublished typescript, TA#50221.

13. David E. Kucharsky to Van Der Puy, April 20, 1959, Folder 6, Box 5, CTI Records (emphasis Kucharsky's). Used with permission.

14. V. R. Edman, book jacket of *Dayuma Story*, 1st edition.

15. Cornell Capa, foreword to *Kinsman*, 14. Portions of the following discussion are based on Kathryn T. Long, "Cameras 'Never Lie': The Role of Photography in Telling the Story of American Evangelical Missions," *Church History* 72, no. 4 (2003): 846–51.

16. LaVerne Kohl, review of *The Savage My Kinsman*, by Elisabeth Elliot, *Library Journal*, May 1, 1961, 1779.

17. *Kinsman*, 101, 104.

18. Ibid., 158.

19. Ibid., 151.

20. Ibid., 155–56.

21. Ibid., 159.

22. Ibid., 18.

23. Elisabeth Elliot, epilogue (1981) to *The Savage My Kinsman* (Ann Arbor, MI: Vine Books, 1996), 145.

24. R. Saint to Townsend, January 29, 1959, TA#17272.

25. *Kinsman* (1961), 63, see also 19.

26. Ibid., 59, 63, 76, 81–82, 94, 104, 145, 156.

27. "Operation Auca: Four Years after Martyrdoms," *Christianity Today*, January 4, 1960, 32.

28. E. Elliot to Folks, June 6, 1961, Folder 9, Box 4, EHE Papers.

29. Russell T. Hitt, "Photojournalism at Its Very Best," review of *The Savage My Kinsman*, by Elisabeth Elliot, *Eternity*, June 1961, 43.

30. Alan M. Fletcher, "A Feature-Length Book Review" of *The Savage My Kinsman*, by Elisabeth Elliot, *SST*, April 22, 1961, 323–24 (7–8).

31. Hitt, "Photojournalism," 44.

32. "Letter from Betty Elliot," *SST*, December 3, 1960, 948 (6).

33. Derr to Charles Mellis, October 20, 1960, Folder 23, Box 6, MAF Records.

34. *Gates of Splendor*, 254.

35. Derr to Truxton, September 2, 1959, Folder 78, Box 5, MAF Records.

36. Townsend to Allyn R. Bell Jr., May 13, 1960, TA#18372.

37. James D. Cockcroft, *Latin America: History, Politics and U.S. Foreign Policy*, 2nd ed. (Chicago: Nelson-Hall, 1996), 440.

38. Glen D. Turner, "Report of Interview with President Velasco Ibarra," n.d. [September 23, 1960], TA#40008. SIL's first accord with the government of Ecuador was signed in June 1952, when Galo Plaza Lasso was president; by the time the first SIL staff arrived in early 1953, Velasco Ibarra had succeeded him.

39. Townsend, "Excerpts from Letter from W. C. Townsend to Elaine Townsend," February 14, 1961, TA#20006.

40. R. Saint to Townsend, February 1961, TA#20301.

41. *Unstilled Voices*, 123.

42. Saint to Townsend, February 1961, TA; W. Cameron Townsend, "Director's Column," *Translation*, Summer 1961, 12.

43. Townsend and Jim Wilson, "Notes on the Visit Made to the President of Brasil [*sic*], Dr. Janio Quadros," unpublished typescript, May 16, 1961, TA#19864.

44. Kenneth L. Pike to Townsend, May 1, 1961, TA#20240.

45. Two reports by Townsend's wife, Elaine, document the content of the conversation during the August luncheon and Velasco Ibarra's interest in the work of SIL. See "Extra: The Philadelphia Informant," unpublished typescript, TA#40002, as well as notes filed as TA#40006, both undated but apparently written in August 1961.

46. Saint to Townsend, February 1961, TA.

47. Townsend, "Director's Column," 12.

48. R. Saint quoted in Elaine Townsend, "Extra," TA.

49. "Rage, Revenge, Religion," 480.

50. Ibid., 483.

51. *Tell Them We Are Not Auca; We are Waorani* (Dallas, TX: Summer Institute of Linguistics, 1988), videocassette. In the film, Guequita also expresses remorse for his role in killing the five missionaries. "I really did badly. . . . They were trying to do good."

52. T. E. McCully, "A Father Visits His Son's Killers," *Action*, March 1962, 14, copy in Folder 9, Box 11, Edman Records.

53. Derr to Charles Mellis, September 10, 1961, Folder 69, Box 6, MAF Records.

54. Schneider to Dick Pittman, November 25, 1958, TA#15533; Schneider to Townsend, May 16, 1959, TA#17122.

55. R. Saint to Johnson, December 30, 1961, TA#20386.

56. Derr to Mellis, October 20, 1960, MAF Records.

57. Elisabeth [Elliot] Gren, interview with author, June 27, 2001, Magnolia, MA.

58. E. Elliot to Folks, February 6, 1961, Folder 9, Box 4, EHE Papers; see also E. Elliot to Folks, May 1, 1961, Folder 9, Box 4, EHE Papers.

59. Betty Elliot, "A Visit to 'Palm Beach' on the Curaray," *SST*, September 30, 1961, 771–72 (15–16).

60. Saint's response quoted in E. Elliot to Folks, November 13, 1961, Folder 9, Box 4, EHE Papers.

61. E. Elliot to Mother, April 4 and April 8, 1961, both in Folder 9, Box 4, EHE Papers.

62. Elliot to Folks, November 13, 1961, EHE Papers.

63. Van Der Puy to David Kucharsky, June 19, 1959, Folder 6, Box 5, CTI Records.

64. Johnson to Townsend and members of the Board, "Re: Auca Situation," November 21, 1961, TA #20069.

65. David Howard, interview with author, May 31, 2000, Wheaton, IL.

66. R. Saint to Townsend, January 1, 1962, TA#21126.

67. R. Saint to Johnson, "Copied from K. L. Pike File," November 8, 1961, TA #20421; see also E. Elliot, "To a few who are intimately concerned," November 6, 1961, letter enclosed in Derr to Parrott, November 16, 1961, Folder 69, Box 6, MAF Records; E. Elliot to Folks, November 20, 1961, Folder 9, Box 4, EHE Papers.

68. Saint to Johnson, November 8, 1961, TA. Elliot had earlier noted that Catherine Peeke was beginning graduate work in linguistics and would focus on the Wao language, another reason Elliot felt her language work was no longer necessary. Elliot to Mother, April 4, 1961, EHE Papers.

69. Saint to Townsend, January 1, 1962, TA.

70. E. Elliot to Folks, November 29, 1961, Folder 9, Box 4, EHE Papers.

71. Saint to Townsend, January 1, 1962, TA.

72. Kenneth Pike to Townsend, December 14, 1961, TA#20052.

73. Elisabeth Elliot, *These Strange Ashes* (New York: Harper & Row, 1975; Ann Arbor, MI: Servant Publications, 1998), 119, 124–25, 144–45. Citations refer to the Servant edition. Elliot was a missionary among the Tsáchila (Colorado) people from September 1952 to June 1953.

74. The Christian tradition of the "Holy Fool" is rooted in 1 Corinthians 3:18 and 4:10.

75. Elliot, epilogue (1981), 146–47.

76. Ibid., 148.

77. Phillip Howard to Townsend, December 6, 1961, TA#19723.

78. Townsend to Phillip Howard, December 13, 1961, TA#19722; Johnson to Townsend and Board, November 21, 1961, TA.

79. Townsend to Howard, December 13, 1961, TA.

80. Gren, interview with author.

81. Ibid.

82. "'God's Carving' for the Aucas," *Translation*, Summer 1960, 14; Derr to Charles Mellis, November 25, 1961, Folder 69, Box 6, MAF Records.

83. Rachel Saint, "Six Years Later, 1956–1962," *Translation*, Spring 1962, 11.

CHAPTER 8

1. R. Saint "To our praying friends," January 10, 1969, "Auca History 1956–1969" Folder, EBC-SIL.

2. R. Saint to Special Friends [newsletter recipients], August 30, 1962, TA#21195; "Five Living Killers of Palm Beach," *Translation*, Summer–Fall 1964, 5.

3. James A. Yost, email message to author, May 3, 2006.

4. Ibid.

5. Peeke to Townsend, July 15, 1962, TA#20998.

6. R. Saint to Elaine and Cameron Townsend, October 18, 1962, TA#20923.

7. Elisabeth [Elliot] Gren, interview with author, June 27, 2001, Magnolia, MA.

8. Saint to Special Friends, August 30, 1962, TA; Saint to Townsends, October 18, 1962, TA.

9. R. Saint to Townsend, March 1, 1962, TA#21069.

10. Ethel Wallis, "What Happened to the Aucas?," *Translation*, Summer–Fall 1964, 2. Wallis was a gifted writer (and ghostwriter), with an ear for the key emphases of Townsend and WBT. Her column closely echoes Townsend's comments on other occasions.

11. "People of Forest," 99.

12. In the early 1960s there were four main groups of Waorani, each located in a different region of territory that represented about 8,100 square miles of rainforest.

13. R. Saint to Family and Friends, May 17, 1966, TA#24591.

14. For the different Wao groups and their locations, see "Twenty Years," 679. Catholic efforts to reach the Waorani are narrated in *Ultimos Huaorani*. David Stoll provides a succinct account of the evangelical-Catholic rivalry, generally critical toward Rachel Saint and SIL, in "The Huaorani Go to Market," chap. 9 in *Fishers of Men*, especially 293–97.

15. R. Saint to Peeke, November 30, 1966, annotated copy, TA#24367.

16. *Fishers of Men*, 294.

17. *Ultimos Huaorani*, 20–48, 219.

18. Although generally balanced in tone, *Ultimos Huaorani* was written by members of the Capuchín order and reflects the Catholic perspective. *Fishers of Men* follows this account.

19. For example, "Piden Patrullaje Militar en Toda Zona de Dominio Auca," *Ultimas Noticias*, May 22, 1964, TA#44034.

20. *Ultimos Huaorani*, 49 (translation mine).

21. Ibid., 51.

22. [Peeke] memorandum to Santa Ana [California headquarters of Wycliffe Bible Translators, Inc.], May 25, 1964, with excerpts from R. Saint notes, Peeke Papers. Connections between the CIA and members of Ecuador's ruling junta may have helped SIL's chances, according to Stoll, *Fishers of Men*, 294.

23. [Peeke] memorandum, May 25, 1964, with Saint excerpts, Peeke Papers.

24. *Ultimos Huaorani*, 52.

25. Johnson to Peeke and Ethel Wallis, June 30, 1964, Peeke Papers.

26. Ethel Emily Wallis, *Aucas Downriver: Dayuma's Story Today* (New York: Harper & Row, 1973), 22, 24, 26.

27. Rachel Saint, "I Am Oncaye," *Translation*, Summer–Fall 1964, 6. This was one of the earliest published accounts.

28. Wallis, *Aucas Downriver*, 31.

29. Rachel Saint, "Ten Years after the Massacre," *Decision*, January 1966, 11.

30. R. Saint, "Excerpts from Quemo's prayer on Easter Sunday, 1965, when the Gospel of Mark in AUCA was received," typed report, n.d., TA#23004; Ethel Wallis, "WBT Conference Report," *Translation*, Summer–Fall 1965, 10; R. Saint, "The Month of May in Tewæno—1965," typescript, "Auca History 1956–1969" Folder, EBC-SIL; *Unstilled Voices*, 145. All accounts refer to the dedication taking place on Easter Sunday 1965, which was April 18. In one typewritten report, Saint refers to May 2 as Easter Sunday. She apparently confused the dates.

31. Robert C. Savage, draft news release, n.d., enclosed with Van Der Puy to David Kucharsky, July 13, 1965, Folder 6, Box 5, CTI Records.

32. Editor [V. R. Edman], "The Aucas: Ten Years Later," *The Alliance Witness*, January 5, 1966, 6–7; V. Raymond Edman, "A Lesson from the Aucas," *Wheaton Alumni*, March 1966, 7.

33. "Copy of Report on World Congress for Evangelization in Berlin . . . sent to Santa Ana by George Cowan, Oct. 31, 1966," TA#24410; see also R. Saint to Townsend, February 27, 1967, TA #25505.

34. Saint to Townsend, February 27, 1967, TA.

35. Ibid.

36. Townsend to James W. Reapsome, December 6, 1966, TA#23434.

37. R. Saint to Lindskoog, January 21, 1966, "Auca History 1956–1969" Folder, EBC-SIL.

38. Ibid.; for the earlier attempts, see Rachel Saint, "Ten Years Later," in Ethel Emily Wallis, *The Dayuma Story* (1960; New York: Harper and Row, 1965 edition only), 296–98, 302; *Unstilled Voices*, 143–44; *Fishers of Men*, 295.

39. Saint identified a young man named Páa as Oncaye's suitor. R. Saint to Lindskoog, February 14, 1966, "Auca History 1956–1969" Folder, EBC-SIL. In correspondence with Lindskoog, Rachel referred to Oncaye by a code name, "Jean d'Arc."

40. Peeke to Praying Friends [newsletter recipients], February 11, 1965, TA#23326. According to Saint, the first attempt was canceled because the group lost the trail and Oncaye was in pain from her injuries the summer before; the second group turned back when torrential rains made river crossings impossible. Stoll, *Fishers of Men*, 295, suggests that the Tewæno Waorani simply weren't ready to risk a potentially violent encounter.

41. Saint to Lindskoog, February 14, 1966, EBC-SIL.

42. The narrative in this and the following paragraphs, including quotations, is based on R. Saint, "Auca Report," February 22, 1966, TA#39994.

43. See, e.g., Saint to Lindskoog, February 14, 1966, EBC-SIL.

44. Lindskoog to R. Saint, "Re: Uncle Cam's letter," April 30, 1966, TA#23652.

45. Estimates vary, but according to Franklin Barriga López, *Las Culturas Indígenas Ecuatorianas y el Instituto Lingüístico de Verano* [Ecuadorian indigenous cultures and the Summer Institute of Linguistics] (Buenos Aires: Ediciones Amauta, 1992), 141, in 1973 the lowland Quichua population in eastern Ecuador was about forty thousand.

46. "Report from Rachel Saint" [from Tewæno], February 17, 1966, TA#24697.

47. R. Saint to George Cowan, May 9, 1966, TA#24607.

48. R. Saint to Lindskoog and Johnson, August 16, 1967, "Auca History 1956–1969" Folder, EBC-SIL.

49. Lindskoog to Townsend, January 19, 1968, TA#26443.

50. *Unstilled Voices*, 162; Wallis, *Aucas Downriver*, 59.

51. R. Saint to Townsend, April 30, 1968, TA#26330. An understatement to say the least.

52. Lindskoog to R. Saint, March 25, 1968, "Auca History 1956–1969" Folder, EBC-SIL.

53. Lindskoog, "Ecuador Branch Director's Report: 1969 Corporation Conference," n.d., "Various Branch Reports 1960–1993" Folder, EBC-SIL.

CHAPTER 9

1. R. Saint, "CRIME—It's [*sic*] Cause and Cure—as seen in Auca Land," typed report, August 14, 1968, "Auca History 1956–1969" Folder, EBC-SIL.

2. Ibid.

3. These "cross-cousin" marriages were acceptable, in contrast to prohibited marriages with "parallel cousins," children of a father's brothers marrying children of a mother's sisters.

4. Saint, "CRIME," August 14, 1968, EBC-SIL.

5. Ibid. The Waorani also believed in partible paternity, meaning that "all of the men sexually involved with a woman around the time of her pregnancy were considered as the fathers of her child." See Stephen Beckerman et al., "Supporting Information," 1, to "Life Histories, Blood Revenge, and Reproductive Success among the Waorani of Ecuador," *PNAS* 106, no. 20 (2009), doi: 10.1073/pnas.0901431106, http://www.pnas.org/content/suppl/2009/05/11/0901431106. DCSupplemental/0901431106SI.pdf.

6. Peeke to Lindskoog, August 16, 1968, "Auca History 1956–1969" Folder, EBC-SIL.

7. "Twenty Years," 685; "People of Forest," 102; "Rage, Revenge, Religion," 481.

8. R. Saint, "Auca Epidemic Report," form letter, early April 1969, Peeke Papers.

9. R. Saint to Lindskoog, handwritten note, n.d.; see also R. Saint, "Baiwa Contact Report," July 1969; both in "Auca History 1956–1969" Folder, EBC-SIL.

10. In mid-1968 the Capuchín friars decided to call off their own "operación aucas," but Saint seemed unaware of that decision. Cabodevilla, *LH*, 392.

11. Catherine Peeke, interview with James Hefley, transcript, n.d. [probably 1980], copy in author's possession. Used with permission.

12. "Auca Missionary Is Weaverville Native," *Presbyterian Journal*, September 13, 1978, 6–8.

13. Peeke, interview with Hefley; Schneider to Townsend, February 21, 1959, TA#17232.

14. Schneider to Dick Pittman, November 25, 1958, TA#15533; Schneider to Peeke, November 9, 1958, TA#15565; Peeke to Schneider, November 11, 1958, TA#15566.

15. Peeke, interview with Hefley; Johnson to Townsend, June 14, 1962, TA#23019; Catherine Peeke, interview with author, July 3, 2000, Weaverville, NC.

16. Peeke, "'Round & 'Round," unpublished essay, n.d., copy sent to the author by Peeke as an email attachment, February 10, 2005.

17. Lindskoog, "Ecuador Branch Director's Report: 1969 Corporation Conference," n.d., "Various Branch Reports 1960–1993" Folder, EBC-SIL.

18. Peeke, "'Round & 'Round."

19. Ibid.

20. Peeke to Lindskoog, extensive flight report, October 5, 1968, "Auca History 1956–1969" Folder, EBC-SIL.

21. It is true, as critics have charged, that Wycliffe Bible Translators US used stories of the Waorani work for fundraising purposes. Little or none of that money came back to Ecuador or Rachel Saint.

22. Lindskoog, "Ecuador Branch Director's Report," EBC-SIL.

23. Peeke to Lindskoog, October 5, 1968, EBC-SIL.

24. Peeke to Lindskoog, October 9, 1968 ("appendix" to October 5 report), "Auca History 1956–1969" Folder, EBC-SIL (emphasis Peeke's).

25. Peeke to Lindskoog, October 5, 1968, EBC-SIL.

26. Cabodevilla, *LH*, 390–91, was one of the few who did.

27. Lindskoog to [multiple recipients including R. Saint, Peeke, the Executive Committee, and others], March 31, 1969, "Auca History 1956–1969" Folder, EBC-SIL; Benjamin F. Elson to Fred B. Morris, May 5, 1971, "Auca Correspondence—Oil" Folder, EBC-SIL.

28. Elson to Morris, May 5, 1971, EBC-SIL.

29. R. Saint to Praying Friends [newsletter recipients], January 10, 1969, "Auca History 1956–1969" Folder, EBC-SIL; George Cowan, February 24, 1969, quoted in Peeke, "Basket to Location 7, Flight over Ridge, and Follow-ups," report dated February 17–24, 1969, "Auca History 1956–1969" Folder, EBC-SIL.

30. Lindskoog to Hans J. Tanner, January 24, 1969, "Auca Correspondence—Oil" Folder, EBC-SIL.

31. Peeke to Lindskoog, January 24, 1969, "Auca History 1956–1969" Folder, EBC-SIL.

32. R. W. Craig to Lindskoog, November 26, 1970, "Auca Correspondence—Oil" Folder, EBC-SIL. One sucre equaled about four cents USD.

33. The account of the rescue in this and preceding paragraphs, as well as quotations, is from Peeke, "Rescue Operation by GSI Helicopter in Texaco Concession, March 27, 1969," "Auca History 1956–1969" Folder, EBC-SIL.

34. José María Velasco Ibarra, "Decreta," presidential decree, August 20, 1961, "Auca Land Map" Folder, EBC-SIL.

35. Ecuador's 1937 Law of Communes/Townships (Ley de Comunas) required indigenous communities to form local governments with town councils to attain legal status. The law was based on the practices of indigenous people in the highlands, the majority of Ecuador's indigenous population. Allen Gerlach, *Indians, Oil, and Politics: A Recent History of Ecuador* (Wilmington, DE: Scholarly Resources, 2003), 66.

36. Velasco Ibarra, "Decreta." Acronym is from the Spanish: El Instituto Ecuatoriano de Reforma Agraria y Colonización.

37. Lindskoog to Gay Schenck, December 1, 1972, "Auca Contact History 1970–1980" Folder, EBC-SIL.

38. Gustavo Medina López to Lindskoog and R. Saint, November 9, 1967, "Auca Land Map" Folder, EBC-SIL.

39. Lindskoog to R. Saint, January 22, 1969, "Auca History 1956–1969" Folder, EBC-SIL.

40. Saint, "Baiwa Contact Report," EBC-SIL.

41. R. Saint, "Report on Use of Electronic Basket at Auca House December 7, 1968," January 10, 1969, "Auca History 1956–1969" Folder, EBC-SIL.

42. "People of Forest," 102.

43. Wallace Swanson, "Polio Strikes the Aucas," transcript for slide series, n.d., 7, copy in author's possession; "Reports from Tewæno via Ruth Choisser [notes by c peeke]," excerpts from August 28 to September 15, 1969, Peeke Papers; Ethel Emily Wallis, *Aucas Downriver: Daymua's Story Today* (New York: Harper & Row, 1973), 94–100; *Unstilled Voices*, 172–77; *Fishers of Men*, 297. Specific dates vary by a day or two in these accounts, but all agree the first case was reported between August 30 and September 2, 1969.

44. "Reports from Tewæno," Peeke Papers.

45. Kingsland, *SAS*, 130. No cases of polio were ever documented among the missionary community prior to the outbreak.

46. Lindskoog to Ben Elson and Dale Kietzman, September 20, 1969, "Auca History 1956–1969" Folder, EBC-SIL.

47. Ibid.

48. "People of Forest," 110–11; James Yost, interview with author, March 15, 2001, Wheaton, IL.

49. R. Saint to Dave Osterhouse, Lloyd and Linda Rogers, and Frank and Martha Kollinger, October 15, 1969, Peeke Papers.

50. JY field notes, August 22, 1975, Yost Papers.

51. Saint to Osterhouse et al., October 15, 1969, Peeke Papers.

52. The unsubstantiated poisoning story came from one of the sons of Mincaye and implicated Dayomæ. Cabodevilla, *LH*, 400–401.

53. Kingsland, *SAS*, 129.

54. "Rage, Revenge, Religion," 484.

55. *Unstilled Voices*, 175.

56. [R. Saint], "COPY from R. Saint, around Dec. 1, 1969," single-page copy of excerpts from letters and reports by Saint on polio epidemic and decision of Baiwa's group to leave Tewæno, Peeke Papers. Unattributed comment among quotations by Saint probably from Lindskoog.

57. Peeke, interview with author.

58. Peeke to Kelley, January 21, 1970, Peeke Papers.

59. Lindskoog to Elson and Kietzman, September 20, 1969, EBC-SIL.

60. Ibid.

61. Wallis, *Aucas Downriver*, 82–83. Oncaye and Dawa were involved, in part because Wepe was Oncaye's father, and Dawa's sister Cawo was there.

62. "Toñæ Wodi's [the late Toñæ's] last note," trans. R. Saint or Peeke, n.d., Peeke Papers.

63. Wallis, *Aucas Downriver*, 104.

64. There were other instances when Tewæno Waorani attempted to contact relatives they had not seen since they were small children and their identities were questioned, especially if the Waorani wore Western clothing.

65. Wallis, *Aucas Downriver*, 120; "Rage, Revenge, Religion," 483.

66. Peeke to R. Saint, September 12, 1970, Peeke Papers.

67. Ibid.

CHAPTER 10

1. The extent to which Saint may have pressured the Baiwaidi to return is unclear. She certainly moved heaven and earth, including the Baiwaidi and oil workers, to organize a complicated evacuation (eight trips by oil company helicopter to airlift the group to the Curaray River, two days'

travel in motorized canoes, followed by a second airlift). Peeke to "Dear Lois," January 26, 1971, Peeke Papers.

2. "Ecuador Praise and Prayer," prayer newsletters, December 1970 and January 1971, EBC-SIL.

3. Johnson, "Ecuador Branch Report, Corporation Conference 1971," "E.C. [Executive Committee] Minutes (Ecuador)—Highlights," folder, EBC/SIL.

4. Jerry Bledsoe, "Saint," *Esquire*, July 1972, 127; see also "Warlike Aucas Now Preach Peace," *Milwaukee Sentinel*, March 27, 1971; "Killer of Missionary Changed," *Daily Northwestern* [Oshkosh, WI], March 18, 1971.

5. Townsend to Clyde Taylor, March 13, 1968, TA#26169.

6. Townsend to Ethel Wallis, March 16, 1968, TA#26142.

7. Townsend to Frank Sherrill and Mel Graham, April 13, 1971, TA#28325.

8. Bledsoe, "Saint," 128.

9. Peeke to R. Saint, September 12, 1970, "Auca Contact History 1970–1980" Folder, EBC-SIL.

10. *Unstilled Voices*, 188.

11. World Council of Churches Programme to Combat Racism, "Declaration of Barbados," January 30, 1971, https://www.iwgia.org/images/publications//0110_01Barbados.pdf, 3.

12. Ibid., 5–6.

13. Bledsoe, "Saint," 147, 127.

14. Laurie Hart, "Pacifying the Last Frontiers: Story of the Wycliffe Translators," *NACLA's Latin America & Empire Report* 7, no. 10 (1973): 15–31. For the Waorani, see 25. See also Brady Tyson, "NACLA as Coalition," *NACLA Newsletter*, March 1967, 4.

15. Todd Hartch, *Missionaries of the State: The Summer Institute of Linguistics, State Formation, and Indigenous Mexico, 1935–1985* (Tuscaloosa: University of Alabama Press, 2006), 147. For an in-depth discussion of anti-SIL sentiment among anthropologists, in Mexico and more broadly, see Hartch, chapter 10.

16. Hart, "Pacifying the Last Frontiers," 15. Like almost everyone at the time, Hart conflated the Wycliffe Bible Translators and the Summer Institute of Linguistics.

17. Hartch, *Missionaries of the State*, 159–60. My research on SIL in Ecuador supports Hartch's conclusion.

18. *North American Protestant Ministries Overseas*, 9th ed. (Monrovia, CA: MARC, 1970), 156.

19. Bill Eddy, "Event: Bill tells Rachel Saint about latest oil company plans for exploring Auca territory," form letter to constituency in US, February 1971, "Auca Correspondence—Oil" Folder, EBC-SIL.

20. Fred B. Morris to Wycliffe Bible Translators, April 25, 1971, "Auca Correspondence—Oil" Folder, EBC-SIL, used with permission; Gay Schenck to Johnson, November 15, 1972, "Auca Contact History 1970–1980" Folder, EBC-SIL.

21. Benjamin R. Elson to Fred B. Morris, May 5, 1971, "Auca Contact History 1970–1980" Folder, EBC-SIL.

22. Lindskoog to Gay Schenck, December 1, 1972, "Auca Contact History 1970–1980" Folder, EBC-SIL.

23. Ibid. (emphasis Lindskoog's).

24. Peeke to Libba [her sister, Elizabeth Peeke], July 12, 1971, Peeke Papers.

25. Erwin Patzelt, *Los Huaorani: Los Ultimos Hijos Libres del Jaguar* [The Waorani: The last free children of the jaguar] (Quito: Banco Central del Ecuador, 2002), 22–23.

26. Ibid., 26 (translation mine).

27. Peeke to Dan and Ruth Choisser et al., September 20, 1971, Peeke Papers; Patzelt, *Los Huaorani*, 26–27. Peeke's and Patzelt's accounts differ on the date of the encounter and on whether Sam Padilla was present, but both agree that Peeke was angry to find Patzelt with the Waorani.

28. Patzelt, *Los Huaorani*, 30.

29. Quoted in ibid.

30. Peeke, "Frases en el Idioma Auca," *TS*, n.d., "Auca Contact History 1970–1980" Folder, EBC-SIL; Lindskoog, "Auca Work Strategy," memorandum, March 19, 1973, "Auca Contact History 1970–1980" Folder, EBC-SIL.

31. Peeke to R. Saint, March 25, 1972, Peeke Papers; Johnson to Townsend, November 29, 1971, "Auca Contact History 1970–1980" Folder, EBC-SIL.

32. Peeke to R. Saint, April 9, 1972, Peeke Papers.

33. Johnson to Townsend, November 29, 1971, EBC-SIL.

34. Erwin Patzelt, *Libre como el jaguar: Los Aucas y su enigmático mundo* [Free like the jaguar: The aucas and their enigmatic world] (Quito: Editorial Las Casas, 1976), 71–73. This version was also included in Patzelt's 2002 photo book, *Los Huaorani*, 117–18.

35. See, e.g., Gerard Colby and Charlotte Dennett, *Thy Will Be Done: The Conquest of the Amazon: Nelson Rockefeller and Evangelism in the Age of Oil* (New York: HarperCollins, 1995), 289–90; also, *Fishers of Men*, 306, for Patzelt's role in the accusations. Wao accounts that mention Nampa suggest that the bullet that hit him was part of a struggle and not the kind of cold-blooded killing Patzelt claimed.

36. Patzelt, *Los Huaorani*.

37. Peeke to Peter B. Ostlund, January 3, 1971 [1972], Peeke Papers; Peeke, "Auca Report, Ecuador Branch Conference, March 1972" [draft], Peeke Papers. For Patzelt's account of "the kidnapping of the Wepe family," see *Los Huaorani*, 35. I have found no evidence to support this story.

38. Peeke to Saint, April 9, 1972, Peeke Papers.

39. Peter Baumann and Erwin Patzelt, *Menschen im Regenwald: Expedition Auka* [Man in the rainforest: Expedition auca] (Düsseldorf: Droste, 1975), 96; Cabodevilla, *LH*, 399. One incident reported by Saint in 1966—two years before Wiñame arrived in Tewæno—might have played into the "mission prison" idea. According to Saint, Gomoque, a young Wao woman, attacked Dayomæ while Dayomæ was alone with two small children in her manioc garden. Dayomæ was beaten severely around the head with a thick manioc stalk. Her husband, Come, later found Gomoque, administered his own beating, and tied her up. A few hours later Saint untied Gomoque and lectured her about what she had done. Based on Saint's account, the conflict was between Waorani and provoked by Gomoque. See R. Saint to Lindskoog, January 24, 1966, "Auca History 1956–1969" Folder, EBC-SIL.

40. Peeke, "Introduction to Auca Report 1972" [draft], Peeke Papers.

41. [R. Saint], "COPY from R. Saint, around Dec. 1, 1969." Other Waorani who left described Tewæno as a "place of death." Cabodevilla, *LH*, 393.

42. Cabodevilla, *LH*, 403–4. Wiñame was a widow with a daughter when Dayomæ invited her to Tewæno. Traditionally consent from either party was not a prerequisite for Waorani marriages.

43. Peeke to Saint, March 25, 1972, Peeke Papers.

44. Kelley, "Auca Literacy Report, Ecuador Branch 1973," "Auca Contact History 1970–1980" Folder, EBC-SIL.

45. Patricia M. Kelley, "Appendix A: Summary of Literacy Materials," in "Literacy Materials," 133. Copies of literacy booklets available in SIL Language and Culture Archives.

46. "Literacy Materials," 57.

47. R. Saint to [Peeke], November 22, 1972, Peeke Papers.

48. "Twenty Years," 701.

49. "Literacy Materials," 54.

50. Peeke, "Introduction to Auca Report 1972," Peeke Papers.

51. Peeke to "Dear Friends," January 1972, Peeke Papers.

52. Peeke, ". . . and the blind see," *TS*, n.d., Peeke Papers.

53. R. Saint to George [no surname], February 16, 1973, Peeke Papers.

54. *Daibæidi* in the Wao language means "the clay group," referring to the images the Catholics made and used. James A. Yost, note to author, March 30, 2015.

55. Saint to [Peeke], November 22, 1972, Peeke Papers.

56. Lindskoog, "Auca Work Strategy," March 19, 1973, EBC-SIL.

57. Ibid. (emphasis Lindskoog's).

58. Ibid.

CHAPTER 11

1. Thomas N. Headland, SIL International, email to author, December 12, 2011.

2. James A. Yost, interview with author, March 15, 2001, Wheaton, IL.

3. Ibid.; James A. Yost, conversation with author, March 30, 2015, Wheaton, IL.

4. Yost family [James A. Yost, Kathie Yost, and Rachelle Yost Dell], joint interview with author, May 5, 2005, Kremmling, CO.

5. Ibid. Yost kept handwritten field notes in small notebooks any time he was with the Waorani. An assistant at SIL later made a typed copy of notes written between December 1973 and September 1979, plus the listing of the 1980 Wao census. All subsequent citations to the Yost field notes (hereafter JY field notes) are from this typescript, James A. Yost Papers, private collection, copy in author's possession (Yost Papers).

6. Yost family, joint interview.

7. Ibid.

8. Ibid.

9. Ibid.

10. Ibid.

11. JY field notes, March 15, 1974, Yost Papers.

12. JY field notes, October 31, 1975, August 12, 1974, Yost Papers. All quotations from Yost notes used with permission.

13. JY field notes, January 28, 1974, Yost Papers.

14. James A. Yost, personal notes (handwritten), February 22, 1974, Yost Papers.

15. James A. Yost in Yost family, joint interview.

16. James A. Yost, interview with author, May 2, 2005, Kremmling, CO.

17. JY field notes, October 16, 1974, Yost Papers.

18. JY field notes, July 29, 1974, Yost Papers.

19. JY field notes, August 18, 1975, Yost Papers (emphasis Yost's).

20. Ibid. (emphasis Yost's).

21. Peter Baumann and Erwin Patzelt, *Menschen im Regenwald: Expedition Auka* (Düsseldorf: Droste, 1975); other books included Erwin Patzelt, *Libre como el jaguar: Los Aucas y su enigmático mundo* (Quito: Editorial Las Casas, 1976) and Karl Dieter Gartelmann, *El Mundo Perdido de los Aucas* [The lost world of the aucas] ([Quito]: Imprinta Mariscal, 1977).

22. Pat Kelley, interview with author, August 10, 2004, Dallas, TX.

23. I am indebted to Sarah Miglio for this insight, identifying it as a form of Orientalism.

24. JY field notes, September 7, 1975, Yost Papers.

25. JY field notes, August 14, 1974, Yost Papers.

26. JY field notes, January 6, 1974, Yost Papers.

27. JY field notes, June 16, 1974, Yost Papers.

28. James A. Yost and Patricia M. Kelley, "Shotguns, Blowguns, and Spears: The Analysis of Technological Efficiency," in *Adaptive Responses of Native Amazonians*, ed. Raymond B. Hames and William T. Vickers (New York: Academic Press, 1983), 193.

29. JY field notes, September 18, 1975, Yost Papers.

30. JY field notes, December 21, 1975, Yost Papers.

31. James A. Yost, conversation with author, March 31, 2015, Wheaton, IL.

32. JY field notes, July 14, 1974, Yost Papers.

33. Yost, interview, May 2, 2005.

34. Yost, "Preliminary Reactions to Auca Situation: Report for the Director of Ecuador, Not for distribution or publication," April 8, 1974, "Auca Contact History 1970–1980" Folder, EBC-SIL. Used with permission.

35. Ibid.

36. Ibid.

37. Ibid.

38. R. Saint to Peeke, April 27, 1974, Peeke Papers (emphasis Saint's).

39. Ibid.

40. R. Saint to Lindskoog, December 31, 1974, Yost Papers.

41. Peeke to R. Saint, June 1, 1974, Yost Papers.

42. Ibid.

43. Lindskoog to Auca team members, May 30, 1974, Yost Papers.

44. Ibid.

45. Dayomæ to Lindskoog [tape-recorded report re: spearing at Chapana, translated and summarized by Peeke], October 10, 1974, and Yost to Lindskoog, October 10, 1974, both in "Auca Contact History 1970–1980" Folder, EBC-SIL.

CHAPTER 12

1. Johnson to Townsend, June 14, 1962, TA#21819.

2. Peeke to Lindskoog, July 13, 1975, Peeke Papers.

3. Lindskoog to Townsend, January 19, 1968, TA#26443.

4. Jim Yost, telephone interview with author, March 26, 2001.

5. See, e.g., P. Curtine, "Does Billy [Graham] Approve?," *Universal Challenger*, October 1967, 8–9.

6. R. Saint to the Auca team, director, and present EC [Executive Committee], January 25, 1975, Yost Papers.

7. Rosi Jung, interview with author, June 18, 2009, Holzhausen, Germany.

8. Yost, personal notes, February 22, 1974, Yost Papers.

9. JY field notes, February 7, 1974, Yost Papers.

10. JY field notes, February 12, 1974, Yost Papers.

11. Saint to Auca team et al., January 25, 1975, Yost Papers.

12. JY field notes, March 17, 1974, Yost Papers.

13. James Yost, interview with author, May 2, 2005, Kremmling, CO. By the early 1970s Dayomæ and Dawa each received a modest monthly stipend from North American supporters of SIL's work among the Waorani. Although the amount was never large, no other Waorani had access to US dollars.

14. JY field notes, February 2, 1974, Yost Papers.

15. JY field notes, January 13, 1974, March 3, 1974, Yost Papers.

16. JY field notes, February 19, 1974, Yost Papers.

17. JY field notes, March 3, 1974, Yost Papers.

18. Yost, personal notes, February 22, 1974, Yost Papers.

19. JY field notes, February 24, 1974; see also entries for January 6 and 13, 1974, Yost Papers.

20. JY field notes, June 6, August 4, and August 11, 1974, Yost Papers.

21. "Twenty Years," 695.

22. Jim Yost, comment to author, May 5, 2005, Kremmling, CO.

23. "Excerpts from Rachel Saint's letter of January 31, 1974," TA#31190.

24. R. Saint to Peeke, July 7, 1974, Peeke Papers.

25. JY field notes, November 4, 1975, Yost Papers.

26. Ibid. (emphasis Yost's).

27. Lindskoog to Yost, May 17, 1974, Yost Papers.

28. Ibid.

29. Saint to Peeke, July 7, 1974, Peeke Papers, refers to a letter.

30. Ibid.

31. Saint to Auca team et al., January 25, 1975, Yost Papers.

32. Ibid.

33. Peeke to R. Saint, March 20, 1975, Yost Papers.

34. Ibid.

35. R. Saint to Lindskoog, December 31, 1974, Peeke Papers.

36. JY field notes, May 14, 1975, October 24, 1975, Yost Papers.

37. Kingsland, SAS, 134–35; Peeke to Judy Maxwell, January 14, 1973, Peeke Papers.

38. R. Saint, "Auca Report," June 13, 1975, "Auca Contact History 1970–1980" Folder, EBC-SIL.

39. Lindskoog, "The Auca Situation Today," January 1976, "Auca Contact History 1970–1980" Folder, EBC-SIL.

40. [Lindskoog], "After 20 Years . . . 1956–1976," news release, n.d., "Auca Contact History 1970–1980" Folder, EBC-SIL.

41. Lindskoog to "Inquirers re: Auca Supplement," January 8, 1976, "Auca Contact History 1970–1980" Folder, EBC-SIL.

42. Clarence Church to Lindskoog [re: Auca Situation], April 21, 1976, Yost Papers.

43. Yost to Clarence Church, April 30, 1976, Yost Papers.

44. Lindskoog to Clarence Church, May 5, 1976, "Auca Contact History 1970–1980" Folder, EBC-SIL.

45. Jim Yost, interview with author, March 15, 2001, Wheaton, IL.

46. Yost, interview, May 2, 2005.

47. Kelley to Lindskoog, January 8, 1975, Peeke Papers. Kelley questioned the effectiveness of this approach.

48. Bill Eddy to R. Saint, June 28, 1976, Yost Papers.

49. Johnson to R. Saint, February 20, 1977, Yost Papers.

50. This at least was Saint's understanding of Johnson's decision. See R. Saint to Peeke, January 16, 1978, Peeke Papers. Peeke to John and Carrie Lindskoog and Wao team, June 11, 1976, Yost Papers, noted the ongoing conflicts between Rachel and Dayomæ.

51. Phil Saint to "Brothers and Sisters in Christ involved in the work among the Aucas," December 17, 1975, Yost Papers; R. Saint to Peeke, December 24, 1980, Peeke Papers.

52. Board Committee on Personnel, SIL, Inc., typed summary of committee motion/decision, November 5, 1980, Yost Papers. Apparently the governing board for the US Division of SIL supported the decision the next year. Bernie May to Jerry Elder, July 16, 1981, Yost Papers.

53. Yost, interview, March 26, 2001.

54. *La viejita que rejuvenecio, El Fracaso de la Búsqueda de la Fuente de la Juventud: Leyenda auca según la versión del Tío Giquita, or The Old Woman Who Became Young Again, The Lost Quest for the Fountain of Youth: An Auca legend as Told by Uncle Gikita*, trans. Rachel Saint and Walter del Aguila (Ecuador: Summer Institute of Linguistics, 1975), https://www.sil.org/resources/ archives/48248; *Auca Childbirth Legend, as Told by Uncle Gikita, or Leyenda de Cómo Nacen los Niños Aucas, Según la versión del Tío [sic] Gikita*, trans. Rachel Saint and Hortensia Balarezo (Ecuador: Summer Institute of Linguistics, 1975), https://www.sil.org/resources/archives/ 52660; *Los Aucas y los canibales: Como Llegaron los Aucas al Ecuador, Según la versión del Tío [sic] Gikita, or Aucas and Cannibals: How the Aucas Came to Ecuador, as Told by Uncle Gikita*, trans. Rachel Saint and Eudofilia Arboleda Reyes (Oklahoma: Summer Institute of Linguistics, 1964), https://www.sil.org/resources/archives/56861. Saint translated from Wao to English; the other translator from English to Spanish.

55. James A. Yost, "Community Development and Ethnic Survival: The Wao Case" (paper presented, Community Development for Minority Language Groups symposium at the Society for Applied Anthropology, Mérida, Yucatán, Mexico, April 1978), 7, Yost Papers; Yost, interview, March 26, 2001; Saint to Peeke, July 7, 1974, Peeke Papers.

56. JY field notes, September 15, 1975, Yost Papers.

57. For an example of this sort of characterization, see Wade Davis, *One River: Explorations and Discoveries in the Amazon Rain Forest* (New York: Simon & Schuster, 1996), 288, where he describes Rachel as having "built a little empire in the forest."

58. Yost, interview, March 26, 2001.

59. According to Pat Kelley, one SIL official went so far as to describe Saint's impact on her coworkers as "devastating." See Kelley to Peeke, n.d. [probably 1977], Peeke Papers.

CHAPTER 13

1. David E. Weaver, "Transforming Universities: The Expediency of Interculturality for Indigenous Superior Education in Ecuador" (master's thesis, Tulane University, 2008), 39–40, ProQuest (#1455699).

2. *Fishers of Men*, 298, paraphrasing economist Fernando Velasco.

3. Ibid.; Lindskoog, "The Report of the Ecuador Branch to the International Conference 1975," "Various Branch Reports 1960–1993" Folder, EBC-SIL.

4. Lindskoog, "Report of the Ecuador Branch," EBC-SIL.

5. Roy Armes, *Third World Film Making and the West* (Berkeley: University of California Press, 1987), 304.

6. Thomas Waugh, "Ecuador: *¡Fuera de Aquí!*," in *South American Cinema: A Critical Filmography, 1915–1994*, ed. Timothy Barnard and Peter Rist (New York: Garland, 1996), 266.

7. Franklin Barriga López, *Las Culturas Indígenas Ecuatorianas y el Instituto Lingüístico de Verano* (Buenos Aires: Ediciones Amauta, 1992), 294.

8. Ibid., 293–95.

9. James W. Larrick et al., "Patterns of Health and Disease among the Waorani Indians of Eastern Ecuador," *Medical Anthropology* 3, no. 2 (1979): 147–89, especially 176, 181.

10. James A. Yost and Patricia M. Kelley, *Consideraciones Culturales del Terreno: El Caso Huaorani* [Cultural considerations of land: The case of the Waorani], Cuadernos Etnolingüísticos, no. 20 (Quito: Instituto Lingüístico de Verano, 1992), 17, http://www.sil.org/resources/archives/17550.

11. John Perkins, *Confessions of an Economic Hit Man* (New York: Plume, 2006), 167. I found no evidence that SIL ever caused a "diarrhea epidemic," one of the most far-fetched rumors about the organization.

12. Bertha Fuentes C., *Huaomoni, Huarani, Cowudi: Una aproximación a los Huaorani en la práctica multi-étnica ecuatoriana* [Us, others, outsiders: An approach to the Waorani in multi-ethnic Ecuadorian political practice] (Quito: Ediciones Abya-Yala, 1997), 172–73.

13. Ibid., 170.

14. Todd Hartch, *Missionaries of the State: The Summer Institute of Linguistics, State Formation, and Indigenous Mexico, 1935–1985* (Tuscaloosa: University of Alabama Press, 2006), 150–51.

15. Philip Harnden, "Today's Wycliffe Version," *The Other Side*, May 1977, 5.

16. Ethel Emily Wallis, "Sharper Than Any Two-Edged Spear," *In Other Words*, January 1976, 4–5.

17. Harnden, "Today's Wycliffe Version," 29, 47–48.

18. Yost, newsletter to supporters, April 2, 1977, Yost Papers; see also Larrick et al., "Patterns of Health," 175.

19. Sol Tax, "Action Anthropology," *Current Anthropology* 16, no. 4 (1975): 515.

20. James A. Yost, "Community Development and Ethnic Survival: The Wao Case" (paper presented, Community Development for Minority Language Groups symposium at the Society for Applied Anthropology, Mérida, Yucatán, Mexico, April 1978), 8, Yost Papers.

21. Yost, newsletter to supporters, February 1980, Yost Papers.

22. Yost, "Community Development," 8.

23. This study is reported in four published articles: Larrick et al., "Patterns of Health," 147–89; Jonathan E. Kaplan et al., "Infectious Disease Patterns in the Waorani, an Isolated Amerindian Population," *American Journal of Tropical Medicine and Hygiene* 29, no. 2 (1980): 298–312; James W. Larrick, James A. Yost, and Jon Kaplan, "Snake Bite among the Waorani Indians of Eastern Ecuador," *Transactions of the Royal Society of Tropical Medicine and Hygiene* 72, no. 5 (1978): 542–43; Jonathan E. Kaplan, James W. Larrick, and James A. Yost, "Workup on the Waorani," *Natural History*, September 1984, 68–74. The first two essays are more technical and detailed, the third is a summary of research on snakebite, and "Workup on

the Waorani" is accessible to a popular audience. Decades later the study was invoked to support accusations of imperialist subjugation and of identifying the Waorani as the "Other" on
the part of the researchers and SIL. This was seen as a first step toward later, unrelated research
by scientists with no connection to SIL that critics have considered "biopiracy." See Hanna
Dahlstrom, "God, Oil, and the Theft of Waorani DNA: A Tale of Biopiracy in Ecuador," *Upside
Down World*, November 8, 2012, http://upsidedownworld.org/main/ecuador-archives-49/
3961-god-oil-and-the-theft-of-waorani-dna-a-tale-of-biopiracy-from-ecuador.

24. Larrick et al., "Patterns of Health," 151; Kaplan, Larrick, and Yost, "Workup on the
Waorani," 70–71, 73.

25. Larrick et al., "Patterns of Health," 162; Kaplan, Larrick, and Yost, "Workup on the
Waorani," 70.

26. Kaplan, Larrick, and Yost, "Workup on the Waorani," 70; Larrick et al., "Patterns of
Health," 179.

27. Larrick et al., "Patterns of Health," 175.

28. Ibid.; Clayton Robarchek and Carole Robarchek, *Waorani: The Contexts of Violence and
War* (Fort Worth, TX: Harcourt Brace, 1998), 79.

29. Larrick et al., "Patterns of Health," 173.

30. SIL staff charged full price for small items, half price for more expensive medicines, and
only a small percentage for the costly but much needed antivenin serum and for medical flights
and hospitalization. Older people and newcomers were not expected to pay. Peeke, "Wao Tribe
Report, Conference, 1976," Peeke Papers.

31. Yost to Peeke and Kelley, October 11, 1979, Peeke Papers.

32. Peeke to director, Executive Committee, [and] Wao tribal workers, September 20, 1976,
Peeke Papers.

33. Peeke, "Wao Report to Conference, 1977, Linguistic and Medical Supplement," Peeke
Papers.

34. Peeke to Yost, October 22, 1979, Yost Papers. Donations to SIL for the Waorani regularly
went to the almost always depleted Wao medical fund.

35. Kaplan, Larrick, and Yost, "Workup on the Waorani," 74.

36. Larrick et al., "Patterns of Health," 165.

37. Ibid., 160. Some 93 percent of those examined had received measles vaccine, a finding that
raised questions in light of the subsequent measles epidemic.

38. Kaplan et al., "Infectious Disease Patterns," 310; Larrick et al., "Patterns of Health," 168–72.

39. Kelley, Peeke, Jim and Kathie Yost, "Waorani Report 1980: Communication, Health,
Translation," Peeke Papers; also "Report to Administration, Waodani [*sic*] Tribe—October 1980,"
"Various Branch Reports 1960–1993" Folder, EBC-SIL. Most potential paramedics completed
three ten-day courses in basic healthcare; others had received some prior training by Saint or Jung.

40. Peeke, "Ecuador Praise and Prayer," October 1980, "Praise and Prayer—Ecuador," EBC-SIL.

41. Jim and Kathie Yost, newsletter, November 21, 1976, Yost Papers; JY field notes, July 5, 1976,
July 5, 1979, Yost Papers; Lois Pederson to Peeke, May 30, 1979, Peeke Papers.

42. Kelley to Peeke and Kathie and Jim Yost, April 3, 1978, Peeke Papers.

43. This account abridged from Kelley, "Wentæ's Story," March 1978, copies in both Peeke
Papers and Yost Papers.

44. "Report to Administration," EBC-SIL.

45. "Waodani (Auca) Tribal Report, Ecuador Branch Conference for January–December 1978," "Various Branch Reports 1960–1993" Folder, EBC-SIL.

46. Kelley to Peeke, August 23, 1978, Peeke Papers.

47. Both Tañe and Gaba lost sight in one eye—and Tañe the eye itself—because the cheaply made shotguns malfunctioned. See "Tañe," n.d., Peeke Papers. For Gaba, see Kelley to Peeke, August 29, 1980, Peeke Papers. Cogui lost two fingers and an eye in a dynamite accident. Kelley to Peeke and R. Saint, August 18, 1974, Peeke Papers.

48. Larrick, Yost, and Kaplan, "Snake Bite," 542. About 45 percent of all Waorani had been bitten at least once.

49. Ibid.

50. *Kinsman*, 102.

51. Kelley to Peeke, April 24, 1977, Peeke Papers; Rosi Jung, interview with author, June 18, 2009, Holzhausen, Germany.

52. Larrick et al., "Patterns of Health," 180.

CHAPTER 14

1. Daan Vreugdenhil, telephone interview with author, August 8, 2008. The Spanish name of the Ecuadorian agency was Departamento de Parques Nacionales y Vida Silvestre. See also Allen D. Putney et al., *Fortalecimiento del Servicio Forestal, Ecuador: Informe Final* [Strengthening the Forestry Service, Ecuador: Final report], unpublished report (Quito, February 1976), http://www.birdlist.org/downloads/parks/estrategia_conservacion_areas_silvestres_sobresalientes_ecuador.pdf.

2. Office de la Recherche Scientifique et Technique d'Outre-Mer (ORSTOM) is today known as the IRD, the French Research Institute for Development.

3. Peeke, "Report re: Huao [*sic*] territory," February 17, 1976, *TS*, Peeke Papers; Vreugdenhil, interview, August 8, 2008.

4. James A. Yost, "Community Development and Ethnic Survival: The Wao Case" (paper presented, Community Development for Minority Language Groups symposium at the Society for Applied Anthropology, Mérida, Yucatán, Mexico, April 1978), 2–3, Yost Papers.

5. Joe Kane, "With Spears from all Sides," *New Yorker*, September 27, 1983, 63; Douglass Southgate, Robert Wasserstrom, and Susan Reider, "Oil Development, Deforestation, and Indigenous Populations in the Ecuadorian Amazon" (paper presented, Latin American Studies Association, Rio de Janeiro, Brazil, June 11–14, 2009), 2–3, http://www.theamazonpost.com/wp-content/uploads/Southgate_Wasserstrom_Reider_LASA_2009.pdf. Southgate, Wasserstrom, and Reider argue that the influx of settlers into the Ecuadorian Amazon was a direct result of pro-colonization government policies and government support of infrastructure development, especially roads.

6. James A. Yost and Patricia M. Kelley, *Consideraciones Culturales del Terreno: El Caso Huaorani*, Cuadernos Etnolingüísticos, no. 20 (Quito: Instituto Lingüístico de Verano, 1992), 8–10, http://www.sil.org/resources/archives/17550.

7. Ibid., 9, 13.

8. Ibid., 13.

9. "People of Forest," 107.

10. Yost and Kelley, *Consideraciones Culturales*, 18–19. The potential for flooding continues to the present.

11. William T. Vickers, "Indian Policy in Amazonian Ecuador," in *Frontier Expansion in Amazonia*, ed. Marianne Schmink and Charles H. Wood (Gainesville: University of Florida Press, 1984), 10, 25. The Spanish name was Comisión Interinstitucional del Ministerio de Agricultura y Ganadería, although it was sometimes called the Comisión Asesora Interinstitucional de Asuntos Nativos (Interinstitutional Advisory Commission for Indigenous Affairs).

12. Yost, no salutation, form letter, December 31, 1980, Yost Papers; Vickers, "Indian Policy," 25; Bertha Fuentes C., *Huaomoni, Huarani, Cowudi: Una aproximación a los Huaorani en la práctica política multi-étnica ecuatoriana* (Quito: Ediciones Abya-Yala, 1997), 208.

13. Kelley to Yost, February 22, [1980], "Team Correspondence" Folder, Yost Papers; Peeke to Glen D. Turner, Yost, November 17, 1978, "Team Correspondence" Folder, Yost Papers; and Peeke to Yost, Turner, and Walter del Aguila, November 21, 1978, Peeke Papers.

14. [Peeke], "Noted in Passing," typed reflections sent to Yost per handwritten name, Summer 1983, "Team Correspondence" Folder, Yost Papers; also Peeke, "My report . . . re Waodani Land Grant," April 29, 1983, "Wao Committees—Land" Folder, Yost Papers.

15. Lawrence Ziegler-Otero, *Resistance in an Amazonian Community: Huaorani Organizing against the Global Economy* (New York: Berghahn Books, 2004), 88.

16. Southgate, Wasserstrom, and Reider, "Oil Development," 2.

17. Come Yete et al. to Enrique Vela [transcript of letter in English], n.d., Yost Papers.

18. "Literacy Materials," 23.

19. Ibid., 40, citing an assessment by James A. Yost in Barbara F. Grimes, "Comprehension and Language Attitudes in Relation to Language Choice for Literature and Education in Pre-literate Societies," *Journal of Multilingual and Multicultural Development* 6, no. 2 (1985): 180.

20. David Miller and Marilyn Miller, interview with author, January 6, 2007, Rome, GA.

21. Ibid.

22. Ibid. Despite Miller's confidence in Spanish-only instruction, it was not easy. See Kelley to Peeke and Lois Pederson, March 12, [1974], Peeke Papers.

23. Lloyd Rogers, "Shell [Ecuador]," prayer calendar report for Day 25, *Christian Missions in Many Lands* [Plymouth Brethren magazine], December 1978, 6. Lloyd Rogers used the name Daniel in Ecuador because Spanish speakers had difficulty pronouncing "Lloyd." However, Rogers used his actual name in his written correspondence and in communication with English speakers.

24. Lloyd Rogers and Linda Rogers, interview with author, March 18, 2006, Wheaton, IL.

25. "Report to Administration, Waodani [*sic*] Tribe—October 1980," "Various Branch Reports 1960–1993" Folder, EBC-SIL.

26. Peeke to Lloyd Rogers, Wao team, Glen Turner, and Technical Affairs Department, "Further thoughts re Meeting regarding Toñampare [*sic*] School," September 27, 1979, "Team Correspondence" Folder, Yost Papers; [Unsigned SIL staff] to Lloyd Rogers, October 11, 1979, "Team Correspondence" Folder, Yost Papers. It is not clear why Dayomæ pushed out her own daughter.

27. "Report to Administration," EBC-SIL; Yost, "Census [Wao] 1980," from JY field notes, Yost Papers.

28. Kelley to Yost (Wadeca), n.d., "Team Correspondence" Folder, Yost Papers; "Report to Administration," EBC-SIL; "Waorani Tribe Report, Conference 1980," Peeke Papers.

29. "Literacy Materials," 47.

30. Ibid., 49.

31. For a nuanced discussion of *Wao tededo* as a language better suited to a phonemic rather than a phonetic orthography, see ibid., 47–51.

32. [Peeke], "Noted in Passing," Yost Papers. The SIL team did use the Spanish alphabet for official documents, such as Wao names on national identity cards and birth certificates. Kelley to Lloyd Rogers, n.d., "Team Correspondence" Folder, Yost Papers.

33. "Literacy Materials," 51.

34. Ibid., 54, 61, 133.

35. Ibid., 59–60. For the aquatic life booklet, see www.sil.org/resources/archives/10386.

36. This account is from "Literacy Materials," 24.

37. Kelley to Walter del Aguila, February 12, 1980, "Team Correspondence" Folder, Yost Papers.

38. Ibid.

39. Ibid.

40. Kelley's classes were criticized because students did not attend all day. Kelley to Peeke, February 24, 1974, Peeke Papers.

41. Laura Rival, *Trekking through History: The Huaorani of Amazonian Ecuador* (New York: Columbia University Press, 2002), 154.

42. "Report to Administration," EBC-SIL.

43. For more on Olga and on Zoila Wiñame, see Cabodevilla, *LH*, 398–99, 403–5, 409n52; "Twenty Years," 682.

44. Peeke to Ruth Shalanko, September 24, 1982, "Team Correspondence" Folder, Yost Papers; "Twenty Years," 682; JY field notes, March 14, 1974, Yost Papers.

45. Dayomæ to Lindskoog [tape-recorded report re: spearing at Chapana, translated and summarized by Peeke], October 10, 1974, and Yost to Lindskoog, October 10, 1974, both in "Auca Contact History 1970–1980" Folder, EBC-SIL; Peeke to Wao team director, November 6, 1974, "Team Correspondence" Folder, Yost Papers.

46. Yost to Lindskoog, October 10, 1974, EBC-SIL.

47. JY field notes, October 29, 1974, Yost Papers; Peeke to R. Saint, October 20, 1974, Peeke Papers.

48. JY field notes, January 30, 1974, February 8, 1974, July 18, 1974, April 6, 1976, April 7, 1976, Yost Papers; Kelley to Peeke and Pederson, March 12, [1974], Peeke Papers.

49. JY field notes, September 16 and 17, 1975, Yost Papers; see also JY field notes, January 6, 1979, Yost Papers.

50. Peeke to Jim and Kathie Yost, February 28, 1980, "Team Correspondence" Folder, Yost Papers.

51. *Kinsman*, 100–101.

52. James A. Yost and Patricia M. Kelley, "Shotguns, Blowguns, and Spears: The Analysis of Technological Efficiency," in *Adaptive Responses of Native Amazonians*, ed. Raymond B. Hames and William T. Vickers (New York: Academic Press, 1983), 202.

53. Ibid., 191.

54. Ibid., 221.

55. Suzana Sawyer, *Crude Chronicles: Indigenous Politics, Multinational Oil, and Neoliberalism in Ecuador* (Durham, NC: Duke University Press, 2004), 65; JY field notes, January 6, 1979, Yost Papers.

56. JY field notes, July 28, 1974, September 18, 1975, Yost Papers.

57. JY field notes, July 29, 1974, Yost Papers.

58. JY field notes, August 14 and 31, 1975, Yost Papers.

59. Peeke, "Not as we expected . . . Auca Bible Conference 1975," newsletter report, Peeke Papers.

60. JY field notes, December 31, 1978, January 6, 1979, June 1, 1979, July 29, 1979, Yost Papers. The trend continued into the 1980s. "Report to Administration," EBC-SIL.

61. Soren Hvalkof and Peter Aaby, eds., *Is God an American? An Anthropological Perspective on the Missionary Work of the Summer Institute of Linguistics* (Copenhagen: International Work Group for Indigenous Affairs; London: Survival International, 1981).

62. JY field notes, March 27, 1976, Yost Papers (emphasis Yost's).

63. JY field notes, July 19, 1976, Yost Papers; Kelley to "Dear You All," September 12, 1977, Peeke Papers.

64. Allen Gerlach, *Indians, Oil, and Politics: A Recent History of Ecuador* (Wilmington, DE: Scholarly Resources, 2003), 8. In 1998, of the approximately 250 people in Toñæmpade, 45 percent were either Quichuas or part Quichua. Pat Kelley, email to author, December 16, 2016.

65. "Report to Administration," EBC-SIL.

66. Yost, "Waodani Report 1980: As of Summer 1980," Peeke Papers.

67. Peeke to Lloyd and Linda Rogers, March 18, 1981, "Team Correspondence" Folder, Yost Papers.

68. Yost, "Waodani Report 1980."

69. JY field notes, July 18, 1974, Yost Papers.

70. [Peeke], "Noted in Passing," Yost Papers.

71. Cabodevilla, *LH*, 411, fig. 390. Texaco was the primary oil producer between 1964 and 1992. Sawyer, *Crude Chronicles*, 13.

72. Sawyer, *Crude Chronicles*, 65.

73. Cabodevilla, *LH*, 414, 416–18; "Franceses suspenden trabajos petroleros en territorio auca" [French suspend petroleum work in auca territory], *El Comercio* (Quito), November 15, 1977.

CHAPTER 15

1. As indicated in the notes that follow, the story of Labaca and the Capuchín mission is based on several sources written by Labaca and fellow members of the Capuchín Order. These include Cabodevilla, *LH*; *Arriesgar la Vida*; *Crónica Huaorani*; and *Los Ultimos Huaorani*. All direct quotations are my translations. Biographical information about Labaca and background on the Capuchíns, a renewal order of missionary friars, historically an offshoot of the Franciscans, are from *Arriesgar la Vida*, 15, 22, 28, 31, 36, 42.

2. For a brief timeline of Labaca's life that differs slightly from Grández, see *Crónica Huaorani*, 11. For the boundaries of the prefecture, see *Arriesgar la Vida*, 83.

3. *Arriesgar la Vida*, 78.

4. *Ultimos Huaorani*, 219.

5. For more details on these efforts, see ibid., 65–70.

6. "Decree on the Missionary Activity of the Church: Vatican II, *Ad Gentes Divinitus*, 7 December, 1965," in *Documents of Vatican II*, ed. Austin P. Flannery (Grand Rapids, MI: William B. Eerdmans, 1975), chap. 2, art. I, para. 11; see also *Arriesgar la Vida*, 90.

7. *Arriesgar la Vida*, 96–97. Labaca's memory of the pope's words is quoted from *Crónica Huaorani*, 108.

8. *Arriesgar la Vida*, 97–98. The Cessna 185 later was traded for a Cessna 209, before the Capuchíns gave up their plane. *Ultimos Huaorani*, 76–77.

9. These Waorani were also known as the Piyæmoidi (Piyæmo's group).

10. *Ultimos Huaorani*, 77.

11. Cabodevilla, *LH*, 417.

12. *Crónica Huaorani*, 23.

13. Ibid.

14. Ibid., 27.

15. Ibid., 31.

16. Ibid., 32.

17. Ibid., 34.

18. Ibid., 26, 51, 145; see also Cabodevilla, *LH*, 420.

19. Labaca suggested this on numerous occasions and offered various ideas for its implementation. See, e.g., [Capuchín Monsignor Jesús Landarica Olagüe?], "Misioneros plantean medidas en defense de los indígenas auca" [Missionaries establish measures in defense of indigenous aucas], *El Comercio* (Quito), November 13, 1977, partially reprinted in *Crónica Huaorani*, 192, where Labaca is credited as the editor. Newspaper clipping of article in Peeke Papers.

20. *Crónica Huaorani*, 41.

21. Ibid., 42–44.

22. *Arriesgar la Vida*, 140, specifically makes the connection with St. Francis.

23. Ibid., 148. Sometimes Labaca was "Capitán Alex" or "Capitán Arex."

24. *Crónica Huaorani*, 58–59.

25. Ibid., 59–60.

26. Ibid., 67–68.

27. Ibid., 63–64.

28. Ibid., 37, 45, 68, 57.

29. A paraphrase of Romans 13:12.

30. *Crónica Huaorani*, 62.

31. Ibid., 69.

32. For examples, see ibid., 29, 57, 63, 157.

33. Ibid., 29.

34. Ibid., 57–58, 63, 150.

35. Ibid., 70.

36. Ibid., 64.

37. Ibid., 84; *Ultimos Huaorani*, 105.

38. *Ultimos Huaorani*, 88, 90; Cabodevilla, *LH*, 423–24; *Arriesgar la Vida*, 150. The names of the three slain workers were Segundo Ribera Proaño, Pablo Huarnizo, and Isaías Paredes.

39. *Ultimos Huaorani*, 111.

40. *Crónica Huaorani*, 88.

41. Clayton Robarchek and Carol Robarchek, *Waorani: The Contexts of Violence and War* (Fort Worth, TX: Harcourt Brace, 1998), 26; "Rage, Revenge, Religion," 475.

42. Jesús Langarica Olágüe (Prefectura Apostolica de Aguarico), "Solicita del Supremo Gobierno Nacional del Ecuador," open letter to government, November 10, 1977, copy in "Wao Communities—Land" Folder, Yost Papers; also reprinted in *Crónica Huaorani*, 193.

43. *Ultimos Huaorani*, 110–13. There is some discrepancy between the accounts of meetings recorded in *Ultimos Huaorani* and in *Crónica Huaorani* in terms of dates and agendas. The content of the narratives remains largely the same.

44. *Ultimos Huaorani*, 110.

45. *Crónica Huaorani*, 96, 97, for this and the previous paragraph.

46. La Congregación de las Misioneras de María Inmaculada y Santa Catalina de Sena (Madre Laura) is a missionary order of women religious founded in Colombia and generally known as Madres Laurítas after their founder, Laura Montoya.

47. *Crónica Huaorani*, 131, 133.

48. Ibid., 138–39, 144, 167.

49. Ibid., 114.

50. Jim Yost, "Update on Wao Raids," email to author, November 17, 2017.

51. *Ultimos Huaorani*, 154, indicates that Adabæ married Obæ and Æguinto [Agnænto, correct name uncertain] married Yaye, both from groups of Waorani who lived along the Cononaco River.

52. *Crónica Huaorani*, 174.

53. Juan Santos Ortíz, "Appendix I," in *Crónica Huaorani*, 177. "Appendix I," a letter from Santos Ortíz to Labaca, provides an early, brief sketch of this visit. For a more detailed account, see *Ultimos Huaorani*, 152–77.

54. *Ultimos Huaorani*, 156.

55. Ibid., 159.

56. Ibid., 168. The site is more commonly known as Garzacocha.

57. Ibid., 164–77.

58. Ibid., 178.

59. Ibid., 191.

CHAPTER 16

1. Larry Montgomery to Townsend, n.d. [probably late February 1958], TA#14883; R. Saint to Townsend, March 3, 1958, TA#15337; Saint to Townsend, December 12, 1958, TA#14923.

2. *Kinsman*, 74, quotes Dayomæ saying that she wants to put her son in school. Kingsland, *SAS*, 119, writes that it was Rachel Saint who encouraged Sam Padilla's education in Quito. See also R. Saint to Johnson, June 14, 1965, "Auca History 1956–1969" Folder, EBC-SIL, where Saint refers to Dayomæ's desire that Sam get a "COMPLETE education" and also mentions discrimination (emphasis Saint's).

3. Jerry Bledsoe, "Saint," *Esquire*, July 1972, 152.

4. Rachel Saint, "To our Praying Friends," January 10, 1969, "Auca History 1956–1969" Folder, EBC-SIL.

5. Bledsoe, "Saint," 152.

6. Erwin Patzelt, *Libre como el jaguar: Los Aucas y su enigmático mundo* (Quito: Editorial Las Casas, 1976), 5, 9; Erwin Patzelt, *Los Huaorani: Los Ultimos Hijos Libres del Jaguar* (Quito: Banco Central del Ecuador, 2002), 22.

7. R. Saint, "Auca Report," June 13, 1975, "Auca Contact History 1970–1980" Folder, EBC-SIL.

8. Patzelt, introduction to *Libre como el jaguar*, n.p.

9. Bledsoe, "Saint," 154.

10. "Ceantu [*sic*]: El retorno a la vida y a la libertad de la selva" [Cænto: The return to the life and freedom of the forest], *El Comercio* (Quito), February 5, 1978, clipping in Peeke Papers.

11. Ibid.

12. For a 1987 feature story on Padilla as a man of the rainforest who only reluctantly lived in Quito, see Fernando Villarroel G., "Cænto no ha dejado la selva" [Cænto has not left the forest behind], *Familia*, June 28, 1987, clipping in Peeke Papers.

13. *Fishers of Men*, 309–11; "Report to Administration: Waodani [*sic*] Tribe—October, 1980," "Various Branch Reports 1960–1993" Folder, EBC-SIL.

14. JY field notes, March 28, 1976, Yost Papers.

15. Peter Broennimann, *Auca on the Cononaco: Indians of the Ecuadorian Rain Forest* (Basel: Birkhäuser, 1981); John Man, *Jungle Nomads of Ecuador: The Waorani* (Amsterdam: Time-Life Books, 1982).

16. Broennimann, *Auca on the Cononaco*, 55.

17. Ibid., 179.

18. "Report to Administration," EBC-SIL.

19. For the text of both letters, from Padilla Cænto to Labaca and Labaca's reply, see Cabodevilla, *LH*, 422. Only the year, 1980, was given to date Padilla's letter. Cabodevilla indicated it was part of an exchange between Sam Padilla and Peter Broennimann with Labaca during 1980–81. Originals are in the Archivo del Vicariato de Aguarico, Aguarico, Ecuador.

20. Cabodevilla, *LH*, 422.

21. Ibid.

22. Peeke to Yost, July 16, 1979, "Team Correspondence" Folder, Yost Papers.

23. JY field notes, August 1, 1980, Yost Papers. Yost's census, July 1980, reported a total of 648 Waorani who were permanent residents of their territory. This number excluded the Tagæidi, any other unknown groups, and Waorani who lived among outsiders.

24. Centro de Investigaciones y Estudios Socio Económicos.

25. *Ecuador ILV/WBT: Entre el Etnocídio y la Alfabetización* ([Quito]: CIESE, Departamento de Antropologia, PUCE, AEDA, March 1980); Jorge Trujillo, *Los Obscuros Designios de Dios y del Imperio: El Instituto Lingüístico de Verano en el Ecuador* (Ecuador: Publicaciones CIESE, 1981); Ginette Cano et al., *Los Nuevos Conquistadores: El Instituto Lingüístico de Verano en América Latina* (Quito: CEDIS and FENOC, 1981), originally published as *Die frohe Botschaft unserer Zivilisation: Evangelikale Indianermission in Lateinamerika* (Göttingen: Gesellschaft für bedrohte Völker, 1979).

26. *Ecuador ILV/WBT*, 4–5.

27. Trujillo, *Los Obscuros Designios*, 9–10, 12.

28. "El mítico oriente y la loca empresa del hermano Townsend."

29. Trujillo, *Los Obscuros Designios*, 47, 51, 53, 56.

30. Ibid., 65.

31. Peeke quoted in R. Saint to Dale Kietzman, September 23, 1971, Peeke Papers.

32. Cabodevilla, *LH*, 421.

33. Franklin Barriga López, *Las Culturas Indigenas Ecuatorianas y el Instituto Lingüístico de Verano* (Buenos Aires: Ediciones Amauta, 1992), 316, 423.

34. Bertha Fuentes C., *Huaomoni, Huarani, Cowudi: Una aproximación a los Huaorani en la práctica política multi-étnica ecuatoriana* (Quito: Ediciones Abya-Yala, 1997), 170.

35. For example, SIL's report in pamphlet form, *La Obra Civilizadora del Instituto Lingüístico de Verano entre los Aucas* [The civilizing task of the Summer Institute of Linguistics among the Aucas] (Quito: [ILV], 1969).

36. For the text of the decree, see Trujillo, *Los Obscuros Designios*, 135–38.

37. Trujillo, *Los Obscuros Designios*, 128.

38. J. Yost, unpublished newsletter, September 13, 1979, Yost Papers.

39. John Maust, "Jungle Identity Crisis: Auca Country Revisited," *Christianity Today*, January 4, 1980, 48–50.

40. Ken Fleming, "High Stakes, High Risks, High Calling," *Christian Missions in Many Lands*, January 1981, 3, 10.

41. Including previous books about Wycliffe Bible Translators: James C. Hefley, *Peril by Choice: The Story of John and Elaine Beekman, Wycliffe Bible Translators in Mexico* (Grand Rapids, MI: Zondervan, 1968) and James C. Hefley and Marti Hefley, *Dawn over Amazonia: The Story of Wycliffe Bible Translators in Peru* (Waco, TX: Word Books, 1972).

42. James C. Hefley to Victor Oliver, March 15, 1980, copy in author's possession. Used with permission.

43. Lindskoog to Jim and Marti Hefley, March 10, 1980, copy in author's possession.

44. James C. Hefley to Victor Oliver, March 15, March 16, and May 26, 1980, copies in author's possession. Quote from May 26 letter, used with permission.

45. William R. Barbour Jr., to Mr. and Mrs. James C. Hefley, June 6, 1980, copy in author's possession.

46. James Hefley and Marti Hefley, *Unstilled Voices* (Chappaqua, NY: Christian Herald Books, 1981).

47. Stoll would later become known for *Is Latin America Turning Protestant? The Politics of Evangelical Growth* (Berkeley: University of California Press, 1990), and for *Rigoberta Menchú and the Story of All Poor Guatemalans* (Boulder, CO: Westview, 1999).

48. *Fishers of Men*, 13.

49. Ibid., 14–16.

50. Ibid., vii.

51. Ibid., 12.

52. Ibid., 278.

53. Ibid., 279.

54. Ibid., 281.

55. Ibid., 299.

56. Ibid., 285.

57. Ibid., 294.

58. Ibid., 302–3, 314.

59. David M. Howard, review of *Fishers of Men or Founders of Empire? The Wycliffe Bible Translators in Latin America*, by David Stoll, *Missiology* 12, no. 3 (1984): 380–82; John A. Lapp, review of *Fishers of Men or Founders of Empire? The Wycliffe Bible Translators in Latin America*, by David Stoll, *Fides et Historia* 17, no. 1 (1984): 92–94; Charles R. Taber, review of *Fishers of Men or Founders of Empire? The Wycliffe Bible Translators in Latin America*, by David Stoll, *International Bulletin of Missionary Research* 8, no. 1 (1984): 34–35; all sources available at ATLA Religion Database.

60. David Stoll, "Wycliffe Bible Translators: Not Telling the Whole Story," *The Other Side*, February 1983, 20–25; James Yost, "We Have a Mandate," *The Other Side*, February 1983, 25, 38–39.

61. Yost, "We Have a Mandate," 38.

62. Ibid.

63. Ibid.

64. Ibid., 39.

65. Johnson, "Director's Report, Ecuador Branch Conference 1981," January 18–27, 1982, "Various Branch Reports 1960–1993" Folder, EBC-SIL.

66. Memorandum from Dianne Parkhurst to Hyatt Moore, May 5, 1993, "Various Branch Reports 1960–1993" Folder, EBC-SIL.

67. Ibid.

68. Roy and Rita Peterson, "Thanks from the Top," *In Other Words*, July–August 1992, 7.

69. James A. Yost, interview with author, May 2, 2005, Kremmling, CO.

CHAPTER 17

1. *Arriesgar la Vida*, 199–200. Most of Labaca's story in this chapter is based on Rufino María Grández, *Arriesgar la Vida*, and on Cabodevilla, *LH*. Both authors are Capuchín friars. Grández's book is a conventional martyrology, while Cabodevilla places Labaca's life in the context of Wao history. A third book, by a Colombian journalist, Germán Castro Caycedo, *Hágase tu Voluntad* [Thy will be done] (Bogotá: Planeta Colombiana Editorial, 1998), has helpful quotations from interviews but is marred by sensationalism and inaccuracies.

2. Castro Caycedo, *Hágase tu Voluntad*, 329.

3. *Arriesgar la Vida*, 219.

4. Ibid., 220–21.

5. Ibid., 185; see also Appendix III in *Crónica Huaorani*, 187–208.

6. Cabodevilla, *LH*, 429.

7. *Arriesgar la Vida*, 163.

8. Cabodevilla, *LH*, 429.

9. "Iglesia pide protección para parcialidad de Aucas" [The Church requests protection for the benefit of the aucas], *El Comercio* (Quito), June 15, 1985, citing Labaca, quoted in Cabodevilla, *LH*, 430.

10. Cabodevilla, *LH*, 431–32, 442n54. Most of this narrative is based on Cabodevilla, *LH*, 429–32 and corresponding endnotes.

11. Cabodevilla, *LH*, and *Arriesgar la Vida*, respectively.

12. Fruit of the Ungurahua palm tree. Kelley to Yost [Cawo to Wadeca], n.d. [probably 1980], "Team Correspondence" Folder, Yost Papers.

13. Peeke for team to Glen Turner and Yost, November 17, 1978, "Team Correspondence" Folder, Yost Papers.

14. Ibid.; see also Wänguï to Wadeca and Co. [Peeke to Yost and others], February 25, 1980, "Team Correspondence" Folder, Yost Papers.

15. To Yost from Janet [no last name] for Dave Underwood [memorandum to Yost re: Visit with Vela], September 3, 1981, "Land" Folder, Yost Papers.

16. "Administrador de Limoncocha fue expulsado por indígenas," *El Comercio* (Quito), February 12, 1983, quoted in Cabodevilla, *LH*, 431.

17. Ronn Pineo, *Ecuador and the United States: Useful Strangers* (Athens: University of Georgia Press, 2007), 199. For the "Wild West" atmosphere in Quito during the Febres Cordero presidency, see 199–204.

18. Cabodevilla, *LH*, 443n61.

19. Pineo, *Ecuador and the United States*, 203; see also Cabodevilla, *LH*, 433.

20. Cabodevilla, *LH*, 431.

21. These included Braspetro, Petrocanadá, and Conoco. Cabodevilla, *LH*, 432.

22. Ibid. For a slightly different version of this story, see *Arriesgar la Vida*, 238–39.

23. Cabodevilla, *LH*, 433.

24. Monsignor Mario Ruiz, interview in *Diario Hoy* (Quito), July 23, 1987, quoted in Cabodevilla, *LH*, 432. Castro Caycedo, *Hágase tu Voluntad*, 344, places this comment just before Labaca's fatal attempt at contact and in response to Vela's imminent plans to go overland to seek the Tagæidi.

25. Cabodevilla, *LH*, 432.

26. *Arriesgar la Vida*, 226.

27. Ibid., 223.

28. Ibid.,158.

29. Ibid., 119. Although it leans toward hagiography, a helpful account of Arango's life is in *Arriesgar la Vida*, 107–23. Arango was given the name María Nieves (Sister María de las Nieves de Medellín), but she later went back to using her family name, Inés Arango Velásquez. Alejandro Labaca Ugarte had done the same.

30. *Crónica Huaorani*, 130–31, 135.

31. Inés Arango to Superior General, Mother Elena Echavarren, March 27, 1987, quoted in *Arriesgar la Vida*, 229.

32. *Arriesgar la Vida*, 233–34.

33. Arango to Echavarren, March 27, 1987, quoted in *Arriesgar la Vida*, 228.

34. Inés Arango to Sister Myriam Mercado, April 12, 1987, quoted in *Arriesgar la Vida*, 231.

35. *Arriesgar la Vida*, 227.

36. Alejandro Labaca, "Informe a Cepe" [Report to CEPE], July 17, 1987, Archive of the Aguarico Vicariate, quoted in Cabodevilla, *LH*, 433.

37. Cabodevilla, *LH*, 433.

38. *Arriesgar la Vida*, 241.

39. Ibid., 242–44.

40. Castro Caycedo, *Hágase tu Voluntad*, 347.

41. José Miguel Goldárez, "Hace 25 Años" [Twenty-five years ago], Hermanos Menores Capuchinos, n.d. [likely around 2012], accessed January 21, 2018, http://capuchinosdelecuador.org/index.php/noticias/generales/722-hace-25-anos-jose-miguel-goldarez.

42. This and the following paragraph are based on *Arriesgar la Vida*, 247–49.

43. Ibid., 249.

44. In an account twenty-five years later, Goldárez would report that Labaca was killed with seventeen spears and Arango with four. Goldárez, "Hace 25 Años."

45. Castro Caycedo, *Hágase tu Voluntad*, 356, which was unfortunately repeated by Mary Ellen Fieweger in an otherwise excellent review and analysis of Joe Kane's popular book, *Savages* (1995). See Fieweger, "Narcissus and the Noble Savage: The Huaorani Packaged and Sold," *Liberarte* 3, no. 2 (2009): 49–71 [electronic publication of the Universidad San Francisco de Quito], http://

www.usfq.edu.ec/publicaciones/liberarte/Documents/Liberarte_Vol_3_No_2_Septiembre_
Diciembre_2009.pdf.

46. See Cabodevilla, *LH*, 434, for the photograph; *Arriesgar la Vida*, 254.

47. *Arriesgar la Vida*, 253.

48. Ibid., 252–53.

49. Ibid., 255–57. Grández reported that the priest who prepared the bodies for burial counted a higher number: 67 on Arango and 160 on the bishop. The Waorani often stabbed a victim repeatedly with the same spear (ibid., 258).

50. Raúl Borja, "Hoaranis [*sic*]: El derecho a resistirse" [Waorani: The right to resist], *Revista Familiar*, [magazine supplement to] *El Comercio* (Quito), August 2, 1987.

51. Ibid.

52. Juan Cueva Jaramillo, "La muerte en la selva" [Death in the jungle], *Diario Hoy* (Quito), July 29, 1987. As with many others, this article contains numerous factual errors.

53. Andres Oppenheimer, "'Killer' Indians Resist Advance of Civilization," *Miami Herald*, August 23, 1987.

54. Ibid.

55. "Misioneros recibieron decenas de lanzazos" [Missionaries speared tens of times], *El Comercio* (Quito), July 24, 1987.

56. Cabodevilla, *LH*, 436–38.

CHAPTER 18

1. Peeke did preliminary translation work in 1977 and 1978 but was officially assigned to Bible translation for the Waorani in 1979. Peeke to "Dear Family in Christ," newsletter, August 26, 1979, Peeke Papers; see also Peeke, "Wao Report to Conference, 1977, Linguistic and Medical Supplement," Peeke Papers; Kelley, "Waodani (Auca) Tribal Report, Ecuador Branch Conference for January–December 1978," "Various Branch Reports 1960–1993" Folder, EBC-SIL.

2. Peeke to Catherine McHale, May 5, 1994, Peeke Papers.

3. Letter from R. Saint to Peeke, May 8, 1973, in Peeke to Sarah Gudschinsky, May 24, 1973, Peeke Papers; Memorandum by Rachel Saint to Sarah Gudschinsky, "Re: Changes in Auca Orthography," August 25, 1972, Peeke Papers. Saint's memo was a seven-page typewritten document in which she explained and defended her orthography.

4. Peeke to Bruce [Moore], November 26, 1974, Peeke Papers.

5. See correspondence between David L. Pearson and Lindskoog, June 1971–May 1972, "Visitors to LC—Scientists" Folder, EBC-SIL.

6. Peeke to Elizabeth Peeke, July 11, 1975, Peeke Papers. All Peeke letters to family members used with permission. See also Peeke to Church Family, June 11, 1975, Peeke Papers.

7. Rosi Jung, interview with author, June 17–18, 2009, Holzhausen, Germany. Unless otherwise indicated the following narrative and quotations are from this extensive interview.

8. Ibid.

9. Ibid.

10. Ibid.

11. Peeke to Elizabeth Peeke, January 20, 1985, Peeke Papers.

12. Jung, interview.

13. Ibid.

14. Catherine Peeke, "One Supreme God," unpublished explanation of how the concept was translated into *Wao tededo*, copy sent to author by Peeke as an email attachment, March 3, 2005.

15. Ibid. The Waorani apparently also had a fish named *wængongui*. To solve that problem, they renamed the fish.

16. Genesis 41.

17. Jung, interview.

18. Peeke to Judy [Maxwell], March 16, 1989, Peeke Papers.

19. SIL had used the term "language informant." However, in the political context of the 1970s and 1980s, the "words smack[ed] of espionage." Peeke recommended "native helper," "language helper," or "language teacher." Catherine Peeke, typed corrections to "Auca Missionary Is Weaverville Native," *Presbyterian Journal*, September 13, 1978, 6–8, Peeke Papers.

20. Peeke, "Update on the Auca's[*sic*]/Waorani," newsletter, n.d., Peeke Papers.

21. Ibid.

22. Peeke, "Wao People," unpublished biographical sketches, n.d., Peeke Papers.

23. Ibid.

24. John 9:1–41; Jung, interview.

25. Pat Kelley, interview with author, August 10, 2004, Dallas, TX.

26. Residents of Toñæmpade, where loyalty to Rachel Saint and the orthography she had created with Dayomæ ran high, were one source of criticism. See Peeke to Wanda Peeke Teague, June 11, 1988, Peeke Papers, where Peeke refers to the criticisms in the context of a change of heart.

27. [Peeke], "Oba," unfinished poem, n.d., Peeke Papers; Kelley, interview; Stephen R. Manock et al., "An Outbreak of Fulminant Hepatitis Delta in the Waorani, an Indigenous People of the Amazon Basin of Ecuador," *American Journal of Tropical Medicine and Hygiene* 63, nos. 3–4 (2000): 209–13, explores causes behind an earlier outbreak.

28. Peeke to "Dear Christian Friend," newsletter, October 16, 1985, Peeke Papers; "Waorani Prayer and Praise, Christmas 1991," staff circular, Peeke Papers.

29. Bruce Moore, "Translation Progress Report for Waodani," June 4, 1991, Peeke Papers, lists books of the New Testament translated by each linguist.

30. Peeke to "Blossoms plucked from the TWIG [absent staff members of SIL's Ecuador "Branch"]," newsletter, February 24, 1984, Peeke Papers.

31. Peeke to Claude and Jane [probably Dodds, not identified], April 14, 1988, Peeke Papers.

32. Peeke, "Waodani Conference Report: March 1988 to February 1989," Peeke Papers.

33. Peeke to "Dear Choise [*sic*] Servants of the Lord" [Dan and Ruth Choisser], July 27, 1985, Peeke Papers.

34. "Auca Missionary Is Weaverville Native," *Presbyterian Journal*, September 13, 1978, 8, copy in Peeke Papers.

35. Peeke, typed corrections to "Auca Missionary" (emphasis Peeke's).

36. Catherine Peeke, interview with author, July 3, 2000, Weaverville, NC.

37. Peeke to Libba [Elizabeth Peeke], March 1, 1987, Peeke Papers.

38. Peeke to Wanda [Wanda Peeke Teague], July 7, 1991, Peeke Papers.

39. James A. Yost, interview with author, May 3, 2005, Kremmling, CO. Christians may also have been concerned because Wao contact with Quichuas and an increasing desire to appeal to tourists had led some Waorani to view jaguar fathers as spiritual figures with powers beyond those associated with hunting.

40. Peeke, "Meeting in August 1990 to discuss Key Terms in Scripture," unpublished report, Peeke Papers. Except where otherwise indicated, the story of this meeting is based on Peeke's report and follows Peeke's spelling of Wao words and phrases.

41. Jung, interview.

42. Peeke, "Meeting . . . to discuss," Peeke Papers.

43. Ibid.

44. Quoted by Jung, interview.

45. Peeke, "Meeting . . . to discuss," Peeke Papers.

46. Peeke, "Waodani Conference Report," Peeke Papers; Memorandum by Glen Turner to Rosi [Jung], Cathie [Peeke], Pat [Kelley], "Waodani orthography for the New Testament," November 13, 1991, Peeke Papers.

47. Peeke, "Waorani Conference Report: March 1990–February 1991," Peeke Papers.

48. Peeke to Ruth [probably Choisser, not identified], December 2, 1989, Peeke Papers.

49. Turner to Rosi et al., "Waodani orthography," November 13, 1991, Peeke Papers. Turner provided a helpful historical summary of the issues surrounding the Wao orthography.

50. Ibid.

51. "Waorani Prayer and Praise, Christmas 1991," Peeke Papers.

52. Peeke, "Waorani Tribe Report" [draft], April 3, 1992, Peeke Papers.

53. A second and earlier innovation was the increasing use and portability of the tape recorder. See "Auca Missionary," 7.

54. [Peeke], "Waorani New Testament Funding," information sheet, n.d., Peeke Papers; also [Peeke], "Waorani New Testament Dedication Plans," information sheet, n.d., Peeke Papers.

55. Peeke and Rosi Jung, "Waorani New Testament Dedication: 11 and 13 June 1992," unpublished report, Peeke Papers.

56. Ibid.; see also Dave Underwood, "Press Release: Waorani Receive Their New Testament," June 11, 1992, Peeke Papers.

57. Underwood, "Press Release"; Peeke and Jung, "Waorani New Testament," Peeke Papers.

58. "Jim Elliot's Legacy Continues," *Christianity Today*, August 17, 1992, 52; Norm Bomer, "At Last: The Afternoon Service," *World*, July 18, 1992, 12–13. *World* did publish A.H.M. [Arthur H. Matthews], "World's Most Watched Translation Reaches Testament Publication Stage," April 25, 1992, 9–11, one of the few articles that featured Peeke and Jung, although the story still began with "the Auca martyrs." For WBT/SIL coverage, see Pat Kelley, "Waorani: In Print and in Person," *In Other Words*, July–August 1992, 4.

59. Harold Goerzen, "The Aucas: 36 Years Later," *Around the World* [HCJB publication], Autumn 1992, 9.

60. Peeke remained an active SIL staff member until 1998, working from her home in North Carolina and making regular trips to Ecuador.

61. Peeke to Hyatt Moore, April 30, 1988, Peeke Papers.

62. Martin Huyett to "Dear Friends," November 23, 1994, Peeke Papers.

63. Peeke, handwritten comments on Huyett to "Dear Friends," November 23, 1994, Peeke Papers.

64. In 2001 King University in Bristol, Tennessee, named the Peeke School of Christian Mission after M. Catherine Peeke in honor of her missionary work among the Waorani. Peeke received a Bachelor of Arts in education from King in 1947.

CHAPTER 19

1. Nate Saint's oldest son, Steve, and his family spent a year with the Waorani in 1995 and made periodic visits before and after that time. In some ways, they attempted to follow the earlier immersion model but were unable to relocate permanently. Steve Saint, *End of the Spear: A True Story* (Carol Stream, IL: Tyndale House, 2005).

2. Jon Christensen, "Big Oil Taps the Rain Forest," Pacific News Service, October 1–5, 1990, copy in Peeke Papers.

3. *Rights Violations in the Ecuadorian Amazon: The Human Consequences of Oil Development* (New York: Center for Economic and Social Rights, 1994), 5, http://www.cesr.org/sites/default/files/Rights_Violation_in_the_Ecuadorian_Amazon_The_Human_Consequences_of_Oil_Development_1_1.pdf; *Amazon Crude*, 43.

4. "Yasuní," 6. Despite some inaccuracies in tracing missionary-Waorani history, the article is an excellent overview. See also Douglas Southgate, Robert Wasserstrom, and Susan Reider, "Oil Development, Deforestation, and Indigenous Populations in the Ecuadorian Amazon" (paper presented, Latin American Studies Association, Rio de Janeiro, Brazil, June 11–14, 2009), 6.

5. Alan Kovski, "Conoco Adopts Tactful Approach to Drilling in Ecuadoran Forest," *Oil Daily*, September 11, 1990, HighBeam Research, www.highbeam.com/doc/1G1-8885180.html.

6. *Amazon Crude*, 52.

7. "Yasuní," 1, 4, 8–9.

8. Some of the groups that were involved in Ecuador, and a few that were founded there in the context of Yasuní-Conoco, include Acción Ecológica, Campaña Amazonía por la vida, Fundación Natura, Tierra Viva, and Corporación Defensa de la Vida.

9. *Amazon Crude*, xxix, 89; Pamela L. Burke, "Embedded Private Authority: Multinational Enterprises and the Amazonian Indigenous Peoples Movement in Ecuador," in *Private Authority and International Affairs*, ed. A. Claire Cutler, Virginia Haufler, and Tony Porter (Albany: SUNY Press, 1999), 239.

10. Christensen, "Big Oil Taps the Rain Forest."

11. Kovski, "Conoco Adopts Tactful Approach."

12. *Amazon Crude*, 48.

13. Ibid. Dirección General de Medio Ambiente (Head Office of the Environment) and Dirección Nacional de Medio Ambiente (National Office of the Environment), respectively.

14. *Amazon Crude*, 48, 112n15.

15. "Conoco Ecuador Ltd.," informational flier released by Conoco, January 14, 1991, copy in Peeke Papers; also Kovski, "Conoco Adopts Tactful Approach."

16. Kovski, "Conoco Adopts Tactful Approach."

17. CONFENIAE is the Spanish acronym for the Confederación de Nacionalidades Indígenas de la Amazonia Ecuatoriana.

18. For a summary of CONFENIAE in the context of other indigenous organizations of the Ecuadorian Amazon, see Burke, "Embedded Private Authority," 235–48. The combined Shuar and Quichua population in the Oriente was about one hundred thousand.

19. In 1998 the reserve was increased to 613,750 hectares (a total of about 1.52 million acres), and in 2001 the Waorani were awarded an additional 29,019 hectares (71,708 acres). See Anthony Stocks et al., "Deforestation and Waodani Lands in Ecuador: Mapping and Demarcation amidst Shaky Politics," in *Deforestation around the World*, ed. Paulo Moutinho

(Rijeka, Croatia: InTech, 2012), 190, doi: 10.5772/1979; Laura Rival, "Huaorani y Petróleo," in *Naufragos del Mar Verde: La resistencia de los Huaorani a una integracíon impuesta* [Sailors of the Green Sea: The resistance of the Waorani to an enforced integration], ed. Giovanna Tassi (Quito: Ediciones Abya-Yala, CONFENIAE, 1992), 133.

20. *Amazon Crude*, 87, 89–90.

21. Pat Kelley, interview with author, August 10, 2005, Dallas, TX; Form letter from the Yosts, December 31, 1980, Yost Papers.

22. Vawter Parker to Stanley L. Whittemore, April 1, 1991, Yost Papers.

23. Ibid.

24. "Judith Kimerling Recipient of 2007 Parker/Gentry Award" [Newsmakers interview], City University of New York, podcast audio, October 25, 2007, www1.cuny.edu/mu/podcasts/2007/10/25/judith-kimerling-recipient-of-2007-parkergentry-award/; see also S. Jacob Scherr, foreword to *Amazon Crude*, xxvii.

25. James Brooke, "Oil and Tourism Don't Mix, Inciting Amazon Battle," *New York Times*, September 26, 1993, http://www.nytimes.com/1993/09/26/world/oil-and-tourism-don-t-mix-inciting-amazon-battle.html?pagewanted=all.

26. *Amazon Crude*, 85.

27. Joe Kane, *Savages*, 1st Vintage Books edition (1995; New York: Vintage, 1996), 72; see also Joe Kane, "With Spears from All Sides," *New Yorker*, September 27, 1993, 60. Kane explains the Conoco episode in much greater detail.

28. Kane, *Savages*, 74.

29. Ibid., 72–73.

30. Kane, "With Spears," 62; see also Kane, *Savages*, 71–74.

31. Kane, *Savages*, 8–9.

32. Yost, "Assessment of the Impact of Road Construction and Oil Extraction upon the Waorani Living on the Yasuní" (unpublished report for Conoco Ecuador Limited, April 1989), Yost Papers.

33. Yost, "Present Status of the Waorani in Ecuador's Oriente and Their Reaction to Oil Exploration, Report of survey made by Jim Yost and Douglas McMeekin, November 18–30, 1989" (unpublished report written for Unocal), Yost Papers, 2, 5.

34. Yost to Ed Davies (general manager of Conoco), August 29, 1990, Yost Papers.

35. Dianne Dumanoski, "Probe of Oil Firms Asked in Reversal of Amazon Drilling Curb," *Boston Globe*, May 16, 1991, HighBeam Research, www.highbeam.com/doc/1P2-7660406.html; see also Alan Kovski, "Oil Companies Charged with Pressuring Ecuador," *Oil Daily*, May 16, 1991, HighBeam Research, www.highbeam.com/doc/1G1-10734386.html.

36. Alan Kovski, "Conoco Decides to Pull Out of Ecuador," *Oil Daily*, October 14, 1991, High Beam Research, www.highbeam.com/doc/1G1-11357712.html. Companies that remained in the consortium, in addition to Maxus, were Murphy Ecuador Oil Co., of El Dorado, Arkansas; Nomemco Ecuador Oil Co., of Jackson, Michigan; Canam Offshore Ltd., of New Orleans; and the Overseas Petroleum & Investment Corp. of Taiwan. See also Kane, *Savages*, 76.

37. Kane, "With Spears," 62 (emphasis in original).

38. There had been coffee table books and other publications that emphasized the exotic nature of Wao life and culture, such as those by Peter Broennimann and John Man cited earlier. The Waorani were also the subjects of several films made in the early 1980s, including *Nomads of the Rain Forest* (WGBH, Nova, 1983), *Waorani: The Last People* (BBC, 1988), and *Waorani* (ABC, 1983). All three

films were made from footage shot in 1983 by a three-person BBC film crew that accompanied a five-person expedition, led by Grant G. Behrman of the Explorers Club, with Jim Yost as consultant. The group spent a month with a Wao man, Cæmpæde, and his family group on the Cononaco River in eastern Ecuador. Neither these films nor the books had the political and social agenda of the works discussed in this chapter. Nor were their authors or producers activists as these authors were. See Susan Heller Anderson and Maurice Carrell, "New York Day by Day; Technology and Trekking," *New York Times*, October 1, 1983, www.nytimes.com/1983/10/01/nyregion/new-york-day-by-day-technology-and-trekking.html; see also Adrian Warren, "Waorani: The Last People," *Last Refuge, Ltd.*, accessed January 22, 2018, www.lastrefuge.co.uk/data/articles/waorani_p1.html.

39. Lawrence Ziegler-Otero, *Resistance in an Amazonian Community: Huaorani Organizing against the Global Economy* (New York: Berghahn Books, 2004), 79; "Social Trans."

40. Muratorio is best known for her book *The Life and Times of Grandfather Alonso: Culture and History in the Upper Amazon* (New Brunswick, NJ: Rutgers University Press, 1991).

41. "Social Trans.," 3–5, 8.

42. Ibid., 7.

43. Ibid., 6, 390; Randy Smith, *Drama Bajo el Manto Amazónico: El turismo y otros problemas de los Huaorani en la actualidad / Crisis under the Canopy: Tourism and Other Problems Facing the Present Day Huaorani* [Spanish and English text] (Quito: Abya-Yala, 1993), 271. It is not clear how many people were Quichuas and how many were Waorani.

44. Smith, *Crisis under the Canopy*, 335.

45. "Twenty Years"; "People of Forest."

46. For Rival's involvement, see Ziegler-Otero, *Resistance*, 81–82. Much of Yost's involvement was during the 1980s, preliminary to the actual founding. However, see Yost, "Report of ONHAE Waorani Initial Organizational Meeting" (unpublished manuscript, December 22, 1990), Yost Papers.

47. For example, Laura Rival, "The Growth of Family Trees: Understanding Huaorani Perceptions of the Forest," *Man*, new series, 28, no. 4 (1993): 635–52, www.jstor.org/stable/2803990.

48. "Social Trans.," 167.

49. Stephen Beckerman et al., "Life Histories, Blood Revenge, and Reproductive Success among the Waorani of Ecuador," *PNAS* 106, no. 20 (2009): 8135, doi: 10.1073/pnas.0901431106. I contributed historical context information to this essay.

50. "Social Trans.," 186.

51. Ibid., 170–71.

52. "People of Forest," 107–8; John Man, *Jungle Nomads of Ecuador: The Waorani* (Amsterdam: Time-Life Books, 1982). The photographs in *Jungle Nomads* are by John Wright, and Yost served as consultant for the volume. The first photo essay in the book, "Raising Crops in the Wilderness," 38–45, focused on the Waorani as horticulturists. A subsequent photo essay, "Gathering the Forest's Bounty," 78–87, shows the Waorani gathering edible foods from the forest.

53. Flora E. Lu [Holt], "The Common Property Regime of the Huaorani Indians of Ecuador: Implications and Challenges to Conservation," *Human Ecology* 29, no. 4 (2001): 426.

54. "Social Trans.," 231–33.

55. Ibid., 252–53.

56. Peeke to Wanda [Peeke Teague], June 18, 1989, Peeke Papers.

57. "Social Trans.," 2, 21, 240; James A. Yost and Patricia M. Kelley, "Shotguns, Blowguns, and Spears: The Analysis of Technological Efficiency," in *Adaptive Responses of Native Amazonians*, ed. Raymond B. Hames and William T. Vickers (New York: Academic Press, 1983), 202. One Wao man, Monca, had a shotgun as early as 1972; Zoila Wiñame's husband, Dabo, may also have had one at that time. R. Saint to Peeke, October 24, 1972, Peeke Papers.

58. "Social Trans.," 195.

59. Ibid., 351–52.

60. Elisabeth Elliot, "Recent News from Betty Elliot," *SST*, December 13, 1958, 920 (6).

61. "Social Trans.," 20, 248, 360.

62. James A. Yost, telephone interview with author, May 20, 2012.

63. Ibid.

64. "Social Trans.," 360. When Pat Kelley began literacy work in the early 1970s, she chose not to incorporate chants into her teaching. This was not because she thought chants were evil but "because so little was known about the music." She did not want to use it inappropriately. "Literacy Materials," 109, 109n*.

65. JY field notes, February 26, 1974, Yost Papers.

66. Various native musicians, "Ecuador, Auca [*sic*] Indians, 1965 [sound recording collected by Rachel Saint]," recorded in Ecuador, September 1965, four sound tape reels, Archives of Traditional Music, Indiana University, Bloomington; see also Various unidentified native musicians, "Ecuador, Tewæno, Auca [*sic*] Indians, 1962 [sound recording collected by Catherine Peeke]," recorded Tewæno, Ecuador, July 1962, four sound tape reels, Archives of Traditional Music, Indiana University. Other recordings are dated 1958–60 and 1963–65.

67. Wade Davis, *One River: Explorations and Discoveries in the Amazon Rain Forest* (New York: Simon & Schuster, 1996), 267–95, see especially 281 and 286–87.

68. "Social Trans.," 101, 40n12.

69. Peeke, "Report re: Huao territory," February 17, 1976, "Auca Contact History, 1970–1980" Folder, EBC-SIL. SIL tried to keep families together as much as possible. When Wepe, a key figure from the ridge, relocated, Peeke noted, "Wepe brought his two wives, his children, a married son and wife, and the grandchildren." Peeke to Peter B. Ostlund, January 3, 1971 [1972], Peeke Papers.

70. "Social Trans.," 255n3.

71. See, e.g., Judith Kimerling, "Disregarding Environmental Law: Petroleum Development in Protected Natural Areas and Indigenous Homelands in the Ecuadorian Amazon," *Hastings International and Comparative Law Review* 14, no. 4 (1991): 878.

72. "Know Your Missionaries, No. 26," insert, *Christian Missions in Many Lands*, December 1980, n.p.; Andrew Rennie, "Ecuador: Land of Contrasts," *Christian Missions in Many Lands*, November 1985, 5–6; see also Lloyd and Linda Rogers, interview with author, March 18, 2006, Wheaton, IL.

73. Lamin Sanneh, *Translating the Message: The Missionary Impact on Culture* (Maryknoll, NY: Orbis Books, 1989), 29.

74. Rival, "Growth of Family Trees"; for work directed toward popular audiences, see Rival, "Huaorani y Petróleo."

CHAPTER 20

1. Jim Sugarman and Holley Knaus, "Environmental Sell-Out," *Multinational Monitor*, May 1991, http://multinationalmonitor.org/hyper/issues/1991/05/lines.html.

2. The title literally means "the right to make noise." Judith Kimerling, *El Derecho del Tambor: Derechos Humanos y Ambientales en los Campos Petroleros de la Amazonía Ecuatoriana* [The right to beat the drum: Human and environmental rights in the oil fields of Amazonian Ecuador], trans. David Padilla D. [first article] and Mary Ellen Fieweger [second article] (Quito: Ediciones Abya-Yala, 1996).

3. Judith Kimerling, "Dislocation, Evangelization, and Contamination: Amazon Crude and the Huaorani People," in *Ethnic Conflict and Governance in Comparative Perspective*, Latin American Program Working Paper Series 215 (Washington, DC: Woodrow Wilson International Center for Scholars, 1995), 82.

4. *Amazon Crude*, 79; see also Kimerling, "Dislocation," 83n48.

5. Gene Jordan (MAF vice president of personnel), email to author, December 6, 2014. Jordan served as an MAF pilot in Shell, Ecuador, from August 1978 to July 2000.

6. *Amazon Crude*, 39; also Kimerling, "Dislocation," 83. The term "ethnocide" was taken from anthropologist Norman E. Whitten Jr., *Ecuadorian Ethnocide and Indigenous Ethnogenesis: Amazonian Resurgence amidst Andean Colonialism*, IWGIA [International Work Group for Indigenous Affairs] Document 23 (Copenhagen: IWGIA, 1976), 24, quoted in *Amazon Crude*, 39 and in Judith Kimerling, "Indigenous Peoples and the Oil Frontier in Amazonia: The Case of Ecuador, ChevronTexaco, and *Aguinda v. Texaco*," *New York University Journal of International Law and Politics* 38, no. 3 (2006): 427n43; see also *Amazon Crude*, 85, 87, where Kimerling translates a report by the Ecuadorian national oil company that identified SIL with a "policy of ethnocide."

7. James W. Larrick et al., "Patterns of Health and Disease among the Waorani Indians of Eastern Ecuador," *Medical Anthropology* 3, no. 2 (1979): 151. The population of Tewaeno is often said to have reached 525; however, this number refers to the entire Wao population in the protectorate in the mid-1970s. Tewæno peaked at about 300 people in 1971.

8. Alison Brysk, *From Tribal Village to Global Village: Indian Rights and International Relations in Latin America* (Stanford, CA: Stanford University Press, 2000), 172.

9. Joe Kane, *Running the Amazon* (New York: Knopf, 1989).

10. Joe Kane, *Savages*, 1st Vintage Books edition (1995; New York: Vintage, 1996), 11.

11. Ibid., 10.

12. Ibid., 18.

13. Ibid., 146.

14. Ibid., 145–46.

15. Ibid., 104.

16. David Miller, interview with author, January 6, 2007, Rome, GA.

17. Kane, *Savages*, 155.

18. Ibid., 103.

19. Ibid., 117.

20. Joe Kane, "Moi Goes to Washington," *New Yorker*, May 2, 1994.

21. *Trinkets and Beads*, directed by Christopher Walker (New York: Faction Films, distributed by First Run/Icarus Films, 1996), DVD.

22. Kane, *Savages*, 40.

23. Ibid., 48.

24. Ibid., 83.

25. Ibid., 135.

26. Ibid., 134. Cæwædi Ono was founded by Moi's father, Ñamæ, from a desire to be near good hunting territory and in the context of a conflict with other community members in Dayono. "Social Trans.," 6.

27. Kane, *Savages*, 155–56.

28. "Literacy Materials," 52.

29. Peeke to Wanda [Peeke Teague], June 18, 1989, Peeke Papers.

30. Kane, *Savages*, 235.

31. Ibid., 138.

32. Ibid., 200, 218.

33. *Savages* had an initial first printing of forty thousand copies; on January 7, 1996, the book ranked tenth on the *New York Times* Business Best Sellers list, www.nytimes.com/1996/01/07/business/the-new-york-times-business-best-sellers.html; "Savages, by Joe Kane," *Kirkus Reviews*, July 15, 1995, posted online May 20, 2010, www.kirkusreviews.com/book-reviews/joe-kane/savages.

34. "Bleeding Heart of Darkness," *Harper's Magazine*, October 1, 1994, https://harpers.org/archive/1994/10/bleeding-heart-of-darkness/.

35. W. C. Hutton and M. M. Skaggs Jr., "Renewable Resource Development in the Ecuadorian Rainforest" (paper presented, Society of Petroleum Engineers 70th Annual Technical Conference, Dallas, TX, October 22–25, 1995). For a summary of accusations against Maxus, see Camapania [*sic*] Amazonia por la Vida, "Maxus and the Ecuadorian Amazon," to email mailing list, April 21, 1995, http://abyayala.nativeweb.org/ecuador/huaorani/huao8.html.

36. *Resoluciones del Congreso de la Organización de la Nacionalidad Huaorani de la Amazonia del Ecuador* (ONHAE) [Resolutions from the Assembly of the Organization of the Huaorani People of Amazonian Ecuador], Shiripuno, December 6–9, 1991, Yost Papers. The document consisted of eleven resolutions passed in the assembly. Resolution 11 called for at least a ten-year moratorium on outside activities coming into Wao territory. This would include building of roads, colonization, and the presence of oil workers, lumber extractors, and miners, among others. See also Resolution 4.

37. Kane, *Savages*, 228.

38. Maxus Ecuador Inc., *Manual de Procedimientos en Territorio Huaorani, Programa de Orientación y Relaciones Comunitarias* [Manual of procedures in Wao territory, program for orientation and community relations] (Quito: [Maxus Ecuador Inc.], 1994), quoted in Iván Narváez Quiñónez, *Huaorani vs Maxus: Poder étnico Poder transnacional* [Waorani vs. Maxus: Ethnic power, transnational power] (Quito: Fundación Ecuatoriana de Estudios Sociales, 1996), 63. An initial contract with Maxus, dated September 9, 1992, and signed by Nanto was repudiated by other Waorani. Nanto denied the existence of such an accord. Lawrence Ziegler-Otero, *Resistance in an Amazonian Community: Huaorani Organizing against the Global Economy* (New York: Berghahn Books, 2004), 82–83; see also Kane, *Savages*, 104.

39. Clayton Robarchek and Carole Robarchek, *Waorani: The Contexts of Violence and War* (Fort Worth, TX: Harcourt Brace, 1998), 62–66.

40. Patricio Trujillo Montalvo, *Salvajes, Civilizados y Civilizadores: La Amazonia Ecuatoriana* [Savages, civilized, and civilizers: The Ecuadorian Amazon] (Quito: Fundación de Investigaciones Andino-Amazónicas, Ediciones Abya-Yala, 2001), 106–7. The accord also affirmed that Maxus and ONHAE would develop two- and five-year plans reflecting the self-identified needs of the Waorani. All oil-related projects within Wao territory would have trained community relations personnel to meet with the Waorani. All oil workers would be trained in company policies and expectations in Wao territory.

41. Ibid., 107.

42. Gregg Jones, "When Worlds Collide: On Delicate Ground: Maxus Trying to Reach Oil without Destroying Rainforest Tribe," *Dallas Morning News*, March 13, 1994. The anthropologist Lawrence Ziegler-Otero claimed, in contrast, that as of 1995, Maxus had "not spent more than a few thousand dollars in fulfillment of its promises." Ziegler-Otero, *Resistance*, 84.

43. Gregg Jones, "Primitive Tribe Strikes Controversial Deal with Oilmen for Black Gold in Rain Forest: Bewildered Waorani Trying to Find Their Way in a Forbidding World That Is Closing in," *Buffalo (NY) News*, April 3, 1994, HighBeam Research, www.highbeam.com/doc/1P2-22610160.html.

44. Jason Feer, "Maxus's Oil Project in Ecuador Encounters Delays, Rising Costs," *Oil Daily*, September 12, 1994, HighBeam Research, www.highbeam.com/doc/1G1-15741331.html.

45. Hutton and Skaggs, "Renewable Resource Development," 442.

46. Miriam Gebb (HCJB nurse), interview with author, Tadangado, Ecuador, July 28, 2005.

47. Kane, *Savages*, 120–21, 156, 231, 233; Robarchek and Robarchek, *Waorani*, 63.

48. "Yasuní," 9.

49. This account is based on Kane, *Savages*, 232–33, and the documentary film *Trinkets and Beads* (1996).

50. *Trinkets and Beads* (1996). While Kane describes the exchange, he did not include the phrase "trinkets and beads" as part of Wiznitzer's response. The film includes videotape of those words.

51. The former is Joe Kane, "With Spears from All Sides," *New Yorker*, September 27, 1993, 54–79; the latter, Kane, "Moi Goes to Washington," 74–81.

52. Kane, "Moi Goes to Washington," 81.

53. Chris Jochnick, "Amazon Oil Offensive," *Multinational Monitor*, January–February 1995, http://www.multinationalmonitor.org/hyper/issues/1995/01/mm0195_07.html.

54. Ibid.; Kane, *Savages*, 251.

55. Brysk, *From Tribal Village*, 274.

56. Hutton and Skaggs, "Renewable Resource Development," 442.

57. Stephen F. Saint, "Nimo Woody" [Rachel has gone from here], open letter to family and friends, n.d. [ca. 1994], copy in author's possession.

58. Peeke to Friends, September 7, 1996, Peeke Papers.

59. Peeke to "Dear Literate Friends," February 1995, Peeke Papers.

60. Kelley, "Waorani Scripture Recording Project," newsletter, January 1997, Peeke Papers.

61. Ziegler-Otero, *Resistance*, 86–87.

62. Peeke, "Waorani Acculturation: Casual Observations," unpublished typescript, May 1994, Peeke Papers.

63. JY field notes, July 22, 1979, Yost Papers.

64. Peeke, "Re Missionaries: Casual Observations," unpublished typescript, May 1994, Peeke Papers.

65. Ibid.

EPILOGUE

1. This paragraph is from Kathryn Long, "More than Meets the Eye: History and 'The End of the Spear,'" *Books and Culture*, May–June 2006, 16. Used with permission. See also Elisabeth Elliot, *No Graven Image* (New York: Harper & Row, 1966).

2. Steve Saint, *End of the Spear: A True Story* (Carol Stream, IL: Tyndale House, 2005), 102, 199. Most information about Saint and his family is based on this book. Background on the name Nemompade based on *End of the Spear* and email comments from Jim Yost to the author, March 30, 2015.

3. Stephen E. Saint, "The Unfinished Mission to the 'Aucas,'" *Christianity Today*, March 2, 1998, 44; Rick Wood, "Fighting Dependency among the 'Aucas': An Interview with Steve Saint," *Mission Frontiers Bulletin*, May–June 1998, 12.

4. Wood, "Fighting Dependency," 8.

5. Steve Saint, *The Great Omission: Fulfilling Christ's Commission Completely* (Seattle: YWAM, 2001), 60.

6. Tim Stafford, "The Maverick," *Christianity Today*, September 2010, 56.

7. Ibid., 57.

8. "I-FILM: I-TEC's Digital Film School," I-Tec, accessed January 27, 2018, http://itecusa.org/i-film.html.

9. Jim Yost, email to author, March 30, 2015.

10. Miriam Gebb, interview with author, Tadangado, Ecuador, July 28, 2005.

11. See, e.g., JY field notes, July 5, 1979, Yost Papers, for Limoncocha dental training, attended by at least one, and perhaps two, Waorani.

12. See Stephen R. Manock et al., "An Outbreak of Fulminant Hepatitis Delta in the Waorani, an Indigenous People of the Amazon Basin of Ecuador," *American Journal of Tropical Medicine and Hygiene* 63, nos. 3–4 (2000): 209–13. No hepatitis D vaccine existed when the Waorani were vaccinated against other diseases during the earlier years.

13. The earliest accounts do not identify Mincaye as Nate Saint's killer. However, given the Waorani practice of multiple attackers spearing each victim, it is possible that he participated or, as Steve Saint records in *End of the Spear*, 58, dealt the final blow. Not surprisingly, given the chaos of the scene, Mincaye's own accounts of the Palm Beach attack have varied over the years. Compare, e.g., E. Elliot, "The Palm Beach Story, according to Mincaye, one of the killers. Taped, transcribed, translated—May 1961," Folder 9, Box 4, EHE Papers with *Gentle Savage*, 167–78.

14. Mark Moring, "From Film Neophyte to Movie Mogul," *Christianity Today* [web-only edition], April 26, 2005, http://www.ctlibrary.com/ct/2005/aprilweb-only/martgreen.html.

15. Ibid.

16. Ibid. The name Mincayani is a combination of Mincaye, plus the plural indicator "-ani," similar to Wao (singular) and Waorani. It indicated a character based on Mincaye, but on others as well. See also *Beyond the Gates of Splendor*, directed by Jim Hanon (Beverly Hills, CA: Twentieth Century Fox Home Entertainment, 2005), DVD; *End of the Spear*, directed by Jim Hanon (Beverly Hills, CA: Twentieth Century Fox Home Entertainment, 2006), DVD; Lisa Ann Cockrel, film review of *End of the Spear*, *Christianity Today* [web-only edition], January 20, 2006, http://www.ctlibrary.com/ct/2006/januaryweb-only/endofthespear.html.

17. Brian Mansfield, "Chapman Show's High Note Is Salute to Reconciliation," *USA Today*, April 18, 2002, http://usatoday30.usatoday.com/life/music/2002/2002-04-18-chapman.htm.

18. Steven Curtis Chapman, *Declaration*, Sparrow Records, 2001, compact disc.

19. Saint, *End of the Spear*, 330–31; Ted Olsen, "Amsterdam 2000 Called the Most Multinational Event Ever," *Christianity Today* [web-only edition], August 2, 2000, http://www.ctlibrary.com/ct/2000/julyweb-only/32.0d.html.

20. Marian Rizzo, "A Pilgrim's Progress: Stephenie Saint, 20, Called 'a Woman after God's Own Heart,'" *Ocala (FL) Star-Banner*, July 28, 2000.

21. Adelle M. Banks, "Shuttle Mission to Include Missionary History," *Christianity Today* [web-only edition], August 28, 2009, http://www.ctlibrary.com/ct/2009/augustweb-only/134-51.0.html.

22. For Bradford Johnson's website, see "Bradford Johnson," bradfordajohnson.net; website accessed January 29, 2018.

23. "Pilipinto" (Butterfly) was the Quichua name given to Valerie Elliot. She went by the same name among the Waorani. Valerie Shepard, *Pilipinto's Happiness: The Jungle Childhood of Valerie Elliot* (San Antonio, TX: Vision Forum, 2012), 17; *Torchlighters: The Jim Elliot Story* [short film], (Worcester, PA: Christian History Institute; distributed by Vision Video, 2005), DVD.

24. Portions of the analysis in this and the following two paragraphs were first published in Long, "More than Meets the Eye," 16. For *End of the Spear* box office and DVD figures, see Sharon Waxman, "Fox Unveils a Division for Religious-Oriented Films," *New York Times*, September 20, 2006, http://www.nytimes.com/2006/09/20/movies/fox-unveils-a-division-for-religiousoriented-films.html.

25. "Death Worked Backwards," interview with Steve Saint by Mark Moring, *Christianity Today* [web-only edition], January 18, 2006, http://www.ctlibrary.com/ct/2006/januaryweb-only/stevesaint.html.

26. Saint, *End of the Spear*, 337.

27. *Unfolding Destinies*, 234, 235.

28. Saint, *End of the Spear*, 335–36. In a separate interview with the author, Yowe said he saw lights (not people) and heard singing, although he did not understand the words. Yowe, interview with author, July 23, 2005, Tewæno, Ecuador.

29. Elisabeth [Elliot] Gren, interview with author, June 27, 2001, Magnolia, MA.

30. Catherine Peeke, email to author, February 21, 2006, and subsequent conversation with author, n.d.

31. "Death Worked Backwards," interview with Saint.

32. *Gentle Savage*.

33. "Yasuní," 8.

34. Flora E. Lu [Holt], "The Common Property Regime of the Huaorani Indians of Ecuador: Implications and Challenges to Conservation," *Human Ecology* 29, no. 4 (2001): 432. The Yasuní region, including the Waorani Ethnic Reserve and the Yasuní National Park, together designated as the Yasuní Man and Biosphere Reserve, has been described as a "complicated array of overlapping protected areas, indigenous reserves and extractive concessions." "Yasuní," 2.

35. Lu, "Common Property," 430–31.

36. Jim Wyss [*Miami Herald* reporter], "In the Amazon, a Mystery of Murderous Revenge and Greed," *Waorani*, posted July 11, 2004, http://www.waorani.com/massacre.html.

37. "Yasuní," 10–11.

38. Bethany Horne, "'After All the People We Killed, We Felt Dizzy,'" *Newsweek*, January 2, 2014, http://www.newsweek.com/2014/01/03/after-all-people-we-killed-we-felt-dizzy-245008.html.

39. Ibid. The best sources in English are the *Newsweek* article cited here, and Inter-American Commission on Human Rights, "Admissibility, Tagaeri and Taromenani Indigenous Peoples in Isolation; Ecuador," Report No. 96/14, Petition 422-06, November 6, 2014, http://www.oas.org/en/iachr/decisions/2014/ECAD422-06EN.pdf. This petition was presented before the IACHR of the Organization of American States. I also had access to an unpublished report by Yost, "Wao Update," n.d., Yost Papers. At the invitation of the Waorani, Yost spent two weeks in Ecuador, arriving on March 24, 2013, a day before the retaliatory raid and massacre. The most helpful source in Spanish is Miguel Angel Cabodevilla and Milagros Aguirre, *Una Tragedia Oculta* [A concealed tragedy], (Quito: CICAME, 2013), http://www.pensamientocritico.org/masmar1113.pdf. Numerous interviews, documentaries, and reports are also on YouTube.

40. Jim Yost, email to author, March 31, 2015; Yost, "Wao Update," Yost Papers; Horne, "After All the People."

41. Matt Finer, Remi Moncel, and Clinton N. Jenkins, "Leaving the Oil under the Amazon: Ecuador's Yasuní-ITT Initiative," *Biotropica* 42, no. 1 (2010): 63–66, doi: 10.1111/j.1744-7429.2009.00587.x.

42. Shaira Panela, "Deforestation Ramping Up in Yasuni as Ecuador Sets to Open Up National Park to Drilling," *Mongabay: News & Inspiration from Nature's Frontline*, July 29, 2014, https://news.mongabay.com/2014/07/deforestation-ramping-up-in-yasuni-as-ecuador-sets-to-open-up-national-park-to-drilling/; Kevin Koenig, "Drilling towards Disaster: Ecuador's Aggressive Amazonian Oil Push," News & Multimedia, *Amazon Watch*, April 6, 2016, http://amazonwatch.org/news/2016/0406-drilling-towards-disaster-ecuadors-aggressive-amazonian-oil-push.

43. Matt Finer et al., "High Resolution Satellite Imagery Reveals Petroamazonas Violated Environmental Impact Study by Building Road into Yasuní National Park," Geoyasuni.org, May 2014, http://www.geoyasuni.org/wp-content/uploads/2014/06/Yasuni-Technical-Report_bloque31.pdf; Panela, "Deforestation Ramping Up."

44. Jonathan Kaiman, "Controversial Ecuador Oil Deal Lets China Stake an $80-Million Claim to Pristine Amazon Rainforest," *Los Angeles Times*, January 29, 2016, http://www.latimes.com/world/mexico-americas/la-fg-ecuador-china-oil-20160129-story.html; Koenig, "Drilling towards Disaster."

45. "Yasuní," 9.

46. Pete Oxford et al., *Yasuni, Tiputini and the Web of Life* (Quito: INGWE Press, 2012), 39.

47. Maria Aguinda Salazar was one of the original plaintiffs in this class action lawsuit. The most careful legal analysis of the lawsuit is a series of essays by Judith Kimerling, including "Lessons from the Chevron Ecuador Litigation: The Proposed Intervenors' Perspective," *Stanford Journal of Complex Litigation* 1, no. 2 (2013): 241–94, and others cited earlier, despite occasional incorrect or misleading statements regarding SIL. For other accounts of the suit and the drama surrounding it, see Michael D. Goldhaber, *Crude Awakening: Chevron in Ecuador* ([New York]: RosettaBooks, 2014), Kindle ebook; Paul M. Barrett, *Law of the Jungle: The $19 Billion Legal Battle over Oil in the Rain Forest and the Lawyer Who'd Stop at Nothing to Win* (New York: Crown, 2014).

48. Kimerling, "Lessons from Chevron Ecuador," 245.

49. Paul M. Barrett, "Chevron Defends Its RICO Victory in the Epic Ecuadorian Oil Pollution Case," *Bloomberg Businessweek*, October 3, 2014, www.businessweek.com/articles/2014-10-03/chevron-defends-rico-victory-in-ecuadorian-oil-pollution-case.

50. *Crude: The Real Price of Oil*, directed by Joe Berlinger (New York: First Run Features/Crude Productions, 2009), DVD.

51. Kimerling, "Lessons from Chevron Ecuador," 241, 241n1, 286.

52. Ibid., 284, 284n134, 269. Kimerling cites Wao elders in her statement that the relocation period was a time "when new diseases sickened and killed many people" (ibid., 269). As mentioned, the Waorani suffered through numerous contact illnesses, but apart from the polio epidemic there were no records or reports of dramatic population loss or widespread deaths.

53. For a description of the lodge and controversies over how profits are distributed, see Megan Alpert, "'They Come, They Photograph, but Don't Help': How Ecotourism in the Amazon Shortchanges the Locals," The Guardian, March 11, 2015, https://www.theguardian.com/environment/2015/mar/11/ecotourism-amazon-shortchanges-locals-ecuador.

54. Much of this paragraph is informed by Casey High, "Oil Development, Indigenous Organisations, and the Politics of Egalitarianism," Cambridge Journal of Anthropology 26, no. 2 (2006–7): 34–46.

55. Kimerling, "Lessons from Chevron Ecuador," 286n136.

56. Logan A. Hennessy, "Discursive Spearpoints: Contentious Interventions in Amazonian Indigenous Environments," in Contentious Geographies: Environmental Knowledge, Meaning, Scale, ed. Michael K. Goodman, Maxwell T. Boykoff, and Kyle T. Evered (Aldershot, UK: Ashgate, 2008), 107–8.

57. Nate Dell, "Personal Perspective on the Waodani Church," unpublished reflections by Dell occasioned by the fiftieth anniversary of the missionaries' deaths, n.d., copy in author's possession. Dell's observations are similar to those of the author during a visit to the communities of Tewæno, Tarangado, and Acado during late July and early August 2005.

58. This and the following paragraph based on Peggy Covert and Ken Fleming, "Following Jesus on the Curaray," Christian Missions in Many Lands, March 2006, 3–6.

59. Clint Rainey, "Five-Man Legacy," World Magazine, January 28, 2006, https://world.wng.org/2006/01/five_man_legacy.

60. Ibid. I use the phrase in a different context than Rainey.

61. Casey High, "'A Little Bit Christian': Memories of Conversion and Community in Post-Christian Amazonia," American Anthropologist 118, no. 2 (2016): 274.

62. See, e.g., Gentle Savage; Carla Seidl, The Sophisticated Savage (Huntington, NY: Inner Hearth Books, 2009).

GLOSSARY

ᴑ

Acawo (Akawo)   Dayomæ's mother and Guequita's sister.

Æncædi (Enqueri)   Son of Mincaye, second president of ONHAE, and key figure in Joe Kane's *Savages*.

Ana   Dayomæ's half sister, early Wao health worker, and Rosi Jung's translation assistant.

Arajuno   Lowland Quichua community, Brethren mission station on the edge of Wao territory, and staging area for "Operation Auca." Home of Ed and Marilou McCully, later of Wilfred and Gwen Tidmarsh. Point of departure for Dayomæ, Rachel Saint, and Elisabeth Elliot as they sought to make peaceful contact with Dayomæ's kinship group.

Arango Velásquez, Sister Inés   Colombian nun serving as a missionary in Ecuador with the Capuchín Tertiary Sisters. Along with Alejandro Labaca, she was speared to death by the Tagæidi in 1987.

Ayebæ   Daughter of Yowe and Oba, early Wao health worker, translation assistant for Rosi Jung.

Baiwaidi   "Baiwa's bunch" or "Bai's bunch," Waorani kinship group, living to the east of the protectorate, and identified with the Wao man "Bai" or "Baiwa" (same person).

Cæmpæde (Quemperi)   Prominent male member of Wao kinship group living along the banks of the Cononaco River.

Cæwæidi Ono   River name and Wao settlement on the Shiripuno River, founded in late 1989 by Ñamæ and others from Dayono. Location of anthropologist Laura Rival's fieldwork. Village is the home of Ñamæ's son Moi Enomenga and his family.

Capuchín friars   Members of the Order of Capuchín Friars Minor, a Catholic missionary order in the Franciscan tradition. Capuchín friars were assigned as missionaries to the Apostolic Vicariate of Aguarico, Ecuador (a provisional territory not yet organized as a diocese), which included ancestral lands claimed by the Waorani.

CEPE/Petroecuador   Corporación Estatal Petrolera Ecuatoriana, the Ecuadorian State Petroleum Corporation; name changed to Petroecuador in 1990.

CGG   Compagnie Générale du Géophysique (General Company of Geophysics), a French geophysical company under contract to CEPE to direct initial seismic exploration of rainforest areas that were potential oil fields.

Christian and Missionary Alliance   A denomination influenced by the faith missions tradition. Founded in 1887, ten years later it was one of the first evangelical denominations to send missionaries to Ecuador. From about 1973 to 1987, missionary David Miller supervised a primary school for Wao children in Dayono.

Christian Missions in Many Lands   A US missions agency that handles finances and other logistical details for independent Brethren missionaries, who are sent to the mission field by their local assemblies (churches). Jim and Elisabeth Elliot, Ed and Marilou McCully, Pete and Olive Fleming, Wilfred and Gwen Tidmarsh, and Lloyd and Linda Rogers were Brethren missionaries with some part in the outreach to the Waorani.

CIESE   Centro de Investigaciones y Estudios Socio Económicos (Center for Research and Socioeconomic Studies), part of the anthropology department at PUCE, the Universidad Católica (Catholic University) in Quito.

Come (Kome)   Guequita's son and Dayomæ's husband; attended the World Congress on Evangelism, 1966, in Berlin; influential figure in Toñæmpade.

come   Thick cotton cord traditionally worn around the hips by Waorani men and women as their only clothing; referred to as a hip-cord or G-string. To wear a *come* was to be "dressed."

CONFENIAE   Confederación de Nacionalidades Indígenas de la Amazonia Ecuatoriana (Confederation of Indigenous Nationalities of the Ecuadorian Amazon). Founded in 1980 by indigenous groups in Amazonian Ecuador, CONFENIAE lobbied the Ecuadorian government for Wao land that would become the Waorani Ethnic Reserve. The group never truly represented the Waorani, which became clear after the founding of the independent Wao association ONHAE in 1990.

Cordavi   Ecuadorian environmental group; the name is a shortened form for Corporación de la Defensa de la Vida (Corporation for the Defense of Life).

cowode   *Wao tededo* for "outsider" or "foreigner"; traditionally the Waorani thought *cowodi* were cannibals or subhuman.

Dawa   The first Wao after Dayomæ to convert to Christianity, Dawa (c. 1938–2018) became an influential figure in Tewæno and later in Tzapino, a clearing established in the early 1970s by Dawa and her husband, Quemo.

Dayomæ (Dayuma)   Wao woman (c. 1931–2014), who became one of the most influential people in recent Wao history. In 1944 Dayomæ fled Waorani violence and was taken to Carlos Sevilla's Hacienda Ila, where she became a field hand in conditions much like slavery. Rachel Saint met Dayomæ at the hacienda in 1955, and over time she became Rachel's language informant, the first Wao Christian, and the broker who facilitated peaceful contact between her kinship group (the Guequitaidi) and missionaries Rachel Saint and Elisabeth Elliot.

Dayono (Dayuno)   Village founded in 1971 by Zoila Wiñame in an acrimonious split with Dayomæ. Wiñame was a Wao woman who had spent years among the Quichua. She wanted to reestablish her Quichua contacts and to get away from what she viewed as the oppressive Christianity practiced in Tewæno.

faith missions   Independent, often nondenominational, mission agencies first founded in the late nineteenth century by people dissatisfied by what they saw as the bureaucracy and rigid requirements of denominational mission boards. Faith missions selected potential missionaries based on the strength of their sense of calling from God and their willingness to trust God to provide the finances they needed rather than being funded by a denomination or board.

FEINE   Federación Ecuatoriana de Indígenas Evangélicos (Ecuadorian Federation of Indigenous Evangelicals), organized in November 1980 among evangelical Quichuas in the Ecuadorian highlands, FEINE later became a national political organization.

Gospel Missionary Union   Now Avant Ministries, a conservative faith mission founded in 1892 out of the Kansas City YMCA to prepare young people for missionary service. Missionaries first arrived in Ecuador in 1896, and in 1953, Roger and Barbara Youderian were assigned by Gospel Missionary Union to work among the Shuar in the southeastern rainforests of Amazonian Ecuador.

Guequita (Geketa, Gikita)   Dayomæ's uncle (1916–97); senior member of the original kinship group in Tewæno and respected Wao warrior. One of the leaders in killing the five missionaries, Guequita stopped spearing enemies when he accepted Christianity.

Guequitaidi (Geketaidi)   "Guequita's bunch," name of the kinship group Dayomæ belonged to and the first Waorani encountered by missionaries. Six Guequitaidi men killed the five missionaries in 1956; Dayomæ convinced the group to relocate in 1958 to the Tewæno clearing, where they made peaceful contact with Elisabeth Elliot and Rachel Saint.

Guiimadi (Gimari)   Dayomæ's sister; "Delilah" of Palm Beach.

HCJB Global   See **World Radio Missionary Fellowship.**

ido   One who curses others. Among the Waorani, an *ido* had access to malevolent spirits that caused illness or death; if found out, the *ido* could be killed.

IERAC   Instituto Ecuatoriano de Reforma Agraria y Colonización (Ecuadorian Institute of Agrarian Reform and Colonization), the state agency responsible for granting land titles.

ILV   Instituto Lingüístico de Verano. Spanish acronym and name for the Summer Institute of Linguistics. See **SIL.**

Iniwa (Eniwa)   Male member of a Waorani kinship group living along the Dicado River; Iniwa became Alejandro Labaca's "adopted" Wao father.

Intangible Zone   Portions of the Waorani Ethnic Reserve and the Yasuní National Park designated by the Ecuadorian government in 2007 as a "safe zone" for the Tagæidi and the Taadomenani, Wao subgroups, to live in voluntary isolation.

JAARS   Jungle Aviation and Radio Service, founded in 1948 to provide air service and other technical support for Summer Institute of Linguistics staff.

jaguar father, jaguar mother   Wao man or woman who could communicate with jaguar spirits and divine the location of herds of peccary (wild pigs) for hunters.

Labaca Ugarte, Alejandro   Spanish Capuchín priest and naturalized Ecuadorian citizen who was a missionary to indigenous people living both north and south of the Napo River, including the Waorani. In 1965 Labaca was named apostolic prefect of the Catholic missionary district of Aguarico in Amazonian Ecuador; after several other assignments, he was named bishop of the same apostolic vicariate. Labaca also was a missionary who made peaceful contact with Waorani living near the Dicado (Yasuní) River. Labaca and Inés Arango were killed by the Tagæidi in 1987.

Limoncocha SIL jungle base in Ecuador, located just north of Pompeya and the Napo River. Opened in the mid-1950s, the base offered a location where linguists and indigenous people could work together on Bible translation without interruption or receive community development training. JAARS planes and pilots serving SIL in Ecuador flew out of Limoncocha. A medical clinic served both SIL staff and indigenous people. SIL left Limoncocha in 1982.

Mæncamo (Maengamo, Mankamu) Dayomæ's aunt, Guequita's wife; early language informant for Elisabeth Elliot.

MAF Mission Aviation Fellowship, known in Ecuador as Alas de Socorro (Wings of "Aid" or "Relief"), a faith mission founded in 1944 of ground personnel and pilots who used aviation to support missionaries in remote locations. In 1948 Nate Saint began the MAF work in Ecuador.

Maxus Ecuador, Inc. Ecuadorian subsidiary of the Dallas-based Maxus Energy Corporation. In 1991 Maxus purchased Conoco's share of a major oil concession in what was known as Block 16 on Waorani land. Maxus built a controversial road across national park territory, drilled wells in Block 16, and made efforts to fund community development for the Waorani. In 1995 the Maxus share of Block 16 was purchased by the Argentine company Yacimientos Petrolíferos Fiscales.

Mincaye (Minkaye, Menkaye) Dayomæ's half brother and one of the six Wao men who participated in the Palm Beach killings. Mincaye traveled widely with Steve Saint on speaking tours during the 1990s and 2000s, witnessing to the change Christianity had brought his people.

Mintaca (Mintaka) Dayomæ's aunt, who with Guiimadi and Nænquiwi made peaceful contact with the five missionaries on Palm Beach; early language informant for Elisabeth Elliot.

Moipa (Moi) Enomenga As a young man in Cæwædi Ono, founded by his father, Ñamæ, Moi helped anthropologist Laura Rival with her fieldwork; he later held a number of offices in ONHAE, including president. Moi was a central figure in Joe Kane's book *Savages* as the ideal Waorani. He later helped found the Huaorani Ecolodge and has been active in environmental issues.

Nampa Dayomæ's younger brother. Together with Guequita, Nampa incited anger and helped to lead the Palm Beach attack on the five missionaries in 1956. Nampa was wounded in a struggle on the beach during the attack and died either a few months or a few weeks afterward. Circumstances surrounding the shot that wounded Nampa have been a source of controversy.

Nantowæ (Nanto) First president of ONHAE; one of the young Waorani men profiled in Joe Kane's *Savages*.

NAWE Nacionalidad Waorani del Ecuador (Waorani Nationality of Ecuador), a political organization that in 2007 replaced ONHAE. It is unclear how much power or influence NAWE has among the Waorani.

Nemonca One of the six Waorani men who participated in the Palm Beach attack.

NRDC Natural Resources Defense Council, the US environmental group that hired (and later fired) Judith Kimerling. Before the falling out, NRDC published Kimerling's 1991 book, *Amazon Crude*. The organization later antagonized other environmental groups by its decision to support efforts by Conoco DuPont to engage in oil extraction on ancestral Wao territory.

Oba   Dayomæ's sister, Yowe's wife, and one of Catherine Peeke's primary language assistants.

Oncaye (Onkaye)   Young woman from the Piyæmoidi who was wounded and captured in 1964 by Ecuadorian settlers near the town of Coca. Oncaye became the focus of conflict between Rachel Saint and the Capuchín missionaries, each of whom wanted her to help make contact with her relatives. Rachel "won," Oncaye went to Tewæno, and she later did help contact the Piyæmoidi.

ONHAE   Organización de la Nacionalidad Huaorani de la Amazonia Ecuatoriana (Organization of the Huaorani Nation of the Ecuadorian Amazon), formed in 1990 by the Waorani to represent their interests in contacts with oil companies and other outsiders. In 2007 ONHAE was replaced by NAWE.

Oriente   Name used for Ecuador's eastern provinces; a synonym for "Amazonian Ecuador" or the "Ecuadorian rainforest."

Paba (Pawa)   Wao woman, wife of Iniwa, who became Alejandro Labaca's adopted Wao mother.

"Palm Beach"   Sandy bank of the Curaray River where five American missionaries set up camp on January 3, 1956, hoping to make peaceful contact with the Waorani. After an initial successful contact, the missionaries were speared by the Waorani, January 8, 1956, on the same riverbank and later buried nearby.

Pegonca   Yowe and Oba's son; language assistant for translator Rosi Jung; Wao preacher.

Piyæmoidi (Piyaemoiri)   "Piyæmo's bunch," also known as the *ænomenani* or "downriver" Waorani because in the late 1930s they fled downstream along the Napo River to the upper Tiputini watershed to escape retaliatory tribal spearings. In 1968 the majority of Piyæmoidi relocated to the area around Tewæno.

protectorate   Approximately 620 square miles (8 percent) of land in traditional Wao territory reserved for the Waorani. Legally recognized as Wao land in 1969, though the Waorani would not receive title to portions of the land until 1983. The protectorate and the Tewæno community, located within it, served as a refuge for Waorani threatened by oil exploration and extraction. Relocation efforts led to overcrowding, hunger, and illnesses, but initially many Waorani liked the access to the outside world they gained living there.

PUCE   Pontificia Universidad Católica del Ecuador (Pontifical Catholic University of Ecuador), with its main campus in Quito, includes a Department of Anthropology, some of whose faculty were critics of SIL during the 1970s and 1980s.

Quemo (Kimo, Kemo)   One of the participants in the Palm Beach killings, Quemo was an early believer and with his wife, Dawa, became a faithful Christian. Quemo attended the Berlin Congress on World Evangelism in 1966 and participated in the 1971 "Auca Update" tour.

Quichua (Kichwa)   The largest indigenous group in the Americas, including in Ecuador, where the ethnic Quichua population is about 408,000, with some estimates placing the number of Quichua speakers in the country at more than two million. Population reports vary widely. The Quichua (known as Quechua outside of Ecuador) have been in contact with people of European ancestry since the Spanish conquest. They are divided into two broad groupings—the mountain (highland) Quichua and the jungle (lowland) Quichua, each with numerous subgroups. The Quichua language is a family of related but distinct languages and dialects. There are three groups of lowland Quichua, with a total population of forty-two thousand, living near the Waorani in Amazonian Ecuador.

Quichuas represent about 37 percent of the indigenous population of the Oriente, while the Waorani represent 2 percent.

Rainforest Action Network   A US environmental group. Writer Joe Kane was working part time at the office in San Francisco when a letter arrived from ONHAE that launched him on an investigation that led to two *New Yorker* essays and the book *Savages*.

Shell Mera   The village of Mera existed first, located near the Pastaza River, where the mountains met the rainforest. Five miles east was flat land suitable for an air base to support Shell Oil explorations. Named Shell Mera, in 1948 it became the home of Mission Aviation Fellowship in Ecuador and for many years the gateway to the rainforest for travelers.

SIL   Summer Institute of Linguistics, now SIL International, founded in 1934 as a nonprofit, nongovernmental organization whose staff work in the areas of linguistics, sociolinguistics, literacy, and literature development. Although SIL is not a religious organization, its staff have an interest in Bible translation, especially of the New Testament.

Taadomenani   The "lowlanders" or the "meandering ones," a descriptive name for an elusive group of previously unknown Waorani who live in self-imposed isolation in the intangible zone of Yasuní National Park. Their few encounters with outsiders have invariably been violent and tragic, whether the Taadomenani were perpetrators or victims.

Tagæidi   "Tagæ's bunch," a small Wao kinship group, identified with a man named Tagæ, that broke away from the Piyæmoidi in 1968 and sought to remain isolated. Following traditional Waorani practices, the Tagæidi defended their territory with violence. Among those killed by the Tagæidi during the 1970s and the 1980s were Alejandro Labaca and Inés Arango.

Tæmænta   Son of Nænquiwi ("George" of Palm Beach), Wao preacher, and Catherine Peeke's primary translation consultant.

tepæ   Thick, carbohydrate-rich drink made of cooked manioc that is then premasticated. It has a central place in the Wao diet.

Tewæno (Tiwaeno, Tiweno, Tihueno)   Clearing on the Tewæno River, established in 1958 by Dayomæ as the site where her extended family, the Guequitaidi, would live in peace with missionaries Rachel Saint and Elisabeth Elliot.

Toñæ   Known as the first Wao martyr, Toñæ was killed in 1970 as he tried to take the Christian message to members of his extended family group. A gifted, literate young man with a promising future, Toñæ left a wife, Wato, and two small children, Onguimæ and Gaba, who as young adults helped with Bible translation.

Toñæmpade   "Toñæ's stream," a tributary of the Curaray River, also the name of a village established by Dayomæ and her son Sam Padilla Cænto in 1977 to encourage tourism. The village is located on the Curaray River, not far from the riverbank where the five missionaries were killed.

Wængongui   Name chosen by Dayomæ and Rachel Saint for the Christian God. Originally, Wængongui was a benign figure in Wao cosmology with some creative powers; before missionaries arrived, the Waorani had no supreme God. Through teaching about the character of the Christian God, Wængongi came to assume those attributes.

Wao tededo (**a person's speech**) or *Waorani tededo* (**the people's speech**)   The name for the language spoken by the Waorani. Based on research to date, it is a linguistic isolate, unrelated to any other language.

Waorani Ethnic Reserve About 1.5 million acres of ancestral Wao lands; in 1990 Ecuadorian president Rodrigo Borja awarded the Waorani title to the land, although the Ecuadorian state retained rights to petroleum exploration and extraction.

WBT Wycliffe Bible Translators, founded in 1942 by William Cameron Townsend with the goal of translating the Bible (New Testament) into languages that did not have it. Now Wycliffe USA, it is part of the Wycliffe Global Alliance, a group of national organizations that recruit personnel and promote the need for Bible translation. In recent years, Wycliffe staff have moved beyond their traditional support roles to engage in actual Bible translation.

Wepeidi "Wepe's bunch," sometimes referred to as the "Ridge people," lived on the ridges along the Gabado River, far to the east of the protectorate. Some began to relocate to the protectorate in 1971; others moved north to live along the Dicado (Yasuní) River; some moved to the Cononaco River; and a few remained in place.

Wiñame, Zoila Founded Dayono in 1971 after a bitter feud with Dayomæ. Like Dayomæ, Wiñame was a Wao woman who spent her formative years living among the Quichuas on the Hacienda Ila. She, too, had the skills to act as a cultural broker between the Waorani and outsiders.

World Radio Missionary Fellowship Founded in Quito, Ecuador, in 1931 by North American missionaries as an evangelical radio station with the call letters HCJB. World Radio Missionary Fellowship later came to be known as HCJB Global and grew into a far-reaching mass media and healthcare mission. The mission now is known as Reach Beyond.

Yowe (Dyuwi, Dyowi) Youngest (born c. 1940) of the six Waorani who killed the missionaries at Palm Beach, Yowe embraced Christianity and years later wrote the first "hymn" to traditional Wao music. Although he never learned to read, Yowe preached among the Waorani and was known for his prayers. His wife, Oba, was one of Catherine Peeke's language assistants.

INDEX

Figures are indicated by an italic *f* following the page number

427